Admiralty and Maritime Law in the United States

Admiralty and Maritime Law in the United States

Cases and Materials

FOURTH EDITION

The Late David W. Robertson
W. Page Keeton Chair in Tort Law
University Distinguished Teaching Professor
University of Texas School of Law

Steven F. Friedell
Professor of Law
Rutgers Law School

Michael F. Sturley
Fannie Coplin Regents Chair in Law
University of Texas School of Law

Carolina Academic Press
Durham, North Carolina

ISBN: 978-1-5310-1839-9
e-ISBN: 978-1-5310-1840-5
LCCN: 2020935363

Carolina Academic Press
700 Kent Street
Durham, North Carolina 27701
Telephone (919) 489-7486
Fax (919) 493-5668
www.cap-press.com

Printed in the United States of America
2023 Printing

Contents

Table of Cases

Names of principal cases and the page numbers on which they are excerpted are in **bold**.

Preface to the Fourth Edition

The present publication marks the first new edition of this work since the death of our friend and colleague, David W. Robertson, in the final week of 2018. The casebook originated with a set of photocopied materials that David assembled to teach his Admiralty classes in the last millennium. Twenty years ago, he invited the two of us to join him in producing a casebook for formal publication, but it was still very much his casebook. For each edition, he carefully reviewed and edited everything that we contributed, and we inevitably deferred to his wishes.

Our deference was not an abdication of responsibility or blind respect for seniority. On the contrary, we both recognized that David was a consummate teacher who fully understood exactly what he was doing. He knew what would work in the classroom, and he worked hard to ensure that the finished product would be user-friendly for both students and faculty. Over the last two decades, the casebook has stood up well. Not only have generations of students used it successfully, but we as co-authors learned so much working with David. He was such a gentleman, and we miss him.

It would be tempting for us to stop with the third edition, leaving the last version of the casebook that David saw as a monument to his accomplishments—but that is not what David would have done or what he would have wanted. The courts have remained active in the field, and maritime law has continued to evolve. Last year, even the Supreme Court was unusually active in maritime law. Keeping the casebook current, therefore, has required the addition of new principal cases and new substantive notes following the existing principal cases; the updating of many more existing notes; and the deletion of some material from the last edition to keep the overall size manageable. (David always felt strongly that the casebook should not be "too fat." He would be pleased that this new edition is less than 1.5% longer than the third edition, and is still shorter than the first edition.)

Although we have updated the text, we have not changed the fundamental approach or the structure of the previous edition. We have therefore retained the Preface to the Third Edition—exactly as David wrote it five years ago—to explain both the philosophy that has continued to guide our work and the editing conventions that we have continued to follow.

Michael F. Sturley
Austin, Texas

Steven F. Friedell
Camden, New Jersey

May 2020

Preface to the Third Edition

Studying the admiralty field—the field of marine casualties and transactions—necessitates inquiry into issues ranging across much of the basic law school curriculum, including civil procedure, comparative law, conflicts of laws, constitutional law, contracts, creditors' rights, environmental law, federal courts, insurance, international law, legislation, products liability, property, remedies, torts, and workers' compensation.

We do not claim that our book provides the opportunity to teach all of these subjects. But we have tried to select cases with an eye to maximizing the admiralty course's potential for integrating the knowledge the students will have gained from their other courses. In Section I-F's *Thorsteinsson* opinion, for example, U.S. law's commitment to the requirement of physical arrest of the vessel in *in rem* proceedings as an essential element of due process comes into sharp conflict with our country's strong regard for the necessity and wisdom of recognizing the judgments of other countries' courts.

In editing the cases and supplementing them with textual material, we have used the following signals: Omitted text is signaled by three asterisks. Inserted text is enclosed in brackets. Omitted citations are signaled by empty brackets. Our own editorial footnotes to the opinions are labeled as such. (Otherwise, footnote numbers in opinions are the courts' original numbers.) Cross-references within the book refer to the chapter number, the section number, and the sub-section (if any). Thus "Section II-A" means chapter II, section A, and "Section I-G-10" means chapter I, section G, subsection 10.

Because this is a teaching book and not a case reporter or a scholarly reference work, we have felt free to make some changes to the opinions without providing any signal. These include minor changes to the courts' punctuation and typography, correction of obvious spelling errors, and correction of citations and citation form. Unsignaled omissions include the courts' citations to the record, citations to the opinions below, and the courts' footnotes. Occasionally, we found that our editing of an opinion required moving one of the court's footnotes. When we did that, we left the footnote number intact but did not signal the change of position. When it seems historically evocative, we have retained the British spellings in use in the early U.S. materials.

This Third Edition contains a large amount of new material, including a new section on punitive damages and new chapters on piracy and oil pollution. We have tried to condense everything as much as we can, realizing the desirability of keeping the book from getting too fat.

Admiralty and Maritime Law in the United States

Chapter I

The Basics: Admiralty Jurisdiction, Conceptual Structure, and Practice

A. Historical Background

According to Professor Wigmore, "the oldest picture of a sea-going ship of large size"—sculpted on an Egyptian relic in the British Museum—dates from ca. 1500 B.C. and depicts a three-masted vessel owned by Queen Hatshepsut, who just happens to have been the princess who rescued Moses from the bulrushes.[1] However this may be, it seems certain that the Ancient Egyptians engaged in ocean travel and shipping, as did the cities of Carthage, the Greeks, the Romans, and the city states of the Mediterranean.

Over the centuries marine shipping spread from the Levant westward and northward. As it did so, it generated legal problems and consequent mechanisms for their solution. There is evidence for the existence of substantive maritime law at Rhodes (ca. 300 B.C.), Rome (ca. 100 A.D.), Amalfi (ca. 1000), Barcelona (called the Consulado del Mar, ca. 1200), Oleron (ca. 1200), Wisby (ca. 1350), and the Hanse Towns (ca. 1400). See also the Marine Ordinances of Louis XIV of France (ca. 1680). Modern English and U.S. decisions occasionally rely on the more recent of these bodies of law. Translations of the Tablets of Amalfi, the Consulado del Mar, the Laws of Oleron, the Laws of Wisby, the Laws of the Hanse Towns, and the Marine Ordinances of Louis XIV can be found in the venerable English publication *Black Book of the Admiralty*. Somewhat different translations of the last four are in 30 Federal Cases at 1171 et seq.

* * *

The centerpiece of U.S. admiralty is Article III of the United States Constitution, which provides in § 2 that the judicial power of the United States "shall extend ... to all cases of admiralty and maritime jurisdiction." Article III § 1 vests the judicial power of the United States in "one Supreme Court and in such inferior courts as the Congress may from time to time ordain and establish." In the Judiciary Act of 1789, the First Congress saw fit to "ordain and establish" a system of inferior federal courts, consisting at that time of thirteen district courts and three circuit courts. Section 9 of that Act provided that the district courts "shall ... have exclusive original cognizance of all civil causes of admiralty and

1. 3 Wigmore, Panorama of the World's Legal Systems 875–76 (1928).

maritime jurisdiction, ... saving to suitors, in all cases, the right of a common law remedy where the common law is competent to give it."

* * *

The Constitution and the Judiciary Act of 1789 left the courts with the task of working out answers to three large questions: (1) the scope and limits of the federal admiralty jurisdiction; (2) the scope and limits of the concurrent jurisdiction of common law courts over admiralty and maritime cases; and (3) the sources, nature, and ultimately the content of the substantive law applicable in admiralty and maritime cases. The first of these questions is addressed *infra* in Sections I-B through I-E. The second is treated in Section I-F. The third is introduced in Section I-H and gets further treatment at subject-matter-specific junctures throughout the remainder of the book.

The first admiralty-law question faced by United States courts was the meaning of the constitutional and statutory phrase "admiralty and maritime." As is indicated by *DeLovio v. Boit*, *infra* at 5, this issue—i.e., the scope and limits of the federal admiralty power—was played out against the backdrop of the severe limitations on admiralty jurisdiction that we might have inherited from England.

The root of the word *admiral* is the Arabic *amir-al-bahr,* meaning commander of the sea. The title of admiral began being used in England around 1300 to refer to a naval official with administrative and disciplinary command over the vessels, officers, and seamen in a fleet. During the 1300s this official acquired a judicial function. Thus, when the United States Constitution was formulated, the term *admiralty* referred to a court hearing disputes arising from naval and marine matters.

The term *maritime* derives from the Latin word for sea—*mare*—and simply means "of or pertaining to the sea." In his lengthy opinion in *DeLovio* (which is set forth in radically truncated form below) Justice Joseph Story, who became famous for his successful efforts to establish a broad subject matter jurisdiction for the United States District Courts sitting in admiralty,[2] argued that the Framers added the word "maritime" to the "admiralty" grant in order to make sure that the jurisdiction was suitably broad. Others have argued to precisely the opposite effect, *viz.,* that the natural thrust of the term *maritime* was to narrow the grant of jurisdiction to exclude waters that are neither salty nor tidal, thus excluding important rivers and lakes.[3]

Because of the historical ties of the term *admiralty* to a particular court, at one time it was thought appropriate to use that term when referring to courts and to technicalities of jurisdiction and procedure, while confining the term *maritime* to the substantive matters litigated and the substantive law applied in those courts. But nowadays the two terms are treated as synonyms. One sees frequent references to "admiralty law" and to "maritime courts," although a proctor[4] of the 1920s would have regarded either locution as unnatural if not incoherent.

---

2. "It was said of the late Justice Story, that if a bucket of water were brought into his court with a corn cob floating in it, he would at once extend the admiralty jurisdiction of the United States over it." Note, *Extension of Admiralty Jurisdiction Over State Canals*, 37 AMER. L. REV. 911, 916 (1903).

3. Stolz, *Pleasure Boating and Admiralty: Erie at Sea*, 51 CAL. L. REV. 661, 677 (1963) (indicating that "the reasonably clear language" of the *maritime* grant should have excluded inland waters).

4. *Proctor*, a word that means agent and has ecclesiastical overtones, was what an admiralty lawyer was called until the unification of the admiralty rules of procedure with the Federal Rules of Civil Procedure in 1966. See *infra* at 75. Nowadays the Maritime Law Association of the United States uses the term *proctor* as an honorific and has a system of certifying its members' qualifications

DeLovio v. Boit

Circuit Court, D. Mass., 1815
7 Fed. Cas. 418, 2 Gall. 398 (Case No. 3,776)

STORY, Circuit Justice:

This is a libel[5] brought in the district court upon a policy of insurance [that insured a vessel against losses at sea. The district court dismissed the case for lack of subject matter jurisdiction, and the libellant appealed to this court.] * * *

The admiralty is a court of very high antiquity. It has been distinctly traced as early as the reign of Edward the First [1272–1307]. * * * There is strong probability of its existence in the reign of Richard the First [1189–99], since the Laws of Oleron, which were compiled and promulgated by him on his return from the Holy Land, have always been deemed the laws of the admiralty * * *.

What was originally the nature and extent of the jurisdiction of the admiralty cannot now with absolute certainty be known. * * * [But] the forms of its proceedings were borrowed from the civil law, [ ] and the rules by which it was governed, were, as is everywhere avowed, the ancient laws, customs and usages of the seas. [ ] In fact, there can scarcely be the slightest doubt, that the admiralty of England, and the maritime courts of all the other powers of Europe, were formed upon one and the same common model; and that their jurisdiction included the same subjects, as the consular courts of the Mediterranean. * * * [It thus appears that] before and in the reign of Edward the Third [1327–77], the admiralty exercised jurisdiction, 1. Over matters of prize and its incidents. 2. Over torts, injuries, and offences, in ports within the ebb and flow of the tide, on the British seas and on the high seas. 3. Over contracts and other matters regulated and provided for by the Laws of Oleron and other special ordinances, and 4. * * * Over maritime causes in general. * * *

* * *

Such then being the ancient or original jurisdiction of the admiralty, it will be in the next place proper to consider, in what respects it has been altered by statutes and decisions made since the period, of which we have been speaking. [Justice Story went on to discuss two statutes from the reign of Richard II (1377–99). These two statutes were at the center of a struggle for jurisdiction between the common law courts and the admiralty that went on for more than two centuries. The statutes authorized the common law courts to issue writs of prohibition against proceedings in admiralty, and the common law courts used extreme interpretations of the statutes to narrow the admiralty's jurisdiction to the point where little was left, in Justice Story's indignant phrase, beyond "the idle and vain authority to enforce contracts which are made upon the high seas to be executed upon the high seas." Moreover, the common law courts] asserted, that the admiralty has jurisdiction, only when the parties have bound themselves in rem; for, if they have bound themselves personally, its jurisdiction is said to be ousted.

* * *

On the whole, the result of this examination may be summed up in the following propositions. 1. That the jurisdiction of the admiralty, until the statutes of Richard II, extended to all maritime contracts, whether executed at home or abroad, and to all torts,

---

to claim it. Staring, *The Proctor's Dilemma: Certifying Specialties in Admiralty*, 28 J. MAR. L. & COM. 503 (1997).

5. Editors' note: *Libel* was the admiralty term for complaint or petition. The plaintiff was termed the *libellant* or *libelant* and the defendant the *respondent*.

injuries, and offences, on the high seas, and in ports, and havens, as far as the ebb and flow of the tide. 2. That the common law interpretation of these statutes abridges this jurisdiction to things wholly and exclusively done upon the sea. 3. That this interpretation is indefensible, upon principle, and the decisions founded upon it are inconsistent and contradictory. 4. That the [far more plausible] interpretation of the same statutes by the admiralty does not abridge any of its ancient jurisdiction, but leaves to it cognizance of all maritime contracts, and all torts, injuries and offences, upon the high sea, and in ports as far the tide ebbs and flows. 5. That this is the true limit, which upon principle would seem to belong to the admiralty; that it is consistent with the language and intent of the statutes; and is supported by analogous reasoning, and public convenience, and a very considerable weight of authority. 6. That under all the circumstances, the courts of law and of admiralty in England are not so tied down by a uniformity of decisions, that they are not at liberty to entertain the question anew, and to settle the doctrines upon their true principles; and that this opinion is supported by some of the best elementary writers in that kingdom.

But whatever may in England be the binding authority of the common law decisions upon this subject, in the United States we are at liberty to re-examine the doctrines, and to construe the jurisdiction of the admiralty upon enlarged and liberal principles. * * * What is the true interpretation of the [constitutional phrase] "cases of admiralty and maritime jurisdiction?" * * * In all the great maritime nations of Europe, the terms "admiralty jurisdiction" are uniformly applied to the courts exercising jurisdiction over maritime contracts and concerns. [These courts have subject matter jurisdiction over a broad range of marine matters; they] possess[] substantially the same jurisdiction, as the English admiralty in the reign of Edward the Third [1327–77]. * * * [Moreover, it is instructive to examine] the authority and powers of the vice admiralty courts in the United States under the colonial government. In some of the states, and probably in all, the crown established, or reserved to itself the right to establish, admiralty courts; and the nature and the extent of their jurisdictions depended upon the commission of the crown, and upon acts of Parliament conferring additional authorities. The commissions of the crown gave [these vice admiralty courts] a most ample jurisdiction over all maritime contracts, and over torts and injuries, as well in ports as upon the high seas. And acts of parliament enlarged * * * this jurisdiction by giving or confirming cognizance of all seizures for contraventions of the revenue laws. [ ] Tested, therefore, by this exposition, the admiralty jurisdiction of the United States would be as large, as its most strenuous advocates ever contended for.

The clause however of the constitution not only confers admiralty jurisdiction, but the word "maritime" is superadded, seemingly *ex industria* [i.e., designedly], to remove every latent doubt. "Cases of maritime jurisdiction" must include all maritime contracts, torts and injuries, which are in the understanding of the common law, as well as of the admiralty, "causae civiles et maritimae." In this view there is a peculiar propriety in the incorporation of the term "maritime" into the constitution. The disputes and discussions, respecting what the admiralty jurisdiction was, could not but be well known to the framers of that instrument. [ ] One party sought to limit it by locality; another by the subject matter. It was wise, therefore, to dissipate all question by giving cognizance of all "cases of maritime jurisdiction," or, what is precisely equivalent, of all maritime cases. Upon any other construction, the word "maritime" would be mere tautology; but in this sense it has a peculiar and appropriate force. * * * The language of the constitution will therefore warrant the most liberal interpretation; and it may not be unfit to hold, that it had reference to that maritime jurisdiction, which commercial convenience, public policy, and national rights, have contributed to establish, with slight local differences, over all Europe; that jurisdiction, which, under the name of consular courts, first established itself upon the shores of the Mediterranean, and, from the general equity and simplicity of its proceedings, soon commended itself to all the maritime states * * *.

At all events, there is no solid reason for construing the terms of the constitution in a narrow and limited sense, or for ingrafting upon them the restrictions of English statutes, or decisions at common law founded on those statutes, which were sometimes dictated by jealousy, and sometimes by misapprehension, which are often contradictory, and rarely supported by any consistent principle. The advantages resulting to the commerce and navigation of the United States, from a uniformity of rules and decisions in all maritime questions, authorize us to believe that national policy, as well as juridical logic, require the clause of the constitution to be so construed, as to embrace all maritime contracts, torts and injuries, or, in other words, to embrace all those causes, which originally and inherently belonged to the admiralty, before any statutable restriction. * * *

* * *

On the whole, I am, without the slightest hesitation, ready to pronounce, that the delegation of cognizance of "all civil [sic] cases of admiralty and maritime jurisdiction" to the courts of the United States comprehends all maritime contracts, torts, and injuries. The latter branch is necessarily bounded by locality; the former extends over all contracts, (wheresoever they may be made or executed, or whatsoever may be the form of the stipulations,) which relate to the navigation, business or commerce of the sea.

The next inquiry is, what are properly to be deemed "maritime contracts." Happily in this particular there is little room for controversy. All civilians and jurists agree, that in this appellation are included, among other things, charter parties, affreightments, marine hypothecations,[6] contracts for maritime service in the * * * repairing, supplying, and navigating [of] ships; contracts between part owners of ships; contracts and quasi contracts respecting averages, contributions and jettisons; and, what is more material to our present purpose, policies of insurance. [ ] And in point of fact the admiralty courts of other foreign countries have exercised jurisdiction over policies of insurance, as maritime contracts; and a similar claim has been uniformly asserted on the part of the admiralty of England. [ ] There is no more reason why the admiralty should have cognizance of bottomry instruments, as maritime contracts, than of policies of insurance. Both are executed on land, and both intrinsically respect maritime risks, injuries and losses.

My judgment accordingly is, that policies of insurance are within (though not exclusively within) the admiralty and maritime jurisdiction of the United States.[48] I therefore overrule the plea to the jurisdiction * * *.

* * *

6. Editors' note: "Marine hypothecations" were bottomry and respondentia bonds, whereby the master of a vessel in a foreign port could pledge the vessel (bottomry) or the cargo (respondentia) to raise money necessary for the continuation of the voyage.

48. There can be no possible question that the courts of common law have acquired a concurrent jurisdiction, though, upon the principles of the ancient common law, it is not easy to trace a legitimate origin to it.

Notes

1. Justice Story's focus was on the restricted condition of the English admiralty court as of 1789. In 1840—too late to make any appreciable difference in the United States—Parliament restored much of the "natural" jurisdiction of the English admiralty. See generally Wiswall, The Development of Admiralty Jurisdiction and Practice Since 1800 (1970).

2. The *DeLovio* opinion canvasses the most dramatic of the limitations on admiralty jurisdiction that we might have inherited from England. These included a rule limiting the jurisdiction of the admiralty court to actions in rem (against a vessel) and thus not allowing actions in personam (against a shipowner, master, or other person); rules precluding the admiralty court from adjudicating matters arising *infra corpus comitatus* (within the body of a county); similar rules precluding the admiralty court from hearing cases arising on waters that did not show the influence of the tide; a requirement that, to be considered maritime and hence within the admiralty jurisdiction, a contract must be made at sea and call for performance wholly at sea; and rules excluding the admiralty court from hearing cases involving the building of a ship or the sale of a ship. (Another important restriction—one that kept admiralty courts from being able to issue injunctions or provide other equitable remedies—is treated below in Section I-G-8.)

In the United States, the idea that admiralty courts should be restricted to in rem actions got short shrift. See *Manro v. Almeida*, 23 U.S. 473 (1825). As we will see below, the *infra corpus comitatus* and tidewater limitations were also eventually rejected, as was the narrow definition of maritime contracts. But for no good reason the United States adopted and has retained the rules excluding ship-building and ship-sale contracts from admiralty jurisdiction. See *People's Ferry Co. v. Beers*, 61 U.S. 393 (1857) (ship-building contract); *The Ada*, 294 F. 194 (2d Cir. 1918) (ship-sale contract). Nowadays these two anomalies seem entrenched.

The Thomas Jefferson

Supreme Court of the United States, 1825
23 U.S. (10 Wheat.) 428, 6 L. Ed. 358

Mr. Justice STORY delivered the opinion of the unanimous Court.

This is a suit brought in the District Court of Kentucky * * *. The libel claims wages earned on a voyage from Shippingport, in that State, up the river Missouri, and back again to the port of departure;[7] and the question is, whether this case, as stated in the libel, is of admiralty and maritime jurisdiction * * *. The Court below dismissed the libel for want of jurisdiction, and the libellants have appealed from that decree to this Court.

In the great struggles between the Courts of common law and the Admiralty, the latter never attempted to assert any jurisdiction except over maritime contracts. In respect to contracts for the hire of seamen, the Admiralty never pretended to claim, nor could it

7. Editors' note: The 1819 voyage of the 250-ton steamboat *Thomas Jefferson* up the Missouri carried supplies for the Army's Yellowstone exploratory expedition. This was the first such ascent of the Missouri, and it was a financial disaster. Chappell, History of the Missouri River (1905), reported that the steamboat sank on the trip, but that actually happened to a keelboat carrying the cargo farther upstream. Note, *From Judicial Grant to Legislative Power: The Admiralty Clause in the Nineteenth Century* 1214, 1215 (1954).

rightfully exercise any jurisdiction, except in cases where the service was substantially performed, or to be performed, upon the sea, or upon waters within the ebb and flow of the tide. This is the prescribed limit which it was not at liberty to transcend. We say, the service was to be substantially performed on the sea, or on tide water, because there is no doubt that the jurisdiction exists, although the commencement or termination of the voyage may happen to be at some place beyond the reach of the tide. * * * In the present case, the voyage, not only in its commencement and termination, but in all its intermediate progress, was several hundreds of miles above the ebb and flow of the tide; and in no just sense can the wages be considered as earned in a maritime employment.

* * * Whether, under the power to regulate commerce between the States, Congress may not extend the remedy by the summary process of the Admiralty, to the case of voyages on the western waters, it is unnecessary for us to consider. If the public inconvenience, from the want of a process of an analogous nature, shall be extensively felt, the attention of the Legislature will doubtless be drawn to the subject. But we have now only to declare, that the present suit is not maintainable as a cause of admiralty and maritime jurisdiction, upon acknowledged principles of law.

The decree of the [court below], dismissing the libel for want of jurisdiction, is therefore affirmed.

Notes

1. Justice Story's opinion in *Thomas Jefferson* is inconsistent with the tenor and jurisdictional philosophy of the opinion he wrote in *DeLovio*. One explanation of the discrepancy is offered in *The Genesee Chief*, *infra* at 10. Another attempted explanation points to "powerful extra-legal forces playing upon Story and the Court in the 1825 Term," noting that the owners of the steamboat *Thomas Jefferson* were three of the brothers of Senator Richard Johnson of Kentucky, a vigorous opponent of federal jurisdiction. Note, *From Judicial Grant to Legislative Power: The Admiralty Clause in the Nineteenth Century*, 67 Harv. L. Rev. 1214, 1218–19 (1954).

2. *Waring v. Clarke*, 46 U.S. 441 (1847), involved the collision of two steamboats in the Mississippi River near the mouth of Bayou Goula, about 95 miles upriver from New Orleans and 200 river miles from the mouth of the Mississippi. The lower courts found that the influence of the tide could be detected that far upriver and upheld admiralty jurisdiction over the case. The finding that the influence of the tide could be meaningfully discerned at the mouth of Bayou Goula has been ridiculed: "[It was] an occult tide, without ebb or flow." Note, *History of Admiralty Jurisdiction in the Supreme Court of the United States*, 5 Amer. L. Rev. 581, 588 (1871). But the principal issue in the Supreme Court was the argument that, "even if the evidence proved that the collision took place within the ebb and flow of the tide, the [district] court had not jurisdiction, because the locality is *infra corpus comitatus*." A divided Court upheld jurisdiction, holding "that the admiralty jurisdiction of the courts of the United States extends to tide waters, as far as the tide flows, though that may be *infra corpus comitatus*." The Court's explanation for that holding was this:

> We think in the controversy between the courts of admiralty and common law [in England], upon the subject of jurisdiction, that the former have the best of the argument; that they maintain the jurisdiction for which they contend with more learning, more directness of purpose, and without any of that verbal subtilty which is found in the arguments of their adversaries. The conclusions of the admiralty, too, are more congenial with our geographical condition.

Justice Woodbury's opinion for the three *Waring* dissenters was passionately opposed to the perceived expansion of federal power:

> A great principle at the foundation of our political system applies strongly to the present case, and is, that, while supporting all the powers clearly granted to the general government, we ought to forbear interfering with what has been reserved to the States, and, in cases of doubt, to follow where that principle leads, unless prevented by the overruling authority of high judicial decisions. So, under the influence of kindred considerations, in case of supposed improvements or increased convenience by changes of the law, it is an imperative duty on us to let them be made by representatives of the people and the States, through acts of Congress, rather than by judicial legislation. [ ]
>
> * * *
>
> [T]hat same sturdy spirit, which in Magna Charta was unwilling to let the laws of England be changed for a foreign code, proceeded, by the [statutes] of Richard II to denounce and forbid the encroachments of the admirals, and their new forms and code of the civil law, into the bodies of counties and the local business of the realm. It produced those two memorable acts of Parliament, never since departed from * * * except under express statutes, and fixing the limit of jurisdiction for them at the line between the counties and the high seas. And they have ever since retained it there * * * from the highest principles of safety to the common law, English liberties, and the inestimable trial by jury—principles surely no less dear in a republic than a monarchy.[8]

3. It is not too difficult to follow the jury trial and states' rights arguments of the *Waring* dissenters. At this juncture, it may be harder to empathize with the political and cultural overtones of the dissenters' vast respect for the common law and corresponding distrust of "the civil law," by which they meant continental European laws and legal cultures. If may be of use in considering that strand of the debate to remark the scornful tone in which one proponent of expansive admiralty jurisdiction summarized the conflict: "When the admiralty was in its struggle with the common law [in England], ... it was treated as an intruder by a system supposed to be perfect because it began in the woods." Bausman, *Admiralty and Maritime Jurisdiction*, 36 Amer. L. Rev. 182, 183 (1902).

The Genesee Chief v. Fitzhugh

Supreme Court of the United States, 1851
53 U.S. (12 How.) 443, 13 L. Ed. 1058

Mr. Chief Justice TANEY delivered the opinion of the Court.

This is a case of collision on Lake Ontario. The libellants were the owners of the schooner *Cuba*, and the respondents and present appellants the master and owners of the propeller *Genesee Chief*. The libellants state that on the 6th of May, 1847, as the *Cuba* was on her voyage from Sandusky, in the state of Ohio, to Oswego, in the state of New York, the *Genesee Chief*, which was proceeding on a voyage up the lake, ran foul of her and damaged her so seriously that she shortly afterwards sunk, with her cargo on board; and they also allege that the collision was occasioned by the carelessness and mismanagement

8. Justice Daniel's dissent in *Jackson v. Steamboat Magnolia*, 61 U.S. 296, 320–21 (1858), was strikingly close in reasoning and tone to the Woodbury dissent in *Waring*. Indeed, many of the dissents in the early Supreme Court cases expanding admiralty jurisdiction expressed the same general views.

of the officers and crew of the propeller, without any fault of the officers or crew of the *Cuba*. The respondents deny that it was occasioned by the fault of the steamboat, and impute it to the carelessness with which the schooner was managed.

The proceeding is in rem, and in substance as well as in form, a proceeding in admiralty. It was instituted under the [Great Lakes Act] of February 26, 1845 (5 Stat. 726), extending the jurisdiction of the district courts to certain cases upon the lakes and navigable waters connecting the same. [The statute provides:

> The district courts of the United States shall have, possess, and exercise, the same jurisdiction in matters of contract and tort, arising in, upon, or concerning steamboats and other vessels of twenty tons burden and upwards, enrolled and licensed for the coasting trade, and at the time employed in business of commerce and navigation between ports and places in different States and Territories upon the lakes and navigable waters connecting said lakes, as is now possessed and exercised by the said courts in cases of the like steamboats and other vessels employed in navigation and commerce upon the high seas, or tide waters, within the admiralty and maritime jurisdiction of the United States; and in all suits brought in such courts in all such matters of contract or tort, the remedies, and the forms of process, and the modes of proceeding, shall be the same as are or may be used by such courts in cases of admiralty and maritime jurisdiction; and the maritime law of the United States, so far as the same is or may be applicable thereto, shall constitute the rule of decision in such suits, in the same manner, and to the same extent, and with the same equities, as it now does in cases of admiralty and maritime jurisdiction; saving, however, to the parties the right of trial by jury of all facts put in issue in such suits, where either party shall require it; and saving also to the parties the right of a concurrent remedy at the common law, where it is competent to give it, and any concurrent remedy which may be given by the State laws, where such steamer or other vessel is employed in such business of commerce and navigation.[9]]

The District Court decreed in favor of the libellants, and the decision was affirmed in the Circuit Court, from which * * * this appeal has been taken.

Before * * *we can look into the merits of the dispute there is [a] question of jurisdiction which meets us at the threshold. When the act of Congress was passed, under which these proceedings were had, serious doubts were entertained of its constitutionality. The language and decision of this court, whenever a question of admiralty jurisdiction had come before it, seemed to imply that under the Constitution of the United States, the jurisdiction was confined to tidewaters. Yet the conviction that this definition of admiralty powers was narrower than the Constitution contemplated, has been growing stronger every day with the growing commerce on the lakes and navigable rivers of the western states. And the difficulties which the language and decisions of this court had thrown in the way, of extending it to these waters, have perhaps led to the inquiry whether the law in question could not be supported under the power granted to Congress to regulate commerce. * * *

The law, however, contains no regulations of commerce; nor any provision in relation to shipping and navigation on the lakes. It merely confers a new jurisdiction on the district

9. Editors' note: Justice Story drafted this statute. Early in 1845 he submitted the draft to all of the Supreme Court justices then in Washington for their comments, and then "sent the bill to Congress, where it was approved in six days. Lame-duck President Tyler signed the measure on February 26, 1845." D. Robertson, Admiralty and Federalism 112 (1970). Justice Story died later that year.

courts; and this is its only object and purpose. * * * It is evident * * * from the title ["an act extending the jurisdiction of the district courts to certain cases upon the lakes and navigable waters connecting the same"] as well as the body of the law, that Congress, in passing it, did not intend to exercise their power to regulate commerce; nor to derive their authority from that article of the Constitution. * * *

* * *

Nor can the jurisdiction of the courts of the United States be made to depend on regulations of commerce. They are entirely distinct things, having no necessary connection with one another, and are conferred in the Constitution by separate and distinct grants. The extent of the judicial power is carefully defined and limited, and Congress cannot enlarge it to suit even the wants of commerce * * *. [T]he limits fixed by the Constitution to the judicial authority of the courts of the United States, would form an insuperable objection to this law, if its validity depended upon the commercial power.

* * *

If this law, therefore, is constitutional, it must be supported on the ground that the lakes and navigable waters connecting them are within the scope of admiralty and maritime jurisdiction, as known and understood in the United States when the Constitution was adopted.

If the meaning of these terms was now for the first time brought before this court for consideration, there could, we think, be no hesitation in saying that the lakes and their connecting waters were embraced in them. These lakes are in truth inland seas. Different states border on them on one side, and a foreign nation on the other. A great and growing commerce is carried on upon them between different states and a foreign nation, which is subject to all the incidents and hazards that attend commerce on the ocean. Hostile fleets have encountered on them, and prizes been made; and every reason which existed for the grant of admiralty jurisdiction to the general government on the Atlantic seas, applies with equal force to the lakes.

* * *

The only objection made to this jurisdiction is that there is no tide in the lakes or the waters connecting them; and it is said that the admiralty and maritime jurisdiction, as known and understood in England and this country at the time the Constitution was adopted, was confined to the ebb and flow of the tide.

Now there is certainly nothing in the ebb and flow of the tide that makes the waters peculiarly suitable for admiralty jurisdiction, nor any thing in the absence of a tide that renders it unfit. If it is a public navigable water, on which commerce is carried on between different states or nations, the reason for the jurisdiction is precisely the same. * * *

In England, undoubtedly the writers upon the subject, and the decisions in its courts of admiralty, always speak of the jurisdiction as confined to tidewater. And this definition in England was a sound and reasonable one, because there was no navigable stream in the country beyond the ebb and flow of the tide * * *.

At the time the Constitution of the United States was adopted, and our courts of admiralty went into operation, the definition which had been adopted in England was equally proper here. In the old thirteen states the far greater part of the navigable waters are tidewaters. And in the states which were at that period in any degree commercial, and where courts of admiralty were called on to exercise their jurisdiction, every public river was tidewater to the head of navigation. And, indeed, until the discovery of steamboats, there could be nothing like foreign commerce upon waters with an unchanging current resisting the upward passage. The courts of the United States, therefore, naturally adopted the English mode of defining a public river, and consequently the boundary of admiralty jurisdiction. It measured it by tidewater. And that definition having found its way into our courts, became, after a time, the familiar mode of describing a public river, and was repeated, as cases occurred, without particularly examining whether it was as universally applicable in this country as it was in England. * * * It was under the influence of these precedents and this usage, that the case of *The Thomas Jefferson* [*supra* at 8] was decided in this court; and the jurisdiction of the courts of admiralty of the United States declared to be limited to the ebb and flow of the tide. * * *

It is the decision in the case of *The Thomas Jefferson* which mainly embarrasses the court in the present inquiry. We are sensible of the great weight to which it is entitled. But at the same time we are convinced that, if we follow it, we follow an erroneous decision into which the court fell, when the great importance of the question as it now presents itself could not be foreseen; and the subject did not therefore receive that deliberate consideration which at this time would have been given to it by the eminent men who presided here when that case was decided. For the decision was made in 1825, when the commerce on the rivers of the west and on the lakes was in its infancy, and of little importance, and but little regarded compared with that of the present day.

* * *

It is evident that a definition that would at this day limit public rivers in this country to tidewater rivers is utterly inadmissible. We have thousands of miles of public navigable water, including lakes and rivers in which there is no tide. And certainly there can be no reason for admiralty power over a public tidewater, which does not apply with equal force to any other public water used for commercial purposes and foreign trade. The lakes and the waters connecting them are undoubtedly public waters; and we think [they] are within the grant of admiralty and maritime jurisdiction in the Constitution of the United States.

* * *

* * * [A]s we are convinced that [*The Thomas Jefferson*] was founded in error, and that the error, if not corrected, must produce serious public as well as private inconvenience and loss, it becomes our duty not to perpetuate it.

* * *

The decree of the Circuit Court must therefore be affirmed with costs.

Note

Justice Daniel was the only dissenter.

The Eagle

Supreme Court of the United States, 1868
75 U.S. (8 Wall.) 15, 19 L. Ed. 365

Mr. Justice NELSON delivered the opinion of the unanimous Court.

[The tug *Eagle*, towing a brig and a barge, grounded the brig on a shoal in the Detroit River, causing the barge to collide with the grounded brig. The brig was on a voyage from Saginaw, Michigan, to Buffalo, New York, when the accident occurred. The owners of the brig filed a libel in the United States District Court for the Eastern District of Michigan against both the tug and the barge. The district court held the tug liable and exonerated the barge. The circuit court affirmed. The case came to the Supreme Court limited to the issue of the district court's subject matter jurisdiction. The tug argued that jurisdiction was lacking because there were no allegations and no evidence that the tug was "enrolled and licensed for the coasting trade," nor was it shown to be engaged in interstate towage. Instead, it towed "from the lower end of Lake Huron to the upper end of Lake Erie. Both termini are within the waters of the State of Michigan."]

[The argument] that the case was not brought within the requirements of the [Great Lakes Act] of 1845, so as to give the District Court jurisdiction [is] untenable.

This act of 1845 * * * has occasioned a good deal of embarrassment * * *. It is quite clear, under [*The Genesee Chief* that] in the absence of that act, the district courts would possess general jurisdiction in admiralty over the lakes, and the waters connecting them; and, hence, there would be no more difficulty in the administration of the law than in cases upon the high seas, or bays, or rivers navigable from the sea.

At the time [the 1845 act]was passed, tidewater was the limit of admiralty jurisdiction, and the act was intended to remove this restriction upon the court, as it respected these lakes, and to extend the jurisdiction to them, thereby making these waters an exception as to the tidewater limit. The power conferred by the act, however, was not that of general admiralty jurisdiction, but was limited to cases of "contract and tort, arising in, upon, or concerning steamboats, and other vessels, of twenty tons burden and upwards, enrolled and licensed for the coasting trade, and at the time employed in the business of commerce and navigation between ports and places of different States." The better opinion, we think, is, that the act does not embrace, but necessarily excludes, cases of prize. These are neither cases of contract or tort, and the vessels engaged in making the seizure, as prize of war, which are ships of the navy, or privateers, are not employed at the time, in the business of commerce and navigation. We think it also a matter of grave doubt if the act confers jurisdiction in cases of salvage, jettison, or general average. These are not matters of contract, according to the most eminent commentators on the subject, and they certainly are not cases of tort.

[The question is] whether, since the decision of *The Genesee Chief*, which opens the lakes and the waters connecting them to the general jurisdiction of the district courts in admiralty, they can entertain this jurisdiction in cases outside of that conferred by [the 1845 act]. * * *

The history and operation of this act of 1845 are peculiar. It is "an act extending the jurisdiction of the district courts to certain cases upon the lakes and navigable waters connecting the same." At the time it was enacted it had the effect expressed and intended, and so continued for some seven years, when the case of *The Genesee Chief* was decided. From that time, its effect ceased as an enabling act; and has been no longer regarded as such. It is no longer considered by this court as conferring any jurisdiction in admiralty upon the district courts over the lakes, or the waters connecting them. That is regarded as having been conferred by the grant of general admiralty jurisdiction by the ninth section of the act of 1789 to these courts. The original purpose of the [1845] act, therefore, has ceased, and is of no effect; and, in order to give it any, instead of construing it as extending the jurisdiction in admiralty, it must be construed as limiting it—the very reverse of its object and intent, as expressed on its face. * * *

[W]e are satisfied, that since the decision of the case of *The Genesee Chief*, the court must regard the district courts as having conferred upon them a general jurisdiction in admiralty upon the lakes and the waters connecting them, by the ninth section of the original act of 1789; and the enabling act of 1845, therefore, has become inoperative and ineffectual as a grant of jurisdiction; and, as it was an act, on the face of it, and as intended, in its purpose and effect, to extend the admiralty jurisdiction to these waters, we cannot, without utterly disregarding this purpose and intent, give effect to it as a limitation or restriction upon it. We must, therefore, regard it as obsolete and of no effect, with the exception of the clause which gives to either party the right of trial by jury when requested * * *.

Notes

1. A remnant of the Great Lakes statute of 1845 is still on the books. 28 U.S.C. § 1873 provides:

> In any case of admiralty and maritime jurisdiction relating to any matter of contract or tort arising upon or concerning any vessel of twenty tons or upward, enrolled and licensed for the coasting trade, and employed in the business of commerce and navigation between places in different states upon the lakes and navigable waters connecting said lakes, the trial of all issues of fact shall be by jury if either party demands it.

2. The story that unfolds in the foregoing cases has its technical fascinations, but do not forget that it was a hotly political story as well. It implicated state and local rights and interests, the revered institution of the jury, and tensions between the legal cultural values of the common versus the civilian law. It had potential impact on a 19th century economic competition between water and land transportation and on disputes about the rate structures on state-owned and operated canals. See Stolz, *Pleasure Boating and Admiralty: Erie at Sea*, 51 CAL. L. REV. 661, 675 n.54 (1963). And some analysts have sought to demonstrate that the admiralty jurisdictional struggle both reflected and affected the pervasive and corrosive ferment over the issue of slavery. See Stolz at 671–83.

B. The "Navigable Waters" Issue

The tidewater restriction is gone, but admiralty jurisdiction does not exist unless the matter in suit had a sufficient involvement with waters that are *navigable*. In a wide variety of other contexts as well, courts frequently confront the issue of whether a particular body of water is to be regarded as navigable for some particular legal purpose.[1] It may seem obvious that the term "navigable" will have a different meaning—i.e., that the test for navigability will be different—in different contexts.[2] But that truism is sometimes overlooked in the busy world of legal practice. "For if in this stage of our jurisprudential development it is no longer necessary to assert that the same words may have different

---

1. *Kaiser Aetna v. United States*, 444 U.S. 164, 171–72 (1979), provided four examples of contexts giving rise to navigability issues—the federal navigational servitude, Congress' regulatory authority under the Commerce Clause, the authority of the Corps of Engineers under the Rivers and Harbors Appropriation Act of 1899, and admiralty jurisdiction. See also *PPL Montana, LLC v. Montana*, 132 S. Ct. 1215 (2012) (treating navigability concepts relevant to issues of state title to riverbeds and Federal Energy Regulatory Commission licensing of hydroelectric dams). Both cases emphasize that the criteria for navigability will properly differ from context to context.

2. "[The] assumption that the same verbal form means the same thing wherever it is used [is] false to everyday life...." Black, *Admiralty Jurisdiction: Critique and Suggestions*, 50 COLUM. L. REV. 259, 274 (1950).

meanings in different contexts, the fact remains that there is still a tendency on the part of the bench and the bar to ignore the obvious and to carry over the meaning given to a phrase in one situation to solve problems which are entirely distinct."[3]

LeBlanc v. Cleveland

United States Court of Appeals, Second Circuit, 1999
198 F.3d 353, 2000 AMC 609

PARKER, Circuit Judge:

On July 4, 1994, Etoile LeBlanc and Stephen Ossen suffered personal injuries when the kayak they were paddling on the Hudson River was struck by a recreational motor boat operated by Terry Cleveland and owned by Robert Grant. LeBlanc and Ossen had rented their kayak from JRD Retailers, Ltd., d/b/a Syd & Dusty's Outfitters ("JRD"). The collision occurred approximately 29 miles upstream of Fort Edward, near Lake Luzerne.

On March 29, 1995, LeBlanc and Ossen sued Grant and Cleveland * * *, invoking federal admiralty jurisdiction. They alleged that Grant and Cleveland negligently caused the collision and their resulting injuries. * * * Cleveland and Grant then brought third-party complaints against JRD. Pursuant to Rule 14(c) of the Federal Rules of Civil Procedure, these third-party complaints allowed the case to proceed as if LeBlanc and Ossen had sued JRD as well as Cleveland and Grant.

On July 22, 1997, JRD moved to dismiss the complaint filed by LeBlanc and Ossen for lack of subject matter jurisdiction. See Fed. R. Civ. P. 12(b)(1). On October 1, 1997, the district court granted the motion, finding that the Hudson River is not "navigable in fact" at the location at which the accident took place and that, consequently, the court lacked admiralty jurisdiction over the lawsuit. The court acknowledged that the Hudson River below Fort Edward is a navigable waterway because it permits passage to the open sea. Nonetheless, the court found that the "part of the Hudson [where the accident took place] cannot ... be accessed from Fort Edward due to the presence of numerous areas of rapids, ... [nine] dams, and at least three major waterfalls of 30 feet or more in height." As a result, the court concluded that "[n]othing in the records suggests that the Hudson north of Fort Edward is now, or has ever been, an artery of maritime commerce" sufficient to support a finding of navigability necessary to the exercise of federal admiralty jurisdiction. LeBlanc and Ossen timely appealed.

* * *

Appellants first contend that the district court applied an incorrect legal standard in finding admiralty jurisdiction lacking. Specifically, they argue for a jurisdictional test that focuses on the historic navigability of the waterway in question, without reference to present-day artificial obstructions, rather than on its contemporary navigability, including artificial dams. Under an historic navigability test, the argument continues, the district court erred in refusing to take into account the fact that, prior to 1951 and before the construction of several impassable dams, the logging industry regularly used the Hudson River upstream of Fort Edward to float logs to timber mills. For the reasons discussed below, appellants' argument fails.

* * *

---

3. Kurland, *The Romero Case and Some Problems of Federal Jurisdiction*, 73 Harv. L. Rev. 817, 834 (1960).

The district court, like virtually every other court to consider the question of navigability for admiralty jurisdiction purposes, applied the definition of navigable waters first articulated in *The Daniel Ball*, 77 U.S. 557 (1870):

> Those rivers must be regarded as public navigable rivers in law which are navigable in fact. And they are navigable in fact when they are used, or are susceptible of being used, in their ordinary condition, as highways for commerce, over which trade and travel are or may be conducted in the customary modes of trade and travel on water. And they constitute navigable waters of the United States within the meaning of the acts of Congress, in contradistinction from the navigable waters of the States, when they form in their ordinary condition by themselves, or by uniting with other waters, a continued highway over which commerce is or may be carried on with other States or foreign countries in the customary modes in which such commerce is conducted by water.

* * * The district court found, and the parties did not dispute, that the Hudson River downstream of Fort Edward can be and is used as a continuous highway for interstate commerce because it permits passage beyond New York both to the south, where it empties into the Atlantic, and to the north, via the Champlain Canal (which begins near Fort Edward) and the St. Lawrence. However, the court found that the accident site is separated from Fort Edward, and therefore from any interstate or international waterway, by numerous impassable rapids, falls, and artificial dams.

Appellants do not dispute that *The Daniel Ball* sets forth the basic navigability test for purposes of admiralty jurisdiction. Instead, they first contend that by focusing on whether rivers are navigable "in their ordinary condition," the *Daniel Ball* test required the district court to measure navigability by reference to the river's historic, unimproved state, rather than its present, improved state.

This argument is foreclosed by subsequent Supreme Court caselaw. In *United States v. Appalachian Electric Power Co.*, 311 U.S. 377, 407 (1940), the Court found that "ordinary condition" as used in *The Daniel Ball* refers not to the absence of human interference with the course of the river, but "to volume of water, the gradients and the regularity of the flow" of the waterway. [ ] Thus, under the *Daniel Ball* test, an otherwise unnavigable river may not be rendered navigable simply because, in extraordinary conditions, its waters rise high enough to support forms of transportation normally impossible. 1 STEVEN F. FRIEDELL, BENEDICT ON ADMIRALTY § 142, at 9-6 (7th ed. 1998) ("It is not enough that a fishing skiff or gunning canoe can be made to float at high water ... or that logs, poles and rafts are floated down in high waters."). But nothing in *The Daniel Ball* indicates that an historically navigable river remains navigable for admiralty jurisdiction purposes when it is made impassable by an artificial obstruction.

Perhaps recognizing that their interpretation of *The Daniel Ball* lacks legal support, appellants next rely on *The Montello*, 87 U.S. 430 (1874), claiming that it "refined" the *Daniel Ball* test discussed above. In *The Montello*, the Supreme Court was called upon to determine whether Congress had the authority under the Commerce Clause to regulate steamships plying the waters of Wisconsin's Fox River. Congress's power to regulate activity on the Fox River turned on whether the river was navigable. Setting forth the standard of navigability applicable in this context, the Court wrote:

> The capability of use by the public for purposes of transportation and commerce affords the true criterion of the navigability of a river, rather than the extent and manner of that use. If it be capable in its natural state of being used for purposes

> of commerce, no matter in what mode the commerce may be conducted, it is navigable in fact, and becomes in law a public river or highway. [ ]

Appellants contend that by referencing the "natural state" of the river in question, the *Montello* Court made clear that navigability should be judged without reference to artificial obstructions. Indeed, the Supreme Court has since specifically held that, for purposes of defining Congress's power to regulate under the Commerce Clause, an otherwise navigable river cannot be rendered unnavigable by the construction of artificial dams. See, e.g., *Economy Light & Power Co. v. United States*, 256 U.S. 113, 123 (1921).

Nonetheless, appellants' reliance on *The Montello* and its progeny is misplaced. As noted above, *The Montello* did not define navigable waters for purposes of establishing the limits of admiralty jurisdiction; instead, it defined navigable waters for the purpose of delimiting Congress's power to regulate under the Commerce Clause. * * * Careful appraisal of the purposes for which the *Montello* Court invoked the concept of navigability reveals that the same definition should not be used to determine the limits of the federal judicial power under Article III or 28 U.S.C. § 1331(1). As the Ninth Circuit put it [in *Adams v. Montana Power Co.*, 528 F.2d 437, 440–41 (9th Cir. 1975)]:

> The definitions of navigability may vary because, as in the present case, the purposes served by the commerce clause and admiralty jurisdiction may vary. Congress's commerce power is designed in part to preserve and protect the nation's waterways which, in their natural condition, are navigable in interstate commerce. By virtue of this power, Congress may prevent or regulate obstruction of these waterways by the states through which they pass. The damming of a previously navigable waterway by a state cannot divest Congress of its control over a potentially useful artery of commerce, since such obstructions may always be removed. Hence the courts have reasonably held that a navigable river is not rendered non-navigable by artificial obstruction.
>
> However, if the damming of a waterway has the practical effect of eliminating commercial maritime activity, no federal interest is served by the exercise of admiralty jurisdiction over the events transpiring on that body of water, whether or not it was originally navigable. No purpose is served by application of a uniform body of federal law, on waters devoid of trade and commerce, to regulate the activities and resolve the disputes of pleasure boaters. Only the burdening of federal courts and the frustrating of the purposes of state tort law would be thereby served.

Recognizing the distinction between legislative authority under the Commerce Clause and admiralty jurisdiction, every circuit court to confront the question has rejected the historic navigability jurisdictional test when determining admiralty jurisdiction. * * *

As their final argument in favor of an historic navigability standard, appellants point us to *Adirondack League Club, Inc. v. Sierra Club*, 706 N.E.2d 1192 (N.Y. 1998). In *Adirondack League*, the New York Court of Appeals used an historic navigability standard for the purpose of identifying those "waterways [that] are of such practical utility that private ownership from the time of the original grant from the State or sovereign is subject to an easement for public travel." [ ] *Adirondack League*, of course, had nothing whatsoever to do with admiralty jurisdiction in the federal courts. Moreover, to state the purpose for which *Adirondack League* utilized the historic navigability standard is to distinguish it from the purpose admiralty jurisdiction serves. By its very nature, the process of determining which waterways are subject to public easements dating from a land grant by the State requires an historic navigability standard; under a contemporary navigability standard, the present-day owner of riparian rights could defeat a public easement merely by erecting an impassable obstacle in the waterway. This, of course, would defeat the purpose of the public easement doctrine. In contrast, and as discussed above, the purpose of federal admiralty jurisdiction is best served if the test for navigability is determined with reference to present-day artificial obstructions.

Thus, in light of the policies served by federal admiralty jurisdiction, we hold that a waterway at the situs in issue is navigable for jurisdictional purposes if it is presently used, or is presently capable of being used, as an interstate highway for commercial trade or travel in the customary modes of travel on water. Natural and artificial obstructions that effectively prohibit such commerce defeat admiralty jurisdiction.

* * *

Notes

1. In the trial court, 979 F. Supp. 142 (N.D.N.Y. 1998), most of the evidence of the river's condition above Fort Edward came from a document the court cited as Army Corps of Engineers, *Determination of Navigability for Hudson River, New York* (May 21, 1975). The parties did not dispute that the river was navigable below Fort Edward, and the court remarked that "[i]ndeed, large vessels are often visible from the windows of the court's chambers plying the Hudson en route to points north and south of Albany."

2. *Lockheed Martin Corp. v. Morganti*, 412 F.3d 407, 409–13 (2d Cir. 2005), relied on the *LeBlanc* analysis to hold that Cayuga Lake, New York, is "navigable waters of the United States" as that term is used in the Longshore and Harbor Workers' Compensation Act, 33 U.S.C. § 903(a). "Cayuga Lake is one of the finger lakes of Central New York, and is connected at its north end to the Erie Canal system, which means that a boat can theoretically sail from Cayuga Lake to any ocean-connected port in the world. * * * [Lockheed argues] that the topography of Cayuga Lake and the economic conditions of the surrounding area make commercial shipping unprofitable, and that the lake is therefore not susceptible of being used for commercial shipping, and thus is not navigable. * * * In [*LeBlanc*] we focused on the federal interest in ensuring that events on the waterway in question were governed by a uniform body of law. In the instant case, where the waterway is not physically obstructed but only economically inactive, the federal interest remains. Because Cayuga Lake is physically capable of supporting shipping, it is possible at any time for an interstate commercial vessel to enter the lake. * * * If we were now to withdraw federal jurisdiction from Cayuga Lake, we would have to extend it again the moment that an interstate commercial ship entered the lake. In contrast, basing such jurisdictional changes on major events like damming or other physical alterations that make it physically impossible for a commercial vessel to travel on the waterway presents few difficulties."

3. In *The Daniel Ball*, the issue was not admiralty jurisdiction but the meaning of the term "navigable waters of the United States" in a statute requiring steamboats to submit to federal inspection and licensing. Nevertheless, the Court's language has long been "the accepted definition of navigable waters for the purpose of determining admiralty jurisdiction." MARAIST, GALLIGAN & MARAIST, ADMIRALTY IN A NUTSHELL 22 (6th ed. 2010).

4. The key sentence of *The Daniel Ball* discussed what "constitute[d] navigable waters of the United States." The "of the United States" qualifier appeared in the Court's language because it appeared in the statute the Court was construing. The qualifier has no legitimate

role on the issue of subject matter jurisdiction in admiralty, which extends to the high seas as well as to the territorial waters of other countries. See, e.g., *Sanchez v. Loffland Brothers Co.*, 626 F.2d 1228 (5th Cir. 1980) (exercising admiralty jurisdiction over an action arising from an accident on a vessel in Lake Maracaibo, Venezuela). Cases like *Dunham v. Hotelera Canco S.A.*, 933 F. Supp. 543, 547 (E.D. Va. 1996)—in which the court denied admiralty jurisdiction over an accident in Mexican territorial waters because it did not occur on "navigable waters of the United States"—are aberrations.

5. The *LeBlanc* court's test—present capability "of being used as an interstate highway for commercial trade or travel in the customary modes of travel on water"—leaves it somewhat indefinite what "commercial" and "customary" mean, *viz.*, how big the notional commercial boats must be. *Lynch v. McFarland*, 808 F. Supp. 559, 563 (W.D. Ky. 1992), held that a "trickle" that might "at best" accommodate canoe and raft traffic (between Kentucky and Tennessee) was not enough. *Tundidor v. Miami-Dade County*, 831 F.3d 1328 (11th Cir. 2016), held that a water control structure was enough to keep a canal from being navigable even though portage around the structure was feasible and indeed had easily been done on occasion.

6. The court's statement that navigability during "extraordinary [high water] conditions" does not qualify a body of water for admiralty jurisdiction refers to waters on which "transportation [is] normally impossible." Conversely, seasonal nonnavigability does not defeat a body of water's general navigability status. *Sanders v. Placid Oil Co.*, 611 F. Supp. 841 (W.D. La. 1985), *aff'd*, 861 F.2d 1374 (5th Cir. 1988), held that Catahoula Lake, Louisiana, qualifies as navigable because during some high-water seasons one could take a sizable boat from the lake into the Black River and thence eventually to the Gulf of Mexico. The court noted that bodies of water that freeze in winter (e.g., parts of the Great Lakes) do not thereby lose their navigability status. By the same token, drying up in summer should not necessarily defeat navigability status.

C. The "Vessel" Issue

Like the navigable waters issue, the issue of what constitutes a *vessel* pervades admiralty and maritime law. Examples of questions implicating the criteria for vessel status include the following: (a) The Admiralty Extension Act, 46 U.S.C. § 30101, extends the federal courts' admiralty jurisdiction over "cases of injury or damage, to person or property, caused by a vessel on navigable water." (b) Neither a maritime lien nor a preferred ship mortgage can attach to tangible property that is not a vessel (or cargo). (c) The "owner of a vessel" benefits from a unique right of Limitation of Vessel Owner's Liability, 46 U.S.C. § 30505. (d) The personal injury doctrines available to seamen—the Jones Act, 46 U.S.C. § 30104, and the maritime common-law doctrines of unseaworthiness and maintenance and cure—require the injured worker to establish that he or she was a member of a crew of a vessel. (e) A worker who is "a member of a crew of any vessel" is not entitled to workers' compensation under the Longshore and Harbor Workers' Compensation Act, 33 U.S.C. § 902(3)(G).

Until the *Stewart* decision, it was generally thought that criteria for vessel status could properly differ from context to context. *Stewart* was a sea change. In contrast, *Lozman* is best regarded as tinkering at the margins of the vessel status issue.

Stewart v. Dutra Construction Co.

Supreme Court of the United States, 2005
543 U.S. 481, 125 S. Ct. 118, 160 L. Ed. 2d 932, 2005 AMC 609

Justice THOMAS delivered the opinion of the unanimous Court.[1]

The question in this case is whether a dredge is a "vessel" under § 2(3)(G) of the Longshore and Harbor Workers' Compensation Act (LHWCA), 33 U.S.C. § 902(3)(G). We hold that it is.

I.

As part of Boston's Central Artery/Tunnel Project, or "Big Dig," the Commonwealth of Massachusetts undertook to extend the Massachusetts Turnpike through a tunnel running beneath South Boston and Boston Harbor to Logan Airport. The Commonwealth employed respondent Dutra Construction Company to assist in that undertaking. At the time, Dutra owned the world's largest dredge, the *Super Scoop*, which was capable of digging the 50-foot-deep, 100-foot-wide, three-quarter-mile-long trench beneath Boston Harbor that is now the Ted Williams Tunnel.

The *Super Scoop* is a massive floating platform from which a clamshell bucket is suspended beneath the water. The bucket removes silt from the ocean floor and dumps the sediment onto one of two scows that float alongside the dredge. The *Super Scoop* has certain characteristics common to seagoing vessels, such as a captain and crew, navigational lights, ballast tanks, and a crew dining area. But it lacks others. Most conspicuously, the *Super Scoop* has only limited means of self-propulsion. It is moved long distances by tugboat. (To work on the Big Dig, it was towed from its home base in California through the Panama Canal and up the eastern seaboard to Boston Harbor.) It navigates short distances by manipulating its anchors and cables. When dredging the Boston Harbor trench, it typically moved in this way once every couple of hours, covering a distance of 30-to-50 feet each time.

Dutra hired petitioner Willard Stewart, a marine engineer, to maintain the mechanical systems on the *Super Scoop* during its dredging of the harbor. At the time of Stewart's accident, the *Super Scoop* lay idle because one of its scows, Scow No. 4, had suffered an engine malfunction and the other was at sea. Stewart was on board Scow No. 4, feeding wires through an open hatch located about 10 feet above the engine area. While Stewart was perched beside the hatch, the *Super Scoop* used its bucket to move the scow. In the process, the scow collided with the *Super Scoop*, causing a jolt that plunged Stewart headfirst through the hatch to the deck below. He was seriously injured.

Stewart sued Dutra in the United States District Court for the District of Massachusetts under the Jones Act [46 U.S.C. § 30104], alleging that he was a seaman injured by Dutra's negligence. * * *

Dutra moved for summary judgment * * *, arguing that Stewart was not a seaman. The company acknowledged that Stewart was "a member of the [*Super Scoop's*] crew," that he spent "[n]inety-nine percent of his time while on the job" aboard the *Super Scoop*, and that his "duties contributed to the function" of the *Super Scoop*. Dutra argued only that the *Super Scoop* was not a vessel for purposes of the Jones Act. Dutra pointed to the Court of Appeals' en banc decision in *DiGiovanni v. Traylor Brothers, Inc.*, 959 F.2d 1119 (1st Cir. 1992), which held that "if a barge or other float's purpose or primary business

1. Editors' note: Chief Justice Rehnquist did not participate.

is *not* navigation or commerce, then workers assigned thereto for its shore enterprise are to be considered seamen only when it is in actual navigation or transit" at the time of the plaintiff's injury. The District Court granted summary judgment to Dutra, because the *Super Scoop*'s primary purpose was dredging rather than transportation and because it was stationary at the time of Stewart's injury. * * * [T]he Court of Appeals affirmed * * *.

* * *

II.

Prior to the passage of the Jones Act, general maritime law usually entitled a seaman who fell sick or was injured both to maintenance and cure (or the right to be cared for and paid wages during the voyage) [ ], and to damages for any "injuries received in consequence of the unseaworthiness of the ship" [ ]. Suits against shipowners for negligence, however, were barred. * * * Congress enacted the Jones Act [46 U.S.C. §30104] in 1920 to remove this bar to negligence suits by seamen [ ]. * * * Although the statute is silent on who is a "seaman," both the maritime law backdrop against which Congress enacted the Jones Act and Congress' subsequent enactments provide some guidance.

First, "seaman" is a term of art that had an established meaning under general maritime law. We have thus presumed that when the [1920 Congress created a negligence cause of action for "a seaman injured in the course of employment"], Congress took the term "seaman" as the general maritime law found it. [ ]

Second, Congress provided further guidance in 1927 when it enacted the LHWCA, which provides scheduled compensation to land-based maritime workers but which also excepts from its coverage "a master or member of a crew of any vessel." 33 U.S.C. §902(3)(G). This exception is simply "a refinement of the term 'seaman' in the Jones Act." *McDermott Int'l, Inc. v. Wilander*, 498 U.S. 337, 347 (1991). Thus the Jones Act and the LHWCA are complementary regimes that work in tandem: The Jones Act provides tort remedies to *sea*-based maritime workers, while the LHWCA provides workers' compensation to *land*-based maritime employees. [ ]

Still, discerning the contours of "seaman" status, even with the general maritime law and the LHWCA's language as aids to interpretation, has not been easy. [ ] We began clarifying the definition of "seaman" in a pair of cases, *McDermott Int'l, Inc. v. Wilander*, *supra*, and *Chandris, Inc. v. Latsis*, 515 U.S. 347 (1995) [*infra* at 189], that addressed the relationship a worker must have to a vessel in order to be a "master or member" of its crew. We now turn to the other half of the LHWCA's equation: how to determine whether a watercraft is a "vessel."

A.

Just as Congress did not define the term "seaman" in the Jones Act, it did not define the term "vessel" in the LHWCA itself. However, Congress provided a definition elsewhere. At the time of the LHWCA's enactment, §§1 and 3 of the Revised Statutes of 1873 specified:

> In determining the meaning of the revised statutes, or of any act or resolution of Congress passed subsequent to [Feb. 25, 1871, the] word "vessel" includes every description of water-craft or other artificial contrivance used, or capable of being used, as a means of transportation on water.

Sections 1 and 3 show that, because the LHWCA is an Act of Congress passed after February 25, 1871, the LHWCA's use of the term "vessel" "includes every description of water-craft or other artificial contrivance used, or capable of being used, as a means of transportation on water."

Section 3's definition, * * * recodified in 1947 as part of the Rules of Construction Act, 1 U.S.C. § 3, has remained virtually unchanged from 1873 to the present. Even now, § 3 continues to supply the default definition of "vessel" throughout the U.S. Code, "unless the context indicates otherwise." 1 U.S.C. § 1. The context surrounding the LHWCA's enactment indicates that § 3 defines the term "vessel" for purposes of the LHWCA.

Section 3 merely codified the meaning that the term "vessel" had acquired in general maritime law. *See* 1 S. Friedell, Benedict on Admiralty § 165 (rev. 7th ed. 2004). In the decades following its enactment, § 3 was regularly used to define the term "vessel" in maritime jurisprudence. Taking only the issue presented here—whether a dredge is a vessel—prior to passage of the Jones Act and the LHWCA, courts often used § 3's definition to conclude that dredges were vessels.

* * *

These early cases show that at the time Congress enacted the Jones Act and the LHWCA in the 1920's, it was settled that § 3 defined the term "vessel" for purposes of those statutes. It was also settled that a structure's status as a vessel under § 3 depended on whether the structure was a means of maritime transportation. [ ] For then, as now, dredges served a waterborne transportation function, since in performing their work they carried machinery, equipment, and crew over water.

* * *

B.

* * * Dutra argues that the Court * * * implicitly narrowed § 3's definition * * * in a pair of cases * * * holding that a drydock [*Cope v. Vallette Dry Dock Co.*, 119 U.S. 625, 630 (1887)] and a wharfboat attached to the mainland [*Evansville & Bowling Green Packet Co. v. Chero Cola Bottling Co.*, 271 U.S. 19, 22 (1926)] were not vessels under § 3, because they were not *practically* capable of being used to transport people, freight, or cargo from place to place. According to Dutra, *Cope* and *Evansville* adopted a definition of "vessel" narrower than § 3's text.

Dutra misreads *Cope* and *Evansville.* In *Cope*, the plaintiff sought a salvage award for having prevented a drydock from sinking after a steamship collided with it.[2] At the time of the accident, the drydock, a floating dock used for repairing vessels, was "moored and lying at [the] usual place" it had occupied for the past 20 years. In those circumstances, the drydock was a "fixed structure" that had been "permanently moored," rather than a vessel that had been temporarily anchored. *Evansville* involved a wharfboat secured by cables to the mainland. Local water, electricity, and telephone lines all ran from shore to the wharfboat, evincing a "permanent location." And the wharfboat, like the drydock in *Cope*, was neither "taken from place to place" nor "used to carry freight from one place to another." As in *Cope*, the Court concluded that the wharfboat "was not practically capable of being used as a means of transportation."[3]

Cope and *Evansville* did no more than construe § 3 in light of the distinction drawn by the general maritime law between watercraft temporarily stationed in a particular location and those permanently affixed to shore or resting on the ocean floor. [ ] Simply

2. Editors' note: Gilmore & Black, The Law of Admiralty 538–541 (2d ed. 1975), points out that the *Cope* Court's assumption that property must be a vessel in order to be subject to the law of salvage has not been followed.

3. Editors' note: The issue in *Evansville* was whether the wharfboat was a vessel for purposes of the Shipowners' Limitation of Liability Act.

put, a watercraft is not "capable of being used" for maritime transport in any meaningful sense if it has been permanently moored or otherwise rendered practically incapable of transportation or movement.

This distinction is sensible: A ship and her crew do not move in and out of Jones Act coverage depending on whether the ship is at anchor, docked for loading or unloading, or berthed for minor repairs, in the same way that ships taken permanently out of the water as a practical matter do not remain vessels merely because of the remote possibility that they may one day sail again. See *Pavone v. Mississippi Riverboat Amusement Corp.*, 42 F.3d 560, 570 (5th Cir. 1995) (floating casino was no longer a vessel where it "was moored to the shore in a semi-permanent or indefinite manner"); *Kathriner v. UNISEA, Inc.*, 975 F.2d 657, 660 (9th Cir. 1992) (floating processing plant was no longer a vessel where a "large opening [had been] cut into her hull," rendering her incapable of moving over the water). Even if the general maritime law had not informed the meaning of § 3, its definition would not sweep within its reach an array of fixed structures not commonly thought of as capable of being used for water transport.

* * *

C.

The Court of Appeals * * * held that the *Super Scoop* is not a "vessel" because its primary purpose is not navigation or commerce and because it was not in actual transit at the time of Stewart's injury. Neither prong of the Court of Appeals' test is consistent with the text of § 3 or the established meaning of the term "vessel" in general maritime law.

Section 3 requires only that a watercraft be "used, or capable of being used, as a means of transportation on water" to qualify as a vessel. It does not require that a watercraft be used *primarily* for that purpose. [ ] As the Court of Appeals recognized, the *Super Scoop*'s "function was to move through Boston Harbor, digging the ocean bottom as it moved." [ ] In other words, the *Super Scoop* was not only "capable of being used" to transport equipment and workers over water—it *was* used to transport those things. Indeed, it could not have dug the Ted Williams Tunnel had it been unable to traverse the Boston Harbor, carrying with it workers like Stewart.

Also, a watercraft need not be in motion to qualify as a vessel under § 3. Looking to whether a watercraft is motionless or moving is the sort of "snapshot" test that we rejected in *Chandris.* Just as a worker does not "oscillate back and forth between Jones Act coverage and other remedies depending on the activity in which the worker was engaged while injured," *Chandris*, 515 U.S. at 363, neither does a watercraft pass in and out of Jones Act coverage depending on whether it was moving at the time of the accident.

Granted, the Court has sometimes spoken of the requirement that a vessel be "in navigation," *id.* at 373–374, but never to indicate that a structure's locomotion at any given moment mattered. Rather, the point was that structures may lose their character as vessels if they have been withdrawn from the water for extended periods of time. [ ] The Court did not mean that the "in navigation" requirement stood apart from § 3, such that a "vessel" for purposes of § 3 might nevertheless not be a "vessel in navigation" for purposes of the Jones Act or the LHWCA. [ ]

Instead, the "in navigation" requirement is an element of the vessel status of a watercraft. It is relevant to whether the craft is "used, or capable of being used" for maritime transportation. A ship long lodged in a drydock or shipyard can again be put to sea, no less than one permanently moored to shore or the ocean floor can be cut loose and made to sail. The question remains in all cases whether the watercraft's use "as a means of transportation on water" is a practical possibility or merely a theoretical one. In some cases that inquiry may involve factual issues for the jury [ ], but here no relevant facts were in dispute. Dutra conceded that the *Super Scoop* was only temporarily stationary while Stewart and others were repairing the scow; the *Super Scoop* had not been taken out of service, permanently anchored, or otherwise rendered practically incapable of maritime transport. * * * Because the *Super Scoop* was engaged in maritime transportation at the time of Stewart's injury, it was a vessel within the meaning of 1 U.S.C. § 3.

* * *

The judgment of the Court of Appeals is reversed, and the case is remanded for further proceedings consistent with this opinion.

Notes

1. Prior to *Stewart*, the prevailing view was that "a single clear test [for vessel status] is hard to discern" in U.S. maritime law. GILMORE & BLACK, THE LAW OF ADMIRALTY 33 (2d ed. 1975). *Stewart*'s holding that 1 U.S.C. § 3 "suppl[ies] the default definition of 'vessel' throughout the U.S. Code" moved admiralty and maritime law a large step toward a single vessel-status test.

2. *Stewart* scrapped the First Circuit's approach to vessel status and required major modifications in the vessel status law of most of the other circuits. See, e.g, *Uzdavines v. Weeks Marine, Inc.*, 418 F.3d 138, 144–45 (2d Cir. 2005) (stating that "*Stewart* supersedes" a body of Second Circuit vessel-status law); *Bunch v. Canton Marine Towing Co.*, 419 F.3d 868, 873 (8th Cir. 2005) (indicating that *Stewart* superseded the vessel status law of the First, Fifth, Seventh, and Eleventh Circuits).

3. Initially the Fifth Circuit seemed reluctant to accept the change. See *Holmes v. Atlantic Sounding Co.*, 429 F.3d 174, 177–88 (5th Cir. 2005):

> The dispositive issue [is] whether an unpowered floatable structure like [defendant's] quarterbarge BT-213, on which Holmes was working when injured, is a *vessel* * * *. We resolved this issue in *Gremillion v. Gulf Coast Catering Co.*, 904 F.2d 290 (5th Cir. 1990). * * * We hold that *Stewart* does not fundamentally alter our "vessel" jurisprudence. * * * *Gremillion* is dispositive [and means that the BT-213 is, as a matter of law, not a vessel.]

The *Holmes* court then granted a petition for rehearing, withdrew its original opinion, and issued a superseding opinion holding that "under *Stewart*'s expanded definition of [the] term 'vessel', the BT-213 is a vessel" as a matter of law. 437 F.3d 441, 449 (5th Cir. 2006).

4. See generally Robertson, *How the Supreme Court's New Definition of "Vessel" is Affecting Seaman Status, Admiralty Jurisdiction, and Other Areas of Maritime Law*, 39 J. MAR. L. & COM. 115 (2008).

Lozman v. City of Riviera Beach

Supreme Court of the United States, 2013
133 S. Ct. 735, 2013 AMC 1

Justice BREYER delivered the opinion of the Court.

The Rules of Construction Act defines a "vessel" as including "every description of watercraft or other artificial contrivance used, or capable of being used, as a means of transportation on water." 1 U.S.C. § 3. The question before us is whether petitioner's floating home (which is not self-propelled) falls within the terms of that definition.

In answering that question we focus primarily upon the phrase "capable of being used." This term encompasses "practical" possibilities, not "merely * * * theoretical" ones. *Stewart v. Dutra Constr. Co.*, 543 U.S. 481, 496 (2005). We believe that a reasonable observer, looking to the home's physical characteristics and activities, would not consider it to be designed to any practical degree for carrying people or things on water. And we consequently conclude that the floating home is not a "vessel."

I

In 2002 Fane Lozman, petitioner, bought a 60-foot by 12-foot floating home. The home consisted of a house-like plywood structure with French doors on three sides. It contained a sitting room, bedroom, closet, bathroom, and kitchen, along with a stairway leading to a second level with office space. An empty bilge space underneath the main floor kept it afloat. After buying the floating home, Lozman had it towed about 200 miles to North Bay Village, Florida, where he moored it and then twice more had it towed between nearby marinas. In 2006 Lozman had the home towed a further 70 miles to a marina owned by the city of Riviera Beach (City), respondent, where he kept it docked.

After various disputes with Lozman and unsuccessful efforts to evict him from the marina, the City brought this federal admiralty lawsuit *in rem* against the floating home. It sought a maritime lien for dockage fees and damages for trespass. [ ] Lozman, acting *pro se*, asked the District Court to dismiss the suit on the ground that the court lacked admiralty jurisdiction. After summary judgment proceedings, the court found that the floating home was a "vessel" and concluded that admiralty jurisdiction was consequently proper. The judge then conducted a bench trial on the merits and awarded the City $3,039.88 for dockage along with $1 in nominal damages for trespass.

On appeal the Eleventh Circuit affirmed. [649 F.3d 1259 (2011).] It agreed with the District Court that the home was a "vessel." In its view, the home was "capable" of movement over water and the owner's subjective intent to remain moored "indefinitely" at a dock could not show the contrary.

Lozman sought certiorari. In light of uncertainty among the Circuits about application of the term "capable" we granted his petition. Compare *De La Rosa v. St. Charles Gaming Co.*, 474 F.3d 185, 187 (5th Cir. 2006) (structure is not a "vessel" where "physically," but only "theoretical[ly]," "capable of sailing," and owner intends to moor it indefinitely as floating casino), with *Board of Comm'rs of Orleans Levee Dist. v. M/V Belle of Orleans*, 535 F.3d 1299, 1311–12 (11th Cir. 2008) (structure is a "vessel" where capable of moving over water under tow, "albeit to her detriment," despite intent to moor indefinitely). See also 649 F.3d at 1267 (rejecting views of circuits that "focus on the intent of the shipowner' ").

* * *

III

A

We focus primarily upon the statutory phrase "capable of being used * * * as a means of transportation on water." 1 U.S.C. § 3. The Court of Appeals found that the home was "capable" of transportation because it could float, it could proceed under tow, and its shore connections (power cable, water hose, rope lines) did not [render it practically incapable of transportation or movement. At least for argument's sake we agree with the Court of Appeals about the last-mentioned point, namely that Lozman's shore connections did not render the home practically incapable of transportation.] But unlike the Eleventh Circuit, we do not find these considerations (even when combined with the home's other characteristics) sufficient to show that Lozman's home was a "vessel."

The Court of Appeals recognized that it had applied the term "capable" broadly. Indeed, it pointed with approval to language in an earlier case, *Burks v. American River Transp. Co.*, 679 F.2d 69, 75 (1982), in which the Fifth Circuit said:

> No doubt the three men in a tub would also fit within our definition, and one probably could make a convincing case for Jonah inside the whale. [ ]

But the Eleventh Circuit's interpretation is too broad. Not *every* floating structure is a "vessel." To state the obvious, a wooden washtub, a plastic dishpan, a swimming platform on pontoons, a large fishing net, a door taken off its hinges, or Pinocchio (when inside the whale) are not "vessels," even if they are "artificial contrivance[s]" capable of floating, moving under tow, and incidentally carrying even a fair-sized item or two when they do so. Rather, the statute applies to an "artificial contrivance * * * capable of being used * * * *as a means of transportation on water.*" 1 U.S.C. § 3 (emphasis added). "[T]ransportation" involves the "conveyance (of things or persons) from one place to another." 18 Oxford English Dictionary 424 (2d ed. 1989) (OED). Accord, N. Webster, An American Dictionary of the English Language 1406 (C. Goodrich & N. Porter eds. 1873) ("[t]he act of transporting, carrying, or conveying from one place to another"). And we must apply this definition in a "practical," not a "theoretical," way. *Stewart*, *supra*, at 496. Consequently, in our view a structure does not fall within the scope of this statutory phrase unless a reasonable observer, looking to the home's physical characteristics and activities, would consider it designed to a practical degree for carrying people or things over water.

B

Though our criterion is general, the facts of this case illustrate more specifically what we have in mind. But for the fact that it floats, nothing about Lozman's home suggests that it was designed to any practical degree to transport persons or things over water. It had no rudder or other steering mechanism. Its hull was unraked, and it had a rectangular bottom 10 inches below the water. It had no special capacity to generate or store electricity but could obtain that utility only through ongoing connections with the land. Its small rooms looked like ordinary nonmaritime living quarters. And those inside those rooms looked out upon the world, not through watertight portholes, but through French doors or ordinary windows.

Although lack of self-propulsion is not dispositive, *e.g., The Robert W. Parsons*, 191 U.S. 17, 31 (1903), it may be a relevant physical characteristic. And Lozman's home differs significantly from an ordinary houseboat in that it has no ability to propel itself. Cf. 33 CFR § 173.3 (2012) ("Houseboat means a *motorized* vessel * * * designed primarily for multi-purpose accommodation spaces with low freeboard and little or no foredeck or cockpit" (emphasis added)). Lozman's home was able to travel over water only by being towed. Prior to its arrest, that home's travel by tow over water took place on only four occasions over a period of seven years. And when the home was towed a significant distance in 2006, the towing company had a second boat follow behind to prevent the home from swinging dangerously from side to side.

The home has no other feature that might suggest a design to transport over water anything other than its own furnishings and related personal effects. In a word, we can find nothing about the home that could lead a reasonable observer to consider it designed to a practical degree for "transportation on water."

C

Our view of the statute is consistent with its text, precedent, and relevant purposes. For one thing, the statute's language, read naturally, lends itself to that interpretation. We concede that the statute uses the word "every," referring to "*every* description of watercraft or other artificial contrivance." [ ] But the term "contrivance" refers to "something contrived for, or employed in contriving to effect a purpose." 3 OED 850 (def. 7). * * *

For another thing, the bulk of precedent supports our conclusion. In *Evansville & Bowling Green Packet Co. v. Chero Cola Bottling Co.*, 271 U.S. 19 (1926), the Court held that a wharfboat was *not* a "vessel." The wharfboat floated next to a dock; it was used to transfer cargo from ship to dock and ship to ship; and it was connected to the dock with cables, utility lines, and a ramp. At the same time, it was capable of being towed. And it was towed each winter to a harbor to avoid river ice. The Court reasoned that, despite the annual movement under tow, the wharfboat "was not used to carry freight from one place to another," nor did it "encounter perils of navigation to which craft used for transportation are exposed."

The Court's reasoning in *Stewart* also supports our conclusion. * * * The basic difference [between *Evansville* and *Stewart*], we believe, is that the dredge [in *Stewart*] was regularly, but not primarily, used (and designed in part to be used) to transport workers and equipment over water while the wharfboat [in *Evansville*] was not designed (to any practical degree) to serve a transportation function and did not do so.

* * *

We recognize that some lower court opinions can be read as endorsing the "anything that floats" approach. [The cases cited here included "Cf. *Holmes v. Atlantic Sounding Co.*, 437 F.3d 441 (5th Cir. 2006) (floating dormitory)."] For the reasons we have stated, we find such an approach inappropriate and inconsistent with our precedents.

* * *

D

The City and supporting *amici* make several important arguments that warrant our response. First, they argue against use of any purpose-based test lest we introduce into "vessel" determinations a subjective element—namely, the owner's intent. That element, they say, is often "unverifiable" and too easily manipulated. Its introduction would "foment unpredictability and invite gamesmanship."

We agree with the City about the need to eliminate the consideration of evidence of subjective intent. But we cannot agree that the need requires abandonment of all criteria based on "purpose." Cf. *Stewart*, 543 U.S., at 495 (discussing transportation purpose). Indeed, it is difficult, if not impossible, to determine the use of a human "contrivance" without some consideration of human purposes. At the same time, we have sought to avoid subjective elements, such as owner's intent, by permitting consideration only of objective evidence of a waterborne transportation purpose. That is why we have referred to the views of a reasonable observer. And this why we have looked to the physical attributes and behavior of the structure, as objective manifestations of any relevant purpose, and not to the subjective intent of the owner. * * *

Second, the City, with support of *amici*, argues against the use of criteria that are too abstract, complex, or open-ended. A court's jurisdiction, *e.g.*, admiralty jurisdiction, may turn on application of the term "vessel." And jurisdictional tests, often applied at the outset of a case, should be "as simple as possible." [ ]

We agree with the last-mentioned sentiment. And we also understand that our approach is neither perfectly precise nor always determinative. * * * Nonetheless, we believe the criterion we have used, taken together with our example of its application here, should offer guidance in a significant number of borderline cases where "capacity" to transport over water is in doubt. Moreover, borderline cases will always exist; they require a method for resolution; we believe the method we have used is workable; and, unlike, say, an "anything that floats" test, it is consistent with statutory text, purpose, and precedent.

* * *

For these reasons, the judgment of the Court of Appeals is reversed.

[In an appendix, the Court reprinted pictures of Lozman's houseboat and the *Evansville* wharfboat. *See* http://www.supremecourt.gov/opinions/12pdf/11-626_p8k0.pdf]

Notes

1. Justice Sotomayor, joined by Justice Kennedy, dissented. The dissenters agreed with the majority that "the subjective intentions of a watercraft's owner or designer play no role in the vessel analysis of 1 U.S.C. § 3." Otherwise, their disagreement was pervasive. Particular points of criticism included the majority's "reasonable observer" centerpiece, which the dissenters said "introduces a subjective component into the vessel-status inquiry" that "gives our vessel test an 'I know it when I see it' flavor. *Jacobellis v. Ohio*, 378 U.S. 184, 197 (Stewart, J., concurring)." The dissenters also strongly criticized the majority's over-emphasis on "lack of self-propulsion" as an indicium of non-vessel status.

2. *Lozman* is exhaustively analyzed and its potential future effects extensively discussed in Robertson & Sturley, *Vessel Status in Maritime Law: Does* Lozman *Set a New Course?*, 44 J. Mar. L. & Com. 393 (2013). In the immediate aftermath of *Lozman*, the lower courts' reactions seemed to fall into three rough groupings. Some courts cited *Lozman* as supportive of vessel status. See, e.g., *Dune Energy, Inc. v. Frogco Amphibious Equipment, LLC.*, 2013 WL 1856058 (E.D. La. Apr. 30, 2013) (indicating that an "amphibious back hoe, also known as a marsh buggy excavator," might qualify for vessel status under *Lozman* because it "seems to have had a steering mechanism and was apparently capable of self-propulsion"). Other courts viewed *Lozman* as importantly anti-vessel status. See, e.g., *Baker v. Director, Office of Workers' Compensation Programs*, 834 F.3d 542, 547 (5th Cir. 2016) (applying "reasonable observer" test); *Martin v. Fab-Con, Inc.*, 9 F. Supp. 3d 642, 648 (E.D. La. 2014) (emphasizing *Lozman*'s criticism of the Fifth Circuit's 2006 opinion in *Holmes*, *supra* at 25 note 3, and taking *Lozman* as having restored the authority of *Gremillion*, *id.*). A third group of opinions suggested that, because of its "borderline cases" caveat, *Lozman* is not of major importance given the existence of large bodies of settled vessel-status jurisprudence in particular contexts. See, e.g., *Warrior Energy Services Corp. v. ATP Titan M/V*, 551 Fed. Appx. 749, 750, 752 n. 5 (5th Cir. 2014) (stating that *Lozman* was of little significance to the court's determination that a floating oil and gas production facility moored on the Outer Continental Shelf miles offshore Louisiana—moored so securely that it would take two months and $42 million to relocate it—was, as a matter of law, not a vessel); *Gautreaux v. Trinity Trading Group, Ltd.*, 2014 WL 1414576 (E.D. La. Apr. 11, 2004 (indicating that Lozman was irrelevant to the court's determination that a "non-self-propelled barge equipped with a conveyor system that performs midstream cargo transfer operations on the Mississippi River" was a vessel as a matter of law).

3. A significant amount of vessel-status litigation in the years immediately before *Lozman* involved riverboat casinos, which are replicas of 19th century vessels. Six states on the Mississippi and Ohio Rivers authorized gambling on such craft. State laws initially required those riverboat casinos to sail when conducting gambling, but the laws were subsequently amended to permit (or require) the casinos to be moored to the shore during gambling operations. Most riverboat casinos have therefore been more-or-less indefinitely moored to the shore since at least 2005. Some have been physically disabled from sailing again as a practical matter, but others are as fully capable of sailing as they ever were. Some pre-*Lozman* courts relied heavily on the owners' professed intent never to sail again to rule against vessel status. After *Lozman*, what is the status of those riverboat casinos that are physically capable without undue difficulty of sailing again? For one answer, see *Caldwell v. St. Charles Gaming Co.*, ___ So.3d ___, 2020 WL 499159, 2020 La. Lexis 222 (La. Jan. 29, 2020).

D. Admiralty Jurisdiction in Tort Cases

Jerome B. Grubart, Inc. v. Great Lakes Dredge & Dock Co.

Supreme Court of the United States, 1995

513 U.S. 527, 115 S. Ct. 1043, 130 L. Ed. 2d 1024, 1995 AMC 913

Justice SOUTER delivered the opinion of the Court.

On April 13, 1992, water from the Chicago River poured into a freight tunnel running under the river and thence into the basements of buildings in the downtown Chicago Loop. Allegedly, the flooding resulted from events several months earlier, when respondent Great Lakes Dredge and Dock Company had used a crane, sitting on a barge in the river next to a bridge, to drive piles into the riverbed above the tunnel. The issue before us is whether a court of the United States has admiralty jurisdiction to determine and limit the extent of Great Lakes's tort liability. We hold this suit to be within federal admiralty jurisdiction.

I.

The complaint, together with affidavits subject to no objection, alleges the following facts. In 1990, Great Lakes bid on a contract with petitioner city of Chicago to replace wooden pilings clustered around the piers of several bridges spanning the Chicago River, a navigable waterway within the meaning of *The Daniel Ball* [*supra* at 17]. [ ] The pilings (called dolphins) keep ships from bumping into the piers and so protect both. After winning the contract, Great Lakes carried out the work with two barges towed by a tug. One barge carried pilings; the other carried a crane that pulled out old pilings and helped drive in new ones.

In August and September 1991, Great Lakes replaced the pilings around the piers projecting into the river and supporting the Kinzie Street Bridge. After towing the crane-carrying barge into position near one of the piers, Great Lakes's employees secured the barge to the riverbed with spuds, or long metal legs that project down from the barge and anchor it. The workers then used the crane on the barge to pull up old pilings, stow them on the other barge, and drive new pilings into the riverbed around the piers. About seven months later, an eddy formed in the river near the bridge as the collapsing walls or ceiling of a freight tunnel running under the river opened the tunnel to river water, which flowed through to flood buildings in the Loop.

After the flood, many of the victims brought actions in state court against Great Lakes and the city of Chicago, claiming that in the course of replacing the pilings Great Lakes had negligently weakened the tunnel structure, which Chicago (its owner) had not properly maintained. Great Lakes then brought this lawsuit in the United States District Court, invoking federal admiralty jurisdiction. Count I of the complaint seeks the protection of the Limitation of Vessel Owner's Liability Act (Limitation Act), [46 U.S.C. § 30501 et seq.], a statute that would, in effect, permit the admiralty court to decide whether Great Lakes committed a tort and, if so, to limit Great Lakes's liability to the value of the vessels (the tug and two barges) involved if the tort was committed "without the privity or knowledge" of the vessels' owner [46 U.S.C. § 30505(b)]. Counts II and III of Great Lakes's complaint ask for indemnity and contribution from the city for any resulting loss to Great Lakes.

The city, joined by petitioner Jerome B. Grubart, Inc., one of the state court plaintiffs, filed a motion to dismiss this suit for lack of admiralty jurisdiction. Fed. R. Civ. P. 12(b)(1). The District Court granted the motion, the Seventh Circuit reversed, and we granted certiorari. We now affirm.

II.

The parties do not dispute the Seventh Circuit's conclusion that jurisdiction as to Counts II and III (indemnity and contribution) hinges on jurisdiction over the Count I claim. [ ] Thus, the issue is simply whether or not a federal admiralty court has jurisdiction over claims that Great Lakes's faulty replacement work caused the flood damage.

A.

* * *

The traditional test for admiralty tort jurisdiction asked only whether the tort occurred on navigable waters. If it did, admiralty jurisdiction followed; if it did not, admiralty jurisdiction did not exist. [ ] This ostensibly simple locality test was complicated by the rule that the injury had to be "wholly" sustained on navigable waters for the tort to be within admiralty. *The Plymouth*, 70 U.S. 20, 34 (1866) (no jurisdiction over tort action brought by the owner of warehouse destroyed in a fire that started on board a ship docked nearby). Thus, admiralty courts lacked jurisdiction over, say, a claim following a ship's collision with a pier insofar as it injured the pier, for admiralty law treated the pier as an extension of the land. [ ]

This latter rule was changed in 1948, however, when Congress enacted the Extension of Admiralty Jurisdiction Act, 62 Stat. 496. [This Act provides:

> The admiralty and maritime jurisdiction of the United States extends to and includes cases of injury or damage, to person or property, caused by a vessel on navigable waters, even though the injury or damage is done or consummated on land. (46 U.S.C. § 30101(a).)]

The purpose of the Act was to end concern over the sometimes confusing line between land and water, by investing admiralty with jurisdiction over [cases] where the injury was caused by a ship or other vessel on navigable water, even if such injury occurred on land. [ ]

After this congressional modification to gather the odd case into admiralty, the jurisdictional rule was qualified again in three decisions of this Court aimed at keeping a different class of odd cases out. In the first case, *Executive Jet Aviation, Inc. v. Cleveland*, 409 U.S. 249 (1972), tort claims arose out of the wreck of an airplane that collided with a flock of birds just after takeoff on a domestic flight and fell into the navigable waters of Lake Erie. We held that admiralty lacked jurisdiction to consider the claims. We wrote that "a purely mechanical application of the locality test" was not always "sensible" or "consonant with the purposes of maritime law," as when (for example) the literal and universal application of the locality rule would require admiralty courts to adjudicate tort disputes between colliding swimmers. We held that "claims arising from airplane accidents are not cognizable in admiralty" despite the location of the harm, unless "the wrong bear[s] a significant relationship to traditional maritime activity."

The second decision, *Foremost Ins. Co. v. Richardson*, 457 U.S. 668 (1982), dealt with tort claims arising out of the collision of two pleasure boats in a navigable river estuary. We held that admiralty courts had jurisdiction, even though jurisdiction existed only if "the wrong" had "a significant connection with traditional maritime activity." We conceded that pleasure boats themselves had little to do with the maritime commerce lying at the heart of the admiralty court's basic work, but we nonetheless found the necessary relationship in

> [t]he potential disruptive impact [upon maritime commerce] of a collision between boats on navigable waters, when coupled with the traditional concern that admiralty law holds for navigation.

In the most recent of the trilogy, *Sisson v. Ruby*, 497 U.S. 358 (1990), we held that a federal admiralty court had jurisdiction over tort claims arising when a fire, caused by a defective washer/dryer aboard a pleasure boat docked at a marina, burned the boat, other boats docked nearby, and the marina itself. We elaborated on the enquiry exemplified in *Executive Jet* and *Foremost* by focusing on two points to determine the relationship of a claim to the objectives of admiralty jurisdiction. We noted, first, that the incident causing the harm, the burning of docked boats at a marina on navigable waters, was of a sort "likely to disrupt [maritime] commercial activity." Second, we found a "substantial relationship" with "traditional maritime activity" in the kind of activity from which the incident arose, "the storage and maintenance of a vessel ... on navigable waters."

After *Sisson*, then, a party seeking to invoke federal admiralty jurisdiction pursuant to 28 U.S.C. § 1333(1) over a tort claim must satisfy conditions both of location and of connection with maritime activity. A court applying the location test must determine whether the tort occurred on navigable water or whether injury suffered on land was caused by a vessel on navigable water. [46 U.S.C. § 30101(a).]. The connection test raises two issues. A court, first, must "assess the general features of the type of incident involved" to determine whether the incident has "a potentially disruptive impact on maritime commerce." Second, a court must determine whether "the general character" of the "activity giving rise to the incident" shows a "substantial relationship to traditional maritime activity." We now apply the tests to the facts of this suit.

B.

The location test is, of course, readily satisfied. If Great Lakes caused the flood, it must have done so by weakening the structure of the tunnel while it drove in new pilings or removed old ones around the bridge piers. * * * The place in the river where the barge sat, and from which workers directed the crane, is in the "navigable waters of the United States." [ ] Thus, if Great Lakes committed a tort, it must have done it while on navigable waters.

It must also have done it "by a vessel." Even though the barge was fastened to the river bottom and was in use as a work platform at the times in question, at other times it was used for transportation. Petitioners do not here seriously dispute the conclusion of each court below that the Great Lakes barge is, for admiralty tort purposes, a "vessel." * * *

* * * Both Grubart and Chicago nonetheless ask us to subject the Extension Act to limitations not apparent from its text. * * * They contend that, to be within the Act, the damage must be close in time and space to the activity that caused it: that it must occur "reasonably contemporaneously" with the negligent conduct and no "farther from navigable waters than the reach of the vessel, its appurtenances and cargo." For authority, they point to this Court's statement in *Gutierrez v. Waterman S.S. Corp.*, 373 U.S. 206 (1963), that jurisdiction is present when the "impact" of the tortious activity "is felt ashore at a time and place not remote from the wrongful act."

The demerits of this argument lie not only in its want of textual support for its non-remoteness rule, but in its disregard of a less stringent but familiar proximity condition tied to the language of the statute. The Act uses the phrase "caused by," which more than one Court of Appeals has read as requiring what tort law has traditionally called "proximate causation." [ ] This classic tort notion normally eliminates the bizarre, cf. *Palsgraf v. Long Island R. Co.*, 248 N.Y. 339 (1928), and its use should obviate not only the complication but even the need for further temporal or spatial limitations. Nor is reliance on familiar proximate causation inconsistent with *Gutierrez*, which used its nonremote language, not to announce a special test, but simply to distinguish its own facts (the victim having slipped on beans spilling from cargo containers being unloaded from a ship) from what the Court called "[v]arious far-fetched hypotheticals," such as injury to someone slipping on beans that continue to leak from the containers after they had been shipped from Puerto Rico to a warehouse in Denver. [ ]

The city responds by saying that, as a practical matter, the use of proximate cause as a limiting jurisdictional principle would undesirably force an admiralty court to investigate the merits of the dispute at the outset of a case when it determined jurisdiction. The argument, of course, assumes that the truth of jurisdictional allegations must always be determined with finality at the threshold of litigation, but that assumption is erroneous. Normal practice permits a party to establish jurisdiction at the outset of a case by means of a nonfrivolous assertion of jurisdictional elements [ ], and any litigation of a contested subject matter jurisdictional fact issue occurs in comparatively summary procedure before a judge alone (as distinct from litigation of the same fact issue as an element of the cause of action, if the claim survives the jurisdictional objection). * * *

C.

We now turn to the maritime connection enquiries, the first being whether the incident involved was of a sort with the potential to disrupt maritime commerce. In *Sisson*, we described the features of the incident in general terms as "a fire on a vessel docked at a marina on navigable waters" and determined that such an incident "plainly satisf[ied]" the first maritime connection requirement, because the fire could have "spread to nearby commercial vessels or ma[d]e the marina inaccessible to such vessels" and therefore "[c]ertainly" had a "potentially disruptive impact on maritime commerce." We noted that this first prong went to potential effects, not to the "particular facts of the incident," noting that in both *Executive Jet* and *Foremost* we had focused not on the specific facts at hand but on whether the "general features" of the incident were "likely to disrupt commercial activity."

The first *Sisson* test turns, then, on a description of the incident at an intermediate level of possible generality. To speak of the incident as "fire" would have been too general to differentiate cases; at the other extreme, to have described the fire as damaging nothing but pleasure boats and their tie-up facilities would have ignored, among other things, the capacity of pleasure boats to endanger commercial shipping that happened to be nearby. We rejected both extremes and instead asked whether the incident could be seen within a class of incidents that posed more than a fanciful risk to commercial shipping.

Following *Sisson*, the "general features" of the incident at issue here may be described as damage by a vessel in navigable water to an underwater structure. So characterized, there is little question that this is the kind of incident that has a "potentially disruptive impact on maritime commerce." As it actually turned out in this suit, damaging a structure beneath the riverbed could lead to a disruption in the water course itself (eddy formed above the leak); and, again as it actually happened, damaging a structure so situated could lead to restrictions on the navigational use of the waterway during required repairs. See Pet. for Cert. in No. 93-1094, p. 22a (District Court found that after the flood "[t]he river remained closed for over a month," "[r]iver traffic ceased, several commuter ferries were stranded, and many barges could not enter the river system ... because the river level was lowered to aid repair efforts"). [ ]

In the second *Sisson* enquiry, we look to whether the general character of the activity giving rise to the incident shows a substantial relationship to traditional maritime activity. We ask whether a tortfeasor's activity, commercial or noncommercial, on navigable waters is so closely related to activity traditionally subject to admiralty law that the reasons for applying special admiralty rules would apply in the suit at hand. Navigation of boats in navigable waters clearly falls within the substantial relationship, *Foremost*, 457 U.S. at 675; storing them at a marina on navigable waters is close enough, *Sisson*, 497 U.S. at 367; whereas in flying an airplane over the water, *Executive Jet*, 409 U.S. at 270–271, as in swimming, *id.* at 255–256, the relationship is too attenuated.

On like reasoning, the "activity giving rise to the incident" [ ] in this suit should be characterized as repair or maintenance work on a navigable waterway performed from a vessel. Described in this way, there is no question that the activity is substantially related to traditional maritime activity, for barges and similar vessels have traditionally been engaged in repair work similar to what Great Lakes contracted to perform here. [ ]

The city argues, to the contrary, that a proper application of the activity prong of *Sisson* would consider the city's own alleged failure at properly maintaining and operating the tunnel system that runs under the river. If this asserted proximate cause of the flood victims' injuries were considered, the city submits, its failure to resemble any traditional maritime activity would take this suit out of admiralty.

The city misreads *Sisson*, however, which did not consider the activities of the washer/dryer manufacturer, who was possibly an additional tortfeasor, and whose activities were hardly maritime; the activities of *Sisson*, the boat owner, supplied the necessary substantial relationship to traditional maritime activity. Likewise, in *Foremost*, we said that "[b]ecause the 'wrong' here involves the negligent operation of a vessel on navigable waters, we believe that it has a sufficient nexus to traditional maritime activity to sustain admiralty jurisdiction...." By using the word "involves," we made it clear that we need to look only to whether one of the arguably proximate causes of the incident originated in the maritime activity of a tortfeasor: as long as one of the putative tortfeasors was engaged in traditional maritime activity the allegedly wrongful activity will "involve" such traditional maritime activity and will meet the second nexus prong. Thus, even if we were to identify the "activity giving rise to the incident" as including the acts of the city as well as Great Lakes, admiralty jurisdiction would nevertheless attach. That result would be true to *Sisson*'s requirement of a "substantial relationship" between the "activity giving rise to the incident" and traditional maritime activity. *Sisson* did not require, as the city in effect asserts, that there be a complete identity between the two. The substantial relationship test is satisfied when at least one alleged tortfeasor was engaging in activity substantially related to traditional maritime activity and such activity is claimed to have been a proximate cause of the incident.

Petitioners also argue that we might get a different result simply by characterizing the "activity" in question at a different level of generality, perhaps as "repair and maintenance," or as "pile driving near a bridge." The city is, of course, correct that a tortfeasor's activity can be described at a sufficiently high level of generality to eliminate any hint of maritime connection, and if that were properly done *Sisson* would bar assertion of admiralty jurisdiction. But to suggest that such hypergeneralization ought to be the rule would convert *Sisson* into a vehicle for eliminating admiralty jurisdiction. Although there is inevitably some play in the joints in selecting the right level of generality when applying the *Sisson* test, the inevitable imprecision is not an excuse for whimsy. The test turns on the comparison of traditional maritime activity to the arguably maritime character of the tortfeasor's activity in a given case; the comparison would merely be frustrated by eliminating the maritime aspect of the tortfeasor's activity from consideration.

Grubart makes an additional claim that *Sisson* is being given too expansive a reading. If the activity at issue here is considered maritime-related, it argues, then virtually "every activity involving a vessel on navigable waters" would be "a traditional maritime activity sufficient to invoke maritime jurisdiction." But this is not fatal criticism. This Court has not proposed any radical alteration of the traditional criteria for invoking admiralty jurisdiction in tort cases, but has simply followed the lead of the lower federal courts in rejecting a location rule so rigid as to extend admiralty to a case involving an airplane, not a vessel, engaged in an activity far removed from anything traditionally maritime. See *Executive Jet,* 409 U.S. at 268–274; see also *Peytavin v. Government Employees Ins. Co.*, 453 F.2d 1121, 1127 (5th Cir. 1972) (no jurisdiction over claim for personal injury by motorist who was rear-ended while waiting for a ferry on a floating pontoon serving as the ferry's landing); *Chapman v. Grosse Pointe Farms*, 385 F.2d 962 (6th Cir. 1967) (no admiralty jurisdiction over claim of swimmer who injured himself when diving off pier into shallow but navigable water). In the cases after *Executive Jet,* the Court stressed the need for a maritime connection, but found one in the navigation or berthing of pleasure boats, despite the facts that the pleasure boat activity took place near shore, where States have a strong interest in applying their own tort law, or was not on all fours with the maritime shipping and commerce that has traditionally made up the business of most maritime courts. *Sisson*, 497 U.S. at 367; *Foremost,* 457 U.S. at 675. Although we agree with petitioners that these cases do not say that every tort involving a vessel on navigable waters falls within the scope of admiralty jurisdiction no matter what, they do show that ordinarily that will be so.[5]

III.

Perhaps recognizing the difficulty of escaping the case law, petitioners ask us to change it. In cases "involving land based parties and injuries," the city would have us adopt a condition of jurisdiction that

5. Because we conclude that the tort alleged in Count I of Great Lakes's complaint satisfies both the location and connection tests necessary for admiralty jurisdiction under 28 U.S.C. § 1333(1), we need not consider respondent Great Lakes's alternative argument that the Extension of Admiralty Jurisdiction Act, [46 U.S.C. § 30101], provides an independent basis of federal jurisdiction over the complaint.

> the totality of the circumstances reflects a federal interest in protecting maritime commerce sufficiently weighty to justify shifting what would otherwise be state court litigation into federal court under the federal law of admiralty.

Grubart and the city say that the Fifth Circuit has applied a somewhat similar "four-factor test" looking to "the functions and roles of the parties; the types of vehicles and instrumentalities involved; the causation and the type of injury; and traditional concepts of the role of admiralty law." *Kelly v. Smith*, 485 F.2d 520, 525 (5th Cir. 1973); see also *Molett v. Penrod Drilling Co.*, 826 F.2d 1419, 1426 (5th Cir. 1987) (adding three more factors: the "impact of the event on maritime shipping and commerce"; "the desirability of a uniform national rule to apply to such matters"; and "the need for admiralty 'expertise' in the trial and decision of the case"). Although they point out that *Sisson* disapproved the use of four-factor or seven-factor tests "where all the relevant entities are engaged in similar types of activity," this rule implicitly left the matter open for cases like this one, where most of the victims, and one of the tortfeasors, are based on land. * * * The city argues that there is a good reason why cases like this one should get different treatment. Since the basic rationale for federal admiralty jurisdiction is "protection of maritime commerce through uniform rules of decision," the proposed jurisdictional test would improve on *Sisson* in limiting the scope of admiralty jurisdiction more exactly to its rationale. A multiple-factor test would minimize, if not eliminate, the awkward possibility that federal admiralty rules or procedures will govern a case, to the disadvantage of state law, when admiralty's purpose does not require it. [ ].

Although the arguments are not frivolous, they do not persuade. It is worth recalling that the *Sisson* tests are aimed at the same objectives invoked to support a new multifactor test, the elimination of admiralty jurisdiction where the rationale for the jurisdiction does not support it. If the tort produces no potential threat to maritime commerce or occurs during activity lacking a substantial relationship to traditional maritime activity, *Sisson* assumes that the objectives of admiralty jurisdiction probably do not require its exercise, even if the location test is satisfied. If, however, the *Sisson* tests are also satisfied, it is not apparent why the need for admiralty jurisdiction in aid of maritime commerce somehow becomes less acute merely because land-based parties happen to be involved. Certainly Congress [in enacting the Extension Act] did not think a land-based party necessarily diluted the need for admiralty jurisdiction or it would have kept its hands off the primitive location test.

* * *

Nor are these the only objections to the city's position. Contrary to what the city suggests, exercise of federal admiralty jurisdiction does not result in automatic displacement of state law. It is true that "[w]ith admiralty jurisdiction comes the application of substantive admiralty law." *East River S.S. Corp. v. Transamerica Delaval Inc.*, 476 U.S. 858, 864 (1986) [*infra* at 140]. But, to characterize that law, as the city apparently does, as "federal rules of decision" * * * is "a destructive oversimplification of the highly intricate interplay of the States and the National Government in their regulation of maritime commerce. It is true that state law must yield to the needs of a uniform federal maritime law when this Court finds inroads on a harmonious system. But this limitation still leaves the States a wide scope." *Romero v. International Terminal Operating Co.*, 358 U.S. 354, 373 (1959) [*infra* at 105]. See *East River*, 476 U.S. at 864–865 ("Drawn from state and federal sources, the general maritime law is an amalgam of traditional common-law rules, modifications of those rules, and newly created rules"). Thus, the city's proposal to synchronize the jurisdictional enquiry with the test for determining the applicable substantive law would discard a fundamental feature of admiralty law, that federal admiralty courts sometimes do apply state law. See, e.g., *American Dredging Co. v. Miller*, 510 U.S. 443, 451–52 (1994) [*infra* at 113]; see also 1 Friedell, Benedict on Admiralty § 112, p. 7–49 (7th ed. 1994).

Finally, on top of these objections going to the city's premises there is added a most powerful one based on the practical consequences of adopting a multifactor test. Although the existing case law tempers the locality test with the added requirements looking to potential harm and traditional activity, it reflects customary practice in seeing jurisdiction as the norm when the tort originates with a vessel in navigable waters, and in treating departure from the locality principle as the exception. For better or worse, the case law has thus carved out the approximate shape of admiralty jurisdiction in a way that admiralty lawyers understand reasonably well. As against this approach, so familiar and relatively easy, the proposed four- or seven-factor test would be hard to apply, jettisoning relative predictability for the open ended rough-and-tumble of factors, inviting complex argument in a trial court and a virtually inevitable appeal.

* * *

Reasons of practice, then, are as weighty as reasons of theory for rejecting the city's call to adopt a multifactor test for admiralty jurisdiction for the benefit of land-based parties to a tort action.

Accordingly, we conclude that the Court of Appeals correctly held that the District Court had admiralty jurisdiction over the respondent Great Lakes's Limitation Act suit. The judgment of the Court of Appeals is affirmed.

Justice Stevens and Justice Breyer took no part in the decision.

Justice O'CONNOR, concurring.

I concur in the Court's judgment and opinion. The Court properly holds that, when a court is faced with a case involving multiple tortfeasors, some of whom may not be maritime actors, if one of the putative tortfeasors was engaged in traditional maritime activity alleged to have proximately caused the incident, then the supposedly wrongful activity "involves" traditional maritime activity. The possible involvement of other, non-maritime parties does not affect the jurisdictional inquiry as to the maritime party. I do not, however, understand the Court's opinion to suggest that, having found admiralty jurisdiction over a particular claim against a particular party, a court must then exercise admiralty jurisdiction over all the claims and parties involved in the case. Rather, the court should engage in the usual supplemental jurisdiction and impleader inquiries. See 28 U.S.C. § 1367; [ ]. I find nothing in the Court's opinion to the contrary.

Justice THOMAS, with whom Justice Scalia joins, concurring in the judgment.

I agree with the majority's conclusion that 28 U.S.C. § 1333(1) grants the District Court jurisdiction over the great Chicago flood of 1992. But I write separately because I cannot agree with the test the Court applies to determine the boundaries of admiralty and maritime jurisdiction. Instead of continuing our unquestioning allegiance to the multifactor approach of *Sisson v. Ruby*, I would restore the jurisdictional inquiry to the simple question whether the tort occurred on a vessel on the navigable waters of the United States. If so, then admiralty jurisdiction exists. This clear, bright-line rule, which the Court applied until recently, ensures that judges and litigants will not waste their resources in determining the extent of federal subject matter jurisdiction.

I.

This action requires the Court to redefine once again the line between federal admiralty jurisdiction and state power due to an ambiguous balancing test. The fact that we have had to revisit this question for the third time in a little over 10 years indicates the defects of the Court's current approach. The faults of balancing tests are clearest, and perhaps most destructive, in the area of jurisdiction. Vague and obscure rules may permit judicial power to reach beyond its constitutional and statutory limits, or they may discourage judges from hearing disputes properly before them. Such rules waste judges' and litigants' resources better spent on the merits, as this action itself demonstrates. * * *

* * *

Although the majority makes an admirable attempt to clarify what *Sisson* obscures, I am afraid that its analysis cannot mitigate the confusion of the *Sisson* test. Thus, faced with the "potential to disrupt maritime commerce" prong, the majority must resort to "an intermediate level of possible generality" to determine the " 'general features' " of the incident here. The majority does not explain the origins of "levels of generality," nor, to my knowledge, do we employ such a concept in other areas of jurisdiction. We do not use "levels of generality" to characterize residency or amount in controversy for diversity purposes, or to determine the presence of a federal question. Nor does the majority explain why an "intermediate" level of generality is appropriate. It is even unclear what an intermediate level of generality is, and we cannot expect that district courts will apply such a concept uniformly in similar cases. It is far from obvious how the undefined intermediate level of generality indicates that the "incident" for *Sisson* purposes is that of a vessel damaging an underwater structure.

The majority also applies levels of generality to the next prong of *Sisson*—whether the tortfeasor is engaged in "activity" that shows a "substantial relationship to traditional maritime activity." The majority decides that the activity is repair work by a vessel on a navigable waterway. But, as the petitioners rightly argue, the "activity" very well could be bridge repair or pile driving. One simply cannot tell due to the ambiguities intrinsic to *Sisson* and to the uncertainty as to the meaning of levels of generality. The majority's response implicitly acknowledges the vagueness inherent in *Sisson*: "Although there is inevitably some play in the joints in selecting the right level of generality when applying the *Sisson* test, the inevitable imprecision is not an excuse for whimsy." The Court cannot provide much guidance to district courts as to the correct level of generality; instead, it can only say that any level is probably sufficient so long as it does not lead to "whimsy." When it comes to these issues, I prefer a clearer rule, which this Court has demanded with respect to federal question or diversity jurisdiction. Indeed, the "play in the joints" and "imprecision" that the Court finds "inevitable" easily could be avoided by returning to the test that prevailed before *Foremost*. In its effort to create an elegant, general test that could include all maritime torts, *Sisson* has only disrupted what was once a simple inquiry.

II.

It should be apparent that this Court does not owe *Sisson* the benefit of *stare decisis*. As shown above, *Sisson* and *Foremost* themselves overextended *Executive Jet* and deviated from a long tradition of admiralty jurisprudence. More importantly, the new test of *Sisson* and *Foremost* did not produce greater clarity or simplicity in exchange for departing from a century of undisturbed practice. Instead, as discussed earlier, the two cases have produced only confusion and disarray in the lower courts and in this Court as well. It would seem that in the area of federal subject matter jurisdiction, vagueness and ambiguity are grounds enough to revisit an unworkable prior decision.

* * * Because *Sisson* departed from a century of precedent, is unworkable, and is easily replaced with a bright line rule, I concur only in the judgment.

Notes

1. **The locality test.** Prior to 1972 it was fairly well-established that the only test of maritime jurisdiction for torts was locality. See, e.g., *The Plymouth*, 70 U.S. 20, 36 (1865): "Every species of tort, however occurring, and whether on board a vessel or not, if upon the high seas or navigable waters, is of admiralty cognizance." Erasmus Benedict, author of an admiralty treatise, doubted the soundness of this view, wondering if there ought to be required some relationship of the parties and the tort to a vessel. BENEDICT, THE LAW OF AMERICAN ADMIRALTY 173 (1850). Doubts were also expressed in England. *The Queen v. The Judge of the City of London Court*, [1892] 1 Q.B. 273, 294 (C.A.). Although the Supreme Court expressed some reservations in *Atlantic Transport Co. v. Imbrovek*, 234 U.S. 52 (1914), it later returned to the orthodox view in *The Admiral Peoples*, 295 U.S. 649 (1935) (holding that disembarking passenger's fall from gangplank to dock was located on the vessel and therefore within admiralty jurisdiction).

The Plymouth described the locality rule as follows: "[T]he wrong and injury complained of must have been committed wholly upon the high seas or navigable waters, or, at least, the substance and consummation of the same must have taken place upon these waters to be within the admiralty jurisdiction." 70 U.S. at 35. The "substance and consummation" language has been translated into an "impact" inquiry that focuses neither on the place of the wrongful conduct nor the place of ultimate injury but rather upon the point at which the wrongful conduct meaningfully came to bear upon the victim. See *T. Smith & Son v. Taylor*, 276 U.S. 179 (1928) (no admiralty jurisdiction when longshoreman was knocked from pier into the water, where he was later found dead); *Minnie v. Port Huron Terminal Co.*, 295 U.S. 647 (1935) (admiralty jurisdiction when longshoreman was knocked from the deck of a vessel onto a pier). The "impact" inquiry is well illustrated by *Executive Jet Aviation, Inc. v. Cleveland*, 448 F.2d 151 (6th Cir. 1971), *aff'd on other grounds*, 409 U.S. 249 (1972). An airplane taking off from Burke Lakefront Airport in Cleveland struck seagulls over the runway and then crashed into the lake. Holding that there was no admiralty jurisdiction over the plane owner's property damage suit against the operator of the airport, the court held that the "impact" of the alleged negligence occurred when the gulls disabled the plane's engines over the land.

2. **Criticisms of the locality test.** The Supreme Court set forth three "indictment[s]" of the locality test in *Executive Jet Aviation, Inc. v. Cleveland*, 409 U.S. 249, 259 (1972): (a) It sometimes produces "perverse and casuistic" distinctions (instancing *T. Smith & Son v. Taylor* and *Minnie v. Port Huron*, *supra* note 1); (b) it is sometimes over-inclusive, bringing "absurd" claims into admiralty (instancing "a swimmer at a public beach injured by another swimmer or by a submerged object on the bottom" and "a piece of machinery [that] sustains water damage by being dropped into a harbor by a land-based crane"); and (c) it is sometimes under-inclusive, requiring "the federal courts and the Congress, in the interests of justice, ... to create exceptions to it [for situations in which] the tort has no maritime locality, but does bear a relationship to maritime service, commerce, or navigation") (instancing the Admiralty Extension Act as well as *O'Donnell v. Great Lakes Dredge & Dock Co.*, 318 U.S. 36 (1943), which held that a seaman's action against his

employer under the Jones Act, 46 U.S.C. 30104, will lie in admiralty regardless of the location of the injury).

3. **Locality plus nexus.** Despite its criticisms of the locality test, the *Executive Jet* court did not abandon it. Instead, it added on a requirement that in airplane negligence cases "the wrong [must] bear a significant relationship to traditional maritime activity." 409 U.S. at 268. The Court did not hold that all aircraft cases fail to satisfy the nexus requirement, although the one before it (crash into Lake Erie of a plane bound from Ohio to Maine) clearly failed. And it said that Congress can make exceptions to the nexus requirement, as it has in the case of the Death on the High Seas Act, 46 U.S.C. §§ 30301–30308. In a limited holding the Court said:

> [W]e hold that, in the absence of legislation to the contrary, there is no federal admiralty jurisdiction over aviation tort claims arising from flights by land-based aircraft between points within the continental United States.

409 U.S. at 274

4. The locality rule is satisfied when conduct on land causes injury on navigable waters. For example, if smoke from a mill obstructs navigation so as to cause a collision on a navigable river, the tort claim against the mill is maritime. *Kelly v. United States*, 531 F.2d 1144 (2d Cir. 1976). But it was not satisfied in the converse situation, when conduct on water caused injury on land. See *The Plymouth*, 70 U.S. 20 (1866) (denying admiralty jurisdiction over an action for damage to a wharf and storage buildings caused by a fire that originated on a ship docked near the wharf). The discrepancy produced "inequities" in situations where a vessel and land-based party such as a bridge owner had cross-claims against each other. As a Senate Report observed, "the owner of the bridge, being denied a remedy in admiralty, is barred by contributory negligence from any recovery in an action at law. But the owner of the vessel may by a suit in admiralty recover ... damages from the bridge, contributory negligence operating merely to reduce the recovery." Sen. Rep. No. 1593, 80th Cong., 2d Sess, *reprinted in* 1948 U.S. Code Cong. Serv. 1898. The Admiralty Extension Act, 46 U.S.C. § 30101, was intended to eliminate the discrepancy.

5. Where does the "impact" occur if a seaman is blacklisted or wrongfully discharged? More generally, if a defendant intentionally interferes with a maritime contract, isn't the impact of the tort also felt on navigable waters? Compare *Carroll v. Protection Maritime Ins. Co.*, 512 F.2d 4 (1st Cir. 1975) (upholding jurisdiction in blacklisting case); *Miller v. Penobscot Bay Medical Associates*, 836 F. Supp. 31 (D. Me. 1993) (exercising admiralty jurisdiction over suit against shore-based physician whose erroneous medical report caused a seaman to get fired) with *J. Lauritzen A/S v. Dashwood Shipping, Ltd.*, 65 F.3d 139 (9th Cir. 1995) (rejecting *Carroll*); *Kuehne & Nagel (Ag & Co.) v. Geosource, Inc.*, 874 F.2d 283 (5th Cir. 1989) (same). See also *Smith v. Atlas Off-Shore Boat Service, Inc.*, 653 F.2d 1057 (5th Cir. 1981)(holding that a wrongfully discharged seaman had a maritime tort claim without addressing the jurisdictional issue). Should these claims be viewed as breach of implied contracts? Alternatively, if these are not maritime claims might state law provide a remedy? See *Robinson v. Alter Barge Line, Inc.*, 513 F.3d 668, 2008 AMC 297 (7th Cir. 2008).

6. **The potential to disrupt maritime commerce.** When the Supreme Court first announced the potential-to-disrupt-maritime-commerce test, it did not appear to perform much of an independent screening function. See, e.g., Robertson & Sturley, *Recent Developments in Admiralty and Maritime Law*, 30 Tul. Mar. L.J. 195, 267 n.513 (2006) (describing requirement as "famously easy to satisfy"). In recent years, however, it has more often been a contentious issue. See, e.g., *In re Christopher Columbus*, 872 F.3d 130, 136-

137 (3d Cir. 2017); *Hargus v. Ferocious & Impetuous, LLC*, 840 F.3d 133, 136-138 (3d Cir. 2016); *Petrobras America, Inc. v. Vicinay Cadenas, S.A.*, 815 F.3d 211 (5th Cir. 2016).

Petrobras America provides a wonderful illustration of the manipulability of the *Grubart* test in general and the potential-to-disrupt-maritime-commerce test in particular. An underwater tether chain on a Gulf of Mexico oil-and-gas facility broke, causing massive damage to a pipeline riser and related equipment, and causing the plaintiff to suspend oil-and-gas operations in the area to investigate the failure. It also caused an "enormous" buoyancy can to rise to the surface and float 36 miles away. The magistrate judge thought that the accident had the potential to disrupt maritime commerce "either by causing the can to collide with a vessel or by requiring ships to take alternative routes." 2015 WL 12940016, at *3 (S.D. Tex. Aug. 25, 2015). The district court agreed but the court of appeals reversed, holding that the failure did not have the potential to disrupt maritime commerce. The court reasoned that the focus needs to be on the potential impact on the navigability of the waterways. The court considered the potential effects of the release of the buoyancy can to be *de minimis*.

7. One may be tempted to read the *Grubart* opinion as suggesting that the concept of "proximate cause" helps to define the types of cases that can be brought within the Admiralty Extension Act. Your editors think the term "caused by a vessel" in the statute refers to factual causation rather than legal causation and that the concept of legal causation is a poor jurisdictional tool. Robertson & Sturley, *The Admiralty Extension Act Solution*, 34 J. MAR. L. & COM. 209 (2003); Friedell, *The Proximate Cause Paradox in The Admiralty Extension Act*, 31 J. MAR. L. & COM. 139 (2000).

8. Some (mistakenly in our opinion) have interpreted the majority in *Grubart* as extending admiralty jurisdiction to all parties in the case when it said, "The substantial relationship test is satisfied when at least one alleged tortfeasor was engaging in activity substantially related to traditional maritime activity...." Despite the cogency of Justice O'Connor's explanation, some have read the majority's language literally and out of context. In *Scarborough v. Clemco Industries*, 391 F.3d 660 (5th Cir. 2004), the court held that admiralty jurisdiction over an offshore oil-and-gas worker's suit against his Jones Act employer automatically entailed admiralty jurisdiction over claims against other defendants who manufactured safety equipment. *Scarborough* is criticized in Robertson, *Admiralty Jurisdiction Over One Co-Tortfeasor Cannot Effectuate Admiralty Jurisdiction Over Another*, 37 J. MAR. L. & COM. 161 (2006).

Taghadomi v. United States

United States Court of Appeals, Ninth Circuit, 2005
401 F.3d 1080, 2005 AMC 958

O'SCANNLAIN, Circuit Judge:

* * *

I.

This case arises from an accident at sea. Manouchehr Monazzami Taghadomi (a U.S. citizen) and his wife Nahid Davoodabadi (a citizen of Iran) rented a kayak during their honeymoon in Maui. Their boat was buffeted by harsh wind and waves, and Nahid was tossed overboard, attacked by a shark, and died. Monazzami washed up on an island and was stranded for three days before he was rescued. He was hospitalized for several days.

While the couple was still in the foundering kayak, a witness on land noticed it through his binoculars. Concerned, he telephoned the Coast Guard's Maui office and gave a description of the kayak and its location. About twenty minutes after receiving the call, the Maui office contacted the Coast Guard Operations Center in Honolulu. The Operations Center, in turn, contacted a Coast Guard cutter—the *Kiska*—and directed it toward the kayak. The *Kiska* conducted a brief search, but darkness soon fell, and at about seven o'clock that evening the search was called off.

This lawsuit followed. Monazzami originally filed a complaint, individually and as special administrator of the estate of Nahid, against Extreme Sports Maui, the company that rented the kayak to Taghadomi. In subsequent amended complaints the estate and Nahid's parents were each added as separate plaintiffs and the United States was added as a defendant.[2] The plaintiffs (collectively, the "survivors") seek damages from the United States for wrongful death and emotional distress. They allege that the Coast Guard was negligent both in carrying out its rescue operation and in failing to contact local authorities who had access to better rescue equipment that might have been able to save the couple. The United States moved to dismiss or, in the alternative, for summary judgment. * * * The district court granted the United States' motion for summary judgment, holding that the survivors' claims are not cognizable, and denied as futile the survivors' motion to amend. The court entered judgment for the United States and this appeal timely followed. We review the grant of summary judgment de novo. [ ]

II.

[The issue before the court is whether the plaintiffs can maintain a suit under the Federal Torts Claims Act (FTCA). That statute does not apply to] "any claim for which a remedy is provided" by either of the other two statutes relevant to this case. 28 U.S.C. § 2680(d). These are the Public Vessels Act ("PVA"), [46 U.S.C. §§ 31101–31113] and the Suits in Admiralty Act ("SAA") [46 U.S.C. §§ 30901–30918].

* * *

A.

The first question we must answer is whether the survivors' claims * * * fall within federal admiralty jurisdiction. For the PVA and the SAA are relevant only to maritime claims and thus pose no obstacle to asserting non-maritime claims under the FTCA.

The survivors seek to bring two different claims against the United States. First, they claim that the Coast Guard cutter *Kiska*'s search for the kayakers was negligently carried out * * *. Second, they claim that the two Coast Guard officers (in Maui and Honolulu) who knew about the kayak in distress negligently failed to contact the Maui Fire Department or any other local agency with access to a helicopter or other rescue vessels. * * *

No one disputes that the negligent search claim is maritime in nature. The survivors argue, however, that the failure-to-communicate claim is not maritime and therefore not within the scope of the SAA or the PVA. Thus, they conclude, it is the proper subject of an action under the FTCA.

* * *

2. The plaintiffs have settled their dispute with Extreme Sports Maui, and the United States is the only remaining defendant.

1.

With regard to the locality test, the survivors argue that because the Coast Guard's actions * * * took place entirely on land, the alleged negligence did not occur on navigable waters. This contention is unavailing, however, because it ignores the clear law of our circuit that the situs of a tort for the purpose of determining admiralty jurisdiction is the place where the injury occurs.

* * *

* * * The survivors do not claim that the injuries occurred anywhere but at sea. Thus, the locality requirement is satisfied.

2.

We turn, then, to the nexus requirement. The survivors argue that the land-based Coast Guard's failure to communicate with the land-based Maui Fire Department is insufficiently related to maritime activity to support admiralty jurisdiction. The Supreme Court's opinion in *Grubart* describes the two relevant inquiries:

> The connection test raises two issues. A court, first, must "assess the general features of the type of incident involved" to determine whether the incident has "a potentially disruptive impact on maritime commerce." Second, a court must determine whether "the general character" of the "activity giving rise to the incident" shows a "substantial relationship to traditional maritime activity." *Grubart* [*supra* at 32], 513 U.S. at 534.

As to the first inquiry, the "type of incident involved" is to be considered at an "intermediate" level of generality. In *Grubart*, for example, the Court described the incident (which specifically involved the faulty replacement of wooden pilings supporting bridges) as "damage by a vessel in navigable water to an underwater structure." So described, the incident clearly posed a danger to maritime commerce.

A corresponding description of the "type of incident involved" in this case would thus be something such as "injury to boaters whose vessel capsizes at sea because of a potential rescuer's negligence in carrying out its rescue operation." One could quibble about precisely how to frame the question, but it is clear that at any reasonable level of generality the incident had a "potentially disruptive impact on maritime commerce." *See, e.g.*, *Polly v. Estate of Carlson*, 859 F. Supp. 270, 272 (E.D. Mich. 1994) ("That men were overboard in an emergency situation by itself is likely to disrupt commercial activity...."). The efficacy of search-and-rescue operations has a direct effect on the health and lives of seamen. While the kayakers in this case were engaged in recreational and not commercial activity, there is no reason to regard that fact as relevant to the nature of the Coast Guard's activity, which would presumably have been the same no matter the purpose of the kayakers' excursion at sea. *Cf. Sisson v. Ruby* [*supra* at 32] ("The relevant "activity" is defined not by the particular circumstances of the incident, but by the general conduct from which the incident arose."). Search-and-rescue operations also affect the vessels themselves: insofar as the rescuer can preserve the vessel, it prevents economic loss to the vessel's owner.

The second inquiry within the nexus test requires us to decide whether the "general character of the activity giving rise to the incident shows a substantial relationship to traditional maritime activity." [ ] A preliminary question arises: what constitutes the "activity giving rise to the incident"? The survivors ask us to follow the path carved out in *Delta Country Ventures, Inc. v. Magana*, 986 F.2d 1260 (9th Cir. 1993). That case dealt with a claim against the owner of a houseboat by a guest who dove off the boat, hit an object in the water, and was paralyzed. The guest sued the owner for negligently situating the boat. The owner asserted admiralty jurisdiction so it could invoke the Limitation of Liability Act, [46 U.S.C. § 30505], to limit its liability to the value of the boat. We held that there was no admiralty jurisdiction because the "activity giving rise to the incident" had no relationship to traditional maritime activity. We did so, however, because we conceived of the "activity" in question as the guest's diving into the water, and held that recreational diving has no relation to traditional maritime activity. [ ] It would be inappropriate, we held, to look past the immediate event surrounding the injury to a more remote cause such as the boat owner's negligent placement of the boat near an underwater object. *But see* id. at 1264 (Kozinski, J., dissenting).

Were we bound by the approach of the *Delta County Ventures* majority, the survivors' argument might have some merit: the activity in question could be defined as recreational kayaking, which (arguably, though not obviously) does not bear a sufficient relationship to traditional maritime activity. But the *Delta County Ventures* approach is flatly inconsistent with the Supreme Court's subsequent decision in *Grubart* and hence is no longer good law. * * * The Court held in *Grubart* that

> we need to look only to whether one of the arguably proximate causes of the incident originated in the maritime activity of a tortfeasor: as long as one of the putative tortfeasors was engaged in traditional maritime activity the allegedly wrongful activity will "involve" such traditional maritime activity and will meet the second nexus prong. 513 U.S. at 541.

The activity at issue, then, is not merely the event immediately surrounding the injury; it is the behavior of any "putative tortfeasor[ ]" (here, the Coast Guard) that is an "arguably proximate cause[ ]" of the injury. In this case, then, the relevant question is whether the Coast Guard's search-and-rescue operation shows a substantial relationship to traditional maritime activity.

It assuredly does. *See Berg v. Chevron U.S.A.*, 759 F.2d 1425, 1429 (9th Cir. 1985) ("The law of admiralty has always sought to encourage and induce men of the sea to go to the aid of life and property in distress." (citations and internal quotation marks omitted)); *Kelly v. United States*, 531 F.2d 1144, 1147 (2d Cir. 1976) ("Rescue operations of the Coast Guard conducted on navigable waters do in fact bear a significant relationship to traditional maritime activities for purposes of admiralty jurisdiction."); *see also Sisson*, 497 U.S. at 367 ("The need for uniform rules of maritime conduct and liability is not limited to navigation, but extends at least to any other activities traditionally undertaken by vessels, commercial or noncommercial."). The Supreme Court emphasized in *Grubart* that the nexus test is not meant to exclude broad swathes of activity; it wrote approvingly of the notion that "virtually every activity involving a vessel on navigable waters would be a traditional maritime activity sufficient to invoke maritime jurisdiction."

Thus, the locality test and both subprongs of the nexus test are satisfied in this case. It follows that all of the survivors' claims fall within federal admiralty jurisdiction.

[The court concluded that because the PVA and SAA provided remedies for the types of torts raised, the survivors' claims were not cognizable under the FTCA. It therefore affirmed the district court's grant of summary judgment.]

Notes

1. Some plaintiffs in *Taghadomi* were U.S. citizens and some were Iranians. The U.S. plaintiffs were unable to recover under either the PVA or the SAA because they failed to file a timely complaint. The Iranian plaintiffs had no remedy under the PVA because that statute allows suits by foreign nationals only if their countries allow similar suits by U.S. citizens and Iran does not do so. *See* 46 U.S.C. § 31111. The court held that the PVA's reciprocity requirement also barred the Iranian plaintiff's claim under the SAA. (For further attention to these statutes, see *infra* Chapter XIII.)

2. In *Delta Country Ventures*, disapproved by *Taghadomi*, the court focused on the injured victim's activity and found that it did not bear a substantial relationship to traditional maritime activity. In that case a 15-year old boy became quadriplegic when he dove into the water from a houseboat. The vessel's owner brought suit in federal court seeking protection under the Limitation of Liability Act, 46 U.S.C. §§ 30505–30512, which has generally been held to be inapplicable to accidents that fall outside admiralty jurisdiction. See *infra* at 50 note 3. Because the majority of the court determined that the case was not within the admiralty jurisdiction, the vessel owner was not entitled to limit its liability. In his dissent, 986 F.2d at 1264–67, Judge Kozinski wrote:

> I fear the compelling facts of this case have led my colleagues to formulate far too narrow a definition of our admiralty jurisdiction. * * * What we must examine under the second prong of *Sisson* is whether the injury took place on or about a vessel engaged in traditional maritime activity. The injury in *Executive Jet* did not, so admiralty jurisdiction did not attach; the injuries in *Foremost* and *Sisson* did, so admiralty jurisdiction attached. This does not, as the majority suggests, reinstate the maritime locality test. Many things that take place on or about vessels wouldn't support admiralty jurisdiction. *See, e.g., Penton v. Pomano Constr. Co., Inc.*, 976 F.2d 636 (11th Cir. 1992) (construction worker injured while building a jetty by operating a crane on a barge); *David Wright Charter Serv. v. Wright*, 925 F.2d 783, 784 (4th Cir. 1991) (per curiam) (explosion of boat stored in shed 75 feet away from water); *Myhran v. Johns-Mansville Corp.*, 741 F.2d 1119 (9th Cir. 1984) (pipefitter's exposure to asbestos while repairing vessel); *Ozzello v. Peterson Builders, Inc.*, 743 F. Supp. 1302 (E.D. Wis. 1990) (construction employee injured by hose while working on deck).

In other limitation of liability cases some courts have made questionable determinations that the federal courts lacked subject matter jurisdiction. E.g., *Tandon v. Captain's Cove Marina of Bridgeport, Inc.*, 752 F.3d 239, 2014 AMC 1581 (2d Cir. 2014) (altercation by recreational boaters in water and on permanent dock surrounded by water that caused serious personal injury; type of incident posed no realistic threat to maritime commerce); *H20 Houseboat Vacations Inc. v. Hernandez*, 103 F.3d 914, 1997 AMC 390 (9th Cir. 1996) (renters of houseboat tied to dock suffered injuries from carbon monoxide while inside the boat; incident did not have potential to disrupt maritime commerce); *Hickam v. Segars*, 905 F. Supp. 2d 835 (M.D. Tenn. 2012) (line connecting jet ski to inner tube snapped and caused serious injury to victim on land; case failed both prongs of nexus test).

3. **Particular determinations**. Many courts have held that product liability claims by shipyard workers against manufacturers of asbestos are nonmaritime. E.g., *Eagle-Picher Indus. v. United States*, 846 F.2d 888 (3d Cir. 1988). Most of these decisions were based on pre-*Grubart* law and some courts have begun to apply maritime law in these situations.

E.g., *Conner v. Alfa Laval, Inc.*, 799 F. Supp. 2d 455, 2012 AMC 2846 (E.D. Pa. 2011) (multidistrict litigation).

Claims relating to seamen's injuries will usually pass the nexus tests. See, e.g., *Taylor v. Kennedy Engine, Inc.*, 861 F.2d 127 (5th Cir. 1988) (defendant's land-based crane damaged ladder on vessel causing seaman to fall on vessel while the vessel was at dock undergoing repairs and was apparently not able to proceed under its own power); *Miles v. Melrose*, 882 F.2d 976 (5th Cir. 1989) (action against labor union for referring a violent crew member to a shipowner without warning of his dangerous propensities). But see *Harrison v. Glendel Drilling Co.*, 679 F. Supp. 1413 (W.D. La. 1988) (rejecting admiralty jurisdiction over shipowner's indemnity claim against doctor for alleged onshore malpractice following seaman's injury at sea).

Suits by passengers have been held to be maritime even when there has been nothing uniquely maritime about the circumstances of the injury. See, e.g., *McDonough v. Royal Caribbean Cruises, Ltd.*, 48 F.3d 256 (7th Cir. 1995) (steward pushed dolly over passenger's foot while the two were standing in a cruise ship's elevator); *Friedman v. Cunard Line Ltd.*, 996 F. Supp. 303 (S.D.N.Y. 1998) (fall during aerobics class while ship was at anchor) (reviewing cases).

Many of these cases were decided under some version of a test first announced in *Kelly v. Smith*, 485 F.2d 520 (5th Cir. 1973), that was rejected by *Grubart*. See *supra* at 36.

4. In *East River S.S. Corp. v. Transamerica Delaval, Inc.*, 476 U.S. 858, 864 (1986) (*infra* at 140), the Court held strict liability tort claims against a manufacturer of engines for commercial vessels were within the admiralty jurisdiction. The Court explained:

> We need not reach the question whether a maritime nexus also must be established when a tort occurs on the high seas. Were there such a requirement, it clearly was met here, for these ships were engaged in maritime commerce, a primary concern of admiralty law.

5. A week after deciding *East River*, the Court held that the crash of a helicopter ferrying workers from offshore structures on the high seas satisfies the nexus requirement. It wrote:

> Here, admiralty jurisdiction is expressly provided under [the Death on the High Seas Act] because the accidental deaths occurred beyond a marine league from shore. See [46 U.S.C. § 30302]. Even without this statutory provision, admiralty jurisdiction is appropriately invoked here under traditional principles because the accident occurred on the high seas and in furtherance of an activity bearing a significant relationship to a traditional maritime activity. See *Executive Jet* [ ]. Although the decedents were killed while riding in a helicopter and not a more traditional maritime conveyance, that helicopter was engaged in a function traditionally performed by waterborne vessels: the ferrying of passengers from an "island," albeit an artificial one, to the shore.

Offshore Logistics, Inc. v. Tallentire, 477 U.S. 207, 218–219 (1986).

6. The courts have maintained separate tests for torts and contract claims even when they overlap. For example, in *East River*, the Court held that the contract claims for products liability were outside the admiralty jurisdiction because contracts to build vessels are non-maritime. By contrast, the related tort claims were maritime. Sometimes the contract claim is maritime but the tort claim is not. See, e.g., *Thompson v. Chesapeake Yacht Club*, 255 F. Supp. 555 (D. Md. 1966) where a person fell through a hole on an extension to a pier. The tort was non-maritime because the locality requirement was not met, but the contract claim for failure to provide a safe dock was maritime.

7. What about a products liability tort claim against the manufacturer of a jet ski for death resulting from a collision with an anchored vessel? The Supreme Court's entire discussion of the jurisdictional issue in *Yamaha Motor Corp. v. Calhoun*, 516 U.S. 199, 206 (1996) (*infra* at 246) consisted of the following sentence: "Because this case involves a watercraft collision on navigable waters, it falls within admiralty's domain." The Court cited *Foremost* and *Sisson* for support. Notice that those cases were not products liability cases. Have the justices who concurred in *Grubart* won?

8. Should courts continue to impose the nexus requirements when a vessel causes the injury? Recall that in footnote 5 the *Grubart* court left that question open. Consider the next case.

Tagliere v. Harrah's Illinois Corp.

United States Court of Appeals, Seventh Circuit, 2006
445 F.3d 1012, 2006 AMC 1290

POSNER, Circuit Judge:

The defendant owns and operates a riverboat casino that at the time of the plaintiff's accident had for the previous two years been moored to a pier on a navigable portion of the Des Plaines River in Illinois; Illinois law permits a casino boat to be moored indefinitely. The plaintiff was playing a slot machine when the stool she was leaning against collapsed and she fell, injuring herself. The boat was stationary when the accident occurred rather than rocking back and forth in the wash of a passing boat. Nevertheless the plaintiff filed suit in federal district court under the admiralty law. The defendant moved to dismiss the suit on the ground that it was not within the admiralty jurisdiction. The district court granted the motion.

Had the casino been located on the pier rather than in a boat moored to it, there would be no argument that the plaintiff's claim was an admiralty claim. Since the boat was moored indefinitely, it could be thought the equivalent of landfill, and an accident occurring on landfill adjacent to navigable waters is not within the admiralty jurisdiction unless (as we'll see) the accident involved the boat's colliding with or otherwise damaging something on the land. The accident in our case had nothing to do with the fact that the casino was on a boat afloat on a navigable stream rather than sitting on dry land. And so whatever distinctive rules of liability admiralty courts have developed would be no better suited, and perhaps would be worse suited, to the resolution of this accident case than ordinary state tort law would be. There is, therefore, common-sense appeal to the district court's ruling that the suit is not within the admiralty jurisdiction.

But the most important requirement of a jurisdictional rule is not that it appeal to common sense but that it be clear. [ ] It is very unfortunate when parties are not sure which court they should be litigating their dispute in, as the case at hand illustrates. The plaintiff brought suit within the three-year statute of limitations applicable to admiralty tort suits, [46 U.C. § 30106] [ ], but the statute of limitations applicable to personal-injury suits under Illinois law is only two years [ ], so that if the ruling stands the plaintiff is barred from any judicial relief because she sued more than two years after the accident.

Congress has extended the admiralty jurisdiction to ["cases of injury or damage, to person or property, caused by a vessel on navigable waters." Extension of Admiralty Jurisdiction Act, 46 U.S.C. § 30101(a).]. Since "vessel" has been interpreted to include the vessel's fixtures, furniture, and other "appurtenances," [*Grubart, supra* at 30, 513 U.S. at 535] [ ], the injury resulting from the defective stool in this case was an injury caused by a vessel. [ ] The vessel was on navigable waters, moreover, and while the Supreme Court has now held that a boat that "has been permanently moored or otherwise rendered practically incapable of transportation or movement" is not a "vessel" for purposes of admiralty jurisdiction, *Stewart v. Dutra Const. Co.* [*supra* at 21, 543 U.S. at 494], there has been no showing that the boat in our case, though stationary for the past two years, is permanently moored in the Court's sense (disabled from sailing) and is thus the equivalent of landfill.

To subject to the admiralty jurisdiction an accident that occurs on a vessel afloat on a navigable body of water, and that is caused by the vessel or by some object in or attached to it, is a natural application of the Extension of Admiralty Jurisdiction Act. *St. Hilaire Moye v. Henderson*, 496 F.2d 973, 979 (8th Cir.1974); 1 Robert Force & Martin J. Norris, The Law of Maritime Personal Injuries § 1:17 (5th ed.2005); David W. Robertson & Michael F. Sturley, "The Admiralty Extension Act Solution," 34 J. Mar. L. & Comm. 209, 239–43, 269–73, 297 (2003); Russell J. Smith, *Note, Congress Giveth and the Fifth Circuit Taketh Away: Post Executive Jet Viability of the Admiralty Extension Act*, 6 U.S.F. Mar. L.J. 609 (1994). But this is on the assumption that the Act is indeed, as its title and language suggest, an independent basis of federal jurisdiction—independent, that is, of the basic grant of admiralty jurisdiction in 28 U.S.C. § 1333(1). And so the Eighth Circuit held in the *St. Hilaire* case, cited above, though the Supreme Court left the question open in [*Grubart, supra* at 35 n.5, 513 U.S. at 543 n.5] as it had earlier done in *Sisson v. Ruby*, 497 U.S. 358, 359 n.1 (1990). But the Fifth and Eleventh Circuits have rejected (though without citing) *St. Hilaire. Sohyde Drilling & Marine Co. v. Coastal States Gas Producing Co.*, 644 F.2d 1132, 1135–36 (5th Cir.1981); *Crotwell v. Hockman-Lewis, Ltd.*, 734 F.2d 767, 768 (11th Cir.1984). They have done this on the basis of legislative history. That history indicates that the Act's purpose was merely to make clear that accidents caused by boats on navigable waters are within the admiralty jurisdiction even if the damage caused by the accident was to something on the land. H.R.Rep. No. 1523, 80th Cong., 2d Sess. (1948); S.Rep. No. 1593, 80th Cong., 2d Sess. (1948).

We do not think that the legislative history should override the broad statutory language, which provides a clear and simple jurisdictional test for cases like this, in contrast to the vague "maritime nexus" (or "connection") test * * * that is used to determine jurisdiction under section 1333(1), which confers but does not define admiralty jurisdiction. But our case would pass that test as well; vagueness has it uses.

The main practical use of the "connection" test has been to expel from the admiralty jurisdiction freak cases. Thus, in describing the application of the test the Supreme Court in *Grubart* cited a case involving a plane crash in which a portion of the wreckage slid into navigable waters, *Executive Jet Aviation, Inc. v. City of Cleveland*, 409 U.S. 249 (1972), the case of a swimmer diving off a pier into navigable waters, *Chapman v. City of Grosse Pointe Farms*, 385 F.2d 962 (6th Cir.1967), and the case of a motorist rear-ended while waiting for a ferry on the ferry's landing, which happened to be a floating pontoon. *Peytavin v. Government Employees Ins. Co.*, 453 F.2d 1121 (5th Cir.1972). *Grubart* itself involved the flooding of tunnels and basements in Chicago caused by the fact that months earlier a crane sitting on a barge had driven piles too far into a riverbed above a tunnel.

Yet unusual as were the facts in *Grubart*, the case was about an appurtenance (the crane) of a boat (a barge) afloat on navigable waters and an accident, albeit on land, caused by the handling of the appurtenance. A passage in the Court's opinion suggests that the Court thought the case rather simple: "This Court has not proposed any radical alteration of the traditional criteria for invoking admiralty jurisdiction in tort cases, but has simply followed the lead of the lower federal courts in rejecting a location rule so rigid as to extend admiralty to a case involving an airplane, not a vessel, engaged in activity far removed from anything traditionally maritime." 513 U.S. at 542. The "location" rule at its broadest was that any accident that occurs on navigable waters is within the admiralty jurisdiction. *The Plymouth*, 70 U.S. (3 Wall.) 20, 36 (1865). That would have encompassed the airplane, swimmer, and motorist cases, and the Court made clear in *Grubart* that it wouldn't go that far. When a boat is involved, however, the location rule is not only thoroughly compatible with the language of the Extension of Admiralty Jurisdiction Act, but appears to have survived *Grubart* and thus to be the test under the general admiralty jurisdiction conferred by 28 U.S.C. § 1333(1), as well.

Weaver v. Hollywood Casino-Aurora, Inc., 255 F.3d 379, 386–87 (7th Cir.2001), found even the "connection" test of *Grubart* and *Sisson* satisfied in a case like the present one, the main difference being that the injury was to a crewmember of the gambling boat rather than to a passenger. An injury to a crewmember is somewhat more likely to affect maritime commerce than an injury to a passenger, because the crewmember might be vital to the operation of the boat and difficult to replace immediately. Yet even an injury to a passenger could have a disruptive effect, if the boat had to make an unscheduled stop to get him to a hospital (not that that could have happened here, since the boat was moored), or if the injury revealed a dangerous condition that required time-consuming repairs. We do not think it necessary to split these hairs—especially since effect on maritime commerce is not necessary to admiralty jurisdiction.

We acknowledge that the distinctive substantive and procedural features of admiralty law, such as the longer statute of limitations and the absence of a right to a jury trial, were not designed for the kind of accident that occurred here, an accident that owed nothing to its maritime setting. So our suggested rule encroaches on a regulatory domain that might well be thought to belong more properly to state courts and legislatures than to federal admiralty courts. But to decide in each case whether admiralty law or state law would make a better fit with the particular circumstances of the accident that had given rise to the suit would make the determination of jurisdiction hopelessly uncertain. It is not a price worth paying for the slightly better match of law to fact that would result.

* * *

* * * We conclude that the district court erred in dismissing the suit, though it is open to the defendant to show on remand, if it can, that its boat was permanently rather than merely indefinitely moored when the accident occurred and was therefore no longer a "vessel" for purposes of admiralty jurisdiction. The difference between "permanently" and "indefinitely" in this context is vague and has not been explored by the parties. The *Stewart* case suggests that the boat must be permanently incapacitated from sailing. Yet maybe—by analogy to the difference between domicile and residence—a boat also is "permanently" moored when its owner intends that the boat will never again sail, while if he has not yet decided its ultimate destiny it is only "indefinitely" moored. These are matters for exploration on remand.

Reversed and remanded.

Notes

1. Courts have held that injury is "caused by a vessel" when injury results from a seaman's wrongful act committed on board the vessel. One case involved a "booze cruise"

when a passenger was served too many drinks and injured another passenger after disembarking. In *Duluth Superior Excursions v. Makela*, 623 F.2d 1251 (8th Cir. 1980), the court held that it had admiralty jurisdiction over a car accident that occurred six minutes after docking. What if the victims were not passengers on the vessel? See *Young v. Players Lake Charles, L.L.C.*, 47 F. Supp. 2d 832 (S.D. Tex. 1999) (admiralty jurisdiction against riverboat casino). See also *White v. Sabatino*, 526 F. Supp. 2d 1135 (D. Hawaii 2007) (admiralty law governs the effect of a settlement between a vessel owner and the estate of an accident victim on non-settling defendants). A questionable case is *Doe v. Celebrity Cruises, Inc.*, 394 F.3d 891 (11th Cir. 2004) (holding that the locality requirement was satisfied when a crew member raped a passenger ashore at a port of call).

2. Restitution claims present their own set of problems. In *Archawski v. Hanioti*, 350 U.S. 532 (1956), the plaintiffs sought restitution of passage money. They were would-be passengers who had paid in advance; the defendant then abandoned the voyage and refused to refund the money. The Second Circuit held that the claim was nonmaritime because the implied promise to repay the money was nonmaritime. But the Supreme Court reversed, saying:

> The truth is that in a case such as the present one there is neither an actual promise to repay the passage moneys nor a second contract. The problem is to prevent unjust enrichment from a maritime contract. See Morrison, *The Remedial Powers of the Admiralty*, 43 YALE L.J. 1, 27 (1933). A court that prevents a maritime contract from being exploited in that way does not reach beyond the domain of maritime affairs. We conclude that, so long as the claim asserted arises out of a maritime contract, the admiralty court has jurisdiction over it.

350 U.S. at 628.

Some restitution claims do not involve a contract between the parties, such as when one person confers a benefit on another by fulfilling that party's obligation. See *Peninsular & Oriental Steam Navigation Co. v. Overseas Oil Carriers, Inc.*, 553 F.2d 830 (2d Cir.1977) (exercising admiralty jurisdiction over claims for reimbursement of expenses incurred in rescuing an ill seaman while at sea). See *infra* at 404. Another type of restitution claim would be that a defendant has gained an unjust benefit by using another's property without permission. We think that the claim for restitution in this latter type of case would be maritime if a tort claim against the defendant under these circumstances would be maritime.

3. **Statutes that supply a stand-alone basis for admiralty jurisdiction.** *Tagliere* suggests that the Admiralty Extension Act, 46 U.S.C. § 30101, supplies an alternative route (*i.e.*, an alternative to 28 U.S.C. § 1333) to admiralty tort jurisdiction. *Executive Jet* (*supra* at 31) repeatedly indicates that the Death on the High Seas Act, 46 U.S.C. § 30302, is another such statute. *See* 409 U.S. at 263–64, 271 n. 20. The thrust of *Panama R. Co., infra* at 152, and *O'Donnell, infra* at 159, is that the Jones Act, 46 U.S.C. § 301014, extends admiralty jurisdiction over all occurrences within its coverage.

Numerous modern lower-court cases hold that the Limitation Act, 46 U.S.C. § 30511, does *not* supply an independent basis for admiralty jurisdiction, but *Richardson v. Harmon*, 222 U.S. 96 (1911), suggests the contrary. In *Sisson v. Ruby*, 497 U.S. 358, 359 n.1 (1990), the Supreme Court declined to reach the issue.

4. **The coverage of DOHSA.** DOHSA covers "death ... caused by wrongful act, neglect, or default occurring on the high seas...." 46 U.S.C. § 30302. Courts have read that language to require focus on where the fatal accident occurred (rather than on where the victim

eventually died or where the defendant's causal wrongful conduct occurred). See, e.g., *Motts v. M/V Green Wave*, 210 F.3d 565 (5th Cir. 2000), where DOHSA was held to cover a situation in which a land-based provider of medical advice negligently caused inappropriate treatment of a patient at sea, leading to the patient's subsequent death on land. Compare the cases treated in the second paragraph of note 1 following *Grubart*, *supra* at 39.

The DOHSA term "high seas" does not prevent the application of DOHSA to fatal accidents in foreign territorial waters. See, e.g., *Howard v. Crystal Cruises, Inc.*, 41 F.3d 527, 529 (9th Cir. 1994) (collecting cases and other authorities).

E. Admiralty Jurisdiction in Contract Cases

Most of the nineteenth-century Supreme Court decisions working out the boundaries of admiralty jurisdiction over contract cases reflected the political issues sketched in section I-A, *supra* at 5–15. At the doctrinal level, the Court was concerned with (a) assessing (and for the most part rejecting) the English limitations and (b) trying to articulate a general test or formula for determining which contracts are maritime enough to be cognizable in admiralty. *Insurance Co. v. Dunham*, 78 U.S. 1 (1870), is perhaps the most important of those decisions. In the course of a unanimous opinion seconding Justice Story's *DeLovio v. Boit* reasoning (and asserting Story's "great erudition," *id.* at 35), the Court held that admiralty jurisdiction extends over marine insurance policies. Helpful precedents—earlier decisions bringing discrete types of contracts into admiralty—included *New Jersey Steam Navigation Co. v. Merchant's Bank*, 47 U.S. 344 (1848) (carriage of goods); *The Moses Taylor* 71 U.S. 411 (1867) [*infra* at 66] (carriage of passengers); and *The Belfast*, 74 U.S. 624 (1868) (intrastate carriage of goods). The *Dunham* Court gave a one-sentence policy argument:

> [T]he contract of insurance, and the rights of the parties arising therefrom, are affected by and mixed up with all the questions that can arise in maritime commerce—jettison, abandonment, average, salvage, capture, prize, bottomry, &c.

And it embarked on an extended and entertaining analogy between marine insurance policies and contracts for the carriage of goods:

> It is objected that [a marine insurance policy] is not a maritime contract because it is made on the land and is to be performed (by payment of the loss) on the land. * * * So the contract of affreightment is also made on land, and is to be performed on the land by the delivery of the goods and payment of the freight. It is true that in the latter case a maritime service is to be performed in the transportation of the goods. But if we carefully analyze the contract of insurance we shall find that, in effect, it is a contract, or guaranty, on the part of the insurer, that the ship or goods shall pass safely over the sea, and through its storms and its many casualties, to the port of destination; and if they do not pass safely, but meet with disaster from any of the misadventures insured against, the insurer will pay the loss sustained. So in the contract of affreightment, the master guarantees that the goods shall be safely transported (dangers of the sea excepted) from the port of shipment to the port of delivery, and there delivered. The contract of the one guarantees against loss from the dangers of the sea, the contract of the other against loss from all other dangers. Of course, these contracts do not always run precisely parallel to each other * * *; special terms are inserted

> in each at the option of the parties. But this statement shows the general nature of the two contracts. And how a fair mind can discern any substantial distinction between them on the question whether they are or are not, maritime contracts, is difficult to imagine.

The *Dunham* Court was sure it was right about marine insurance policies, but when it came to articulating a general rule for determining admiralty's contract jurisdiction, arguably it displayed much less confidence:

> It * * * appears that in each case the decision of the court and the reasoning on which it was founded have been based upon the fundamental inquiry whether the contract was or was not a maritime contract. If it was, the jurisdiction was asserted; if it was not, the jurisdiction was denied. And whether maritime or not maritime depended, not on the place where the contract was made, but on the subject-matter of the contract. If that was maritime the contract was maritime. This may be regarded as the established doctrine of the court.

Professor Charles Black famously criticized the rules for admiralty contract jurisdiction with the observation that they have "about as much principle as there is in a list of irregular verbs." Black, *Admiralty Jurisdiction: Critique and Suggestions*, 50 COLUM. L. REV. 259, 264 (1950). The practical solution, he explained, was that "the contracts involved tend to fall into a not-too-great number of stereotypes, the proper placing of which can be learned, like irregular verbs, and errors in grammar thus avoided." *Id.*

North Pacific Steamship Co. v. Hall Brothers Marine Railway & Shipbuilding Co.

Supreme Court of the United States, 1919
249 U.S. 119, 39 S. Ct. 221, 63 L. Ed. 510

Mr. Justice PITNEY delivered the opinion of the unanimous Court.

This is a direct appeal involving only the question whether the cause was within the admiralty jurisdiction of a District Court of the United States.

Both parties are corporations of the state of California. Appellee, which for convenience may be referred to as the "Shipbuilding Company," filed its libel in personam against appellant, which we may call the "Steamship Company," to recover a balance claimed to be due for certain work and labor done, services rendered, and materials furnished in and about the repairing of the steamship *Yucatan*. The Steamship Company filed an answer denying material averments of the libel, and a cross-libel setting up a claim for damages for delay in the making of the repairs. The cause having been heard upon the pleadings and proofs, there was a decree for a recovery in favor of the Shipbuilding Company and a dismissal of the cross-libel. After this the Steamship Company filed a motion to arrest and vacate the decree and to dismiss the cause for want of jurisdiction. The motion * * * was denied, and the present appeal followed.

The facts were these: In the month of May, 1911, the Steamship Company was the owner of the American steamer *Yucatan*, which then lay moored or tied up at dock upon the waters of Puget Sound at Seattle, in the state of Washington. The vessel, which was of steel construction, was in need of extensive repairs. She had been wrecked, and had remained submerged for a long time; ice floes had torn away the upper decks, and some of her bottom plates also needed to be replaced. She was under charter for an Alaskan voyage, to be commenced as soon as the repairs could be completed. * * * Under these circumstances it was agreed between the parties that the Shipbuilding Company should tow the vessel from where she lay to the shipyard, haul her out as required upon the marine railway to a position on dry land adjacent to the machine shop—the place being known as the "dry dock," and the hauling out being described as "docking"—and should furnish mechanics, laborers, and foremen as needed, who were to work with other men already in the employ of the Steamship Company, and under its superintendence * * *.

The vessel was docked and repaired in the manner contemplated by the agreement; she was brought to the shipyard on the 27th of May, and lay in the water alongside of the dock there until the 17th of June, during which time upper decks and beams were put in and other work of a character that could be done as well while she was afloat as in the dry dock. On June 17th she was hauled out and remained in dry dock for about two weeks while her bottom plates were renewed. During the same period the propeller was removed to permit of an examination of the tail shaft, and as the shaft showed deterioration a new one was ordered to be supplied by a concern in San Francisco. Upon completion of the work upon the bottom plates, and on the 5th of July, the vessel was returned to the water and lay there for about two weeks awaiting arrival of the new tail shaft. When this arrived the vessel was again hauled out, the tail shaft and propeller were fitted, and the remaining repairs completed. Libellant's claim was for work and labor performed, services rendered, and materials furnished under the circumstances mentioned, and was based upon the agreed scale of compensation.

The question in dispute is whether a claim thus grounded is the subject of admiralty jurisdiction; appellant's contention being that the contract, or at least an essential part of it, was for the use by appellant of libelant's marine railway, shipyard, equipment, and laborers in such manner as appellant might choose to employ them, and that it called for the performance of no maritime service by libelant.

* * *

It must be taken to be the settled law of this court that while the civil jurisdiction of the admiralty in matters of tort depends upon locality, whether the act was committed upon navigable waters, in matter of contract it depends upon the subject-matter, the nature and character of the contract, and that the English rule, which conceded jurisdiction, with a few exceptions, only to contracts made and to be executed upon the navigable waters, is inadmissible; the true criterion being the nature of the contract, as to whether it have reference to maritime service or maritime transactions. [ ] *Insurance Co. v. Dunham*, 78 U.S. 1, 26 (1870) [*supra* at 51].

In some of the earlier cases the influence of the English rule may be discerned, in that the question whether a contract was to be performed upon the navigable waters was referred to as pertinent to the question whether the contract was of a maritime nature (*The Thomas Jefferson*, 23 U.S. 428, 429 (1825) [*supra* at 8]); but a careful examination of the opinions shows that the place of performance was dealt with as an evidential circumstance bearing with more or less weight upon the fundamental question of the nature of the contract. If they go beyond this, they must be deemed to be overruled by *Insurance Co. v. Dunham, supra.*

Neither in jurisdiction nor in the method of procedure are our admiralty courts dependent alone upon the theory of implied hypothecation; it being established that in a civil cause of maritime origin involving a personal responsibility the libelant may proceed in personam if the respondent is within reach of process. [ ]

* * *

It is settled that a contract for building a ship or supplying materials for her construction is not a maritime contract. *People's Ferry Co. v. Beers*, 61 U.S. (20 How.) 393 (1857) [ ]. In *People's Ferry*, the court said:

> So far from the contract being purely maritime, and touching rights and duties appertaining to navigation (on the ocean or elsewhere), it was a contract made on land, to be performed on land.

But the true basis for the distinction between the construction and the repair of a ship, for purposes of the admiralty jurisdiction, is to be found in the fact that the structure does not become a ship, in the legal sense, until it is completed and launched.

> A ship is born when she is launched, and lives so long as her identity is preserved. Prior to her launching she is a mere congeries of wood and iron—an ordinary piece of personal property—as distinctly a land structure as a house, and subject * * * to mechanics' liens created by state law enforceable in the state courts. In the baptism of launching she receives her name, and from the moment her keel touches the water she is transformed, and becomes a subject of admiralty jurisdiction. (*Tucker v. Alexandroff*, 183 U.S. 424, 438 (1902).)

In *The Robert W. Parsons*, 191 U.S. 17, 33, 34 (1903), it was held that the admiralty jurisdiction extended to an action for repairs put upon a vessel while in dry dock; but the question whether this would apply to a vessel hauled up on land for repairs was reserved, the language of the court, by Mr. Justice Brown, being:

> Had the vessel been hauled up by ways upon the land and there repaired a different question might have been presented, as to which we express no opinion; but as all serious repairs upon the hulls of vessels are made in dry dock, the proposition that such repairs are made on land would practically deprive the admiralty courts of their largest and most important jurisdiction in connection with repairs.

In *The Steamship Jefferson*, 215 U.S. 130 (1909), it was held that the admiralty jurisdiction extends to a claim for salvage service rendered to a vessel while undergoing repairs in a dry dock.

What we have said sufficiently indicates the decision that should be reached in the case at bar. The contract as made contemplated the performance of services and the furnishing of the necessary materials for the repairs of the steamship *Yucatan*. It was an entire contract, intended to take the ship as she was and to discharge her only when completely repaired and fit for the Alaskan voyage. It did not contemplate, as is contended by appellant, either a lease, or a contract for use in the nature of a lease, of the libelant's marine railway and machine shop. The use of these was but incidental; the vessel being hauled out, when consistent with the progress of other work of the Shipbuilding Company, for the purpose of exposing the ship's bottom to permit of the removal and replacement of the broken plates and the examination of the propeller and tail shaft. In *The Planter* (*Peyroux v. Howard*), 32 U.S. 324, 327, 341 (1833), the vessel, requiring repairs below the water line as well as above, was to be and in fact was hauled up out of the water; and it was held that the contract for materials furnished and work performed in repairing her under these circumstances was a maritime contract. We think the same rule must be applied to the case before us; that the doubt intimated in *The Robert W. Parsons* must be laid aside; and that there is no difference in character as to repairs made upon the hull of a vessel dependent upon whether they are made while she is afloat, while in dry dock, or while hauled up by ways upon land. The nature of the service is identical in the several cases, and the admiralty jurisdiction extends to all.

This is recognized by the Act of Congress of June 23, 1910 (chapter 373, 36 Stat. 604 [Comp. St. § 7783]), which declares that "any person furnishing repairs, supplies, or other necessaries, including the use of dry dock or marine railway, to a vessel, whether foreign or domestic," upon the order of a proper person, shall have a maritime lien upon the vessel.

* * *

Decree affirmed.

Notes

1. Did the Court's statement of a general test for contract jurisdiction improve upon *Dunham*'s?

2. Factually *Peyroux v. Howard* was squarely on point. But the decision was not viewed as dispositive, presumably because the *Peyroux* Court's attention had not been directed to the potential significance of the fact that a good part of the repairs took place on land.

3. What weight should the Court have given to the 1910 statute? Does a congressional declaration that repairs on a marine railway create a maritime lien necessarily either assume the existence of admiralty jurisdiction or create admiralty jurisdiction?

4. **Shipbuilding.** It has been suggested that excluding shipbuilding contracts from the admiralty jurisdiction causes no real harm since the parties know the law and can safeguard their interests, and that the federal courts can exercise supplemental jurisdiction in appropriate cases. See AMERICAN LAW INSTITUTE, STUDY OF THE DIVISION OF JURISDICTION BETWEEN STATE AND FEDERAL COURTS 228 (1969). Judge Posner argued that such contracts involve damage at a fixed locale and that most "do not involve safety or other distinctively maritime issues at all." *In re Oil Spill by the Amoco Cadiz*, 699 F.2d 909, 914 (7th Cir. 1983).

5. **Sale of vessels.** It is well established in the lower courts that contracts to sell a vessel are non-maritime. E.g., *Lynnhaven Dolphin Corp. v. E.L.O. Enterprises*, 776 F.2d 538 (5th Cir. 1985). Does the sale of a vessel relate to maritime commerce? For purposes of jurisdiction must courts treat contracts to sell a vessel the same as contracts to build a vessel? Does the agreement to build a vessel necessarily include an agreement to sell it?

The traditional rule that contracts for the sale of a vessel are nonmaritime has long been criticized. See, e.g., *Jack Neilson, Inc. v. Tug Peggy*, 428 F.2d 54, 58 (5th Cir. 1970) (Wisdom, J.) ("the petrified rule that ship-sale contracts are not within admiralty jurisdiction ... 'arose as an analogy to a case [*People's Ferry Co. v. Beers*, quoted *supra* at 54] which is inconsistent with basic principles governing the admiralty jurisdiction of United States courts.'") (quoting Note, *Admiralty Jurisdiction and Ship-Sale Contracts*, 6 STAN. L. REV. 540, 540 (1954)) (footnote omitted). In 2008, a district court held that the "broad language" of *Norfolk Southern Railway Co. v. James N. Kirby, Pty Ltd.*, *infra* at 60, and its progeny "support the demise" of the traditional rule. *Kalafrana Shipping v. Sea Gull Shipping Co.*, 591 F. Supp. 2d 505, 509 (S.D.N.Y. 2008). But no other court was willing to follow that lead. What policies might justify adhering to the traditional rule?

6. **Ship mortgages.** As is discussed *infra* at 434, the Ship Mortgage Act of 1920 gives maritime lien status to certain ship mortgages. Previously ship mortgages had been treated as nonmaritime contracts.

7. **Products liability contract claims.** The influence of the ship-building and ship-sale exclusions means that claims for breach of warranty involving ship construction are non-

maritime. See *East River S.S. Corp. v. Transamerica Delaval, Inc., infra* at 140. The *East River* Court noted that the Uniform Commercial Code, adopted in 49 states, would apply. The Court held that the tort claims for products liability were maritime.

Kossick v. United Fruit Co.

Supreme Court of the United States, 1961
365 U.S. 731, 81 S. Ct. 886, 6 L. Ed. 2d 56, 1961 AMC 833

Mr. Justice HARLAN delivered the opinion of the Court.

This case calls in question the propriety of a dismissal before trial of the first cause of action in a seaman's diversity complaint. Dismissal was on the ground that the allegations of the complaint are deficient by reason of the New York Statute of Frauds.

The allegations of the complaint, which for present purposes must be taken as true, are in substance as follows: Petitioner, while employed as chief steward on one of the vessels of respondent, United Fruit Company, suffered a thyroid ailment, not attributable to any fault of the respondent, but with respect to which it concededly had a legal duty to provide him with maintenance and cure. *The Osceola*, 189 U.S. 158 (1903). Respondent insisted that petitioner undergo treatment at a United States Public Health Service Hospital. Petitioner, however, considering on the basis of past experience that such treatment would prove unsatisfactory and inadequate, notified respondent that he wished to be treated by a private physician who had agreed to take care of him for $350, which amount petitioner insisted would be payable by the respondent in fulfillment of its obligation for maintenance and cure.

Respondent, the complaint continues, declined to accede to this course, but agreed that if petitioner would enter a Public Health Service Hospital (where he would receive free care) it would assume responsibility for all consequences of improper or inadequate treatment. Relying on that undertaking, and being unable himself to defray the cost of private treatment, petitioner underwent treatment at a Public Health Service Hospital. The Public Health Service Hospital and private physician alluded to were both located in New York.

Finally, it is alleged that by reason of the improper treatment received at such hospital, petitioner suffered grievous unwonted bodily injury, for which the respondent, because of its undertaking, is liable to the petitioner for damages in the amount of $250,000.

The District Court dismissed the complaint, considering that the agreement sued on was void under the New York Statute of Frauds, * * * there being no allegation that such agreement was evidenced by any writing. The Court of Appeals affirmed. We brought the case here because it presented novel questions as to the interplay of state and maritime law.

* * *

With respect to respondent's alleged agreed undertaking, as the case comes to us, petitioner, on the one hand, does not deny the contract's invalidity under the New York Statute of Frauds, if state law controls, nor, on the other hand, can its validity well be doubted, though the alleged agreement was not reduced to writing, if maritime law controls. For it is an established rule of ancient respectability that oral contracts are generally regarded as valid by maritime law. In this posture of things two questions must be decided: First, was this alleged contract a maritime one? Second, if so, was it nevertheless of such a "local" nature that its validity should be judged by state law?

I.

The boundaries of admiralty jurisdiction over contracts—as opposed to torts or crimes—being conceptual rather than spatial, have always been difficult to draw. Precedent and usage are helpful insofar as they exclude or include certain common types of contract: a contract to repair [ ] or to insure a ship [ ] is maritime, but a contract to build a ship is not. [ ] Without doubt a contract for hire either of a ship or of the sailors and officers to man her is within the admiralty jurisdiction. [ ] A suit on a bond covering cargo on general average is governed by admiralty law [ ], while an agreement to pay damages for another's breach of a maritime charter is not [ ]. The closest analogy we have found to the case at hand is a contract for hospital services rendered an injured seaman in satisfaction of a shipowner's liability for maintenance and cure, which has been held to be a maritime contract. *Methodist Episcopal Hospital v. Pacific Transport Co.*, 3 F.2d 508 (N.D. Cal. 1920). The principle by reference to which the cases are supposed to fall on one side of the line or the other is an exceedingly broad one. "The only question is whether the transaction relates to ships and vessels, masters and mariners, as the agents of commerce...." I BENEDICT, ADMIRALTY, 131.

The Court of Appeals here held:

> The contract sued on is not a maritime contract, since it was merely a promise to pay money, on land, if the former seaman should suffer injury at the hands of the United States Public Health Service personnel, on land, in the course of medical treatment. * * * For all that appears in the complaint, it may well be that the contract sued on was allegedly made after the maritime contract of employment of the plaintiff had been terminated. It really makes no difference whether this was so or not. All that remained was the performance by the shipowner of its undisputed obligation to supply maintenance and cure. The shipowner supplied plaintiff with a master's certificate, which was used by him to obtain admittance as a patient in the United States Public Health Service Hospital. * * * That took care of the obligation to furnish "cure." * * * [ ]

With respect to the learned judges below, we think that is too narrow a view of the matter. It can as well be argued that the alleged contract related to and stood in place of a duty created by and known only in admiralty as a kind of fringe benefit to the maritime contract of hire. [ ] The Court of Appeals and respondent are certainly correct in considering that a shipowner's duty to provide maintenance and cure may ordinarily be discharged by the issuing of a master's certificate carrying admittance to a public hospital, and that a seaman who refuses such a certificate or the free treatment to which it entitles him without just cause, cannot further hold the shipowner to his duty to provide maintenance and cure. [ ] But without countenancing petitioner's intemperate aspersions against Public Health Service Hospitals, * * * we nevertheless are clear that the duty to afford maintenance and cure is not simply and as a matter of law an obligation to provide for entrance to a public hospital. The cases which respondent cites hold no more than that a seaman who can receive adequate and proper care free of charge at a public hospital may not "deliberately refuse the hospital privilege, and then assert a lien upon his vessel for the increased expense which his whim or taste has created." [ ] Presumably if a seaman refuses to enter a public hospital or, having entered, if he leaves to undergo treatment elsewhere, he may recover the cost of such other treatment upon proof that "proper and adequate" cure was not available at such hospital. [ ]

No matter how skeptical one may be that such a burden of proof could be sustained, or that an indigent seaman would be likely to risk losing his rights to free treatment on the chance of sustaining that burden, since we should not exclude that possibility as a matter of law as the Court of Appeals apparently did, it must follow that the contract here alleged should be regarded as an agreement on the part of petitioner to forego a course of treatment which might have involved respondent in some additional expense, in return for respondent's promise to make petitioner whole for any consequences of what appeared to it at the time as the cheaper alternative. In other words, the consideration for respondent's alleged promise was petitioner's good faith forbearance to press what he considered—perhaps erroneously—to be the full extent of his maritime right to maintenance and cure. [ ] So viewed, we think that the alleged agreement was sufficiently related to peculiarly maritime concerns as not to put it, without more, beyond the pale of admiralty law.

* * *

II.

[The Court went on to hold that state law would not be applied and so the contract was not barred by the statute of frauds. See *infra* at 124.]

[Justices Frankfurter, Whittaker, and Stewart dissented.]

Notes

1. **Preliminary contracts.** At least until recently, it was generally thought that certain contracts that lead up to a maritime contract are not maritime. Under this view, for example, although a marine insurance policy is maritime, a contract to procure such a policy was not. Similarly, a charterparty is maritime, but a contract to procure a person to make one was not. See 1 BENEDICT ON ADMIRALTY § 183. Judge Addison Brown justified the preliminary contract doctrine in *The Thames*, 10 F. 848 (S.D.N.Y. 1881), as follows:

> The distinction between preliminary services leading to a maritime contract and such contracts themselves * * * furnishes a distinction capable of somewhat easy application. If it be broken down, I do not perceive any other dividing line for excluding from the admiralty many other sorts of claims which have a reference, more or less near or remote, to navigation and commerce. If the broker of a charter-party be admitted, the insurance broker must follow—the drayman, the expressman, and all others who perform services having reference to a voyage either in contemplation or executed.

In *Minturn v. Maynard*, 58 U.S. 477 (1855), the Supreme Court held that an agent who had advanced funds for repairs and supplies necessary for a vessel could not bring a claim in admiralty against the vessel's owners. Lower courts interpreted *Minturn* as establishing a *per se* rule excluding agency contracts from admiralty. In *Exxon Corp. v. Central Gulf Lines, Inc.*, 500 U.S. 603 (1991), however, the Court overruled *Minturn* and held that "lower courts should look to the subject matter of the agency contract and determine whether the services performed under the contract are maritime in nature." The Court reasoned that Exxon's contract to provide fuel to vessels was maritime in nature whether Exxon furnished the fuel itself or bought the fuel from a third party and had the third party deliver to the vessels.

Does *Exxon* undermine the preliminary contract doctrine? The *Exxon* Court declared that it did not reach the issue:

> [T]he District Court regarded the services performed by Exxon * * * as "preliminary" and characterized the rule excluding agency contracts from admiralty

> as "a subset" of the preliminary contract doctrine. [ ] This Court has never ruled on the validity of the preliminary contract doctrine, nor do we reach that question here. However, we emphasize that *Minturn* has been overruled and that courts should focus on the nature of the services performed by the agent in determining whether an agency contract is a maritime contract.

In the wake of *Exxon,* several courts have concluded that contracts with insurance brokers to procure marine insurance are within the admiralty jurisdiction. See, e.g., *Fernandez v. Haynie*, 120 F. Supp. 2d 575 (E.D. Va. 2000), *aff'd*, 31 Fed. Appx. 816 (4th Cir. 2002) (per curiam).

2. In a case decided before *Exxon*, the Second Circuit exercised admiralty jurisdiction over a contract between a shipper and a freight forwarder that called for the latter to prepare, obtain, and process shipping documents including a bill of lading. *Ingersoll Milling Mach. Co. v. M/V Bodena*, 829 F.2d 293 (2d Cir. 1987). The court said that the services were not preliminary to a voyage but were essential to it because "[w]ithout these, there can be no voyage." Is that a coherent explanation?

3. Contracts to load and unload vessels are maritime. *American Stevedores v. Porello*, 330 U.S. 446 (1947). The lease of shipping containers is maritime. *CTI-Container Leasing Corp. v. Oceanic Operations Corp.*, 682 F.2d 377 (2d Cir. 1982). What about a contract to watch a vessel? See *Port Welcome Cruises, Inc. v. S.S. Bay Belle*, 215 F. Supp. 72 (D. Md.) (maritime), *aff'd* 324 F.2d 954 (4th Cir. 1963); *The Seguranca*, 58 F. 908 (S.D.N.Y. 1893) (maritime); *The Sirius*, 65 F. 226 (N.D. Cal. 1895) (not maritime).

4. **Mixed contracts.** Courts and commentators have long declared that a contract is not within the admiralty jurisdiction unless it is "wholly maritime." See, e.g., *Rea v. The Eclipse*, 135 U.S. 599, 608 (1890) (contract jurisdiction "is limited to contracts, claims and services purely maritime"); *Grant v. Poillon*, 61 U.S. (20 How.) 162, 168 (1858) ("whole contract must, in its essence, be maritime"); Gilmore & Black, The Law of Admiralty 28 & n.95 (2d ed. 1975). Thus a contract to perform some maritime and some non-maritime services or an insurance policy that covers some maritime and some non-maritime risks, to take two simple examples, would traditionally have been considered a "mixed contract" that is not subject to admiralty jurisdiction.

For over a century, the courts recognized two exceptions to the "wholly maritime" requirement. When the maritime and non-maritime elements are "separable," an admiralty court can exercise jurisdiction over the maritime portion. And if the non-maritime element of the contract is "incidental," the court can exercise admiralty jurisdiction over the entire claim.

What happens if a charterparty includes an option to purchase? The charter of a vessel is maritime but the sale of a vessel is not. Courts have tried to determine which agreement predominated. In *The Ada*, 250 F. 194 (2d Cir. 1918), for example, the lease ran for six months and the charterer had the right to purchase the vessel at the end of the six months for the amount paid to charter it. The charterer exercised the option. The court held that the agreement was not cognizable in admiralty. But in *Flota Maritima Browning De Cuba, Sociadad Anonima v. Snobl*, 363 F.2d 733 (4th Cir. 1965), the court held that the two charter agreements before it were separable from the option to purchase. The charters were to run for periods of seven and fifteen years, "the rentals were not so unreasonably high as to suggest a disguised sale," and neither party had converted the contract into a sale.

5. How should the mixed contract doctrine apply in the context of multimodal contracts for the carriage of goods over both sea and land? Until 2004, the lower courts uniformly

denied admiralty jurisdiction when a contract of carriage included a land transport segment that was more than "incidental." See, e.g., *Hartford Fire Ins. Co. v. Orient Overseas Containers Lines (UK) Ltd.*, 230 F.3d 549, 555–556 (2d Cir. 2000); *Berkshire Fashions, Inc. v. The M.V. Hakusan II*, 954 F.2d 874, 880–881 (3d Cir.1992); *Kuehne & Nagel (Ag & Co) v. Geosource, Inc.*, 874 F.2d 283, 290 (5th Cir. 1989). Consider how the Supreme Court resolved the issue in the following case.

Norfolk Southern Railway Co. v. James N. Kirby, Pty Ltd.

Supreme Court of the United States, 2004
543 U.S. 14, 125 S. Ct. 385, 160 L. Ed. 2d 283, 2004 AMC 2705

Justice O'CONNOR delivered the opinion for a unanimous Court.

This is a maritime case about a train wreck. A shipment of machinery from Australia was destined for Huntsville, Alabama. The intercontinental journey was uneventful, and the machinery reached the United States unharmed. But the train carrying the machinery on its final, inland leg derailed, causing extensive damage. The machinery's owner sued the railroad. The railroad seeks shelter in two liability limitations contained in contracts that upstream carriers negotiated for the machinery's delivery.

I.

* * * Respondent James N. Kirby, Pty Ltd. (Kirby), an Australian manufacturing company, sold 10 containers of machinery to the General Motors plant located outside Huntsville, Alabama. Kirby hired International Cargo Control (ICC), an Australian freight forwarding company, to arrange for delivery by "through" (*i.e.*, end-to-end) transportation. (A freight forwarding company arranges for, coordinates, and facilitates cargo transport, but does not itself transport cargo.) To formalize their contract for carriage, ICC issued a bill of lading to Kirby (ICC bill). The bill designates Sydney, Australia, as the port of loading, Savannah, Georgia, as the port of discharge, and Huntsville as the ultimate destination for delivery.

In negotiating the ICC bill, Kirby had the opportunity to declare the full value of the machinery and to have ICC assume liability for that value. [ ] Instead, and as is common in the industry [ ], Kirby accepted a contractual liability limitation for ICC below the machinery's true value, resulting, presumably, in lower shipping rates. The ICC bill sets various liability limitations for the journey from Sydney to Huntsville. For the sea leg, the ICC bill invokes the default liability rule set forth in the Carriage of Goods by Sea Act.[1] * * * For the land leg, in turn, the bill limits the carrier's liability to a higher amount. So that other downstream parties expected to take part in the contract's execution could benefit from the liability limitations, the bill also contains a so-called "Himalaya Clause."[2] It provides:

> These conditions [for limitations on liability] apply whenever claims relating to the performance of the contract evidenced by this [bill of lading] are made against any servant, agent or other person (including any independent contractor) whose services have been used in order to perform the contract.

---

1. Editors' note: The Carriage of Goods by Sea Act (COGSA) is excerpted in the Statutory Supplement and discussed in chapter III, *infra* at 280–324. COGSA § 4(5) sets a default limitation of the carrier's liability of $500 per package. See *infra* at 309.

2. Editors' note: A Himalaya clause generally extends the benefits of a carrier's defenses and limitations of liability to third parties performing the carrier's duties under the contract of carriage. See *infra* at 319–324 & n.16.

Meanwhile, Kirby separately insured the cargo for its true value. * * *

Having been hired by Kirby, and because it does not itself actually transport cargo, ICC then hired Hamburg Südamerikanische Dampfschifffahrts-Gesellschaft Eggert & Amsinck (Hamburg Süd), a German ocean shipping company, to transport the containers. To formalize their contract for carriage, Hamburg Süd issued its own bill of lading to ICC (Hamburg Süd bill). That bill designates Sydney as the port of loading, Savannah as the port of discharge, and Huntsville as the ultimate destination for delivery. It adopts COGSA's default rule in limiting the liability of Hamburg Süd, the bill's designated carrier, to $500 per package. [ ] It also contains a clause extending that liability limitation beyond the "tackles"—that is, to potential damage on land as well as on sea. Finally, it too contains a Himalaya Clause extending the benefit of its liability limitation to "all agents ... (including inland) carriers ... and all independent contractors whatsoever."

Acting through a subsidiary, Hamburg Süd hired Petitioner Norfolk Southern Railroad (Norfolk) to transport the machinery from the Savannah port to Huntsville. Delivery failed. The Norfolk train carrying the machinery derailed en route, causing an alleged $1.5 million in damages. Kirby's insurance company reimbursed Kirby for the loss. Kirby and its insurer then sued Norfolk in the United States District Court for the Northern District of Georgia, asserting diversity jurisdiction and alleging tort * * * claims. In its answer, Norfolk argued, among other things, that Kirby's potential recovery could not exceed the amounts set forth in the liability limitations contained in the bills of lading for the machinery's carriage.

The District Court granted Norfolk's motion for partial summary judgment, holding that Norfolk's liability was limited to $500 per container. Upon a joint motion from Norfolk and Kirby, the District Court certified its decision for interlocutory review pursuant to 28 U.S.C. § 1292(b).

A divided panel of the Eleventh Circuit reversed. It held that Norfolk could not claim protection under the Himalaya Clause in the first contract, the ICC bill. It construed the language of the clause to exclude parties, like Norfolk, that had not been in privity with ICC when ICC issued the bill. The majority also suggested that "a special degree of linguistic specificity is required to extend the benefits of a Himalaya clause to an inland carrier." As for the Hamburg Süd bill, the court held that Kirby could be bound by the bill's liability limitation "only if ICC was acting as Kirby's agent when it received Hamburg Süd's bill." And, applying basic agency law principles, the Court of Appeals concluded that ICC had not been acting as Kirby's agent when it received the bill. Based on its opinion that Norfolk was not entitled to benefit from the liability limitation in either bill of lading, the Eleventh Circuit reversed the District Court's grant of summary judgment for the railroad. We granted certiorari to decide whether Norfolk could take shelter in the liability limitations of either bill, and now reverse.

II.

[Respondents emphasize] that, at bottom, this is a diversity case involving tort and contract claims arising out of a rail accident somewhere between Savannah and Huntsville. We think, however, borrowing from Justice Harlan, that "the situation presented here has a more genuinely salty flavor than that." *Kossick*, *infra* at 125, 365 U.S. at 742. * * *

This suit was properly brought in diversity, but it could also be sustained under the admiralty jurisdiction by virtue of the maritime contracts involved.[3] * * * Our cases do

3. Editors' note: The Court's statement is not strictly accurate. Kirby sued Norfolk in tort. As we saw in Section I-D, *supra* at 32, there would be no basis for admiralty tort jurisdiction on these facts.

not draw clean lines between maritime and non-maritime contracts. We have recognized that "[t]he boundaries of admiralty jurisdiction over contracts—as opposed to torts or crimes—being conceptual rather than spatial, have always been difficult to draw." [ ] To ascertain whether a contract is a maritime one, we cannot look to whether a ship or other vessel was involved in the dispute, as we would in a putative maritime tort case. [ ] Nor can we simply look to the place of the contract's formation or performance. Instead, the answer "depends upon ... the nature and character of the contract," and the true criterion is whether it has "reference to maritime service or maritime transactions." *North Pacific* [*supra* at 53], 249 U.S. at 125 (citing *Ins. Co. v. Dunham* [*supra* at 51], 11 Wall. (78 U.S.) at 26. See also *Exxon Corp. v. Central Gulf Lines* [*supra* at 58], 500 U.S. at 611 ("[T]he trend in modern admiralty case law ... is to focus the jurisdictional inquiry upon whether the nature of the transaction was maritime").

The ICC and Hamburg Süd bills are maritime contracts because their primary objective is to accomplish the transportation of goods by sea from Australia to the eastern coast of the United States. See G. Gilmore & C. Black, Law of Admiralty 31 (2d ed. 1975) ("Ideally, the [admiralty] jurisdiction [over contracts ought] to include those and only those things principally connected with maritime transportation" (emphasis deleted)). To be sure, the two bills call for some performance on land; the final leg of the machinery's journey to Huntsville was by rail. But under a conceptual rather than spatial approach, this fact does not alter the essentially maritime nature of the contracts.

In *Kossick*, for example, we held that a shipowner's promise to assume responsibility for any improper treatment his seaman might receive at a New York hospital was a maritime contract. The seaman had asked the shipowner to pay for treatment by a private physician, but the shipowner, preferring the cheaper public hospital, offered to cover the costs of any complications that might arise from treatment there. We characterized his promise as a "fringe benefit" to a shipowner's duty in maritime law to provide " 'maintenance and cure.' " [ ] Because the promise was in furtherance of a "peculiarly maritime concer[n]," [ ] it folded into federal maritime law. It did not matter that the site of the inadequate treatment—which gave rise to the contract dispute—was in a hospital on land. Likewise, Norfolk's rail journey from Savannah to Huntsville was a "fringe" portion of the intercontinental journey promised in the ICC and Hamburg Süd bills.

We have reiterated that the "fundamental interest giving rise to maritime jurisdiction is 'the protection of maritime *commerce*.' " [ ] The conceptual approach vindicates that interest by focusing our inquiry on whether the principal objective of a contract is maritime commerce. While it may once have seemed natural to think that only contracts embodying commercial obligations between the "tackles" (*i.e.*, from port to port) have maritime objectives, the shore is now an artificial place to draw a line. Maritime commerce has evolved along with the nature of transportation and is often inseparable from some land-based obligations. The international transportation industry "clearly has moved into a new era—the age of multimodalism, door-to-door transport based on efficient use of all available modes of transportation by air, water, and land." [ ] The cause is technological change: Because goods can now be packaged in standardized containers, cargo can move easily from one mode of transport to another. [ ]

But the Court's real point is that the contract of carriage was "maritime" because an action on that contract—such as a declaratory judgment action by the railroad to establish the limit of its liability—could have been sustained under the admiralty jurisdiction.

Contracts reflect the new technology, hence the popularity of "through" bills of lading, in which cargo owners can contract for transportation across oceans and to inland destinations in a single transaction. [ ] Put simply, it is to Kirby's advantage to arrange for transport from Sydney to Huntsville in one bill of lading, rather than to negotiate a separate contract—and to find an American railroad itself—for the land leg. The popularity of that efficient choice, to assimilate land legs into international ocean bills of lading, should not render bills for ocean carriage nonmaritime contracts.

Some lower federal courts appear to have taken a spatial approach when deciding whether [multimodal] transportation contracts for intercontinental shipping are maritime in nature. They have held that admiralty jurisdiction does not extend to contracts which require maritime and nonmaritime transportation, unless the nonmaritime transportation is merely incidental—and that long-distance land travel is not incidental. [ ] As a preliminary matter, it seems to us imprecise to describe the land carriage required by an intermodal transportation contract as "incidental"; realistically, each leg of the journey is essential to accomplishing the contract's purpose. In this case, for example, the bills of lading required delivery to Huntsville; the Savannah port would not do.

Furthermore, to the extent that these lower court decisions fashion a rule for identifying maritime contracts that depends solely on geography, they are inconsistent with the conceptual approach our precedent requires. [ ] Conceptually, so long as a bill of lading requires substantial carriage of goods by sea, its purpose is to effectuate maritime commerce—and thus it is a maritime contract. Its character as a maritime contract is not defeated simply because it also provides for some land carriage. Geography, then, is useful in a conceptual inquiry only in a limited sense: If a bill's *sea* components are insubstantial, then the bill is not a maritime contract.

[The Court proceeded to consider whether the case was governed by maritime law, see *infra* at 127, and then to decide the case on the merits, see *infra* at 320.]

Notes

1. Did the *Kirby* Court fairly characterize the lower court decisions holding that multimodal contracts of carriage are non-maritime? Does the application of the mixed contract doctrine necessarily require a "spatial" approach? Did the *Kirby* Court treat the two bills of lading as mixed contracts?

2. What is the status of the mixed contract doctrine after *Kirby*? Should *Kirby* be limited to the multimodal carriage context? Or does it apply more broadly when evaluating any contract that might be considered maritime? In *Folksamerica Reinsurance Co. v. Clean Water of New York, Inc.*, 413 F.3d 307 (2d Cir. 2005), the Second Circuit applied *Kirby* in a marine insurance context to uphold admiralty contract jurisdiction over a policy in which some of the coverages were maritime and others were not. The court noted that the mixed contract doctrine would have defeated admiralty jurisdiction prior to *Kirby*. In *Sentry Select Insurance Co. v. Royal Insurance Co.*, 481 F.3d 1208 (9th Cir. 2007), the Ninth Circuit generally followed the Second Circuit's approach (applying *Kirby* in a marine insurance context) but on the particular facts before it held that there was no admiralty jurisdiction when the maritime obligations of the policy were a small part of the overall coverage.

3. Does *Kirby* establish a rule that all multimodal contracts of carriage including a sea leg are maritime contracts? If not, what is the test for distinguishing maritime from non-maritime multimodal contracts?

4. The federal courts within the Fifth Circuit have issued over a hundred reported decisions addressing whether contracts for services in the offshore oil-and-gas industry are "maritime." (The answer to that question very often determines whether an indemnity provision in the contract is enforceable, and thus who is responsible for compensating the victims of offshore accidents.) In *In re Larry Doiron, Inc.*, 879 F.3d 568 (5th Cir. 2018) (en banc), the full Fifth Circuit unanimously overruled its pre-*Kirby* standard and adopted a "more straight-forward test" that it described as "consistent with the Supreme Court's decision in [*Kirby*]." *Id.* at 569. Only two questions are relevant under the new test:

> First, is the contract one to provide services to facilitate the drilling or production of oil and gas on navigable waters? * * * Second, if the answer to the above question is "yes," does the contract provide or do the parties expect that a vessel will play a substantial role in the completion of the contract? If so, the contract is maritime in nature.

Id. at 576. Do you agree that the Fifth Circuit's new test is consistent with *Kirby*? Is it consistent with the Supreme Court's decision in *Herb's Welding v. Gray*, *infra* at 224, which held that the "exploration and development of the Continental Shelf are not themselves maritime commerce"? Should the presence of a "vessel" be dispositive for admiralty contract jurisdiction? To what extent is the presence of a "vessel" relevant in deciding admiralty tort jurisdiction? In *Barrios v. Centaur, L.L.C.*, 942 F.3d 670 (5th Cir. 2019), a Fifth Circuit panel extended the *Doiron* test by modifying the first question to apply to all activity on navigable waters. Is that extended test consistent with *Kirby*?

F. The Exclusive Jurisdiction of the Federal Admiralty Courts and the Concurrent Jurisdiction of "Common Law" Courts

Article III of the Constitution creates a Supreme Court and gives it original jurisdiction over "all cases affecting ambassadors, other public ministers and consuls, and those in which a state shall be party." All other federal courts are creatures of Congress,[1] and all of the categories of federal jurisdiction set out in Article III (except for the category comprising the Supreme Court's original jurisdiction) are subject to congressional control. Obviously Congress cannot bestow more federal jurisdiction than is authorized by Article III. Subject to that overarching limitation, Congress has authority over the extent of the Supreme Court's appellate jurisdiction; over whether a system of lower federal courts should exist and what that system's structure should be; and over the extent of the original and appellate jurisdiction of the lower federal courts.[2]

Article III has nothing directly to say about the exclusivity of any of the categories of federal jurisdiction. Presumably any category could be vested exclusively in the federal courts if Congress chose. But the accepted view is that no category of federal jurisdiction is exclusive "unless Congress chooses to make it so, either expressly or by fair implication."[3]

---

1. Article III § 1 vests the judicial power of the United States in the Supreme Court and "in such inferior courts as the Congress may from time to time ordain and establish." Article I § 8 cl. 9 empowers Congress "to constitute tribunals inferior to the Supreme Court."

2. See generally WRIGHT, LAW OF FEDERAL COURTS §§ 4, 8, and 10 (5th ed. 1994).

3. *Id.* at § 10, p. 43.

The congressional grant of general "admiralty or maritime" jurisdiction to the federal district courts is facially ambiguous as to the exclusivity of that jurisdiction. But in specific subcategories of admiralty, Congress has spoken clearly—or at least, clearly enough—and made the jurisdiction of the federal admiralty courts exclusive. Thus, the shipowner's petition for exoneration or limitation of liability under the Limitation of Liability Act, 46 U.S.C. § 30511, can be brought only in a federal admiralty court, *viz.*, a United States District Court exercising its admiralty and maritime jurisdiction. An action to foreclose a preferred ship mortgage can be brought only in a federal admiralty court. Suits against the United States under the Suits in Admiralty Act, 46 U.S.C. §§ 30901–30918, can be maintained only in a federal admiralty court. The same is true of suits against the United States under the Public Vessels Act, 46 U.S.C. §§ 31101–31113.[4]

Turning now to the central difficulty in this area, the key datum is the general congressional grant of admiralty and maritime jurisdiction to the federal district courts. The original grant was § 9 of the Judiciary Act of 1789, which provided in pertinent part as follows:

> [The federal] district courts ... shall ... have exclusive original cognizance of all civil causes of admiralty and maritime jurisdiction, ... saving to suitors, in all cases, the right of a common law remedy where the common law is competent to give it.

The present version of that provision, dating from 1948, is 28 U.S.C. § 1333(1), which states:

> The district courts shall have original jurisdiction, exclusive of the Courts of the States, of [a]ny civil case of admiralty or maritime jurisdiction, saving to suitors in all cases all other remedies to which they are otherwise entitled.

Straightforwardly enough, the initial clause of the statute provides for exclusive federal-court jurisdiction over "all" (or "any") admiralty cases. But the clause that follows—known in admiralty lore as the *saving clause* or *saving-to-suitors clause*—imports an immediate contradiction by contemplating concurrent "common law" jurisdiction in some undefined set of admiralty cases. (The 1948 reenactment of the statute changed the wording of the saving clause to omit the historically crucial "common law" phrase. However, in the present context we can largely ignore that change, because the *Madruga* decision, *infra* at 72, stands for the proposition that the present language does not alter the meaning of the statute. Even though the literal wording of the present saving clause is virtually open-ended, the authoritative view has been that it means "the same thing as the old" saving clause. Gilmore & Black, The Law of Admiralty 39 (2d ed. 1975).)

The question then becomes, what is "exclusive" and what is "saved"? The cases and notes that follow explore these questions and provide this general answer: What is exclusive is the action in rem against the vessel or cargo; everything else—*viz.*, all in personam litigation (subject to the statutory exceptions noted above)—is cognizable in nonadmiralty courts at the option of the "suitor" (i.e., plaintiff).

That general answer is helpful but insufficient. The following cases and notes try to take the inquiry three levels deeper: (1) What is the nature of the admiralty action in rem? I.e., what is there about the admiralty action in rem that distinguishes it from all other actions? (2) Why should an admiralty court be empowered to enforce such a powerful

4. There are also a number of important procedural devices that are available only in admiralty proceedings. See *infra* at 78.

remedial device? (3) Why should state courts be precluded from hearing admiralty actions in rem? If state courts can't do that, can they do anything similar?

The Moses Taylor

Supreme Court of the United States, 1867
71 U.S. (4 Wall.) 411, 18 L. Ed. 397

Mr. Justice FIELD delivered the opinion of the unanimous Court.

[The owner of the steamship *Moses Taylor* agreed for a consideration of $100 to transport a man called Hammons to San Francisco as a steerage passenger. When Hammons arrived in San Francisco, he went before a justice of the peace and initiated a proceeding against the steamship, alleging breach of the contract of passage and seeking $200 in damages. The principal grounds constituting the alleged breach were unwholesome food and unhealthful crowding, without sufficient room or air, in consequence of an excessively large number of steerage passengers aboard.]

[The proceeding instituted by Hammons was authorized by a statute of California providing that a passenger harmed by breach of a passage contract had a lien against the vessel for the damages resulting from the breach. The statute explicitly provided that the lien could be enforced in an action brought directly against the vessel, designating the vessel by name as defendant. It further provided that the vessel would be seized as security for the satisfaction of any judgment that may be rendered, and that—if the owner did not post a bond to secure the release of the vessel—it would be sold by the sheriff and the proceeds used to satisfy any judgment recovered by the plaintiff.]

[The agent of the vessel defended the proceeding on the ground that the justice of the peace had no jurisdiction, because the cause of action, being one against the vessel herself, was one of which the federal courts of admiralty had exclusive jurisdiction. The justice decided that he had jurisdiction and gave judgment for $200. The case was appealed to the county court, which affirmed.] The amount of the judgment was too small to enable the owner of the steamer to take the case by appeal to the Supreme Court of the State. * * * The decision of the County Court was the decision of the highest court in the State which had jurisdiction of the matter in controversy. From that court, therefore, the case is brought here by writ of error.

The case presented is clearly one within the admiralty and maritime jurisdiction of the Federal courts. The contract for the transportation of the plaintiff was a maritime contract. As stated in the complaint, it related exclusively to a service to be performed on the high seas, and pertained solely to the business of commerce and navigation. There is no distinction in principle between a contract of this character and a contract for the transportation of merchandise. The same liability attaches upon their execution both to the owner and the ship. The passage-money in the one case is equivalent to the freight-money in the other. A breach of either contract is the appropriate subject of admiralty jurisdiction.

The action against the steamer by name, authorized by the statute of California, is a proceeding in the nature and with the incidents of [an in rem] suit in admiralty. The distinguishing and characteristic feature of such suit is that the vessel or thing proceeded against is itself seized and impleaded as the defendant, and is judged and sentenced accordingly. It is this dominion of the suit in admiralty over the vessel or thing itself which gives to the title made under its decrees validity against all the world. By the common law process, whether of mesne attachment or execution, property is reached only through a personal defendant, and then only to the extent of his title. Under a sale, therefore, upon a judgment in a common law proceeding the title acquired can never be better than that possessed by the personal defendant. It is his title, and not the property itself, which is sold.

The statute of California, to the extent in which it authorizes actions in rem against vessels for causes of action cognizable in the admiralty, invests her courts with admiralty jurisdiction, and so the Supreme Court of that State has decided in several cases. * * *

* * *

The cognizance of civil causes of admiralty and maritime jurisdiction vested in the District Courts by the ninth section of the Judiciary Act * * * has been made exclusive by Congress. * * *

The case before us is not within the saving clause of the ninth section. That clause only saves to suitors "the right of a common-law remedy, where the common law is competent to give it." It is not a remedy in the common-law courts which is saved, but a common-law remedy. A proceeding in rem, as used in the admiralty courts, is not a remedy afforded by the common law * * *.

It follows, from the views expressed, that the judgment of the County Court must be reversed, and the cause remanded, with directions to dismiss the action for want of jurisdiction.

Notes

1. In *The Hine v. Trevor*, 71 U.S. 555 (1867) (which was handed down the same day as *The Moses Taylor*) the Court noted that "nearly all the states—perhaps all whose territories are penetrated or bounded by rivers capable of floating a steamboat—have statutes authorizing their courts, by proceedings in rem, to enforce contracts or redress torts." Despite the resulting wide "extent of the interests to be affected by our decision," the Court concluded that such statutes are invalid when they purport to allow state courts to provide "a remedy partaking of all the essential features of an admiralty proceeding in rem."

2. What are "the essential features of an admiralty proceeding in rem"? *The Moses Taylor* gave its answer in the paragraph beginning with the sentence: "The action against the steamer by name, authorized by the statute of California, is a proceeding in the nature and with the incidents of [an in rem] suit in admiralty." It helps to understand that paragraph to know that a "mesne attachment" occurs during the course of a proceeding. An attachment for "execution" occurs to satisfy a judgment. *The Moses Taylor* opinion says that when a common law court sells property that it has seized—whether by mesne attachment or execution—what is sold is the defendant's "title, and not the property itself." This proposition—that a purchaser at a common law judicial sale acquires only the judgment debtor's interest or title in the thing sold, and that the property acquired is thus subject to existing liens and encumbrances—is still blackletter law. See generally 47 Am.Jur.2d *Judicial Sales* § 243 (1995); 25 Am.Jur.2d *Ejectment* § 12 (1996); 30 Am.Jur.2d *Ejectment* § 560 (1994).

3. In *The Rock Island Bridge*, 73 U.S. 213 (1867), a steamboat owner whose vessels were damaged by striking a bridge sought to bring an in rem action in admiralty against the bridge. Affirming the lower courts' determination that admiralty has no in rem jurisdiction over a bridge, the Court tied the availability of the admiralty in rem remedy tightly to the existence of a maritime lien, stating:

> A maritime lien * * * confers * * * upon its holder such a right in the thing that he may subject it to condemnation and sale to satisfy his claim * * *. The only object of the proceeding in rem is to [enforce such a lien]. * * * The lien and the proceeding in rem are, therefore, correlative—where one exists the other can be taken, and not otherwise.
>
> * * *
>
> A maritime lien can only exist upon movable things engaged in navigation, or upon things which are the subjects of commerce on the high seas or navigable waters. It may arise with reference to vessels, steamers, and rafts, and upon goods and merchandise carried by them. But it cannot arise upon anything which is fixed and immovable, like a wharf, a bridge, or real estate of any kind.

Rounds v. Cloverport Foundry & Machine Co.

Supreme Court of the United States, 1915
237 U.S. 303, 35 S. Ct. 596, 59 L. Ed. 966

Mr. Justice HUGHES delivered the opinion of the unanimous Court.

The Cloverport Foundry & Machine Company * * * brought this suit against F. T. Rounds and S. A. Jesse, of Owensboro, Kentucky, in the Breckinridge circuit court of that state, to recover the sum of $5,668.65 for work and materials furnished under a contract to repair and rebuild a steamboat formerly known as the "R. D. Kendall," and renamed the "Golden Girl." The defendants were the owners of the vessel. A specific attachment was issued under §§ 2480 to 2486 of the Kentucky Statutes, which provided for a lien upon watercraft for work and supplies, etc., and the defendants procured a release of the boat by executing a forthcoming bond. By special demurrer, the defendants challenged the jurisdiction of the court to entertain the action upon the ground that the subject-matter was exclusively cognizable in the admiralty. The demurrer was overruled, and the defendants, reasserting the absence of authority in the court, answered, denying the allegations of the petition, and setting up a counterclaim for damages alleged to have been caused by defective work and by delay in completion. Upon the trial, the counterclaim was dismissed and [Cloverport] had judgment against the defendants for the amount demanded in its petition; it was further adjudged that, by virtue of the attachment and the applicable law, [Cloverport] had a lien upon the vessel for the payment of the judgment, and the vessel was ordered to be sold and the proceeds applied to the debt. The court of appeals of the state affirmed the judgment.

The question presented on this writ of error relates solely to the jurisdiction of the state court. It is contended by [Rounds and Jesse] that the contract in suit was for repairs on the vessel, and therefore was maritime in character; that the proceeding was in rem and beyond the competency of the local tribunal. [ ] On the other hand, [Cloverport] denies that the contract was maritime, contending that the old boat was dismantled, its identity destroyed, and a new boat built, and that the case in this aspect falls within the decisions relating to contracts for the original construction of a vessel. [ ] Further, it is urged in support of the judgment that the proceeding was in personam, and not in rem; that the attachment and direction for sale were incidental to the suit against the owners and for the purpose of securing satisfaction of the personal judgment. Accordingly, it is said, the proceeding was within the scope of the "common-law remedy" saved to suitors by the judiciary act.

As the last point is plainly well taken, it is unnecessary to go further. It is well settled that in an action in personam the state court has jurisdiction to issue an auxiliary attachment against the vessel; and, whether or not the contract in suit be deemed to be of a maritime nature, it cannot be said that the state court transcended its authority. The proceeding in rem which is within the exclusive jurisdiction of admiralty is one essentially against the vessel itself as the debtor or offending thing, in which the vessel is itself "seized and impleaded as the defendant, and is judged and sentenced accordingly." By virtue of dominion over the thing all persons interested in it are deemed to be parties to the suit; the decree binds all the world, and under it the property itself passes, and not merely the title or interest of a personal defendant. [ ] Actions in personam with a concurrent attachment to afford security for the payment of a personal judgment are in a different category. [ ] And this is so not only in the case of an attachment against the property of the defendant generally, but also where it runs specifically against the vessel under a state statute providing for a lien, if it be found that the attachment was auxiliary to the remedy in personam. [ ]

* * *

In the present case, as we have said, the suit was in personam and the attachment was in that suit. It had no other effect than to provide security for the payment of the personal judgment which was recovered, and it was for the purpose of satisfying this judgment that, in the same proceeding and by the terms of the judgment, the vessel was directed to be sold. It was within the scope of the common-law remedy to sell the property of the judgment debtors to pay their debt. We are not able to find any encroachment upon the exclusive jurisdiction vested in the Federal court in admiralty.

Judgment affirmed.

Notes

1. The "forthcoming bond" whereby defendants got the vessel released during the litigation was presumably "a bond to the sheriff, with surety conditioned to the effect that [defendants] would not send the property out of the jurisdiction of the court nor make any improper use of it, and that [they] would faithfully present the same in case such should be the decree of the court." *Leon v. Galceran*, 78 U.S. 185, 189 (1870).

2. In its Supreme Court argument, Cloverport offered the Court two plausible bases for upholding the state courts' jurisdiction. Did the Court take the easier route?

Thorsteinsson v. M/V Drangur

United States Court of Appeals, Eleventh Circuit, 1990
891 F.2d 1547, 1990 AMC 2478

FAY, Circuit Judge:

This admiralty appeal involves two seamen, plaintiffs-appellants Thorsteinsson and Havardsson, who brought suit in rem [in the Southern District of Florida] asserting various maritime liens against their vessel, the *M/V Drangur*, after it had been bought by Utvegsbanki Islands HF ("Bank") at a judicial sale in Iceland. * * * The district court found that the Icelandic judicial sale had extinguished all prior liens against the *Drangur* and entered final summary judgment in favor of [the defendant]. * * *

The *M/V Drangur* is a vessel of Icelandic registry, originally owned by an Icelandic corporation, Drangur Inc., and operated by Vikur Shipping, an Icelandic entity, through its American subsidiary, Vikur Shipping U.S.A. The *Drangur* carried cargo in and around Central America, the Caribbean and the United States. [Havardsson was hired to work on the *Drangur* on May 10, 1987. His employment on the *Drangur* continued through February 22, 1988. Thorsteinsson was hired to work on the *Drangur* on February 5, 1986, and remained a crew member until July 15, 1987.]

In their complaint, plaintiffs-appellants made claims against the *Drangur* * * * for unpaid wages, reimbursement of personal expenditures made on behalf of the vessel, repatriation costs for Havardsson, and maintenance and cure for medical treatment received by Thorsteinsson while employed by Vikur. The district court issued a warrant of arrest in rem on February 25, 1988, to preserve plaintiffs-appellants' interest in the vessel and to perfect the jurisdiction of the district court over the vessel. The *Drangur* was seized on February 26, 1988.

On February 29, 1988, the Bank entered a Claim of Owner with the court, securing the right of defending against plaintiffs-appellants on behalf of the *Drangur*. The Bank simultaneously posted a cash bond to procure the release of the *Drangur*. [In its answer to the complaint, the Bank alleged that it had purchased the *Drangur* in an Icelandic judicial sale on December 18, 1987, free and clear of all liens.]

All the parties agree on the procedural facts of the Icelandic sale. In late 1987, various Icelandic creditors, not including the Bank, filed claims against the *Drangur* in the court in Akureyri, Iceland. The Icelandic court, possessing general admiralty jurisdiction, had specific jurisdiction over the *Drangur* [under Icelandic law] by virtue of the fact that the *Drangur* was registered in the district in which the court was located. Upon initiation of the action, the Icelandic court gave the requisite general notice of the action against the *Drangur* by publication in an Icelandic legal gazette, as well as specific notice to the owners, registered mortgage holders, and other lienholders of the *Drangur* known to the court. The court need not, and usually does not, give notice to the crew members, and [in Iceland] a vessel does not have to be arrested for the court to have jurisdiction. No official means of notice exists for non-registered lienholders outside of Iceland at the time the action is filed.

Though the Bank was not an original participant in the Icelandic suit, it received notice as a preferred mortgage holder of the *Drangur*. At the auction of the *Drangu*r [the Bank was the highest bidder and obtained the vessel.] * * *

Based on the judicial sale in Iceland, the Bank moved the district court for summary judgment * * *, arguing that the district court had an obligation to recognize the Icelandic judicial sale and its effect of discharging all liens not previously asserted, including the claims presented by plaintiffs-appellants. * * *

In opposition to [defendant's] motion for summary judgment, plaintiffs-appellants maintained that a condition precedent to recognition by American courts of foreign judicial sales in admiralty is the actual arrest of the vessel. Without such seizure to give due notice to all lienholders, plaintiffs-appellants contended, the judicial sale lacked due process and American courts would not uphold the foreign judgment. * * *

The district court granted summary judgment for [defendant], holding that the law of the United States acknowledges that "the sale of a vessel, made pursuant to the decree of a foreign court of admiralty, will vest a clear and indefeasible title in the purchaser," and that "a judgment in rem that adjudicates the title to a ship is valid everywhere."

* * *

[The district court determined] that the judicial sale of the *Drangu*r that took place in Iceland destroyed all interests not asserted in the Icelandic action and that the Bank took title to the vessel free and clear of all liens. The district court rejected plaintiffs-appellants' contention that our courts should not recognize the judgment of the Icelandic court because its admiralty procedures lacked sufficient notice to fulfill the due process required for American courts to give effect to foreign decrees. We find that plaintiffs-appellants' reasoning has merit and that the district court misconstrued the law regarding recognition of foreign admiralty judgments.

The district court correctly cited *The Trenton*, 4 F. 657 (E.D. Mich. 1880), for the proposition that "the sale of a vessel, made pursuant to the decree of a foreign court of admiralty, will be held valid in every other country, and will vest a clear and indefeasible title in the purchaser...." * * * The court also noted that *The Trenton* accorded validity to such foreign judgments in rem when the foreign courts have " 'a rightful jurisdiction, founded upon the actual, rightful, or constructive possession of the subject-matter.' " The district court applied these statements by the *Trenton* court to find that the Icelandic court had rightful jurisdiction over the *Drangur*, constructively possessing the vessel through possession of the *Drangur*'s registration papers as required by Icelandic law, and that actual seizure of the vessel was not necessary for recognition of the Icelandic judgment in American courts.

The *Trenton* decision continues, however, by discussing grounds on which interested persons may impeach a foreign admiralty sale. One such ground is a showing "that the court or officer making the sale had no jurisdiction of the subject-matter by actual seizure and custody of the thing sold." Later in the opinion, the *Trenton* court held that "[w]hen the courts of such country have obtained jurisdiction of the *res* by actual seizure, they have full power to dispose of the property and to transfer the title, and such transfer will ordinarily be respected in every other country." *The Trenton* thus does not support the district court's conclusion that the Icelandic court had rightful jurisdiction over the *Drangur* nor that the Icelandic sale vested clear title in the Bank effective in our courts.

The Supreme Court explained the rationale underlying the prerequisite of seizure for a valid in rem judgment to issue in *The Mary*, 13 U.S. 126, 144 (1815):

> The whole world, it is said, are parties in an admiralty cause; and, therefore, the whole world is bound by the decision. The reason on which this dictum stands will determine its extent. Every person may make himself a party, and appeal from the sentence; but notice of the controversy is necessary in order to become a party, and it is a principle of natural justice, of universal obligation, that before the rights of an individual be bound by a judicial sentence, he shall have notice, either actual or implied, of the proceedings against him. Where these proceedings are against the person, notice is served personally, or by publication; where they are in rem, notice is served upon the thing itself. This is necessarily notice to all those who have any interest in the thing, and is reasonable because it is necessary, and because it is part of common prudence for all those who have any interest in it, to guard that interest by persons who are in a situation to protect it.

* * *

In cases following *The Mary*, foreign judgments which resulted from proceedings lacking other forms of notice required by American courts have been upheld. * * * No foreign judgment regarding admiralty and maritime issues, however, has been given effect by American courts absent arrest in rem of the vessel. * * * [See] *Todd Shipyards Corp. v. F/V Maigus Luck*, 243 F. Supp. 8, 14 (D. C.Z. 1965) (sale of vessel in Panamanian foreclosure proceeding without seizure of vessel does not divest liens, even when lienholder had actual notice of foreclosure).

The Bank therefore did not and could not have established as a matter of law that the mere existence of the Icelandic judgment bars plaintiffs-appellants' claims before the district court. The district court erred in entering summary judgment in favor of [defendant] solely based on the force of the Icelandic decree in admiralty.

* * *

Notes

1. *Thorsteinsson* provoked a significant amount of critical commentary. See, e.g., Ward, *Thorsteinsson v. The Drangur: The Eleventh Circuit's Unnecessary Scuttling of a Foreign Admiralty In Rem Judgment*, 27 Tex. Int'l L.J. 507 (1992) (arguing that the Eleventh Circuit gave short shrift to the principles of international comity set forth in *Hilton v. Guyot*, 159 U.S. 113 (1895)). But the decision has its staunch defenders, those who remain persuaded by *The Mary* and thus believe that physical arrest is little enough in the way of notice to creditors who are about to lose their security.

2. Do the *Trenton*, *Mary*, and *Thorsteinsson* opinions suggest reasons why state courts should not be empowered to give the kind of in rem judgments and decrees that admiralty courts can give?

Madruga v. Superior Court

Supreme Court of the United States, 1954
346 U.S. 556, 74 S. Ct. 298, 98 L. Ed. 290, 1954 AMC 405

Mr. Justice BLACK delivered the opinion of the Court.

This case for sale of a vessel and partition of the proceeds pursuant to a California statute began in the Superior Court of San Diego, the home port of the vessel. The plaintiffs were eight individuals including Edward, Anthony, and Joseph Madruga. The defendant was Manuel Madruga on whom personal service was had by summons. The defendant owned a 15% interest and the eight plaintiffs owned undivided interests aggregating 85% in a ship certificated under the maritime laws of the United States. The defendant 15% owner challenged the jurisdiction of the San Diego court on the ground that only the United States district court sitting in admiralty could take jurisdiction to consider such a case. The San Diego court decided it had jurisdiction and was upheld by the State Supreme Court which declined to issue a writ of prohibition. Certiorari was granted to consider the state court's jurisdiction.

First. Article III, § 2, of the Constitution extends the judicial power to "all Cases of admiralty and maritime Jurisdiction * * *." And since the first Judiciary Act, United States district courts have had jurisdiction of all civil cases of "admiralty or maritime jurisdiction * * *." 28 U.S.C. § 1333. Whether this grants United States district courts power to sell ships for partition of the proceeds has never been squarely decided by this Court. * * * We think, however, that the power of admiralty, as Congress and the courts have developed it over the years, is broad enough for United States district courts to order vessels sold for partition. This brings us to the contention that this federal admiralty power is exclusive.

Second. Had Congress simply granted district courts "admiralty or maritime jurisdiction exclusive of the states" California might not have power to order partition of a ship. But Congress did not stop there. It went on in the first Judiciary Act to say "saving to suitors, in all cases, the right of a common law remedy, where the common law is competent to give it." [ ][12] Viewed superficially the clause giving United States district courts exclusive admiralty or maritime jurisdiction appears inconsistent with the clause which permits persons to sue on maritime claims in common law courts. But former decisions of this Court have clarified this seeming conflict. Admiralty's jurisdiction is "exclusive" only as to those maritime causes of action begun and carried on as proceedings in rem, that is, where a vessel or thing is itself treated as the offender and made the defendant by name or description in order to enforce a lien. See, e.g., *The Moses Taylor* [*supra* at 64]. It is this kind of in rem proceeding which state courts cannot entertain. But the jurisdictional act does leave state courts "competent" to adjudicate maritime causes of action in proceedings "in personam," that is, where the defendant is a person, not a ship or some other instrument of navigation. *Rounds v. Cloverport Foundry & Machine Co.* [*supra* at 68]. * * *.

The proceedings in this California partition case were not in rem in the admiralty sense. The plaintiffs' quarrel was with their co-owner, not with the ship. Manuel Madruga, not the ship, was made defendant. Thus the state court in this proceeding acts only upon the interests of the parties over whom it has jurisdiction in personam, and it does not affect the interests of others in the world at large, as it would if this were a proceeding in rem to enforce a lien. The California court is "competent" to give this partition remedy and it therefore has jurisdiction of the cause of action.

* * *

Affirmed.

Mr. Justice Reed concurs in the judgment of the Court.

Mr. Justice FRANKFURTER, whom Mr. Justice Jackson joins, dissenting.

For one reason or another, eight co-owners having eighty-five percent interest in a vessel wished to terminate the enterprise but found the present petitioner, owner of the remaining fifteen percent, opposed to sale. Accordingly they asked a California State court for judicial sale of the vessel and appropriate distribution of the proceeds among all the owners. This is the only claim the plaintiffs made. There was no claim to enforce a personal right against the petitioner; no claim of any sort for which the levy on the ship as security was sought for some personal obligation owing from the petitioner. The jurisdiction of the State court was invoked exclusively for the sale of [the] vessel.

If this is not an action against the thing, in the sense in which that has meaning in the law, then the concepts of a *res* and an in rem proceeding have an esoteric meaning which I do not understand. From the terms of the complaint for partition through the opinion of this Court authorizing the State court to grant it, there is not the remotest suggestion that we are dealing with a remedy to enforce a separate underlying personal claim. Here the ship's the thing—not a claim outside the ship for which an ancillary remedy against the ship is sought. [ ] Is it to be doubted that if California procedure required the proceeding to be brought by name against the *Oil Screw Vessel Liberty*, Official No. 256332, or if the action had in fact been so entitled, it would inescapably be deemed an action in rem? To make the existence of State power depend on such tenuous formalities is to make questions of jurisdiction in matters maritime, as between federal and State courts, turn on distinctions much too frail.

* * *

12. The 1948 and 1949 revisions of 28 U.S.C. § 1333 amended the above clause. It now reads: "saving to suitors in all cases all other remedies to which they are otherwise entitled." We take it that this change in no way narrowed the jurisdiction of the state courts under the original 1789 Act.

The Supreme Court of California * * * reached the result it did, because it found that the "saving clause," descended from the First Judiciary Act [ ], had been drastically modified by the 1948 revision of the Judicial Code. 28 U.S.C. § 1333. The Reviser's notes completely refute this view. And since this Court does not adopt the construction given § 1333 by the California Supreme Court, the argument against it need not be elaborated.

Once it is established that the federal courts have jurisdiction and that the remedy here sought in a State court has "all the essential features of an admiralty proceeding in rem," *The Hine v. Trevor* [*supra* at 67, note 1], the disposition of this case is clearly controlled by decisions of this Court.

* * *

Were Congress to authorize the States to exercise jurisdiction for the partition of vessels, we would of course have a very different question than the one now before us, the more so because one may assume that such a statute would differentiate between small craft plying within a limited area and ocean-going vessels. This Court cannot on its own initiative make such differentiations, regarding the power of State courts, as between small vessels and large. Whatever power may be exercised by Congress in ceding national maritime jurisdiction to the States, it is not for this Court to allow State courts to have concurrent jurisdiction in rem * * *.

Notes

1. Who had the better of the argument?

2. Gilmore & Black, The Law of Admiralty 39 (2d ed. 1975) says the *Madruga* Court used "main force" to interpret the 1948 version of the saving clause to mean the same thing as the old one. Do you see the points in the two opinions where the force was applied?

3. A significant exception to the rule that state courts cannot exercise jurisdiction in proceedings that are "in rem in the admiralty sense" was established in *C.J. Hendry Co. v. Moore*, 318 U.S. 133 (1942), which holds that state courts can order the sale or forfeiture of vessels or other maritime property in actions brought by state or local law enforcement agencies to punish violations of state laws regulating fishing, navigation, water quality, and the like. These proceedings are plainly in rem in the admiralty sense—a decree of forfeiture or sale in these circumstances would clearly dispose of all interests in the property—but the majority concluded that a law-enforcement exception is justified. Justice Black dissented.

4. We have now come full circle. Why should only an admiralty court be able to judicially sell a vessel so as to convey a clear title? Doctrinal explanations do not satisfy. For example, Chief Justice Marshall once addressed the matter by stating: "The decisions of a Court of exclusive jurisdiction are necessarily conclusive on all other Courts, because the subject matter is not examinable in them." *The Mary*, 13 U.S. 126 (1815). From the present vantage point, this seems a highly formalistic and circular observation.

Somewhat more helpfully, Gilmore & Black, The Law of Admiralty 39 (2d ed. 1975), indicates that state courts are excluded from entertaining in rem proceedings on "the square and sole ground that such proceedings are not 'common law remedies.'" As the authors acknowledge, this explanation is less than fully satisfactory, for two reasons. First, it is inconsistent with cases holding that state courts can "exercis[e] jurisdiction in proceedings of an *equitable* nature, dealing with maritime subject matter." *Id.* at 38. Second, since 1948 the saving clause has been bereft of "common law" references.

When the doctrinal explanation for a particular legal rule seems evasive or incoherent, this often signals that the rule needs to be changed. Is that true here? Or do the materials in this section suggest policy justifications for the present structure?

G. The Distinctiveness of the Federal Admiralty Court and Some Fundamental Features of Its Procedure

1. Admiralty Procedure before 1966

The First Judiciary Act (1789) provided that the constitutionally-mandated Supreme Court of the United States would consist of six justices. It went on to create thirteen district courts, each with one judge, and three circuit courts, each made up of two Supreme Court justices plus the district judge for the district. (The Supreme Court justices complained about having to "ride circuit," and in 1793 Congress responded by providing that only one justice had to attend each circuit court session.) The district courts were given original jurisdiction over several categories of cases, including "all civil[1] causes of admiralty and maritime jurisdiction." The circuit courts (which also had some appellate jurisdiction) were given original jurisdiction over several categories of cases, including "suits ... at common law or in equity" in which the parties were of diverse citizenship. Congress did not bestow the constitutionally permissible "arising under" (federal question) jurisdiction on the lower federal courts until 1875.

These nineteen judges confronted the task of devising rules of procedure for the trial of cases in the brand-new United States judicial system. Congress provided only a very general blueprint. The constitutional grant of federal judicial power (Art. III, § 2) was viewed as comprising three broad categories of cases—"law," "equity," and "admiralty." Congress decided that in "law" cases, federal-court procedure would follow state procedural law. In equity and admiralty cases, the federal courts would look to "the course of the civil law." "Law" cases would be tried to juries. Equity and admiralty cases would be tried to the bench.[2]

The Supreme Court issued rules of procedure for equity proceedings in 1822, 1842, and 1912. It issued rules of admiralty procedure in 1844[3] and 1920.[4] The admiralty rules were broad and general,[5] and periodic amendments were piecemeal and unsystematic.

---

1. The word "civil" in this context means "as opposed to criminal." In other contexts it means "as distinguished from common law." In still others it has occasionally meant "as distinguished from admiralty."

2. The key statutes were Judiciary Act of Sept. 24, 1789, c. 20, §§ 9, 12, 30, 1 Stat. 73 *et seq.*; Judiciary Act of Sept. 29, 1789, c. 21, § 2, 1 Stat. 93. See also Process Act of May 8, 1792, c. 36, § 2, 1 Stat. 275.

3. The 1844 rules were written by Justice Story. They went into effect on September 1, 1845, and can be found at 44 U.S. iii (1845). These same rules, as amended through ca. 1900, are an appendix to PUGH, FORMS OF PROCEDURE IN THE COURTS OF ADMIRALTY OF THE UNITED STATES OF AMERICA (1903).

4. 254 U.S. 673.

5. See CONKLING, ADMIRALTY JURISDICTION, LAW, AND PRACTICE 7 (1857) ("little more than a skeleton"); WISWALL, THE DEVELOPMENT OF ADMIRALTY JURISDICTION AND PRACTICE SINCE 1800 at 53 (1970) ("codification of previously accumulated customs").

For answers to admiralty procedural issues not covered by the Supreme Court's rules, the lower federal courts looked for guidance to England and to each other.

In the early 20th century the legal profession's attention began turning to the need for unification and systematization of federal-court procedure. Many judges and lawyers had come to the view that, while admiralty and equity procedure were in relatively decent shape, common-law federal procedure was crippled by the required conformity to state law. In an important address to the Chicago Bar Association in 1921, Chief Justice William Howard Taft went further:

> [We need] a simplification of the procedure in all cases in the Federal trial courts. We still retain in those courts the distinction between suits at law, suits in equity, and suits in admiralty. The Constitution refers specifically to them, and in deference to that separation in the Constitution, the distinction is preserved in the Federal practice. It seems to me that there is no reason why this distinction, so far as actual practice is concerned, should not be wholly abolished, and what are now suits in law, in equity and in admiralty, should not be conducted in the form of one civil action.[6]

The Chief Justice's strong pronouncement soon began to bear fruit. In 1934, Congress passed the Rules Enabling Act,[7] authorizing the Supreme Court to issue procedural rules for common-law cases to unify common law and equity procedure. Admiralty went unmentioned. The Court appointed an advisory committee to draft a set of unified procedural rules to govern law and equity cases. The eventual result was "that law and equity were merged under a single set of simple and effective rules,"[8] the Federal Rules of Civil Procedure, which went into effect on September 16, 1938.

Admiralty procedure continued to be governed by the 1920 rules, which were amended from time to time to incorporate piecemeal provisions of the Federal Rules of Civil Procedure. It became increasingly evident that unification of admiralty procedure with that of law and equity was the only sensible step. The American Bar Association and the Maritime Law Association of the United States began working in that direction, and a substantial unification was eventually achieved. Effective July 1, 1966, an order of the Supreme Court rescinded the 1920 admiralty rules, promulgated amendments to the Federal Rules of Civil Procedure designed to accommodate the inclusion of admiralty cases, and provided that admiralty cases would thenceforth be governed by the Federal Rules of Civil Procedure.

2. Admiralty Procedure since 1966: The Big Picture

According to Professor Charles Alan Wright—long regarded as the foremost authority on the matter—the 1938 Federal Rules of Civil Procedure (FRCP) brought about huge improvements:

---

6. Taft, *Three Needed Steps of Progress*, 8 A.B.A.J. 34, 35 (1922).

7. Act of June 19, 1934, c. 651, 48 Stat. 1064. The present version of the Rules Enabling Act is 28 U.S.C. §§2071–2077. It spells out a process whereby the Judicial Conference (a body consisting of the Chief Justice, the chief judge of each circuit, the chief judge of the Court of International Trade, and a district judge from each circuit, see 28 U.S.C. §331) recommends rules and amendments to the Court, which (after making whatever changes it wishes) then transmits them to Congress. Congress has seven months to disapprove or make changes. Thereafter, the rules go into effect.

8. Wright, Law of Federal Courts 428 (5th ed. 1994).

> The success of the Federal Rules of Civil Procedure has been quite phenomenal. They provide for the federal courts a uniform procedure in civil actions. This in itself would be a fine accomplishment, but the rules go beyond this to create a uniform procedure that is flexible, simple, clear, and efficient.

WRIGHT, LAW OF FEDERAL COURTS 429 (5th ed. 1994). It is generally thought that the FRCP's 1966 absorption of admiralty has been similarly successful.

The FRCP rules that are relevant to the absorption include Rules 1, 2, 8(a)(1), 9(h), 38(e), 82, and Supplemental Rules A through F. Rule 1 states that "[t]hese rules govern the procedure in all civil [i.e., noncriminal] actions and proceedings in the United States district courts." Rule 2 provides: "There is one form of action—the civil action." Rule 8(a)(1) states: "A pleading that states a claim for relief must contain a short and plain statement of the grounds for the court's [subject matter] jurisdiction...." The linchpin of the FRCP's absorption of admiralty is Rule 9(h), which provides:

> **(h) Admiralty or Maritime claim.**
>
> *(1) How Designated.* If a claim for relief is within the admiralty or maritime jurisdiction and also within the court's subject-matter jurisdiction on some other ground, the pleading may designate the claim as an admiralty or maritime claim for purposes of Rules 14(c), 38(e), and 82 and the Supplemental Rules for Admiralty or Maritime Claims and Asset Forfeiture Actions. A claim cognizable only in the admiralty or maritime jurisdiction is an admiralty or maritime claim for those purposes, whether or not so designated.
>
> *(2) Designation for Appeal.* A case that includes an admiralty or maritime claim within this subdivision (h) is an admiralty case within 28 U.S.C. § 1292(a)(3).

The Note of the Advisory Committee that oversaw the drafting of FRCP 9(h)—explaining the rule's intended function and operation—is set forth just below. Remember that the committee was writing on the eve of enactment of the 1966 unification provisions, so that words like "now" or "present" mean pre-unification.

Advisory Committee Note

28 U.S.C.A., Federal Rules of Civil Procedure, Rule 9(h) (1966)

Certain distinctive features of the admiralty practice must be preserved for what are now suits in admiralty. This raises the question: After unification, when a single form of action is established, how will the counterpart of the present suit in admiralty be identifiable? In part the question is easily answered. Some claims for relief can only be suits in admiralty, either because the admiralty jurisdiction is exclusive or because no nonmaritime ground of federal jurisdiction exists. Many claims, however, are cognizable by the district courts whether asserted in admiralty or in a civil action, assuming the existence of a nonmaritime ground of jurisdiction. Thus at present the pleader has power to determine procedural consequences by the way in which he exercises the classic privilege given by the saving-to-suitors clause (28 U.S.C. § 1333) or by an equivalent statutory provision. For example, a longshoreman's claim for personal injuries suffered by reason of the [negligence] of a vessel may be asserted in a suit in admiralty or, if diversity of citizenship exists, in a civil action. One of the important procedural consequences is that in the civil action either party may demand a jury trial, while in the suit in admiralty there is no right to jury trial except as provided by statute.

It is no part of the purpose of unification to inject a right to jury trial into those admiralty cases in which that right is not provided by statute. Similarly as will be more specifically noted below, there is no disposition to change the present law as to interlocutory appeals in admiralty, or as to the venue of suits in admiralty; and, of course, there is no disposition to inject into the civil practice as it now is the distinctively maritime remedies (maritime attachment and garnishment, actions in rem, possessory, petitory and partition actions and limitation of liability). The unified rules must therefore provide some device for preserving the present power of the pleader to determine whether these historically maritime procedures shall be applicable to his claim or not; the pleader must be afforded some means of designating his claim as the counterpart of the present suit in admiralty, where its character as such is not clear.

The problem is different from the similar one concerning the identification of claims that were formerly suits in equity. While that problem is not free from complexities, it is broadly true that the modern counterpart of the suit in equity is distinguishable from the former action at law by the character of the relief sought. This mode of identification is possible in only a limited category of admiralty cases. In large numbers of cases the relief sought in admiralty is simple money damages, indistinguishable from the remedy afforded by the common law. This is true, for example, in the case of the longshoreman's action for personal injuries stated above. After unification has abolished the distinction between civil actions and suits in admiralty, the complaint in such an action would be almost completely ambiguous as to the pleader's intentions regarding the procedure invoked. The allegation of diversity of citizenship might be regarded as a clue indicating an intention to proceed as at present under the saving-to-suitors clause; but this, too, would be ambiguous if there were also reference to the admiralty jurisdiction, and the pleader ought not be required to forego mention of all available jurisdictional grounds.

Other methods of solving the problem were carefully explored, but the Advisory Committee concluded that the preferable solution is to allow the pleader who now has power to determine procedural consequences by filing a suit in admiralty to exercise that power under unification, for the limited instances in which procedural differences will remain, by a simple statement in his pleading to the effect that the claim is an admiralty or maritime claim. * * *

Note

Rule 9(h) provides a checklist of the eight ways in which modern admiralty procedure differs from procedure in other federal-court cases. Rule 14(c) describes a distinctive form of impleader (third party practice). Rule 38(e) states that "[t]hese rules do not create a right to a jury trial on issues in a claim that is an admiralty or maritime claim under Rule 9(h)." Rule 82 provides that "[a]n admiralty or maritime claim under Rule 9(h)" is not subject to the venue requirements that govern other actions. 28 U.S.C. § 1292(a)(3) preserves a broader right to interlocutory appeal in admiralty cases. Supplemental Rules A through F of the FRCP include detailed procedures to be followed in distinctive types of admiralty proceedings including actions in rem; actions involving a distinctive process of attachment and/or garnishment of the defendant's property; possessory, petitory, and partition actions; and shipowners' petitions for limitation of liability. We examine some of these distinctive features of admiralty procedure in the following subsections.

3. Bench Trial Versus Jury Trial in Seamen's Actions

The *Romero* Case

In *Romero v. International Terminal Operating Co.*, 358 U.S. 354 (1959), the Court was confronted with difficult issues respecting the availability of jury trial in actions by injured seamen against employers and shipowners. Justice Frankfurter wrote the opinion for the five-justice majority.

The case arose when Francisco Romero, a seaman working aboard the Spanish-flagged vessel *S.S. Guadalupe* as a member of its crew, was injured at work on the deck of the vessel while it was berthed at Pier 2, Hoboken, New Jersey. Romero brought an action in the Southern District of New York against the shipowner/employer, Compania Transatlantica. (International Terminal was a peripheral defendant, of no present relevance.) Romero's complaint asserted causes of action based on United States law. It alleged that the injury resulted from Compania's negligence and from the unseaworthiness of the *S.S. Guadalupe*, and that regardless of whether there was any fault on Compania's or the vessel's part, the accident entitled Romero to maintenance (room and board) and cure (medical care) at Compania's expense. These three counts—negligence, unseaworthiness, and maintenance and cure—all arose from a single accident and were so closely interrelated that as a practical matter they needed to be tried together.

Romero could have brought about a single unified trial in a bench-trial proceeding under the district court's admiralty jurisdiction, 28 U.S.C. § 1333. But Romero wanted a jury trial. The saving-to-suitors clause would have authorized Romero to seek a unified jury trial in state court. But Romero wanted to be in federal, not state, court. The saving-to-suitors clause would have authorized Romero to seek a unified jury trial in federal court provided the requisites for diversity jurisdiction, 28 U.S.C. § 1332, could be shown. But Romero and Compania were both citizens of Spain, so diversity jurisdiction was out of the question. So, a unified federal-court jury trial could be had *only* if the case could be lodged under the district court's federal question ("arising under") jurisdiction, 28 U.S.C. 1331. And that is how Romero pleaded his case.

At first blush, Romero's jurisdictional strategy appeared promising. He asserted that the negligence action against Compania was created by the Jones Act, 46 U.S.C. § 30104, which states that an injured seaman may assert his employer's negligence in "a civil action at law, with the right of trial by jury." Straightforwardly enough, this language describes an action falling under 28 U.S.C. § 1331. But the district court dismissed Romero's Jones Act count for lack of subject matter jurisdiction, reasoning that the Jones Act did not apply to an action by a Spanish seaman against a Spanish shipowner for an injury incurred aboard a vessel registered and flagged in Spain. The Second Circuit affirmed.

The Supreme Court disagreed with the dismissal of the Jones Act count on subject matter grounds. It explained that the issue of the Jones Act's applicability to actions brought by foreign seamen was a transnational choice-of-law issue, not a subject matter jurisdiction issue:

> As frequently happens where jurisdiction depends on subject matter, the question whether jurisdiction exists has been confused with the question whether the complaint states a cause of action. [Romero] asserts a substantial claim that the Jones Act affords him a right of recovery for the negligence of his employer. Such assertion alone is sufficient to empower the district court to assume jurisdiction

> over the case and determine whether, in fact, the Act does provide the claimed rights. A cause of action under our law was asserted here, and the court had power to determine whether it was or was not well founded in law and in fact.[9]

The Supreme Court went on to hold that the district court and Second Circuit were correct in concluding that Romero's unseaworthiness and maintenance-and-cure claims did not fall within the coverage of 28 U.S.C. § 1331. Unlike the Jones Act claim, these two claims had no statutory basis but instead arose under *general maritime law* (a form of federal common law). After detailed deliberation the five-justice majority concluded that 28 U.S.C. § 1331 does not confer subject matter jurisdiction over claims rooted in general maritime law.

The logic of the Court's ruling that the two general maritime counts did not fall within § 1331's coverage meant that only the Jones Act count could go forward; the general maritime counts would have to be abandoned or handled elsewhere.[10] But the *Romero* majority did not choose to follow the logic of its § 1331 ruling:

> Rejection of [Romero's] reading of § 1331 does not preclude consideration of [his general maritime claims.] These claims cannot, we have seen, be justified under § 1331. However, the district court may have jurisdiction of them "pendent" to its jurisdiction under the Jones Act. Of course the considerations which call for the exercise of pendent jurisdiction of a state claim related to a pending federal cause of action ... are not the same when, as here, what is involved are related claims based on the federal maritime law. We perceive no barrier to the exercise of "pendent jurisdiction" in the very limited circumstances before us. Here we merely decide that a district court has jurisdiction to determine whether a cause of action has been stated if that jurisdiction has been invoked by a complaint at law rather than by a libel in admiralty, as long as the complaint also properly alleges a claim under the Jones Act. We are not called upon to decide whether the district court may submit to the jury the "pendent" claims under the general maritime law in the event that a cause of action be found to exist.

Notes

1. The question "whether the district court may submit to the jury the 'pendent' claims" was answered affirmatively in *Fitzgerald*, just below.

2. The *Romero* Court felt that it should not reach that question because it went on to determine that, under the prevailing transnational choice-of-law analysis that had recently crystallized in *Lauritzen v. Larsen*, 345 U.S. 571 (1953), Romero's entire case against Compania should be governed by Spanish, not U.S., law and therefore dismissed on the merits. Justices Black and Douglas dissented from this holding. (Transnational choice-of-law analysis is treated *infra* at 550, 553 notes 8 and 9.)

---

9. 354 U.S. at 359 (citations and internal quotation marks omitted).

10. Presumably Romero could have refiled the general maritime claims in admiralty or in state court. (Remember, there was no basis for diversity jurisdiction.) This would have produced an inherently messy two-trial treatment of what was in all practical respects a single case; Romero would have lost the unified trial treatment that he sought (and that the nature of the case demanded). Alternatively, he could presumably have dismissed the Jones Act § 1331 action and refiled the whole case in admiralty or in state court.

3. The Court's reasons for concluding that Romero's general maritime claims did not fall within the coverage of 28 U.S.C. § 1331 are treated *infra* at 102–05.

4. Justice Brennan dissented from the Court's use of the "pendent jurisdiction" concept to justify bringing the nonstatutory claims to the law side as tag-alongs to the Jones Act claim. In Justice Brennan's view, the pendent jurisdiction doctrine was inapplicable here because it was "limited to cases where claims arising under state law, over which there was no independent jurisdiction in the federal court, have been [so] intertwined with federal claims" that it was necessary for the federal court to hear them. 358 U.S. at 412.

The pendent jurisdiction doctrine itself has subsequently been replaced. 28 U.S.C. § 1367 was enacted in 1990 to create a concept of "supplemental jurisdiction" that combines and broaden the fields formerly known as "pendent" and "ancillary" jurisdiction. The device invented by the *Romero* Court bears little resemblance to the former concept of pendent jurisdiction and perhaps even less to the new supplemental jurisdiction concept. Nevertheless, Justice Frankfurter's invention retains validity and continues to go by the name of "*Romero*-pendent" jurisdiction. It is confined to the specific context in which it arose: seamen's actions combining Jones Act, unseaworthiness, and maintenance and cure claims.

Fitzgerald v. United States Lines Co.

Supreme Court of the United States, 1963

374 U.S. 16, 83 S. Ct. 1646, 10 L. Ed. 2d 720, 1963 AMC 1083

Mr. Justice BLACK delivered the opinion of the Court.

[Andres San Martin, a seaman, brought this action in the District Court for the Southern District of New York against the respondent United States Lines Company. (Martin died while his appeal was pending, and an administrator was substituted for him.) Alleging that he had twisted and strained his back while working for respondent on its ship, Martin asserted three causes of action: the Jones Act, 46 U.S.C. § 30104, which provides that a seaman injured in the course of employment by his employer's negligence "may elect to bring a civil action at law, with the right of trial by jury, against the employer;" the general maritime doctrine of unseaworthiness; and the general maritime doctrine of maintenance and cure. Respecting the Jones Act claim, Martin based subject matter jurisdiction on the Act's language and 28 U.S.C. § 1331. Respecting the two general maritime law claims, he asserted subject matter jurisdiction under the "pendent" jurisdiction recognized in *Romero, supra* at 79.]

[Martin's complaint demanded a jury trial for all the issues growing out of the single accident. The trial judge granted a jury trial for the Jones Act and the unseaworthiness issues but held the question of recovery under maintenance and cure in abeyance to try to the bench after jury trial of the other two issues. The jury returned a verdict for United States Lines on the negligence and unseaworthiness issues; the court then, after hearing testimony in addition to that presented to the jury, awarded Martin $224 for maintenance and cure. Martin appealed, arguing that he was entitled to jury trial on his maintenance and cure claim. Rejecting Martin's argument, the Second Circuit affirmed.]

For years it has been a common, although not uniform, practice of District Courts to grant jury trials to plaintiffs who join in one complaint their Jones Act, unseaworthiness, and maintenance and cure claims when all the claims, as here, grow out of a single transaction or accident. This practice of requiring issues arising out of a single accident to be tried by a single tribunal is by no means surprising. Although remedies for negligence, unseaworthiness, and maintenance and cure have different origins and may on occasion call for application of slightly different principles and procedures, they nevertheless, when based on one unitary set of circumstances, serve the same purpose of indemnifying a seaman for damages caused by injury, depend in large part upon the same evidence, and involve some identical elements of recovery. Requiring a seaman to split up his lawsuit, submitting part of it to a jury and part to a judge, unduly complicates and confuses a trial, creates difficulties in applying doctrines of res judicata and collateral estoppel, and can easily result in too much or too little recovery. * * * In the absence of some statutory or constitutional obstacle, an end should be put to such an unfortunate, outdated, and wasteful manner of trying these cases. Fortunately, there is no such obstacle.

While this Court has held that the Seventh Amendment does not require jury trials in admiralty cases, neither that Amendment nor any other provision of the Constitution forbids them. Nor does any statute of Congress or Rule of Procedure, Civil or Admiralty, forbid jury trials in maritime cases. Article III of the Constitution vested in the federal courts jurisdiction over admiralty and maritime cases, and, since that time, the Congress has largely left to this Court the responsibility for fashioning the controlling rules of admiralty law. This Court has long recognized its power and responsibility in this area and has exercised that power where necessary to do so. Where, as here, a particular mode of trial being used by many judges is so cumbersome, confusing, and time consuming that it places completely unnecessary obstacles in the paths of litigants seeking justice in our courts, we should not and do not hesitate to take action to correct the situation. Only one trier of fact should be used for the trial of what is essentially one lawsuit to settle one claim split conceptually into separate parts because of historical developments. And since Congress in the Jones Act has declared that the negligence part of the claim shall be tried by a jury, we would not be free, even if we wished, to require submission of all the claims to the judge alone. Therefore, the jury, a time-honored institution in our jurisprudence, is the only tribunal competent under the present congressional enactment to try all the claims. Accordingly, we hold that a maintenance and cure claim joined with a Jones Act claim must be submitted to the jury when both arise out of one set of facts. The seaman in this case was therefore entitled to a jury trial as of right on his maintenance and cure claim.

[The case was remanded for jury trial on the maintenance and cure claim. Justice Harlan dissented.]

Note

Plainly, *Fitzgerald* validates the *Romero*-pendent device. Many authorities believe it goes further and authorizes jury trial in seamen's admiralty actions seeking "the procedural advantages of [the] inherent admiralty claims for unseaworthiness and maintenance and cure" along with the jury trial authorized by the Jones Act. *Haskins v. Point Towing Co.*, 395 F.2d 737, 741 (3d Cir. 1968). See also *Peace v. Fidalgo Island Packing Co.*, 419 F.2d 371 (9th Cir. 1969); 9 Wright & Miller, Federal Practice & Procedure § 2315. This reading of *Fitzgerald* makes good practical sense, and it finds support in Fed. R. Civ. P. Rules 1, 2, 8(e), and 18(a). It is important to note, though, that a seaman's complaint seeking the benefit of this reading of *Fitzgerald* needs to be carefully crafted so as to avoid "designat[ing] the [Jones Act] claim as an admiralty and maritime claim" within the meaning of Rule 9(h).

4. Bench Trial Versus Jury Trial in Other Maritime Actions

In re Lockheed Martin Corp.

United States Court of Appeals for the Fourth Circuit, 2007
503 F.3d 351, 2007 AMC 3304, *cert. denied*, 553 U.S. 1017 (2008)

TRAXLER, Circuit Judge:

* * *

Lockheed owned a ship that was damaged at sea in June 2001. The ship was insured by National Casualty Company. In April 2005, Lockheed submitted a claim for more than $2,600,000 in damages. Lockheed informed National that it intended to file suit by July 29, 2005, unless National acknowledged that the policy established a six-year statute of limitations.

On July 22, 2005, National preemptively filed a declaratory judgment action[11] seeking a declaration that Lockheed's claims were time-barred under the policy. In accordance with the rules governing admiralty claims, National designated its action as a non-jury admiralty claim. National later amended its complaint, seeking in the alternative a declaration of Lockheed's amount of loss. Lockheed filed an answer and asserted a counterclaim seeking payment for the damage to the ship. [As the district judge noted, this was "a counterclaim for breach of contract predicated on this Court's diversity jurisdiction."] Lockheed requested a jury trial on its counterclaim.

Lockheed later filed a motion for judgment on the pleadings. Lockheed asserted that National's first request for declaratory relief (that the claims were untimely) should be dismissed because Lockheed's claim was timely under the policy. Lockheed then argued that the district court should * * * dismiss National's second request for declaratory relief (for a determination of the amount of loss), so that Lockheed's counterclaim (which raised the same issue) could be tried by a jury.

The district court concluded that the policy established a six-year limitations period, and the court therefore dismissed National's first request for declaratory relief. The district court, however, concluded that Lockheed did not have a right to a jury trial. The court therefore declined to dismiss National's second request for declaratory relief, and the court struck Lockheed's jury demand. Lockheed then filed this petition for a writ of mandamus, arguing that the district court's ruling improperly deprived it of its right to a jury trial.

* * *

In this circuit, a petition for a writ of mandamus is the proper way to challenge the denial of a jury trial. * * *; see also *Beacon Theatres, Inc. v. Westover*, 359 U.S. 500, 511 (1959) ("[T]he right to grant mandamus to require jury trial where it has been improperly

11. Editors' note: The Declaratory Judgment Act provides in pertinent part: "In a case of actual controversy within its jurisdiction, ... any court of the United States, upon the filing of an appropriate pleading, may declare the rights and other legal relations of any interested party seeking such declaration, whether or not further relief is or could be sought." 28 U.S.C. § 2201(a).

denied is settled."). Because Lockheed's petition for a writ of mandamus is a proper vehicle for challenging the district court's decision, we now turn to the merits of Lockheed's claims.

* * *

[The Seventh Amendment guarantees the right to a jury trial "[i]n suits at common law," a category that does not include admiralty cases. Thus, in general terms, the Seventh Amendment creates no constitutional right to a jury trial of admiralty claims. However, the "saving to suitors" clause of 28 U.S.C. § 1333 enables most maritime plaintiffs to bring in personam proceedings at law in a state court or (provided there is a basis for federal subject matter jurisdiction other than admiralty) in a United States district court. The most important aspect of a maritime plaintiff's right to proceed "at law" in state or federal court is the right to demand a jury trial.]

* * * Lockheed argues that because it asserted an in personam counterclaim against National, the parties are diverse, and the amount-in-controversy requirement is satisfied, it has the right under the saving-to-suitors clause to demand a jury trial on the counterclaim. Lockheed also contends that it has a right to a jury trial under *Beacon Theatres*, in which the Supreme Court held that the right to a jury trial in a declaratory judgment action depends on whether there would have been a right to a jury trial had the action proceeded without the declaratory judgment vehicle.

As to Lockheed's counterclaim argument, National contends that Lockheed's counterclaim is not a true counterclaim, but is merely the flip side of National's declaratory judgment claim. National seeks a declaration that there is no coverage and a declaration of the amount owed if there is coverage, and Lockheed asserts in the counterclaim that there is coverage and that the loss amount is more than National will admit. National argues that if this kind of in-name-only counterclaim is enough to require a jury trial in an admiralty case, then the plaintiff's historic right to decide whether to proceed in admiralty will be eviscerated. And even if Lockheed's counterclaim is a true counterclaim, National argues that its Rule 9(h) admiralty designation is controlling and prevents Lockheed from obtaining a jury trial. As to Lockheed's *Beacon Theatres* argument, National contends that Beacon Theatres involved common law claims for which there is a Seventh Amendment right to a jury trial and that the Supreme Court's decision in that case was driven by a need to protect the defendant's constitutional right to a jury trial. This case, by contrast, involves admiralty claims, for which there is no constitutional right to a jury trial. National thus contends that *Beacon Theatres* is simply inapplicable to this case.

At the heart of National's position is its view that the Seventh Amendment is inapplicable to admiralty claims. While it is correct that the Seventh Amendment does not create a right to a jury trial on [admiralty] claims, we believe that National's position oversimplifies the matter.

As discussed above, the effect of the saving-to-suitors clause is to permit maritime in personam claims to be pursued in federal court as [admiralty] (and thus non-jury) claims, in state court as legal claims, or in federal court as legal claims (for which a jury trial is available) if an independent basis for federal court jurisdiction exists. If [a maritime] claim is tried "at law," the claim nonetheless remains [a maritime claim subject to maritime substantive law. Its maritime nature] does not mean that the Seventh Amendment is inapplicable.

In *Atlantic and Gulf Stevedores, Inc. v. Ellerman Lines, Ltd.*, 369 U.S. 355 (1952), a longshoreman injured while unloading cargo brought suit against the owners of the ship carrying the cargo. Diversity jurisdiction existed, and the plaintiff designated the action as one at law and demanded a jury trial. The vessel owners impleaded the stevedore for whom the longshoreman worked, arguing that the stevedore was negligent as to the manner in which the vessel was unloaded and that the stevedore should indemnify the vessel owners if they were found liable to the longshoreman. Answering special interrogatories, the jury found the vessel owners liable but found no fault on the part of the stevedore. On appeal, the circuit court affirmed the jury's verdict against the vessel owners but reversed the judgment in favor of the stevedore, concluding that the stevedore was negligent as a matter of law.

The Supreme Court reversed the decision of the circuit court. The Court explained that "[t]he requirements of the Seventh Amendment were brought into play in this case, even though a stevedoring contract is a maritime contract." The Court held that "[t]his suit being in the federal courts by reason of diversity of citizenship carried with it, of course, the right to trial by jury," and that the manner in which the circuit court rejected the jury verdict violated the Seventh Amendment's prohibition against the re-examination of facts found by a jury. [The Seventh Amendment provides: "In suits at common law, where the value in controversy shall exceed twenty dollars, the right of trial by jury shall be preserved, and *no fact tried by a jury, shall be otherwise re-examined in any Court of the United States, than according to the rules of the common law.*"]

In our view, *Ellerman* makes it clear that the Seventh Amendment applies to [maritime] claims that are tried "at law" by way of the saving-to-suitors clause. [ ] There is an important difference, however, between *Ellerman* and the case at bar. Whereas in *Ellerman* the plaintiff elected to proceed at law, the plaintiff here [National] elected to proceed in admiralty. We do not believe, at least in this case, that this factual difference is relevant.

Generally speaking, the right to determine whether a [maritime] claim will proceed as an admiralty claim (without a jury) or as a common law claim (with a jury) belongs strictly to the plaintiff. That is, if a plaintiff designates his claim as a Rule 9(h) [admiralty] claim, the saving-to-suitors clause does not permit a defendant to trump that designation and demand a jury trial. [ ] While this principle governs simple proceedings—*e.g.*, proceedings where the defendant does not assert any counterclaims or implead third parties—there is some dispute about its application to more complex cases.

In cases involving counterclaims or cross-claims that could proceed at law, courts are divided on the question of whether the plaintiff's Rule 9(h) admiralty designation prevents the defendant from obtaining a jury trial. Some courts have concluded that the plaintiff's Rule 9(h) designation is controlling and that no jury trial is permitted. [ ] Other courts, however, have concluded that a plaintiff's Rule 9(h) designation cannot trump the defendant's Seventh Amendment right to a jury trial on a legal counter- or cross-claim. [ ]

In our view, allowing a plaintiff's Rule 9(h) designation to preclude a jury trial on compulsory legal counter- or cross-claims effectively and improperly elevates the traditional mode of trial in admiralty (a bench trial) to a right *not* to proceed before a jury. While the Constitution does not give an admiralty plaintiff the right to a jury trial, it likewise does not give the plaintiff a right to a bench trial. See *Fitzgerald*, [*supra* at 81], 374 U.S. at 20. To permit the plaintiff's choice of a customary but not constitutionally required mode of trial to prevent a defendant from taking advantage of his constitutionally guaranteed mode of trial is inconsistent with the Supreme Court's admonition that the Seventh Amendment right to a jury trial must be preserved "wherever possible." *Beacon Theatres*, 359 U.S. at 510.

As noted above, however, National contends that the counterclaims asserted by Lockheed are not true counterclaims. National contends that Lockheed's claims are simply the flip side of National's own claims and add no new issue to the litigation. National argues that permitting a jury trial on the basis of such claims would eviscerate the admiralty plaintiff's traditional right to control the manner in which his claims will be tried. We agree with National that permitting such counterclaims to effectively undo the plaintiff's Rule 9(h) designation would be inconsistent with the historic admiralty practice of giving the plaintiff the power to determine the manner in which his claims would be tried. We need not decide, however, whether the counterclaims asserted by Lockheed are "true" counterclaims, nor need we decide how a defendant's jury demand would be resolved if his counterclaims were not true counterclaims. We need not consider these issues because we agree with Lockheed that *Beacon Theatres* requires a jury trial in this case, even if no counterclaims had been filed.

In *Beacon Theatres*, Beacon notified Fox West Coast Theatres that it believed Fox was violating the Sherman Act. Fox thereafter brought a declaratory judgment action seeking a declaration that its conduct did not violate the Sherman Act. Beacon answered and counterclaimed, seeking treble damages under the Sherman Act and demanding a jury trial. The district court concluded that Fox's declaratory judgment claims were equitable in nature and that a bench trial on the issues raised in Fox's complaint would be held *before* a jury considered Beacon's treble-damages claim. The Supreme Court held that the district court erred by viewing Fox's claims as equitable. The Court explained that the Declaratory Judgment Act,

> while allowing prospective defendants to sue to establish their nonliability, * * * preserves the right to jury trial for both parties. *It follows that if Beacon would have been entitled to a jury trial in a treble damage suit against Fox it cannot be deprived of that right merely because Fox took advantage of the availability of declaratory relief to sue Beacon first.* Since the right to trial by jury applies to treble damage suits under the antitrust laws, and is, in fact, an essential part of the congressional plan for making competition rather than monopoly the rule of trade, the Sherman and Clayton Act issues on which Fox sought a declaration were essentially jury questions.

This case, like *Beacon Theatres*, involves a declaratory judgment action commenced by the party that, but for the existence of the declaratory judgment procedure, would have been the defendant. Although the action sounds in admiralty, that is only because National won the race to the courthouse door and made the Rule 9(h) designation first. *Beacon Theatres* * * * requires us to ignore National's status as the declaratory judgment plaintiff and to instead look to how the action otherwise would have proceeded. Without the declaratory judgment vehicle, Lockheed would have sued National for breach of the insurance policy, a claim over which admiralty and "law" courts have concurrent jurisdiction. As the plaintiff, Lockheed would have been entitled under the saving-to-suitors clause to designate its claim as a legal one as to which there is a Seventh Amendment right to jury trial.

* * *

At issue in this case is a dispute over whether an insurer is obligated to indemnify its insured for damage sustained by an insured vessel. In the usual course of events—that is, without the declaratory judgment vehicle—Lockheed would have sued National for breach of the insurance contract. And under the saving-to-suitors clause, Lockheed would have been entitled to a jury trial on that claim. Accordingly, under *Beacon Theatres*, Lockheed cannot lose its right to a jury trial simply because National initiated the declaratory judgment action. * * * We therefore grant Lockheed's petition for the issuance of a writ of mandamus and we direct the district court on remand to try the case before a jury.

Notes

1. The court's doubt as to whether Lockheed's was a "true" counterclaim (as opposed to a "in name only" counterclaim) is puzzling. Lockheed's counterclaim did not merely seek an amount-of-loss declaration; it sought money damages for breach of contract. Because Lockheed asserted diversity as the basis for subject matter jurisdiction over its counterclaim, it was plainly entitled to a jury trial on the counterclaim, a Seventh Amendment right that trumped National's Rule 9(h) right to a bench trial.

2. The fact that Lockheed's counterclaim was "compulsory" within the meaning of FRCP Rule 13 meant that if National's declaratory action had been bench tried to judgment, the judgment would have had preclusive (res judicata) effect on the amount-of-loss issue; Lockheed would have entirely lost its constitutional right. There was no way to accommodate both National's statutory right to a bench trial and Lockheed's constitutional right to a jury trial; in such circumstances, it seemed obvious that the constitutional right must prevail.

3. Two of this book's editors agree with the Fourth Circuit's view that the *Beacon Theatres* argument was alone strong enough to support the court's resolution of the Seventh Amendment-Rule 9(h) conflict. For a contrary view on that point, see Friedell, *Expert Commentary*, available at the Lexis report of 503 F.3d 351 (2008).

4. It is often said that no concept "is more fundamental to the American judicial system than the right to trial by jury." *Sphere Drake Ins. Co. v. J. Shree Corp.*, 184 F.R.D. 258, 261 (S.D.N.Y. 1999). That argument has maximum appeal when made by a litigant like Lockheed, who seeks to steer clear of admiralty procedures in order to secure its constitutional right. It is less powerful when made by a litigant who wants to combine a right to jury trial with procedures available only in admiralty. Nevertheless, at least two courts of appeals have held that plaintiffs may combine in rem claims (justiciable only in admiralty) and diversity-based in personam claims arising from a single accident and have the whole case tried to the jury. *Luera v. M/V Alberta*, 635 F.3d 181 (5th Cir. 2011); *Ghotra v. Bandila Shipping, Inc.*, 113 F.3d 1050 (9th Cir. 1996). Cf. *Vodusek v. Bayliner Marine Corp.*, 71 F.3d 148 (4th Cir.1995); *Blake v. Farrell Lines, Inc.*, 417 F.2d 264 (3d Cir. 1969).

5. The range of procedural situations entailing conflict or tension between the Seventh Amendment and the Rule 9(h) bench-trial right is fairly broad, and the issues can become complex. See generally Friedell, *When Worlds Collide: The In Rem Jury and Other Marvels of Modern Admiralty*, 35 J. MAR. L. & COM. 143 (2004); Dyer, *Note, the Jury on the Quarterdeck: The Effect of Pleading Admiralty Jurisdiction When a Proceeding Turns Hybrid*, 63 TEX. L. REV. 533 (1984).

5. Impleader under Rule 14(c)

The general rule of impleader (third-party practice)—applicable in both admiralty and nonadmiralty cases—is set forth in FRCP 14(a), which provides that the defendant can bring into the lawsuit "a nonparty who is or may be liable to [defendant] for all or part of the claim against it." By contrast, FRCP 14(c)(1) states that the defendant in an admiralty action may, "as a third-party plaintiff, bring in a third-party defendant who may be wholly or partly liable—either to the plaintiff or to the third-party plaintiff—for remedy over, contribution, or otherwise on account of the same transaction, occurrence, or series of transactions or occurrences." FRCP 14(c)(2) adds: "The third-party plaintiff may demand judgment in the plaintiff's favor against the third-party defendant. In that event, the third-party defendant must defend under Rule 12 against the plaintiff's claim as well as the third-party plaintiff's claim; and the action proceeds as if the plaintiff had sued both the third-party defendant and the third-party plaintiff."

6. Possessory, Petitory, and Partition Actions, Including Actions to Try Title to Vessels

FRCP Supplemental Rule D and the jurisprudence establish that all of the captioned actions are commenced by *arresting* the ship. *Arrest* is typically the language of the action in rem. See generally *Dluhos v. Floating & Abandoned Vessel*, 162 F.3d 63 (2d Cir. 1998). Other actions in which a vessel or other property is seized use the differentiating term *attachment*. See FRCP Supplemental Rule B.

The actions treated by Supplemental Rule D are usually not in rem in the true admiralty sense, because they typically seek to affect the rights of only those parties and interests that are brought into the proceedings. See *Madruga*, *supra* at 72. But a plaintiff who specifically pleads that he seeks to establish his title good against all the world is bringing a true in rem action. *Dluhos*, 162 F.3d at 72–73.

7. Limitation of Liability Proceedings

These are governed by FRCP Supplemental Rule F and 46 U.S.C. §§ 30501–30512. We take up this highly specialized subject in Chapter IX.

8. Equitable Remedies in Admiralty Cases

Among the many restrictions on the jurisdiction of the English admiralty court as of 1789 was a crippling separateness from the realm of equity, entailing a lack of authority to issue an injunction, decree specific enforcement of a contract, administer or enforce a trust, hear an action for an accounting, reform or cancel a contract, or grant other equitable relief. For no good reason, our Supreme Court signed off on the view that the U.S. admiralty courts were similarly restricted. Admiralty and equity were two different systems, thought the Court, so it seemed to follow that admiralty courts could not provide the remedies in which equity courts specialized. *Rea v. The Eclipse*, 135 U.S. 599 (1890). No one defended this broad restriction on any principled basis. To the contrary, it was well and often criticized. See Black, *Admiralty Jurisdiction: Critique and Suggestions*, 50 Colum. L. Rev. 259, 275 (1950) ("the least defensible feature of the present structure . . . , one that crumbles at the touch of reasonable evaluation"); Morrison, *The Remedial Powers of the Admiralty*, 43 Yale L.J. 1 (1933). The 1966 merger seems to have done away with the restriction, in toto. *Farrell Lines Inc. v. Ceres Terminal Inc.*, 161 F.3d 115 (2d Cir. 1998), so holds, citing like-minded cases from the First and Fifth Circuits. The Fifth Circuit's declaration to this effect was ebullient:

> The Chancellor is no longer fixed to the woolsack. He may stride the quarterdeck of maritime jurisprudence and, in the role of admiralty judge, dispense, as would his landlocked brother, that which equity and good conscience impels.

Lewis v. S.S. Baume, 534 F.2d 1115, 1121 (5th Cir. 1976).

9. Service of Process

A federal-court lawsuit "is commenced by filing a complaint with the court" (FRCP 3), but the lawsuit cannot accomplish anything without service of process on the defendant. The term *service of process* is sometimes used broadly to refer to the delivery of any court order or other document that a party or witness is entitled to receive, but here we are using it to mean the initial official notice (FRCP 4 calls this the "summons") to the defendant of the filing of a lawsuit against it.

For federal-court cases generally, FRCP 4 requires the complaint and summons to be served together and sets forth a variety of methods for accomplishing formal service. And Rule 4(d) enables the plaintiff to write a letter to the defendant, enclosing a copy of the complaint and requesting the defendant to waive formal service. Defendants located in the United States who refuse without good cause to waive formal service are assessed with costs of service and related attorneys' fees.

For cases brought under admiralty jurisdiction, Supplemental Rules B, C, and E describe additional methods of service that are sometimes available. Rule B(1)(a) provides that a maritime defendant who "is not found within the district" can be served by attachment or garnishment of the defendant's tangible or intangible personal property. Rule C(3)(a)(i) provides that maritime liens can be enforced by in rem process consisting in "the arrest of the vessel or other property that is the subject of the action." Rule E(3)(a) sets forth a crucial limitation:

> In admiralty and maritime proceedings process in rem or of maritime attachment and garnishment may be served only within the district.

10. Personal Jurisdiction

Properly serving the summons and complaint on the individual, corporation, or vessel being sued is but one of the requisites to a valid judgment. Another, as we have seen in previous sections, is the existence of subject matter jurisdiction. In this subsection we are concerned with a third requisite, which has at least four labels. Court sometimes inquire into the defendant's "amenability to service [of process],"[12] sometimes into "jurisdiction in personam,"[13] sometimes into whether there is "jurisdiction over the person" of the defendant,[14] and sometimes into the existence of "personal jurisdiction" over the defendant.[15] *Personal jurisdiction* is the simplest of these synonyms and is preferable provided one remembers that it is proper to speak of "personal" jurisdiction over a corporation or a vessel.

There are two fundamental requirements for personal jurisdiction to exist over the defendant in a federal court. First, there must be a federal legislative authorization for the exercise of jurisdiction over the defendant.[16] Second, there must be enough of a relationship between the defendant and the forum to justify the conclusion that the defendant can be "haled into court"[17] there without offending the constitutional guarantees of due process. This constitutional principle is sometimes called the "minimum contacts" requirement.

---

12. *Omni Capital International, Ltd. v. Rudolf Wolff & Co., Ltd.*, 484 U.S. 97, 103 & n.6 (1987).
13. *Shaffer v. Heitner*, 433 U.S. 186, 207 (1977).
14. *Insurance Corp. of Ireland, Ltd. v. Compagnie des Bauxites de Guinee*, 452 U.S. 694, 716 n.6 (1982) (Powell, J., concurring).
15. *Id.*
16. *Omni*, 484 U.S. at 108–11.
17. *World-Wide Volkswagen Corp. v. Woodson*, 444 U.S. 286, 297 (1980).

The term comes from *International Shoe Co. v. Washington*, 326 U.S. 310, 316 (1945), which remains the seminal case on the general subject of personal jurisdiction.

In addition to their provisions detailing permissible methods of serving process, FRCP 4 and Supplemental Rules B and C also serve as legislative authorizations for the exercise of federal-court personal jurisdiction. The materials below treat five such authorizations: FRCP 4(k)(1)(A), authorizing personal jurisdiction over a defendant "who is subject to the jurisdiction of a court of general jurisdiction in the state where the [federal] district court is located"; FRCP 4(k)(1)(B), authorizing personal jurisdiction over an impleaded (via Rule 14) or compulsorily joined party (under Rule 19) who "is served within a judicial district of the United States and not more than 100 miles from where the summons was issued"; FRCP 4(k)(2), authorizing personal jurisdiction over defendants sued under federal law who have significant nationwide contacts but who are not "subject to jurisdiction in any state's courts of general jurisdiction"; FRCP Rule B, maritime attachment and garnishment; and FRCP Rule C, actions in rem.

In re Rationis Enterprises of Panama

United States Court of Appeals, Second Circuit, 2001
261 F.3d 264, 2001 AMC 2610

WINTER, Circuit Judge:

* * *

On November 24, 1997, the *M/V MSC Carla*, a ship carrying more than 1600 shipping containers, broke in half en route from France to the United States. Half of the vessel sank, along with her cargo. [The cargo included such items as cheese, ceramic tile, razor blades, heavy machinery, beer, perfume, automobile parts, furniture, porcelain dishes, limestone, and personal effects, destined for various ports and consignees. Hyundai Mipo Dockyard Co., Ltd. ("HMD"), a Korean shipyard,] had elongated the *Carla* in 1984 by installing a mid-body insert. When the *Carla* split, she did so near one of the seams joining the original hull with HMD's insert.

On December 9, 1997, the ship's owner filed a petition under the Limitation of Shipowners' Liability Act [46 U.S.C. §§30501–30512] in the Southern District of New York. That Act provides a procedure in the exercise of admiralty jurisdiction that allows a single federal court to determine all relevant issues related to liability and limits the shipowner's liability to the salvage value of the vessel plus the value of freight then pending, should exoneration be denied.

HMD was brought into this action in January 1998, when the approximately 1000 cargo claimants in the limitation proceeding put the shipyard on notice that they intended to hold it jointly and severally responsible for the casualty. HMD responded by seeking a declaratory judgment of non-liability from the Ulsan District Court of Korea in June 1998. In the Korean action, HMD served only three of the 1000 cargo claimants, namely, the three appellees in this appeal. * * *.

In September 1998, various cargo claimants began serving third-party complaints on HMD, at HMD's New Jersey office. In November 1999, appellees — the three cargo claimants sued by HMD in Korea — moved in the Southern District to enjoin HMD's Korean action against them.

The district court granted the injunction. The grounds primarily relied on were that: (i) the "unusual size and complexity" of the case made it preferable that all claims be settled "in one action to the extent possible," and (ii) the fact that HMD brought its Korean action against only three of the 1000 cargo claimants might create difficult problems of collateral estoppel unless the court "enjoin[ed] the risk of the[ir] occurring."

The district court also found no merit in HMD's claim that the court lacked personal jurisdiction over it. The court found that

> HMD with its sales office in Englewood Cliffs, New Jersey, as observed, right across the Hudson River from New York City, and a New York (Manhattan) telephone listing in the White Pages, has been served in this proceeding, filed an answer, and participated in the case, has not moved to dismiss for lack of personal jurisdiction, and has availed itself of the United States at large.

It therefore held that personal jurisdiction had been properly established because HMD had sufficient contacts in the "bulge area." [FRCP 4(k)(1)(B) provides that "[s]erving a summons ... establishes personal jurisdiction over a defendant ... who is a party joined under Rule 14 or 19 and is served within a judicial district of the United States and not more than 100 miles from where the summons was issued."] "The circuit courts have uniformly concluded that if a party delineated in Rule 4(k)(1)(B) has minimum contacts with the bulge area, the district court in the forum state gains personal jurisdiction over him through service of process pursuant to Rule 4." [ ] The district court also noted that HMD had participated in discovery in the United States.

This appeal followed. [HMD contests personal jurisdiction and the propriety of the anti-suit injunction.]

(a) Forfeiture of Objections to the Exercise of Personal Jurisdiction

The cargo claimants contend that HMD has forfeited its lack of personal jurisdiction defense. [ ] Specifically, appellees argue that HMD missed the deadline imposed by a magistrate judge's scheduling order for filing motions to dismiss. However, the scheduling order is ambiguous. * * *

Appellees also claim that, even if HMD did not miss the filing deadline, it otherwise forfeited its jurisdictional defense under standards set out in our decision in *Hamilton v. Atlas Turner, Inc.*, 197 F.3d 58 (2d Cir. 1999). In *Hamilton*, we held that a defendant forfeited its lack of personal jurisdiction defense when the defendant's answer asserted the court's lack of personal jurisdiction, but the defendant did not move to dismiss on those grounds until four years later. We found that "[c]onsiderable pretrial activity," including discovery and settlement conferences, had occurred during the four-year interval, and that the defendant had "several clear opportunities" to make its motion earlier.

Appellees argue that HMD has both engaged in full discovery and foregone opportunities to raise the lack of personal jurisdiction. * * * As in the case of the scheduling order, we simply cannot determine on the record before us whether HMD forfeited its objections to the exercise of personal jurisdiction over it.

On remand, therefore, the district court should determine whether HMD missed the filing deadline and/or whether it forfeited its defense by participating in the litigation.

(b) The Need for an Evidentiary Hearing

HMD also argues that the district court erred by issuing the injunction without first holding an evidentiary hearing on jurisdiction. We agree. Should the district court on remand conclude that HMD did not forfeit its jurisdictional defense, we believe that a hearing will then be required on the merits of that defense before another injunction may be considered. * * * [E]ssential facts relating to the court's personal jurisdiction over HMD remain[] in dispute.

The district court concluded here that it had personal jurisdiction over HMD on the grounds that HMD had a sales office in New Jersey, a Manhattan White Pages listing, and "has availed itself of the United States at large." HMD, however, claims that the telephone listing referenced does not belong to it, and appellees do not contradict that assertion. Moreover, HMD disputes that its contacts in New Jersey—its local sales office—sufficed to establish the court's jurisdiction. While a local office may constitute a "continuous and systematic" contact sufficient to allow a court to hold that a defendant subjected itself to the general jurisdiction of the forum state, [ ] the presence of such an office is not dispositive. [ ] The district court made no findings regarding whether HMD had sufficient minimum contacts apart from the fact that HMD had a local office and a White Pages listing.[4]

* * *

Appellees contend HMD's contacts sufficed; HMD contends otherwise. There is no evidence in the record concerning the nature of HMD's business in New Jersey, and it now appears that the district court's reliance on the telephone listing was misplaced. Appellate review is not possible under these circumstances, and essential facts clearly remain in dispute. An evidentiary hearing will therefore be required on jurisdiction before the court can reach the merits on remand, should it wish to do so.

* * *

We therefore vacate the injunction and remand for further proceedings not inconsistent with this opinion.

Note

On remand, the district court announced that HMD had voluntarily suspended the Korean declaratory action, thereby mooting the injunction issue. It again found that HMD had forfeited its personal jurisdiction defense, conducted a bench trial, and held HMD liable. Reversing, the Second Circuit concluded that HMD was protected against liability by a Korean statute of repose providing that "the right to claim damages resulting from an unlawful act shall lapse by prescription if ten years have elapsed from the time when the unlawful act was committed." *Rationis Enterprises Inc. v. Hyundai Mipo Dockyard Co.*, 426 F.3d 580, 588 & n. 4 (2d Cir. 2005).

4. The district court did not specify whether it determined that it had personal jurisdiction over HMD based on specific or general jurisdiction theories. Specific jurisdiction exists when a state exercises personal jurisdiction over a defendant in a suit arising out of or related to the defendant's contacts with the forum; a court's general [personal] jurisdiction, on the other hand, is based on the defendant's general business contacts with the forum state and permits a court to exercise its power in a case where the subject matter of the suit is unrelated to those contacts. HMD argues that the claims relating to its lengthening of the *Carla* do not relate to any activities in the United States and, therefore, only general jurisdiction theories may be used to establish personal jurisdiction over it. Although appellees do not appear to contend otherwise, we do not decide whether specific jurisdiction theories might be applicable, because the district court did not find facts adequate to support a finding of jurisdiction under either set of theories. [Citation and internal quotation marks omitted.]

Submersible Systems, Inc. v. Perforadora Central, S.A. De C.V.

United States Court of Appeals, Fifth Circuit, 2001
249 F.3d 413, 2001 AMC 1873

DAVIS, Circuit Judge:

* * *

I.

[Submersible Systems, Inc. ("SSI") is a Louisiana corporation that operates small remotely-operated submersible vehicles used in underwater inspection, construction, and surveying. In the latter part of 1996, SSI contracted with Quantum Ingenieros, S.A. de C.V. ("Quantum") to provide the submersible vehicles for Quantum's inspection of certain oil and gas pipelines located in Mexican waters. As part of this project, Quantum also contracted with Perforadora Central, S.A. de C.V. ("Central") to transport the equipment, including SSI's submersible vehicles, and the personnel to be used to inspect the pipelines. To carry out this contract, in November 1966 Central dispatched its vessel, the *M/V Don Francisco*, to Morgan City, Louisiana, to pick up SSI's equipment and transport it to its destination in Mexico.]

Quantum was late paying both SSI and Central * * *. By early June of 1997 Quantum owed both SSI and Central substantial sums for their services on the pipeline inspection project. As a result of Quantum's indebtedness, Quantum and Central agreed to end the charter of the *Don Francisco* on June 23, 1997 and on that day the *Don Francisco* returned to the port of Dos Bocas, Mexico. At that time, SSI had two employees, one of its submersible vehicles, and some other related equipment on board the *Don Francisco.* All of SSI's equipment was clearly marked as belonging to SSI.

At about 9 am on the morning of the 23rd, the captain of the *Don Francisco* woke the two SSI employees and told them that SSI's equipment had been seized to force Quantum to pay Central what it was owed for the charter of its vessel. Shortly thereafter, one of Central's agents boarded the vessel and inspected the immigration papers of the two SSI employees. Seeing that they were out of order, the agent reported the two men to the Mexican immigration authorities. The two SSI employees then left the vessel and spent the day getting their immigration papers in order. While they were gone, Central offloaded SSI's equipment from the *Don Francisco* and put it into a locked yard at the port.

Wolfgang Burnside, the owner of SSI, arrived in Mexico on June 26, 1997 to demand the release of SSI's equipment. Central refused to release the equipment and instead deposited it with the Mexican Ministerio Publico. In later proceedings before the Ministerio Publico, Central asserted that the seized equipment belonged to Quantum and should be held pending an investigation of Quantum for its failure to pay its debts. Central was eventually appointed custodian of SSI's equipment for the Ministerio Publico and moved the equipment to Central's yard in Ciudad del Carmen, Mexico, where it was exposed to the elements.

After SSI filed this lawsuit, Central released the equipment in March of 1999 and SSI transported it back to the United States. However, because of prolonged exposure to the elements, the equipment had been rendered worthless.

II.

While it was attempting to get Central to return its property, SSI discovered that Central was building a marine drilling rig at the TDI Halter shipyard in Pascagoula, Mississippi.

SSI then filed [this] suit in the southern district of Mississippi, in May of 1998, for the conversion of its equipment by Central. SSI's suit invoked both the admiralty jurisdiction and the diversity jurisdiction of the district court. SSI prayed for attachment of the rig, pursuant to Rule B of the Supplemental Rules for Certain Admiralty and Maritime Claims. [Rule B(1)(a) provides: "If a defendant is not found within the district when a verified complaint praying for attachment and the affidavit required by Rule B(1)(b) are filed, a verified complaint may contain a prayer for process to attach the defendant's tangible or intangible personal property—up to the amount sued for—in the hands of garnishees named in the process." Rule B(1)(b) provides: "The plaintiff or the plaintiff's attorney must sign and file with the complaint an affidavit stating that, to the affiant's knowledge, or on information and belief, the defendant cannot be found within the district."] * * *.

Central responded to the suit by moving to dismiss for lack of personal jurisdiction. Central argued that given the nature of the suit, it had insufficient contacts with Mississippi to subject it to suit in Mississippi. Central argued against attachment of its rig pursuant to Rule B by arguing that the district court had no admiralty jurisdiction, or in the alternative that [Central] could be found within the southern district of Mississippi and so attachment under Rule B would be improper. * * *

The district court * * * ruled that the nature of Central's contacts with Mississippi made it subject to suit in Mississippi. The district court ruled that admiralty jurisdiction existed in this case, but denied attachment under Rule B on two separate grounds. The district court first held that as Central was subject to jurisdiction in the southern district of Mississippi, it could also be ["found within"] the southern district of Mississippi [within the meaning of rule B.] The district court next held, in the alternative, that SSI had not filed the affidavit required by Rule B regarding SSI's efforts to locate Central within the southern district of Mississippi. * * *

Following a three day bench trial, the district court found that Central had converted SSI's equipment. The district court awarded SSI [compensatory and punitive damages totaling more than $4.25 million.]

* * *

III.

[Central's appeal challenges the district court's personal jurisdiction. Because the facts concerning Central's contacts with Mississippi and the United States are undisputed, the issue of personal jurisdiction in this case presents a question of law that we review *de novo.*]

A. [FRCP 4(k)(1)(A)]

Absent a federal statute that provides for more expansive personal jurisdiction, the personal jurisdiction of a federal district court is coterminous with that of a court of general jurisdiction of the state in which the district court sits. [Fed. R. Civ. P. 4(k)(1)(A) provides: "Serving a summons or filing a waiver of service establishes personal jurisdiction over a defendant who is subject to the jurisdiction of a court of general jurisdiction in the state where the district court is located."] For a federal district court in a particular state to exercise personal jurisdiction over a defendant, that exercise of jurisdiction must first be proper under that state's long-arm statute. If the state long-arm statute allows the district court to exercise personal jurisdiction, the exercise of personal jurisdiction must also be proper under the due process clause of the Fourteenth Amendment.

* * *

* * * [We conclude that] Central is not subject to the personal jurisdiction of the Mississippi courts under the [terms of the] Mississippi long-arm statute. * * *

Nor would a district court's exercise of personal jurisdiction over Central in Mississippi comport with the requirements of the due process clause of the Fourteenth Amendment. Due process requires that a foreign corporate defendant "establish sufficient contacts or ties with the state of the forum to make it reasonable and just according to our traditional conception of fair play and substantial justice to permit the state to enforce the obligations which [the defendant] has incurred there." *International Shoe Co. v. Washington*, 326 U.S. 310, 320 (1945); *Shaffer v. Heitner*, 433 U.S. 186, 207 (1977). An exercise of personal jurisdiction, even when a foreign corporate defendant has established sufficient contacts with a forum, must also be reasonable in light of the forum's interest in the litigation in question. *Asahi Metal Indus. Co. v. Superior Court*, 480 U.S. 102, 113–14 (1987).

The extent of the contacts that a foreign corporate defendant must establish with a forum to satisfy due process concerns differs depending on the nature of the litigation. In this case, Central's contacts with the state of Mississippi are wholly unrelated to SSI's claim that Central converted SSI's equipment in Mexico. When a plaintiff's claim does not arise out of a defendant's contacts with a forum, then the defendant's contacts with the forum must be "continuous and systematic" to satisfy the requirements of due process. *Helicopteros Nacionales de Colombia v. Hall*, 466 U.S. 408, 416 (1984) [ ].

As commentators have recognized, the continuous and systematic contacts test is a difficult one to meet, requiring extensive contacts between a defendant and a forum. [ ] The Supreme Court has upheld an exercise of personal jurisdiction when the suit was unrelated to the defendant's contacts with a forum only once. [This was in *Perkins v. Benguet Consolidated Mining Co.*, 342 U.S. 437 (1952).] Purchasing equipment in a forum and traveling to that forum on related business are, without more, insufficient to confer personal jurisdiction when the plaintiff's cause of action does not arise out of those purchasing activities. *Helicopteros*, 466 U.S. at 417.

Central's only contacts with the state of Mississippi grow out of its construction of a marine drilling rig at the TDI Halter shipyard in Pascagoula. Central contracted with TDI Halter for the construction of the rig, and also maintained an office at the shipyard with three employees to monitor the construction. These are not the sort of continuous and systematic contacts that would allow the district court to take jurisdiction over Central in this case.[2]

* * *

* * * [Central's] contacts with Mississippi are even less substantial than those of the Colombian company with Texas in *Helicopteros*. * * *

---

2. SSI has argued that Central conceded personal jurisdiction in its opposition to attachment of the drilling rig under Rule B. Central did admit, as part of that opposition, to the contacts with Mississippi which are discussed above. Central argued that those contacts meant that it could be found within the Southern District of Mississippi and so attachment under Rule B would be improper. However, Central specifically stated that it was not thereby conceding the issue of personal jurisdiction outside of the context of Rule B attachment. Central stated [that it] "does not dispute that the presence of the rig in the district itself is sufficient to satisfy general personal jurisdiction in the district for the purposes of Rule B *as Rule B is not subject to common law due process constraints. Maritime attachment warrants consideration of a more flexible application of the doctrines of due process consistent with its historical functions*" (emphasis added). Whether Central is correct or not concerning what due process requires in the Rule B attachment context, Central cannot be said to have conceded the issue of personal jurisdiction."

B. [FRCP 4(k)(2)]

SSI argues, as an alternative ground for supporting the judgment entered by the district court in its favor, that [FRCP 4(k)(2)] authorized the district court to assume jurisdiction over Central. [Rule 4(k)(2) provides:

> For a claim that arises under federal law, serving a summons or filing a waiver of service establishes personal jurisdiction over a defendant if:
>
> (A) the defendant is not subject to jurisdiction in any state's courts of general jurisdiction; and
>
> (B) exercising jurisdiction is consistent with the United States Constitution and laws.]

Our court has previously held that claims falling within the admiralty jurisdiction of the federal courts are claims arising under federal law for the purposes of Rule 4(k)(2). [ ]

Rule 4(k)(2) applies to actions in which a federal court draws its authority directly from federal law, and does not borrow it from state law. The due process required in federal cases governed by Rule 4(k)(2) is measured with reference to the Fifth Amendment, rather than the Fourteenth Amendment. That is, Rule 4(k)(2) requires us to consider Central's contacts with the United States as a whole, and not just Central's contacts with the state of Mississippi. [ ] If Central has sufficient contacts with the United States, then the district court could have exercised jurisdiction over Central pursuant to Rule 4(k)(2).

In analyzing Central's contacts with the United States, we must keep in mind that this case does not arise out of Central's contacts with the United States. All the events constituting Central's conversion of SSI's equipment—the seizure aboard the *Don Francisco*, the unloading of the equipment at the port of Dos Bocas, and the proceedings before the Mexican Ministerio Publico—took place in Mexico. Therefore, Central's contacts with the United States must be "continuous and systematic" to have allowed the district court to take jurisdiction over Central pursuant to Rule 4(k)(2). [ ]

The record reflects very few contacts between Central and the United States other than those related to the construction of the rig in Pascagoula. Central has an account at a Houston bank and sends some employees to an offshore drilling conference in Houston every year. Central has purchased spare parts and vessels in the United States, though to what extent is not clear from the record. Central's vessels have also occasionally called on United States ports. These contacts with the United States are, at best, sporadic and of small consequence. Central conducts no operations in the United States, maintains no office in the United States (other than the one which is maintained solely to oversee construction in Pascagoula), and owns no real or personal property located in the United States.

Because Central's contacts with the United States are not continuous and systematic, the district court had no authority to assume jurisdiction over Central pursuant to Rule 4(k)(2).

C. [FRCP Supp. Rule B]

[Rule B (quoted above in the first paragraph of section II of this opinion) allows a district court to take jurisdiction over a defendant in an admiralty or maritime action by attaching property of the defendant provided the defendant "is not found within the district." A defendant is "found within the district" for Rule B purposes only if it has both "minimum contacts" and an agent for service of process within the district. *Heidmar, Inc. v. Anomina Ravennate*, 132 F.3d 264, 268 (5th Cir. 1998); *LaBlanca v. Ostermunchner*, 664 F.2d 65, 67 (5th Cir. 1981).]

The district court gave two grounds for denying SSI's motion to attach [Central's rig under construction] pursuant to Rule B. The district court held that Central could be found within the southern district of Mississippi because its contacts with Mississippi made it subject to jurisdiction there. The district court also held that SSI did not submit the affidavit required by Rule B stating that Central could not be found within the southern district of Mississippi. As discussed above, we disagree with the district court's conclusion that Central's contacts were sufficient to permit it to exercise jurisdiction over this action. Thus, the district court erred in concluding that Central [could] be found within the southern district of Mississippi for the purposes of Rule B. However, that conclusion does not mean that the district court erred in refusing to attach Central's rig pursuant to Rule B.

Rule B requires that a plaintiff seeking attachment pursuant to Rule B file an affidavit, as well as a verified complaint, concerning the presence of the defendant within the district in which the action is filed. As the district court held, and as our review of the record confirms, SSI did not file the required affidavit with its verified complaint when it sought attachment of Central's drilling rig. * * *

The affidavit required by Rule B serves a useful purpose: it assures the district court that the plaintiff has been diligent in searching for the defendant within the district in which the action is filed. [ ]. As the district court said, the contacts that Central had with Mississippi raised questions about whether Central could be found within the southern district of Mississippi. Thus, it was especially important that SSI demonstrate that it had been diligent about searching for Central and that SSI was not seeking attachment merely for purposes of security or harassment. There was good reason for the district court to enforce Rule B as written and refuse to attach Central's rig.

IV.

For the reasons discussed above, Central was not subject to the personal jurisdiction of the district court. * * * Therefore, the judgment of the district court is vacated and this case is remanded with instructions to dismiss this case for lack of jurisdiction.

Notes

1. The court's ruling that maritime law is "federal law" within the meaning of Rule 4(k)(2) has been generally accepted. The initial doubts stemmed from the holding in *Romero, supra* at 79–80, that maritime law is not federal law for purposes of assertions of jurisdiction under 28 U.S.C. § 1331.

2. For a further demonstration of the difficulty of establishing a defendant's "continuous and systematic" business contacts with the United States for purposes of general personal jurisdiction under Rule 4(k)(2), see *Porina v. Marward Shipping Co.*, 521 F.3d 122 (2d Cir. 2008) (holding that the owner of a cargo vessel that made regular voyages to U.S. ports—60 in the four years preceding defendant's purchase of the ship and at least 16 in the 18 months following the purchase—was not subject to personal jurisdiction because the vessel's charterers decided where the ship would go and the owner merely reaped the profits). See also *DeLeon v. Shih Wei Nav. Co.*, 268 Fed. Appx. 487 (5th Cir. 2008).

3. How does a plaintiff go about satisfying Rule 4(k)(2)'s requirement that the defendant is not "subject to the jurisdiction of the courts of general jurisdiction of any state"? Must the plaintiff "traipse through the 50 states, asking whether each could entertain the suit"? Not at all, says the Seventh Circuit in *ISI Int'l, Inc. v. Borden Ladner Gervais, LLP*, 256 F.3d 548, 552 (7th Cir. 2001):

> Constitutional analysis for each of the 50 states is eminently avoidable by allocating burdens sensibly. A defendant who wants to preclude use of Rule 4(k)(2) has only to name some other state in which suit could proceed. Naming a more appropriate state would amount to a consent to personal jurisdiction there (personal jurisdiction, unlike federal subject-matter jurisdiction, is waivable). If, however, the defendant contends that he cannot be sued in the forum state and refuses to identify any other where suit is possible, then the federal court is entitled to use Rule 4(k)(2).

For similarly reasoned cases, see *Touchcom, Inc. v. Bereskin & Parr*, 547 F.3d 1403, 1413 (Fed. Cir. 2009); *Adams v. Unione Mediterranea Di Scurta*, 364 F.3d 646, 651 (5th Cir. 2004); *United States v. Swiss American Bank*, 191 F.3d 30, 41–42 (1st Cir. 1999); *Ogden v. GlobalSantaFe Offshore Services*, 31 F. Supp. 3d 832 (E.D. La. 2014).

Grand Bahama Petroleum Co. v. Canadian Transp. Agencies, Ltd.

United States District Court for the Western District of Washington, 1978
450 F. Supp. 447, 1978 AMC 789

BEEKS, District Judge:

[Grand Bahama Petroleum Company, a Bahamian corporation, seeks to recover the value of fuel oil and other incidental services supplied to the Soviet flag vessel *M/V Kuibshevges* while under charter to defendants, citizens of Canada. Jurisdiction is based upon Supplemental Rule B(1) of the Federal Rules of Civil Procedure and the garnishment of a bank account on deposit with garnishee Seattle-First National Bank. Defendants seek dismissal alleging lack of personal jurisdiction. They contend that the nonmaritime decision in *Shaffer v. Heitner*, 433 U.S. 186 (1977), means that jurisdiction based on attachment is no longer permissible without the presence of minimum contacts. The only contact which the defendants appear to have with this district is the existence of the Seattle-First bank account.]

[Plaintiff maintains a fueling facility in Freeport, Grand Bahama Island. In early July, 1977, *Kuibshevges*, * * * under charter to defendants, called at Grand Bahama's facility to take on bunkers. Plaintiff avers that it agreed to provide approximately 330 metric tons at a specified price upon the promise of defendants to contemporaneously deposit $45,000 with plaintiff, any excess to be refunded. Grand Bahama supplied the vessel with 2,296 barrels of fuel on or about July 6 and charged defendants $40,363.68. Defendants apparently failed to make the required deposit and have not paid the amount due, or any part thereof.]

Grand Bahama filed suit [on] August 3, 1977, to recover this debt from defendants. Since none of the defendants could be found within this district, Grand Bahama sought to attach any of their property which could be so found pursuant to Rule B(1). [Defendants have filed a motion to dismiss the action for lack of jurisdiction. On the basis of *Shaffer*, they contend that Rule B(1) violates the due process clause of the fifth amendment because it would permit this court to exercise jurisdiction despite the absence of sufficient contacts among the defendants, the litigation, and this district. *Shaffer* holds that in cases involving a non-resident defendant, the jurisdiction of a state court is to be measured by the minimum contacts standard enunciated in *International Shoe Co. v. Washington*, 326 U.S. 310 (1945). In other words, where a non-resident defendant is involved, *in rem* and *quasi-in-rem* jurisdiction are merged into *in personam* jurisdiction.]

[The *Shaffer* Court was persuaded by the following argument: The case for applying to jurisdiction in rem the same test of "fair play and substantial justice" as governs assertions of jurisdiction in personam is simple and straightforward. It is premised on recognition that the phrase, "judicial jurisdiction over a thing," is a customary elliptical way of referring to jurisdiction over the interests of persons in a thing. This recognition leads to the conclusion that in order to justify an exercise of jurisdiction in rem, the basis for jurisdiction must be sufficient to justify exercising jurisdiction over the interests of persons in a thing. The standard for determining whether an exercise of jurisdiction over the interests of persons is consistent with the Due Process Clause is the minimum-contacts standard elucidated in *International Shoe*.]

[Certainly this action bears some similarity to *Shaffer*. The primary purpose of the Delaware sequestration statute at issue in *Shaffer* and Supplemental Rule B(1) is to compel the personal appearance of a non-resident defendant to answer and defend a suit brought against him through the seizure of any property which might be found in the geographical area over which the court has jurisdiction.]

[Notwithstanding the similarities, I am not persuaded that *Shaffer* invalidates admiralty *quasi-in-rem* jurisdiction. The autonomy of admiralty from the common law is of constitutional magnitude.] The justification for maintaining the autonomy of admiralty jurisprudence derives from the maritime context in which admiralty is set. Admiralty deals with circumstances generally different from those of the common law:

> Courts of admiralty are established for the settlement of disputes between persons engaged in commerce and navigation, who, on the one hand, may be absent from their homes for long periods of time, and, on the other hand, often have property or credits in other places. In all nations, as observed by an early writer, such courts "have been directed to proceed at such times, and in such manner, as might best consist with the opportunities of trade, and least hinder or detain men from their employments." [ ] In the same spirit this court has more than once said: "Courts of admiralty have been found necessary in all commercial countries, for the safety and convenience of commerce and the speedy decision of controversies, where delay would often be ruin." [ ] To compel suitors in admiralty (when the ship is abroad and cannot be reached by a libel in rem) to resort to the home of the defendant, and to prevent them from suing him in any district in which he might be served with a summons or his goods or credits attached, would not only often put them to great delay, inconvenience and expense, but would in many cases amount to a denial of justice.

In re Louisville Underwriters, 134 U.S. 488, 493 (1890). *See also Comm'l Transport. Co. v. Fitzhugh*, 66 U.S. (1 Black.) 574, 580–81 (1862).

* * *

I am convinced that maritime attachment is constitutionally permissible. The recognized autonomy of admiralty jurisprudence, although not absolute, and the long constitutional viability of maritime attachment compel me to conclude that *Shaffer* does not reach Rule B(1) attachment.

* * *

Notes

1. The courts of appeals that have considered the impact of *Shaffer* on Rule B jurisdiction have agreed with the conclusion and general reasoning in *Grand Bahama*. See *Trans-Asiatic Oil Ltd. v. Apex Oil Co.*, 743 F.2d 956, 960 (1st Cir. 1984); *Polar Shipping v. Oriental Shipping Corp.*, 686 F.2d 627, 637 (9th Cir. 1982); *Amoco Overseas Oil Co. v. C.N.A.N.*, 605 F.2d 648, 655 (2d Cir. 1979).

2. "The 'jurisdiction' at issue in a Rule B attachment proceeding is *quasi in rem*, rather than *in personam* or *in rem*. In Rule B attachment proceedings, jurisdiction is predicated on the presence within the court's territorial reach of property in which the Rule B defendant has an interest. [ ] Because of the requirement that the defendant not be 'found' within the district where the action is brought, Rule B contemplates that a court will lack *in personam* jurisdiction over the defendant when it orders that a writ of attachment be issued. In such a proceeding, the court's coercive authority is coterminous with the scope of its jurisdiction, and limited to the extent of the defendant's interest in the attached property; that authority does not extend to the exercise of *in personam* jurisdiction over a Rule B defendant." *Shipping Corp. of India Ltd. v. Jaldhi Overseas Pte. Ltd.*, 585 F.3d 58, 69 n. 12 (2d Cir. 2009).

Personal Jurisdiction in Actions In Rem under Rule C

The judicial consensus that Rule B attachment is under no threat from *Shaffer* has meant, *a fortiori*, that Rule C jurisdiction is safe. As was explained in *Merchants National Bank v. Dredge General G.L. Gillespie*, 663 F.2d 1338, 1350 & n.18 (5th Cir. 1981):

> [In rem] jurisdiction is asserted on the basis of the presence of the vessel within the district. Rule E(3)(a) states that process in rem "shall be served only within the district." In *Shaffer* ... the Supreme Court held that, in a nonmaritime action, assertion of in rem or quasi in rem jurisdiction, as well as personal jurisdiction, requires that a defendant have certain minimum contacts with the forum such that the maintenance of the suit does not offend traditional notions of fair play and substantial justice. Under the strict personification theory of admiralty in rem actions, jurisdiction is asserted over the vessel under the same circumstances that jurisdiction could be asserted over an individual. *Shaffer* thus results in no change in the admiralty context. [ ]
>
> * * * [A] foreign ship may be sued even though it would not satisfy the "minimum contacts" test developed out of *International Shoe Co. v. Washington*, 326 U.S. 310 (1945). The theory of the ship's own liability is sufficient to confer in rem jurisdiction without regard to the contacts its owner may have with the district. It is clear that the due process questions in admiralty are significantly different than in attachment proceedings commenced in state courts.

The "strict personification theory" refers to the doctrines whereby the holder of a maritime lien can use in rem process to force a judicial sale of the vessel regardless of the owner or charterer's personal liability for the debt or even presence in the litigation. This theory had perhaps its sharpest illustration in *The China*, 74 U.S. 53 (1868) [*infra* at 361]. The *China*, a British ship, was leaving the port of New York under the command of a harbor pilot when she ran into the *Kentucky*, a U.S. ship, and sank her. The owners of the *Kentucky* brought a libel in rem. Moving to dismiss, the owners of the *China* showed that they were compelled by New York law to use the pilot and that the fault was exclusively that of the pilot; there was no fault of the master or crew of the *China*. The Supreme Court accepted the *China* owners' factual showing as well as their legal argument that there would have been no liability under English law. Nevertheless, the Court held the *China* liable, stating: "A damaging vessel is [not] excused because she was compelled to obey.... The only question in all such cases is, was she in fault?" *Id.* at 68–69.

The personification theory is sometimes characterized as a legal fiction, and it has been said that *Continental Grain Co. v. Barge FBL-585*, 364 U.S. 19 (1960), questioned the fiction's continued vitality. See, e.g., Adrignolo, *Navigating the Channels of Due Process: Admiralty Rule C Arrests Without Minimum Contacts*, 4 SETON HALL CONST. L.J. 705, 750–51 (1994). On another view, *Continental* neither disparaged nor trumpeted the theory. Holding that an in rem action in which the shipowner has provided a bond or undertaking to secure the vessel's release can be transferred (pursuant to 28 U.S.C. § 1404(a)) to a more convenient venue, the *Continental* Court (364 U.S. at 22–23) stated:

> [There is] a long-standing admiralty fiction that a vessel may be assumed to be a person for the purpose of filing a lawsuit and enforcing a judgment. The fiction ... has not been without its critics even in the field it was designed to serve. It has been referred to as "archaic," "an animistic survival from remote times," "irrational," and "atavistic." Perhaps this is going too far since the fiction is one that certainly had real cause for its existence in its context and in the day and generation in which it was created. A purpose of the fiction, among others, has been to allow actions against ships where a person owning the ship could not be reached, and it can be very useful for this purpose still. We are asked here, however, to transplant this ancient salt-water admiralty fiction into the dry-land context of forum non conveniens, where its usefulness and possibilities for good are questionable at best. In fact, the fiction appears to have no relevance whatever in a District Court's determination of where a case can most conveniently be tried. A fiction born to provide convenient forums should not be [transformed] into a weapon to defeat that very purpose.

The simple idea of *Merchants National Bank*—that an in rem action against a vessel is above successful due process challenge because the offender is being sued where it (she?) is located—gained potential support from the nonmaritime decision in *Burnham v. Superior Court*, 495 U.S. 604 (1990), holding that the Fourteenth Amendment is not offended when an individual is "tagged" with service of process and thereby subjected to personal jurisdiction in a state that he happens to be passing through. It seems an obvious argument that an in rem suit against a personified vessel is insulated from due process challenge by the *Burnham* principle. Oddly enough, no cases can be found saying that. We suspect this is because the admiralty courts had already put the *Shaffer* question to rest before *Burnham* came along.

11. Venue

FRCP 82 provides that "[a]n admiralty or maritime claim under Rule 9(h) is not a civil action for purposes of [the federal-court venue statute, 28 U.S.C. § 1391]." What this means is that in cases classified as admiralty under Rule 9(h), "venue is proper ... in any district where the parties are subject to personal jurisdiction and can be served with process." *I & M Rail Link v. Northstar Navigation*, 21 F. Supp. 2d 849, 857 (N.D. Ill. 1998). If the plaintiff initiates the suit in a venue that is allowed by this liberal rule but is nevertheless inappropriate, the case can be transferred to the appropriate federal court under 28 U.S.C. § 1404(a). As we saw *supra* at 100–01, *Continental Grain* held that even an in rem action can be transferred once the vessel has been released from arrest and a bond or letter of undertaking furnished in its stead.

12. Removal of Maritime Cases

The focus of this subsection is maritime lawsuits that "suitors" (plaintiffs) have chosen—pursuant to the saving-to-suitors clause of 28 U.S.C. § 1333(1)—to institute in state court. It will lend clarity to the discussion if we term such lawsuits "saving clause cases."

When can defendants remove saving-clause cases to federal court? The traditional short answer has been, only when there is some basis for federal subject-matter jurisdiction in addition to admiralty. An even shorter way to say it: *No removal into admiralty.* The statutory basis for that rule is hard to discern, but the saving clause itself—long regarded as "the sort of quasi-constitutional statutory law, change in which (despite theoretical susceptibility to the usual processes of amendment and repeal) one feels it almost impious to contemplate"[18]—is often cited as a prohibition against removal into admiralty. If defendants could freely remove into admiralty, the only maritime cases that could be heard in state courts would be the presumably minuscule few in which the parties are agreed to state jurisdiction. That would be a severe affront to a fundamental premise of *Romero*, just below.

Romero v. International Terminal Operating Co.

Supreme Court of the United States, 1959
358 U.S. 354, 79 S. Ct. 468, 3 L. Ed. 2d 368, 1959 AMC 832

Mr. Justice FRANKFURTER delivered the opinion of the Court.

[Romero, a seaman injured on the deck of a vessel berthed in the harbor at Hoboken, New Jersey, brought a personal injury action in the Southern District of New York against Compania Transatlantica, the shipowner/employer. Romero sought recovery under the Jones Act, 46 U.S.C. § 30104, and under the general maritime doctrines of unseaworthiness and maintenance and cure. Subject matter jurisdiction was predicated solely on 28 U.S.C. § 1331. By seeking to pursue the unseaworthiness and maintenance and cure claims on the law side of federal court, plaintiff presented a question of first impression in this Court: whether actions arising under the general (nonstatutory) federal maritime law are "actions arising under the Constitution, laws, or treaties of the United States" within the meaning of 28 U.S.C. § 1331. The district court and Second Circuit held no. The First Circuit has taken a different view. We granted certiorari because of the conflict among Courts of Appeals as to the proper construction of the relevant provision of the Judiciary Act of 1875 (now 28 U.S.C. § 1331). Such conflict in the construction of an old and important statute calls for a full exposition of the problem. For the reasons set forth below, we conclude that the Second Circuit's interpretation of § 1331 is correct.]

Abstractly stated, the problem is the ordinary task of a court to apply the words of a statute according to their proper construction. But "proper construction" is not satisfied by taking the words as if they were self-contained phrases. So considered, the words do not yield the meaning of the statute. The words we have to construe are not only words with a history. They express an enactment that is part of a serial, and a serial that must be related to Article III of the Constitution, the watershed of all judiciary legislation, and to the enactments which have derived from that Article. Moreover, Article III itself has its sources in history. These give content and meaning to its pithy phrases. Rationally construed, the Act of 1875 must be considered part of an organic growth—part of the

18. Black, *Admiralty Jurisdiction: Critique and Suggestions*, 50 COLUM. L. REV. 259, 260 (1950).

evolutionary process of judiciary legislation that began September 24, 1789, and projects into the future.

Article III §2, cl. 1 (3d provision) of the Constitution and section 9 of the Act of September 24, 1789, have from the beginning been the sources of jurisdiction in litigation based upon federal maritime law. Article III impliedly contained three grants. (1) It empowered Congress to confer admiralty and maritime jurisdiction on the "tribunals inferior to the Supreme Court" which were authorized by Art. I. §8, cl. 9. (2) It empowered the federal courts in their exercise of the admiralty and maritime jurisdiction which had been conferred on them, to draw on the substantive law "inherent in the admiralty and maritime jurisdiction" [ ] and to continue the development of this law within constitutional limits. (3) It empowered Congress to revise and supplement the maritime law within the limits of the Constitution. [ ]

Section 9 of the First Judiciary Act granted the District Courts maritime jurisdiction. This jurisdiction has remained unchanged in substance to the present day. Indeed it was recognition of the need for federal tribunals to exercise admiralty jurisdiction that was one of the controlling considerations for the establishment of a system of lower federal courts.[8] Such a system is not an inherent requirement of a federal government. There was strong opposition in the Constitutional Convention to any such inferior federal tribunals. No comprehensive system of lower federal courts has been established in Canada or Australia. Congress could leave the enforcement of federal rights to state courts,[10] and indeed the state courts, in large measure, now exercise concurrent jurisdiction over a wide field of matters of federal concern, subject to review of federal issues by the Supreme Court.

Section 9 not only established federal courts for the administration of maritime law; it recognized that some remedies in matters maritime had been traditionally administered by common-law courts of the original States. This role of the States in the administration of maritime law was preserved in the famous "saving clause"—"saving to suitors, in all cases, the right of a common law remedy, where the common law is competent to give it." Since the original Judiciary Act also endowed the federal courts with diversity jurisdiction, common-law remedies for maritime causes could be enforced by the then Circuit Courts when the proper diversity of parties afforded access.

Up to the passage of the Judiciary Act of 1875 these jurisdictional bases provided the only claim for jurisdiction in the federal courts in maritime matters. The District Courts, endowed with "exclusive original cognizance of all civil causes of admiralty and maritime jurisdiction," sat to enforce the comprehensive federal interest in the law of the sea which had been a major reason for their creation. This jurisdiction was exercised according to the historic procedure in admiralty, by a judge without a jury. In addition, common-law remedies were, under the saving clause, enforcible in the courts of the States and on the

8. See 1 FARRAND, RECORDS OF THE FEDERAL CONVENTION (1911) 124; 2 *id.* at 46. * * * In THE FEDERALIST, No. 80 [Lodge ed. 1908, at 497–498], Hamilton wrote: "The most bigoted idolizers of State authority have not thus far shown a disposition to deny the national judiciary the cognizance of maritime causes. These so generally depend on the laws of nations, and so commonly affect the rights of foreigners, that they fall within the considerations which are relative to the public peace. The most important part of them are, by the present Confederation, submitted to federal jurisdiction."

10. Thus Rutledge argued against the establishment of inferior federal tribunals, saying "that the State Tribunals might and ought to be left in all cases to decide in the first instance, the right of appeal to the supreme national tribunal being sufficient to secure the national rights & uniformity of Judgmts." 1 FARRAND, RECORDS OF THE FEDERAL CONVENTION (1911) 124. [ ]

[law] side of the lower federal courts when the diverse citizenship of the parties permitted. Except in diversity cases, maritime litigation brought in state courts could not be removed to the federal courts.[16]

The Judiciary Act of 1875 effected an extensive enlargement of the jurisdiction of the lower federal courts. For the first time their doors were opened to "all suits of a civil nature at common law or in equity, * * * arising under the Constitution or laws of the United States, or treaties made, or which shall be made, under their authority * * *." From 1875 to 1950 there is not to be found a hint or suggestion to cast doubt on the conviction that the language of that statute was taken straight from Art. III § 2, cl. 1 [1st provision], extending the judicial power of the United States "to all cases, in law and equity, arising under this Constitution, the laws of the United States, and treaties made, or which shall be made, under their authority." Indeed what little legislative history there is affirmatively indicates that this was the source. Thus the Act of 1875 drew on the scope of this [1st] provision of clause 1, just as the Judiciary Act of 1789 reflected the constitutional authorization of [the 3d provision of clause 1], which extended the judicial power "to all cases of admiralty and maritime jurisdiction."

These provisions of Article III are two of the nine separately enumerated classes of cases to which "judicial power" was extended by the Constitution and which thereby authorized grants by Congress of "judicial power" to the "inferior" federal courts. The vast stream of litigation which has flowed through these courts from the beginning has done so on the assumption that, in dealing with a subject as technical as the jurisdiction of the courts, the Framers, predominantly lawyers, used precise, differentiating and not redundant language. * * *

This lucid principle of constitutional construction * * * was never brought into question until [two First Circuit cases in 1950 and 1952]. It had been treated as black-letter law in leading treatises. It was part of the realm of legal ideas in which the authors of the Act of 1875 moved. Certainly the accomplished lawyers who drafted the Act of 1875 drew on the language of the constitutional grant on the assumption that they were dealing with a distinct class of cases, that the language incorporated in their enactment precluded "identity" with any other class of cases contained in Article III. Thus the grant of jurisdiction over "suits of a civil nature at common law or in equity ... arising under the Constitution or laws of the United States" in the Act of 1875, as derived from Article III, could not reasonably be thought of as comprehending an entirely separate and distinct class of cases—"cases of admiralty and maritime jurisdiction."

* * *

Not only does language and construction point to the rejection of any infusion of general maritime jurisdiction into the Act of 1875, but history and reason powerfully support that rejection. The far-reaching extension of national power resulting from the victory of the North, and the concomitant utilization of federal courts for the vindication of that power in the Reconstruction Era, naturally led to enlarged jurisdiction of the federal courts over federal rights. But neither the aim of the Act of 1875 to provide a forum for the vindication of new federally created rights, nor the pressures which led to its enactment, suggest, even remotely, the inclusion of maritime claims within the scope

16. The removal provisions of the original Judiciary Act of 1789, 1 Stat. 79, conferred a limited removal jurisdiction, not including cases of admiralty and maritime jurisdiction. In none of the statutes enacted since that time have saving-clause cases been made removable.

of that statute. The provision of the Act of 1875 with which we are concerned was designed to give a new content of jurisdiction to the federal courts, not to reaffirm one long-established, smoothly functioning since 1789. We have uncovered no basis for finding the additional design of changing the method by which federal courts had administered admiralty law from the beginning. The federal admiralty courts had been completely adequate to the task of protecting maritime rights rooted in federal law. There is not the slightest indication of any intention, or of any professional or lay demands for a change in the time-sanctioned mode of trying suits in admiralty without a jury, from which it can be inferred that by the new grant of jurisdiction of cases "arising under the Constitution or laws" a drastic innovation was impliedly introduced in admiralty procedure, whereby Congress changed the method by which federal courts had administered admiralty law for almost a century. To draw such an inference is to find that a revolutionary procedural change had undesignedly come to pass.

* * *

Not only would the infusion of general maritime jurisdiction into the Act of 1875 disregard the obvious construction of that statute. Important difficulties of judicial policy would flow from such an interpretation, an interpretation which would have a disruptive effect on the traditional allocation of power over maritime affairs in our federal system.

Thus the historic option of a maritime suitor pursuing a common-law remedy to select his forum, state or federal, would be taken away by an expanded view of § 1331, since saving-clause actions would then be freely removable * * * The interpretation of the Act of 1875 contended for would have consequences more deeply felt than the elimination of a suitor's traditional choice of forum. By making maritime cases removable to the federal courts it would make considerable inroads into the traditionally exercised concurrent jurisdiction of the state courts in admiralty matters—a jurisdiction which it was the unquestioned aim of the saving clause of 1789 to preserve. * * * The role of the States in the development of maritime law is a role whose significance is rooted in the Judiciary Act of 1789 and the decisions of this Court. Recognition of the part the States have played from the beginning has a dual significance. It indicates the extent to which an expanded view of the Act of 1875 would eviscerate the postulates of the saving clause, and it undermines the theoretical basis for giving the Act of 1875 a brand new meaning.

Although the corpus of admiralty law is federal in the sense that it derives from the implications of Article III evolved by the courts, to claim that all enforced rights pertaining to matters maritime are rooted in federal law is a destructive oversimplification of the highly intricate interplay of the States and the National Government in their regulation of maritime commerce. It is true that state law must yield to the needs of a uniform federal maritime law when this Court finds inroads on a harmonious system. But this limitation still leaves the States a wide scope. * * * [I]f one thing is clear it is that the source of law in saving-clause actions cannot be described in absolute terms. Maritime law is not a monistic system. The State and Federal Governments jointly exert regulatory powers today as they have played joint roles in the development of maritime law throughout our history. This sharing of competence in one aspect of our federalism has been traditionally embodied in the saving clause of the Act of 1789. Here, as is so often true in our federal system, allocations of jurisdiction have been carefully wrought to correspond to the realities of power and interest and national policy. To give a novel sweep to the Act would disrupt traditional maritime policies and quite gratuitously disturb a complementary, historic interacting federal-state relationship.

* * *

Notes

1. The no-removal-into-admiralty rule is not immediately self-evident from the text of the removal statute. According to the leading federal courts treatise, "[t]here does not appear to be any statutory reason for denying a defendant ... the right to remove a state initiated maritime action brought under the savings clause. The language of [28 U.S.C. § 1441(a)] is applicable." 14A Wright, Miller & Cooper, Federal Practice and Procedure: Jurisdiction and Related Matters § 3674, at 630–31 (2013). But for six decades, courts and nearly all commentators have read *Romero* as precluding removal into admiralty. See, e.g., *id.* at 634 (describing the no-removal-into-admiralty rule as "preferable ... from a policy perspective, and ... most consistent with ... the law").

2. The Federal Courts Jurisdiction and Venue Clarification Act (JVCA), Pub. L. No. 112–63, 125 Stat. 758 (2011), which amended the removal statute, persuaded some district courts that saving-clause cases can now be removed on the basis of admiralty jurisdiction alone. In *Ryan v. Hercules Offshore, Inc.*, 945 F. Supp. 2d 772, 775–76 (S.D. Tex. 2013), the court acknowledged that Congress probably did not mean for the JVCA to eviscerate *Romero.* But it concluded that when Congress amended the statute to expressly limit the "forum defendant" rule in 28 U.S.C. § 1441(b)(2) to diversity cases, it eliminated the only barrier to removal into admiralty. For a critique of *Ryan*, see Sturley, *Removal into Admiralty: The Removal of State-Court Maritime Cases to Federal Court*, 46 J. Mar. L. & Com. 105, 116–19 (2015).

3. In the thirteen months immediately after *Ryan*, some district courts in Louisiana and Texas followed its reasoning. Every other court to address the issue—including all of the Louisiana and Texas district courts that have addressed the issue more recently—disagreed with *Ryan.* See, e.g., *Cassidy v. Murray*, 34 F. Supp. 3d 579, 584 (D. Md. 2014):

> [T]he removal of admiralty cases without an independent [i.e., nonadmiralty] jurisdictional basis permits the very occurrence the Supreme Court attempted to avoid in *Romero*—the evisceration of the saving[] clause. The purpose of the clause is to preserve the traditional role of the states in the administration of common-law remedies for maritime cases. Permitting defendants to remove these cases without an independent jurisdictional basis not only disrupts decades of maritime precedent but also renders the saving clause null and void.

Courts disagreeing with *Ryan* have handled the statutory construction issue in three different ways. *Cassidy* and a number of similarly reasoned cases have simply said that if Congress wants "to reject decades of well-established law" it must provide a clearer signal than the JVCA's. Several courts have suggested that Congress has indeed "expressly provided" against removal into admiralty in the saving clause itself. And at least one has said that the "original jurisdiction" referred to in § 1441(a) "evaporate[s] when [a maritime plaintiff] file[s] his action in state court." *Figueroa v. Marine Inspection Services*, LLC, 28 F. Supp. 3d 677, 680 (S.D. Tex. 2014); *cf. Paduano v. Yamashita Kisen Kabushiki Kaisha*, 221 F.2d 615, 620–21 (2d Cir. 1955) (Dimock, J., concurring).

13. Admiralty Appeals

Nineteenth century admiralty appeals were conceptualized as *de novo* proceedings in which the appellate courts could receive new evidence and owed no deference to the trial courts' findings of fact. But the authority to take new evidence on appeal was seldom used. And long before the 1966 unification, most of the courts of appeals had announced their intention to give trial court findings of fact the same deference in admiralty as in other classes of cases. (In Learned Hand's words, they had come to realize that "all modern procedural tendencies ... seek to center responsibility for the decision of the facts upon the trial [court]." *Petterson Lighterage & Towing Corp. v. New York Central R Co.*, 126 F.2d 992, 996 (2d Cir. 1942).) By 1954, the Supreme Court could announce that the assimilation was complete: "No greater scope of review is exercised by the appellate tribunals in admiralty cases than they exercise under Rule 52(a) of the Federal Rules of Civil Procedure." *McAllister v. United States*, 348 U.S. 19, 20 (1954).

The 1966 unification swept away any vestigial differences between the scope of appellate review in admiralty and other cases in federal court. On questions of law, review is *de novo*. A trial judge's findings of fact "must not be set aside unless clearly erroneous, and the reviewing court must give due regard to the trial court's opportunity to judge the witnesses' credibility." FRCP 52(a)(6). A jury's findings of fact should not be reversed on appeal unless there is no evidence in the record on which a reasonable juror could base the finding.

One special feature of admiralty appellate procedure has survived unification. Rule 9(h)(2) states that "[a] case that includes an admiralty or maritime claim within this subdivision (h) is an admiralty case within 28 U.S.C. § 1292(a)(3)." 28 U.S.C. § 1292(a)(3) provides in pertinent part that "the courts of appeals shall have jurisdiction of appeals from ... [i]nterlocutory decrees of [the] district courts or the judges thereof determining the rights and liabilities of the parties to admiralty cases in which appeals from final decrees are allowed." Nobody quite knows what § 1292(a)(3) means.[19] Its "original purpose ... was to allow appeals after a determination of liability and before a determination of damages in proceedings before a commissioner."[20] It has acquired a somewhat broader meaning, but there is dispute as to how much broader. Courts frequently announce a policy of strict construction of the provision, but there is no consistent application. For example, quite a broad view of § 1292(a)(3) was taken in *In re Patton-Tully Transportation Co.*, 715 F.2d 219, 222 (5th Cir. 1983), which allowed an appeal from an order increasing the amount of the fund setting a provisional ceiling on a shipowner's potential liability in a limitation of liability proceeding. At the other end of the spectrum, perhaps, is *Slatton v. Martin K. Eby Constr. Co.*, 491 F.2d 707, 709 (8th Cir. 1974), which invoked "the universal policy against piecemeal appeals" in refusing to hear an appeal from an order granting a new trial solely on the amount of damages. One recurring question has been whether § 1292(a)(3) permits an interlocutory appeal when a district court has permitted a defendant to limit its potential liability but has not yet decided whether the defendant is actually liable. *Compare, e.g., Wallis v. Princess Cruises, Inc.*, 306 F.3d 827, 830 (9th Cir. 2002) (permitting appeal), *with, e.g., SCF Waxler Marine, L.L.C. v. Aris T M/V*, 902 F.3d 461, 468 (5th Cir. 2018) (dismissing appeal).

Professor Wright states that, while "[t]he admiralty bar continues to find interlocutory appeals [under § 1292(a)(3)] useful, ... the *Slatton* case shows [that] the courts of appeals do not like them."[21] It may be that § 1292(a)(3) is no longer necessary, given the present applicability in all federal-court noncriminal cases (including admiralty) of the interlocutory appeal effects of FRCP 54(b) and 28 U.S.C. § 1292(b).

---

19. It is clear at least that § 1292(a)(3) applies only in admiralty cases. See, e.g., *Buccina v. Grimsby*, 889 F.3d 256 (6th Cir. 2018) (dismissing appeal under § 1292(a)(3) because maritime case had been filed in diversity).

20. 16 Wright, Miller & Cooper, Federal Practice and Procedure § 3927 (1996).

21. Wright, Law of Federal Courts 749 n.4 (5th ed. 1994).

H. Sources of Controlling Law in Admiralty and Maritime Cases

Preceding sections of this chapter have afforded frequent glimpses of a multifaceted issue to which we now turn directly: When a federal or state court decides an admiralty or maritime case, where does it find (or how does it construct) the governing law? Inquiry here sensibly begins with the Supremacy Clause, Article VI cl. 2, which provides:

> This Constitution, and the laws of the United States which shall be made in pursuance thereof; and all treaties made, or which shall be made, under the authority of the United States, shall be the supreme law of the land; and the judges in every state shall be bound thereby, any thing in the constitution or laws of any state to the contrary notwithstanding.

Plainly enough, a valid Act of Congress that speaks clearly to an issue in litigation must control. This is true regardless of whether the issue arises in federal or state court, regardless of whether the issue is characterized as substantive or procedural, and regardless of whether the federal statute is in competition with preexisting federal case law, a state statute, or state decisional law.

1. Separation of Powers: The Relationship Between Congress and the Supreme Court in the Admiralty and Maritime Field

The phrase "valid Act of Congress" in the preceding subsection glosses over some intermittently sensitive separation-of-powers wrangles. On at least two occasions, the Supreme Court has found federal maritime legislation to be unconstitutional under the Admiralty Clause, Article III § 2 cl. 3.[1] Moreover, while the Court has almost always ended up upholding the constitutionality of federal maritime statutes, some of the opinions have been grudging in tone, carrying the implication that Congress ought to be diffident when venturing into territory that the Court regards as primarily its own domain.[2] In the view of some admiralty experts, this pride-of-judicial-turf tone[3] gains plausibility from the fact that Article I of the Constitution includes no express grant of congressional authority to issue admiralty or maritime legislation. The accepted view today—traceable to *Butler v. Boston & S.S. Co.*, 130 U.S. 527 (1889), and *In re Garnett*, 141 U.S. 1 (1891)—is that Congress gets its admiralty and maritime authority from Article III § 2 cl. 3 by

1. *Washington v. W.C. Dawson & Co.*, 264 U.S. 219 (1924); *Knickerbocker Ice Co. v. Stewart*, 253 U.S. 149 (1920).

2. See *Detroit Trust Co. v. Barlum S.S. Co.*, 293 U.S. 21, 50–52 (1934); *Crowell v. Benson*, 285 U.S. 22, 53–63 (1932); *Genesee Chief v. Fitzhugh*, 53 U.S. 443, 451–52, 458–60 (1851).

3. See *McDermott, Inc. v. AmClyde*, 511 U.S. 202, 207 (1994) ("the Judiciary has traditionally taken the lead in formulating flexible and fair remedies in the law maritime"); *Northwest Airlines, Inc. v. Transport Workers Union*, 451 U.S. 77, 96 (1981) ("in admiralty, ... the federal judiciary's lawmaking power may well be at its strongest"); *Mitchell v. Trawler Racer, Inc.*, 362 U.S. 539, 550 (1960) ("No area of federal law is judge-made at its source to such an extent as is the law of admiralty.") (Frankfurter, J., dissenting); *Wilburn Boat Co. v. Fireman's Fund Ins. Co.*, 348 U.S. 310, 323 (1955) ("the preponderant body of maritime law comes from this Court and not from Congress") (Frankfurter, J., concurring).

way of the Necessary and Proper Clause.[4] Thus, it is possible to make the (formalistic?) argument that judicial admiralty authority stems directly and immediately from Article III whereas congressional admiralty authority is in some sense oblique or secondary.

The jurisprudence and secondary literature offer a broad range of views on the proper relationship between Congress and the courts in the admiralty and maritime field. At the extreme deference-to-legislature end of the range is Justice O'Connor's opinion for the Court in *Miles v. Apex Marine Corp.*, 498 U.S. 19, 32, 36 (1990) (*infra* at 241), expressly relegating the admiralty courts' authority to declare rules of substantive maritime law to a subservient "place in the constitutional scheme" and stating (somewhat inaccurately) that "[m]aritime tort law is now dominated by federal statute." At the extreme judicial-dominance end is Judge John R. Brown's criticism of *Miles:*

> [A]dmiralty judges have enunciated principles of maritime law that provide both certainty to commercial shipping and protection to those who risk life or property at sea. Moreover, the image of the great maritime judges and their opinions have been a beacon to judges in other areas of the law.... [But] the Supreme Court [in *Miles*] has ... abandoned its Constitutional duty of enunciating maritime law.... Apparently admiralty judges should now assume the role of followers rather than leaders. Have admiralty judges become flotsam on the sea of maritime law?
>
> * * *
>
> [Admiralty] is the only grant of [judicial] jurisdiction in the Constitution that identifies an area of substantive law. Federal authority over admiralty and maritime law is addressed only in the Judicial Article.... [T]he Constitution does not confer a similar grant of specific authority to Congress over admiralty and maritime law.
>
> The grant of judicial power to the federal courts in Article III of the Constitution also imposes the duty on admiralty judges to exercise that power. This duty requires that the admiralty judges declare the governing principles of maritime law.
>
> * * *
>
> Congressional efforts [in the maritime field] have been repeatedly scrutinized by the admiralty judges to insure harmony [with] the principles of maritime law incorporated in the United States Constitution.... When Congress legislates ... in [a maritime] area, the statute should not be read as varying or repealing the existing general maritime law. There must be something inconsistent or repugnant to the maritime law principle before the statute impugns a doctrine that is Constitutionally based. [T]he Court should endeavor to construe all Congressional enactments consistently with the governing principles of the general maritime law.

Brown, *Admiralty Judges: Flotsam on the Sea of Maritime Law?*, 24 J. MAR. L. & COM. 249, 251, 254, 264, 271 (1993) (citations omitted).

On the broad issue of the proper relationship between Congress' and the Supreme Court's authority in the admiralty and maritime field, over the decades the Court has swung back and forth like a pendulum between assertions of judicial dominance and

4. Article I § 8 cl. 18: "The Congress shall have power ... to make all laws which shall be necessary and proper for carrying into execution the foregoing powers, and all other powers vested by this Constitution in the government of the United States, or in any department or officer thereof."

comparatively meek acquiescence in congressional primacy.[5] The Court's most recent articulation finds a pragmatic middle ground: "[Federal maritime law] falls within a federal court's jurisdiction to decide in the manner of a common law court, subject to the authority of Congress to legislate otherwise if it disagrees with the judicial result." *Exxon Shipping Co. v. Baker*, 554 U.S. 471, 489–90 (2008).

2. An Important Note on Terminology

In discussing the separation-of-powers issue treated just above and the federalism issue treated in the subsection below, courts and scholars have often made no distinction between the terms *displacement* and *preemption*, using them interchangeably. Recently, however, an extremely useful distinction has begun emerging and put into practice.[6] In the separation-of-powers context—i.e., when talking about when an Act of Congress will trump federal maritime common law—the proper term is *displacement*. So, for example, *Miles* is best described as treating the Jones Act's *displacement* (not preemption) of federal common law. In the federalism context—i.e., when talking about when federal maritime law will trump state law—the proper term is *preemption*. So, for example, *Romero. supra* at 79–80, 102–05, discusses the *preemption* (not displacement) of state law.

3. Federalism: When Will Federal Maritime Law Preempt State Substantive Law?

At some risk of oversimplification, we will begin by setting procedural issues aside with this generalization: On matters that are purely procedural, the state courts can be expected to (and properly do) follow state law, while the federal courts follow the FRCP.[7]

A general answer to the question asked in the subtitle is difficult to come by. That is because the question is genuinely difficult.[8] Some of the difficulties are doctrinal, conceptual, and historical in nature. See e.g. the discussion in *Romero*, *supra* at 102–05. Some—see generally *supra* Section I-A—are political. In a usefully realistic sense, there will always be a political dimension to a federal court's ruling that the federal admiralty power triumphs over state legislative or judicial authority. To borrow the phrasing in Judge Brown's *Flotsam* essay, *supra* at 109, our hundreds of federal judges are all "admiralty judges" who at least potentially regard themselves as duty-bound to declare and apply preemptive rules of federal maritime law as needed. These men and women have vast power and life tenure. Moreover, their compensation is not subject to diminution. In the

---

5. See Robertson, *Our High Court of Admiralty and Its Sometimes Peculiar Relationship With Congress*, 55 St. Louis U.L.J. 491 (2011).

6. See e.g. Galligan & Bush, *Displacement and Preemption*, 42 Cum. L. Rev. 1 (2012).

7. Distinguishing between the substantive and procedural nature of legal questions can be difficult at the margins, but we can all recognize core examples of each category. Whether recovery in negligence actions is barred by the victim's fault is indisputably a substantive issue. Statutes of limitation are also substantive. How and when a defense to personal jurisdiction may be waived is indisputably a procedural issue.

8. See generally D. Currie, *Federalism and the Admiralty: "The Devil's Own Mess"*, 1960 Sup. Ct. Rev. 158; Robertson, *Displacement of State Law by Federal Maritime Law*, 26 J. Mar. L. & Com. 325 (1995); Robertson, *The Applicability of State Law in Maritime Cases After* Yamaha Motor Corp. v. Calhoun, 21 Tul. Mar. L.J. 507 (1996).

quiet words of Professor Wright, they are "puissant figure[s]."[9] In the curmudgeonly parlance of Professor J.W. Moore, "if a federal judge is not courageous he was born a coward."[10]

Ballard Shipping Co. v. Beach Shellfish

United States Court of Appeals, First Circuit, 1994
32 F.3d 623, 1994 AMC 2705

BOUDIN, Circuit Judge:

This appeal presents the question whether federal maritime law preempts Rhode Island legislation affording expanded state-law remedies for oil pollution damage. In an able opinion, the district court held that the remedies were preempted. Discerning the law in this area is far from easy; one might tack a sailboat into a fog bank with more confidence. Yet guided in part by an important Supreme Court decision rendered after the district court's decision, we are constrained to reverse in part and to remand for further proceedings.

The basic facts of the case are not in dispute. On June 23, 1989, the *M/V World Prodigy*, an oil tanker owned by Ballard Shipping Co., ran aground in Narragansett Bay, Rhode Island, spilling over 300,000 gallons of heating oil into the bay. * * * The oil slick prompted the State of Rhode Island to close Narragansett Bay to all shellfishing activities for a period of two weeks during and after cleanup operations.

State authorities charged the captain of the ship with entering the bay without a local pilot on board in violation of state law. Both the captain and Ballard also pleaded guilty to criminal violations of the Federal Water Pollution Control Act, see 33 U.S.C. § 1319(c). The captain and owner were fined a total of $30,500 and $500,000, respectively. In addition, Ballard agreed to pay $3.9 million in compensation for federal cleanup costs, $4.7 million for state cleanup costs and damage to natural resources, $500,000 of which was to be available to compensate individuals, and $550,000 to settle claims for lost wages by local shellfishermen.[11]

* * *

[Ballard Shipping filed a petition in the district court invoking admiralty jurisdiction pursuant to 28 U.S.C. § 1333 and seeking the protection of the Limitation of Liability Act, 46 U.S.C. §§ 30501–12]. The claimants in the present appeal are a group of shellfish dealers who [seek recovery from Ballard for] severe economic losses arising from the two-week hiatus in shellfishing activities, which suspended their operations during the busiest time of the shellfishing season. They allege[] negligence under the general maritime law and the common law of Rhode Island, as well as a claim for economic losses pursuant to the Rhode Island Environmental Injury Compensation Act [ ].

* * * Ballard moved to dismiss the shellfish dealers' claims on the basis of the Supreme Court's decision in *Robins Dry Dock & Repair Co. v. Flint*, 275 U.S. 303 (1927), which held that compensation for economic losses standing alone is unavailable in admiralty cases. The district court granted the motion, holding that *Robins* preempted the contrary provisions

9. Wright, Law of Federal Courts 693 (5th ed. 1994).

10. Moore, *Conflict of Jurisdiction*, 23 La. L. Rev. 29, 33 (1962).

11. Editors' note: Presumably Ballard settled with the shellfishermen under the pressure of a widely accepted rule that commercial fishermen are "favorites of admiralty" who enjoy an exception from the *Robins Dry Dock* rule. See *Union Oil Co. v. Oppen*, 501 F.2d 558 (9th Cir. 1974).

of the state's Compensation Act, which expressly provides for recovery of purely economic losses arising from an oil spill [ ]. The dealers now appeal from that dismissal.

We first address the federal claims brought under the general maritime law. The Constitution grants the federal courts authority to hear "all cases of admiralty and maritime jurisdiction." [ ] The parties agree that the dealers' * * * claims fall within this group because the spill occurred on navigable waters and arose out of traditional maritime activity. [ ] Admiralty jurisdiction brings with it a body of federal jurisprudence, largely uncodified, known as maritime law. [ ]

The dealers assert that their businesses were injured when the *World Prodigy* spill prevented local fishermen from harvesting shellfish in Narragansett Bay and thereby precluded the dealers from purchasing the shellfish and reselling them to restaurants and other buyers. The dealers' maritime-law claims are thus purely for economic losses, unaccompanied by any physical injury to their property or person. Those federal claims, as the district court held, are squarely foreclosed by *Robins Dry Dock.* * * * [This] appeal thus turns upon the extent to which *Robins* bars the states from permitting a different result under *state* law pursuant to the exercise of the state's police powers.

[Under 28 U.S.C. § 1333 and its saving-to-suitors clause, most cases falling within the admiralty jurisdiction can be brought in federal or state court, at the plaintiff's option. Regardless of whether the case is in] a federal court or a state forum, "the extent to which state law may be used to remedy maritime injuries is constrained by a so-called 'reverse-*Erie*' doctrine which requires that the substantive remedies afforded by the states conform to governing federal maritime standards." *Offshore Logistics, Inc. v. Tallentire*, 477 U.S. 207, 223 (1986). How far this conformity requirement extends, and whether it preempts the dealers' state-law claims, are the central issues in this case.

On appeal, the dealers mainly stress their claims under Rhode Island's Compensation Act. The Compensation Act provides generally that owners or operators of seagoing vessels may be held liable for harms arising from negligence of the owner, operator or agents or from the violation of Rhode Island pilotage and water pollution laws.] * * * For the purposes of this appeal only, Ballard concedes that the dealers would have a valid cause of action under this statute * * *. We think that the statutory claims effectively subsume state common law claims since the Compensation Act appears to go as far and further than common law in departing from *Robins.* Thus, we focus upon the statute.

[Ballard insists], and the district court agreed, that the state claims are preempted under the doctrine of *Southern Pacific Co. v. Jensen*, 244 U.S. 205 (1917) [*infra* at 116]. *Jensen*, in a now famous passage, held that state legislation affecting maritime commerce is invalid "if it contravenes the essential purpose expressed by an act of Congress, or works material prejudice to the characteristic features of the general maritime law, or interferes with the proper harmony and uniformity of that law in its international and interstate relations." [ ]

Jensen, however, was by its own terms something less than a rule of automatic and mechanical preemption. "It would be difficult, if not impossible," said the Court, "to define with exactness just how far the general maritime law may be changed, modified, or affected by state legislation. That this may be done to some extent cannot be denied." [ ] What is even more telling is that the Supreme Court after *Jensen*, without ever repudiating its language, upheld the application of state law in a number of maritime-related cases despite the existence of a direct conflict between maritime rules and state law. * * * A familiar example is *Just v. Chambers*, 312 U.S. 383 (1941), where the Court permitted a state law claim for personal injury occurring on board a ship against the estate of the vessel's owner, despite a contrary maritime rule that a shipowner's liability [did] not survive his death. This year, in *American Dredging Co. v. Miller*, 510 U.S. 443 (1994), the Court upheld a Louisiana open-forum statute, making the forum non conveniens doctrine unavailable in [saving] clause cases, even though forum non conveniens is a part of federal maritime law.

American Dredging assertedly reaffirms *Jensen*'s three-prong test for preemption quoted above. Since no act of Congress directly governs our case, the first prong (contravention) is irrelevant to our case. The third prong ("proper harmony and uniformity") we reserve for consideration below. What is of immediate concern is the second ("material prejudice") prong; and here, *American Dredging* gave the famous language a twist that could not easily have been anticipated by the litigants in this case or by the district court.

Judged by the bare language of *Jensen*, the Compensation Act might easily seem to do "material prejudice" to a "characteristic feature" of maritime law, since *Robins* is the governing maritime rule and the Compensation Act rejects *Robins* in everything but name. But the word "characteristic" has different shadings, and *American Dredging*, in its first and most important holding, gives the "characteristic feature" language a definitive meaning: it reads the phrase to apply—and apparently only to apply—to a federal rule that either "originated in admiralty" or "has exclusive application there."

* * *

* * * [W]e have found no evidence that *Robins*' denial of recovery for purely economic losses originated in admiralty. * * * Nor has the doctrine forbidding recovery of such losses had "exclusive" application in admiralty. * * * Thus, we hold that Rhode Island's decision to depart from *Robins* does not materially prejudice a rule that originated in or is exclusive to general maritime law.

Even absent prejudice to a characteristic feature of admiralty, state legislation is preempted if (under *Jensen*'s third test) it "interferes with the proper harmony and uniformity" of maritime law. [ ] As Justice Scalia observed in considering this question [in *American Dredging*], "[i]t would be idle to pretend that the line separating permissible from impermissible state regulation is readily discernible in our admiralty jurisprudence, or indeed is even entirely consistent within our admiralty jurisprudence." [ ] He did not, however, articulate a definitive test of harmony and uniformity, holding only that there is no preemption where the relevant state law is procedural rather than substantive. [ ] In our case, the Rhode Island statute is indisputably substantive.

Where substantive law is involved, we think that the Supreme Court's past decisions yield no single, comprehensive test as to where harmony is required and when uniformity must be maintained. Rather, the decisions however couched reflect a balancing of the state and federal interests in any given case. * * * In balancing the state interest in regulation against a potential overriding federal need for harmony or uniformity, we start with Rhode Island's interest in implementing its Compensation Act. No one can doubt that the state's interest in avoiding pollution in its navigable waters and on its shores, and in redressing injury to its citizens from such pollution, is a weighty one.

* * *

The federal interest in limiting remedies is more subtle but also not without importance. The Compensation Act does not regulate the out-of-court behavior of ships or sailors—what is sometimes called "primary conduct;" rather the act is concerned with the liability imposed for conduct that is already unlawful. State regulation of primary conduct in the maritime realm is not automatically forbidden [ ], but such regulation presents the most direct risk of conflict between federal and state commands, or of inconsistency between various state regimes to which the same vessel may be subject.[4]

Instead, the question here is the familiar one of burden. At some point, a regime of liability, or a diversity of regimes, could impose or threaten such heavy costs that maritime commerce may itself be impaired. Initially such costs are borne by shipowners but in the end they affect every business that uses ships or receives raw materials by ship and every citizen who, as a worker or consumer, depends upon such commerce. A regime may also be so difficult to administer as to prevent the efficient and predictable resolution of maritime disputes. These are not trivial or irrelevant concerns, for "the fundamental interest giving rise to maritime jurisdiction is the protection of maritime commerce." *Exxon Corp. v. Central Gulf Lines*, 500 U.S. 603, 606–08 (1991) [*supra* at 58 note 1].

Indeed, these very concerns—with the burden of liability and of administration—underpin the *Robins* rule itself * * *. But it is one thing to say that a federal court, largely responsible for shaping the common law of admiralty, should follow a longstanding liability rule to govern a federal cause of action. It is quite another to say that a state remedy, presumptively preserved under the [saving to suitors] clause, is potentially so disruptive as to be unconstitutional. Where as here the state remedy is aimed at a matter of great and legitimate state concern, a court must act with caution.

The question, then, is whether absent the *Robins* rule there remain limitations on the scope of recovery under the Compensation Act adequate to limit the burden it imposes on maritime commerce. The Compensation Act has yet to be construed by the Rhode Island courts. We nevertheless assume that its extension of liability to cover all "loss of income or diminution of profit … *as a result of* damage to the natural resources of the state of Rhode Island *caused* by the violation of [Rhode Island pilotage or pollution laws]" incorporates the familiar tort limitations of foreseeability and proximate cause. These principles do in some measure limit the burden imposed on maritime shipping.

Foreseeability may extend some distance [ ], and "remoteness" is scarcely a sharply defined concept. [ ] We cannot be sure how Rhode Island courts will develop these concepts in the context of oil pollution cases. Depending on Rhode Island's solutions, the burdens imposed by the Compensation Act, financial and administrative, may be substantial but they may also be tolerable. One might say that the case for preemption at this stage is subject to the Scotch verdict—not proven.

Having said all this, we think one final consideration tips the scales in favor of the Compensation Act's validity. Congress has recently enacted the Oil Pollution Act [of 1990], 33 U.S.C. § 2701 et seq., which * * * provides for recovery of purely economic damages in oil spill cases. * * * The act also expressly provides that it does not preempt state imposition of additional liability requirements. 33 U.S.C. § 2718(a).

* * *

The new federal statute does not apply retroactively to govern the present case [ ]. But we think that the statute is compelling evidence that Congress does not view either

4. *O'Melveny & Myers v. Federal Deposit Ins. Corp.*, 512 U.S. 79, 88 (1994) (suggesting that uniformity is most important where the rule at issue is one governing primary conduct); *American Dredging*, 510 U.S. at 454 (noting that "forum non conveniens does not bear upon the substantive right to recover, and is not a rule upon which maritime actors rely in making decisions about primary conduct").

expansion of liability to cover purely economic losses or enactment of comparable state oil pollution regimes as an excessive burden on maritime commerce. Given the Congress' superior ability to weigh the very practical considerations relating to such a judgment, we give Congress' conclusion substantial weight. For this purpose, the non-retroactivity of the statute is irrelevant.

We hold, then, that Rhode Island's Compensation Act as reasonably construed and applied is not preempted by the admiralty clause of the Constitution. We express no judgment on whether claimants' particular injuries were reasonably foreseeable or proximately caused by the grounding of the *M/V World Prodigy*, or whether claimants' claims are otherwise viable under the Rhode Island statute. That determination is for the district court in the first instance or for the state courts. *Robins Dry Dock* remains the rule in this circuit for federal [maritime] claims; we simply hold that Rhode Island is free to chart a different course.

Because of the Oil Pollution Act, it may well be that the immediate problem with which we have wrestled at length in this case is a transient one; the legal regime for oil pollution accidents after August 18, 1990, will largely be a creature of the new statute. But the case before us, like all cases, is important to the litigants, and the governing legal standards have application elsewhere. Applying an imprecise federal preemption standard to a little construed state statute is no easy task. For the present, assuming that the Rhode Island statute is providently construed and applied, we think that it is not unconstitutional.

The decision of the district court dismissing plaintiffs' federal claims is affirmed; the dismissal of plaintiffs' state claims is reversed and the case is remanded for further proceedings consistent with this opinion.

Notes

1. The term "reverse-*Erie*" refers to *Erie R. Co. v. Tompkins*, *infra* at 119. The *Ballard* court used the phrase "reverse-*Erie* doctrine" (*supra* at 112) to refer broadly to the obligation of all courts to apply federal substantive maritime law in cases of admiralty jurisdiction. Properly speaking, the term "reverse-*Erie*" has a narrower meaning, referring to the obligation of state courts in saving clause cases to apply the same substantive law that a federal admiralty court would apply. What the *Ballard* court meant to say was "*Jensen* doctrine."

2. The *Ballard* opinion does not explicitly say so, but it reflects a prevailing assumption that the *Jensen* doctrine finds its basis in the Supremacy Clause. The Supreme Court has so stated only once. See *Kossick v. United Fruit Co.*, *infra* at 124. But the courts of appeals seem routinely to assume that federal maritime statutes (obviously) and judge-made federal maritime law (less obviously) constitute "laws of the United States" within the meaning of the Supremacy Clause. See *Wahlstrom v. Kawasaki Heavy Industries*, 4 F.3d 1084, 1087 (2d Cir. 1993); *Purnell v. Norned Shipping*, 804 F.2d 248, 249–50 (3d Cir. 1986); *Linton v. Great Lakes Dredge & Dock Co.*, 964 F.2d 1480, 1487 (5th Cir. 1992).

3. In their efforts to comply with the reverse-*Erie* doctrine, state courts look to the decisions of the lower federal courts for guidance. But it is important to note that they are not bound by them. See, e.g., *Penrod Drilling Corp. v. Williams*, 868 S.W.2d 294, 296 (Tex. 1993): "While Texas courts may certainly draw upon the precedents of the Fifth Circuit, or any other federal or state court, in determining the appropriate federal [maritime] rule of decision, they are obligated to follow only higher Texas courts and the

United States Supreme Court." Cf. *Lockhart v. Fretwell*, 506 U.S. 364, 376 (1993) (Thomas, J., concurring) ("[N]either federal supremacy nor any other principle of federal law requires that a state court's interpretation of federal law give way to a federal court's interpretation. In our federal system, a state trial court's interpretation of federal law is no less authoritative than that of the federal court of appeals in whose circuit the trial court is located."); Hart, *The Relations Between State and Federal Law*, 54 Colum. L. Rev. 489, 510 (1954) ("The suggestion seems never to have been seriously made that the courts of the states are formally bound by the decisions of federal district courts or even of federal courts of appeal on questions of federal law.").

4. In *United States v. Locke*, 529 U.S. 89 (2000) (popularly known as the *Intertanko* case), the unanimous Court struck down statutes regulating oil tanker operations that were enacted by the state of Washington in response to the 1989 incident in which the supertanker *Exxon Valdez* ran aground in Prince William Sound, Alaska, and spilled eleven million gallons of crude oil. The basis for the *Intertanko* holding that federal law preempted these statutes was the Oil Pollution Act of 1990 (OPA), 33 U.S.C. § 2701 et seq. The Court indicated that OPA leaves room for "state laws which, rather than imposing substantive regulation of a vessel's primary conduct, establish liability rules and financial requirements relating to oil spills" (529 U.S. at 105) but that—subject to very narrow exceptions—"only the Federal Government may regulate the 'design, construction, alteration, repair, maintenance, operation, equipping, personnel qualification, and manning' of tanker vessels" (*id.* at 111).

Southern Pacific Co. v. Jensen

Supreme Court of the United States, 1917
244 U.S. 205, 37 S. Ct. 524, 61 L. Ed. 1086, 1996 AMC 2076

Mr. Justice McREYNOLDS delivered the opinion of the Court.

[Christen Jensen, an employee of the Southern Pacific Company, was killed on August 15, 1914, while engaged in unloading one of the company's steamships. The fatal injury occurred when Jensen tried to back a small electric freight truck into the hatchway of the vessel. He struck his head on the top of the hatchway and suffered a broken neck. Jensen's widow and two small children sought workers' compensation benefits under New York law. The New York Workmen's Compensation Commission determined that Jensen's average weekly wage was $19.60 and awarded Mrs. Jensen $5.87 a week during her widowhood and each child $1.96 a week until reaching the age of eighteen. Southern Pacific appealed the award, contending that the New York workmen's compensation statute is unconstitutional. The state courts rejected Southern Pacific's constitutional arguments and affirmed the award.]

[Six weeks ago, we handed down our decision in *New York C. R. Co. v. White*, 243 U.S. 188 (1917), holding that the New York workmen's compensation statute does not violate the 14th Amendment guaranties of due process and equal protection. Southern Pacific's remaining argument here is that, as applied to injuries incurred on the navigable waters of the United States, the statute is unconstitutional under the Admiralty Clause, Article III § 2 cl. 3.]

Article III § 2 of the Constitution extends the judicial power of the United States "to all cases of admiralty and maritime jurisdiction;" and article I § 8 confers upon the Congress power "to make all laws which shall be necessary and proper for carrying into execution the foregoing powers and all other powers vested by this Constitution in the government of the United States or in any department or officer thereof." Considering our former opinions, it must now be accepted as settled doctrine that, in consequence of these provisions, Congress has paramount power to fix and determine the maritime law which shall prevail throughout the country. [ ] And further, that, in the absence of some controlling statute, the general maritime law, as accepted by the federal courts, constitutes part of our national law, applicable to matters within the admiralty and maritime jurisdiction. [ ]

* * *

By § 9, Judiciary Act of 1789 [ ], the district courts of the United States were given "exclusive original cognizance of all civil causes of admiralty and maritime jurisdiction, ... saving to suitors, in all cases, the right of a common-law remedy, where the common law is competent to give it." * * *

In view of these constitutional provisions and the [Judiciary Act] it would be difficult, if not impossible, to define with exactness just how far the general maritime law may be changed, modified, or affected by state legislation. That this may be done to some extent cannot be denied. A lien upon a vessel for repairs in her own port may be given by state statute [ ]; pilotage fees fixed [ ], and the right given to recover in death cases [ ]. Equally well established is the rule that state statutes may not contravene an applicable act of Congress or affect the general maritime law beyond certain limits. They cannot authorize proceedings in rem according to the course in admiralty [ ]; nor create liens for materials used in repairing a foreign ship [ ]. And plainly, we think, no such legislation is valid if it contravenes the essential purpose expressed by an act of Congress, or works material prejudice to the characteristic features of the general maritime law, or interferes with the proper harmony and uniformity of that law in its international and interstate relations. This limitation, at the least, is essential to the effective operation of the fundamental purposes for which such law was incorporated into our national laws by the Constitution itself. * * *

A similar rule in respect to interstate commerce, deduced from the grant to Congress of power to regulate it, is now firmly established. "Where the subject is national in its character, and admits and requires uniformity of regulation, affecting alike all the states, such as transportation between the states, including the importation of goods from one state to another, Congress can alone act upon it and provide the needed regulations. The absence of any law of Congress on the subject is equivalent to its declaration that commerce in that matter shall be free." [ ] And the same character of reasoning which supports this rule, we think, makes imperative the stated limitation upon the power of the states to interpose where maritime matters are involved.

The work of a stevedore, in which the deceased was engaging, is maritime in its nature; his employment was a maritime contract; the injuries which he received were likewise maritime; and the rights and liabilities of the parties in connection therewith were matters clearly within the admiralty jurisdiction. [ ]

If New York can subject foreign ships coming into her ports to such obligations as those imposed by her Compensation Statute, other states may do likewise. The necessary consequence would be destruction of the very uniformity in respect to maritime matters which the Constitution was designed to establish; and freedom of navigation between the states and with foreign countries would be seriously hampered and impeded. * * * The legislature exceeded its authority in attempting to extend the statute under consideration to conditions like those here disclosed. So applied, it conflicts with the Constitution and to that extent is invalid.

Exclusive jurisdiction of all civil cases of admiralty and maritime jurisdiction is vested in the Federal district courts, "saving to suitors in all cases the right of a common-law remedy where the common law is competent to give it." The remedy which the Compensation Statute attempts to give is of a character wholly unknown to the common law, incapable of enforcement by the ordinary processes of any court, and is not saved to suitors from the grant of exclusive jurisdiction. * * *

* * *

Mr. Justice HOLMES, dissenting.

* * *

No doubt there sometimes has been an air of benevolent gratuity in the admiralty's attitude about enforcing state laws. But of course there is no gratuity about it. Courts cannot give or withhold at pleasure. If the claim is enforced or recognized it is because the claim is a right, and if a claim depending upon a state statute is enforced, it is because the state had constitutional power to pass the law. Taking it as established that a state has constitutional power to pass laws giving rights and imposing liabilities for acts done upon the * * * seas when there were no such rights or liabilities before, what is there to hinder its doing so in the case of a maritime tort? Not the existence of an inconsistent law emanating from a superior source, that is, from the United States. There is no such law. The maritime law is not a corpus juris—it is a very limited body of customs and ordinances of the sea. * * *

* * * I recognize without hesitation that judges do and must legislate, but they can do so only interstitially; they are confined from molar to molecular motions. A common-law judge could not say, "I think the doctrine of consideration a bit of historical nonsense and shall not enforce it in my court." No more could a judge, exercising the limited jurisdiction of admiralty, say, "I think well of the common-law rules of master and servant, and propose to introduce them here en bloc." Certainly he could not in that way enlarge the exclusive jurisdiction of the district courts and cut down the power of the states. If admiralty adopts common-law rules without an act of Congress, it cannot extend the maritime law as understood by the Constitution. It must take the rights of the parties from a different authority, just as it does when it enforces a lien created by a state. The only authority available is the common law or statutes of a state. * * *

The common law is not a brooding omnipresence in the sky, but the articulate voice of some sovereign or quasi sovereign that can be identified * * *.

* * * [I]t is too late to say that the mere silence of Congress excludes the statute or common law of a state from supplementing the wholly inadequate maritime law of the time of the Constitution, in the regulation of personal rights, and I venture to say that it never has been supposed to do so, or had any such effect.

* * *

[Justice Pitney "concurr[ed] substantially" in the Holmes dissent and also wrote a lengthy one of his own. Justices Brandeis and Clarke concurred in both dissenting opinions.]

Note

One major implication of *Jensen* was made explicit the following year in *Chelentis v. Luckenbach S.S. Co.*, 247 U.S. 372, 384 (1918) [*infra* at 151], which held that a federal court exercising its diversity jurisdiction in a seaman's-injury case removed to it from state court could not apply state law but had to follow general maritime law. Justice McReynolds's opinion for the Court stated:

> [U]nder the saving clause a right sanctioned by the maritime law may be enforced through any appropriate remedy recognized at common law; but we find nothing therein which reveals an intention to give the complaining party an election to determine whether the defendant's liability shall be measured by common-law standards rather than those of the maritime law.

Erie Railroad Co. v. Tompkins

Supreme Court of the United States, 1938
304 U.S. 64, 58 S. Ct. 817, 82 L. Ed. 1188

Mr. Justice BRANDEIS delivered the opinion of the Court.

The question for decision is whether the oft-cited doctrine of *Swift v. Tyson*, 41 U.S. 1 (1842), shall now be disapproved.

Tompkins, a citizen of Pennsylvania, was injured on a dark night by a passing freight train of the Erie Railroad Company while walking along its right of way at Hughestown in that state. He claimed that the accident occurred through negligence in the operation, or maintenance, of the train; that he was rightfully on the premises as licensee because on a commonly used beaten footpath which ran for a short distance alongside the tracks; and that he was struck by something which looked like a door projecting from one of the moving cars. To enforce that claim he brought an action in the federal court for Southern New York, which had jurisdiction because the company is a corporation of that state. It denied liability; and the case was tried by a jury.

The Erie insisted that its duty to Tompkins was no greater than that owed to a trespasser. It contended, among other things, that its duty to Tompkins, and hence its liability, should be determined in accordance with the Pennsylvania law; that under the law of Pennsylvania, as declared by its highest court, persons who use pathways along the railroad right of way—that is, a longitudinal pathway as distinguished from a crossing—are to be deemed trespassers; and that the railroad is not liable for injuries to undiscovered trespassers resulting from its negligence, unless it be wanton or willful. Tompkins denied that any such rule had been established by the decisions of the Pennsylvania courts; and contended that, since there was no statute of the state on the subject, the railroad's duty and liability is to be determined in federal courts as a matter of general law.

The trial judge refused to rule that the applicable law precluded recovery. The jury brought in a verdict of $30,000; and the judgment entered thereon was affirmed by the Circuit Court of Appeals, which held that it was unnecessary to consider whether the law of Pennsylvania was as contended, because the question was one not of local, but of general, law, and that [under the rule of *Swift v. Tyson*] "upon questions of general law the federal courts are free, in absence of a local statute, to exercise their independent judgment as to what the law is; and it is well settled that the question of the responsibility of a railroad for injuries caused by its servants is one of general law. * * * Where the public has made open and notorious use of a railroad right of way for a long period of time and without objection, the company owes to persons on such permissive pathway a duty of care in the operation of its trains. * * *."

The Erie [contends] that application of the Pennsylvania rule was required * * * by section 34 of the Federal Judiciary Act of September 24, 1789, which provides: "The laws of the several States, except where the Constitution, treaties, or statutes of the United States otherwise require or provide, shall be regarded as rules of decision in trials at common law, in the courts of the United States, in cases where they apply."

Because of the importance of the question whether the federal court was free to disregard the alleged rule of the Pennsylvania common law, we granted certiorari.

First. *Swift v. Tyson* held that federal courts exercising jurisdiction on the ground of diversity of citizenship need not, in matters of general jurisprudence, apply the unwritten law of the state as declared by its highest court; that they are free to exercise an independent judgment as to what the common law of the state is—or should be; and that, as there stated by Mr. Justice Story:

> [T]he true interpretation of the 34th section limited its application to state laws, strictly local, that is to say, to the positive statutes of the state, and the construction thereof adopted by the local tribunals, and to rights and titles to things having a permanent locality, such as the rights and titles to real estate, and other matters immovable and intra-territorial in their nature and character. It never has been supposed by us, that the section did apply, or was designed to apply, to questions of a more general nature, not at all dependent upon local statutes or local usages of a fixed and permanent operation, as, for example, to the construction of ordinary contracts or other written instruments, and especially to questions of general commercial law, where the state tribunals are called upon to perform the like functions as ourselves, that is, to ascertain, upon general reasoning and legal analogies, what is the true exposition of the contract or instrument, or what is the just rule furnished by the principles of commercial law to govern the case.

* * * [Under *Swift v. Tyson*, the] federal courts assumed, in the broad field of "general law," the power to declare rules of decision which Congress was confessedly without power to enact as statutes. Doubt was repeatedly expressed as to the correctness of the construction given section 34 [by *Swift*], and as to the soundness of the rule which [*Swift*] introduced. But it was the * * * research of a competent scholar, who examined the original document, which established that the construction given to [section 34] by the [*Swift*] Court was erroneous; and that the purpose of the section was merely to make certain that, in all matters except those in which some federal law is controlling, the federal courts exercising jurisdiction in diversity of citizenship cases would apply as their rules of decision the law of the state, unwritten as well as written.[5]

* * *

Second. Experience in applying the doctrine of *Swift v. Tyson*, [has] revealed its defects, political and social; and the benefits expected to flow from the rule did not accrue. Persistence of state courts in their own opinions on questions of common law [has] prevented uniformity; and the impossibility of discovering a satisfactory line of demarcation between the province of general law and that of local law [has] developed a new well of uncertainties.

* * *

The injustice and confusion incident to the doctrine of *Swift v. Tyson* have been repeatedly urged as reasons for abolishing or limiting diversity of citizenship jurisdiction. Other legislative relief has been proposed. If only a question of statutory construction were involved, we should not be prepared to abandon a doctrine so widely applied throughout nearly a century. But the unconstitutionality of the course pursued has now been made clear, and compels us to do so.

---

5. Charles Warren, *New Light on the History of the Federal Judiciary Act of 1789*, 37 Harv. L. Rev. 49, 51–52, 81–88, 108 (1923).

Third. Except in matters governed by the Federal Constitution or by acts of Congress, the law to be applied in any case is the law of the state. And whether the law of the state shall be declared by its legislature in a statute or by its highest court in a decision is not a matter of federal concern. There is no federal general common law. Congress has no power to declare substantive rules of common law applicable in a state whether they be local in their nature or "general," be they commercial law or a part of the law of torts. And no clause in the Constitution purports to confer such a power upon the federal courts. * * *

The fallacy underlying the rule declared in *Swift v. Tyson* is made clear by Mr. Justice Holmes [in his dissenting opinions in cases applying the *Swift* rule]. The doctrine rests upon the assumption that there is "a transcendental body of law outside of any particular State but obligatory within it unless and until changed by statute," that federal courts have the power to use their judgment as to what the rules of common law are; and that in the federal courts "the parties are entitled to an independent judgment on matters of general law."

"But law in the sense in which courts speak of it today does not exist without some definite authority behind it. The common law so far as it is enforced in a State, whether called common law or not, is not the common law generally but the law of that State existing by the authority of that State without regard to what it may have been in England or anywhere else. * * * The authority and only authority is the State, and if that be so, the voice adopted by the State as its own (whether it be of its Legislature or of its Supreme Court) should utter the last word."

Thus the doctrine of *Swift v. Tyson* is, as Mr. Justice Holmes said, "an unconstitutional assumption of powers by the Courts of the United States which no lapse of time or respectable array of opinion should make us hesitate to correct." In disapproving that doctrine we do not hold unconstitutional section 34 of the Federal Judiciary Act of 1789 or any other act of Congress. We merely declare that in applying the doctrine this Court and the lower courts have invaded rights which in our opinion are reserved by the Constitution to the several states.

* * *

Reversed [and remanded to the Court of Appeals to decide the liability question under Pennsylvania law].

[Justices Butler and McReynolds dissented. Justice Cardozo did not participate.]

Notes

1. Section 34 of the 1789 Judiciary Act is known as the Rules of Decision Act. The present version, 28 U.S.C. § 1652, provides: "The laws of the several states, except where the Constitution or treaties of the United States or Acts of Congress otherwise require or provide, shall be regarded as rules of decision in civil actions in the courts of the United States, in cases where they apply." The change from "trials at common law" to "civil actions" occurred in 1948 and was meant to "clarify" the applicability of the Act to "suits in equity." 28 U.S.C.A. § 1652, *Historical and Statutory Notes, 1948 Acts.*

2. What Charles Warren discovered (see footnote 5 in *Erie)* was an earlier draft of the Rules of Decision Act providing that "the Statute law of the several States in force for the time being and their unwritten or common law now in use, whether by adoption from the common law of England, the ancient statutes of the same or otherwise" should be

rules of decision in federal court. Senator Oliver Ellsworth, the main drafter of the First Judiciary Act, deleted the quoted phrase and substituted "laws of the several States." Warren concluded that Ellsworth's phrase was just a more economical expression of the idea in the earlier draft. 37 HARV. L. REV. at 84–88. Professor Wright notes that "[o]ther commentators have been less confident that this is the inevitable conclusion from the facts found by Warren." WRIGHT, LAW OF FEDERAL COURTS 372 (5th ed. 1994).

3. Professor Wright also notes: "It is impossible to overstate the importance of the *Erie* decision. It announces no technical doctrine of procedure or jurisdiction, but goes to the heart of the relations between the federal government and the states and returns to the states a power that had for nearly a century been exercised by the federal government." *Id.* at 377. Now let us see whether what is true in Wright's world has been true in admiralty.

Pope & Talbot, Inc. v. Hawn

Supreme Court of the United States, 1953
346 U.S. 406, 74 S. Ct. 202, 98 L. Ed. 143, 1954 AMC 1

Mr. Justice BLACK delivered the opinion of the Court.

The respondent Charles Hawn sustained severe physical injuries when he slipped and fell through an uncovered hatch hole on the petitioner Pope & Talbot's vessel. The ship was then berthed at a pier located in Pennsylvania waters of the Delaware River. Loading of the vessel with grain for a voyage had been temporarily interrupted to make minor repairs on the grain loading equipment. Hawn was doing carpentry work on this equipment to make it spread grain evenly and thereby balance the ship's load to make the coming voyage safer. He was not an employee of Pope & Talbot's but of the respondent Haenn Ship Ceiling and Refitting Company which had been hired to make these repairs. Hawn brought this [diversity] action in a United States District Court to recover damages for his injuries. His complaint charged that his injuries resulted from the vessel's unseaworthiness and from Pope & Talbot's negligence. In answering, Pope & Talbot denied both charges and set up contributory negligence as a defense to each. * * * A jury found that the ship was unseaworthy, that Pope & Talbot had been negligent, * * * and that Hawn's own negligence had contributed 17½% of his damages. On this basis, the court entered judgment for Hawn against Pope & Talbot for $29,700, 17½% less than the $36,000 at which the jury had fixed his damages. * * * The Court of Appeals affirmed Hawn's judgment against Pope & Talbot. * * *

* * *

* * * Petitioner urges that the jury finding of contributory negligence should have been accepted as a complete bar to Hawn's recovery. The contention appears to rest on two separate bases: (a) Admiralty has not developed any definite rule as to the effect of contributory negligence, and therefore the common-law rule under which contributory negligence bars recovery should govern in admiralty, (b) Pennsylvania law controls this case and under that state's law any contributory negligence of an injured person is an insuperable bar to his recovery.

(a) The harsh rule of the common law under which contributory negligence wholly barred an injured person from recovery is completely incompatible with modern admiralty policy and practice. Exercising its traditional discretion, admiralty has developed and now follows its own fairer and more flexible rule which allows such consideration of contributory negligence in mitigation of damages as justice requires. [ ] Petitioner presents no persuasive arguments that admiralty should now adopt a discredited doctrine which automatically destroys all claims of injured persons who have contributed to their injuries in any degree, however slight.

(**b**) Nor can we agree that Hawn's rights must be determined by the law of Pennsylvania, under which, it is said, any contributory negligence would bar all recovery in this personal injury action. True, Hawn was hurt inside Pennsylvania and ordinarily his rights would be determined by Pennsylvania law. But he was injured on navigable waters while working on a ship to enable it to complete its loading for safer transportation of its cargo by water. Consequently, the basis of Hawn's action is a maritime tort, a type of action which the Constitution had placed under national power to control in "its substantive as well as its procedural features...." * * * While states may sometimes supplement federal maritime policies, a state may not deprive a person of any substantial admiralty rights as defined in controlling acts of Congress or by interpretative decisions of this Court. These principles have been frequently declared and we adhere to them. * * *

Another argument is that Pennsylvania law must govern here because the District Court's jurisdiction was rested on diversity of citizenship under 28 U.S.C. § 1332. For this contention the principle established in *Erie R. Co. v. Tompkins* [*supra* at 119] is invoked. That case decided that federal district diversity courts must try state-created causes of action in accordance with state laws. This ended a longstanding federal court practice under which the outcome of lawsuits to enforce state created causes of action often depended on whether they were tried in a state courthouse or a federal courthouse. *Erie R. Co. v. Tompkins* was thus designed to ensure that litigants with the same kind of case would have their rights measured by the same legal standards of liability. It appears to be contended here, however, that one injured on navigable waters who sues in federal court under diversity jurisdiction somehow jeopardizes his right to have as full a recovery as he otherwise would. It is certainly contended that one who sues on the "law side" of the docket has much less chance to recover than one who sues on the "admiralty side." Thus we are asked to use the *Erie-Tompkins* case to bring about the same kind of unfairness it was designed to end. Once again, the substantial rights of parties would depend on which courthouse, or even on which "side" of the same courthouse, a lawyer might guess to be in the best interests of his client. We decline to depart from the principle of equal justice embodied in the *Erie-Tompkins* doctrine. Of course the substantial rights of an injured person are not to be determined differently whether his case is labelled "law side" or "admiralty side" on a district court's docket. [ ] The District Court and Court of Appeals correctly refused to deny Hawn's federal right of recovery by applying the Pennsylvania contributory negligence rule.

* * *

[Justice Frankfurter concurred in the result. Justices Jackson, Reed, and Burton dissented, believing that Hawn's exclusive remedy was the workers' compensation benefits provided by the Longshore and Harbor Workers' Compensation Act (LHWCA), 33 U.S.C. §§ 901–950.]

Notes

1. In 1972 the LHWCA was amended to provide that nonseamen can no longer sue on the basis of unseaworthiness. See *infra* Section II-C.

2. Some scholars have contended that federal admiralty courts' long-asserted authority to declare and apply preemptive rules of federal maritime law is unconstitutional under

Erie. See Young, *Preemption at Sea*, 57 GEO. WASH. L. REV. 273 (1999). On this view, *Pope & Talbot* is unpersuasive because the Court failed to examine its "underlying premise—that the [Constitution's] grant of admiralty jurisdiction, unlike the grant of diversity jurisdiction, gives federal courts the power to formulate federal common-law rules of decision." *Id.* at 311–12. That premise is badly and maybe even dangerously wrong, says Professor Young, who can find no legitimate basis for "a broad rule of preemption that allows federal courts to preempt state regulatory authority without grounding their decisions in a federal statute or constitutional provision." Young, *The Last Brooding Omnipresence*, 43 ST. LOUIS U.LJ. 1349, 1350 (1999). Young's articles offer a number of reasons for his belief that the admiralty grant in Article III § 2 is no more a legitimate source of preemptive federal common law than the diversity grant.

Maritime lawyers have generally been skeptical of Young's and like-minded scholarship. Addressing the Centennial Meeting of the Maritime Law Association of the United States in 1999, Professor Robert Force described Young's work as an "attack [on the] general maritime law as a legal institution." See Symposium, *The Federal Common Law in Admiralty*, 43 ST. LOUIS U. L. J. 1337 (1999), in which Professor Young summarizes his thesis and Professors Force, Friedell, and Goldstein stand up for the traditional admiralty view.

Kossick v. United Fruit Co.

Supreme Court of the United States, 1961

365 U.S. 731, 81 S. Ct. 886, 6 L. Ed. 2d 56, 1961 AMC 833

Mr. Justice HARLAN delivered the opinion of the Court.

[The facts, the rulings of the lower courts, and the reasoning of the Supreme Court on the admiralty jurisdiction issue are set forth *supra* at 56–58. Having determined that the contract in suit was maritime and thus within admiralty jurisdiction, the Court then turned to the source-of-law issue.]

This brings us, then, to the remaining, and what we believe is the controlling, question: whether the alleged contract, though maritime, is "maritime and local" [ ] in the sense that the application of state law would not disturb the uniformity of maritime law, *Southern Pacific Co. v. Jensen* [*supra* at 116].

Although the doctrines of the uniformity and supremacy of the maritime law have been vigorously criticized [ ], the qualifications and exceptions which this Court has built up to that imperative doctrine have not been considered notably more adequate. [ ] Perhaps the most often heard criticism of the supremacy doctrine is this: the fact that maritime law is—in a special sense at least, *Romero v. International Terminal Operating Co.* [*supra* at 79, 102]—federal law and therefore supreme by virtue of Article VI of the Constitution carries with it the implication that wherever a maritime interest is involved, no matter how slight or marginal, it must displace a local interest, no matter how pressing and significant. But the process is surely rather one of accommodation, entirely familiar in many areas of overlapping state and federal concern, or a process somewhat analogous to the normal conflict of laws situation where two sovereignties assert divergent interests in a transaction as to which both have some concern. Surely the claim of federal supremacy is adequately served by the availability of a federal forum in the first instance and of review in this Court to provide assurance that the federal interest is correctly assessed and accorded due weight.

Thus, for instance, it blinks at reality to assert that because a longshoreman, living ashore and employed ashore by shoreside employers, performs seaman's work, the State with these contacts must lose all concern for the longshoreman's status and well-being. In allowing state wrongful death statutes, *The Tungus v. Skovgaard*, 358 U.S. 588 (1959), and state survival of actions statutes, *Just v. Chambers*, 312 U.S. 383 (1941), respectively, to grant and to preserve a cause of action based ultimately on a wrong committed within the admiralty jurisdiction and defined by admiralty law, this Court has attempted an accommodation between a liability dependent primarily upon the breach of a maritime duty and state rules governing the extent of recovery for such breach. Since the chance of death foreclosing recovery is necessarily a fortuitous matter, and since the recovery afforded the disabled victim of an accident need be no less than that afforded to his family should he die, the intrusion of these state remedial systems need not bring with it any undesirable disuniformity in the scheme of maritime law.

* * *

Turning to the present case, we think that several considerations point to an accommodation favoring the application of maritime law. It must be remembered that we are dealing here with a contract, and therefore with obligations, by hypothesis, voluntarily undertaken, and not, as in the case of tort liability or public regulations, obligations imposed simply by virtue of the authority of the State or Federal Government. This fact in itself creates some presumption in favor of applying that law tending toward the validation of the alleged contract. [ ] As we have already said, it is difficult to deny the essentially maritime character of this contract without either indulging in finespun distinctions in terms of what the transaction was *really* about, or simply denying the alleged agreement that characterization by reason of its novelty. Considering that sailors of any nationality may join a ship in any port, and that it is the clear duty of the ship to put into the first available port if this be necessary to provide prompt and adequate maintenance and cure to a seaman who falls ill during the voyage, [ ] it seems to us that this is such a contract as may well have been made anywhere in the world, and that the validity of it should be judged by one law wherever it was made. On the other hand we are hard put to perceive how this contract was "peculiarly a matter of state and local concern," [ ] unless it be New York's interest in not lending her courts to the accomplishment of fraud, something which appears to us insufficient to overcome the countervailing considerations. Finally, since the effect of the application of New York law here would be to invalidate the contract, this case can hardly be analogized to cases such as * * * *Just v. Chambers*, where state law had the effect of supplementing the remedies available in admiralty for the vindication of maritime rights. Nor is *Wilburn Boat Co. v. Fireman's Fund Ins. Co.*, 348 U.S. 310 (1955) [*infra* at 461], apposite. The application of state law in that case was justified by the Court on the basis of a lack of any provision of maritime law governing the matter there presented. A concurring opinion and some commentators have preferred to refer the decision to the absurdity of applying maritime law to a contract of insurance on a houseboat established in the waters of a small artificial lake between Texas and Oklahoma. [ ] Needless to say the situation presented here has a more genuinely salty flavor than that.

* * *

Reversed.

Mr. Justice FRANKFURTER, whom Mr. Justice Stewart joins, dissenting.

Certainly no decision in the Court's history has been the progenitor of more lasting dissatisfaction and disharmony within a particular area of the law than *Southern Pacific Co. v. Jensen* [*supra* at 116]. The mischief it has caused was due to the uncritical application of the loose doctrine of observing "the very uniformity in respect to maritime matters which the Constitution was designed to establish." [ ] The looser a legal doctrine, like that of the duty to observe "the uniformity of maritime law," the more incumbent it is upon the judiciary to apply it with well-defined concreteness. It can fairly be said that the *Jensen* decision has not been treated as a favored doctrine. Quite the contrary. It has been steadily narrowed in application * * *.

The Court today, relying as it does on *Jensen*, reinvigorates that "ill-starred decision." [ ] The notion that if such a limited and essentially local transaction as the contract here in issue were allowed to be governed by a local statute of frauds it would "disturb the uniformity of maritime law" is, I respectfully submit, too abstract and doctrinaire a view of the true demands of maritime law. I would affirm the judgment below.

Mr. Justice WHITTAKER, dissenting.

Like the Court of Appeals, I think the oral contract here claimed by petitioner was not a maritime but a New York contract and barred by its statute of frauds. I therefore dissent.

Notes

1. The phrase "maritime and local" originated in *Western Fuel Co. v. Garcia*, 257 U.S. 233, 242 (1924), in which the Court held that an admiralty action for the wrongful death of a longshoreman killed while working in the hold of a ship anchored in San Francisco Bay was barred by California's one-year statute of limitations. Often rendered as "maritime but local," the phrase has been touted as a guide to the Court's maritime-law preemption cases. But it is too conclusory to be a good guide. See Robertson, *The Applicability of State Law in Maritime Cases After Yamaha Motor Corp. v. Calhoun*, 21 TUL. MAR. L. J. 81, 91–97 (1996).

2. Do Justice Harlan's "process of ... accommodation" and "analog[y] to the normal conflict of laws situation where two sovereignties assert divergent interests in a transaction" represent a change from the approach taken in *Jensen* and *Pope & Talbot*? On their face, the quoted phrases assert that the federal-state conflict of laws problem with which we are concerned—a *vertical* choice-of-law issue, with the Supremacy Clause perched heavily on the federal side of the scales—should be solved with the same tools courts use in the *horizontal* (state-state, country-country) choice of law arena. It is common ground that horizontal choice-of-law thinking, at least in the United States, incorporates a decided preference for the law of the forum. Under this line of thought, admiralty courts would appropriately lean toward applying federal maritime law—so far so good, perhaps—and state courts toward applying state law, which is completely antithetical to the reverse-*Erie* doctrine, *supra* at 115 note 1.

3. To what extent did Justice Harlan actually "accommodate" New York? Does his approach bear any resemblance to the "air of benevolent gratuity" decried by Justice Holmes in his *Jensen* dissent?

4. In thinking about the "balancing" that went on in *Ballard* and *Kossick*, it may be useful to consider the analogous interest-balancing vocabulary the Court has used in some nonmaritime cases to decide whether the commerce clause invalidates state law, as to which Justice Scalia noted:

> This process is ordinarily called "balancing," but the scale analogy is not really appropriate, since the interests on both sides are incommensurate. It is more like judging whether a particular line is longer than a particular rock is heavy.

Bendix Autolite Corp. v. Midwesco Enterprises, Inc. 486 U.S. 888, 897 (1988) (Scalia, J. concurring) (citation omitted).

5. The Court's fifty-plus maritime preemption decisions are summarized in tabular form in Robertson, *supra* note 1, 21 TUL. MAR. L.J. at 89–97. When that article was written, the two most recent decisions presenting the preemption issue were *American Dredging Co. v. Miller*, which is discussed in *Ballard*, *supra* at 113, and *Yamaha Motor Corp. v. Calhoun*, 516 U.S. 199 (1996) (*infra* at 246), a unanimous holding that the federal judge-made law of wrongful death did not displace state remedies in a products liability action in admiralty court arising from the death of a recreational boater. *Kirby*, just below, is the newest addition.

Norfolk Southern Railway Co. v. James N. Kirby, Pty Ltd.

Supreme Court of the United States, 2004
543 U.S. 14, 125 S. Ct. 385, 160 L. Ed. 2d 283, 2004 AMC 2705

Justice O'CONNOR delivered the opinion for a unanimous Court.

[The facts, the rulings of the lower courts, and the Supreme Court's reasoning on the admiralty jurisdiction issue are set forth *supra* at 60.]

Our authority to make decisional law for the interpretation of maritime contracts stems from the Constitution's grant of admiralty jurisdiction to federal courts. * * * Indeed, for federal common law to apply in these circumstances, this suit *must* also be sustainable under the admiralty jurisdiction. * * *

Having established that the ICC and the Hamburg Süd bills [of lading] are maritime contracts [and thus within admiralty jurisdiction], we must clear a second hurdle before applying federal law in their interpretation. Is this case inherently local? For not "every term in every maritime contract can only be controlled by some federally defined admiralty rule." *Wilburn Boat Co. v. Fireman's Fund Ins. Co.*, 348 U.S. 310, 313 (1955) [*infra* at 461] (applying state law to maritime contract for marine insurance because of state regulatory power over insurance industry). A maritime contract's interpretation may so implicate local interests as to beckon interpretation by state law. *See Kossick* [*supra* at 124]. Respondents have not articulated any specific Australian or state interest at stake, though some are surely implicated. But when state interests cannot be accommodated without defeating a federal interest, as is the case here, then federal substantive law should govern. *See Kossick*, 365 U.S. at 739 (the process of deciding whether federal law applies "is surely one of accommodation, entirely familiar in many areas of overlapping state and federal concern, or a process somewhat analogous to the normal conflict of laws situation where two sovereignties assert divergent interests in a transaction") [ ].

Here, our touchstone is a concern for the uniform meaning of maritime contracts like the ICC and Hamburg Süd bills. We have explained that Article III's grant of admiralty jurisdiction "must have referred to a system of law coextensive with, and operating uniformly in, the whole country. It certainly could not have been the intention to place the rules and limits of maritime law under the disposal and regulation of the several States, as that would have defeated the uniformity and consistency at which the Constitution aimed on all subjects of a commercial character affecting the intercourse of the States with each other or with foreign states." *American Dredging Co. v. Miller*, 510 U.S. 433, 451 (1994) (quoting *The Lottawanna*, 88 U.S. (21 Wall.) 558, 576 (1875)). See also *Yamaha Motor Corp. v. Calhoun*, 516 U.S. 199, 210 (1996) [*infra* at 246] ("[I]n several contexts, we have recognized that vindication of maritime policies demanded uniform adherence to a federal rule of decision" [ ]); *Romero v. International Terminal Operating Co.* [*supra* at 102–05] ("[S]tate law must yield to the needs of a uniform federal maritime law when this Court finds inroads on a harmonious system[,] [b]ut this limitation still leaves the States a wide scope").

Applying state law to cases like this one would undermine the uniformity of general maritime law. The same liability limitation in a single bill of lading for international intermodal transportation often applies both to sea and to land * * *. Confusion and inefficiency will inevitably result if more than one body of law governs a given contract's meaning. As we said in *Kossick*, when "a [maritime] contract ... may well have been made anywhere in the world," it "should be judged by one law wherever it was made." [ ] Here, that one law is federal.

[The Court proceeded to decide the case on the merits. See *infra* at 320.]

Notes

1. The Court undergirded its decision to apply federal maritime law by asserting that "[i]n protecting the uniformity of federal maritime law, we also buttress the liability regime Congress established in COGSA [the Carriage of Goods by Sea Act]." 543 U.S. at 29. We consider COGSA in Chapter III, *infra* at 277.

2. In *American Dredging* and *Yamaha*, the Court seemed to go out of its way to proclaim a lack of clarity as to the principles determining when federal maritime law preempts state law. Justice Scalia's opinion for the *American Dredging* Court stated (510 U.S. at 452–53, citations omitted):

> It would be idle to pretend that the line separating permissible from impermissible state regulation is readily discernible in our admiralty jurisprudence, or indeed is even entirely consistent within our admiralty jurisprudence. Compare *Kossick* (state law cannot require provisions of maritime contract to be in writing) with *Wilburn Boat* (state law can determine effect of breach of warranty in marine insurance policy). Happily, it is unnecessary to wrestle with that difficulty today.

In *Yamaha*, Justice Ginsburg quoted Justice Scalia's "idle to pretend" sentence and went on to say:

> We attempt no grand synthesis or reconciliation of our precedent today. * * * We * * * reserve for another day reconciliation of the maritime personal injury decisions that rejected state substantive liability standards, and the maritime wrongful death cases in which state law has held sway.

3. In *American Dredging*, Justice Stevens wrote a concurring opinion arguing that *Jensen* should be overruled: "In my view, *Jensen* is just as untrustworthy a guide in an admiralty case today as *Lochner v. New York*, 198 U.S. 45 (1905), would be in a case under the Due Process Clause." 510 U.S. at 458. Justice Scalia responded for the majority that the parties and amici had couched their arguments in Jensenian terms and stating: "Since we ultimately find that the Louisiana law meets the standards of *Jensen* anyway, we think it inappropriate to overrule *Jensen* in dictum, and without argument or even invitation." *Id.* at 447 n.1.

4. Meanwhile—while we are waiting to see what, if anything, the Supreme Court will do about the many doubts it has countenanced—the state and lower federal courts struggle with the task of divining the Court's avowedly vague and wavering line. *Morrow v. Marinemax, Inc.*, 731 F. Supp. 2d 390, 393 (D.N.J. 2010), aptly illustrates the situation. The question in *Morrow*—*res nova* in the Third Circuit—was whether "the exclusive

remedy provision of a state's workers' compensation law [can] bar a plaintiff's general maritime tort claim against his employer." This is a highly important and recurrent issue, and the *Morrow* opinion is quietly but firmly critical of the lack of Supreme Court guidance. It documents that the Fifth and Ninth Circuits have held that state employer-immunity statutes are preempted by general maritime law, whereas the Eleventh Circuit and Virginia Supreme Court have upheld the applicability of such statutes. (The Supreme Court denied certiorari in all three of the court of appeals cases.) Ultimately, after a considerable struggle, the *Morrow* court elected to follow the Fifth and Ninth Circuit decisions.

Chapter II

Personal Injury, Death, and Tortious Harm to Property

A. The Basic Maritime Tort Law

In many spheres of maritime activity, the courts, with some help from Congress, have developed specialized bodies of law to control recurrent issues. For example, collisions between vessels and allisions between vessels and stationary objects are governed in major part by a specialized body of tort law (see Chapter IV). A specialized body of law governs injuries to seamen (Section II-B), and another governs injuries to maritime workers who do not qualify as seamen (Section II-C). The responsibility of a maritime carrier of goods to the shipper of the goods is governed by a specialized body of law that is an amalgam of contract and tort principles (Chapter III). The responsibility of tug and tow to one another and to third parties likewise turns in significant part on the application of specialized body of law combining principles of contract and tort (Chapter V). In this section, we look at selected features of the general law of maritime tort, *viz.*, the tort law that applies in maritime cases falling outside the aforementioned discrete areas or in the interstices of cases within those areas.

Kermarec v. Compagnie Generale Transatlantique

Supreme Court of the United States, 1959

358 U.S. 625, 79 S. Ct. 406, 3 L. Ed. 2d 550, 1959 AMC 597

Mr. Justice STEWART delivered the opinion of the unanimous Court.

On November 24, 1948, the respondent's vessel, the *S. S. Oregon*, was berthed at a pier in the North River, New York City. About noon on that day Joseph Kermarec came aboard to visit Henry Yves, a member of the ship's crew. The purpose of the visit was entirely personal, to pay a social call upon Yves and to give him a package to be delivered to a mutual friend in France. In accordance with customary practice permitting crew members to entertain guests aboard the vessel, Yves had obtained a pass from the executive officer authorizing Kermarec to come aboard. As he started to leave the ship several hours later, Kermarec fell and was injured while descending a stairway.

On the theory that his fall had been caused by the defective manner in which a canvas runner had been tacked to the stairway, Kermarec brought an action for personal injuries in the District Court for the Southern District of New York, alleging unseaworthiness of the vessel and negligence on the part of its crew. Federal jurisdiction was invoked by reason of the diverse citizenship of the parties, and a jury trial was demanded.

The district judge was of the view that the substantive law of New York was applicable. Accordingly, he eliminated the unseaworthiness claim from the case and instructed the jury that Kermarec was "a gratuitous licensee" who could recover only if the defendant had failed to warn him of a dangerous condition within its actual knowledge, and only if Kermarec himself had been entirely free of contributory negligence.

The jury returned a verdict in Kermarec's favor. Subsequently the trial court granted a motion to set the verdict aside and dismiss the complaint, ruling that there had been a complete failure of proof that the shipowner had actually known that the stairway was in a dangerous or defective condition. A divided Court of Appeals affirmed. The opinion of that court does not make clear whether affirmance was based upon agreement with the trial judge that New York law was applicable, or upon a determination that the controlling legal principles would in any event be no different under maritime law. Certiorari was granted to examine both of these issues.

The District Court was in error in ruling that the governing law in this case was that of the State of New York. Kermarec was injured aboard a ship upon navigable waters. It was there that the conduct of which he complained occurred. The legal rights and liabilities arising from that conduct were therefore within the full reach of the admiralty jurisdiction and measurable by the standards of maritime law. [ ] If this action had been brought in a state court, reference to admiralty law would have been necessary to determine the rights and liabilities of the parties. [ ] Where the plaintiff exercises the right conferred by diversity of citizenship to choose a federal forum, the result is no different, even though he exercises the further right to a jury trial. Whatever doubt may once have existed on that score was effectively laid to rest by *Pope & Talbot, Inc., v. Hawn* [*supra* at 122]. It thus becomes necessary to consider whether prejudice resulted from the court's application of the substantive law of New York.

In instructing the jury that contributory negligence on Kermarec's part would operate as a complete bar to recovery, the district judge was clearly in error. The jury should have been told instead that Kermarec's contributory negligence was to be considered only in mitigation of damages. [ ] It is equally clear, however, that this error did not prejudice Kermarec. By returning a verdict in his favor, the jury necessarily found that Kermarec had not in fact been guilty of contributory negligence "even in the slightest degree."

The district judge refused to submit the issue of unseaworthiness to the jury for the reason that an action for unseaworthiness is unknown to the common law of New York. Although the basis for its action was inappropriate, the court was correct in eliminating the unseaworthiness claim from this case. Kermarec was not a member of the ship's company, nor of that broadened class of workmen to whom the admiralty law has latterly extended the absolute right to a seaworthy ship. [See *infra* Sections II-B and II-C.] Kermarec was aboard not to perform ship's work, but simply to visit a friend.

It is apparent, therefore, that prejudicial error occurred in this case only if the maritime law imposed upon the shipowner a standard of care higher than the duty which the district judge found owing to a gratuitous licensee under the law of New York. If, in other words, the shipowner owed Kermarec the duty of exercising ordinary care, then upon this record

Kermarec was entitled to judgment, the jury having resolved the factual issues in his favor under instructions less favorable to him than should have been given. Stated broadly, the decisive issue is thus whether admiralty recognizes the same distinctions between an invitee and a licensee as does the common law.

It is a settled principle of maritime law that a shipowner owes the duty of exercising reasonable care towards those lawfully aboard the vessel who are not members of the crew. [ ] But this Court has never determined whether a different and lower standard of care is demanded if the ship's visitor is a person to whom the label "licensee" can be attached. The issue must be decided in the performance of the Court's function in declaring the general maritime law, free from inappropriate common-law concepts. [ ]

The distinctions which the common law draws between licensee and invitee were inherited from a culture deeply rooted to the land, a culture which traced many of its standards to a heritage of feudalism. In an effort to do justice in an industrialized urban society, with its complex economic and individual relationships, modern common-law courts have found it necessary to formulate increasingly subtle verbal refinements, to create subclassifications among traditional common-law categories, and to delineate fine gradations in the standards of care which the landowner owes to each. Yet even within a single jurisdiction, the classifications and subclassifications bred by the common law have produced confusion and conflict. As new distinctions have been spawned, older ones have become obscured. Through this semantic morass the common law has moved, unevenly and with hesitation, towards "imposing on owners and occupiers a single duty of reasonable care in all the circumstances."

For the admiralty law at this late date to import such conceptual distinctions would be foreign to its traditions of simplicity and practicality. [ ] The incorporation of such concepts appears particularly unwarranted when it is remembered that they originated under a legal system in which status depended almost entirely upon the nature of the individual's estate with respect to real property, a legal system in that respect entirely alien to the law of the sea. We hold that the owner of a ship in navigable waters owes to all who are on board for purposes not inimical to his legitimate interests the duty of exercising reasonable care under the circumstances of each case. It follows that in the present case the judgment must be vacated and the case remanded to the District Court with instructions to reinstate the jury verdict and enter judgment accordingly.

* * *

Notes

1. Note how easily state law was swept aside. Note how comfortable the Court seemed with its "function in declaring the general maritime law, free from inappropriate common-law concepts."

2. The holding in *Kermarec*—"the owner of a ship in navigable waters owes to all who are on board for purposes not inimical to his legitimate interests the duty of exercising reasonable care under the circumstances of each case"—is fairly broad. And *Kermarec* quickly came to stand for the much broader principle that all maritime actors presumptively owe one another a duty of reasonable care. As such, *Kermarec* sets forth a general principle of negligence liability that supplies the default rule—the rule applicable when specialized statutory or caselaw doctrines do not obtain—for maritime cases of physical injury to persons and property. All of the cases in this section of Chapter II fall under the mantle of *Kermarec*.

3. In *Air & Liquid Systems Corp. v. DeVries*, 139 S. Ct. 986, 995 (2019), the Supreme Court addressed a claim that the manufacturers of pumps, blowers, turbines, and similar machinery installed on Navy ships had a duty to warn of the dangers associated with the asbestos that was required for that machinery to function even if they did not themselves provide the asbestos. The manufacturers, asserting the so-called "bare metal" defense, argued that they were not liable under maritime law for injuries caused by products that they did not make, sell, or distribute. Rejecting the defense, the Court could have resolved the case by applying the general rule derived from *Kermarec*: the manufacturers owed a duty of reasonable care to those who would use the machinery. The Court instead announced a specific rule for duty-to-warn cases in the bare-metal context that clarified what was reasonable under the circumstances:

> In the maritime tort context, a product manufacturer has a duty to warn when (i) its product requires incorporation of a part, (ii) the manufacturer knows or has reason to know that the integrated product is likely to be dangerous for its intended uses, and (iii) the manufacturer has no reason to believe that the product's users will realize that danger.

Brotherhood Shipping Co. v. St. Paul Fire & Marine Insurance Co.

United States Court of Appeals, Seventh Circuit, 1993
985 F.2d 323, 1993 AMC 2729

POSNER, Circuit Judge:

The *M/V Capetan Yiannis*, a freighter, was damaged and temporarily put out of service in an accident in the Port of Milwaukee on Lake Michigan. The owner of the ship, Brotherhood Shipping Company, brought suit against * * * the City of Milwaukee, which owns the port, * * * seeking damages for the damage to the ship and for the loss of revenues from the ship's being out of service because of the accident. The plaintiff designated the suit as one in admiralty, in accordance with Rule 9(h) of the Federal Rules of Civil Procedure. * * * The district judge granted the city's motion for summary judgment and dismissed the shipowner's claims against it. * * *

The only issue for us is whether, viewing the evidence obtained through pretrial discovery as favorably to the shipowner as reason allows, we can say that no reasonable trier of fact could conclude that the city had been even a little bit negligent. * * * [The city argues] that, even if the city was negligent, the captain of the *Capetan Yiannis*, and other persons who may * * * have been the shipowner's agents, were themselves negligent—and far more so than the city.

The * * * point is * * * irrelevant. * * * The rule in admiralty, when property damage results from a collision between two ships, or, as here, between ship and shore, is comparative negligence (equivalently, relative fault). The plaintiff's negligence reduces the amount of damages that he can collect, but is not a defense to liability. [ ] Now in many states that embrace comparative negligence the plaintiff's negligence remains a defense to liability if he fails to prove that the defendant's negligence was more than 50 percent responsible for the accident.[1] Wisconsin is such a state. Wis.Stat. § 895.045. And the appellees urge us to apply Wisconsin's rule. But admiralty is not merely a basis of ju-

1. Editors' note: As to Wisconsin, the phrase "more than 50 percent" is a mistake. It should read "at least 50 percent." See Wis. Stat. § 895.045 (providing that a plaintiff whose assessed fault is "not greater than" the defendant's is not barred).

risdiction, like diversity of citizenship. It is a body of substantive principles as well, or more precisely a grant of power to federal judges to create a body of admiralty law * * *. One of the judge-made substantive admiralty rules is the doctrine of comparative negligence * * *. The admiralty doctrine of comparative negligence, unlike some state comparative-negligence statutes, has never had a threshold above which a plaintiff's negligence barred all recovery. We do not understand the city to be arguing that we should create such a threshold. It argues, erroneously, that we should apply Wisconsin law, which contains the threshold; but it does not argue that if we reject Wisconsin law we should create a new doctrine of admiralty law. As we are given no reason to depart from the "pure" comparative negligence standard, [ ] we shall assume that if the plaintiff's negligence is deemed 99 percent responsible for the accident in this case and the defendant's negligence 1 percent responsible, the plaintiff is entitled to 1 percent of its damages.

* * *

* * * The sole issue for us is whether, viewed as favorably to the plaintiff as is reasonable, the evidence gathered in pretrial discovery would, were the same evidence to constitute the entire record at trial, warrant a finding that the city was negligent. In answering that question, we apply the standard of negligence laid down by Judge Hand in the famous admiralty case of *United States v. Carroll Towing Co.*, 159 F.2d 169, 173 (2d Cir. 1947) * * *. Under that standard, a defendant is negligent if the burden (cost) of the precautions that he could have taken to avoid the accident (B in Hand's formula) is less than the loss that the accident could reasonably be anticipated to cause (L), discounted (i.e., multiplied) by the probability that the accident would occur unless the precautions were taken. So: B<PL. The cost-justified level of precaution (B)—the level that the defendant must come up to on penalty of being found to have violated his duty of due care if he does not—is thus higher, the likelier the accident that the precaution would have prevented was to occur (P) and the greater the loss that the accident was likely to inflict if it did occur (L). Looked at from a different direction, the formula shows that the cheaper it is to prevent the accident (low B), the more likely prevention is to be cost-justified and the failure to prevent therefore negligent. Negligence is especially likely to be found if B is low and both P and L (and therefore PL, the expected accident cost) are high.

We now have a framework for analyzing the facts. The Port of Milwaukee has a breakwater, with, of course, a gap in it to allow ships to go in and out of the harbor. Two of the slips in the harbor, where ships berth, are directly opposite the gap in the breakwater. As a result of this geometry, and the occasional violence of Lake Michigan storms, surprising to strangers to the Great Lakes, a northeast gale—and such gales are common on Lake Michigan—can afflict these slips with two severe patterns of wave action, which the parties refer to as "cross-slapping" and "over-topping." Waves from the open water surge through the gap in the breakwater, strike the wall on the other side, recoil, and collide with the next surge, creating a wave twice as high as the other waves stirred up in the harbor by the gale. This is cross-slapping. Over-topping occurs when waves in this area of the harbor become so violent that they spill over the wall of the slip at which a ship is berthed. The concern with these unusual conditions is not an academic one. Between 1964 and 1979, nine ships were damaged while berthed in the outer harbor (that is, in the area of the breakwater—there are safer berths in an inner harbor). One of them [the *E.M. Ford*] sank. That disaster occurred in 1979, and the [*E.M. Ford*] had been berthed in the slip next to that in which the *Capetan Yiannis* became the tenth victim of cross-slapping and over-topping, in 1987. As early as 1951 the city had commissioned a study of wave conditions in the outer harbor that found those conditions to be unsafe.

A series of additional studies, the last shortly before the accident that damaged the *Capetan Yiannis*, confirmed the hazard and recommended measures, such as the construction of a baffle device, that would reduce the violence of the waves in the outer harbor. The city did nothing.

Well, not quite nothing. After the *E.M. Ford* sank in 1979 * * * the city had the following notice inserted in the U.S. Coastal Pilot, the manual that mariners use in unfamiliar ports: "Vessels moored in the outer harbor [of the Port of Milwaukee] may be subject to severe surging when there are strong NNE to ENE winds." The city continued to promote the Port as a "harbor of refuge," adding that the Port provides "everything you'd expect a major world port to have," though in fact tugs and pilots are not available around the clock, as they are, at least according to some of the evidence, at other major ports. This evidence suggests, as we are about to see, that the master of the plaintiff's ship may have been induced to rely on nonexistent safety features of the Port of Milwaukee.

In December 1987, the *Capetan Yiannis*, a 590-foot ocean-going freighter owned by a Greek company and captained by a Greek mariner named Konstadinos, was ordered to the Port of Milwaukee to pick up a cargo for South Africa. Konstadinos berthed the ship, pursuant to directions by a lessee that a trier of fact might find was the city's agent, in one of the two slips opposite the gap in the breakwater. At noon the following day, while the ship was being loaded, Konstadinos heard (or was told about) a report on the radio that a gusty northeaster was brewing. He made some inquiries—not as yet from the city, however—and was reassured that he could ride out the storm. At 4 p.m., an hour after hearing a weather report similar to the one at noon, the city's harbor master received a Coast Guard report predicting waves five to twelve feet high and winds of 35 to 40 knots out of the northeast. He wrote this information, together with the expected duration of the storm (36 hours), at the bottom of a "weather notice." This is a printed form that states in its entirety:

> The Weather Bureau has warned the Milwaukee area that a North and/or Northeast storm is imminent.
>
> The resultant wave action can be very severe, causing your vessel to pitch, roll and yaw. These actions may be separate or simultaneous. This may result in damage to your vessel and/or the dock structure.
>
> This is not an order to vacate the berth. This is information to assist you in determining your course of action.

The harbor master waited till he left for home at 5 p.m. to deliver the weather notice to Konstadinos, who, receiving it at 5:30 and becoming alarmed, sent for a pilot to direct the ship to a safer berth. The pilot, however, had—despite the stormy weather, which might have been expected to alert him to a possible emergency need for his services—already left for the day and was en route to his home in Chicago. Even if Konstadinos had wanted to take his chances on leaving the berth without a pilot, he couldn't have done so, because there were no tugs or linesmen available at that hour. By the time the pilot arrived, at 11:30 p.m., the storm was too severe for the ship to leave the berth. Conditions continued to worsen and at 6:15 a.m. the stern ropes broke and the stern of the ship was dashed against the wall of the slip. The plaintiff estimates its total damages—the cost of repairs plus lost revenue while the ship was out of commission—at $4.5 to $5 million. * * *

Evaluating these facts with the aid of the Hand formula, we note first that L in the formula—the magnitude or gravity of the loss that an accident that the precautions the defendant failed to take would have averted could be expected to inflict—was substantial.

The ships that dock at the Port of Milwaukee are expensive machines carrying expensive goods. Moreover, an accident to such a ship, even while the ship is berthed, could endanger human life. The loss to the shipowner in this case has merely been alleged, not as yet determined, but there is nothing implausible in the claim that it is in the millions. The ship could have sunk, like the *E.M. Ford*, in which event the loss might easily have exceeded $5 million. * * * As for the likelihood of such an accident (P), it could not be reckoned small, given the history of accidents to ships at the two exposed slips in the outer harbor. So PL, the expected accident cost, was substantial and therefore imposed on the defendant a duty of taking substantial precautions.

At least three types of precaution were possible. One was a structural alteration to the harbor that would have eliminated the problem once and for all, or, more realistically, have greatly reduced the risk of accident. The second possible precaution was to have pilots, tugs, and linesmen available round the clock in the winter to remove endangered ships from the slips at short notice. The third was to give the masters of the ships berthed at the "bad" slips (a characterization offered by one of the city's own employees) sufficient early warning to enable them to obtain a pilot, tugs, and linesmen before the close of business on the day of a storm. The city did none of these things. It did not build a baffle or other device that would have prevented cross-slapping and over-topping. It did not arrange for pilots, tugs, and linesmen to stand by after 5 p.m. during the winter in case there was a storm. It did not include an explicit warning in the U.S. Coastal Pilot—the note on weather conditions makes no reference to the bad slips. It did not direct the *Capetan Yiannis* to an empty slip (if there was one) in a less exposed position. And it made no effort to communicate a clear and effective warning to Captain Konstadinos as soon as the harbor master found out that a dangerous northeaster was approaching.

Maybe every one of these precautions would have cost more than the benefit in averting the accident. But on that subject all that the city says is that it doesn't employ any pilots—they are independent contractors who deal directly with the ship's crew. This is hardly responsive. It is not beyond the city's power to make an arrangement with the pilots' association under which the association would undertake to have a pilot on stand-by status after 5 p.m. But this is not an issue worth pursuing here. Clearly the cheapest precaution was to include a candid, comprehensive explanation in U.S. Coastal Pilot. Second cheapest was to give a prompt warning if and when a storm was expected. In some cases the warning would come too late. But here the city's harbor master knew by 3 p.m. and probably earlier that a northeaster was approaching, and when he received the Coast Guard report at 4 p.m. he knew everything a reasonable person would have had to know to have a duty to warn the master of the *Capetan Yiannis* immediately that he must make arrangements to clear the slip at short notice. The printed weather notice was inexplicit but in any event was delivered too late.

Given the unpredictability of Lake Michigan storms and the vagaries of a notice system, sole reliance on such a system to protect mariners, many of whom like Captain Konstadinos are foreigners unfamiliar with Lake Michigan, might not suffice to fulfill the city's duty of care, provided one of the alternatives—a structural alteration to the harbor or the provision of stand-by rescue services—would be less costly than the expected accident cost that would remain once the notice system was in place. The U.S. Coastal Pilot warning, even if far more explicit than it was, might have been deemed inadequate if, in conjunction with the city's promotional literature, it left the impression that adequate rescue services were available on a stand-by basis, which they were not. But we need not get into any of these issues. They may or may not become important on remand. For purposes of this appeal it is enough that the plaintiff has raised a genuine issue of material fact concerning the adequacy of the precautions that the City of Milwaukee took to prevent the type of serious, and by no means remotely unlikely, accident that occurred. In so saying we do not deny the possibility that the accident might have been prevented had Captain Konstadinos been more alert [or] more cautious * * *. Or perhaps the captain should have been more daring, and have left the berth without waiting for a pilot and tugs and linesmen. But to repeat an earlier point, the issue of the parties' relative fault is not before us. There is evidence from which a reasonable trier of fact could infer that the city was negligent and that the accident would not have occurred had it not been. No more need be decided to require that the judgment of the district court be reversed.

Note

Judge Posner's opinion in *Brotherhood* uses Learned Hand's famous *Carroll Towing* "formula"—turning the determination whether particular conduct was negligent on the question, B<PL?—to flesh out the meaning of the "reasonable care under the circumstances" standard laid down in *Kermarec*. In *Carroll*, Judge Hand used the "formula" to help him conclude that the owner of a barge that was caused to break loose from its mooring by nearby activity was negligent in failing to have a watchman aboard "during the working hours of daylight." *United States v. Carroll Towing Co.*, 159 F.2d 169, 174 (2d Cir. 1947). The B<PL "formula"—which now lies at the heart of the law of negligence of most of the states—is interestingly foreshadowed in Judge Hand's opinion in another maritime case, *The Glendola*, 47 F.2d 206 (2d Cir. 1931). Judge Posner is a strong proponent of its usefulness. In his opinion for the court in *United States Fidelity & Guaranty Co. v. Plovidba*, 683 F.2d 1022, 1026 (7th Cir. 1982), he stated:

> Though mathematical in form, the Hand formula does not yield mathematically precise results in practice; that would require that B, P, and L all be quantified, which so far as we know has never been done in an actual lawsuit. Nevertheless, the formula is a valuable aid to clear thinking about the factors that are relevant to a judgment of negligence and about the relationship among those factors. It gives federal district courts in maritime cases ... a useful framework for evaluating proposed jury instructions, for deciding motions for directed verdict and for judgment notwithstanding the verdict, and, in nonjury cases, for preparing Rule 52(a) findings. * * * We do not want to force the district courts into a straitjacket, so we do not hold that they must use the Hand formula in all maritime negligence cases. We merely commend it to them as a useful tool.

The E.M. Ford Litigation

Winter storms on the Great Lakes are nightmarish for marine interests but potentially kind to admiralty lawyers. Consider the lengthy litigation generated by the sinking of the *E.M. Ford* in Milwaukee harbor on Christmas Eve, 1979. Initially the trial judge assessed the defendant city's negligence at 4% and the vessel's at 96%. The court of appeals found that allocation to be clearly erroneous and assessed the city with 1/3 of the fault and the vessel with 2/3. *Cement Division v. Milwaukee*, 915 F.2d 1154 (7th Cir. 1990).

The costs of repairing the vessel exceeded $6.5 million. After the court of appeals decision, the vessel accepted the city's payment of $1.79 million as a discharge of the city's liability for the principal sum, but the parties could not agree on the issue of prejudgment interest and submitted that issue to the trial court for decision. The trial court correctly set forth the general rule—in admiralty cases prejudgment interest is normally owed, running from the date of the accident until the date of judgment[2]—but invoked its discretion to deny such interest on equitable grounds, reasoning that a party guilty of 2/3 fault should not be entitled to prejudgment interest. The court of appeal reversed and laid down a rule of law that "the mutual fault of the parties in an admiralty collision case does not constitute a peculiar circumstance justifying the denial of prejudgment interest." *Cement Division v. Milwaukee*, 31 F.3d 581, 586 (7th Cir. 1994).

On the basis of a "deepen[ing] ... circuit split regarding the criteria for denying prejudgment interest in maritime collision cases," the Supreme Court granted certiorari and affirmed the court of appeals' decision that the city owed prejudgment interest, stating:

> Although Congress has enacted a statute governing the award of postjudgment interest in federal court litigation, see 28 U.S.C. § 1961, there is no comparable legislation regarding prejudgment interest. Far from indicating a legislative determination that prejudgment interest should not be awarded, however, the absence of a statute merely indicates that the question is governed by traditional judge-made principles. Those principles are well developed in admiralty, where the Judiciary has traditionally taken the lead in formulating flexible and fair remedies.
>
> * * *
>
> [The] general rule [is] that prejudgment interest should be awarded in maritime collision cases, subject to a limited exception for "peculiar" or "exceptional" circumstances. The essential rationale for awarding prejudgment interest is to ensure than an injured party is fully compensated for its loss. * * * Although we have never attempted to exhaustively catalog the circumstances that will justify the denial of interest, and do not do so today, the most obvious example is the plaintiff's responsibility for undue delay in prosecuting the lawsuit.
>
> * * *
>
> [I]t might appear somewhat inequitable to award a large sum of prejudgment interest against a relatively innocent party [such as the City, here assessed with only 1/3 of the fault]. But any unfairness is illusory, because the relative fault of the parties has already been taken into consideration in calculating the amount of the loss for which the City is responsible. * * * [D]enying prejudgment interest on the basis of mutual fault would seem to penalize a party twice for the same mistake. Such a double penalty is commended neither by logic nor by fairness.

Milwaukee v. Cement Division, 515 U.S. 189, 194, 195–96, 198–99 (1995) (citations and internal quotation marks omitted).

The case then took its third trip through the trial court, where the amount of prejudgment interest had to be calculated. The trial judge wrote a detailed opinion, eventually concluding that the city owed interest at the prime rate from the date of the accident (Dec. 24, 1979) through the date of entry of judgment (Jan. 31, 1997),

2. Postjudgment interest, i.e., interest on judgments, is governed by 28 U.S.C. § 1961. Admiralty's rule on prejudgment interest is court-made. While the Seventh Circuit and Supreme Court opinions in *Cement Division* are limited by their terms to collision cases, the resulting rule—that a plaintiff assessed with a percentage of fault, even a big one, can still get prejudgment interest—is applicable to other types of maritime cases as well.

compounded annually. *Cement Division v. Milwaukee*, 950 F. Supp. 904 (E.D. Wis. 1996). Affirming, the Seventh Circuit noted that the prejudgment interest award came to $6,497,651. 144 F.3d 1111, 1113 (7th Cir. 1998).

East River Steamship Corp. v. Transamerica Delaval

Supreme Court of the United States, 1986

476 U.S. 858, 106 S. Ct. 2295, 90 L. Ed. 2d 865, 1986 AMC 2027

Justice BLACKMUN delivered the opinion of the unanimous Court.

In this admiralty case, we must decide whether a cause of action in tort is stated when a defective product purchased in a commercial transaction malfunctions, injuring only the product itself and causing purely economic loss. The case requires us to consider preliminarily whether admiralty law, which already recognizes a general theory of liability for negligence, also incorporates principles of products liability, including strict liability. Then, charting a course between products liability and contract law, we must determine whether injury to a product itself is the kind of harm that should be protected by products liability or left entirely to the law of contracts.

I.

In 1969, Seatrain Shipbuilding Corp. (Shipbuilding), a wholly owned subsidiary of Seatrain Lines, Inc. (Seatrain), announced it would build the four oil-transporting supertankers in issue—the *T.T. Stuyvesant*, *T.T. Williamsburgh*, *T.T. Brooklyn*, and *T.T. Bay Ridge*. * * * Shipbuilding in turn contracted with respondent, now known as Transamerica Delaval Inc. (Delaval), to design, manufacture, and supervise the installation of turbines (costing $1.4 million each) that would be the main propulsion units for the 225,000-ton $125 million supertankers. When each ship was completed, [it was chartered] to one of the [four] petitioners, also subsidiaries of Seatrain. * * *. Each petitioner operated under a bareboat charter, by which it took full control of the ship for 20 or 22 years as though it owned it, with the obligation afterwards to return the ship to the real owner. * * *

The *Stuyvesant* sailed on its maiden voyage in late July 1977. On December 11 of that year, as the ship was about to enter the Port of Valdez, Alaska, steam began to escape from the casing of the high-pressure turbine. That problem was temporarily resolved by repairs, but before long, while the ship was encountering a severe storm in the Gulf of Alaska, the high-pressure turbine malfunctioned. The ship, though lacking its normal power, was able to continue on its journey to Panama and then San Francisco. In January 1978, an examination of the high-pressure turbine revealed that the first-stage steam reversing ring virtually had disintegrated and had caused additional damage to other parts of the turbine. The damaged part was replaced with a part from the *Bay Ridge*, which was then under construction. In April 1978, the ship again was repaired, this time with a part from the *Brooklyn*. Finally, in August, the ship was permanently and satisfactorily repaired with a ring newly designed and manufactured by Delaval.

The *Brooklyn* and the *Williamsburgh* were put into service in late 1973 and late 1974, respectively. In 1978, as a result of the *Stuyvesant*'s problems, they were inspected while in port. Those inspections revealed similar turbine damage. Temporary repairs were made, and newly designed parts were installed as permanent repairs that summer.

When the *Bay Ridge* was completed in early 1979, it contained the newly designed parts and thus never experienced the high-pressure turbine problems that plagued the other three ships. [But] the *Bay Ridge* experienced a unique problem. In 1980, when the ship was on its maiden voyage, the engine began to vibrate with a frequency that increased even after speed was reduced. It turned out that the astern guardian valve, located between the high-pressure and low-pressure turbines, had been installed backwards. Because of that error, steam entered the low-pressure turbine and damaged it. After repairs, the *Bay Ridge* resumed its travels.

II.

The [four] charterers' * * * complaint, filed in the United States District Court for the District of New Jersey, invokes admiralty jurisdiction. It [alleges] tortious conduct on the part of respondent Delaval and seeks an aggregate of more than $8 million in damages for the cost of repairing the ships and for income lost while the ships were out of service. * * * Delaval * * * moved for summary judgment, contending that the charterers' actions were not cognizable in tort.

The District Court granted summary judgment for Delaval, and the Court of Appeals for the Third Circuit, sitting en banc, affirmed. The Court of Appeals held that damage solely to a defective product is actionable in tort if the defect creates an unreasonable risk of harm to persons or property other than the product itself, and harm materializes. Disappointments over the product's quality, on the other hand, are protected by warranty law. [ ] The charterers were dissatisfied with product quality: the defects involved gradual and unnoticed deterioration of the turbines' component parts, and the only risk created was that the turbines would operate at a lower capacity. [ ] Therefore, neither the negligence claim nor the strict-liability claim was cognizable.

* * *

Judge Becker largely agreed with the majority's approach, but would permit recovery for a "near miss," where the risk existed but no calamity occurred. He felt that the first count, concerning the *Stuyvesant*, stated a cause of action in tort. The exposure of the ship to a severe storm when the ship was unable to operate at full power due to the defective part created an unreasonable risk of harm.

We granted certiorari to resolve a conflict among the Courts of Appeals sitting in admiralty.

III.

* * *

The torts alleged * * * clearly fall within the admiralty jurisdiction. The claims satisfy the traditional "locality" requirement—that the wrong must have occurred on the high seas or navigable waters. [ ] The [complaint alleges] that the injury to the *Stuyvesant*'s high-pressure turbine and the *Bay Ridge*'s low-pressure turbine occurred while the ships were sailing on the high seas. The damage to the *Williamsburgh* and the *Brooklyn* * * * occurred at sea, and was discovered in port, also a maritime locale. [ ]

When torts have occurred on navigable waters within the United States, the Court has imposed an additional requirement of a "maritime nexus"—that the wrong must bear "a significant relationship to traditional maritime activity." [ ] We need not reach the question whether a maritime nexus also must be established when a tort occurs on the high seas. Were there such a requirement, it clearly was met here, for these ships were engaged in maritime commerce, a primary concern of admiralty law.

* * *

With admiralty jurisdiction comes the application of substantive admiralty law. [ ] Absent a relevant statute, the general maritime law, as developed by the judiciary, applies. [ ] Drawn from state and federal sources, the general maritime law is an amalgam of traditional common-law rules, modifications of those rules, and newly created rules. [ ] This Court has developed a body of maritime tort principles, see, e.g., *Kermarec* [*supra* at 131], and is now asked to incorporate products-liability concepts, long a part of the common law of torts, into the general maritime law. [ ]

The Courts of Appeals sitting in admiralty overwhelmingly have adopted concepts of products liability, based both on negligence [ ] and on strict liability [ ]. Indeed, the Court of Appeals for the Third Circuit previously had stated that the question whether principles of strict products liability are part of maritime law "is no longer seriously contested." [ ]

We join the Courts of Appeals in recognizing products liability, including strict liability, as part of the general maritime law. This Court's precedents relating to injuries of maritime workers long have pointed in that direction. See *Seas Shipping Co. v. Sieracki*, 328 U.S. 85, 94 (1946) (strict liability for unseaworthiness) * * *. The Court's rationale in those cases—that strict liability should be imposed on the party best able to protect persons from hazardous equipment—is equally applicable when the claims are based on products liability. [ ] And to the extent that products actions are based on negligence, they are grounded in principles already incorporated into the general maritime law. See *Kermarec* [*supra* at 131]. Our incorporation of products liability into maritime law, however, is only the threshold determination to the main issue in this case.

IV.

Products liability grew out of a public policy judgment that people need more protection from dangerous products than is afforded by the law of warranty. See *Seely v. White Motor Co.*, 403 P.2d 145, 149 (Cal. 1965). It is clear, however, that if this development were allowed to progress too far, contract law would drown in a sea of tort. [ ] We must determine whether a commercial product injuring itself is the kind of harm against which public policy requires manufacturers to protect, independent of any contractual obligation.

A.

The paradigmatic products-liability action is one where a product "reasonably certain to place life and limb in peril," distributed without reinspection, causes bodily injury. See, e.g., *MacPherson v. Buick Motor Co.*, 217 N.Y. 382 (1916). The manufacturer is liable whether or not it is negligent because "public policy demands that responsibility be fixed wherever it will most effectively reduce the hazards to life and health inherent in defective products that reach the market." [ ]

For similar reasons of safety, the manufacturer's duty of care was broadened to include protection against property damage. [ ] Such damage is considered so akin to personal injury that the two are treated alike. [ ]

In the traditional "property damage" cases, the defective product damages other property. In this case, there was no damage to "other" property. Rather, the [complaint alleges] that each supertanker's defectively designed turbine components damaged only the turbine itself. Since each turbine was supplied by Delaval as an integrated package, each is properly regarded as a single unit. "Since all but the very simplest of machines have component parts, [a contrary] holding would require a finding of 'property damage' in virtually every case where a product damages itself. Such a holding would eliminate the distinction between warranty and strict products liability." * * * Obviously, damage to a product itself has certain attributes of a products-liability claim. But the injury suffered—the failure of the product to function properly—is the essence of a warranty action, through which a contracting party can seek to recoup the benefit of its bargain.

B.

The intriguing question whether injury to a product itself may be brought in tort has spawned a variety of answers. At one end of the spectrum, the case that created the majority land-based approach, *Seely v. White Motor Co.* [ ] (defective truck), held that preserving a proper role for the law of warranty precludes imposing tort liability if a defective product causes purely monetary harm. [ ]

At the other end of the spectrum is the minority land-based approach, whose progenitor, *Santor v. A & M Karagheusian, Inc.*, 207 A.2d 305 (N.J. 1965) (marred carpeting), held that a manufacturer's duty to make nondefective products encompassed injury to the product itself, whether or not the defect created an unreasonable risk of harm. [ ] The courts adopting this approach, including the majority of the Courts of Appeals sitting in admiralty that have considered the issue, [ ] find that the safety and insurance rationales behind strict liability apply equally where the losses are purely economic. These courts reject the *Seely* approach because they find it arbitrary that economic losses are recoverable if a plaintiff suffers bodily injury or property damage, but not if a product injures itself. They also find no inherent difference between economic loss and personal injury or property damage, because all are proximately caused by the defendant's conduct. Further, they believe recovery for economic loss would not lead to unlimited liability because they think a manufacturer can predict and insure against product failure. [ ]

Between the two poles fall a number of cases that would permit a products-liability action under certain circumstances when a product injures only itself. These cases attempt to differentiate between "the disappointed users ... and the endangered ones," [ ] and permit only the latter to sue in tort. The determination has been said to turn on the nature of the defect, the type of risk, and the manner in which the injury arose. * * *

We find the intermediate and minority land-based positions unsatisfactory. The intermediate positions, which essentially turn on the degree of risk, are too indeterminate to enable manufacturers easily to structure their business behavior. Nor do we find persuasive a distinction that rests on the manner in which the product is injured. We realize that the damage may be qualitative, occurring through gradual deterioration or internal breakage. Or it may be calamitous. [ ] But either way, since by definition no person or other property is damaged, the resulting loss is purely economic. Even when the harm to the product itself occurs through an abrupt, accident-like event, the resulting loss due to repair costs, decreased value, and lost profits is essentially the failure of the purchaser to receive the benefit of its bargain—traditionally the core concern of contract law. [ ]

We also decline to adopt the minority land-based view espoused by *Santor* * * *. Such cases raise legitimate questions about the theories behind restricting products liability, but we believe that the countervailing arguments are more powerful. The minority view fails to account for the need to keep products liability and contract law in separate spheres and to maintain a realistic limitation on damages.

C.

Exercising traditional discretion in admiralty, see *Pope & Talbot* [*supra* at 122], we adopt an approach similar to *Seely* and hold that a manufacturer in a commercial relationship has no duty under either a negligence or strict products-liability theory to prevent a product from injuring itself.[6]

"The distinction that the law has drawn between tort recovery for physical injuries and warranty recovery for economic loss is not arbitrary and does not rest on the "luck" of one plaintiff in having an accident causing physical injury. The distinction rests, rather, on an understanding of the nature of the responsibility a manufacturer must undertake in distributing his products." *Seely* [ ]. When a product injures only itself the reasons for imposing a tort duty are weak and those for leaving the party to its contractual remedies are strong.

The tort concern with safety is reduced when an injury is only to the product itself. When a person is injured, the "cost of an injury and the loss of time or health may be an overwhelming misfortune," and one the person is not prepared to meet. [ ] In contrast, when a product injures itself, the commercial user stands to lose the value of the product, risks the displeasure of its customers who find that the product does not meet their needs, or, as in this case, experiences increased costs in performing a service. Losses like these can be insured. [ ] Society need not presume that a customer needs special protection. The increased cost to the public that would result from holding a manufacturer liable in tort for injury to the product itself is not justified. [ ]

Damage to a product itself is most naturally understood as a warranty claim. Such damage means simply that the product has not met the customer's expectations, or, in other words, that the customer has received "insufficient product value." [ ] The maintenance of product value and quality is precisely the purpose of express and implied warranties.[7] [ ] Therefore, a claim of a nonworking product can be brought as a breach-of-warranty action. * * *

Contract law, and the law of warranty in particular, is well suited to commercial controversies of the sort involved in this case because the parties may set the terms of their own agreements. The manufacturer can restrict its liability, within limits, by disclaiming warranties or limiting remedies. [ ] In exchange, the purchaser pays less for the product. Since a commercial situation generally does not involve large disparities in bargaining power, [ ] we see no reason to intrude into the parties' allocation of the risk.

* * *

In products-liability law, where there is a duty to the public generally, foreseeability is an inadequate brake. [ ] Permitting recovery for all foreseeable claims for purely economic loss could make a manufacturer liable for vast sums. It would be difficult for a manufacturer to take into account the expectations of persons downstream who may encounter its product. In this case, for example, if the charterers—already one step removed from the transaction—were permitted to recover their economic losses, then the companies that subchartered the ships might claim their economic losses from the delays, and the charterers' customers also might claim their economic losses, and so on. "The law does not spread its protection so far." *Robins Dry Dock & Repair Co. v. Flint*, 275 U.S. 303, 309 (1927).

* * *

---

6. We do not reach the issue whether a tort cause of action can ever be stated in admiralty when the only damages sought are economic. [ ] But see *Robins Dry Dock & Repair Co. v. Flint*, 275 U.S. 303 (1927).

7. If the charterers' claims were brought as breach-of-warranty actions, they would not be within the admiralty jurisdiction. Since contracts relating to the construction of or supply of materials to a ship are not within the admiralty jurisdiction, [ ] neither are warranty claims grounded in such contracts. [ ] State law would govern the actions. [ ] In particular the Uniform Commercial Code, which has been adopted by 49 States, would apply.

D.

For the first three [tankers], the defective turbine components allegedly injured only the turbines themselves. Therefore, a strict products-liability theory of recovery is unavailable to the charterers. * * *

* * *

Similarly, in the [*Bay Ridge*] count, alleging the reverse installation of the astern guardian valve, the only harm was to the propulsion system itself rather than to persons or other property. Even assuming that Delaval's supervision was negligent, as we must on this summary judgment motion, Delaval owed no duty under a products-liability theory based on negligence to avoid causing purely economic loss. [ ] Thus, whether stated in negligence or strict liability, no products-liability claim lies in admiralty when the only injury claimed is economic loss.

[W]e affirm the entry of judgment for Delaval.

* * *

Notes

1. Is the Court's statement that "[w]ith admiralty jurisdiction comes the application of substantive admiralty law" fully borne out by the materials in Section I–H, *supra* at 108–29?

2. The Court's holding is limited to "product[s] purchased in ... commercial transaction[s]," but most lower courts have concluded that it should apply against consumer plaintiffs as well. See, e.g., *Stanton v. Bayliner Marine Corp.*, 866 P.2d 15 (Wash. 1993).

3. The *East River* holding—precluding a tort action for damage to "the product itself"—invites litigation as to the precise identity of the product. See, e.g., *Sea-Land Service, Inc. v. General Electric Co.*, 134 F.3d 149 (3d Cir. 1998) (holding that a damaged diesel engine, rather than the component connecting rod that failed and damaged the rest of the engine, was the product, precluding tort recovery). The Supreme Court tackled this issue in *Saratoga Fishing Co.* v. *J.M. Martinac & Co.*, 520 U.S. 875 (1997), where a divided Court (6–3) held that fishing gear added to a vessel by the initial purchaser was not part of the "product itself" in the hands of a subsequent purchaser, although this gear would have been part of the product itself if it had been installed by the manufacturer. Dissenting, Justice Scalia said the majority probably got the wrong answer—he called his dissent on this point "diffident[ ]"—but stressed as his major point the inappropriateness of the grant of certiorari:

> The present case involves a relative detail of application of the *East River* holding. * * * It would have been better * * * not to grant certiorari in this case. By the time *East River* was decided, we had a wealth of lower-court development to draw upon. * * * We could be confident in our decision, knowing that it broke little new ground. * * * In the present case, by contrast, the Court sets sail into uncharted seas. * * * I would feel less uncomfortable about our plying these unknown waters if we were skilled navigators. But unlike state courts, we have little first-hand experience in the development of new common-law rules of tort and contract. * * * Better to have followed some state-court pilots than to proceed on our own—and even, perhaps, to lead state courts aground.

520 U.S. at 885–886.

4. As the *East River* Court's footnote 6 suggests, the prohibition against recovery in tort for damage to the product itself can be seen as part of a larger principle that some courts believe derives from the 1927 decision in *Robins Dry Dock.* (Recall the discussion of *Robins* in *Ballard Shipping, supra* at 111.) In *Robins,* the opinion of Justice Holmes for the Court held that a time charterer of a vessel could not recover loss-of-use damages from a dry dock that had the ship in for repairs and negligently damaged it. The narrow holding of *Robins* was that a defendant (the drydock) who negligently damages the plaintiff (the time charterer) only through interfering with the plaintiff's contractual arrangement with a third party (the shipowner) is not liable in tort. But in many courts *Robins* has been taken to stand for a much broader proposition, that there can be no recovery in negligence for economic loss from an accident that does not cause physical damage to the plaintiff's person or property. See, e.g., *Louisiana v. M/V Testbank,* 752 F.2d 1019 (5th Cir. 1985) (en banc).

B. Injuries to Seamen

1. Historical Introduction

The reported decisions indicate that nineteenth-century seamen led miserable lives. For insubordination, they might be flogged,[1] beaten,[2] locked up in irons,[3] or set ashore on a remote island.[4] When injured and disabled while doing their dangerous work, they might be thrown into a cramped bunk and left essentially unattended for weeks or even months until the vessel arrived at a convenient port.[5] If they came down with a contagious disease, they might be simply abandoned on a barren shore and left to die.[6] If they deserted, they could be arrested by public authorities and forcibly returned to the vessel.[7]

Congress took steps to ameliorate some of the worst abuses. It outlawed "cruel and unusual punishment" of sailors in 1835,[8] and in 1850 it abolished "flogging in the navy and

1. *Sheridan v. Furbur,* 21 Fed. Cas. 1266 (S.D.N.Y. 1834) (No. 12,761) ("seized up to the rigging ... and a dozen blows inflicted ... with a nine-thread rattling").

2. *Elwell v. Martin,* 8 Fed. Cas. 584 (D. Me. 1824) (No. 4,425) (dislocated shoulder). In *Gould v. Christianson,* 10 F.Cas. 857 (S.D.N.Y. 1836) (No. 5,636), the court deplored the necessity for corporal punishment of seaman and held that it should not have been inflicted on "a gentleman's son" who had ignored his father's advice and decided to sample the seafaring life.

3. *Jay v. Almy,* 13 Fed. Cas. 387 (C.C.D. Mass. 1846) (No. 7,236).

4. *Id.* (suspected mutineer put in irons and then left locked in a fort on an island in the Indian Ocean).

5. *The Rolph,* 293 F. 269, 272 (N.D. Cal. 1923) (after receiving a savage beating from a mate whom the court described as a "ferocious giant," the blinded victim requested medical treatment and was "brutally refused"); *The Margharita,* 140 F. 820 (5th Cir. 1905) (seaman who lost his leg to a "shark or other marine monster" was not taken to any accessible port for medical treatment but forced to wait four months until the ship had completed its voyage); *The Troop,* 118 F. 769, 770 (D. Wash. 1902) (cramming a seaman with a broken arm and a broken leg into a tiny bunk and leaving him to suffer there unattended was "a shocking instance of man's inhumanity to man"); *The City of Carlisle,* 39 F. 807, 811–12 (D. Ore. 1889) (master's treatment of 16-year-old apprentice seaman with a serious skull fracture was "brutal and indecent" and "simply inhuman").

6. *Tomlinson v. Hewett,* 24 Fed. Cas. 29 (D. Cal. 1872) (No. 14,087) (smallpox sufferer was tricked into going ashore at a place with no medical facilities and abandoned there).

7. *Robertson v. Baldwin,* 165 U.S. 275 (1897) (holding that statutes authorizing the arrest and forced return of deserters were not in conflict with the Thirteenth Amendment).

8. Act of March 3, 1835, 4 Stat. 777.

on board vessels of commerce."[9] Eventually it repealed the statutes authorizing the arrest of deserters. (Other legislation sought to require vessels to carry sufficient and wholesome food and suitable emergency medical supplies.) Today a master or officer who "flogs, beats, wounds, or without justifiable cause, imprisons any of the crew of [the] vessel, or withholds from them suitable food and nourishment, or inflicts upon them any corporal or other cruel and unusual punishment, shall be fined ... or imprisoned not more than five years, or both." 8 U.S.C. §2191. (The modern master does have statutory authority to confine disobedient seamen and to put them on limited rations. 46 U.S.C. §11501(4) and (5).) Today, the punishment for desertion is forfeiture of all wages. 46 U.S.C. §§10509. 11501(1).

The main protectors of seamen have been the federal admiralty courts. In *Harden v. Gordon*, 11 Fed. Cas. 480 (C.C.D. Me. 1823) (No. 6,047), Circuit Justice Story looked to Articles VI and VII of the Laws of Oleron[10] as authority for holding that "the expenses of sick seamen shall be borne by the ship." In the course of establishing this obligation and admiralty courts' authority and duty to enforce it, Story laid down a broad "wards of the admiralty" theme that has been a significant influence in the entire body of seamen's-injury jurisprudence:

> [The doctrine requiring shipowners to meet the medical needs of injured and ill seamen] appears to me so consonant with humanity, with sound policy, and with national interests, that it commends itself to my mind quite as much by its intrinsic equity, as by the sanction of its general authority. Seamen are by the peculiarity of their lives liable to sudden sickness from change of climate, exposure to perils, and exhausting labour. They are generally poor and friendless, and acquire habits of gross indulgence, carelessness, and improvidence. If some provision be not made for them in sickness at the expense of the ship, they must often in foreign ports suffer the accumulated evils of disease, and poverty, and sometimes perish from the want of suitable nourishment. Their common earnings in many instances are wholly inadequate to provide for the expenses of sickness; and if liable to be so applied, the great motives for good behaviour might be ordinarily taken away by pledging their future as well as past wages for the redemption of the debt. * * * On the other hand, if these expenses are a charge upon the ship, the interest of the owner will be immediately connected with that of the seamen. The master will watch over their health with vigilance and fidelity. He will take the best methods, as well to prevent diseases, as to ensure a speedy recovery from them. He will never be tempted to abandon the sick to their forlorn fate; but his duty, combining with the interest of his owner, will lead him to succor their distress, and shed a cheering kindness over the anxious hours of suffering and despondency. Beyond this, is the great public policy of preserving this important class of citizens for the commercial service and maritime defence of the nation. Every act of legislation which secures their healths, increases their comforts, and administers to their infirmities, binds them more strongly to their

9. Act of Sept. 28, 1850, 9 Stat. 515.

10. Article VI of the Laws of Oleron, 30 Fed. Cas. 1174: "* * * [I]f by the master's orders and commands any of the ship's company be in the service of the ship, and thereby happen to be wounded or otherwise hurt, in that case they shall be cured and provided for at the costs and charges of the said ship." Article VII: "If it happens that sickness seizes on any one of the mariners, while in the service of the ship, the master ought to set him ashore, to provide lodging and candlelight for him, and also to spare him one of the shipboys, or hire a woman to attend him, and likewise to afford such diet as is usual in the ship * * *"

country; and the parental law, which relieves them in sickness by fastening their interests to the ship, is as wise in policy, as it is just in obligation. Even the merchant himself derives an ultimate benefit from what may seem at first an onerous charge. It encourages seamen to engage in perilous voyages with more promptitude, and at lower wages. It diminishes the temptation to plunderage upon the approach of sickness; and urges the seamen to encounter hazards in the ship's service, from which they might otherwise be disposed to withdraw.

* * *

* * * Every court should watch with jealousy an encroachment upon the rights of seamen, because they are unprotected and need counsel; because they are thoughtless and require indulgence; because they are credulous and complying; and are easily overreached. But courts of maritime law have been in the constant habit of extending towards them a peculiar, protecting favor and guardianship. They are emphatically the wards of the admiralty; and though not technically incapable of entering into a valid contract, they are treated in the same manner, as courts of equity are accustomed to treat young heirs, dealing with their expectancies, wards with their guardians, and cestuis que trust with their trustees. They are considered as placed under the dominion and influence of men, who have naturally acquired a mastery over them; and as they have little of the foresight and caution belonging to persons trained in other pursuits of life, the most rigid scrutiny is instituted into the terms of every contract, in which they engage. If there is any undue inequality in the terms, any disproportion in the bargain, any sacrifice of rights on one side which are not compensated by extraordinary benefits on the other, the judicial interpretation of the transaction, is that the bargain is unjust and unreasonable, that advantage has been taken of the situation of the weaker party, and that pro tanto the bargain ought to be set aside as inequitable.

The Supreme Court has called seamen "wards of admiralty" in at least 24 decisions[11] (most recently in *Atlantic Sounding Co. v. Townsend*, 337 U.S. 404, 417 (2009)) (see *infra* at 259). See also *Air & Liquid Systems Corp. v. DeVries*, 139 S. Ct. 986, 995 (2019) (not using the term "wards of admiralty" but relying heavily on maritime law's "'special solicitude for the welfare' of those who undertake to 'venture upon hazardous and unpredictable sea voyages.'") (quoting *American Export Lines, Inc. v. Alvez*, 446 U.S. 274, 285 (1980)); but see *Dutra Group v. Batterton*, *infra* at 267 (describing seamen as historically having been "wards of the admiralty" but minimizing the current importance of the "special solicitude" doctrine).

The Osceola

Supreme Court of the United States, 1903
189 U.S. 158, 23 S. Ct. 463, 47 L. Ed. 760, 2000 AMC 1207

Mr. Justice BROWN delivered the opinion of the unanimous Court.

This was a libel in rem filed in the district court for the eastern district of Wisconsin, in admiralty, against the propeller *Osceola*, to recover damages for a personal injury

11. Robertson, *Punitive Damages in Maritime Law*, 70 La. L. Rev. 463, 479 n. 107 (2010).

sustained by one Patrick Shea, a seaman on board the vessel, through the negligence of the master.

The case resulted in a decree for the libellant, from which an appeal was taken by the owners to the circuit court of appeals, which certified to this court certain questions * * *.

* * * In the month of December, 1896, the vessel was on a voyage bound for the port of Milwaukee, and when within 3 miles of that port, and while in the open lake, the master of the vessel ordered the forward port gangway to be hoisted by means of the derrick, in order that the vessel might be ready to discharge cargo immediately upon arrival at her dock. At this time the vessel was proceeding at the rate of 11 miles an hour against a head wind of 8 miles an hour. Under the supervision of the mate, the crew, including the appellee, Patrick Shea, who was one of the crew, proceeded to execute the order of the master. The derrick was set in place to raise the gangway. As soon as the gangway was swung clear of the vessel, the front end was caught by the wind and turned outward broadside to the wind, and by the force of the wind was pushed aft and pulled the derrick over, which in falling struck and injured [Shea]. The negligence, if any there was, consisted solely in the order of the master that the derrick should be used and that the gangway should be hoisted while the vessel was yet in the open sea, when the operation might be impeded and interfered with by the wind. * * *

The questions of law upon which [the court of appeals] desired the advice and instruction of the Supreme Court are:

"First. Whether the vessel is responsible for injuries happening to one of the crew by reason of an improvident and negligent order of the master in respect of the navigation and management of the vessel.

"Second. Whether in the navigation and management of a vessel the master of the vessel and the crew are fellow servants.

"Third. Whether, as a matter of law, the vessel or its owners are liable to the appellee, Patrick Shea, who was one of the crew of the vessel, for the injury sustained by him by reason of the improvident and negligent order of the master of the vessel in ordering and directing the hoisting of the gangway at the time and under the circumstances declared; that is to say, on the assumption that the order so made was improvident and negligent."

* * *

In the view we take of this case, we find it necessary to express an opinion only upon the first and third questions * * *.

* * *

The statutes of the United States contain no provision upon the subject of the liability of the ship or her owners for damages occasioned by the negligence of the captain to a member of the crew; but in all but a few of the more recent cases the analogies of the English and Continental Codes have been followed, and the recovery limited to the wages and expenses of maintenance and cure. * * *

In *The Edith Godden*, 23 F. 43 (S.D.N.Y. 1885), the vessel was held liable in rem for personal injuries received from the neglect of the owner to furnish appliances adequate to the place and occasion where used; in other words, for unseaworthiness. This is * * * in line with English and American authorities holding owners to be responsible to the seamen for the unseaworthiness of the ship and her appliances. * * *

Upon a full review * * * of English and American authorities upon these questions, we think the law may be considered as settled upon the following propositions:

1. That the vessel and her owners are liable, in case a seaman falls sick, or is wounded, in the service of the ship, to the extent of his maintenance and cure, and to his wages, at least so long as the voyage is continued.

2. That the vessel and her owner are, both by English and American law, liable to an indemnity for injuries received by seamen in consequence of the unseaworthiness of the ship, or a failure to supply and keep in order the proper appliances appurtenant to the ship. *Scarff v. Metcalf*, 107 N. Y. 211, 13 N. E. 796 (1887).

3. That all the members of the crew, except, perhaps, the master, are, as between themselves, fellow servants, and hence seamen cannot recover for injuries sustained through the negligence of another member of the crew beyond the expense of his maintenance and cure.

4. That the seaman is not allowed to recover an indemnity for the negligence of the master, or any member of the crew, but is entitled to maintenance and cure, whether the injuries were received by negligence or accident.

It will be observed in these cases that a departure has been made from the Continental Codes in allowing an indemnity beyond the expense of maintenance and cure in cases arising from unseaworthiness. This departure originated in England in the merchants' shipping act of 1876, [ ] and in this country, in a general consensus of opinion among the circuit and district courts, that an exception should be made from the general principle before obtaining, in favor of seamen suffering injury through the unseaworthiness of the vessel. We are not disposed to disturb so wholesome a doctrine by any contrary decision of our own.

* * *

It results that the first and third questions must be answered in the negative.

Notes

1. By 1900, the land-based tort law in England and the United States had developed a set of doctrines that precluded most injured workers from any recovery from their employers. These included a very robust version of the defensive doctrine of proximate cause plus what was sometimes called the "unholy trinity" of affirmative defenses—assumption of risk, contributory negligence, and fellow servant. In response to the fact that tort law had little to offer them, injured industrial workers in Germany and England had been given the protection of workers' compensation statutes. See generally Epstein, *The Historical Origins and Economic Structure of Workers' Compensation Law*, 16 Ga. L. Rev. 775 (1982). And a movement toward adopting workers' compensation statutes was afoot in some of the United States. Seamen had something roughly comparable to workers' compensation in the maintenance and cure doctrine. The *Osceola* Court evidently felt that such protection—together with the nascent "indemnity" for unseaworthiness—was adequate.

2. But U.S. law soon took a different turn. At the same time that most industrial workers were coming under workers' compensation regimes, railroad workers were succeeding with another route to reform. In 1906 Congress passed the first version of an act designed to provide such workers with a relatively liberal negligence action against their employers. This act was declared unconstitutional—as beyond Congress's authority to regulate interstate commerce—in the *Employers' Liability Cases (Howard v. Illinois Central R. Co.)*, 207 U.S. 463 (1908). Congress rewrote the statute in 1908 to meet the Court's objections, and this

time it passed muster. *Second Employers' Liability Cases (Mondou v. N.Y., N.H. & H. R. Co.)*, 223 U.S. 1 (1912). Key portions of this statute, known as the Federal Employers Liability Act or FELA, 45 U.S.C. §§ 51–60, are set forth in the Statutory Supplement.

3. With some land-based workers getting a "modern" workers' compensation remedy and railroad workers getting a first-class tort remedy, seamen might have been falling behind. Congress seemed to think so. Section 20 of the Act to Promote the Welfare of American Seamen, approved March 4, 1915, c. 153, 38 Stat. 1164, 1185, provided:

> That in any suit to recover damages for any injury sustained on board vessel or in its service seamen having command shall not be held to be fellow servants with those under their authority.

This provision had only one conceivable purpose: to overrule *The Osceola* and thereby permit seamen to sue their employers for negligent injury. But, as the next case indicates, the Court had other ideas.

Chelentis v. Luckenbach Steamship Co.

Supreme Court of the United States, 1918
247 U.S. 372, 38 S. Ct. 501, 62 L. Ed. 1171

Mr. Justice McREYNOLDS delivered the opinion of the Court.

In December, 1915, petitioner was employed by respondent, a Delaware corporation, as fireman on board the steamship *J. L. Luckenbach*, which it then operated and controlled. While at sea, twenty-four hours out from New York, the port of destination, petitioner undertook to perform certain duties on deck during a heavy wind; a wave came aboard, knocked him down and broke his leg. He received due care immediately; when the vessel arrived at destination he was taken to the marine hospital, where he remained for three months; during that time it became necessary to amputate his leg. After discharge from the hospital, claiming that his injuries resulted from the negligence and an improvident order of a superior officer, he instituted a common-law action in Supreme Court, New York county, demanding full indemnity for damage sustained. The cause was removed to the United States District Court because of diverse citizenship. Counsel did not question seaworthiness of ship or her appliances, and announced that no claim was made for maintenance, cure, or wages. At conclusion of plaintiff's evidence the court directed verdict for respondent, and judgment thereon was affirmed by the Circuit Court of Appeals. * * *

* * *

[U]nless in some way there was imposed upon the owners a liability different from that prescribed by maritime law [under the rules laid down in *The Osceola*], petitioner could properly demand only wages, maintenance and cure. * * *

* * *

Section 20 of the [Act to Promote the Welfare of American Seamen] declares "seamen having command shall not be held to be fellow servants with those under their authority," and full effect must be given this whenever the relationship between such parties becomes important. But the maritime law imposes upon a shipowner liability to a member of the crew injured at sea by reason of another member's negligence without regard to their relationship; it was of no consequence therefore to petitioner whether or not the alleged negligent order came from a fellow servant; the statute is irrelevant. The language of the section discloses no intention to impose upon shipowners the same measure of liability for injuries suffered by the crew while at sea as the common law prescribes for employers in respect of their employees on shore.

The judgment of the court below is affirmed.

Mr. Justice Holmes concurs in the result.

Mr. Justice Pitney, Mr. Justice Brandeis, and Mr. Justice Clarke dissent.

Notes

1. Gilmore and Black characterize *Chelentis* as "giv[ing] Congress a lesson on 'how to read a case' [*The Osceola*] of a type familiar to any first term law student." GILMORE & BLACK, THE LAW OF ADMIRALTY 325 (2d ed. 1975).

2. In 1920 Congress responded to the lesson by enacting the statute presently known as the Jones Act. The Jones Act is set out in the Statutory Supplement. It is presently codified as 46 U.S.C. § 30104, which provides:

> A seaman injured in the course of employment, or, if the seaman dies from the injury, the personal representative of the seaman may elect to bring a civil action at law, with the right of trial by jury, against the employer. Laws of the United States regulating recovery for personal injury to, or death of, a railway employee apply to an action under this section.

The "railway employee" laws that the Jones Act incorporates by reference are the FELA, 45 U.S.C. §§ 51–60.

Panama Railroad Co. v. Johnson

Supreme Court of the United States, 1924
264 U.S. 375, 44 S. Ct. 391, 68 L. Ed. 748, 1924 AMC 551

Mr. Justice VAN DEVANTER delivered the opinion of the unanimous Court.[12]

This was an action by a seaman against his employer, the owner of the ship on which he was serving, to recover damages for personal injuries suffered at sea while he was ascending a ladder from the deck to the bridge in the course of his employment—the complaint charging that the injuries resulted from negligence of the employer in providing an inadequate ladder and negligence of the ship's officers in permitting a canvas dodger to be stretched and insecurely fastened across the top of the ladder and in ordering the seaman to go up the ladder. The employer was a New York corporation. [The seaman was a resident of the borough of Brooklyn, city and state of New York.] The ship was a domestic merchant vessel which at the time of the injuries was returning from an Ecuadorian port. The action was brought on the [law] side of a District Court of the United States, and the right of recovery was based expressly on section 20 of the [Act to Promote the Welfare of American Seamen, providing in pertinent part as follows:

> [A]ny seaman who shall suffer personal injury in the course of his employment may, at his election, maintain an action for damages at law, with the right of trial by jury, and in such action all statutes of the United States modifying or extending the common-law right or remedy in cases of personal injury to railway employees shall apply ...].

12. Editors' note: Justice Sutherland did not participate.

The defendant unsuccessfully demurred to the complaint and then answered. The issues were tried to the court and a jury; a verdict for the plaintiff was returned, and a judgment was entered thereon, which the Circuit Court of Appeals affirmed. The defendant prosecutes this writ of error.

* * *

The defendant objects that the statute whereon the plaintiff based his right of action is in conflict with § 2 of Article III of the Constitution, which extends the judicial power of the United States to "all cases of admiralty and maritime jurisdiction." Before coming to the particular grounds of the objection, it will be helpful to refer briefly to the purpose and scope of the constitutional provision as reflected in prior decisions.

As there could be no cases of "admiralty and maritime jurisdiction," in the absence of some maritime law under which they could arise, the provision presupposes the existence in the United States of a law of that character. Such a law or system of law existed in colonial times and during the Confederation, and commonly was applied in the adjudication of admiralty and maritime cases. It embodied the principles of the general maritime law, sometimes called the law of the sea, with modifications and supplements adjusting it to conditions and needs on this side of the Atlantic. The framers of the Constitution were familiar with that system and proceeded with it in mind. Their purpose was not to strike down or abrogate the system, but to place the entire subject—its substantive as well as its procedural features—under national control, because of its intimate relation to navigation and to interstate and foreign commerce. In pursuance of that purpose the constitutional provision was framed and adopted. Although containing no express grant of legislative power over the substantive law, the provision was regarded from the beginning as implicitly investing such power in the United States. Commentators took that view. Congress acted on it, and the courts, including this court, gave effect to it. Practically therefore the situation is as if that view were written into the provision. After the Constitution went into effect, the substantive law theretofore in force was not regarded as superseded or as being only the law of the several states, but as having become the law of the United States—subject to power in Congress to alter, qualify, or supplement it as experience or changing conditions might require. When all is considered, therefore, there is no room to doubt that the power of Congress extends to the entire subject and permits of the exercise of a wide discretion.

But there are limitations which have come to be well recognized. One is that there are boundaries to the maritime law and admiralty jurisdiction which inhere in those subjects and cannot be altered by legislation, as by excluding a thing falling clearly within them or including a thing falling clearly without. * * *

In this connection it is well to recall that the Constitution, by § 1 of Article III, declares that the judicial power of the United States shall be vested in one Supreme Court "and in such inferior courts as the Congress may from time to time ordain and establish," and, by § 8 of Article I, empowers the Congress to make all laws which shall be necessary and proper for carrying into execution the several powers vested in the government of the United States. Mention should also be made of the enactment by the first Congress * * * whereby the District Courts are given exclusive original jurisdiction "of all civil causes of admiralty and maritime jurisdiction, saving to suitors in all cases the right of a common-law remedy where the common law is competent to give it."

The particular grounds on which a conflict with § 2 of Article III is asserted are that the statute enables a seaman asserting a cause of action essentially maritime to withdraw it from the reach of the maritime law and the admiralty jurisdiction, and to have it determined according to the principles of a different system applicable to a distinct and irrelevant field * * *.

The statute is concerned with the relative rights and obligations of seamen and their employers arising out of personal injuries sustained by the former in the course of their employment. Without question this is a matter which falls within the recognized sphere of the maritime law, and in respect of which the maritime rules have differed materially from those of the common law applicable to injuries sustained by employees in nonmaritime service. But, as Congress is empowered by the constitutional provision to alter, qualify or supplement the maritime rules, there is no reason why it may not bring them into relative conformity to the common-law rules or some modification of the latter * * *. Not only so, but the constitutional provision interposes no obstacle to permitting rights founded on the maritime law or an admissible modification of it to be enforced as such through appropriate actions on the common-law side of the courts—that is to say, through proceedings in personam according to the course of the common law. [ ] This was permissible before the Constitution, and it is still permissible [citing the saving-to-suitors clause].

Rightly understood, the statute neither withdraws injuries to seamen from the reach and operation of the maritime law, nor enables the seamen to do so. On the contrary, it brings into that law new rules drawn from another system and extends to injured seamen a right to invoke, at their election, either the relief accorded by the old rules or that provided by the new rules. The election is between alternatives accorded by the maritime law as modified, and not between that law and some nonmaritime system.

The source from which the new rules are drawn contributes nothing to their force in the field to which they are translated. In that field their strength and operation come altogether from their inclusion in the maritime law. [ ] True, they are not in so many words made part of that law; but an express declaration is not essential to make them such. As originally enacted, section 20 was part of an act the declared purpose of which was "to promote the welfare of American seamen." It then provided that in suits to recover damages for personal injuries "seamen having command shall not be held to be fellow-servants with those under their authority," and in *Chelentis* [*supra* at 151] this court treated it as part of the maritime law, but held it did not disclose a purpose "to impose on shipowners the same measure of liability for injuries suffered by the crew while at sea as the common law prescribes for employers in respect of their employees on shore." After that decision the section was re-enacted in the amended form hereinbefore set forth * * *. In that form it makes applicable to personal injuries suffered by seamen in the course of their employment "all statutes of the United States modifying or extending the common-law right or remedy in cases of personal injury to railway employees." Thus its origin, environment and subject matter show that it is intended to, and does, bring the rules to which it refers into the maritime law.

But it is insisted that, even if the statute brings those rules into that law, it is still invalid in that it restricts the enforcement of right founded on them to actions at law, and thereby encroaches on the admiralty jurisdiction intended by the Constitution. It must be conceded that the construction thus sought to be put on the statute finds support in some of its words, and also that if it be so construed a grave question will arise respecting its constitutional validity. But, as this court often has held, "a statute must be construed, if fairly possible, so as to avoid not only the conclusion that it is unconstitutional but also grave doubts upon that score." [ ] The question arises, therefore, whether the statute is fairly open to such a construction. There may be room for diverging opinions about the answer, but we think the better view is that it should be in the affirmative.

The course of legislation, as exemplified in section 9 of the Judiciary Act of 1789 [ ] always has been to recognize the admiralty jurisdiction as open to the adjudication of all maritime cases as a matter of course, and to permit a resort to common-law remedies through appropriate proceedings in personam as a matter of admissible grace. It therefore is reasonable to believe that, had Congress intended by this statute to withdraw rights of action founded on the new rules from the admiralty jurisdiction and to make them cognizable only on the common-law side of the courts, it would have expressed that intention in terms befitting such a pronounced departure—that is to say, in terms unmistakably manifesting a purpose to make the resort to common-law remedies compulsory, and not merely permissible. But this was not done. On the contrary, the terms of the statute in this regard are not imperative but permissive. It says "may maintain" an action at law "with the right of trial by jury," the import of which is that the injured seaman is permitted, but not required, to proceed on the common-law side of the court with a trial by jury as an incident. The words "in such action" in the succeeding clause are all that are troublesome. But we do not regard them as meaning that the seaman may have the benefit of the new rules if he sues on the law side of the court, but not if he sues on the admiralty side. Such a distinction would be so unreasonable that we are unwilling to attribute to Congress a purpose to make it. A more reasonable view, consistent with the spirit and purpose of the statute as a whole, is that the words are used in the sense of "an action to recover damages for such injuries," the emphasis being on the object of the suit rather than the jurisdiction in which it is brought. So we think the reference is to all actions brought to recover compensatory damages under the new rules as distinguished from the allowances covered by the old rules, usually consisting of wages and the expense of maintenance and cure. [ ] In this view the statute leaves the injured seaman free under the general law [ ] to assert his right of action under the new rules on the admiralty side of the court. On that side the issues will be tried by the court, but if he sues on the common-law side there will be a right of trial by jury. So construed, the statute does not encroach on the admiralty jurisdiction intended by the Constitution, but permits that jurisdiction to be invoked and exercised as it has been from the beginning.

* * *

Judgment affirmed.

Notes

1. On the face of the version of the Jones Act quoted in the opinion, what did the words "in such action" refer to? Under the Court's construction of the statute, what do they refer to? Does the language of the present Jones Act (changed incident to the 2006 recodification whereby the Act, formerly 46 U.S.C. app. § 688(a), became the present 46 U.S.C. § 30104) bear the same construction?

2. The paragraph in which the Court treated the words "in such action" begins with a sentence stating that maritime cases go to nonadmiralty courts "as a matter of admissible grace." Can you translate that phrase?

3. Under the Court's reasoning, can Jones Act cases be maintained in state court?

4. The holding and most of the implications of *Panama R. Co.* are good law today. But one implication—that the injured seaman must elect between his traditional maritime

remedies (maintenance and cure and unseaworthiness) and the new Jones Act remedy—did not survive. As we saw *supra* at 81, *Fitzgerald v. United States Lines Co.,* 374 U.S. 16, 18 (1963), confirmed that seamen may "join in one complaint their Jones Act, unseaworthiness, and maintenance and cure claims when all the claims ... grow out of a single transaction or accident."

2. Maintenance and Cure

The happenstance that the United States Government was the defendant in the *Warren* and *Farrell* cases just below has no present relevance or legal significance. The plaintiffs were merchant seamen, not members of the Armed Forces. The Government-owned ships involved were being operated by private employers under agency service agreements with the War Shipping Administration.

Warren v. United States

Supreme Court of the United States, 1951
340 U.S. 523, 71 S. Ct. 432, 95 L. Ed. 503, 1951 AMC 416

Mr. Justice DOUGLAS delivered the opinion of the Court.

Petitioner seeks in this suit maintenance and cure from the United States, as owner of *S. S. Anna Howard Shaw.* Petitioner was a messman who went ashore on leave while the vessel was at Naples in 1944. He and two other members of the crew first did some sightseeing. Then the three of them drank one bottle of wine and went to a dance hall, where they stayed an hour and a half, dancing. There was a room adjoining the dance hall that overlooked the ocean. French doors opened onto an unprotected ledge which extended out from the building a few feet. Petitioner stepped to within 6 inches of the edge and leaned over to take a look. As he did so, he took hold of an iron rod which seemed to be attached to the building. The rod came off and petitioner lost his balance and fell, breaking a leg.

The District Court awarded maintenance. The [Second Circuit] Court of Appeals disallowed it. The case is here on certiorari.

The Shipowners' Liability Convention, [which was ratified by the Senate and made effective by proclamation of the President on October 29, 1939, 54 Stat. 1693, 1704], provides in Art. 2:

1. The shipowner shall be liable in respect of:

    (a) sickness and injury occurring between the date specified in the articles of agreement for reporting for duty and the termination of the engagement;

    (b) death resulting from such sickness or injury.

2. Provided that national laws or regulations may make exceptions in respect of:

    (a) injury incurred otherwise than in the service of the ship;

    (b) injury or sickness due to the wilful act, default or misbehaviour of the sick, injured or deceased person;

    (c) sickness or infirmity intentionally concealed when the engagement is entered into.

Petitioner's argument is twofold. He maintains first that under paragraph 1, a shipowner's duty to provide maintenance and cure is absolute and that the exceptions specified in paragraph 2 are not operative until a statute is enacted which puts them in force. He argues in the second place that, even if paragraph 2 is operative without an Act of Congress, his conduct was not due to a "wilful act, default or misbehaviour" within the meaning of that paragraph. An amicus curiae argues that the injury was not received "in the service of the ship" within the meaning of paragraph 2(a) of Art. 2.

There is support for petitioner's first point [ ]. But we think the preferred view is opposed. Our conclusion is that the exceptions permitted by paragraph 2 are operative by virtue of the general maritime law and that no Act of Congress is necessary to give them force.

The language of paragraph 2, in its ordinary range of meaning, easily permits that construction. It is "national laws or regulations" which may make exceptions. The term law in our jurisprudence usually includes the rules of court decisions as well as legislative acts. That was held in *Erie Railroad Co. v. Tompkins* [*supra* at 119] to be true of the phrase "The laws of the several states" as used in the first Judiciary Act. No reason is apparent why a more restricted meaning should be given "national laws or regulations." The purpose of the Convention would not be served by the narrow meaning. This Convention was a product of the International Labor Organization. Its purpose was to provide an international system of regulation of the shipowner's liability. That international system was aimed at providing a reasonable average which could be applied in any country. We find no suggestion that it was designed to adopt a more strict standard of liability than that which our maritime law provides. The aim indeed was not to change materially American standards but to equalize operating costs by raising the standards of member nations to the American level. * * * Our conclusion is that both paragraph 1 and paragraph 2 of Art. 2 state the standard of liability which legislative and decisional law define in particularity.

The District Court held that petitioner's degree of fault did not bar a recovery for maintenance and cure. The Court of Appeals thought otherwise. The question is whether the injury was "due to the wilful act, default or misbehaviour" of petitioner within the meaning of Art. 2 paragraph 2(b) of the Convention. The standard prescribed is not negligence but wilful misbehavior. In the maritime law it has long been held that while fault of the seaman will forfeit the right to maintenance and cure, it must be "some positively vicious conduct—such as gross negligence or willful disobedience of orders." [ ] In *Aguilar v. Standard Oil Co.*, 318 U.S. 724, 731 (1943), we stated the rule as follows:

> Conceptions of contributory negligence, the fellow-servant doctrine, and assumption of risk have no place in the liability or defense against it. Only some wilful misbehavior or deliberate act of indiscretion suffices to deprive the seaman of his protection.

The exception which some cases have made for injuries resulting from intoxication, see *Aguilar*, 318 U.S. at 731, has no place in this case. As the District Judge ruled, the amount of wine consumed hardly permits a finding of intoxication. Petitioner was plainly negligent. Yet we would have to strain to find the element of wilfulness or its equivalent. He sought to use some care when he looked down from the small balcony, as evidenced by his seizure of the iron bar for a handhold. His conduct did not measure up to a standard of due care under the circumstances. But we agree with the District Court that it was not wilful misbehavior within the meaning of the Convention.

Finally it is suggested that the injury did not occur "in the service of the ship," as that term is used in paragraph 2(a) of Art. 2 of the Convention. We held in *Aguilar* * * * that maintenance and cure extends to injuries occurring while the seaman is departing on or returning from shore leave though he has at the time no duty to perform for the ship. It is contended that the doctrine of that case should not be extended to injuries received during the diversions of the seaman after he has reached the shore. Mr. Justice Rutledge, speaking for the Court in the *Aguilar* case, stated the reasons for extending maintenance and cure to shore leave cases as follows (318 U.S. at 733–34):

> To relieve the shipowner of his obligation in the case of injury incurred on shore leave would cast upon the seaman hazards encountered only by reason of the voyage. The assumption is hardly sound that the normal uses and purposes of shore leave are "exclusively personal" and have no relation to the vessel's business. Men cannot live for long cooped up aboard ship without substantial impairment of their efficiency, if not also serious danger to discipline. Relaxation beyond the confines of the ship is necessary if the work is to go on, more so that it may move smoothly. No master would take a crew to sea if he could not grant shore leave, and no crew would be taken if it could never obtain it. * * * In short, shore leave is an elemental necessity in the sailing of ships, a part of the business as old as the art, not merely a personal diversion.
>
> The voyage creates not only the need for relaxation ashore, but the necessity that it be satisfied in distant and unfamiliar ports. If in those surroundings the seaman, without disqualifying misconduct, contracts disease or incurs injury, it is because of the voyage, the shipowner's business. That business has separated him from his usual places of association. By adding this separation to the restrictions of living as well as working aboard, it forges dual and unique compulsions for seeking relief wherever it may be found. In sum, it is the ship's business which subjects the seaman to the risks attending hours of relaxation on strange surroundings. Accordingly it is but reasonable that the business extend the same protections against injury from them as it gives for other risks of the employment.

This reasoning is as applicable to injuries received during the period of relaxation while on shore as it is to those received while reaching it. To restrict the liability along the lines suggested would be to whittle it down "by restrictive and artificial distinctions" as attempted in the *Aguilar* case. We repeat what we said there, "If leeway is to be given in either direction, all the considerations which brought the liability into being dictate it should be in the sailor's behalf."

Reversed.

Mr. Justice JACKSON and Mr. Justice CLARK dissent on the ground that the injuries were not sustained in the service of the ship. *Aguilar* [ ] held a seaman to be in the ship's service while going to or from the ship over premises at which the ship docked, even if the purpose of being ashore was leave from duty. The route of access was not the choice of the seaman, and access to the ship was held essential to the ship's service. But the choice of places of refreshment and varieties of entertainment are the sailor's own. Unless his employment is a policy of accident insurance while on leave, recovery cannot be sustained in this case. That might be a wise rule of law but we think it one that should depend on legislation.

Mr. Justice FRANKFURTER, dissenting.

* * *

The District Judge concluded that libellant had not acted "in reckless disregard of safety." The Court of Appeals for the Second Circuit unanimously reversed. It thought that "In the case at bar, the risk of serious injury or even death if the seaman should fall over the cliff, was obvious; and the requisite degree of care correspondingly higher. In the face of evident danger, the care which Warren took was very slight—a mere casual glance at the rod which he thought to be a 'lightning arrester or something of that type.' We think that a man who acts as he did under circumstances of danger does not show even a minimal degree of regard for the consequences of his act. Unless his ship is to be an insurer of his safety, he cannot recover against her."

I do not think the judgment of the Court of Appeals that the libellant's conduct was a "deliberate act of indiscretion" [ ] should be disturbed.

Notes

1. **Jurisdiction.** Maintenance and cure actions are not actions in tort, and they are within admiralty jurisdiction regardless of whether the injury or illness occurred on land or water. *O'Donnell v. Great Lakes Dredge & Dock Co.*, 318 U.S. 36, 42–43 (1943).

2. The *Warren* opinion describes the suit as seeking maintenance (room and board) and cure (medical care), but the district court awarded only maintenance. Presumably cure was furnished. Until 1982, the United States Public Health Service hospitals provided medical services to seamen at no cost to shipowners or seamen. At the behest of President Reagan, Congress eliminated these medical services and closed the Public Health Service Hospitals by the Omnibus Budget Reconciliation Act, Pub.L. No. 97-35, § 987, 95 Stat. 603 (1981), codified as amended at 42 U.S.C. § 248b.

3. **Service of the ship.** *Warren's* holding that shore leave is in the service of the ship causes problems in litigation involving "brownwater" seamen[13] such as roustabouts and roughnecks on jack-up rigs and other floatable oil drilling apparatus. Typically these workers serve on the "vessel" (rig) for a week or two and then go home for several days. The Fifth Circuit has determined that their time ashore is not to be analogized to shore leave. See *Baker v. Ocean Systems, Inc.*, 454 F.2d 379 (5th Cir. 1972) (fight in pool hall); *Sellers v. Dixilyn Corp.*, 433 F.2d 446 (5th Cir. 1970) (homeward-bound car trip); *Daughdrill v. Diamond M. Drilling Co.*, 447 F.2d 781 (5th Cir. 1971) (rig-bound car trip). But employer-provided transportation may be in the ship's service. *Vincent v. Harvey Well Service*, 441 F.2d 146 (5th Cir. 1971).

4. **The willful misconduct defense.** Judicial attitudes toward what the *Aguilar* Court called "the traditional instances [of disqualifying misconduct], venereal disease and injuries received as a result of intoxication," have been variable. *Koistinen v. American Export Lines*, 83 N.Y.S.2d 297 (City Court of New York 1948), is famous for its leniency (and attempted levity) respecting sexual misconduct. For a contrasting attitude, see *Ressler v. States Marine Lines, Inc.*, 517 F.2d 579 (2d Cir. 1975).

Cases denying maintenance and cure on the basis of the intoxication defense include *Barlow v. Pan Atlantic S.S. Corp.*, 101 F.2d 697 (2d Cir. 1939); *The S.S. Berwindglen*, 88 F.2d 125 (1st Cir. 1937); *Lortie v. American-Hawaiian S.S. Co.*, 78 F.2d 819 (9th Cir. 1935). But see *Garay v. Carnival Cruise Line*, 904 F.2d 1527 (11th Cir. 1990) (holding that intoxication could not constitute willful misconduct in light of the ship's tacit policy of permitting drunkenness); *The Quaker City*, 1 F. Supp. 840, 843 (E.D. Pa. 1931) (holding that "mere drunkenness does not forfeit the right" to maintenance and cure).

---

13. *Brownwater seamen* is jargon for workers who achieve seaman status through their work on rivers, see, e.g., Ross, As They Say on the River 12 (2d ed. 1997), or their connection with drilling rigs and other unorthodox vessels in the Gulf of Mexico, see, e.g., Maraist, Galligan & Maraist, Admiralty in a Nutshell 212 (6th ed. 2010). See generally *infra* Section II-D.

In the modern cases, the substance allegedly abused by the seaman will fairly often be a drug other than alcohol. See, e.g., *Silmon v. Can Do II, Inc.*, 89 F.3d 240 (5th Cir. 1996) (upholding denial of maintenance and cure on determining that the seaman's back injury was traceable to illegal intravenous drug use).

5. **The intentional concealment defense.** The leading case on the intentional concealment defense is *McCorpen v. Central Gulf S.S. Corp.*, 396 F.2d 547, 548–49 (5th Cir. 1968), which explained the matter as follows (citations omitted):

> Maintenance may be awarded by courts even where the seaman has suffered from an illness pre-existing his employment, but there is a general principle that it will be denied where he knowingly or fraudulently conceals his illness from the shipowner. In cases involving a pre-existing illness or other disability, the courts have made a distinction between nondisclosure and concealment. Where the shipowner does not require a pre-employment medical examination or interview, the rule is that a seaman must disclose a past illness or injury only when in his own opinion the shipowner would consider it a matter of importance. If the shipowner is unable to persuade the court or jury that the seaman could reasonably be expected to have considered his medical history a matter of importance, he will be liable for maintenance. He will be liable if it is found that there exists reasonable grounds for the seaman's good-faith belief that he was fit for duty. On the other hand, where the shipowner requires a seaman to submit to a pre-hiring medical examination or interview and the seaman intentionally misrepresents or conceals material medical facts, the disclosure of which is plainly desired, then he is not entitled to an award of maintenance and cure. Of course, the defense that a seaman knowingly concealed material medical information will not prevail unless there is a causal link between the pre-existing disability that was concealed and the disability incurred during the voyage.

In recent decades the intentional concealment defense has become increasingly litigious and controversial. See, e.g., *McMillan v. Tug Jane A. Bouchard*, 885 F. Supp. 452, 460 (E.D.N.Y. 1995) (discussing disagreement between the Second and Fifth Circuits as to the breadth and strength of the defense); *Brown v. Parker Drilling Offshore Corp.*, 444 F.3d 457 (5th Cir. 2006) (revealing disagreements within the Fifth Circuit over subjective versus objective measures of falsification); *Boudreaux v. Transocean Deepwater, Inc.*, 721 F.3d 723, 726–27 (5th Cir. 2013) (suggesting that *McCorpen* is inconsistent with Supreme Court and circuit-level holdings that a worker's fraud in procuring employment is not a defense to liability in FELA and Jones Act cases); see also Robertson, Sturley & Ammerman, *Recent Developments in Admiralty and Maritime Law*, 42 TUL. MAR. L.J. 373, 466-473 (2018).

6. **Asymptomatic illnesses.** The Shipowners' Liability Convention (*supra* at 156) says maintenance and cure are owed respecting "sickness and injury occurring" during the seaman's employment. *Calmar Steamship Corp. v. Taylor*, 303 U.S. 525, 527–30 (1938), famously proclaimed that the maintenance and cure obligation "does not rest upon negligence or culpability on the part of the owner or master," is not "restricted to those cases where the seamen's employment is the cause of the injury or illness," and thus cover any injury or illness that "*manifests itself* during [the] employment" (emphasis supplied).

For many decades it was taken as settled that the *Calmar* term "manifests itself" means something like "shows symptoms." But *Messier v. Bouchard Transportation*, 688 F.3d 78 (2d Cir. 2012), holds that a maintenance and cure plaintiff who can present medical evidence that the disease from which he is presently suffering *existed* within the plaintiff's body—albeit entirely asymptomatically—during a period of employment by the defendant is entitled to benefits unless the defendant can show that the disease preexisted the employment. *Messier* is likely to inspire quite a bit of litigation. Cf. also note 1 following *Farrell, infra* at 164.

Farrell v. United States

Supreme Court of the United States, 1949
336 U.S. 511, 69 S. Ct. 707, 93 L. Ed. 850, 1949 AMC 613

Mr. Justice JACKSON delivered the opinion of the Court.

Petitioner, a seaman, brought suit in admiralty to recover damages [for his employer's alleged negligence] under the Jones Act [46 U.S.C. § 30104] and [to recover] maintenance [and] cure * * * under [general] maritime law. The issue of negligence was decided against him by both courts below and the claim is abandoned here.

* * *

The facts which occasion maintenance and cure for this seaman are not in dispute. The claimant, 22 years of age and in good health, was a member of the Merchant Marine. He was in the service of the *S.S. James E. Haviland*, a merchant vessel owned and operated by the United States as a cargo and troopship. On February 5, 1944, she was docked at Palermo, Sicily, and Farrell was granted shore leave which required his return to the ship by 6 p.m. of the same day. He overstayed his leave and about eight o'clock began, in rain and darkness, to make his way to the ship. He became lost and was misdirected to the wrong gate, by which he entered the shorefront area about a mile from where the ship lay moored. The area generally was blacked out but petitioner's companion, forty or fifty feet away, saw him fall over a guard chain into a drydock which was lighted sufficiently for night work then in progress. Farrell was grievously injured.

He was treated without expense to himself in various government hospitals until June 30, 1944, when he was discharged at Norfolk, Virginia, as completely disabled. He is totally and permanently blind and suffers post-traumatic convulsions which probably will become more frequent and are without possibility of further cure. From time to time he will require some medical care to ease attacks of headaches and epileptic convulsions. The [United States District Court for the Southern District of New York] concluded that the duty of a shipowner to furnish maintenance and cure does not extend beyond the time when the maximum cure possible has been effected [and the Second Circuit affirmed]. Petitioner contends that he is entitled to maintenance as long as he is disabled, which in this case is for life.

Admittedly there is no authority in any statute or American admiralty decisions for the proposition that he is entitled to maintenance for life. But an argument is based upon the ancient authority of Cleirac, Jugmens d'Oleron, Arts. 6 and 7 and notes by Cleirac [ ], to which American authorities have paid considerable respect. [ ] A translation of the note relied upon reads:

> If in defending himself or fighting against an enemy or corsairs, a mariner is maimed, or disabled to serve on board a ship for the rest of his life, besides the charge of his cure, he shall be maintained as long as he lives at the cost of the ship and cargo. Vide the Hanseatic Law, Art. 35.

Article 35 of the Laws of the Hanse Towns referred to reads:

> Art. XXXV. The seamen are obliged to defend their ship against rovers, on pain of losing their wages; and if they are wounded, they shall be healed and cured at the general charge of the concerned in a common average. If anyone of them is maimed and disabled he shall be maintained as long as he lives by a like average.

We need not elaborate upon the meanings or weight to be given to these medieval pronouncements of maritime law. As they show, they were written when pirates were not operatic characters but were real-life perils of the sea. When they bore down on a ship, all was lost unless the seaman would hazard life and limb in desperate defense. If they saved the ship and cargo, it was something in the nature of salvage and for their sacrifice in the effort a contribution on principles of average may have been justly due. Perhaps more than humanitarian considerations, inducement to stand by the ship generated the doctrine that saving the ship and her cargo from pirates entitles the seaman to lifelong maintenance if he is disabled in the struggle.

But construe the old-time law with what liberality we will, it cannot be made to cover the facts of this case. This ship was not beset but was snug at berth in a harbor that had capitulated to the United States and her allied forces six months before. No sea rovers, pirates or corsairs appeared to have menaced her. It is true that the ship was engaged in warlike operations and was a legitimate target for enemy aircraft or naval vessels, which made her service a war risk, but at that time and place no enemy attack was in progress or imminent. Even if we pass all this and assume the ship always to have been in potential danger and in need of defense, this seaman at the time of his injury had taken leave of her and he is in no position to claim that he was a sacrifice to her salvation. Far from helping to man the ship at the moment, he was unable to find her; he was lost ashore and not able adequately to take care of himself. However patriotic his motive in enlisting in the service and however ready he may have been to risk himself for his country, we can find no rational basis for awarding lifetime maintenance against the ship on the theory that he was wounded or maimed while defending her against enemies.

It is claimed, however, even if the basis for a lifetime award does not exist, that he is entitled to maintenance and cure beyond the period allowed by the courts below. This is based largely upon statements in the opinion of the Court in *Calmar Steamship Corp. v. Taylor*, 303 U.S. 525, 530 (1938). There the question as stated by the Court was whether the duty of a shipowner to provide maintenance and cure for a seaman falling ill of an incurable disease while in its employ, extends to the payment of a lump-sum award sufficient to defray the cost of maintenance and cure for the remainder of his life. The Court laid aside cases where incapacity is caused by the employment and said, "We can find no basis for saying that, if the disease proves to be incurable, the duty extends beyond a fair time after the voyage in which to effect such improvement in the seaman's condition as reasonably may be expected to result from nursing, care, and medical treatment. This would satisfy such demands of policy as underlie the imposition of the obligation. Beyond this we think there is no duty, at least where the illness is not caused by the seaman's service."

It is claimed that when the Court reserved or disclaimed any judgment as to cases where the incapacity is caused "by the employment" or "by the seaman's service" it recognized or created such cases as a separate class for a different measure of maintenance and cure. We think no such distinction exists or was premised in the *Calmar* case. In *Aguilar* [*supra* at 157–158] the Court pointed out that logically and historically the duty of maintenance and cure derives from a seaman's dependence on his ship, not from his individual deserts, and arises from his disability, not from anyone's fault. We there refused to look to the personal nature of the seaman's activity at the moment of injury to determine his right to

[an] award. Aside from gross misconduct or insubordination, what the seaman is doing and why [and] how he sustains injury does not affect his right to maintenance and cure, however decisive it may be as to claims for indemnity or for damages for negligence. He must, of course, at the time be "in the service of the ship," by which is meant that he must be generally answerable to its call to duty rather than actually in performance of routine tasks or specific orders.

It has been the merit of the seaman's right to maintenance and cure that it is so inclusive as to be relatively simple, and can be understood and administered without technical considerations. It has few exceptions or conditions to stir contentions, cause delays, and invite litigations. The seaman could forfeit the right only by conduct whose wrongful quality even simple men of the calling would recognize—insubordination, disobedience to orders, and gross misconduct. On the other hand, the Master knew he must maintain and care for even the erring and careless seaman, much as a parent would a child. For any purpose to introduce a graduation of rights and duties based on some relative proximity of the activity at time of injury to the "employment" or the "service of the ship" would alter the basis and be out of harmony with the spirit and function of the doctrine and would open the door to the litigiousness which has made the landman's remedy so often a promise to the ear to be broken to the hope.

Nor is it at all clear to us what this particular litigant could gain from introduction of the distinction for which contention is made. If we should concede that larger measure of maintenance is due those whose injury is caused by the nature of their employment, it would seem farfetched to hold it applicable here. Claimant was disobedient to his orders and for his personal purposes overstayed his shore leave. His fall into a drydock that was sufficiently lighted for workmen to be carrying on repairs to a ship therein was due to no negligence but his own. These matters have not been invoked to forfeit or reduce his usual seaman's right, but it is difficult to see how such circumstances would warrant enlargement of it. We hold that he is entitled to the usual measure of maintenance and cure at the ship's expense, no less and no more.

* * *

Maintenance and cure is not the only recourse of the injured seaman. In an appropriate case he may obtain indemnity or compensation for injury due to negligence or unseaworthiness and may recover, by trial before court and jury, damages for partial or total disability. But maintenance and cure is more certain if more limited in its benefits. It does not hold a ship to permanent liability for a pension, neither does it give a lump-sum payment to offset disability based on some conception of expectancy of life. Indeed the custom of providing maintenance and cure in kind and concurrently with its need has had the advantage of removing its benefits from danger of being wasted by the proverbial improvidence of its beneficiaries. The Government does not contend that if Farrell receives future treatment of a curative nature he may not recover in a new proceeding the amount expended for such treatment and for maintenance while receiving it.

The need of this seaman for permanent help is great and his plight most unfortunate. But as the evidence has afforded no basis for supplying that need by finding negligence, neither does the case afford a basis for distortion of the doctrine of maintenance and cure. This seaman was in the service of the United States and extraordinary measures of relief while not impossible are not properly addressed to the courts.

* * *

[Justices Douglas, Black, Murphy, and Rutledge dissented.]

Notes

1. **Is the maximum medical recovery rule stable?** The relatively conservative duration rule expressed in *Farrell* remains in place, but it is recurrently controversial. In *Vella v. Ford Motor Co.,* 421 U.S. 1, 5 (1975), the Court held that the "maintenance and cure [obligation] continues until such time as the [seaman's] incapacity is [medically] declared to be permanent." Taking *Vella* as having "reiterated" the maximum medical recovery rule articulated in *Farrell,* the en banc Third Circuit reversed two panel decisions that had allowed maintenance for seamen who, like Farrell, had no expectation of further medical improvement but who needed medical and nursing assistance to alleviate suffering and slow the deterioration process. *Cox v. Dravo Corp.*, 517 F.2d 620, 623 (3d Cir. 1975) (en banc). See also *Whitman v. Miles*, 387 F.3d 68, 72 (1st Cir. 2004) (holding that the employer's obligation ended on the date after which "[t]he testimony of the doctors for both parties leaves no genuine issue of material fact that Whitman's treatment [after that date] would, at best, slow or arrest the procession of her [multiple sclerosis], but would not reverse her symptoms or improve her condition beyond the point of maximum medical recovery.").

But see *Costa Crociere v. Rose*, 939 F. Supp. 1538 (S.D. Fla. 1996), holding that a seaman who needed dialysis or a kidney transplant had not reached maximum medical improvement since both continued dialysis and a transplant would offer the possibility of betterment. *Costa Crociere* well illustrates that the duration issue is recurrently litigious because of "the fuzzy boundary between improvement and palliation." *In re RJF Int'l Corp.*, 354 F.3d 104, 107 (1st Cir. 2004). See also *Haney v. Miller's Launch, Inc.*, 773 F. Supp. 2d 280, 283 (E.D.N.Y. 2010):

> Does medical treatment to reduce pain and suffering come within the definition of "cure?" While the law in this circuit is unclear, and the law of other circuits as well as tradition suggests the answer is "no," changes in the view of the medical profession and the public on the subject of pain amelioration answer "yes." The cost of palliative medical attention to reduce pain, even after physical injuries have been corrected to the extent practicable, should be included in treatment and cure of injured seamen.

Cf. also note 6 following *Warren*, *supra* at 160.

2. **The burden of proof on the maximum medical recovery issue.** Without directly addressing the point, both *Farrell* and *Vella* imply that it is the employer's burden to establish the maximum medical recovery point. Scattered district court decisions looking the other way appear to be outliers.

Maintenance Rates

Maintenance is meant to provide for the cost of food and lodging comparable in quality to what the seaman would have had on the ship. In the 1940s and '50s, courts "fell into the habit" of awarding $8.00 a day. *Incandela v. American Dredging Co.*, 659 F.2d 11, 14 (2d Cir. 1981). Nowadays union contracts often specify a maintenance rate, usually a relatively low one. Most of the circuits have long upheld the validity of such contracts. See *Macedo v. F/V Paul & Michelle*, 868 F.2d 519 (1st Cir. 1989) ($10); *Ammar v. United States*, 342 F.3d 133 (2d Cir. 2003) ($8); *Baldassaro v. United States*, 64 F.3d 206 (5th Cir. 1995) ($8); *Skowronek v. American Steamship Co.*, 505 F.3d 482 (6th Cir. 2007) ($8); *Gardiner v. Sea-Land Service, Inc.*, 786 F.2d 943 (9th Cir. 1986); *Frederick v. Kirby Tankships,*

Inc., 205 F.3d 1277 (11th Cir. 2000) ($15). For almost 30 years, the Third Circuit was the lone holdout. See *Barnes v. Andover Co.*, 900 F.2d 630, 640 (3d Cir. 1990) (holding that "it is inconsistent both with the traditional doctrine of maintenance and with our rejection of preemption of maintenance by the labor laws to hold that the maintenance rate set in the collective bargaining agreement is binding on a seaman who can show higher daily expenses."). In *Joyce v. Maersk Line Ltd.*, 876 F.3d 502, 509-510 (3d Cir. 2017), the Third Circuit rejected *Barnes* and adopted the majority rule.

In cases not constrained by union agreements, courts will receive evidence of the costs of food and lodging. Often the seaman's own testimony suffices. Amounts vary widely. The federal district court in New Orleans recently ordered an employer to raise its voluntary daily rate from $15 to $40.[14] A federal magistrate judge in the Eastern District of New York calculated the lodging costs of a seaman who lived in rural Virginia at $45 per day for a period when he owned a home and had mortgage and utility payments, and at $21 per day for the ensuing period when he lived in rented premises after he lost the house.[15] The federal district court in Massachusetts upheld a jury award that included the full amount of the seaman's mortgage payments ($36.67 per day) plus $58 per day for other expenses.[16]

Damages for Failure to Provide Maintenance and Cure

An employer who erroneously but without negligence or other fault fails to furnish maintenance or cure that a court ultimately determines was due will be held liable only for the unpaid benefits. *Morales v. Garijak, Inc.*, 829 F.2d 1355, 1358 (5th Cir. 1987). Under the "American rule," the attorneys' fees the seaman incurs in this situation are the seaman's own problem. See generally Robertson, *Court-Awarded Attorneys' Fees in Maritime Cases: The "American Rule" in Admiralty*, 27 J. MAR. L. & COM. 507 (1996).

If the employer is negligent in withholding the maintenance and cure—*viz.*, if it turns out that there was no "reasonable defense"—then the liability imposed will include any compensatory damages (e.g., enhancement of the illness or injury, costs of finding alternative medical care, pain and suffering) that the seaman can show proximately resulted from the employer's failure to pay. *Morales*, *supra*, 829 F.2d at 1358; *The Iroquois*, 194 U.S. 240 (1904). Here again, the winning plaintiff's attorneys' fees remain the plaintiff's own problem.

If the employer's failure to provide maintenance or cure was more blameworthy than that—if it was arbitrary, callous, capricious, egregious, indifferent, intentional, recalcitrant, wanton, or willful[17]—then the award can include attorneys' fees, *Vaughan v. Atkinson*, 369 U.S. 527 (1962), and punitive damages, *Atlantic Sounding Co. v. Townsend*, 557 U.S. 404 (2009). See *infra* at 259.

Unearned Wages

Statutes require a seaman's *earned* wages to be paid periodically upon demand and upon termination of the seaman's employment and set forth a penalty of "2 days' wages for each

14. Robertson & Sturley, *Recent Developments in Admiralty and Maritime Law*, 36 TUL. MAR. L.J. 425, 493 (2012).

15. Robertson & Sturley, *Recent Developments in Admiralty and Maritime Law*, 33 TUL. MAR. L.J. 381, 408 (2009).

16. *Id.* at 408–09.

17. These are but some of the "pejorative adjectives" courts have used in this context, all of them aiming at connoting "a wanton and intentional disregard of a seaman's rights." *Kraljic v. Berman Enterprises, Inc.*, 575 F.2d 412, 416 (2d Cir. 1978).

day payment is delayed" without sufficient cause. 46 U.S.C. §§ 10313(g), 10504(c). In *Griffin v. Ocean Contractors, Inc.* 458 U.S. 564 (1982), an employer who lacked sufficient cause for withholding $412.50 was assessed the statutory penalty; it came to more than $300,000.

Unearned wages is a conceptually different matter. "The right to the wages [an injured or ill] seaman would have earned if he had been able to complete the contractual terms of employment, usually to work until the end of the voyage, has been viewed as incident to maintenance and cure and traditionally considered part of the right." *Barnes v. Andover Co.*, 900 F.2d 630, 634 n.2 (3d Cir. 1990). The association of the seaman's rights to maintenance, cure, and unearned wages has been traced as far back as "the seventh article of the laws of Oleron." *Walton v. The Neptune*, 29 Fed. Cas. 142, 142–43 (No. 17,135) (D. Pa. 1800).

In *Farrell, supra* at 161, the Court split on the measure of the unearned wages due the injured seaman. As the majority described the situation, 336 U.S. at 520:

> [The articles of employment signed by Farrell] were on a printed form which left a vacant space subject to the following footnote: "Here the nature of the voyage is to be described and the places named at which the ship is to touch; or if that cannot be done, the general nature and probable length of the voyage is to be stated, and the port or country at which the voyage is to terminate." [For wartime security reasons, the *Haviland*'s articles] did not describe the voyage in such terms but provided, "from the port of Philadelphia, to a port in the Atlantic Ocean to the eastward of Philadelphia and thence to such ports and places in any part of the world as the Master may direct or as may be ordered or directed by the United States Government or any department, commission, or agency thereof ... and back to a final port of discharge in the United States, for a term of time not exceeding 12 (twelve) calendar months."

Farrell signed the articles and joined the vessel on December 16, 1943. His accident occurred on February 5, 1944. The voyage ended at New York on March 28, 1944. The majority determined that the voyage rule applied and meant that unearned wages did not accrue past March 28:

> It is not questioned that the general custom in ships, other than the coastwise trade, is to sign on for a voyage rather than for a fixed period. * * * The contract is not an uncommon form and complied with war-time requirements as to voyage contracts. We think, in the light of the custom of the industry and the condition of the times, there is nothing ambiguous about it and that it obligated the petitioner only for the voyage on which the ship was engaged when he signed on and that, when it terminated at a port of discharge in the United States, he could not have been required to reimbark for a second voyage. The twelve-month period appears as a limitation upon the duration of the voyage and not as a stated period of employment.

The dissenters thought Farrell should have been awarded unearned wages through December 15, 1944:

> If this were a coastwise voyage, there would be little question that Farrell could recover his wages for the entire twelve-month period.... [T]he principle of [the coastwise cases] is likewise applicable to foreign voyages. [ ] Any difference is not apparent. In each [situation] the seaman binds himself for the period. The obligation to pay wages should be coterminous with that responsibility. [ ] The number of voyages made is therefore immaterial. It is the extent of the voyage that could be demanded that is controlling.

3. The Negligence Cause of Action Provided by the Jones Act

As we saw in Section II-B-1, *supra* at 146–56, the Jones Act, 46 U.S.C. § 30104, was enacted in 1920 to overrule the portion of *The Osceola* holding that seamen have no cause of action for injuries resulting from the negligence of their employers. It provides:

> A seaman injured in the course of employment or, if the seaman dies from the injury, the personal representative of the seaman may elect to bring a civil action at law, with the right of trial by jury, against the employer. Laws of the United States regulating recovery for personal injury to, or death of, a railway employee apply to an action under this section.

The second sentence of the Act incorporates by reference the Federal Employers' Liability Act (FELA), 45 U.S.C. §§ 51–60. Remember that *Panama Railroad Co.*, *supra* at 152, holds that the Jones Act plaintiff can sue in admiralty as well as "at law."

The Jones Act and FELA generate abundant litigation, and the decisional law is full of substantive,[18] remedial,[19] and procedural[20] peculiarities. In this subsection we are concerned with the main features of the statutory scheme: the issues of coverage, employer fault, causation, and victim fault.

Jones Act Coverage

The Act's principal coverage limitations are the "seaman" and "course of employment" requirements.[21] Seaman status is treated *infra* in Section II-B-5, at 189–99. Note that there is no requirement that the injury occur on navigable water: *O'Donnell v. Great Lakes Dredge & Dock Co.*, 318 U.S. 36, 41–42, 43 (1943), holds that a vessel's crew member injured while on land engaged in the vessel's work is entitled to the Jones Act remedy because "[f]rom its dawn, the maritime law has recognized the seaman's right to maintenance and cure for injuries suffered in the course of his service to his vessel, whether occurring on sea or on land," and "the Jones Act, in extending a right of recovery to the seaman injured while in the service of his vessel by negligence, has done no more than

---

18. See, e.g., the FELA decisions on emotional injuries: *Norfolk & Western Ry. Co. v. Ayers*, 538 U.S. 135 (2003); *Metro-North Commuter R. Co. v. Buckley*, 521 U.S. 424 (1997); *Consolidated Rail Corp. v. Gottshall*, 512 U.S. 532 (1994). See, e.g., the Jones Act decisions on intentional harms: *Jamison v. Encarnacion*, 281 U.S. 635 (1930); *Cash v. Tidewater Marine, Inc.*, 34 F. Supp. 2d 448 (S.D. Tex. 1999).

19. See, e.g., *Cortes v. Baltimore Insular Line*, 287 U.S. 367 (1932) (holding that a shipowner's tortious breach of the duty to provide medical care to an injured seaman can be litigated under the Jones Act or as a straight maintenance-and-cure action, at the plaintiff's option); *Plamals v. The Pinar Del Rio*, 277 U.S. 151 (1928) (holding that the Jones Act cannot be asserted in an in rem action, i.e., that the Act does not give rise to a maritime lien).

20. See, e.g., Robertson & Sturley, *The Right to a Jury Trial in Jones Act Cases: Choosing the Forum Versus Choosing the Procedure*, 30 J. Mar. L. & Com. 649 (1999) (criticizing cases holding that a Jones Act plaintiff has an indefeasible right to choose between bench and jury trial). See also Robertson & Sturley, *Understanding Panama Railroad Co. v. Johnson: The Supreme Court's Interpretation of the Seaman's Elections Under the Jones Act*, 14 U.S.F. Mar. L.J. 229 (2002).

21. Note that the Act also requires the Jones Act defendant to be the plaintiff's "employer." The point becomes litigious when a vessel's crew member is nominally employed by one entity but actually operating under the direction and control of another entity. See, e.g., *Spinks v. Chevron Oil Co.*, 507 F.2d 216, 225 (5th Cir. 1975) (noting that in such circumstances "a seaman may have more than one Jones Act employer.").

supplement the remedy of maintenance and cure for injuries suffered by the seaman, whether on land or sea."[22]

Braen v. Pfeifer Oil Transportation Co., 361 U.S. 129 (1959), holds that a seaman does not step out of the "course of employment" when temporarily assigned by his employer to a job that is unrelated to his regular vessel-based duties. The *Braen* holding seems unassailable, but the opinion (by Justice Douglas) included a potentially troublesome dictum:

> *Aguilar* [*supra* at 157–58] recognized that a seaman is as much in the service of his ship when boarding it on first reporting for duty, quitting it on being discharged, or going to and from the ship while on shore leave, as he is while on board at high sea. We also held that a seaman injured in a dance hall while on shore leave was in the service of his ship in *Warren* [*supra* at 156]. These two cases were not brought under the Jones Act but involved maintenance and cure. Yet they make clear that the scope of a seaman's employment or the activities which are related to the furtherance of the vessel are not measured by the standards applied to land-based employment relationships. They also supply relevant guides to the meaning of the term "course of employment" under the [Jones] Act since it is the equivalent of the "service of the ship" formula used in maintenance and cure cases.

The proclaimed "equivalen[ce]" of the "course of employment" and "service of the ship" formulas is questionable, so much so that some lower courts have refused to adhere to it. See *Colon v. Apex Marine Corp.*, 832 F. Supp. 508 (D.R.I. 1993), *aff'd per curiam*, 35 F.3d 16 (1st Cir. 1994) (refusing to follow the *Braen* dictum and citing other cases for the view that the Jones Act course-of-employment requirement should be more restrictive than the service-of-ship concept used in maintenance and cure cases).

Gautreaux v. Scurlock Marine, Inc.

United States Court of Appeals, Fifth Circuit, 1997 (en banc)
107 F.3d 331, 1997 AMC 1521

DUHÉ, Circuit Judge:

* * *

Archie Scurlock, as President and owner of Scurlock Marine, Inc., ("Scurlock Marine") purchased the *M/V Brooke Lynn* in May, 1993, and retained Lance Orgeron as her first and permanent captain. Scurlock hired Charles Gautreaux as the *Brooke Lynn*'s relief captain in October, 1993. * * *

The *Brooke Lynn* is * * * equipped with two towing winches on her bow, which are used to secure lines joining the *Brooke Lynn* to the barges in her tow. The starboard side winch is hydraulic, and the port side winch is electric. Upon being hired, Gautreaux was taken to the *Brooke Lynn* and instructed on her operation by Archie Scurlock. Orgeron took Gautreaux on a tour of the vessel, showing him her layout and familiarizing him with her equipment. Orgeron showed Gautreaux the manual crank handle that accompanied the port side electric winch and told him that it was to be used to override the electric switches on the winch if they failed. Orgeron explained that, if the winch became "bound up" and failed to engage by use of the electric ignition switch, the manual

22. *O'Donnell* makes the Jones Act a stand-alone basis for admiralty jurisdiction and extends the Act's coverage to injuries sustained by seamen in the course of their employment while on land.

crank should be attached to the winch motor and turned a few times to "unbind" the winch, and then the electric ignition switch should be used to try to engage the winch. Neither Scurlock nor Orgeron told Gautreaux that if he needed to use the manual crank handle to unbind the winch, he should not leave it on the winch motor when attempting to engage the winch by use of the electric ignition switch.

About four months after he was hired, Gautreaux, serving as captain of the *Brooke Lynn*, relieved the tanker man on duty and began off loading of the barge in tow. As the barge discharged its cargo, it began to rise in the water, eventually causing the towing wires to become taut. Noticing this, Gautreaux attempted to relieve the tension in the wires by unwinding them from the winches. He released the starboard wire first, which caused that side of the *Brooke Lynn* to drop and the port side towing wire to become even tighter. Gautreaux then attempted to release the port side wire, but the electric winch would not work. He attached the manual crank to the winch motor, and began turning the crank while simultaneously pressing the electric ignition switch. When the motor started, the manual crank handle flew off and struck Gautreaux on the right side of his face, crushing his right eye and inflicting other severe injuries.

Gautreaux sued Scurlock Marine, alleging that his injuries were caused by its negligence and the unseaworthiness of the *Brooke Lynn*. Gautreaux's primary complaint was that Scurlock Marine failed to properly train him in the use and operation of the electric towing winch and its manual crank handle, thereby not providing him a safe place to work. Scurlock Marine answered and sought exoneration from or limitation of its liability. After a two-day trial, the jury returned a verdict in favor of Gautreaux on his Jones Act negligence claim, but found the *Brooke Lynn* seaworthy. The jury apportioned fault 95% to Scurlock Marine and 5% to Gautreaux * * *.

The district court entered judgment for Gautreaux * * * for $736,925 * * *. On appeal to this Court, Scurlock Marine argued, inter alia, that in its instructions regarding contributory negligence, the district court erred by charging the jury that a Jones Act seaman need exercise only "slight care" for his own safety. Scurlock Marine maintained that the standard to which Gautreaux, and all seamen, should be held is that of a reasonably prudent person exercising ordinary or due care under like circumstances. Accordingly, Scurlock Marine urged this Court to abandon the slight care standard in Jones Act cases, contending the standard "has evolved from this Court's blind adherence to an incorrect statement of the law." The panel acknowledged that the viability of the slight care standard has recently been questioned but considered it the settled law of this Circuit. It thus refused to hold that the district court erred in giving the "slight care" instruction, noting that "settled law of this Circuit, such as the slight care standard in a Jones Act case, can only be changed, absent action by the United States Supreme Court, by this Court sitting en banc." The panel accordingly affirmed the district court's judgment and this en banc rehearing followed.

* * *

The district court's instruction, consistent with the Fifth Circuit's Pattern Jury Instructions, informed the jurors that "[i]n determining whether the plaintiff was contributorily negligent, you must bear in mind that a Jones Act seaman does not have a duty to use ordinary care under the circumstances for his own safety. A Jones Act seaman is obliged to exercise only slight care under the circumstances for his own safety at the time of the accident." Scurlock Marine asserts that this charge is defective, maintaining that historically, Jones Act seamen had been expressly bound to a standard of ordinary prudence under like circumstances. * * *

We acknowledge there is much confusion in this Circuit as to the proper standard of care by which juries should measure a plaintiff's duty under the Jones Act to protect himself. While some courts have instructed juries that a plaintiff's duty is only one of slight care, as did the district court in the instant case, others charge that the duty is one of ordinary prudence. Admittedly, this Court has been less than clear in its articulation of the proper standard of care to which seamen are bound. * * *

The language chosen by Congress to determine the responsibility of both employers and employees under the Jones Act is simple and direct. Nothing in the statute indicates that Congress intended to hold Jones Act employees to a standard of slight duty of care in the exercise of concern for their own safety. * * *

Under the Jones Act, seamen are afforded rights parallel to those of railway employees under the Federal Employers' Liability Act * * *. [45 U.S.C. § 51] provides, in pertinent part, that "[e]very common carrier by railroad ... shall be liable in damages ... for such injury or death resulting in whole or in part from the negligence of any of the officers, agents, or employees of such carrier." A seaman is entitled to recovery under the Jones Act, therefore, if his employer's negligence is the cause, in whole or in part, of his injury. In their earlier articulations of § 51 liability, courts * * * replaced the phrase "in whole or in part" with the adjective "slightest." * * *

* * * [T]he phrase "in whole or in part" as set forth in the statute, or, as it has come to be known, "slightest," modifies only the causation prong of the inquiry. The phrase does not also modify the word "negligence." The duty of care owed, therefore, under normal rules of statutory construction, retains the usual and familiar definition of ordinary prudence. * * *

* * *. Once the Supreme Court had reduced the statutory language "in whole or in part" to "any part, even the slightest," it was not long before our court further reduced the phrase "any part, even the slightest" to a shorthand expression of "slight negligence" * * *. [And once we began using] the phrase "slight negligence" as shorthand to depict [the] duty of care owed by [the Jones Act] employer to its employee, it was not long before we [were also using] the phrase to represent the plaintiff's duty of care to protect himself from work-related injuries. We did so by rephrasing "slight negligence" to "slight care."

Historically, then, Jones Act employers and seamen were expressly bound to a standard of ordinary prudence; when the phrase "slight negligence" came to stand for the duty of care owed by employers and employees, however, employers were understood to be held to a higher degree of personal responsibility as to their employees, and plaintiff-seamen were understood to be held to a lower degree of personal responsibility for themselves. We hold that the historical interpretation always should have been, and should now be, applied in this Circuit. * * *

* * * [N]othing in the text or structure of the FELA-Jones Act legislation suggests that the standard of care to be attributed to either an employer or an employee is anything different than ordinary prudence under the circumstances. * * *

A seaman, then, is obligated under the Jones Act to act with ordinary prudence under the circumstances. The circumstances of a seaman's employment include not only his reliance on his employer to provide a safe work environment but also his own experience, training, or education. The reasonable person standard, therefore, [in] a Jones Act negligence action becomes one of the reasonable seaman in like circumstances. To hold otherwise would unjustly reward unreasonable conduct and would fault seamen only for their gross negligence, which was not the contemplation of Congress. [ ]

By ascribing to seamen a slight duty of care to protect themselves from the negligence of their employers, [a number of our decisions] are repugnant to the principles we espouse today and are therefore overruled. Moreover, by attributing to Jones Act employers a higher duty of care than that required under ordinary negligence, [others of our cases] repudiate the reasonable person standard and are also overruled.

In light of the foregoing discussion about the appropriate standards of care that should guide employers and employees under the Jones Act, we hold that the jurors in the instant case were improperly instructed as to Gautreaux's duty to exercise care for his own safety. * * * We accordingly * * * vacate the district court's judgment as to comparative fault and remand for proceedings to determine the comparative fault (if any) of the plaintiff and apportionment of the damages consistent with this opinion. * * *

Notes

1. **Symmetrical treatment of the negligent-conduct issues against defendants and plaintiffs.** Scurlock's appeal and application for rehearing focused on the trial court's instructions addressing the *plaintiff-employee's* duty of care. The *Gautreaux* court agreed that the instructions were wrong and held that Jones Act plaintiffs are required to exercise reasonable care for their own safety; *nothing less* than reasonable care is acceptable. The court then went beyond the parties' narrow focus and held that the conduct of Jones Act *defendants* is likewise to be adjudged under the reasonable care standard; *nothing more* than reasonable care is required.

2. **The *Sorrell* case.** The *Gautreaux* court's view that the negligence of Jones Act defendants and Jones Act plaintiffs must be adjudged under the same (reasonable care) criterion gained powerful implicit support from the unanimous holding in *Norfolk Southern Ry. Co. v. Sorrell*, 549 U.S. 158, 171 (2007), that in FELA cases "the same standard of causation applies to railroad negligence ... as to plaintiff contributory negligence." Even though *Gautreaux* was a Jones Act case addressing the negligence (breach of duty) issue while *Sorrell* was a FELA case addressing the causation issue, there is no good reason for believing that the basic decisional principles should differ.

3. **Should Jones Act/FELA defendants be held to a higher standard than traditional common-law reasonable care?** The Second Circuit in *Williams v. Long Island R. Co.*, 196 F.3d 402, 406 (2d Cir. 1999), disagreed with *Gautreaux*'s view that nothing more than reasonable care is required of Jones/FELA defendants and held that FELA/Jones defendants should be held to a higher degree of care than the traditional common-law reasonable care standard. (Writing before *Sorrell*, the court said nothing about adjudging the negligence of FELA/Jones plaintiffs.)

4. **Negating the victim fault defense.** FELA § 3, 45 U.S.C. § 53, provides that an employer who violates an employee-safety statute is not entitled to any reduction on the basis of victim fault. See *Fuszek v. Royal King Fisheries*, 98 F.3d 514 (9th Cir. 1996) (Coast Guard safety regulation); *Roy Crook & Sons v. Allen*, 778 F.2d 1037 (5th Cir. 1985) (same).

There is scattered lower-court authority that seamen may escape the comparative-fault penalty by establishing that their injuries occurred while conducting rescue missions or while obeying supervisors' specific orders.

5. **What is the Jones/FELA causation standard?** The procedural posture of *Sorrell* (*supra* note 2) dissuaded the Court from addressing the issue of what the FELA causation standard should be. This issue is analyzed in *McBride*, just below.

CSX Transportation, Inc. v. McBride

Supreme Court of the United States, 2011

564 U.S. 685, 131 S. Ct. 2630, 180 L. Ed. 2d 637, 2011 AMC 1521

Justice GINSBURG delivered the opinion of the Court.[23]

This case concerns the standard of causation applicable in cases arising under the Federal Employers' Liability Act (FELA), 45 U.S.C. § 51 *et seq.* FELA renders railroads liable for employees' injuries or deaths "resulting in whole or in part from [carrier] negligence." § 51. In accord with the text and purpose of the Act, this Court's decision in *Rogers v. Missouri Pacific R. Co.*, 352 U.S. 500 (1957), and the uniform view of federal appellate courts, we conclude that the Act does not incorporate "proximate cause" standards developed in nonstatutory common-law tort actions. The charge proper in FELA cases, we hold, simply tracks the language Congress employed, informing juries that a defendant railroad caused or contributed to a plaintiff employee's injury if the railroad's negligence played any part in bringing about the injury.

I

Respondent Robert McBride worked as a locomotive engineer for petitioner CSX Transportation, Inc., which operates an interstate system of railroads. On April 12, 2004, CSX assigned McBride to assist on a local run between Evansville, Indiana, and Mount Vernon, Illinois. The run involved frequent starts and stops to add and remove individual rail cars, a process known as "switching." The train McBride was to operate had an unusual engine configuration: two "wide-body" engines followed by three smaller conventional cabs. McBride protested that the configuration was unsafe, because switching with heavy, wide-body engines required constant use of a hand-operated independent brake. But he was told to take the train as is. About ten hours into the run, McBride injured his hand while using the independent brake. Despite two surgeries and extensive physical therapy, he never regained full use of the hand.

Seeking compensation for his injury, McBride commenced a FELA action against CSX in the U.S. District Court for the Southern District of Illinois. He alleged that CSX was * * * negligent [in] requir[ing] him to use equipment unsafe for switching * * *. A verdict for McBride would be in order, the District Court instructed, if the jury found that CSX "was negligent" and that the "negligence caused or contributed to" McBride's injury.

CSX sought additional charges that the court declined to give. One of the rejected instructions would have required "the plaintiff [to] show that ... the defendant's negligence was a proximate cause of the injury." Another would have defined "proximate cause" to mean "any cause which, in natural or probable sequence, produced the injury complained of," with the qualification that a proximate cause "need not be the only cause, nor the last or nearest cause."

Instead, the District Court employed, as McBride requested, the Seventh Circuit's pattern instruction for FELA cases, which reads:

> Defendant 'caused or contributed to' Plaintiff's injury if Defendant's negligence played a part—no matter how small—in bringing about the injury. The mere

---

23. Justices Breyer, Sotomayor, and Kagan joined Justice Ginsburg's opinion. Justice Thomas joined except for Part III-A.

> fact that an injury occurred does not necessarily mean that the injury was caused by negligence.

For this instruction, the Seventh Circuit relied upon this Court's decision in *Rogers*. The jury returned a verdict for McBride, setting total damages at $275,000, but reducing that amount by one-third, the percentage the jury attributed to plaintiff's negligence.

CSX appealed to the Seventh Circuit, renewing its objection to the failure to instruct on "proximate cause." Before the appellate court, CSX "maintain[ed] that the correct definition of proximate causation is a direct relation between the injury asserted and the injurious conduct alleged." A properly instructed jury, CSX contended, might have found that the chain of causation was too indirect, or that the engine configuration was unsafe because of its propensity to cause crashes during switching, not because of any risk to an engineer's hands.

The Court of Appeals approved the District Court's instruction and affirmed the judgment entered on the jury's verdict. * * * We granted certiorari to decide whether the causation instruction endorsed by the Seventh Circuit is proper in FELA cases. That instruction does not include the term "proximate cause," but does tell the jury defendant's negligence must "pla[y] a part—no matter how small—in bringing about the [plaintiff's] injury."

II

A

The railroad business was exceptionally hazardous at the dawn of the twentieth century. As we have recounted, "the physical dangers of railroading ... resulted in the death or maiming of thousands of workers every year," *Consolidated Rail Corporation v. Gottshall*, 512 U.S. 532, 542 (1994), including 281,645 casualties in the year 1908 alone, S. Rep. No. 61–432, p. 2 (1910). Enacted that same year in an effort to "shif[t] part of the human overhead of doing business from employees to their employers," [ ], FELA prescribes:

> "Every common carrier by railroad ... shall be liable in damages to any person suffering injury while he is employed by such carrier ... for such injury or death *resulting in whole or in part* from the negligence of any of the officers, agents, or employees of such carrier...." 45 U.S.C. § 51 (emphasis added).

Liability under FELA is limited in these key respects: Railroads are liable only to their employees, and only for injuries sustained in the course of employment. FELA's language on causation, however, "is as broad as could be framed." [ ] Given the breadth of the phrase "resulting in whole or in part from the [railroad's] negligence," and Congress' "humanitarian" and "remedial goal[s]," we have recognized that, in comparison to tort litigation at common law, "a relaxed standard of causation applies under FELA." *Gottshall*, 512 U.S., at 542–543. In our 1957 decision in *Rogers*, we described that relaxed standard as follows:

> "Under [FELA] the test of a jury case is simply whether the proofs justify with reason the conclusion that employer negligence played any part, even the slightest, in producing the injury or death for which damages are sought." [ ]

As the Seventh Circuit emphasized, the instruction the District Court gave in this case, permitting a verdict for McBride if "[railroad] negligence played a part—no matter how small—in bringing about the injury," tracked the language of *Rogers*. If *Rogers* prescribes the definition of causation applicable under FELA, that instruction was plainly proper. [ ]. While CSX does not ask us to disturb *Rogers*, the railroad contends that lower courts have overread that opinion. In CSX's view, shared by the dissent, *Rogers* was a narrowly focused decision that did not touch, concern, much less displace common-law formulations of "proximate cause."

Understanding this argument requires some background. The *term* "proximate cause" is shorthand for a concept: Injuries have countless causes, and not all should give rise to legal liability. [ ]. "What we ... mean by the word 'proximate,'" one noted jurist has explained, is simply this: "[B]ecause of convenience, of public policy, of a rough sense of justice, the law arbitrarily declines to trace a series of events beyond a certain point." *Palsgraf v. Long Island R. Co.*, 248 N.Y. 339, 352 (1928) (Andrews, J., dissenting). Common-law "proximate cause" formulations varied, and were often both constricted and difficult to comprehend. * * *

CSX contends that the *Rogers* "any part" test displaced only common-law restrictions on recovery for injuries involving contributory negligence or other "multiple causes." *Rogers* "did not address the requisite directness of a cause," CSX argues, hence that question continues to be governed by restrictive common-law formulations.

B

To evaluate CSX's argument, we turn first to the facts of *Rogers*. The employee in that case was injured while burning off weeds and vegetation that lined the defendant's railroad tracks. A passing train had fanned the flames, which spread from the vegetation to the top of a culvert where the employee was standing. Attempting to escape, the employee slipped and fell on the sloping gravel covering the culvert, sustaining serious injuries. A Missouri state-court jury returned a verdict for the employee, but the Missouri Supreme Court reversed. Even if the railroad had been negligent in failing to maintain a flat surface, the court reasoned, the employee was at fault because of his lack of attention to the spreading fire. [ ] As the fire "was something extraordinary, unrelated to, and disconnected from the incline of the gravel," the court felt "obliged to say [that] plaintiff's injury was not the natural and probable consequence of any negligence of defendant."

We held that the jury's verdict should not have been upset. Describing two potential readings of the Missouri Supreme Court's opinion, we condemned both. First, the court erred in concluding that the employee's negligence was the "sole" cause of the injury, for the jury reasonably found that railroad negligence played a part. *Rogers,* 352 U.S., at 504–505. Second, the court erred insofar as it held that the railroad's negligence was not a sufficient cause unless it was the more "probable" cause of the injury. [ ] FELA, we affirmed, did not incorporate any traditional common-law formulation of "proximate causation[,] which [requires] the jury [to] find that the defendant's negligence was the sole, efficient, producing cause of injury." [ ] Whether the railroad's negligent act was the "immediate reason" for the fall, we added, was "an irrelevant consideration." [ ] We then announced the "any part" test, [ ] and reiterated it several times. * * *

Rogers is most sensibly read as a comprehensive statement of the FELA causation standard. * * * Our understanding is informed by the statutory history and precedent on which *Rogers* drew. Before FELA was enacted, the "harsh and technical" rules of state common law had "made recovery difficult or even impossible" for injured railroad workers. [ ] "[D]issatisfied with the [railroad's] common-law duty," Congress sought to "supplan[t] that duty with [FELA's] far more drastic duty of paying damages for injury or death at work due in whole or in part to the employer's negligence." [ ] Yet, *Rogers* observed, the Missouri court and other lower courts continued to ignore FELA's "significan[t]" departures from the "ordinary common-law negligence" scheme, to reinsert common-law formulations of causation involving "probabilities," and consequently to "deprive litigants of their right to a jury determination." [ ] Aiming to end lower court disregard of congressional purpose, the *Rogers* Court repeatedly called the "any part" test the "*single* " inquiry determining causation in FELA cases. [ ] (emphasis added). In short, CSX's argument that the *Rogers* standard concerns only division of responsibility among multiple actors, and not causation more generally, misses the thrust of our decision in that case.

Our subsequent decisions have confirmed that *Rogers* announced a general standard for causation in FELA cases, not one addressed exclusively to injuries involving multiple potentially cognizable causes. * * *

In reliance on *Rogers*, every Court of Appeals that reviews judgments in FELA cases has approved jury instructions on causation identical or substantively equivalent to the Seventh Circuit's instruction. Each appellate court has rejected common-law formulations of proximate cause of the kind CSX requested in this case. * * *

In sum, the understanding of *Rogers* we here affirm "has been accepted as settled law for several decades." [ ]. "Congress has had [more than 50] years in which it could have corrected our decision in [*Rogers*] if it disagreed with it, and has not chosen to do so." [ ]. Countless judges have instructed countless juries in language drawn from *Rogers*. To discard or restrict the *Rogers* instruction now would ill serve the goals of "stability" and "predictability" that the doctrine of statutory *stare decisis* aims to ensure. [ ]

III

CSX nonetheless insists that proximate causation, as captured in the charge and definitions CSX requested, is a concept fundamental to actions sounding in negligence. The *Rogers* "any part" instruction opens the door to unlimited liability, CSX worries, inviting juries to impose liability on the basis of "but for" causation. The dissent shares these fears. But a half century's experience with *Rogers* gives us little cause for concern: CSX's briefs did not identify even *one* trial in which the instruction generated an absurd or untoward award. Nor has the dissent managed to uncover such a case. ([The dissent] cit[es] no actual case but conjur[es] up images of falling pianos and spilled coffee).

While some courts have said that *Rogers* eliminated the *concept* of proximate cause in FELA cases, we think it "more accurate ... to recognize that *Rogers* describes the test for proximate causation applicable in FELA suits." [*Norfolk Southern Railway Co. v. Sorrell*, 549 U.S. 158, 178(2007) (Ginsburg, J., concurring in judgment)]. * * *

A

As we have noted, the phrase "proximate cause" is shorthand for the policy-based judgment that not all factual causes contributing to an injury should be legally cognizable causes. * * * To prevent "infinite liability," [ ], courts and legislatures appropriately place limits on the chain of causation that may support recovery on any particular claim.

The term "proximate cause" itself is hardly essential to the imposition of such limits. It is a term notoriously confusing. * * * And the lack of consensus on any one definition of "proximate cause" is manifest. [ ] * * * Notably, CSX itself did not settle on a uniform definition of the term "proximate cause" in this litigation * * *. In the District Court, CSX requested a jury instruction defining "proximate cause" to mean "any cause which, in natural or probable sequence, produced the injury complained of." On appeal, "CSX maintain[ed] that the correct definition ... is a 'direct relation between the injury asserted and the injurious conduct alleged.'" Before this Court, CSX called for "a demonstration that the plaintiff's injury resulted from the wrongful conduct in a way that was natural, probable, and foreseeable." * * *

Congress, it is true, has written the words "proximate cause" into a number of statutes. But when the legislative text uses less legalistic language, *e.g.*, "caused by," "occasioned by," "in consequence of," or, as in FELA, "resulting in whole or in part from," and the legislative purpose is to loosen constraints on recovery, there is little reason for courts to hark back to stock, judge-made proximate-cause formulations. [ ]

B

FELA's language is straightforward: railroads are made answerable in damages for an employee's "injury or death resulting in whole or in part from [carrier] negligence." 45 U.S.C. § 51. The argument for importing into FELA's text "previous judicial definitions or dicta" originating in nonstatutory common-law actions [ ] misapprehends how foreseeability figures in FELA cases.

"[R]easonable foreseeability of harm" [ ] is indeed "an essential ingredient of [FELA] *negligence*." [ ] (emphasis added). The jury, therefore, must be asked, initially: Did the carrier "fai[l] to observe that degree of care which people of ordinary prudence and sagacity would use under the same or similar circumstances[?]" [ ] In that regard, the jury may be told that "[the railroad's] duties are measured by what is reasonably foreseeable under like circumstances." [ ] Thus, "[i]f a person has no reasonable ground to anticipate that a particular condition ... would or might result in a mishap and injury, then the party is not required to do anything to correct [the] condition." [ ] [If negligence is proved, however, and is shown to have "*played any part, even the slightest, in producing the injury*," [ ] (emphasis added), then the carrier is answerable in damages even if "the extent of the [injury] or the manner in which it occurred" was not "[p]robable" or "foreseeable."

Properly instructed on negligence and causation, and told, as is standard practice in FELA cases, to use their "common sense" in reviewing the evidence, juries would have no warrant to award damages in far out "but for" scenarios. Indeed, judges would have no warrant to submit such cases to the jury. See *Nicholson v. Erie R. Co.*, 253 F.2d 939, 940–941 (C.A.2 1958) (alleged negligence was failure to provide lavatory for female employee; employee was injured by a suitcase while looking for a lavatory in a passenger car; applying *Rogers*, appellate court affirmed lower court's dismissal for lack of causation); *Moody v. Boston and Maine Corp.*, 921 F.2d 1, 2–5 (C.A.1 1990) (employee suffered stress-related heart attack after railroad forced him to work more than 12 hours with inadequate breaks; applying *Rogers*, appellate court affirmed grant of summary judgment for lack of causation). * * *

* * *

For the reasons stated, it is not error in a FELA case to refuse a charge embracing stock proximate cause terminology. Juries in such cases are properly instructed that a defendant railroad "caused or contributed to" a railroad worker's injury "if [the railroad's] negligence played a part—no matter how small—in bringing about the injury." That, indeed, is the test Congress prescribed for proximate causation in FELA cases. [ ]. As the courts below so held, the judgment of the U.S. Court of Appeals for the Seventh Circuit is affirmed.

Chief Justice ROBERTS, with whom Justice SCALIA, Justice KENNEDY, and Justice ALITO join, dissenting.

* * * The Court is wrong to dispense with [the proximate cause] element of an action seeking recovery for negligence, an element "generally thought to be a necessary limitation on liability." [ ] The test the Court would substitute—whether negligence played any part, even the slightest, in producing the injury—is no limit at all. It is simply "but for"

causation. Nothing in FELA itself or our decision in *Rogers* supports such a boundless theory of liability. * * *

When Congress creates * * * a federal tort, "we start from the premise" that Congress "adopts the background of general tort law." [ ] With respect to FELA in particular, we have explained that "[a]bsent express language to the contrary, the elements of a FELA claim are determined by reference to the common law." [ ] * * *FELA expressly abrogated common law tort principles in four specific ways. [ ] As enacted in 1908, the Act abolished the common law contributory negligence rule, which barred plaintiffs whose negligence had contributed to their injuries from recovering for the negligence of another. See Act of Apr. 22, § 3, 35 Stat. 66. FELA also abandoned the so-called fellow-servant rule, § 1, prohibited an assumption of risk defense in certain cases, § 4, and barred employees from contractually releasing their employers from liability, § 5.

But "[o]nly to the extent of these explicit statutory alterations is FELA an avowed departure from the rules of the common law." [ ]. FELA did not abolish the familiar requirement of proximate cause. Because "Congress expressly dispensed with [certain] common-law doctrines" in FELA but "did not deal at all with [other] equally well-established doctrine[s]," I do not believe that "Congress intended to abrogate [the other] doctrine[s] *sub silentio*." *Monessen Southwestern R. Co. v. Morgan*, 486 U.S. 330, 337–338 (1988).

We have [often] applied the standard requirement of proximate cause to actions under federal statutes where the text did not expressly provide for it. * * *

At oral argument, counsel for McBride explained that the correct standard for recovery under FELA is "but-for plus a relaxed form of legal cause." There is no "plus" in the rule the Court announces today. * * * At certain points in its opinion, the Court acknowledges that "[i]njuries have countless causes," not all of which "should give rise to legal liability." But the causation test the Court embraces contains no limit on causation at all.

* * * The Court today takes the "any part, even the slightest" language [of *Rogers*] out of context and views it as a rejection of proximate cause. But *Rogers* was talking about contributory negligence—it said so—and the language it chose confirms just that. * * *

A few of our cases have characterized *Rogers* as holding that "a relaxed standard of causation applies under FELA." [ ] Fair enough; but these passing summations of *Rogers* do not alter its holding. * * * [W]e have never held—until today—that FELA entirely eliminates proximate cause as a limit on liability.

III

The Court is correct that the federal courts of appeals have read *Rogers* to support the adoption of instructions like the one given here. But we do not resolve questions such as the one before us by a show of hands. * * *

Even the Court seems to appreciate that it is creating a troubling gap in the FELA negligence action and ought to do *something* to patch it over. The something it proposes is "[r]easonable foreseeability of harm." Foreseeability as a test for proximate causation would be one thing; foreseeability has, after all, long been an aspect of proximate cause. But that is not the test the Court prescribes. It instead limits the foreseeability inquiry to whether the defendant was negligent in the first place.

The Court observes that juries may be instructed that a defendant's negligence depends on "what a reasonably prudent person would anticipate or foresee as creating a potential for harm." [ ]. That's all fine and good when a defendant's negligence results directly in the plaintiff's injury (never mind that no "reasonable foreseeability" instruction was given in this case). For instance, if I drop a piano from a window and it falls on a person, there is no question that I was negligent and could have foreseen that the piano would hit someone—as, in fact, it did. The problem for the Court's test arises when the negligence does not directly produce the injury to the plaintiff: I drop a piano; it cracks the sidewalk; during sidewalk repairs weeks later a man barreling down the sidewalk on a bicycle hits a cone that repairmen have placed around their worksite, and is injured. Was I negligent in dropping the piano because I could have foreseen "*a* mishap and injury?" Yes. Did my negligence cause "[*the*] mishap and injury" that resulted? It depends on what is meant by cause. My negligence was a "but for" cause of the injury: If I had not dropped the piano, the bicyclist would not have crashed. But is it a legal cause? No.

* * * Where does "foreseeability of harm" as the sole protection against limitless liability run out of steam? An answer would seem only fair to the common law. A railroad negligently fails to maintain its boiler, which overheats. An employee becomes hot while repairing it and removes his jacket. When finished with the repairs, he grabs a thermos of coffee, which spills on his now-bare arm, burning it. Was the risk that someone would be harmed by the failure to maintain the boiler foreseeable? Was the risk that an employee would be burned while repairing the overheated boiler foreseeable? Can the railroad be liable under the Court's test for the coffee burn? According to the Court's opinion, it does not matter that the "manner in which [the injury] occurred was not ... foreseeable," so long as some negligence—any negligence at all—can be established.

* * *

Law has its limits. But no longer when it comes to the causal connection between negligence and a resulting injury covered by FELA. A new maxim has replaced the old: *Caelum terminus est*—the sky's the limit. * * *

Notes

1. In *Ferguson v. Moore-McCormack Lines, Inc.*, 352 U.S. 521, 522 (1957), a Jones Act case on which the *McBride* Court relied, a seaman lost two fingers on his right hand when he used "a sharp butcher knife" to serve ice cream that was too hard to serve with a normal scoop. The district court entered judgment for the injured seaman on a jury verdict. The Second Circuit reversed, at least arguably on the basis of proximate cause, concluding that the employer should have prevailed. 228 F.2d 891, 892 (2d Cir. 1956). The Supreme Court reversed the court of appeals and reinstated the jury verdict. The four-justice plurality applied *Rogers*. Only Justice Harlan dissented on the causation standard. 352 U.S. at 559.

2. For a detailed analysis of *McBride*, see Robertson, *Causation Issues in FELA and Jones Act Cases in the Wake of* McBride, 36 Tul. Mar. L.J. 397 (2012).

4. Seamen's Actions for Injuries Caused by Unseaworthiness

In *The Osceola, supra* at 148–49, the Court proclaimed "[t]hat the vessel and her owner are ... liable to an indemnity for injuries received by seamen in consequence of the unseaworthiness of the ship." The decisions in this subsection explore the implications of that proposition.

Mitchell v. Trawler Racer, Inc.

Supreme Court of the United States, 1960
362 U.S. 539, 80 S. Ct. 926, 4 L. Ed. 2d 941, 1960 AMC 1503

Mr. Justice STEWART delivered the opinion of the Court.

The petitioner was a member of the crew of the Boston fishing trawler *Racer*, owned and operated by the respondent. On April 1, 1957, the vessel returned to her home port from a 10-day voyage to the North Atlantic fishing grounds, loaded with a catch of fish and fish spawn. After working that morning with his fellow crew members in unloading the spawn, the petitioner changed his clothes and came on deck to go ashore. He made his way to the side of the vessel which abutted the dock, and in accord with recognized custom stepped onto the ship's rail in order to reach a ladder attached to the pier. He was injured when his foot slipped off the rail as he grasped the ladder.

To recover for his injuries he filed this action for damages [in the United States District Court for the District of Massachusetts] in a complaint containing three counts: the first under the Jones Act, alleging negligence; the second alleging unseaworthiness; and the third for maintenance and cure. At the trial there was evidence to show that the ship's rail where the petitioner had lost his footing was covered for a distance of 10 or 12 feet with slime and fish gurry, apparently remaining there from the earlier unloading operations.

The district judge instructed the jury that in order to allow recovery upon either the negligence or unseaworthiness count, they must find that the slime and gurry had been on the ship's rail for a period of time long enough for the respondent to have learned about it and to have removed it. Counsel for the petitioner requested that the trial judge distinguish between negligence and unseaworthiness in this respect, and specifically requested him to instruct the jury that notice was not a necessary element in proving liability based upon unseaworthiness of the vessel. This request was denied. The jury awarded the petitioner maintenance and cure, but found for the respondent shipowner on both the negligence and unseaworthiness counts.

An appeal was taken upon the sole ground that the district judge had been in error in instructing the jury that constructive notice was necessary to support liability for unseaworthiness. The [First Circuit] Court of Appeals affirmed, holding that * * * with respect to "an unseaworthy condition which arises only during the progress of the voyage," the shipowner's obligation "is merely to see that reasonable care is used under the circumstances ... incident to the correction of the newly arisen defect." Certiorari was granted to consider a question of maritime law upon which the Courts of Appeals have expressed differing views. [ ]

In its present posture this case * * * presents the single issue whether with respect to so-called "transitory" unseaworthiness the shipowner's liability is limited by concepts of common-law negligence. * * *

The origin of a seaman's right to recover for injuries caused by an unseaworthy ship is far from clear. The earliest codifications of the law of the sea provided only the equivalent of maintenance and cure—medical treatment and wages to a mariner wounded or falling ill in the service of the ship. Markedly similar provisions granting relief of this nature are to be found in the Laws of Oleron * * *, the Laws of Wisbuy * * *, the Laws of the Hanse Towns * * *, and the Marine Ordinances of Louis XIV * * *.

For many years American courts regarded these ancient codes as establishing the limits of a shipowner's liability to a seaman injured in the service of his vessel. [ ] During this early period the maritime law was concerned with the concept of unseaworthiness only with reference to two situations quite unrelated to the right of a crew member to recover for personal injuries. The earliest mention of unseaworthiness in American judicial opinions appears in cases in which mariners were suing for their wages. They were required to prove the unseaworthiness of the vessel to excuse their desertion or misconduct which otherwise would result in a forfeiture of their right to wages. [ ] The other route through which the concept of unseaworthiness found its way into the maritime law was via the rules covering marine insurance and the carriage of goods by sea. [ ]

Not until the late nineteenth century did there develop in American admiralty courts the doctrine that seamen had a right to recover for personal injuries beyond maintenance and cure. During that period it became generally accepted that a shipowner was liable to a mariner injured in the service of a ship as a consequence of the owner's failure to exercise due diligence [to provide a seaworthy vessel]. The decisions of that era for the most part treated maritime injury cases on the same footing as cases involving the duty of a shoreside employer to exercise ordinary care to provide his employees with a reasonably safe place to work. [ ]

Although some courts held shipowners liable for injuries caused by "active" negligence, [ ] it was held in *The City of Alexandria*, 17 F. 390 (S.D.N.Y 1883), in a thorough opinion by Judge Addison Brown, that the owner was not liable for negligence which did not render the ship or her appliances unseaworthy. * * *

This was the historical background behind Mr. Justice [Henry Billings] Brown's much quoted second proposition in *The Osceola* [*supra* at 148–49]: "That the vessel and her owner are, both by English and American law, liable to an indemnity for injuries received by seamen in consequence of the unseaworthiness of the ship, or a failure to supply and keep in order the proper appliances appurtenant to the ship." * * *

It is arguable that the import of the above-quoted second proposition in *The Osceola* was not to broaden the shipowner's liability, but, rather, to limit liability for negligence to those situations where his negligence resulted in the vessel's unseaworthiness. Support for such a view is to be found not only in the historic context in which *The Osceola* was decided, but in the discussion in the balance of the opinion * * *. In any event, with the passage of the Jones Act in 1920, Congress effectively obliterated all distinctions between the kinds of negligence for which the shipowner is liable * * *.

The first reference in this Court to the shipowner's obligation to furnish a seaworthy ship as explicitly unrelated to the standard of ordinary care in a personal injury case appears in *Carlisle Packing Co. v. Sandanger*, 259 U.S. 255 (1922). There it was said "we think the trial court might have told the jury that without regard to negligence the vessel was unseaworthy when she left the dock ... and that if thus unseaworthy and one of the crew received damage as the direct result thereof, he was entitled to recover compensatory damages." [ ] This characterization of unseaworthiness as unrelated to negligence was probably not necessary to the decision in that case, where the respondent's injuries had clearly in fact been caused by failure to exercise ordinary care (putting gasoline in a can labeled "coal oil" and neglecting to provide the vessel with life preservers). Yet there is no reason to suppose that the Court's language was inadvertent.

During the two decades that followed the *Carlisle* decision there came to be a general acceptance of the view that *The Osceola* had enunciated a concept of absolute liability for unseaworthiness unrelated to principles of negligence law. Personal injury litigation based upon unseaworthiness was substantial. [ ] And the standard texts accepted that theory of liability without question. * * *

In 1944 this Court decided *Mahnich v. Southern S.S. Co.*, 321 U.S. 96. * * * *Mahnich* stands as a landmark in the development of admiralty law. Chief Justice Stone's opinion in that case gave an unqualified stamp of solid authority to the view that *The Osceola* was correctly to be understood as holding that the duty to provide a seaworthy ship depends not at all upon the negligence of the shipowner or his agents. Moreover, the dissent in *Mahnich* accepted this reading of *The Osceola* and claimed no more than that the injury in *Mahnich* was not properly attributable to unseaworthiness. [ ]

In *Seas Shipping Co. v. Sieracki*, 328 U.S. 85 (1946), the Court effectively scotched any doubts that might have lingered after *Mahnich* as to the nature of the shipowner's duty to provide a seaworthy vessel. The character of the duty, said the Court, is "absolute." "It is essentially a species of liability without fault, analogous to other well known instances in our law. Derived from and shaped to meet the hazards which performing the service imposes, the liability is neither limited by conceptions of negligence nor contractual in character. * * * It is a form of absolute duty owing to all within the range of its humanitarian policy." The dissenting opinion agreed as to the nature of the shipowner's duty. "[D]ue diligence of the owner," it said, "does not relieve him from this obligation."

From that day to this, the decisions of this Court have undeviatingly reflected an understanding that the owner's duty to furnish a seaworthy ship is absolute [and] completely independent of his duty under the Jones Act to exercise reasonable care. [ ]

There is no suggestion in any of the decisions that the duty is less onerous with respect to an unseaworthy condition arising after the vessel leaves her home port, or that the duty is any less with respect to an unseaworthy condition which may be only temporary. Of particular relevance here is *Alaska Steamship Co. v. Petterson*, 347 U.S. 396 (1954). In that case the Court affirmed a judgment holding the shipowner liable for injuries caused by defective equipment temporarily brought on board by an independent contractor over which the owner had no control. That decision is thus specific authority for the proposition that the shipowner's actual or constructive knowledge of the unseaworthy condition is not essential to his liability. That decision also effectively disposes of the suggestion that liability for a temporary unseaworthy condition is different from the liability that attaches when the condition is permanent.

There is ample room for argument, in the light of history, as to how the law of unseaworthiness should have or could have developed. Such theories might be made to fill a volume of logic. But, in view of the decisions in this Court over the last 15 years, we can find no room for argument as to what the law is. What has evolved is a complete divorcement of unseaworthiness liability from concepts of negligence. To hold otherwise now would be to erase more than just a page of history.

What has been said is not to suggest that the owner is obligated to furnish an accident-free ship. The duty is absolute, but it is a duty only to furnish a vessel and appurtenances reasonably fit for their intended use. The standard is not perfection, but reasonable fitness; not a ship that will weather every conceivable storm or withstand every imaginable peril of the sea, but a vessel reasonably suitable for her intended service. [ ]

The judgment must be reversed, and the case remanded to the District Court for a new trial on the issue of unseaworthiness.

Mr. Justice FRANKFURTER, whom Mr. Justice Harlan and Mr. Justice Whittaker join, dissenting.[24]

No area of federal law is judge-made at its source to such an extent as is the law of admiralty. The evolution of judge-made law is a process of accretion and erosion. We are told by a great master that law is civilized to the extent that it is purposefully conscious. Conversely, if law just "grow'd" like Topsy unreflectively and without conscious design, it is irrational. When it appears that a challenged doctrine has been uncritically accepted as a matter of course by the inertia of repetition—has just "grow'd" like Topsy—the Court owes it to the demands of reason, on which judicial law-making power ultimately rests for its authority, to examine its foundations and validity in order appropriately to assess claims for its extension.

* * *

The birth of the current doctrine of unseaworthiness * * * can be stated precisely: it occurred on May 29, 1922, in *Carlisle Packing Co. v. Sandanger* [ ]. The action was brought in the Washington state courts by Sandanger, an employee of Carlisle, who was injured while working on its motorboat on a six- or eight-hour trip. The injury occurred when he lighted fuel from a can on board marked "coal oil" in order to start a cookstove, and it exploded. It appeared thereafter that the can had mistakenly been filled with gasoline. In a suit based on a claim of negligence, Sandanger won a verdict on a finding of negligence, which was challenged in the Supreme Court of Washington on the ground that the exclusively applicable maritime law did not afford relief by way of compensation for negligent injury of an employee. The Washington court held that an injury caused by a negligently created unseaworthy condition was compensable, even when, under the rule laid down in *The Osceola*, negligent injury without unseaworthiness would not be. [ ]

The matter was dealt with in this Court in the few lines innovating the rule of absolute liability: "We think the trial court might have told the jury that without regard to negligence the vessel was unseaworthy when she left the dock ... and that if ... one of the crew received damage as the direct result thereof, he was entitled to recover compensatory damages." [ ] No explication accompanied this dogmatic pronouncement on an issue not presented by an issue of the affirmed judgment. It was strangely deemed sufficient to rely on the unelaborated citation of two cases in this Court [ ] which were concerned not with the rights of seamen but with the shipowner's liability for cargo damage. The abrupt, unreasoned conclusion was reached without benefit of argument: the parties had presented the case solely on the basis [of] * * * negligence. Neither our own investigation nor that of the parties here has disclosed a single case in an English or an American court prior to *Sandanger* in which the absolute duty to provide a seaworthy vessel for cargo carriage and marine insurance contracts was applied to a seaman's suit for personal injury.[25] *Sandanger* was an unillumined departure in the law of the sea. Reasoned decision of the case before us, in which extension is sought of a rule so dubiously initiated, requires that its rational, historical and social basis be scrutinized and not merely accepted as unquestionable dogma.

* * *

24. Editors' note: Our presentation of Justice Frankfurter's opinion has moved his discussion of *Petterson* from near the beginning to near the end of the opinion.

25. Editors' note: As we will see in Chapter III, *infra* at 277–330, the old "absolute duty to provide [an initially] seaworthy ship for cargo carriage ... contracts" has been reduced by statute to an obligation of due diligence in that respect.

[Moreover, if] *Sandanger* now stood alone, it would be plain that the absolute warranty it announced, [like the warranty involved in the old cargo cases the *Sandanger* Court cited, would be confined to conditions in existence at the beginning of the voyage], and the question now presented—whether the warranty is also absolute as to subsequently arising conditions—would clearly present a novel issue for decision. Subsequent decisions in this Court have not deliberately closed the gap.

It was twenty-two years before the question of the existence and scope of absolute liability came before this Court again. * * * In 1944 this Court decided *Mahnich v. Southern S.S. Co.* The suit was brought by a seaman under the general maritime law (the statute of limitations having run on Jones Act claims) for injuries which he incurred at sea when a rope, with which the staging on which he was working fifteen feet over the deck was rigged, parted and he fell. The mate in charge had taken the rope, which was unused, but at least two years old, from the Lyle Gun (a life-saving device) box. After the accident it appeared that the rope was decayed.

The District Court found that the mate's selection of the rope was negligent but dismissed the libel on the ground that, apart from the Jones Act, negligent injury alone was not compensable and that the vessel, since it had other good rope on board sufficient for the job, was not unseaworthy. The Court of Appeals affirmed. It assumed, without deciding, that the rope was negligently selected * * * and agreed with the District Court's conclusion that the vessel was not unseaworthy. Though it reversed, this Court, too, found it unnecessary to decide the contested question of negligence. It gave as its primary reason that "the exercise of due diligence does not relieve the owner of his obligation to the seaman to furnish adequate appliances." [ ] Although this statement was the critical major premise of an opinion which went on to decide that such absolute liability would not be barred by the mate's intervening negligence, it was rested primarily on [*Sandanger*], without further explanation.

There is no more disclosure in the opinion or history of [*Mahnich*] than there was in *Sandanger* to warrant attributing to this statement a deliberate or authoritative ruling that liability is absolute for all injuries resulting from unseaworthy conditions. Confined to the facts of the case, the decision that intervening negligence would not constitute a defense to an action for injuries resulting from an unseaworthy condition is consistent with the rule of the cargo and insurance cases, confining the absolute warranty to damage resulting from initial unseaworthiness. The rope, which was new, had decayed from overlong or improper storage, not from use, and was, it is right to assume, defective from the start of the voyage. [ ]

Seas Shipping Co. v. Sieracki is no better authority for petitioner's contentions here. The action was instituted by a longshoreman who was injured while loading respondent's vessel, when a forged shackle supporting the vessel's ten-ton boom gave way because of a latent defect in the forging. The defect had existed from the time of the construction of the ship. Both parties conceded that the vessel was unseaworthy, and that if a seaman had been injured in the same way he could have recovered compensatory damages. The District Court gave judgment for the owner on the ground that it was not negligent for it to have failed to discover the defect. [ ] The Court of Appeals reversed, on the ground that Sieracki was entitled to recover under the warranty of seaworthiness. [ ] The turning-point of the case in this Court was whether the warranty of seaworthiness, concededly absolute on the facts, covered longshoremen doing seamen's work.

The Court's extended discussion of the sources and rationale of the warranty is entirely consistent with the history noted above. [ ] Nothing that was said or implied casts any light whatever on the question whether the initial absolute warranty carried over by *Sandanger* from the cargo cases extends to subsequently arising conditions, unless, as in *Mahnich*, the Court's equation of the warranty running to seamen with the [warranty in the old cargo cases] bespeaks its assumption that the warranty was absolute only as to the start of the voyage.

No other case in this Court is further enlightening on the question of the scope of the absolute warranty. * * * The present majority regard the question now presented as foreclosed by *Alaska S.S. Co. v. Petterson.* But *Petterson* was an unrevealing per curiam opinion, itself founded on prior decisions affording no justification for the result here. *Petterson* held a shipowner liable for injuries to a longshoreman caused by defective equipment brought on board his vessel by a contract stevedore for use in loading operations. The owner gave the stevedore permission at his option to substitute his own equipment for that of the vessel, and the equipment which caused the injury was a snatch-block, standard ships' equipment, supplied pursuant to that permission. * * * The defendant did not argue that the vessel was seaworthy at the start of the voyage and that no absolute liability attached to subsequently arising conditions * * *. There is therefore no foundation, either in what the per curiam revealed or in the history of the case, to warrant the inference that the Court was conscious of the distinctions now squarely pressed upon us, much less that it rejected them. Such a conclusion is the more fanciful because, even had the Court considered and accepted the contentions now urged, it might well have found them insufficient to avoid liability and have held that, by giving permission to have substitution made for warranted ships' equipment, the owner adopted the substitute as his own.

* * *

Against this background of prior adjudications it assumes what is required to be established to assert that "[t]here is no suggestion in any of the decisions that the duty is less onerous with respect to an unseaworthy condition arising after the vessel leaves her home port." In fact, there is no overt suggestion in any of our decisions that the duty is not less onerous, and the origin of the duty in cargo and marine insurance cases strongly suggests that it is. * * *

* * *

Mr. Justice HARLAN, whom Mr. Justice Frankfurter and Mr. Justice Whittaker join, dissenting.

In joining my Brother Frankfurter's dissent, I wish to add a few words. I believe the Court's decision not only finds no support in the past cases, but also is unjustified in principle, and is directed at ends not appropriately within our domain. The Second Circuit's decision in *Poignant v. United States*, 225 F.2d 595 (2d Cir. 1955), provides a useful point of departure for what I have to say.

In *Poignant* the libellant, a crew member, slipped on a small piece of garbage lying in a passageway of the ship. The vessel lacked garbage chutes, and the garbage was pulled, in cans, through the passageway to a railing, where it was jettisoned. The Court of Appeals first expressed the view that any unseaworthy condition which existed had in all probability arisen after the voyage had commenced. It said, much as the Court now holds, that [*Petterson*] required it to apply a rule of absolute liability nonetheless. It then put, as the critical issue, the question whether the presence of some garbage in a public passageway constituted an unseaworthy condition, and, finding the matter to turn on an issue of fact, remanded the case for trial. However, it is important to note the manner in which the court dealt with the problem. Although at the outset of the opinion the allegedly unseaworthy condition was assumed to be the presence of garbage in a passageway, [ ] the remand was in fact directed to the question whether the absence of garbage chutes rendered the vessel not reasonably fit for the voyage, and therefore unseaworthy. [ ] This, of course, would be a condition going to the proper outfitting of the vessel for sea travel, and a clear case of initial unseaworthiness. In such event, the injury would have been the proximate result of that unseaworthiness, for it was by reason of the lack of chutes that garbage was carried through the passageways at all.

For me this approach indicates the rule which should govern the case before us. Had the petitioner contended and proved that a properly outfitted trawler of this type should have had a particular device for unloading fish, or an alternative means of facilitating petitioner's egress from the vessel, so that either the railing would not have been slippery or the petitioner would not have been required to use the railing in debarking, the case would have been governed by the absolute liability rule of *Sandanger* and its successors, and respondent's opportunity to remove the spawn from the rail would properly be held immaterial. As the case is decided, however, we are told that even though there is no claim that the vessel should have made different provisions for the unloading of its catch or the debarking of its crew, the shipowner is liable for an injury caused by a temporary unsafe condition arising from the normal operation of the vessel, not the result of fault or mismanagement of anyone on board, and which no one had a reasonable opportunity to remedy. * * * [Such an] imposition of liability seems to me * * * a "hard doctrine," "startlingly opposed to principle." [ ]

The Court is not fashioning a rule designed to protect life, [ ] for there appears no real basis for expectation that today's decision will promote the taking of greater precautions at sea. [ ] The respondent is held liable, without being told that there was something left undone which should have been done, for petitioner is not asked to show, as was the libellant in *Poignant*, that the vessel ought to have been outfitted differently, that is, in a fashion which would have prevented the dangerous condition from arising at all. Nor is the respondent permitted to show that such condition was not due to its fault.

The *sole* interest served by the Court's decision is compensation. Such an interest is, of course, equally present in the case of an undoubted accident, where under the Court's ruling no right of recovery is bestowed, as it is in the present case. But, because of the Court's inherent incapacity to deal with the problem in the comprehensive and integrated manner which would doubtless characterize its legislative treatment [ ], this arbitrary limitation is preserved. This internal contradiction in the rule which the Court has established only serves to highlight a more central point: it is not for a court, even a court of admiralty, to fashion a tort rule solely in response to considerations which underlie workmen's compensation legislation, weighty as such considerations doubtless are as a legislative matter. Citation is not needed to remind one of the readiness of Congress to deal with felt deficiencies in judicial protection of the interests of those who go to sea. We should heed the limitations on our own capacity and authority. [ ]

Notes

1. Before *Mitchell* it had been clear that shipowners were strictly liable to seamen injured by initial unseaworthiness. But which pre-*Mitchell* decision had authoritatively held that this strict liability extended to transitory unseaworthiness? Does Justice Frankfurter persuade you that *Sandanger*, *Mahnich*, *Sieracki*, and *Petterson* were all cases in which initial unseaworthiness could have been found?

2. Justice Frankfurter's discussion of *Sandanger* included the following footnote: "It is not irrelevant to note that the spokesman for the Court was the Justice under whose lead the most unhappy admiralty doctrines were promulgated: *Southern Pacific Co. v. Jensen*, 244 U.S. 205 (1917), and *Knickerbocker Ice Co. v. Stewart*, 253 U.S. 149 (1920)."

3. In Justice Harlan's view, what should the issue be on remand of the case? Under the majority's view what will it be?

4. A ship can be unseaworthy—*viz.*, not "reasonably suitable for her intended service"—by reason of deficiencies in appurtenances, equipment, gear, personnel, or operational methods. See, e.g., *Waldron v. Moore-McCormack Lines, Inc.*, 386 U.S. 724 (1967) (too few men assigned to task); *Michalic v. Cleveland Tankers, Inc.*, 364 U.S. 325 (1960) (worn-out wrench); *Boudin v. Lyles Brothers Steamship Co.*, 348 U.S. 336 (1955) (vicious crew member); *Johnson v. Offshore Express, Inc.*, 845 F.2d 1347 (5th Cir. 1988) (no ladder supplied for making up upper berths); *Reyes v. Vantage Steamship Co.*, 609 F.2d 140 (5th Cir. 1980) (unrestricted sale of beer).

5. In one major respect, the law of unseaworthiness is more liberal (pro-plaintiff) than Jones Act law: It is generally easier to prove a deficiency in the vessel than that the employer was negligent. See, e.g., *Perkins v. American Electric Power Fuel Supply*, 246 F.3d 593 (6th Cir. 2001) (holding that a towboat deckhand injured by a defective tool had failed to prove Jones Act negligence but was nevertheless entitled to recover for unseaworthiness). But this difference is often offset by the fact that liability for unseaworthiness requires a showing of proximate causation, whereas *CSX v. McBride* (*supra* at 172) dispenses with that requirement in FELA and thus presumably Jones Act cases.

6. In maintenance and cure and Jones Act actions, the proper defendant is the seaman's employer. In unseaworthiness actions, it is the owner or operator of the ship. Often the shipowner and employer will be the same entity, but by no means always. See, e.g., *Mahramas v. American Export Isbrandtsen Lines*, 475 F.2d 165 (2d Cir. 1973), in which the injured seaman was aboard the named defendant's vessel as an employee of the House of Albert, a beauty salon operating on the ship.

Usner v. Luckenbach Overseas Corp.

Supreme Court of the United States, 1971
400 U.S. 494, 91 S. Ct. 514, 27 L. Ed. 2d 562, 1971 AMC 277

Mr. Justice STEWART delivered the opinion of the Court.

The petitioner, a longshoreman employed by an independent stevedoring contractor, was injured while engaged with his fellow employees in loading cargo aboard the *S. S. Edgar F. Luckenbach*. He brought this action for damages against the respondents, the owner and the charterer of the ship, in a federal district court, alleging that his injuries had been caused by the ship's unseaworthiness.

In the course of pretrial proceedings the circumstances under which the petitioner had been injured were fully disclosed, and they are not in dispute. On the day in question the ship lay moored to a dock in New Orleans, Louisiana, receiving cargo from a barge positioned alongside. The loading operations were being performed by the petitioner and his fellow longshoremen under the direction of their employer. Some of the men were on the ship, operating the port winch and boom at the No. 2 hatch. The petitioner and others were on the barge, where their job was to "break out" the bundles of cargo by securing them to a sling attached to the fall each time it was lowered from the ship's boom by the winch operator. The loading operations had been proceeding in this manner for some time, until upon one occasion the winch operator did not lower the fall far enough. Finding the sling beyond his reach, the petitioner motioned to the flagman standing on the deck of the ship to direct the winch operator to lower the fall farther. The winch operator then lowered the fall, but he lowered it too far and too fast. The sling struck the petitioner, knocking him to the deck of the barge and causing his injuries. Neither before nor after this occurrence was any difficulty experienced with the winch, boom, fall, sling, or any other equipment or appurtenance of the ship or her cargo.

The respondents moved for summary judgment in the District Court, upon the ground that a single negligent act by a fellow longshoreman could not render the ship unseaworthy. The District Court denied the motion, but granted the respondents leave to take an interlocutory appeal.

The United States Court of Appeals for the Fifth Circuit allowed the appeal and, reversing the District Court, directed that the respondents' motion for summary judgment be granted. It was the appellate court's view that "'[i]nstant unseaworthiness' resulting from 'operational negligence' of the stevedoring contractor is not a basis for recovery by an injured longshoreman." We granted certiorari because of a conflict among the circuits on the basic issue presented.

The development in admiralty law of the doctrine of unseaworthiness as a predicate for a shipowner's liability for personal injuries or death has been fully chronicled elsewhere, and it would serve no useful purpose to repeat the details of that development here. Suffice it to recall that from its humble origin as a dictum in an obscure case in 1922, the doctrine of liability based upon unseaworthiness has experienced a most extraordinary expansion in a series of cases decided by this Court over the last 25 years. The Court's decisions in some of those cases have been severely questioned, by dissenting Justices and by others, on the basis of history, reason, and logic. The present case, however, offers no occasion to re-examine any of our previous decisions. We may accept it as fully settled that a shipowner's liability for an unseaworthy vessel extends beyond the members of the crew and includes a longshoreman like the petitioner. [*Seas Shipping Co. v. Sieracki*, 328 U.S. 85 (1946), so held.] We may accept it as settled, too, that the shipowner is liable though the unseaworthiness be transitory, and though the injury be suffered elsewhere than aboard the ship. But these propositions do not dispose of the case before us. For the question here goes to the very definition of what unseaworthiness is and what it is not.

A major burden of the Court's decisions spelling out the nature and scope of the cause of action for unseaworthiness has been insistence upon the point that it is a remedy separate from, independent of, and additional to other claims against the shipowner, whether created by statute or under general maritime law. More specifically, the Court has repeatedly taken pains to point out that liability based upon unseaworthiness is wholly distinct from liability based upon negligence. The reason, of course, is that unseaworthiness is a condition, and how that condition came into being—whether by negligence or otherwise—is quite irrelevant to the owner's liability for personal injuries resulting from it.

We had occasion to emphasize this basic distinction * * * in *Mitchell.* * * * What has evolved in our case law, we said, is the "complete divorcement of unseaworthiness liability from concepts of negligence."

[*Mitchell*] involved the defective condition of a physical part of the ship itself. But our cases have held that the scope of unseaworthiness is by no means so limited. A vessel's condition of unseaworthiness might arise from any number of circumstances. Her gear might be defective, her appurtenances in disrepair, her crew unfit. The number of men assigned to perform a shipboard task might be insufficient. The method of loading her cargo, or the manner of its stowage, might be improper. For any of these reasons, or others, a vessel might not be reasonably fit for her intended service.

What caused the petitioner's injuries in the present case, however, was not the condition of the ship, her appurtenances, her cargo, or her crew, but the isolated, personal negligent act of the petitioner's fellow longshoreman. To hold that this individual act of negligence rendered the ship unseaworthy would be to subvert the fundamental distinction between unseaworthiness and negligence that we have so painstakingly and repeatedly emphasized in our decisions. In [*Mitchell*] there existed a condition of unseaworthiness, and we held it was error to require a finding of negligent conduct in order to hold the shipowner liable. The case before us presents the other side of the same coin. For it would be equally erroneous here, where no condition of unseaworthiness existed, to hold the shipowner liable for a third party's single and wholly unforeseeable act of negligence. The judgment of the Court of Appeals is affirmed.

Mr. Justice DOUGLAS, with whom Mr. Justice Black and Mr. Justice Brennan concur, dissenting.

* * * We held in *Mahnich* [ ] that the obligation of an owner to furnish a seaworthy ship extends to seaworthy appliances. We also held that the owner was not insulated from liability by the "negligent failure" of his officers or members of the crew to furnish seaworthy appliances. [ ] In *Mahnich*, the staging from which the seaman fell was an unseaworthy appliance because of the defective rope with which it was rigged. There was sound rope on board but defective rope was used. The fact that the mate and boatswain were negligent in selecting defective rope was held to be no defense.

In *Crumady v. The J. H. Fisser*, 358 U.S. 423 (1959), a winch was not inherently defective as was the rope in *Mahnich*. But it was used in a way which made it unsafe and dangerous for the work at hand. While the rigging would take only three tons of stress, the cutoff of the winch, "its safety device," was set at twice that limit. [ ] And so the rope sling broke and injured the seaman. The vessel which paid the damages was allowed to recover over from the stevedores whose negligence with the winch made the vessel pro tanto unseaworthy.

* * *

Changes in membership do change decisions; and those changes are expected at the level of constitutional law. But when private rights not rooted in the Constitution are at issue, it is surprising to find law made by new judges taking the place of law made by prior judges.

* * *

Mr. Justice HARLAN, dissenting.

Past decisions of this Court have expanded the doctrine of unseaworthiness almost to the point of absolute liability. I have often protested against this development. [ ] But I must in good conscience regard the particular issue in this case as having been decided by *Crumady* [ ] even if prior decisions did not inexorably point to that result. As my Brother Douglas states, *Crumady* cannot justly be distinguished from the case before us. Much as I would welcome a thoroughgoing re-examination of the past course of developments in the unseaworthiness doctrine, I fear that the Court's action today can only result in compounding the current difficulties of the lower courts with this area of the law.

Notes

1. The 1946 decision in *Seas Shipping Co. v. Sieracki*—permitting longshoremen to sue for unseaworthiness—was legislatively overruled by the 1972 amendments to § 5(b) of the Longshore and Harbor Workers' Compensation Act (LHWCA), 33 U.S.C. § 905(b). For the most part, today only seamen have that right. (There are scattered decisions holding that certain nonseamen who for some reason are not covered by the LHWCA can still maintain unseaworthiness actions. See, e.g., *Green v. Vermilion Corp.*, 144 F.3d 332 (5th Cir. 1999).) *Usner* involved an injured longshoreman, but the limitation it imposes on the unseaworthiness doctrine is applicable in seamen's cases.

2. Reconciling *Mitchell* and *Usner* is a source of perpetual difficulty in the lower courts. Presumably what is necessary is an understanding of the difference between an *act* and a *condition*, no matter how short-lived. Some have found helpful the following language from *Puddu v. Royal Netherlands S.S. Co.*, 303 F.2d 752, 757 (2d Cir. 1962) (Hays, J., concurring):

> A ship is not unseaworthy because it has glass in a window which might be broken. [That's a condition, but not a defective one.] The injuries of a seaman who negligently breaks such a glass are not the result of unseaworthiness, nor are the injuries of a seaman who is cut by the falling glass. But injury incurred in stepping on the broken glass does result from unseaworthiness.

5. Seaman Status

The combination of the Jones Act, unseaworthiness, and maintenance-and-cure causes of action have traditionally made seamen the most generously-treated personal injury victims in U.S. law. Consequently, seaman status has been hotly contested in case after case after case. The Supreme Court has never explicitly said so (although the *Chandris* opinion comes close), but the lower courts and commentators take it as settled that the criteria for seaman status are the same for Jones Act, unseaworthiness, and maintenance-and-cure purposes.[26]

Chandris Inc. v. Latsis

Supreme Court of the United States, 1995

515 U.S. 347, 115 S. Ct. 2172, 132 L. Ed. 2d 314, 1995 AMC 1840

Justice O'CONNOR delivered the opinion of the Court.

I.

In May 1989, respondent Antonios Latsis was employed by petitioner Chandris, Inc., as a salaried superintendent engineer. Latsis was responsible for maintaining and updating the electronic and communications equipment on Chandris' fleet of vessels, which consisted of six passenger cruise ships. Each ship in the Chandris fleet carried between 12 and 14 engineers who were assigned permanently to that vessel. Latsis, on the other hand, was

26. See, e.g., *Guevara v. Maritime Overseas Corp.*, 59 F.3d 1496, 1499 (5th Cir. 1995) (en banc), overruled on other grounds, *Atlantic Sounding Co. v. Townsend*, 337 U.S. 404 (2009); *Johnson v. Continental Grain Co.*, 58 F.3d 1232, 1236 (8th Cir. 1995); *Harwood v. Partredereit AF 15.5.81*, 944 F.2d 1187, 1192 (4th Cir. 1991).

one of two supervising engineers based at Chandris' Miami office; his duties ran to the entire fleet and included not only overseeing the vessels' engineering departments, which required him to take a number of voyages, but also planning and directing ship maintenance from the shore. Latsis claimed at trial that he spent 72 percent of his time at sea; his immediate supervisor testified that the appropriate figure was closer to 10 percent.

On May 14, 1989, Latsis sailed for Bermuda aboard the *S.S. Galileo* to plan for an upcoming renovation of the ship, which was one of the older vessels in the Chandris fleet. Latsis developed a problem with his right eye on the day of departure, and he saw the ship's doctor as the *Galileo* left port. The doctor diagnosed a suspected detached retina but failed to follow standard medical procedure, which would have been to direct Latsis to see an ophthalmologist on an emergency basis. Instead, the ship's doctor recommended that Latsis relax until he could see an eye specialist when the *Galileo* arrived in Bermuda two days later. No attempt was made to transport Latsis ashore for prompt medical care by means of a pilot vessel or helicopter during the 11 hours it took the ship to reach the open sea from Baltimore, and Latsis received no further medical care until after the ship arrived in Bermuda. In Bermuda, a doctor diagnosed a detached retina and recommended immediate hospitalization and surgery. Although the operation was a partial success, Latsis lost 75 percent of his vision in his right eye.

Following his recuperation, which lasted approximately six weeks, Latsis resumed his duties with Chandris. On September 30, 1989, he sailed with the *Galileo* to Bremerhaven, Germany, where the vessel was placed in drydock for a 6-month refurbishment. After the conversion, the company renamed the vessel the *S.S. Meridian*. Latsis, who had been with the ship the entire time she was in drydock in Bremerhaven, sailed back to the United States on board the *Meridian* and continued to work for Chandris until November 1990, when his employment was terminated for reasons that are not clear from the record.

In October 1991, Latsis filed suit in the United States District Court for the Southern District of New York seeking compensatory damages under the Jones Act for the negligence of the ship's doctor that resulted in the significant loss of sight in Latsis' right eye. * * * The District Court instructed the jury that it could conclude that Latsis was a seaman within the meaning of the statute if it found as follows:

> [T]he plaintiff was either permanently assigned to the vessel or performed a substantial part of his work on the vessel. In determining whether Mr. Latsis performed a substantial part of his work on the vessel, you may not consider the period of time the *Galileo* was in drydock in Germany, because during that time period she was out of navigation. You may, however, consider the time spent sailing to and from Germany for the conversion. Also, on this first element of being a seaman, seamen do not include land-based workers.

The parties stipulated to the District Court's second requirement for Jones Act coverage—that Latsis' duties contributed to the accomplishment of the missions of the Chandris vessels. Latsis did not object to the seaman status jury instructions in their entirety, but only contested that portion of the charge which explicitly took from the jury's consideration the period of time that the *Galileo* was in drydock. The jury returned a verdict in favor of Chandris solely on the issue of Latsis' status as a seaman under the Jones Act.

Respondent appealed to the Court of Appeals for the Second Circuit, which vacated the judgment and remanded the case for a new trial. The court emphasized that its longstanding test for seaman status under the Jones Act required "a more or less permanent connection with the ship," [ ] a connection that need not be limited to time spent on the vessel but could also be established by the nature of the work performed. The court thought that the alternate formulation employed by the District Court (permanent assignment to the vessel or performance of a substantial part of his work on the vessel), which was derived from *Offshore Co. v. Robison*, 266 F.2d 769, 779 (5th Cir. 1959), improperly framed the issue for the jury primarily, if not solely, in terms of Latsis' temporal relationship to the vessel. With that understanding of what the language of the *Robison* test implied, the court concluded that the District Court's seaman status jury instructions constituted plain error under established circuit precedent.[27] The court then took this case as an opportunity to clarify its seaman status requirements, directing the District Court that the jury should be instructed on remand as follows:

> [T]he test of seaman status under the Jones Act is an employment-related connection to a vessel in navigation. The test will be met where a jury finds that (1) the plaintiff contributed to the function of or helped accomplish the mission of, a vessel; (2) the plaintiff's contribution was limited to a particular vessel or identifiable group of vessels; (3) the plaintiff's contribution was substantial in terms of its (a) duration or (b) nature; and (4) the course of the plaintiff's employment regularly exposed the plaintiff to the hazards of the sea.

* * * [T]he Court of Appeals [also] held that the District Court erred in instructing the jury that the time Latsis spent with the ship while she was in drydock could not count in the substantial connection equation. * * *

We granted certiorari to resolve the continuing conflict among the Courts of Appeals regarding the appropriate requirements for seaman status under the Jones Act.

II.

* * * Congress enacted the Jones Act in 1920 to remove the bar to suit for negligence articulated in *The Osceola*, thereby completing the trilogy of heightened legal protections (unavailable to other maritime workers) that seamen receive because of their exposure to the "perils of the sea." See G. Gilmore & C. Black, Law of Admiralty §6-21, at 328–329 (2d ed. 1975); Robertson, *A New Approach to Determining Seaman Status*, 64 Tex. L. Rev. 79 (1985) (hereinafter Robertson). Justice Story identified this animating purpose behind the legal regime governing maritime injuries when he observed that seamen "are emphatically the wards of the admiralty" because they "are by the peculiarity of their lives liable to sudden sickness from change of climate, exposure to perils, and exhausting labour." *Harden v. Gordon* [*supra* at 147–48]. Similarly, we stated in *McDermott Int'l, Inc. v. Wilander*, 498 U.S. 337, 354 (1991)] that "[t]raditional seamen's remedies have been 'universally recognized as ... growing out of the status of the seaman and his peculiar relationship to the vessel, and as a feature of the maritime law compensating or offsetting the special hazards and disadvantages to which they who go down to sea in ships are subjected'" (quoting *Seas Shipping Co. v. Sieracki*, 328 U.S. 84, 104 (1946) (Stone, C.J., dissenting)).

The Jones Act, however, does not define the term "seaman" and therefore leaves to the courts the determination of exactly which maritime workers are entitled to admiralty's special protection. Early on, we concluded that Congress intended the term to have its established meaning under the general maritime law at the time the Jones Act was enacted. * * *

27. Editors' note: Designating the mistaken instruction as "plain error" enabled the court of appeals to fully review it despite Latsis's failure to object to most of it in the trial court.

Congress provided some content for the Jones Act requirement in 1927 when it enacted the Longshore and Harbor Workers' Compensation Act (LHWCA), which provides scheduled compensation (and the exclusive remedy) for injury to a broad range of land-based maritime workers but which also explicitly excludes from its coverage "a master or member of a crew of any vessel." 33 U.S.C. § 902(3)(G). As the Court has stated on several occasions, the Jones Act and the LHWCA are mutually exclusive compensation regimes: " 'master or member of a crew' is a refinement of the term 'seaman' in the Jones Act; it excludes from LHWCA coverage those properly covered under the Jones Act." *Wilander*, 498 U.S. at 347. Indeed, "it is odd but true that the key requirement for Jones Act coverage now appears in another statute." *Ibid.* Injured workers who fall under neither category may still recover under an applicable state workers' compensation scheme or, in admiralty, under general maritime tort principles (which are admittedly less generous than the Jones Act's protections). [ ]

Despite the LHWCA language, drawing the distinction between those maritime workers who should qualify as seamen and those who should not has proved to be a difficult task and the source of much litigation—particularly because "the myriad circumstances in which men go upon the water confront courts not with discrete classes of maritime employees, but rather with a spectrum ranging from the blue-water seaman to the land-based longshoreman." *Brown v. ITT Rayonier, Inc.*, 497 F.2d 234, 237 (5th Cir. 1974). The federal courts have struggled over the years to articulate generally applicable criteria to distinguish among the many varieties of maritime workers, often developing detailed multipronged tests for seaman status. * * *

A.

In *Wilander*, decided in 1991, the Court attempted for the first time in 33 years to clarify the definition of a "seaman" under the Jones Act. Jon Wilander was injured while assigned as a foreman supervising the sandblasting and painting of various fixtures and piping on oil drilling platforms in the Persian Gulf. His employer claimed that he could not qualify as a seaman because he did not aid in the navigation function of the vessels on which he served. Emphasizing that the question presented was narrow, we considered whether the term "seaman" is limited to only those maritime workers who aid in a vessel's navigation. * * * [W]e held that, although "[i]t is not necessary that a seaman aid in navigation or contribute to the transportation of the vessel, ... a seaman must be doing the ship's work." 498 U.S. at 355. We explained that "[t]he key to seaman status is employment-related connection to a vessel in navigation," and that, although "[w]e are not called upon here to define this connection in all details, we believe the requirement that an employee's duties must 'contribut[e] to the function of the vessel or to the accomplishment of its mission' captures well an important requirement of seaman status."

Beyond dispensing with the "aid to navigation" requirement, however, *Wilander* did not consider the requisite connection to a vessel in any detail and therefore failed to end the prevailing confusion regarding seaman status.

B.

Respondent urges us to find our way out of the Jones Act "labyrinth" by focusing on the seemingly activity-based policy underlying the statute (the protection of those who are exposed to the perils of the sea), and to conclude that anyone working on board a vessel for the duration of a "voyage" in furtherance of the vessel's mission has the necessary employment-related connection to qualify as a seaman. Such an approach, however, would run counter to our prior decisions and our understanding of the remedial scheme Congress has established for injured maritime workers. A brief survey of the Jones Act's tortured history makes clear that we must reject the initial appeal of such a "voyage" test and undertake the more difficult task of developing a status-based standard that, although it determines Jones Act coverage without regard to the precise activity in which the worker is engaged at the time of the injury, nevertheless best furthers the Jones Act's remedial goals.

Our Jones Act cases establish several basic principles regarding the definition of a seaman. First, "[w]hether under the Jones Act or general maritime law, seamen do not include land-based workers." [ ] Our early Jones Act decisions had not recognized this fundamental distinction. In *International Stevedoring Co. v. Haverty*, 272 U.S. 50 (1926), we held that a longshoreman injured while stowing cargo, and while aboard but not employed by a vessel at dock in navigable waters, was a seaman covered by the Jones Act. * * * In 1946, the Court * * * recognized that Congress had acted, in passing the LHWCA in 1927, to undercut the Court's reasoning in the *Haverty* line of cases and to emphasize that land-based maritime workers should not be entitled to the seamen's traditional remedies. Our decision in *Swanson v. Mara Brothers, Inc.*, 328 U.S. 1, 7 (1946), acknowledged that Congress had expressed its intention to "confine the benefits of the Jones Act to the members of the crew of a vessel plying in navigable waters and to substitute for the right of recovery recognized by the *Haverty* case only such rights to compensation as are given by (the LHWCA)." [ ] Through the LHWCA, therefore, Congress "explicitly den[ied] a right of recovery under the Jones Act to maritime workers not members of a crew who are injured on board a vessel." *Swanson*, 328 U.S. at 6. And this recognition process culminated in *Wilander* with the Court's statement that, "[w]ith the passage of the LHWCA, Congress established a clear distinction between land-based and sea-based maritime workers. The latter, who owe their allegiance to a vessel and not solely to a land-based employer, are seamen." 498 U.S. at 347.

In addition to recognizing a fundamental distinction between land-based and sea-based maritime employees, our cases also emphasize that Jones Act coverage, like the jurisdiction of admiralty over causes of action for maintenance and cure for injuries received in the course of a seamen's employment, depends "not on the place where the injury is inflicted, but on the nature of the seaman's service, his status as a member of the vessel, and his relationship as such to the vessel and its operation in navigable waters." [ ] Thus, maritime workers who obtain seaman status do not lose that protection automatically when on shore and may recover under the Jones Act whenever they are injured in the service of a vessel, regardless of whether the injury occurs on or off the ship. * * *

Our LHWCA cases also recognize the converse: Land-based maritime workers injured while on a vessel in navigation remain covered by the LHWCA * * *. [See, e.g.,] *Parker v. Motor Boat Sales, Inc.*, 214 U.S. 244 (1941) (upholding LHWCA coverage for a worker testing outboard motors who "was drowned when a motor boat in which he was riding capsized"). [Such] decisions, which reflect our longstanding view of the LHWCA's scope, indicate that a maritime worker does not become a "member of a crew" as soon as a vessel leaves the dock.

It is therefore well settled after decades of judicial interpretation that the Jones Act inquiry is fundamentally status-based; land-based maritime workers do not become seamen because they happen to be working on board a vessel when they are injured, and seamen do not lose Jones Act protection when the course of their service to a vessel takes them ashore. In spite of this background, respondent and Justice Stevens suggest that any maritime worker who is assigned to a vessel for the duration of a voyage—and whose duties contribute to the vessel's mission—should be classified as a seaman for purposes of injuries incurred during that voyage. Under such a "voyage test," which relies principally upon this Court's statements that the Jones Act was designed to protect maritime workers who are exposed to the "special hazards" and "particular perils" characteristic of work on vessels at sea [ ], the worker's activities at the time of the injury would be controlling.

The difficulty with respondent's argument, as the foregoing discussion makes clear, is that the LHWCA repudiated the *Haverty* line of cases and established that a worker is no longer considered to be a seaman simply because he is doing a seaman's work at the time of the injury. Seaman status is not coextensive with seamen's risks. See, e.g., [ ]; Robertson 93 (following "the overwhelming weight of authority in taking it as given that seaman status cannot be established by any worker who fails to demonstrate that a significant portion of his work was done aboard a vessel" and acknowledging that "[s]ome workers who unmistakably confront the perils of the sea, often in extreme form, are thereby left out of the seamen's protections" [footnote omitted]). A "voyage test" would conflict with our prior understanding of the Jones Act as fundamentally status-based, granting the negligence cause of action to those maritime workers who form the ship's company. [ ]

* * *

We believe it is important to avoid "'engrafting upon the statutory classification of a "seaman" a judicial gloss so protean, elusive, or arbitrary as to permit a worker to walk into and out of coverage in the course of his regular duties.'" [ ] In evaluating the employment-related connection of a maritime worker to a vessel in navigation, courts should not employ "a 'snapshot' test for seaman status, inspecting only the situation as it exists at the instant of injury; a more enduring relationship is contemplated in the jurisprudence." [ ] Thus, a worker may not oscillate back and forth between Jones Act coverage and other remedies depending on the activity in which the worker was engaged while injured. [ ] Unlike Justice Stevens, we do not believe that any maritime worker on a ship at sea as part of his employment is automatically a member of the crew of the vessel within the meaning of the statutory terms. Our rejection of the voyage test is also consistent with the interests of employers and maritime workers alike in being able to predict who will be covered by the Jones Act (and perhaps more importantly for purposes of the employers' workers' compensation obligations, who will be covered by the LHWCA) before a particular work day begins.

To say that our cases have recognized a distinction between land-based and sea-based maritime workers that precludes application of a voyage test for seaman status, however, is not to say that a maritime employee must work *only* on board a vessel to qualify as a seaman under the Jones Act. In *Southwest Marine, Inc. v. Gizoni*, 502 U.S. 81 (1991), decided only a few months after *Wilander*, we concluded that a worker's status as a ship repairman, one of the enumerated occupations encompassed within the term "employee" under the LHWCA [ ], did not necessarily restrict the worker to a remedy under that statute. We explained that, "[w]hile in some cases a ship repairman may lack the requisite connection to a vessel in navigation to qualify for seaman status, ... not all ship repairmen lack the requisite connection as a matter of law. This is so because '[i]t is not the employee's particular job that is determinative, but the employee's connection to a vessel.'" Thus, we concluded, the Jones Act remedy may be available to maritime workers who are employed by a shipyard and who spend a portion of their time working on shore but spend the rest of their time at sea.

Beyond these basic themes, which are sufficient to foreclose respondent's principal argument, our cases are largely silent as to the precise relationship a maritime worker must bear to a vessel in order to come within the Jones Act's ambit. We have, until now, left to the lower federal courts the task of developing appropriate criteria to distinguish the "ship's company" from those members of the maritime community whose employment is essentially land-based.

C.

* * *

[A] major body of seaman status law developed in the Court of Appeals for the Fifth Circuit, which has a substantial Jones Act caseload, in the wake of *Offshore Co. v. Robison*, 266 F.2d 769 (5th Cir. 1959). At the time of his injury, Robison was an oil worker permanently assigned to a drilling rig mounted on a barge in the Gulf of Mexico. In sustaining the jury's award of damages to Robison under the Jones Act, the court abandoned the aid in navigation requirement * * * and held as follows:

> [T]here is an evidentiary basis for a Jones Act case to go to the jury: (1) if there is evidence that the injured workman was assigned permanently to a vessel ... or performed a substantial part of his work on the vessel; and (2) if the capacity in which he was employed or the duties which he performed contributed to the function of the vessel or the accomplishment of its mission, or to the operation or welfare of the vessel in terms of its maintenance during its movement or during anchorage for its future trips.

Soon after *Robison*, the Fifth Circuit modified the test to allow seaman status for those workers who had the requisite connection with an "identifiable fleet" of vessels, a finite group of vessels under common ownership or control. [ ] The modified *Robison* formulation * * * [is] the definitive test for seaman status in the Fifth Circuit [and] has been highly influential in other courts as well. See Robertson 95 [ ].

* * * [S]ubsequent developments in the Fifth Circuit's Jones Act jurisprudence added a strictly temporal gloss to the Jones Act inquiry. Under *Barrett v. Chevron, U.S.A., Inc.*, [781 F.2d 1067, 1075 (5th Cir. 1986) (en banc)], if an employee's regular duties require him to divide his time between vessel and land, his status as a crew member is determined "in the context of his entire employment" with his current employer. In *Barrett*, the court noted that the worker "performed seventy to eighty percent of his work on platforms and no more than twenty to thirty percent of his work on vessels" and then concluded that, "[b]ecause he did not perform a substantial portion of his work aboard a vessel or fleet of vessels, he failed to establish that he was a member of the crew of a vessel." Since *Barrett*, the Fifth Circuit consistently has analyzed the problem in terms of the percentage of work performed on vessels for the employer in question—and has declined to find seaman status where the employee spent less than 30 percent of his time aboard ship. [ ]

* * *

D.

From this background emerge the essential contours of the "employment-related connection to a vessel in navigation" [ ] required for an employee to qualify as a seaman under the Jones Act. * * * [W]e think that the essential requirements for seaman status are twofold. First, as we emphasized in *Wilander*, "an employee's duties must 'contribut[e] to the function of the vessel or to the accomplishment of its mission.'" 498 U.S. at 355 (quoting *Robison*, 266 F.2d at 779). The Jones Act's protections, like the other admiralty protections for seamen, only extend to those maritime employees who do the ship's work. But this threshold requirement is very broad: "[A]ll who work at sea in the service of a ship" are *eligible* for seaman status. 498 U.S. at 354.

Second, and most important for our purposes here, a seaman must have a connection to a vessel in navigation (or to an identifiable group of such vessels) that is substantial in terms of both its duration and its nature. The fundamental purpose of this substantial connection requirement is to give full effect to the remedial scheme created by Congress and to separate the sea-based maritime employees who are entitled to Jones Act protection from those land-based workers who have only a transitory or sporadic connection to a vessel in navigation, and therefore whose employment does not regularly expose them to the perils of the sea. [ ] This requirement therefore determines which maritime employees in *Wilander's* broad category of persons eligible for seaman status because they are "doing the ship's work" are in fact entitled to the benefits conferred upon seamen by the Jones Act because they have the requisite employment-related connection to a vessel in navigation.

It is important to recall that the question of who is a "member of a crew," and therefore who is a "seaman," is a mixed question of law and fact. Because statutory terms are at issue, their interpretation is a question of law and it is the court's duty to define the appropriate standard. [ ] On the other hand, "[i]f reasonable persons, applying the proper legal standard, could differ as to whether the employee was a 'member of a crew,' it is a question for the jury." [ ] The jury should be permitted, when determining whether a maritime employee has the requisite employment-related connection to a vessel in navigation to qualify as a member of the vessel's crew, to consider all relevant circumstances bearing on the two elements outlined above.

In defining the prerequisites for Jones Act coverage, we think it preferable to focus upon the essence of what it means to be a seaman and to eschew the temptation to create detailed tests to effectuate the congressional purpose, tests that tend to become ends in and of themselves. * * * In our view, "the total circumstances of an individual's employment must be weighed to determine whether he had a sufficient relation to the navigation of vessels and the perils attendant thereon." [ ] The duration of a worker's connection to a vessel and the nature of the worker's activities, taken together, determine whether a maritime employee is a seaman because the ultimate inquiry is whether the worker in question is a member of the vessel's crew or simply a land-based employee who happens to be working on the vessel at a given time.

Although we adopt the centerpiece of the formulation used by the Court of Appeals in this case—that a seaman must have a connection with a vessel in navigation that is substantial in both duration and nature—we should point out how our understanding of the import of that language may be different in some respects from that of the court below. The Court of Appeals suggested that its test for seaman status "does not unequivocally require a Jones Act seaman to be substantially connected to a vessel" in terms of time if the worker performs important work on board on a steady, although not necessarily on a temporally significant, basis. Perhaps giving effect to this intuition, or perhaps reacting to the temporal gloss placed on the *Robison* language by later Fifth Circuit decisions, the court phrased its standard at one point as requiring a jury to find that a Jones Act plaintiff's contribution to the function of the vessel was substantial in terms of its duration *or* nature. It is not clear which version ("duration or nature" as opposed to "duration and nature") the Court of Appeals intended to adopt for the substantial connection requirement—or indeed whether the court saw a significant difference between the two. Nevertheless, we think it is important that a seaman's connection to a vessel in fact be substantial in both respects.

We agree with the Court of Appeals that seaman status is not *merely* a temporal concept, but we also believe that it necessarily includes a temporal element. A maritime worker who spends only a small fraction of his working time on board a vessel is fundamentally land-based and therefore not a member of the vessel's crew, regardless of what his duties are. Naturally, substantiality in this context is determined by reference to the period covered by the Jones Act plaintiff's maritime employment, rather than by some absolute measure. Generally, the Fifth Circuit seems to have identified an appropriate rule of thumb for the ordinary case: a worker who spends less than about 30 percent of his time in the service of a vessel in navigation should not qualify as a seaman under the Jones Act. This figure of course serves as no more than a guideline established by years of experience, and departure from it will certainly be justified in appropriate cases. As we have said, "[t]he inquiry into seaman status is of necessity fact specific; it will depend on the nature of the vessel and the employee's precise relation to it." [ ] Nevertheless, we believe that courts, employers, and maritime workers can all benefit from reference to these general principles. And where undisputed facts reveal that a maritime worker has a clearly inadequate temporal connection to vessels in navigation, the court may take the question from the jury by granting summary judgment or a directed verdict. [ ]

On the other hand, we see no reason to limit the seaman status inquiry, as petitioners contend, exclusively to an examination of the overall course of a worker's service with a particular employer. When a maritime worker's basic assignment changes, his seaman status may change as well. *See Barrett*, 781 F.2d at 1077 (Rubin, J., dissenting) ("An assignment to work as a crew member, like the voyage of a vessel, may be brief, and the *Robison* test is applicable in deciding the worker's status during any such employment") [ ]. For example, we can imagine situations in which someone who had worked for years in an employer's shoreside headquarters is then reassigned to a ship in a classic seaman's job that involves a regular and continuous, rather than intermittent, commitment of the worker's labor to the function of a vessel. Such a person should not be denied seaman status if injured shortly after the reassignment, just as someone actually transferred to a desk job in the company's office and injured in the hallway should not be entitled to claim seaman status on the basis of prior service at sea. If a maritime employee receives a new work assignment in which his essential duties are changed, he is entitled to have the assessment of the substantiality of his vessel-related work made on the basis of his activities in his new position. [ ] Thus, nothing in our opinion forecloses Jones Act coverage, in appropriate cases, for Justice Stevens' paradigmatic maritime worker injured while reassigned to "a lengthy voyage on the high seas." While our approach maintains the status-based inquiry this Court's earlier cases contemplate, we recognize that seaman status also should not be some immutable characteristic that maritime workers who spend only a portion of their time at sea can never attain.

III.

One final issue remains for our determination: whether the District Court erred in instructing the jurors that, "[i]n determining whether Mr. Latsis performed a substantial part of his work on the vessel, [they could] not consider the period of time the *Galileo* was in drydock in Germany, because during that time period she was out of navigation." We agree with the Court of Appeals that it did.

The foregoing discussion establishes that, to qualify as a seaman under the Jones Act, a maritime employee must have a substantial employment-related connection to a vessel *in navigation.* [ ] Of course, any time Latsis spent with the *Galileo* while the ship was out of navigation could not count as time spent at sea for purposes of that inquiry, and it would have been appropriate for the District Court to make this clear to the jury. Yet the underlying inquiry whether a vessel is or is not "in navigation" for Jones Act purposes is a fact-intensive question that is normally for the jury and not the court to decide. [ ] Removing the issue from the jury's consideration is only appropriate where the facts and the law will reasonably support only one conclusion, and the colloquy between the court and counsel does not indicate that the District Court made any such findings before overruling respondent's objection to the drydock instruction. Based upon the record before us, we think the court failed adequately to justify its decision to remove the question whether the *Galileo* was "in navigation" while in Bremerhaven from the jury.

* * * [I]t is generally accepted that "a vessel does not cease to be a vessel when she is not voyaging, but is at anchor, berthed, or at dockside" [ ], even when the vessel is undergoing repairs. * * *. The general rule among the Courts of Appeals is that vessels undergoing repairs or spending a relatively short period of time in drydock are still considered to be "in navigation" whereas ships being transformed through "major" overhauls or renovations are not. [ ]

Obviously, while the distinction at issue here is one of degree, the prevailing view is that "major renovations can take a ship out of navigation, even though its use before and after the work will be the same." [ ] Our review of the record in this case uncovered relatively little evidence bearing on the *Galileo*'s status during the repairs, and even less discussion of the question by the District Court. On the one hand, the work on the Chandris vessel took only about six months, which seems to be a relatively short period of time for important repairs on oceangoing vessels. [ ] On the other hand, Latsis' own description of the work performed suggests that the modifications to the vessel were actually quite significant, including the removal of the ship's bottom plates and propellers, the addition of bow thrusters, overhaul of the main engines, reconstruction of the boilers, and renovations of the cabins and other passenger areas of the ship. On these facts, * * * it is possible that Chandris could be entitled to partial summary judgment or a directed verdict concerning whether the *Galileo* remained in navigation while in drydock; the record, however, contains no stipulations or findings by the District Court to justify its conclusion that the modifications to the *Galileo* were sufficiently extensive to remove the vessel from navigation as a matter of law. On that basis, we agree with the Court of Appeals that the District Court's drydock instruction was erroneous.

Even if the District Court had been justified in directing a verdict on the question whether the *Galileo* remained in navigation while in Bremerhaven, we think that the court's charge to the jury swept too broadly. Instead of simply noting the appropriate legal conclusion and instructing the jury not to consider the time Latsis spent with the vessel in drydock *as time spent with a vessel in navigation*, the District Court appears to have prohibited the jury from considering Latsis' stay in Bremerhaven *for any purpose.* In our view, Latsis' activities while the vessel was in drydock are at least marginally relevant to the underlying inquiry (whether Latsis was a seaman and not a land-based maritime employee). Naturally, the jury would be free to draw several inferences from Latsis' work during the conversion, not all of which would be in his favor. But the choice among such permissible inferences should have been left to the jury, and we think the District Court's broadly worded instruction improperly deprived the jury of that opportunity by forbidding the consideration of Latsis' time in Bremerhaven at all.

IV.

Under the Jones Act, "[i]f reasonable persons, applying the proper legal standard, could differ as to whether the employee was a 'member of a crew,' it is a question for the jury." [ ] On the facts of this case, given that essential points are in dispute, reasonable fact-finders could disagree as to whether Latsis was a seaman. Because the question whether the *Galileo* remained "in navigation" while in drydock should have been submitted to the jury, and because the decision on that issue might affect the outcome of the ultimate seaman status inquiry, we affirm the judgment of the Court of Appeals remanding the case to the District Court for a new trial.

On remand, the District Court should charge the jury in a manner consistent with our holding that the "employment-related connection to a vessel in navigation" necessary to qualify as a seaman under the Jones Act comprises two basic elements: the worker's duties must contribute to the function of the vessel or to the accomplishment of its mission, and the worker must have a connection to a vessel in navigation (or an identifiable group of vessels) that is substantial in terms of both its duration and its nature. As to the latter point, the court should emphasize that the Jones Act was intended to protect sea-based maritime workers, who owe their allegiance to a vessel, and not land-based employees, who do not. By instructing juries in Jones Act cases accordingly, courts can give proper effect to the remedial scheme Congress has created for injured maritime workers.

Justice STEVENS, with whom Justice Thomas and Justice Breyer join, concurring in the judgment:

The majority has reached the odd conclusion that a maritime engineer, injured aboard ship on the high seas while performing his duties as an employee of the ship, might not be a "seaman" within the meaning of the Jones Act. This decision is unprecedented. It ignores the critical distinction between work performed aboard ship during a voyage—when the members of the crew encounter "the perils of the sea"—and maritime work performed on a vessel moored to a dock in a safe harbor. In my judgment, an employee of the ship who is injured at sea in the course of his employment is always a "seaman." I would leave more ambiguous, shore-bound cases for another day.

* * *

Notes

1. **Bartenders, muleteers, and waiters.** The view expressed in *Wilander* and *Chandris* that in enacting the Jones Act the 1920 Congress "intended the term [seaman] to have its established meaning under the general maritime law at the time" sets a broad initial template for defining the term. An amicus brief in *Wilander* detailed the pre-Jones Act case law on seaman status: "In cases spanning the period 1781–1926 United States admiralty courts accorded seaman status [not only to classic sailors but also to] bartenders, cabin boys, carpenters, chambermaids, clerks, cooks, coopers, divers, doctors, dredge workers, engineers, firemen, fishermen, harpooners, horsemen, masons, muleteers, musicians, pursers, radio operators, seal hunters, stewards, and waiters." Brief of Association of Trial Lawyers of America as Amicus Curiae in Support of Respondents 8–9 (footnotes omitted) (1990). The *Wilander* Court accepted this enumeration, stating that at the time of *The Osceola* and the passage of the Jones Act, seamen included "all persons employed on board ships and vessels during the voyage to assist in their navigation and preservation, or to promote the purposes of the voyage." 498 U.S. at 344.

2. **Member of a crew of any vessel.** The *Swanson/Wilander/Chandris* ruling that the "member of a crew of any vessel" provision in the 1927 LHWCA narrowed the Jones Act's coverage means that workers—regardless of whether they are classic sailors or bartenders, etc.—are Jones Act seamen only if they serve the function or mission of a vessel or fleet

while engaged in a relationship with a vessel or fleet that satisfies the substantial-in-nature and substantial-in-duration requirements.

3. **Attachment to a fleet of vessels.** In *Harbor Tug & Barge Co. v. Papai*, 520 U.S. 548, 557 (1997), the Court emphasized that seaman status cannot be achieved by establishing a substantial relationship with a group of vessels unless the group meets the legal definition of a *fleet*, *viz.*, "an identifiable group of vessels [that are] subject to common ownership or control."

4. In the view of Justices Stevens, Thomas, and Breyer, Antonios Latsis should have been classified as seaman as a matter of law. But the *Chandris* majority did not agree. Nor did two juries. In the Southern District of New York on remand, Judge Preska again submitted the issue of Mr. Latsis's status to the jury, this time under instructions modeled on those laid out in *Chandris.* That jury, like the first one, concluded that Latsis was not a seaman.

5. ***Stewart's* contribution.** *Chandris* is often described as setting forth a two-part test for seaman status, but it is apparent that the key language of *Chandris* included five elements. Under *Chandris*, an employee who aspired to seaman status had to show that the employee worked on, for, or with a vessel (or fleet of vessels); the vessel (or fleet) was in navigation; the employee's duties contributed to the vessel's (or fleet's) function or mission; the employee's connection to the vessel (or fleet) was substantial in duration; and the employee's connection to the vessel (or fleet) was substantial in nature.

Stewart v. Dutra Constr. Co., *supra* at 21, 24, shortened the list to four elements by removing the second element (the "in navigation" element). The *Stewart* Court explained the *Chandris* Court's use of the term "in navigation" as follows:

> [The *Chandris*] Court did not mean that the "in navigation" requirement stood apart from [1 U.S.C.] § 3, such that a "vessel" for purposes of § 3 might nevertheless not be a "vessel in navigation" for purposes of the Jones Act or the LHWCA. Instead, the "in navigation" requirement is an element of the vessel status of a watercraft. It is relevant to whether the craft is "used, or capable of being used" for maritime transportation.

6. **Summarizing the Chandris/Stewart test.** The four-requirement test for seaman status that emerges from *Chandris* and *Stewart* can be summarized as follows:

> a. The worker must work on a vessel (or fleet of vessels). A *vessel* is defined by 1 U.S.C. § 3 and *Stewart* as any "description of watercraft or other artificial contrivance used, or [practically] capable of being used, as a means of transportation on water." This *vessel* requirement keeps crewboat helicopter pilots, fixed-platform workers, and workers on watercraft that have "been taken out of service, permanently anchored, or otherwise rendered practically incapable of maritime transport" [*Stewart*, *supra* at 25] from being seamen.
>
> b. The worker's duties must contribute to the vessel's (or fleet's) function or mission. This *contribution* requirement is intended as a "threshold requirement [that] is very broad" [*Chandris*, 515 U.S. at 368], but it nevertheless keeps amphibious workers who merely ride a vessel to work (for example, on a fixed offshore oil or gas platform) or sleep and eat on a vessel without doing any work there out of seaman status.
>
> c. The worker's connection to the vessel (or fleet) must be substantial in duration. The *substantial-in-duration* requirement (together with the Court's fairly restrictive

definition of a "fleet" as an "identifiable group of vessels under common ownership or control" [*Papai, supra* note 3] keeps everyday longshoremen out of seaman status by generally requiring that the worker must have spent at least 30 percent of his time while working for the current employer (or, if there has been a change of assignment, in the current assignment with the employer) in the service of a particular vessel or fleet of vessels under common ownership or control. The restrictive definition of a "fleet" also excludes pilots from seaman status. See, e.g., *Bach v. Trident Steamship Co.*, 920 F.2d 322, 324-326 (5th Cir. 1991), *reinstated after remand*, 947 F.2d 1290 (5th Cir. 1991).

d. The worker's connection to the vessel (or fleet) must be substantial in nature. The *substantial-in-nature* requirement keeps various sorts of amphibious workers out of seaman status by addressing whether the worker's duties regularly or significantly exposed the worker to the perils of the sea.

C. The Longshore and Harbor Workers' Compensation Act

As we saw in Section II-B-5, *supra* at 192, the Longshore and Harbor Workers' Compensation Act (LHWCA), 33 U.S.C. §§ 901–950, provides a workers' compensation remedy for maritime workers who do not qualify as seamen. The LHWCA was enacted in 1927 and extensively amended in 1972 and 1984. The present version—the relevant portions of which are set out in the Statutory Supplement—is detailed and somewhat complex. Determining whether an employer owes workers' compensation benefits to an ill or injured LHWCA worker—and if so, how much and for how long—is often disputatious. Controversies about workers' compensation benefits under the LHWCA are adjudicated by administrative law judges (ALJs) in the U.S. Department of Labor. ALJ determinations are reviewable by a three-member body called the Benefits Review Board (BRB). BRB determinations are reviewable by the U.S. Courts of Appeals.

We are not concerned with the details of workers' compensation practice, but we do need to know how the LHWCA intersects (on one side, notionally speaking) with the seamen's remedies and (on the other side) with maritime workers' rights under state law. We also need to know how the LHWCA affects LHWCA-covered workers' rights under federal maritime tort law. This subsection therefore addresses three issues: (a) the boundaries (coverage) of the LHWCA; (b) the LHWCA's intersection with the seamen's remedies on one side and state workers' compensation law on the other; and (c) the nature of the tort action that LHWCA-covered workers are permitted to maintain against shipowners.

In studying this and ensuing sections of Chapter II, an obvious (but occasionally overlooked) distinction should be kept firmly in mind: ***the distinction between workers' compensation proceedings*** and ***tort cases.*** The central idea of workers' compensation systems is the immunization of the employer from tort liability in exchange for the obligation to provide workers compensation benefits. (See LHWCA § 5(a), 33 U.S.C. § 905(a).) The vast bulk of the LHWCA (most of which has been edited out of this casebook and Statutory Supplement) deals with workers' compensation proceedings. *Caputo* dealt with workers' compensation proceedings. *Howlett* and *Jones & Laughlin*, on the other hand, are tort cases; they treat the somewhat exceptional tort action made available to LHWCA-covered workers by LHWCA § 5(b), 33 U.S.C. § 905(b).

Northeast Marine Terminal Co. v. Caputo

Supreme Court of the United States, 1977
432 U.S. 249, 97 S. Ct. 2348, 53 L. Ed. 2d 320, 1977 AMC 1037

Mr. Justice MARSHALL delivered the opinion of the unanimous Court.

In 1972 Congress amended the [LHWCA] in substantial part to "extend [the Act's] coverage to protect additional workers." S. Rep. No. 92-1125, at 1 (1972) (hereinafter S. Rep.).[28] In these consolidated cases we must determine whether respondents Caputo and Blundo, injured while working on the New York City waterfront, are entitled to compensation. To answer that question we must determine the reach of the 1972 Amendments.

* * * Specifically at issue here is whether respondents Caputo and Blundo were "employees" within the meaning of [LHWCA § 2(3), 33 U.S.C. § 902(3)] and whether the injuries they sustained occurred on the "navigable waters of the United States" [LHWCA § 3(a), 33 U.S.C. § 903(a)].

I.

At the time of his injury respondent Carmelo Blundo had been employed for five years as a "checker" by petitioner International Terminal Operating Co. (ITO) at its facility in Brooklyn, N.Y., known as the 21st Street Pier. As a checker he was responsible for checking and recording cargo as it was loaded onto or unloaded from vessels, barges, or containers.[2] Blundo was assigned his tasks at the beginning of each day and until he arrived at the terminal he did not know whether he would be working on a ship or on shore. He was reassigned during the day if he completed the task to which he was assigned initially.

On January 8, 1974, ITO assigned Blundo to check cargo being "stripped" or removed from a container on the 19th Street side of the pier. The container Blundo was checking had been taken off a vessel at another pier facility outside of Brooklyn and brought overland unopened by an independent trucking company to the 21st Street Pier. It was Blundo's job to break the seal that had been placed on the container in a foreign port and show it to United States Customs Agents. After the seal was broken, Blundo was to check the contents of the container against a manifest sheet describing the cargo, the consignees, and the ship on, and port from which, the cargo had been transported. He was to mark each item of cargo with an identifying number. After the checking, the cargo was to be placed on pallets, sorted according to consignees, and put in a bonded warehouse pending customs inspection. Blundo was injured as he was marking the cargo stripped from the container, when he slipped on some ice on the pier.

Blundo sought compensation under the LHWCA. The Administrative Law Judge (ALJ) concluded that Blundo satisfied the coverage requirements of the Act and the Benefits Review Board (BRB) affirmed.

Respondent Ralph Caputo was a member of a regular longshoring "gang" that worked for Pittston Stevedoring Co. When his gang was not needed, Caputo went to the waterfront

28. Editors' note: The substantially identical House Report, H. Rep. No. 92-1441, may be found at 1972 *U.S. Code Cong. & Ad. News* 4698.

2. A container is a large metal box resembling a truck trailer without wheels. It can carry large amounts of cargo destined for one or more consignees. If the goods are for a single consignee, the container may be removed from the pier intact and delivered directly to him, but if it carries goods destined for several consignees, it must be unloaded or "stripped" and the goods sorted according to consignee. This operation may be done at the waterfront or inland. The analogous process during the loading phase is called "stuffing."

hiring hall, where he was hired by the day by other stevedoring companies or terminal operators with work available. He had been hired on some occasions by Northeast Stevedoring Co. to work as a member of a stevedore gang on ships at the 39th Street Pier in Brooklyn; on other occasions he had been hired by petitioner Northeast Marine Terminal Co., Inc. (Northeast), for work in its terminal operations at the same location.

On April 16, 1973, Caputo was hired by Northeast to work as a "terminal labor[er]." A terminal laborer may be assigned to load and unload containers, lighters, barges, and trucks. When he arrived at the terminal, Caputo was assigned, along with a checker and forklift driver, to help consignees' truckmen load their trucks with cargo that had been discharged from ships at Northeast's terminal. Caputo was injured while rolling a dolly loaded with cheese into a consignee's truck.

The Administrative Law Judge found that Caputo satisfied the requirements of the Act and awarded him compensation. The BRB affirmed.

The employers in both cases filed petitions to review the decisions and the Court of Appeals for the Second Circuit consolidated the cases. After thorough consideration of the language, history, and purposes of the 1972 Amendments, the court held, one judge dissenting, that the injuries of both respondents were compensable under the LHWCA. In view of the conflict over the coverage afforded by the 1972 Amendments, we granted certiorari to consider both cases. We affirm.

II.

Congress enacted the LHWCA in 1927, after this Court had thwarted the efforts of the States and of Congress to provide compensation for maritime workers injured on navigable waters through state compensation programs. In 1917, the Court [in *Jensen*, *supra* at 116] held that the States were without power to provide a workmen's compensation remedy to longshoremen injured on the gangplank between a ship and a pier. The decision left longshoremen injured on the seaward side of a pier without a compensation remedy while longshoremen injured on the pier were protected by state compensation Acts. [ ] Dissatisfied with the gap in coverage thus created * * *, Congress sought to authorize States to apply their compensation statutes to injures seaward of the *Jensen* line. [But Congress's two attempts to legitimate state workers' compensation coverage of workers hurt on vessels] were struck down as unlawful delegations of congressional power. *Washington v. W.C. Dawson & Co.*, 264 U.S. 219 (1924); *Knickerbocker Ice Co. v. Stewart*, 253 U.S. 149 (1920). Finally, convinced that the only way to provide workmen's compensation for longshoremen and harborworkers injured on navigable water was to enact a federal system, Congress, in 1927, passed the LHWCA.

The [1927 LHWCA] was, in a sense, a typical workmen's compensation system, compensating an employee for injuries "arising out of and in the course of employment." But it was designed simply to be a gapfiller to fill the void created by the inability of the States to remedy injuries on navigable waters. Thus, it provided coverage only for injuries occurring "upon the navigable waters of the United States" and permitted compensation awards only "if recovery ... through workmen's compensation proceedings [could] not validly be provided by state law."

* * * The courts spent the next 45 years trying to ascertain the respective spheres of coverage of the state and federal systems. As two commentators described it, "the relationship between [LHWCA] and the otherwise applicable State Compensation Act [was] shrouded in impenetrable confusion." G. GILMORE & C. BLACK, LAW OF ADMIRALTY 409 (2d ed. 1975). It is unnecessary to examine in detail the Court's efforts to dispel the

confusion. Suffice it to say that while the Court permitted recovery under state remedies in particular situations seaward of the *Jensen* line, see, e.g., *Davis v. Department of Labor and Industries of Washington*, 317 U.S. 249 (1942), the Court made it clear that federal coverage stopped at the water's edge. *Nacirema Operating Co. v. Johnson*, 396 U.S. 212 (1969) [held that longshoremen killed or injured on a pier while attaching cargo to ships' cranes for loading onto the ships were not covered by the LHWCA because they were not injured "upon the navigable waters of the United States" as required by LHWCA § 3(a).]

* * *

[In 1972, Congress amended LHWCA § 3(a) to move the line demarking LHWCA coverage.] The 1972 Amendments were the first significant effort to reform the 1927 Act and the judicial gloss that had been attached to it. The main concern of the 1972 Amendments was not with the scope of coverage but with accommodating the desires of three interested groups: (1) shipowners who were discontented with the decisions allowing many maritime workers to use the doctrine of "seaworthiness" to recover full damages from shipowners regardless of fault; (2) employers of the longshoremen who, under another judicially created doctrine, could be required to indemnify shipowners and thereby lose the benefit of the intended exclusivity of the compensation remedy; and (3) workers who wanted to improve the benefit schedule deemed inadequate by all parties.[18] Congress sought to meet these desires by "specifically eliminating suits against vessels brought for injuries to longshoremen under the doctrine of seaworthiness and outlawing indemnification actions and 'hold harmless' or indemnity agreements [; continuing] to allow suits against vessels or other third parties for negligence [; and raising] benefits to a level commensurate with present day salaries and with the needs of injured workers whose sole support will be payments under the Act." S. Rep. 5.

In increasing the benefits, however, Congress recognized that the disparity between the federal compensation rates and the significantly lower state rates would exacerbate the harshness of the already unpopular [*Nacirema*] line. It also realized that modern tech-

18. The Report of the Senate Committee on Labor and Public Welfare described the need for the bill: "The [LHWCA] was last amended in 1961, at which time the maximum benefit under the Act was set at $70 per week. Clearly, in order to provide adequate income replacement for disabled workers covered under this law a substantial increase in benefits is urgently required. While everyone has agreed since at least the mid-1960's that the benefits under this Act should be raised, there has been some dispute over the years as to whether such benefits should be raised so long as this compensation law was not the exclusive remedy for an injured worker. It has been the feeling of most employers that while they were willing to guarantee payment to an injured worker regardless of fault, they would only do so if the right to such payment was the exclusive remedy and they would not be subject to additional lawsuits because of that injury. Since 1946, due to a number of decisions by the U.S. Supreme Court (starting with *Seas Shipping Co. v. Sieracki*, 328 U.S. 85 (1946)), it has been possible for an injured longshoreman to avail himself of the benefits of the [LHWCA] and to sue the owner of the ship on which he was working for damages as a result of this injury. The Supreme Court has ruled that such ship owner, under the doctrine of seaworthiness, was liable for damages caused by any injury regardless of fault. In addition, (under the ruling of *Ryan Stevedoring Co. v. Pan-Atlantic S. S. Corp.*, 350 U.S. 124 (1956)) shipping companies generally have succeeded in recovering the damages for which they are held liable to injured longshoremen from the stevedore on theories of express or implied warranty, thereby transferring their liability to the stevedore company, the actual employer of the longshoremen. The end result is that, despite the provision in the Act which limits an employer's liability to the compensation and medical benefits provided in the Act, a stevedore-employer is indirectly liable for damages to an injured longshoreman who utilizes the technique of suing the vessel under the unseaworthiness doctrine. The social costs of these law suits, the delays, crowding of court calendars and the need to pay for lawyers' services have seldom resulted in a real increase in actual benefits for injured workers."

nology had moved much of the longshoreman's work onto the land so that if coverage were not extended, there would be many workers who would be relegated to what Congress deemed clearly inadequate state compensation systems. * * *

To remedy these problems, Congress extended the coverage shoreward. It broadened the definition of "navigable waters of the United States" to include "any adjoining pier, wharf, dry dock, terminal, building way, marine railway, or other adjoining area customarily used by an employer in loading, unloading, repairing, or building a vessel." [LHWCA § 3(a), 33 U.S.C. § 903(a).] At the same time, Congress amended the definition of the persons covered by the Act. * * * [W]ith the definition of "navigable waters" expanded by the 1972 Amendments to include such a large geographical area, it became necessary to describe affirmatively the class of workers Congress desired to compensate. It therefore added the requirement that the injured worker be "engaged in maritime employment," which it defined to include "any longshoreman or other person engaged in longshoring operations, and any harbor-worker including a ship repairman, shipbuilder, and ship-breaker * * *." [LHWCA § 2(3), 33 U.S.C. § 902(3).]

The 1972 Amendments thus changed what had been essentially only a "situs" test of eligibility for compensation to one looking to both the "situs" of the injury and the "status" of the injured. We must now determine whether respondents Caputo and Blundo satisfied these requirements.

III.

We turn first to the question whether Caputo and Blundo satisfied the "status" test that is, whether they were "engaged in maritime employment" and therefore "employees" at the time of their injuries. The question is made difficult by the failure of Congress to define the relevant terms—"maritime employment," "longshoremen," "longshoring operations"[25]—in either the text of the Act or its legislative history.

* * *

Nevertheless, we are not without guidance in resolving that question. The language of the 1972 Amendments is broad and suggests that we should take an expansive view of the extended coverage. Indeed, such a construction is appropriate for this remedial legislation. The Act "must be liberally construed in conformance with its purpose, and in a way which avoids harsh and incongruous results." [ ] Consideration of the purposes behind the broadened coverage reveals a clear intent to reach persons such as Blundo and Caputo.

One of the primary motivations for Congress' decision to extend the coverage shoreward was the recognition that "the advent of modern cargo-handling techniques" had moved much of the longshoremen's work off the vessel and onto land. [ ] Noted specifically was the impact of containerization. Unlike traditional break-bulk cargo handling, in which each item of cargo must be handled separately and stored individually in the hold of the ship as it waits in port, containerization permits the time-consuming work of stowage and unstowage to be performed on land in the absence of the vessel. The use of

---

25. As the definition of "employee" makes clear, the category of persons engaged in maritime employment includes more than longshoremen and persons engaged in longshoring operations. It is, however, unnecessary in this case to look beyond these two subcategories.

This case also does not involve the question whether Congress excluded people who would have been covered before the 1972 Amendments; that is, workers who are injured on [actual] navigable water * * *.

containerized ships has reduced the costly time the vessel must be in port and the amount of manpower required to get the cargo onto the vessel. In effect, the operation of loading and unloading has been moved shoreward; the container is a modern substitute for the hold of the vessel. * * * Congress' intent to adapt the LHWCA to modern cargo-handling techniques clearly indicates that these tasks, heretofore done on board ship, are included in the category of "longshoring operations."

It is therefore apparent that respondent Blundo was a statutory "employee" when he slipped on the ice. His job was to check and mark items of cargo as they were unloaded from a container. This task is clearly an integral part of the unloading process as altered by the advent of containerization and was intended to be reached by the Amendments. Indeed, the Committee Reports explicitly state: "[C]heckers, for example, who are directly involved in the loading or unloading functions are covered by the new amendment." [ ] We thus have no doubt that Blundo satisfied the status test.

The congressional desire to accommodate the Act to modern technological changes is not relevant to Caputo's case, since he was injured in the old-fashioned process of putting goods already unloaded from a ship or container into a delivery truck. Another dominant theme underlying the 1972 Amendments, however, assists us in analyzing Caputo's status. Congress wanted a "uniform compensation system to apply to employees who would otherwise be covered by this Act for part of their activity." [ ] It wanted a system that did not depend on the "fortuitous circumstance of whether the injury [to the longshoreman] occurred on land or over water." [ ] It therefore extended the situs to encompass the waterfront areas where the overall loading and unloading process occurs. It is the view of the * * * Director of the [Office of Workers' Compensation Programs in the Department of Labor ("OWCP")] that a uniform system must reach "all physical cargo handling activity anywhere within an area meeting the situs [test]." "[M]aritime employment," in his view, "include[s] all physical tasks performed on the waterfront, and particularly those tasks necessary to transfer cargo between land and water transportation." [ ] Under this theory, it is clear that the Act would cover someone who, like Caputo, was engaged in the final steps of moving cargo from maritime to land transportation: putting it in the consignee's truck.

We need not decide * * * whether the congressional desire for uniformity supports the Director's view and entitles everyone performing a task such as Caputo's to benefits under the Act. * * * It [at least] seems clear * * * that when Congress said it wanted to cover "longshoremen," it had in mind persons whose employment is such that they spend at least some of their time in indisputably longshoring operations and who, without the 1972 Amendments, would be covered for only part of their activity.

That Caputo is such a person is readily apparent. As a member of a regular stevedoring gang, he participated on either the pier or the ship in the stowage and unloading of cargo. On the day of his injury he had been hired by petitioner Northeast as a terminal laborer. In that capacity, he could have been assigned to any one of a number of tasks necessary to the transfer of cargo between land and maritime transportation, including stuffing and stripping containers, loading and discharging lighters and barges, and loading and unloading trucks. Not only did he have no idea when he set out in the morning which of these tasks he might be assigned, but in fact his assignment could have changed during the day. Thus, had Caputo avoided injury and completed loading the consignee's truck on the day of the accident, he then could have been assigned to unload a lighter. Since it is clear that he would have been covered while unloading such a vessel, to exclude him from the Act's coverage in the morning but include him in the afternoon would be to revitalize the shifting and fortuitous coverage that Congress intended to eliminate.

Petitioners * * * seek to avoid these results by proposing a so-called "point of rest" theory. The term "point of rest" is claimed to be a term of art in the industry that denotes the point where the stevedoring operation ends (or, in the case of loading, begins) and the terminal operation function begins (or ends, in the case of loading). Petitioners contend that the "maritime employment of longshoremen" includes only "the stevedoring activity of the longshore gang (and those directly involved with the gang) which, in the case of unloading, takes cargo out of the hold of the vessel, moves it away from the ship's side, and carries it to its point of rest on the pier or in a terminal shed." Since Caputo and Blundo were handling cargo that had already reached its first point of rest, petitioners argue they are not to be covered.

This contention that Congress intended to use the point of rest as the decisive factor in the "status" determination has several fatal weaknesses. First, the term "point of rest" nowhere appears in the Act or in the legislative history. It is difficult to understand why, if Congress intended to stop coverage at this point, it never used the term. The absence of a term that is claimed to be so well known in the industry is both conspicuous and telling.

But it is not simply the term's unexplained absence that undermines petitioners' theory. More fundamentally, the theory is simply too restrictive, failing to accommodate either the language or the intent of the 1972 Amendments. The operations petitioners would cover clearly are "longshoring operations" and are appropriately covered by the Act. But petitioners fail to give effect to the obvious desire to cover longshoremen whether or not their particular task at the moment of injury is clearly a "longshoring operation." The theory does not comport with the Act's focus on occupations and its desire for uniformity. * * * In addition, the theory fails to accommodate the intent to cover those longshoring operations that modern technology had moved onto the land. Coverage that stops at the point of rest excludes those engaged in loading and unloading the modern functional equivalents of the hold of the ship. As we have indicated, Congress clearly intended to cover such operations.

* * *

In view of all this, it is not surprising that the "point of rest" limitation has been rejected by all but one of the Circuits that have considered it and by virtually all the commentators.[41] We too reject it. * * *

IV.

Having established that respondents Blundo and Caputo satisfied the "status" test for coverage under the Act, we consider now whether their injuries occurred on a covered "situs"—"the navigable waters of the United States (including any adjoining pier, wharf, dry dock, terminal, building way, marine railway, or other adjoining area customarily used by an employer in loading, unloading, repairing or building a vessel)." [LHWCA § 3(a), 33 U.S.C. § 903(a).]

There is no dispute with respect to Caputo. The truck he was helping to load was parked inside the terminal area. As petitioner Northeast correctly concedes, this situs "unquestionably met the requirements of § 3(a) of the Act ... because the terminal adjoins navigable waters of the United States and parts of the terminal are used in loading and unloading ships."

---

41. Only one of the commentators ... even thought of the point of rest as a line of demarcation, but he makes no effort to explain why the term was never mentioned in the Act or history. Vickery, *Some Impacts of the 1972 Amendments to the Longshoremen's and Harbor Workers' Compensation Act*, 41 Ins. Counsel J. 63 (1974). * * *.

Blundo's injury was sustained while he was checking a container being stripped on a pier located within a facility known as the 21st Street Pier. The fenced-in facility was located on the water and ran between 19th and 21st Streets. It included two "finger-piers." The pier on the 21st Street end was used to berth ships for purposes of loading and unloading them. The one on the 19th Street end was used only for stripping and stuffing containers and storage. Blundo was working on this latter pier.

Petitioner ITO argues that Blundo was not on a covered situs because the 19th Street Pier was not "customarily used by an employer for loading [or] unloading ... a vessel." The Court of Appeals labeled this argument "halfhearted" and dismissed it in a footnote. We agree that the argument does not merit extended discussion.

First, we agree with the court below that it is not at all clear that the phrase "customarily used" was intended to modify more than the immediately preceding phrase "other areas." * * *

Second, even if we assume that the phrase should be read to modify the preceding terms, we agree with the BRB and the Court of Appeals that Blundo satisfied the situs test in the same way that Caputo did by working in an "adjoining ... terminal ... customarily used ... in loading [and] unloading." The entire terminal facility adjoined the water and one of its two finger-piers clearly was used for loading and unloading vessels.

Accordingly, we conclude that when Congress sought to expand the situs to avoid anomalies inherent in a system that drew lines at the water's edge, it intended to include an area such as the one at issue here. [ ]

Since we find that both Caputo and Blundo satisfied the status and the situs tests, we affirm.

Notes

1. The ALJs, BRB, and Court of Appeals (over one dissent) agreed that Blundo and Caputo were covered. In light of this near-unanimity, why did the employers think it worth taking the case to the Supreme Court?

2. **LHWCA status: additional Supreme Court decisions taking an expansive view of the LHWCA concept "longshoring operations."** The unanimous Court in *P.C. Pfeiffer Co. v. Ford*, 444 U.S. 69, 82–83 (1979), stated that "longshoring operations" means "the process of loading or unloading a ship" and gave an affirmative answer to a question explicitly left open in *Caputo*—whether "everyone performing a task such as Caputo's [satisfies the status requirement of] the Act." The *P.C. Pfeiffer* Court (addressing two LHWCA claimants) held as follows:

> Persons moving cargo directly from ship to land transportation are engaged in [longshoring operations and hence in] maritime employment. [ ] A worker responsible for some portion of that activity is as much an integral part of the process of loading or unloading a ship as a person who participates in the entire process. We therefore hold that Ford [injured at the Port of Beaumont while affixing military vehicles to railroad flatcars, the last step in the movement of the vehicles from ship to land transport] and Bryant [injured at the Port of Galveston while moving cotton from a draywagon into a pier warehouse, the first step in the movement of the cotton from land transport to ship] were engaged in maritime employment because they were engaged in intermediate steps of moving cargo between ship and land transportation.

P.C. Pfeiffer supplies an answer to the *Caputo* question because Ford's and Bryant's work could never have taken them aboard vessels; they were precluded by labor union rules from moving cargo directly to or from ships. The Court sought an outer boundary to its coverage concept by stating: "There is no doubt … that neither the driver of the truck carrying cotton to Galveston nor the locomotive engineer transporting military vehicles from Beaumont was engaged in maritime employment even though he was working on the marine situs." *Id.* at 83.

Chesapeake & Ohio R. Co. v. Schwalb, 493 U.S. 40, 47 (1989), continued the expansive trend by holding that "employees who are injured while maintaining or repairing equipment essential to the loading or unloading process are covered by the Act." Three justices separately concurred, seeking to clarify that a worker who "spends part of his time maintaining or repairing loading equipment" satisfies the status requirement even if injured while doing something else. *Id.* at 50.

3. **Another expansive status decision.** In *Director v. Perini North River Associates*, 459 U.S. 297, 299 n. 3 (1983), the Court answered another question explicitly left open in *Caputo*—"whether congressional addition of the *status* requirement meant that 'Congress excluded people who would have been covered before the 1972 Amendments; that is, workers who are injured on the navigable waters as previously defined' [ ]." The *Perini* Court's answer was no. The claimant in *Perini* (Raymond Churchill) was a construction worker injured on a cargo barge being used to build a sewage treatment plant extending over the Hudson River. Churchill was denied LHWCA benefits by the ALJ, BRB, and Second Circuit Court of Appeals on the view that he was not engaged in maritime employment within the meaning of the Act. Reversing, the Supreme Court held:

> [W]hen a worker is injured on the actual navigable waters in the course of his employment on those waters, he satisfies the status requirement in § 2(3). * * * We consider these employees to be "engaged in maritime employment" not simply because they are injured in a historically maritime locale, but because they are required to perform their employment duties upon navigable waters. * * * Our holding, of course, extends only to those persons "traditionally covered" before the 1972 amendments. We express no opinion whether such coverage extends to a worker injured while transiently or fortuitously upon actual navigable waters. * * * Our decision today should not be read as exempting water-based workers from the * * * status test. Rather, our holding is simply a recognition that a worker's performance of his duties upon actual navigable waters is necessarily a very important factor in determining whether he is engaged in "maritime employment."

459 U.S. at 324 & n.34. The lower courts have found *Perini* to be confusing. See, e.g., *Lockheed Martin Corp. v. Morganti*, 412 F.3d 407, 413–14 (2d Cir. 2005); *Bienvenu v. Texaco, Inc.*, 164 F.3d 901, 908 (5th Cir. 1999) (*en banc*).

4. **A different philosophy regarding the status requirement.** In *Herb's Welding, Inc. v. Gray*, 470 U.S. 414, 416 (1985) (*infra* at 224), a divided Court held that "a welder working on a fixed offshore oil-drilling platform in state territorial waters was [not] entitled to benefits under the Act [because he] was not engaged in maritime employment." The Court explained its philosophy regarding the LHWCA status requirement as follows:

> The LHWCA covers "any person engaged in maritime employment, including any longshoreman or other person engaged in longshoring operations, and any harbor worker including a ship repairman, shipbuilder, and shipbreaker." While "maritime employment" is not limited to the occupations specifically

> mentioned..., neither can it be read to exclude any requirement of a connection with the loading or construction of ships. [Generally speaking, the 1972] Amendments were not meant to cover employees who are not engaged in loading, unloading, repairing, or building a vessel * * *.

Id. at 423–24 & n. 9 (citations and internal quotation marks omitted).

5. **Still more on LHWCA status: who are "harbor workers"?** The *Perini* Court said that Raymond Churchill was not a harbor worker but offered no explanation why not. The *Herb's Welding* Court was also unconcerned with the term's meaning but did hint that it may not cover much beyond the "ship repairman, shipbuilder, and shipbreaker" categories. But "harbor worker" coverage has often been broader than that; many cases hold or assume that marine construction workers—workers engaged in building and repairing docks and other waterfront and harbor facilities—are covered. For an instructive treatment, see *Healy Tibbits Builders, Inc. v. Director, Office of Workers' Compensation Programs*, 444 F.3d 1095, 1100–01 (9th Cir. 2006) (affirming the award of LHWCA benefits to the family of a worker killed while digging a trench for utility lines to submarine berths at Pearl Harbor and holding that the LHWCA term "harbor worker" is not limited to shipbuilding and repair activities).

6. **The situs requirement.** Noting that there has been too much situs litigation in the Fifth Circuit, and that the other circuits have taken varying approaches to the issue, the court in *New Orleans Depot Services v. Director, Office of Workers' Compensation Programs*, 718 F.3d 384 (5th Cir. 2013) (en banc), significantly narrowed its definition of LHWCA situs.[29] The focus of the case was § 3(a)'s "other adjoining area" provision, i.e., the provision extending the Act's geographic coverage to accidents "occurring upon [an area that adjoins navigable water and is] customarily used by an employer in loading, unloading, repairing, dismantling or building a vessel." The claimant in *New Orleans Depot* was injured at work in a container repair facility located about 300 yards from navigable water and surrounded by nonmaritime businesses. The Fifth Circuit defined its new "adjoining area" rule (which it said followed the Fourth Circuit's) as follows:

> [A]n "other adjoining area" must satisfy two distinct situs components: (1) a geographic component (the area must adjoin navigable waters) and (2) a functional component (the area must be "customarily used by an employer in [loading, unloading, repairing, dismantling or building] a vessel. * * * [To "adjoin" navigable water means to] "border on" or "be contiguous with" navigable waters.

Id. at 389, 393–94. The 11-judge majority opinion held that the container repair facility failed the geographic component because it "did not border upon and was not contiguous with navigable waters." *Id.* at 394. Judge Higginson concurred in the result but would have decided the case on the basis of the functional component. Three judges dissented.

7. **Navigable waters "of the United States."** Despite the LHWCA § 3(a), 33 U.S.C. § 903(a) phrase "navigable waters *of the United States*," several of the courts of appeals have held that LHWCA coverage can extend to injuries on the high seas. But *Grennan v. Crowley Marine Services*, 116 P.3d 1024 (Wash. App. 2005)—citing those cases in support of holding that the LHWCA covered injuries incurred by a Seattle-based longshoreman injured while on a temporary assignment in Russian territorial waters—is probably an outlier.

8. **Constitutionality.** Somewhat grudgingly, *Crowell v. Benson*, 285 U.S. 22, 55 (1932), upheld the constitutionality of the 1927 LHWCA, indicating that the Act was constitutional

29. As is not uncommon, the court disagreed with the position taken by the Director of the Office of Workers' Compensation Programs.

only because its coverage was limited to accidents on navigable waters. Is there a constitutional problem with the 1972 amendments' landward extension? Somewhat surprisingly, *Jacksonville Shipyards v. Perdue*, 539 F.2d 533, 545 (5th Cir. 1976), seems to be the courts' last word on that question. The *Jacksonville* court handled *Crowell* simply by ignoring it (citations and internal quotation marks omitted):

> No authority supports the notion that, in enacting a uniform compensation scheme for waterfront employees, Congress must find a "contract" or "tort" peg upon which to hang its legislation. The true analysis to be applied to such statutes is quite different. It must begin with the long-standing judicial recognition of Congress's broad powers to expand the reach of admiralty jurisdiction. * * * [S]uch judicially authorized expansion has often been geographical in nature. See, e.g., *The Genesee Chief* [*supra* at 10], overruling *The Thomas Jefferson* [*supra* at 8] (abandoning former limitation of admiralty jurisdiction to the tidewaters). * * * We have had abundant reason to realize that our experience and new conditions give rise to new conceptions of maritime concerns. * * * Congress could properly determine that new conceptions of maritime concerns justifie[s] the extension of compensation coverage to workers in the immediate waterfront area * * *. Congress was concerned that under the former Act maritime workers were covered over the waters but not covered while performing similar or related work on shore. The inequities of the pre-1972 Act in this regard are obvious, and we feel that this concern was a legitimate reason for Congress to [act]. We also feel that this concern was a "maritime" one within the meaning of the Admiralty Clause. * * * [I]n defining "maritime" concerns, we will not be limited by the rules which apply to tort and contract litigation.

9. **Preemption of state workers' compensation law.** The Supreme Court has moved the *Jensen* line—the line beyond which state workers' compensation statutes cannot constitutionally go—from the water's edge notionally seaward to the limits of some vague "maritime but local" area. See *supra* at 126 note 1; see also *Davis v. Department of Labor*, *supra* at 204 (holding that state workers' compensation coverage is valid in a "twilight zone" that includes some water-based injuries). But *Jensen* presumably still stands for the proposition that some worker injuries are so quintessentially maritime in nature that state workers' compensation relief is constitutionally precluded.

Sun Ship, Inc. v. Pennsylvania, 447 U.S. 715 (1980), discusses the *Jensen* restriction on state workers' compensation coverage in the course of holding that "in the 1972 amendments to the LHWCA ... Congress [did not] alter the accepted understanding that federal jurisdiction would coexist with state compensation laws in that field in which the latter may constitutionally operate under the *Jensen* doctrine." *Id.* at 722. In other words, the LHWCA itself does not preempt state workers' compensation statutes.

Workers injured under circumstances covered by both the LHWCA and a state workers' compensation statute (that validly applies despite *Jensen*) may choose which remedy to pursue. LHWCA § 3(e), 33 U.S.C. § 903(e), recognizes this overlap by providing that "any amounts paid to an employee for the same injury ... for which benefits are claimed under this Act pursuant to any other workers' compensation law ... shall be credited against any liability imposed by this Act."

10. **The intersection of the LHWCA with the seamen's remedies.** As we saw *supra* at 192, the LHWCA § 2(3)(G) phrase "master or member of a crew of any vessel" draws a line separating the theoretically mutually exclusive regimes of the LHWCA and the seamen's remedies. Despite the theoretical mutual exclusivity, as a practical matter many workers

will be injured under circumstances leaving it unclear which regime they fall under. LHWCA § 3(e), 33 U.S.C. § 903(e), recognizes the existence of a functional overlap zone by providing that "any amounts paid to an employee for the same injury ... for which benefits are claimed under this Act pursuant to [the Jones Act] shall be credited against any liability imposed by this Act." The courts have read this provision to mean that the reverse is also true: a Jones Act employer who has paid LHWCA benefits is entitled to a credit against any seaman's benefits paid or ultimately determined to be owed.

It is a common situation for workers injured in the functional overlap zone to accept or seek LHWCA benefits while at the same time asserting seamen's rights and remedies. Such workers must be careful lest their pursuit of LHWCA benefits kill their seamen's lawsuits. If an ALJ adjudicates that a worker's injury fell within LHWCA coverage—which entails the conclusion that the worker was not a "master or member of a crew of any vessel," *viz.*, was not a seaman—such a ruling will likely operate via the doctrine of collateral estoppel (issue preclusion) to cut off the seaman's suit.

Howlett v. Birkdale Shipping Co.

Supreme Court of the United States, 1994
512 U.S. 92, 114 S. Ct. 2057, 129 L. Ed. 2d 78, 1994 AMC 1817

Justice KENNEDY delivered the opinion of the unanimous Court.

* * *

The case arrives after a grant of summary judgment to respondent Birkdale Shipping Co., S.A., so we consider the facts in the light most favorable to petitioner Albert Howlett. Howlett, a longshoreman employed in the Port of Philadelphia by stevedore Northern Shipping Co., was injured while discharging bags of cocoa beans from a cargo hold on the *MV Presidente Ibanez*, a ship owned and operated by Birkdale. During the unloading operation, Howlett and three other longshoremen hooked up a draft, or load, of bags stowed on the tween deck of the hold. When the ship's boom lifted the draft out of the hold, an 8-square-foot area of the tween deck was exposed. Howlett, who was standing on surrounding bags, jumped down about three feet to the deck, where he slipped and fell on a sheet of clear plastic that had been placed under the cargo. As a result of his fall, Howlett sustained serious injuries that have disabled him from returning to work as a longshoreman.

Howlett brought suit against Birkdale under [LHWCA § 5(b), 33 U.S.C. § 905(b)]. Both parties agreed that it is customary to lay paper and plywood on a steel deck to protect a stow of cocoa beans against condensation damage. They also agreed that, for purposes of protecting the beans, it was improper to use plastic, which tends to aggravate condensation damage rather than prevent it. Evidence adduced during pretrial proceedings suggested that the independent stevedore engaged by Birkdale to load the beans in Guayaquil, Ecuador, had placed the plastic on the tween deck. Further evidence showed that the vessel had supplied the Guayaquil stevedore with the plastic, along with other material used in stowing cargo, including paper, plywood, and dunnage. Howlett claimed that before jumping to the deck he did not see the plastic, which was covered by dirt and debris. He charged that Birkdale was negligent in failing to warn Northern and its longshoremen-employees of this dangerous condition.

The United States District Court for the Eastern District of Pennsylvania granted summary judgment in favor of Birkdale. * * * The [Third Circuit] Court of Appeals affirmed without opinion. We granted certiorari to resolve a conflict among the Circuits regarding the scope of the shipowner's duty to warn of latent hazards in the cargo stow * * *.

* * *

The design of [the 1972 enactment of § 5(b), substituting a negligence action for the unseaworthiness remedy,] was to shift more of the responsibility for compensating injured longshoremen to the party best able to prevent injuries: the stevedore-employer. [*Scindia Steam Nav. Co. v. De Los Santos*, 451 U.S. 156, 171 (1981).] Subjecting vessels to suit for injuries that could be anticipated and prevented by a competent stevedore would threaten to upset the balance Congress was careful to strike in enacting the 1972 amendments.

The question whether Howlett produced evidence sufficient to hold Birkdale liable for his injuries turns on the meaning of the term "negligence" in § 5(b). Because Congress did not "specify the acts or omissions of the vessel[30] that would constitute negligence," the contours of a vessel's duty to longshoremen are "left to be resolved through the 'application of accepted principles of tort law and the ordinary process of litigation.'" *Id.* at 165–66.

The starting point in this regard must be our decision in *Scindia Steam*, which outlined the three general duties shipowners owe to longshoremen. The first, which courts have come to call the "turnover duty," relates to the condition of the ship upon the commencement of stevedoring operations. [ ] The second duty, applicable once stevedoring operations have begun, provides that a shipowner must exercise reasonable care to prevent injuries to longshoremen in areas that remain under the "active control of the vessel." [ ] The third duty, called the "duty to intervene," concerns the vessel's obligations with regard to cargo operations in areas under the principal control of the independent stevedore. [ ]

The allegations of Howlett's complaint, and the facts adduced during pretrial proceedings, implicate only the vessel's turnover duty. * * * A vessel must "exercise ordinary care under the circumstances" to turn over the ship and its equipment and appliances "in such condition that an expert and experienced stevedoring contractor, mindful of the dangers he should reasonably expect to encounter, arising from the hazards of the ship's service or otherwise, will be able by the exercise of ordinary care" to carry on cargo operations "with reasonable safety to persons and property." [ ] A corollary to the turnover duty requires the vessel to warn the stevedore "of any hazards on the ship or with respect to its equipment," so long as the hazards "are known to the vessel or should be known to it in the exercise of reasonable care," and "would likely be encountered by the stevedore in the course of his cargo operations[,] are not known by the stevedore[,] and would not be obvious to or anticipated by him if reasonably competent in the performance of his work." [ ] Although both components of the turnover duty are related in various respects, Howlett confines his case to an allegation that Birkdale failed to warn that the tween deck was covered with plastic rather than (as is ordinarily the case) paper and plywood.

Most turnover cases brought under § 5(b) concern the condition of the ship itself or of equipment on the ship used in stevedoring operations. * * * The turnover duty to warn, however, may extend to certain latent hazards in the cargo stow. This is so because an improper stow can cause injuries to longshoremen [ ] and thus is among the "hazards on the ship" to which the duty to warn attaches. [ ]

The precise contours of the duty to warn of latent hazards in the cargo stow must be defined with due regard to the concurrent duties of the stevedore and to the statutory

30. Editors' note: LHWCA § 2(21), 33 U.S.C. § 902(21), defines "vessel" to include its owner, charterer, operator, etc.

scheme as a whole. It bears repeating that the duty attaches only to latent hazards, defined in this context as hazards that would be neither obvious to nor anticipated by a competent stevedore in the ordinary course of cargo operations. In addition, the vessel's duty to warn is confined to latent hazards that "are known to the vessel or should be known to it in the exercise of reasonable care." [ ] Absent actual knowledge of a hazard, then, the duty to warn may attach only if the exercise of reasonable care would place upon the shipowner an obligation to inspect for, or discover, the hazard's existence.

* * *

* * * Howlett's contention that a vessel must make reasonable inspections, both during and after stevedoring operations, to discover defects in the stow contradicts the principles underlying our decision in *Scindia Steam*. The plaintiff longshoreman in *Scindia Steam*, injured by cargo that fell from a defective winch, alleged that the shipowner should have intervened in the stevedoring operations and repaired the winch before permitting operations to continue. The case thus turned not upon the turnover duty but upon the scope of the vessel's duty to intervene once cargo operations have begun. We held that the duty to intervene, in the event the vessel has no knowledge of the hazardous condition, is limited: "[A]bsent contract provision, positive law, or custom to the contrary," a vessel "has no general duty by way of supervision or inspection to exercise reasonable care to discover dangerous conditions that develop within the confines of the cargo operations that are assigned to the stevedore." [ ]

The rule relieving vessels from this general duty rests upon "the justifiable expectations of the vessel that the stevedore would perform with reasonable competence and see to the safety of the cargo operations." * * * The stevedore's obligations in this regard may not be diminished by transferring them to the vessel.

Given the legal and practical realities of the maritime trade, we concluded in *Scindia Steam* that imposing a duty upon vessels to supervise and inspect cargo operations for the benefit of longshoremen then on board would undermine Congress's intent in § 5(b) to terminate the vessel's "automatic, faultless responsibility for conditions caused by the negligence or other defaults of the stevedore," [ ] and to foreclose liability "based on a theory of unseaworthiness or nondelegable duty" [ ]. * * *

The foregoing principles, while taken from *Scindia Steam's* examination of the vessel's duty to intervene, bear as well on the nature of the vessel's turnover duty, and hence on the case before us. We consider first Howlett's view that a vessel must make reasonable inspections during stevedoring operations to ensure a proper stow and to detect any hazards or defects before they become hidden. The beneficiaries of this proposed duty would be longshoremen who unload or otherwise deal with the cargo at later ports. But if, as we held in *Scindia Steam*, a vessel need not supervise or inspect ongoing cargo operations for the benefit of longshoremen then on board, it would make little sense to impose the same obligation for the benefit of longshoremen at subsequent ports. In practical effect, then, adopting Howlett's proposal would impose inconsistent standards upon shipowners as to different sets of longshoremen, and would render much of our holding in *Scindia Steam* an empty gesture.

* * *

We next consider Howlett's view that a vessel must make reasonable inspections after the completion of stevedoring operations to discover hazards in the stow. There is good reason to doubt that adopting this rule would have much practical import. Any hazard uncovered by a shipowner who inspects a completed stow would, as a matter of course, be discovered in a subsequent port by a stevedore "reasonably competent in the performance of his work." * * * [S]hipowners engage a stevedore for its expertise in cargo operations and are entitled to assume that a competent stevedore will be able to identify and cope with defects in the stow. [ ] Once loading operations are complete, it follows that any dangers arising from an improper stow would be "at least as apparent to the [subsequent stevedore] as to the [shipowner]." [ ] Because there can be no recovery under § 5(b) for a vessel's failure to warn of dangers that would be apparent to a longshoreman of reasonable competence [ ], nothing would be accomplished by imposing a duty upon vessels to inspect the stow upon completion of cargo operations. That is reason enough to reject it.

For the purposes of delineating the scope of a shipowner's turnover duty, then, the cargo stow is separate and distinct from other aspects of the ship. When between ports, the vessel and its crew have direct access to (and control over) the ship itself and its gear, equipment, and tools. The vessel's responsibilities to inspect these areas of the ship are commensurate with its access and control, bearing in mind, of course, that negligence, rather than unseaworthiness, is the controlling standard where longshoremen are concerned. Because the vessel does not exercise the same degree of operational control over, and does not have the same access to, the cargo stow, its duties with respect to the stow are limited by comparison. [ ]

In sum, the vessel's turnover duty to warn of latent defects in the cargo stow and cargo area is a narrow one. The duty attaches only to latent hazards, defined as hazards that are not known to the stevedore and that would be neither obvious to nor anticipated by a skilled stevedore in the competent performance of its work. [ ] Furthermore, the duty encompasses only those hazards that "are known to the vessel or should be known to it in the exercise of reasonable care." [ ] Contrary to Howlett's submission, however, the exercise of reasonable care does not require the shipowner to supervise the ongoing operations of the loading stevedore (or other stevedores who handle the cargo before its arrival in port) or to inspect the completed stow.

We turn to the proper disposition of this case. As the Court of Appeals did not issue an opinion, we have before us only the District Court's statement of its reasons for granting summary judgment in favor of Birkdale. The vessel having been under no obligation to supervise and inspect the cargo loading operations, and no other theory for charging the vessel with constructive knowledge having been advanced, the District Court was correct to inquire whether the vessel had actual knowledge of the tween deck's condition. The District Court found it undisputed that there was no actual knowledge. At this stage of the proceedings, however, we cannot conclude that summary judgment can rest on this ground. There is sufficient evidence in the record to support a permissible inference that, during the loading process, some crew members, who might have held positions such that their knowledge should be attributed to the vessel, did in fact observe the plastic on the tween deck. * * *

[T]his does not mean that the vessel is not entitled to summary judgment. Howlett's own witnesses stated that the plastic was visible, even from the top deck, during unloading operations. Howlett must overcome these submissions, for even assuming the vessel had knowledge of the tween deck's condition, he must further demonstrate that the alleged hazard would have been neither obvious to nor anticipated by a skilled and competent stevedore at the discharge port. This contention, however, was not addressed by the District Court and was not explored in detail here. We think it the better course to remand the case to the Court of Appeals so that it, or the District Court, can address in the first instance these and other relevant points upon a review of the entire record made in support of the vessel's motion for summary judgment.

* * *

Notes

1. Judging from the reported cases, the success rate for § 5(b) actions is fairly low. See, e.g., *Reed v. ULS Corp.*, 178 F.3d 988 (8th Cir. 1999) (upholding summary judgment for defendant vessel when its gangway failed and caused a longshoreman to fall, on the view that the vessel's duty of care was satisfied by conducting monthly inspections of the gangway); *Quevedo v. Trans-Pacific Shipping, Inc.*, 143 F.3d 1255, 1258 (9th Cir. 1998) (upholding summary judgment for defendant in suit alleging latent defects in the cargo stow and stating—per retired Justice White, the author of *Scindia Steam*, sitting by designation—that "[i]t is now accepted that shipowners owe [only] three narrow duties to longshoremen"); *United States Fid. & Guar. Co. v. Plovidba*, 683 F.2d 1022 (7th Cir. 1982) (Posner, J.) (upholding judgment on jury verdict for defendant in case in which a longshoreman fell to his death through a hatch cover the ship's crew had left open in a darkened hold).

2. As examples of successful § 5(b) actions, see *Moore v. Angela MV*, 353 F.3d 376, 381 (5th Cir. 2003) (finding ship's crane dangerously defective and stating that even if the danger was "obvious to a longshoreman of reasonable competence," obviousness should not defeat recovery "if the longshoreman's only alternatives to facing the hazard are unduly impracticable or time-consuming or would force him to leave the job"); *England v. Reinauer Transp. Cos.*, 194 F.3d 265 (1st Cir. 1999) (affirming judgment on a jury verdict for the plaintiff and holding that the customs of the Port of Boston require towboat companies—rather than stevedoring contractors—to maintain the proper tension on lines used to moor barges that are being unloaded).

Jones & Laughlin Steel Corp. v. Pfeifer

Supreme Court of the United States, 1983

462 U.S. 523, 103 S. Ct. 2541, 76 L. Ed. 2d 768, 1983 AMC 1881

Justice STEVENS delivered the opinion of the unanimous Court.

Respondent was injured in the course of his employment as a loading helper on a coal barge. As his employer, petitioner was required to compensate him for his injury under [LHWCA § 4, 33 U.S.C. § 904]. As the owner *pro hac vice* of the barge, petitioner may also be liable for negligence under § 5 of the Act [33 U.S.C. § 905]. We granted certiorari to decide whether petitioner may be subject to both forms of liability * * *.

Petitioner owns a fleet of barges that it regularly operates on three navigable rivers in the vicinity of Pittsburgh, Pennsylvania. Respondent was employed for 19 years to aid in loading and unloading those barges at one of petitioner's plants located on the shore of the Monongahela River. On January 13, 1978, while carrying a heavy pump, respondent slipped and fell on snow and ice that petitioner had negligently failed to remove from the gunnels of a barge. His injury made him permanently unable to return to his job with the petitioner, or to perform anything other than light work after July 1, 1979.

In November 1979, respondent brought this action against petitioner, alleging that his injury had been "caused by the negligence of the vessel" within the meaning of § 5(b) of the Act. The District Court found in favor of respondent [, holding] that receipt of compensation payments from petitioner under § 4 of the Act did not bar a separate recovery of damages for negligence. [The Third Circuit Court of Appeal affirmed.]

* * *

Most longshoremen who load and unload ships are employed by independent stevedores, who have contracted with the vessel owners to provide such services. In this case, however, the respondent longshoreman was employed directly by the petitioner vessel owner. Under § 4 of the Act, a longshoreman who is injured in the course of his employment is entitled to a specified amount of compensation from his employer, whether or not the injury was caused by the employer's negligence. Section 5(a) of the Act appears to make that liability exclusive. * * * Since the petitioner was the respondent's employer and paid him benefits pursuant to § 4 of the Act, it contends that § 5(a) absolves it of all other responsibility for damages.

Although petitioner's contention is, indeed, supported by the plain language of § 5(a), it is undermined by the plain language of § 5(b). The first sentence of § 5(b) authorizes a longshoreman whose injury is caused by the negligence of a vessel to bring a separate action against such a vessel as a third party. Thus, in the typical tripartite situation, the longshoreman is not only guaranteed the statutory compensation from his employer; he may also recover tort damages if he can prove negligence by the vessel.[5] The second sentence of § 5(b) makes it clear that such a separate action is authorized against the vessel even when there is no independent stevedore and the longshoreman is employed directly by the vessel owner. That sentence provides: "If such person was employed by the vessel to provide stevedoring services, no such action shall be permitted if the injury was caused by the negligence of persons engaged in providing stevedoring services to the vessel." If § 5(a) had been intended to bar all negligence suits against owner-employers, there would have been no need to put an additional sentence in § 5(b) barring suits against owner-employers for injuries caused by fellow servants.[6]

The history of the Act further refutes petitioner's contention that § 5(a) of the Act bars respondent's suit under § 5(b). Prior to 1972, this Court had construed the Act to authorize a longshoreman employed directly by the vessel to obtain a recovery from his employer in excess of the statutory schedule, even though § 5 of the Act contained the same exclusive liability language as today. *Reed v. The Yaka*, 373 U.S. 410 (1963) [ ]. Although the 1972 Amendments changed the character of the longshoreman's action against the vessel by substituting negligence for unseaworthiness as the basis for liability, Congress clearly intended to preserve the rights of longshoremen employed by the vessel to maintain such an action. The House Committee Report [1972 *U.S. Code Cong. & Ad. News* 4698, 4705] is unambiguous:

The Committee has also recognized the need of special provisions to deal with a case where a longshoreman ... is employed directly by the vessel. In such case, notwithstanding the fact the vessel is the employer, the Supreme Court in *Reed* ... held that the unseaworthiness remedy is available to the injured employee. The Committee believes the rights of an injured longshoremen ... should not depend on whether he was employed directly by the vessel or by an independent contractor.... The Committee's intent is that the same principles should apply in determining the liability of the vessel which

5. The longshoreman cannot receive a double recovery, because the stevedore, by paying him statutory compensation, acquires a lien in that amount against any recovery the longshoreman may obtain from the vessel. See *Edmonds v. Compagnie Generale Transatlantique*, 443 U.S. 256, 269–70 (1979).

6. Of course, § (b) does make it clear that a vessel owner acting as its own stevedore is liable only for negligence in its "owner" capacity, not for negligence in its "stevedore" capacity.

employs its own longshoremen ... as apply when an independent contractor employs such persons.

* * * If respondent had been employed by an independent stevedore at the time of his injury, he would have had the right to maintain a tort action against the vessel. We hold today that he has the same right even though he was in fact employed by the vessel.

* * *

Notes

1. The foregoing is a relatively small portion of the *Jones & Laughlin* opinion, the bulk of which was devoted to damages-calculation issues (inflation and discount to present value).

2. The Court's footnote 6 barely hints at the difficulties of establishing § 5(b) liability against a dual-capacity employer/vessel like *Jones & Laughlin*. Under the prevailing lower-court view, the plaintiff must show that the injury resulted from the defendant's breach of one of the three *Scindia/Howlett* duties and then trace that particular conduct to the defendant's "vessel" activities as opposed to its "employer" activities. In litigation unrelated to the treatment of the seaman-status (vessel definition) issue in *Stewart v. Dutra Const. Co. supra* 20–25, the First Circuit upheld summary judgment against Willard Stewart's dual-capacity § 5(b) action against Dutra, asserting that it was clear that the *Super Scoop*-scow collision resulted from Dutra's "employer" activities as dredger, not from anything properly classified as vessel-operator activities. 343 F.3d 10, 16. The court did not even mention *Jones & Laughlin v. Pfeifer*, much less explain how and why Stewart's dual-capacity case was weaker than Pfeifer's.

D. Offshore Oil and Gas Workers

As we saw in Section II-B-5, many offshore oil and gas workers are seamen. In this section, we are principally concerned with those who lack seaman status. The centrally relevant statutes here are the LHWCA (*supra* section II-C) and the 1953 Outer Continental Shelf Lands Act (OCSLA), 43 U.S.C. §§ 1331–1356a.

OCSLA's geographical coverage is described in § 2(a), 43 U.S.C. § 1331(a) as "all submerged lands lying seaward and outside" the areas placed within coastal state boundaries by the Submerged Lands Act, 43 U.S.C. §§ 1301–1315. Under the Submerged Lands Act, Florida's and Texas's boundaries extend nine geographic miles into the Gulf of Mexico; whereas the seaward boundaries of all other states stop three geographic miles from the coast. "Geographic mile" is another name for nautical mile, ca. 6076 feet. What we generally think of as a mile, 5280 feet, is technically a "statute mile" or an "English mile.") See 43 U.S.C. §§ 1301(b) and 1312. See generally *United States v. Maine*, 420 U.S. 515 (1975); *United States v. Louisiana*, 363 U.S. 1 (1960).

For a fascinating account of the political deliberations that produced OCSLA, see Warren Christopher, *The Outer Continental Shelf Lands Act: Key to a New Frontier*, 6 Stan. L. Rev. 23 (1953). For detailed criticism of the Fifth Circuit's OCSLA jurisprudence, see Robertson, *The Outer Continental Shelf Lands Act's Provisions on Jurisdiction, Remedies, and Choice of Law: Correcting the Fifth Circuit's Mistakes*, 38 J. Mar. L. & Com. 487 (2007).

* * *

Selected OCSLA provisions are set out in the Statutory Supplement. For purposes of the issues treated in this section, the important OCSLA provisions are the following:

> OCSLA § 4(a)(1), 43 U.S.C. § 1333(a)(1): The Constitution and laws and civil and political jurisdiction of the United States are extended to the subsoil and seabed of the outer Continental Shelf and to all artificial islands, and all installations and other devices permanently or temporarily attached to the seabed, which may be erected thereon for the purpose of exploring for, developing, or producing resources therefrom * * *, to the same extent as if the outer Continental Shelf were an area of exclusive Federal jurisdiction located within a State. * * *
>
> OCSLA § 4(a)(2)(A), 43 U.S.C. § 1333(a)(2)(A): To the extent that they are applicable and not inconsistent with this Act or with other Federal laws * * *, the civil and criminal laws of each adjacent State * * * are declared to be the law of the United States for that portion of the subsoil and seabed of the outer Continental Shelf, and artificial islands and fixed structures erected thereon, which would be within the area of the State if its boundaries were extended seaward to the outer margin of the outer Continental Shelf * * *. All of such applicable laws shall be administered and enforced by the appropriate officers and courts of the United States. * * *
>
> OCSLA § 4(b)(1), 43 U.S.C. § 1333(b)(1): With respect to disability or death of an employee resulting from any injury occurring as the result of [oil and gas] operations conducted on the outer Continental Shelf * * *, compensation shall be payable under the provisions of the [LHWCA]. For the purposes of [this] extension of the provisions of the [LHWCA], * * * the term "employee" does not include a master or member of a crew of any vessel * * *
>
> OCSLA § 23(b)(1), 43 U.S.C. § 1349(b)(1): * * * [T]he district courts of the United States shall have jurisdiction of cases and controversies arising out of, or in connection with (A) any operation conducted on the outer Continental Shelf which involves exploration, development, or production of the minerals, of the subsoil and seabed of the outer Continental Shelf, or which involves rights to such minerals, or (B) the cancellation, suspension, or termination of a lease or permit under this Act. * * *

Rodrigue v. Aetna Casualty & Surety Co.

Supreme Court of the United States, 1969
395 U.S. 352, 89 S. Ct. 1835, 23 L. Ed. 2d 360, 1969 AMC 1082

Mr. Justice WHITE delivered the opinion of the unanimous Court.

This case involves two men, Dore and Rodrigue, who met their deaths on artificial island drilling rigs located on the outer Continental Shelf off the Louisiana coast. [Both families brought federal-court tort actions seeking wrongful death damages. Dore was killed while working on a crane mounted on the artificial island and being used to unload a barge. As the crane lifted a load from the barge to place it on the artificial island, the crane collapsed and toppled over onto the barge, killing the worker. Dore's family sued the firms that manufactured, installed, and serviced the crane. Rodrigue was killed while performing a test on a drill pipe. He was high on the derrick rising above the artificial island, and fell from it to his death on the floor of the structure. His family sued the owner and insurer of the drill rig and the owner of the stationary platform.]

[In both actions, the families sought wrongful death damages under the Death on the High Seas Act, 46 U.S.C. §§ 30301–30308 (hereinafter "Seas Act"), and also under Louisiana law assertedly made applicable by the Outer Continental Shelf Lands Act, 43 U.S.C. § 1333(a)(2)(A) (hereinafter "Lands Act"). The district courts held that the Seas Act was the families' exclusive remedy. The Fifth Circuit affirmed. Certiorari was granted in both cases, and they were argued together here.]

* * *

In light of the principles of traditional admiralty law, the Seas Act, and the Lands Act, we hold that petitioners' remedy is under the Lands Act and Louisiana law. The Lands Act makes it clear that federal law, supplemented by state law of the adjacent State, is to be applied to these artificial islands as though they were federal enclaves in an upland State. This approach was deliberately taken in lieu of treating the structures as vessels, to which admiralty law supplemented by the law of the jurisdiction of the vessel's owner would apply. [ ] This was done in part because men working on these islands are closely tied to the adjacent State, to which they often commute and on which their families live, unlike transitory seamen to whom a more generalized admiralty law is appropriate. Since the Seas Act does not apply of its own force under admiralty principles, and since the Lands Act deliberately eschewed the application of admiralty principles to these novel structures, Louisiana law is not ousted by the Seas Act, and under the Lands Act it is made applicable.

I.

The purpose of the Lands Act was to define a body of law applicable to the seabed, the subsoil, and the fixed structures such as those in question here on the outer Continental Shelf. That this law was to be federal law of the United States, applying state law only as federal law and then only when not inconsistent with applicable federal law, is made clear by the language of the Act. [43 U.S.C. § 1332(1)] makes it the "policy of the United States" that the affected areas "appertain to the United States and are subject to its jurisdiction, control, and power of disposition." [43 U.S.C. § 1333(a)(1)] makes the "Constitution and laws and civil and political jurisdiction of the United States" apply "to the same extent as if the outer Continental Shelf were an area of exclusive Federal jurisdiction located within a State." Since federal law, because of its limited function in a federal system, might be inadequate to cope with the full range of potential legal problems, the Act supplemented gaps in the federal law with state law through the "adoption of State law as the law of the United States." Under [43 U.S.C. § 1333(a)(2)(A)], the adjacent State's laws were made "the law of the United States for [the relevant subsoil and seabed] and artificial islands and fixed structures erected thereon," but only to "the extent that they are applicable and not inconsistent with ... other Federal laws."

It is evident from this that federal law is "exclusive" in its regulation of this area, and that state law is adopted only as surrogate federal law.

* * *

The principles that federal law should prevail, and that state law should be applied only as federal law and then only when no inconsistent federal law applied, were adopted by a Congress in which full debate had underscored the issue. Senator Cordon, in presenting the Lands Act to the Senate, noted that the problem addressed by [§ 1333(a)(2)(A)] had been raised by "the fact that the full development of the estimated values in the shelf area will require the efforts and the physical presence of thousands of workers on fixed structures in the shelf area. Industrial accidents, accidental death, peace, and order" present problems requiring a body of law for their solution. Since "as every Member of the Senate knows, the Federal Code was never designed to be a complete body of law in and of itself," the committee decided that state law would have to be referred to in some instances. * * * Senator Cordon * * * added that: "These laws, by the terms of the act, are enacted as Federal law."

The opponents of the Act realized full well that state law was being used only to supplement federal law, and Senator Long introduced an amendment [that would have made state law applicable of its own force. The amendment was rejected.] This legislative history buttresses the Court of Appeals' finding that in view of the inconsistencies between the state law and the Seas Act, the Seas Act remedy would be exclusive if it applied.

II.

However, for federal law to oust adopted state law federal law must first apply. The court below assumed that the Seas Act did apply, since the island was located more than a marine league off the Louisiana coast. But that is not enough to make the Seas Act applicable. The Act redresses only those deaths stemming from wrongful actions or omissions "occurring on the high seas," and these cases involve a series of events on artificial islands. * * * Admiralty jurisdiction has not been construed to extend to accidents on piers, jetties, bridges, or even ramps or railways running into the sea. To the extent that it has been applied to fixed structures completely surrounded by water, this has usually involved collision with a ship and has been explained by the use of the structure solely or principally as a navigational aid. But when the damage is caused by a vessel admitted[ly] in admiralty jurisdiction, the Admiralty Extension Act [46 U.S.C. § 30101] would now make available the admiralty remedy in any event.

The accidents in question here involved no collision with a vessel, and the structures were not navigational aids. They were islands, albeit artificial ones, and the accidents had no more connection with the ordinary stuff of admiralty than do accidents on piers. * * * In these circumstances, the Seas Act—which provides an action in admiralty—clearly would not apply under conventional admiralty principles and, since the Lands Act provides an alternative federal remedy through adopted state law, there is no reason to assume that Congress intended to extend those principles to create an admiralty remedy here. And if the Congress had made the 1920 Seas Act applicable, ousting inconsistent state law, the artificial island worker would be entitled to far less comprehensive remedies in many cases than he is now.

Even if the admiralty law would have applied to the deaths occurring in these cases under traditional principles, the legislative history [of OCSLA] shows that Congress did not intend that result. First, Congress assumed that the admiralty law would not apply unless Congress made it apply, and then Congress decided not to make it apply. The legislative history of the Lands Act makes it clear that these structures were to be treated as island or as federal enclaves within a landlocked State, not as vessels.

In introducing the bill to the Senate, Senator Cordon explained its inception as follows:

> The [Senate Committee on Interior and Insular Affairs] first attempted to provide housekeeping law for the outer shelf by applying [the maritime law of the United States] to the structures necessary for the removal of the minerals in the area … * * * However, further consideration clearly showed that this approach was not an adequate and complete answer to the problem. * * * [Instead, the approach set forth in 43 U.S.C. § 1333(a)(2)(A) was adopted.] [T]he legal situation is comparable to that in the areas owned by the Federal Government under the exclusive

> jurisdiction of the Federal Government and lying within the boundaries of a State in the uplands.

Similarly, Senator Ellender asserted that in the first draft it "was sought to treat the platforms or artificial islands created in the water as ships" but now the "islands are made subject to our domestic law" instead so as to "be treated just as though they were islands created by nature, insofar as the application of our domestic laws is concerned."

* * *

Careful scrutiny of the hearings which were the basis for eliminating from the Lands Act the treatment of artificial islands as vessels convinces us that the motivation for the change, together with the adoption of state law as surrogate federal law, was the view that maritime law was inapposite to these fixed structures. * * *

The committee was aware that it had the power to treat activity on these artificial islands as though it occurred aboard ship. [ ] And the very decision to do so in the initial bill recognized that if it were not adopted explicitly, maritime law simply would not apply to these stationary structures not erected as navigational aids. Moreover, the committee was acutely aware of the inaptness of admiralty law. The bill applied the same law to the seabed and subsoil as well as to the artificial islands, and admiralty law was obviously unsuited to that task.

Although the Assistant Attorney General, Office of Legal Counsel, persisted to the end in his claim that admiralty law should apply, * * * this view obviously did not prevail. Instead, a compromise emerged. The administration's opposition to committing these areas solely to the jurisdiction of state courts, state substantive law, and state law enforcement was recognized in that the applicable law was made federal law enforceable by federal officials in federal courts. But the special relationship between the men working on these artificial islands and the adjacent shore to which they commute to visit their families was also recognized by dropping the treatment of these structures as "vessels" and instead, over the objections of the administration that these islands were not really located within a State, the bill was amended to treat them "as if [they] were [in] an area of exclusive Federal jurisdiction located within a State." State law became federal law federally enforced.

In view of all this, and the disclosure by Senator Cordon to the Senate upon introduction of the bill that the admiralty or maritime approach of the original bill had been abandoned, it is apparent that the Congress decided that these artificial islands, though surrounded by the high seas, were not themselves to be considered within maritime jurisdiction. Thus the admiralty action under the Seas Act no more applies to these accidents actually occurring on the islands than it would to accidents occurring in an upland federal enclave or on a natural island to which admiralty jurisdiction had not been specifically extended. At a minimum, the legislative history shows that accidents on these structures, which under maritime principles would be no more under maritime jurisdiction than accidents on a wharf located above navigable waters, were not changed in character by the Lands Act.

Since the inapplicability of the Seas Act removes any obstacle to the application of state law by incorporation as federal law through the Lands Act, the decisions below are reversed and the causes remanded for proceedings consistent with this opinion.

Notes

1. Note that the Court treated Dore's death as an "accident[] actually occurring on the island" even though he died from a fall from the island to the deck of a floating

barge. Here the Court's thinking reflects the view taken in the cases treated *supra* at 39 note 1.

2. Note that neither the *Dore* nor the *Rodrigue* action was against the worker's employer. These workers' rights against their employers were confined to the provisions of LHWCA made applicable on the OCS by 43 U.S.C. § 1333(b).

3. **Admiralty jurisdiction in OCS cases.** When OCSLA was enacted, the available technology confined offshore oil and gas exploration and production activities primarily to fixed platforms. The industry subsequently developed jack-up rigs, submersible rigs, semi-submersible rigs, and drill ships, all of which are capable of conducting drilling operations while stabilized, and then floating to a new location. As we have seen, these apparatuses are legally characterized as vessels. See *supra* 195; see also footnote 2 in *Herb's Welding, infra* at 224. Most events occurring on floating drilling and production apparatus (i.e., vessels) and on the waters near OCS platforms will naturally fall within admiralty jurisdiction.

As the Court noted, some occurrences on fixed platforms will fall within admiralty jurisdiction by virtue of the Admiralty Extension Act. See, e.g., *Callahan v. Cheramie Boats, Inc.*, 383 F. Supp. 1217, 1221–22 (E.D. La. 1974) Other fixed-platform occurrences will fall within admiralty jurisdiction because the accident victim is a seaman by virtue of his connection with a vessel being used to service or deliver to the platform. See, e.g., *Noble Drilling Corp. v. Smith*, 412 F.2d 952, 956 (5th Cir. 1969).

4. **Choice of law analysis in cases of overlapping OCSLA coverage and admiralty jurisdiction: *displacement*, not preemption.** It should be obvious by this point that many OCS events will naturally fall under both OCSLA coverage and admiralty jurisdiction. In such cases, the courts routinely hold that federal maritime law applies to the exclusion of the state law made surrogate federal law by 43 U.S.C. § 1333(a)(2)(A). See, e.g., *Strong v. B.P. Exploration & Production, Inc.*, 440 F.3d 665 (5th Cir. 2006). It is useful to view these cases as presenting *displacement* rather than *preemption* issues. See *supra* at 110. When a court holds that federal maritime law trumps state/surrogate federal law, it is effectively holding that the "other Federal laws" language of § 1333(a) dictates that federal maritime law should *displace* state/surrogate federal law.

5. **State law as surrogate federal law.** Under OCSLA § 4(a)(2)(A), 43 U.S.C. § 1333(a)(2)(A), state law serves as surrogate federal law on the OCS when it is "applicable and not inconsistent with [OCSLA] or with other Federal laws." In *Parker Drilling Management Services, Ltd. v. Newton*, 139 S. Ct. 1881, 2019 AMC 1548 (2019), the Supreme Court had to decide how broadly § 4(a)(2)(A) applies. Parker Drilling employed Brian Newton to work on two OCS drilling platforms off California's coast. On the platforms, Newton worked 14-day shifts, which consisted of 12 hours on duty and 12 hours of "controlled standby" each day. During the "controlled standby" time he could eat and sleep, but he was required to address problems as they arose, such as responding to alarms. The employer paid Newton for his 12 hours on duty each day and for the time he spent actually responding to incidents that arose during controlled-standby periods, but did not otherwise pay him for that time.

OCSLA § 4(a)(1) indisputably makes the federal Fair Labor Standards Act of 1938 (FLSA), 29 U.S.C. §§ 201–219, applicable on the OCS. The FLSA is a comprehensive wage-and-hour-protection statute. It does not require an employer to pay for stand-by time (even when the employee is not free to leave the workplace), but it does not prohibit paying for stand-by time. Newton therefore sought the benefit of California's more generous wage-and-hour laws, which define the "hours worked" to include stand-by time.

He argued that those California statutes were valid as surrogate federal law because they were (by their own terms) "applicable" and (by a process of comparing them with the comparable FLSA provisions) "not inconsistent with" the FLSA.

The Supreme Court unanimously concluded that state law is not "applicable" when federal law has already addressed the relevant issue. Because the FLSA addresses Newton's claim that he should be paid for his stand-by time, there is no need to incorporate California law as surrogate federal law. That holding follows well-established precedent in the Fifth Circuit (where most OCSLA cases arise).

6. **Some implications of the choice of law.** The choice-of-law decision can control the outcome of a case in a number of different ways. For example, in *Strong v. B.P. Exploration & Production, Inc., supra* note 3, the plaintiff's case was dismissed as untimely when the court held that federal maritime law applied. If Louisiana law had applied, the suit would have been timely. In *Parker Drilling, supra* note 4, the employee would have recovered substantial back pay if California law had applied as surrogate federal law. In *In re Larry Doiron, supra* at 64, note 4, the choice of law determined which of two companies would be responsible for compensating the victim of an offshore accident. Under maritime law, an indemnity provision in the contract between them would have been enforceable, but under Louisiana law it was invalid.

7. **OCSLA jurisdiction.** 43 U.S.C. § 1349(b) sets forth an "arising under" ground of federal-court jurisdiction that includes tort actions arising from OCS occurrences. State courts have concurrent jurisdiction over such actions. *Gulf Offshore Co. v. Mobil Oil Corp.*, 453 U.S. 473 (1981).

Herb's Welding, Inc. v. Gray

Supreme Court of the United States, 1985
470 U.S. 414, 105 S. Ct. 1421, 84 L. Ed. 2d 406 1985 AMC 1700

Justice WHITE delivered the opinion of the Court.

The [LHWCA] provides compensation for the death or disability of any person engaged in "maritime employment" [LHWCA § 2(3), 33 U.S.C. § 902(3)] if the disability or death results from an injury incurred upon the navigable waters of the United States or any adjoining pier or other area customarily used by an employer in loading, unloading, repairing, or building a vessel [LHWCA § 3(a), 33 U.S.C. § 903(a)]. Thus, a worker claiming under the Act must satisfy both a "status" and a "situs" test. The court below held that respondent Robert Gray, a welder working on a fixed offshore oil-drilling platform in state territorial waters, was entitled to benefits under the Act. We reverse for the reason that Gray was not engaged in maritime employment.

I.

Respondent Gray worked for Herb's Welding, Inc., in the Bay Marchand oil and gas field off the Louisiana coast. Herb's Welding provided welding services to the owners of drilling platforms. The field was located partly in Louisiana territorial waters, i.e., within three miles of the shore, and partly on the Outer Continental Shelf. Gray ate and slept on a platform situated in Louisiana waters. He spent roughly three-quarters of his working time on platforms in state waters and the rest on platforms on the Outer Continental Shelf. He worked exclusively as a welder, building and replacing pipelines and doing general maintenance work on the platforms.

On July 11, 1975, Gray was welding a gas flow line on a fixed platform[2] located in Louisiana waters. He burnt through the bottom of the line and an explosion occurred. Gray ran from the area, and in doing so hurt his knee. He sought benefits under the LHWCA for lost wages, disability, and medical expenses. When petitioner United States Fidelity & Guaranty Co., the workers' compensation carrier for Herb's Welding, denied LHWCA benefits, Gray filed a complaint with the Department of Labor. The Administrative Law Judge (ALJ), relying on our decision in *Rodrigue* [*supra* at 219], ruled that because Gray's work was totally involved in the exploration for, and development and transmission of, oil and gas from submerged lands, it was not relevant to traditional maritime law and lacked any significant maritime connection. Gray therefore did not satisfy the LHWCA's status requirement.

The Benefits Review Board reversed on other grounds. By a vote of 2–1, it concluded that irrespective of the nature of his employment, Gray could recover by virtue of [the OCSLA extension of the LHWCA, 43 U.S.C. § 1333(b)]. Although Gray had been injured in state waters, the Board felt that his injury nonetheless could be said to have occurred, in the words of [§ 1333)b)], "as a result of" operations on the outer shelf. It considered his work "integrally related" to such operations. The dissenting Board member argued that the Lands Act provides LHWCA benefits only for injuries actually occurring in the geographic area of the outer shelf.

* * * [P]etitioners sought review in the Court of Appeals for the Fifth Circuit. That court affirmed, relying directly on the LHWCA rather than on the [OCSLA extension thereof]. With regard to the [LHWCA's] situs requirement, it noted that this Court had compared drilling platforms to wharves in *Rodrigue* [ ]. Given that the 1972 Amendments to the LHWCA extended coverage to accidents occurring on wharves, it would be incongruous if they did not also reach accidents occurring on drilling platforms. Also, since workers injured on movable barges, on fixed platforms on the Outer Continental Shelf, or en route to fixed platforms, are all covered, there would be a "curious hole" in coverage if someone in Gray's position was not. [ ] As for Gray's status, the Court of Appeals, differing with the ALJ, held that Gray's work bore "a realistically significant relationship to traditional maritime activity involving navigation and commerce on navigable waters" because it was an integral part of the offshore drilling process, which, the court had held in *Pippen v. Shell Oil Co.*, 661 F.2d 378 (1981), was itself maritime commerce. We granted certiorari.

---

2. Offshore oil rigs are of two general sorts: fixed and floating. *Hearings on S. 2318 et al. before the Subcommittee on Labor of the Senate Committee on Labor and Public Welfare*, 92d Cong., 2d Sess., 395–396, 48–486 (1972) (hereafter *Hearings*). Floating structures have been treated as vessels by the lower courts [ ]. Workers on them, unlike workers on fixed platforms, see *Rodrigue*, enjoy the same remedies as workers on ships. If permanently attached to the vessel as crewmembers, they are regarded as seamen; if not, they are covered by the LHWCA because they are employed on navigable waters. See generally Robertson, *Injuries to Marine Petroleum Workers: A Plea for Radical Simplification*, 55 Tex. L. Rev. 973, 982–992 (1977) (hereinafter *Robertson*). [See also *Perini*, *supra* at 209 note 3.] Gray is not in a position to take advantage of this line of cases. All, or almost all, the platforms in the field were fixed production platforms rather than floating rigs. There has never been any dispute that Gray was injured on a fixed platform, nor any contention that he should be considered to have been on a vessel at the time of his injury. The only question, therefore, is whether Gray is limited to state workers' compensation remedies or may also recover under the LHWCA.

II.

A.

When extractive operations first moved offshore, all claims for injuries on fixed platforms proceeded under state workers' compensation schemes. See *Hearings* at 396, 409, 411. See also *Robertson* 993. With the 1953 passage of the Lands Act, Congress extended LHWCA coverage to oil workers more than three miles offshore. 43 U.S.C. § 1333(b). Because until 1972 the LHWCA itself extended coverage only to accidents occurring on navigable waters [ ], and because stationary rigs were considered to be islands, *Rodrigue* [ ], oil rig workers inside the 3-mile limit were left to recover under state schemes. [ ] Any worker, inside or outside the 3-mile limit, who qualified as a seaman was not covered by the LHWCA, but could sue under the Jones Act * * * and the general maritime law. [ ]

So matters stood when Congress amended the LHWCA in 1972. What is known about the congressional intent behind that legislation has been amply described in our prior opinions [particularly *Caputo, supra* at 202]. The most important of Congress's concerns, for present purposes, was the desire to extend coverage to longshoremen, harborworkers, and others who were injured while on piers, docks, and other areas customarily used to load and unload ships or to repair or build ships, rather than while actually afloat. Whereas prior to 1972 the Act reached only accidents occurring on navigable waters, the amended 33 U.S.C. § 903 expressly extended coverage to "adjoining area[s]." At the same time, the amended definition of an "employee" limited coverage to employees engaged in "maritime employment."

The [LHWCA], as amended, does not mention offshore drilling rigs or the workers thereon. The legislative history of the amendments is also silent, although early in the legislative process, a bill was introduced to extend the [LHWCA] to all offshore oil workers. The bill died in Committee.[5] While hardly dispositive, it is worth noting that the same Committee considered the 1972 Amendments to the LHWCA and the possible extension of the Land Act's application of the LHWCA to [all offshore oil workers] apparently without it ever occurring to anyone that the two might have been duplicative. The concurrent but independent reconsideration of both the Lands Act and the LHWCA, the congressional view that the amendments to the latter involved the "[e]xtension of [c]overage to [s]horeside [a]reas," [ ] and the absence of any mention of drilling platforms in the discussion of the LHWCA, combine to suggest that the 1972 Congress at least did not intentionally extend the LHWCA to workers such as Gray.

B.

The rationale of the Court of Appeals was that offshore drilling is maritime commerce and that anyone performing any task that is part and parcel of that activity is in maritime employment for LHWCA purposes. Since it is doubtful that an offshore driller will pay and maintain a worker on an offshore rig whose job is unnecessary to the venture, this approach would extend coverage to virtually everyone on the stationary platform. We think this construction of the Act is untenable.

---

5. Petitioners view Congress' failure to extend LHWCA coverage to all offshore oil workers as an explicit rejection of the position adopted by the court below. However, it appears that the bill [the so-called "Tower bill," S. 1547, named for Senator John Tower (R.-Tex.)] was designed not so much to increase the benefits of those not covered as to limit the remedies of those workers who could qualify as seamen and so were not confined to the workers' compensation scheme. [ ] The bill was opposed because it would limit recoveries by those who did better without LHWCA coverage. [ ]

The Act does not define the term "maritime employment," but our cases and the legislative history of the amendments foreclose the Court of Appeals' reading. *Rodrigue* [stated that the platforms there involved] "were islands, albeit artificial ones, and the accidents had no more connection with the ordinary stuff of admiralty than do accidents on piers." [ ] Indeed, observing that the Court had previously "held that drilling platforms are not within admiralty jurisdiction," we indicated that drilling platforms were not even suggestive of traditional maritime affairs. [ ]

We also went on to examine the legislative history of the Lands Act and noted (1) that Congress was of the view that maritime law would not apply to fixed platforms unless a statute expressly so provided; and (2) that Congress had seriously considered applying maritime law to these platforms but had rejected that approach because it considered maritime law to be inapposite, a view that would be untenable if drilling from a fixed platform is a maritime operation. The history of the Lands Act at the very least forecloses the Court of Appeals' holding that offshore drilling is a maritime activity and that any task essential thereto is maritime employment for LHWCA purposes.

We cannot assume that Congress was unfamiliar with *Rodrigue* and the Lands Act when it referred to "maritime employment" in defining the term "employee" in 1972. It would have been a significant departure from prior understanding to use that phrase to reach stationary drilling rigs generally.

The Fifth Circuit's expansive view of maritime employment is also inconsistent with our prior cases under the 1972 Amendments to the LHWCA. The expansion of the definition of navigable waters to include rather large shoreside areas necessitated an affirmative description of the particular employees working in those areas who would be covered. This was the function of the maritime employment requirement. But Congress did not seek to cover all those who breathe salt air. Its purpose was to cover those workers on the situs who are involved in the essential elements of loading and unloading; it is "clear that persons who are on the situs but not engaged in the overall process of loading or unloading vessels are not covered." *Caputo* [*supra* at 202, 432 U.S. at 267]. While "maritime employment" is not limited to the occupations specifically mentioned in § 2(3),[9] neither can it be read to eliminate any requirement of a connection with the loading or construction of ships. As we have said, the "maritime employment" requirement is "an occupational test that focuses on loading and unloading." *P.C. Pfeiffer Co. v. Ford* [*supra* at 208 note 2; 444 U.S. at 80]. The Amendments were not meant "to cover employees who are not engaged in loading, unloading, repairing, or building a vessel, just because they are injured in an area adjoining navigable waters used for such activity." [ ] We have never read "maritime employment" to extend so far beyond those actually involved in moving cargo between ship and land transportation. Both *Caputo* and *P.C. Pfeiffer Co.* make this clear and lead us to the conclusion that Gray was not engaged in maritime employment for purposes of the LHWCA.

Gray was a welder. His work had nothing to do with the loading or unloading process, nor is there any indication that he was even employed in the maintenance of equipment used in such tasks. Gray's welding work was far removed from traditional LHWCA activities, notwithstanding the fact that he unloaded his own gear upon arriving at a platform by

9. The LHWCA covers "any person engaged in maritime employment, including any longshoreman or other person engaged in longshoring operations, and any harborworker including a ship repairman, shipbuilder, and shipbreaker." By the use of the term "including," Congress indicated that the specifically mentioned occupations are not exclusive. * * *

boat. He built and maintained pipelines and the platforms themselves. There is nothing inherently maritime about those tasks. They are also performed on land, and their nature is not significantly altered by the marine environment, particularly since exploration and development of the Continental Shelf are not themselves maritime commerce.

The dissent emphasizes that Gray was generally on or near the water and faced maritime hazards. To the extent this is so, it is relevant to "situs," not "status." To hold that Gray was necessarily engaged in maritime employment because he was on a drilling platform would ignore Congress' admonition that not everyone on a covered situs automatically satisfies the status test. [ ] The dissent considers "[t]he maritime nature of the occupation ... apparent from examining its location in terms of the expanded situs coverage of the 1972 Amendments." We recognize that the nature of a particular job is defined in part by its location. But to classify Gray's employment as maritime because he was on a covered situs or in a "maritime environment" would blur together requirements Congress intended to be distinct. We cannot thus read the status requirement out of the statute.

III.

Respondents, and the dissenters, object that denying coverage to someone in Gray's position will result in exactly the sort of inconsistent, checkered coverage that Congress sought to eliminate in 1972. In the words of the court below, it creates a "curious hole" in coverage [ ], because Gray would have been covered had he been injured on navigable waters or on the outer shelf.

We do not find the argument compelling. First, this submission goes far beyond Congress' undoubted desire to treat equally all workers engaged in loading or unloading a ship, whether they were injured on the ship or on an adjoining pier or dock. The former were covered prior to 1972; the latter were not. Both are covered under the 1972 Amendments. Second, there will always be a boundary to coverage, and there will always be people who cross it during their employment. [ ] If that phenomenon was enough to require coverage, the Act would have to reach much further than anyone argues that it does or should. Third, the inconsistent coverage here results primarily from the explicit geographic limitation to the Lands Act's incorporation of the LHWCA. Gray would indeed have been covered for a significant portion of his work-time, but because of the Lands Act, not because he fell within the terms of the LHWCA. Congress' desire to make LHWCA coverage uniform reveals little about the position of those for whom partial coverage results from a separate statute. This is especially true because that statute draws a clear geographical boundary that will predictably result in workers moving in and out of coverage.

As we have said before in this area, if Congress' coverage decisions are mistaken as a matter of policy, it is for Congress to change them. We should not legislate for them. [ ]

* * *

Justice MARSHALL, with whom Justice Brennan, Justice Blackmun, and Justice O'Connor join, dissenting.

Today the Court holds that a marine petroleum worker is not covered by the [LHWCA] when pursuing his occupation on a fixed offshore rig within the 3-mile limit of a State's territorial waters. Although such an individual routinely travels over water as an essential part of his job and performs the rest of his job adjacent to and surrounded by water, he is not covered because, in the Court's view, his occupation is not "maritime employment." [ ] The Court reaches this conclusion even though a worker of the same occupation, working in the same industry, and performing the same tasks on a rig located in the same place, would be covered if that rig were one that was capable of floating. Neither the

Court nor any of the parties have identified any reason why Congress might have desired this distinction. To the contrary, a principal congressional goal behind the 1972 amendments was to rid the [LHWCA] of just such arbitrary distinctions * * *.

* * *

Note

The Court stated (in a footnote not included above): "Throughout these proceedings, Gray has argued that he need not satisfy the [LHWCA] status/situs test because he falls within the Lands Act's incorporation of LHWCA benefits. The [BRB] so held. He repeats that argument in this Court, as he is free to do. However, it has not been fully briefed and argued here and was not discussed by the Court of Appeals. We therefore decline to consider it. It is open to the Court of Appeals on remand."

On remand, the Fifth Circuit held that 43 U.S.C. § 1333(b) did not extend LHWCA coverage to Gray because, in the language of the statute, his injury was not "the result of operations conducted on the outer Continental Shelf." Instead:

> Gray's injury happened on a platform that produced oil from the territorial seabed, not that of the shelf. Even if Herb's Welding had confined its operations solely to the Louisiana part of the oil field, the accident still would have happened. The fact that the platform where Gray was injured might have been indirectly connected to a platform on the shelf by a network of pipelines is unrelated to the accident's causation.

Herb's Welding v. Gray, 766 F.2d 898, 900 (5th Cir. 1985). The court expressly declined to say whether "section 1333(b) can ever apply to an injury that occurs in territorial waters and not on the shelf." In *Mills v. Director, Office of Workers' Compensation Programs*, 877 F.2d 356, 362 (5th Cir. 1989) (en banc), the Fifth Circuit answered no. According to *Valladolid*, just below, *Mills* got the wrong answer.

Pacific Operators Offshore, LLP v. Valladolid

Supreme Court of the United States, 2012

565 U.S. 207, 132 S. Ct. 680, 181 L. Ed. 2d 675, 2012 AMC 1

Justice THOMAS delivered the opinion of the Court.

* * *

Petitioner Pacific Operators Offshore, LLP (Pacific), operates two drilling platforms on the Outer Continental Shelf off the coast of California and an onshore oil and gas processing facility in Ventura County, California. Pacific employed Juan Valladolid as a general manual laborer—known in the trade as a roustabout—in its oil exploration and extraction business. Valladolid spent about 98 percent of his time on one of Pacific's offshore drilling platforms performing maintenance duties, such as picking up litter, emptying trashcans, washing decks, painting, maintaining equipment, and helping to load and unload the platform crane. Valladolid spent the remainder of his time working at Pacific's onshore processing facility, where he also performed maintenance duties, including painting, sandblasting, pulling weeds, cleaning drain culverts, and operating a forklift.

While on duty at the onshore facility, Valladolid died in a forklift accident. His widow, a respondent here, filed a claim for benefits under the LHWCA pursuant to the extension of that Act contained [in 43 U.S.C. § 1333(b)]. After a hearing, an Administrative Law Judge (ALJ) dismissed respondent's claim. The ALJ reasoned that Valladolid's fatal injury was not covered under § 1333(b) because his accident occurred on land, rather than on the Outer Continental Shelf. On appeal, the United States Department of Labor's Benefits Review Board affirmed, concluding that Congress intended to limit the coverage provided by the OCSLA to injuries suffered by employees within the "geographical locale" of the Outer Continental Shelf. [The Ninth Circuit reversed. We granted Pacific's petition for a writ of certiorari to resolve a conflict among the Third, Fifth, and Ninth Circuits over the interpretation of § 1333(b).]

* * *

The question before us is the scope of coverage under § 1333(b). The parties agree that § 1333(b) covers employees, such as oil rig and drilling platform workers, who are injured while working directly on the OCS to extract its natural resources. They disagree, however, whether employees who are involved in extraction operations but who are injured beyond the OCS are also covered under the OCSLA. This dispute focuses on the meaning of the phrase "any injury occurring as the result of operations conducted on the outer Continental Shelf" in § 1333(b).

The Courts of Appeals have offered competing interpretations. In *Curtis v. Schlumberger Offshore Service, Inc.*, [849 F.2d 805, 811 (3d Cir. 1988), the Third Circuit held that, because Congress intended LHWCA coverage to be expansive, § 1333(b) extends to all injuries that would not have occurred "but for" operations on the OCS. The Third Circuit thus concluded that an employee who worked on a semisubmersible drill rig, but who was killed in a car accident on the way to the helicopter that was to fly him to that rig, was eligible for § 1333(b) benefits. The Third Circuit summarized, " 'But for' [Curtis'] travelling to [his drill rig] for the purpose of conducting 'operations' within § 1333(b), employee Curtis would not have sustained injuries in the automobile accident."

In *Mills v. Director*, [877 F.2d 356 (5th Cir. 1989) (en banc)], the Fifth Circuit adopted a narrower interpretation of § 1333(b). The court concluded that Congress intended to establish "a bright-line geographic boundary for § 1333(b) coverage," and held that § 1333(b) extends coverage only to employees engaged in OCS extractive activities who "suffer injury or death on an OCS platform or the waters above the OCS." *Id.* at 362. Applying its "situs-of-injury" test, the Fifth Circuit held that a welder who was injured on land during the construction of an offshore oil platform was not eligible for § 1333(b) benefits.

In the case below, the Ninth Circuit rejected the Fifth Circuit's "situs-of-injury" requirement as unsupported by the text of § 1333(b), and the Third Circuit's "but for" test as too broad to be consistent with Congress' intent. 604 F.3d 1125, 1139 (9th Cir. 2010). Instead, the Ninth Circuit adopted a third interpretation of § 1333(b), holding that a "claimant must establish a substantial nexus between the injury and extractive operations on the shelf" to be eligible for § 1333(b) benefits. To meet the standard," the Ninth Circuit explained, "the claimant must show that the work performed directly furthers outer continental shelf operations and is in the regular course of such operations."

The Solicitor General suggests yet a fourth interpretation of § 1333(b).[1] This interpretation would extend coverage to two categories of injuries: (1) all on-OCS injuries suffered by employees of companies engaged in resource extraction on the OCS; and (2)

---

1. The Director, Office of Workers' Compensation Programs, is a respondent in this case because the Director administers the OCSLA compensation scheme established by § 1333(b).

the off-OCS injuries of those employees who spend a substantial portion of their worktime on the OCS engaging in extractive operations. According to the Solicitor General, this test would provide § 1333(b) coverage for off-OCS injuries only to those employees whose duties contribute to operations on the OCS and who perform work on the OCS itself that is substantial in both duration and nature.

III

Pacific argues that the Fifth Circuit's "situs-of-injury" test presents the best interpretation of § 1333(b). The crux of Pacific's argument is that off-OCS injuries cannot be "the result of operations conducted on the outer Continental Shelf" for purposes of § 1333(b). Pacific asserts that because Valladolid was injured on dry land, his death did not occur as the result of extraction operations conducted on the OCS, and therefore respondent is ineligible for LHWCA workers' compensation benefits. We disagree. * * * Contrary to the view of Pacific and the Fifth Circuit, nothing in [the language of § 1333(b)] suggests that the injury to the employee must occur on the OCS. Section 1333(b) states only two requirements: The extractive operations must be "conducted on the outer Continental Shelf," and the employee's injury must occur "as the result of" those operations.

Despite the lack of a textual "situs-of-injury" requirement in § 1333(b), Pacific argues that it is logically impossible for an off-OCS employee to be injured "as the result of" on-OCS operations. Pacific offers no basis for this assertion, and we find none. Indeed, given that many OCS platforms are physically connected to onshore processing facilities via oil and gas pipelines, it is not difficult to imagine an accident occurring on an OCS platform that could injure employees located off the OCS.

Moreover, if, as Pacific suggests, the purpose of § 1333(b) was to geographically limit the extension of LHWCA coverage to injuries that occurred on the OCS, Congress could easily have achieved that goal by omitting the following six words in § 1333(b)'s text: "as the result of operations conducted." Had Congress done so, the statute would extend LHWCA coverage to the "disability or death of an employee resulting from any injury occurring on the outer Continental Shelf." But that is not the text of the statute Congress enacted.

* * *

IV

The Solicitor General urges us to adopt a status-based inquiry that applies one test to on-OCS injuries and a different test to off-OCS injuries. Specifically, the Government proposes that when a worker is injured on the OCS, he is eligible for workers' compensation benefits if he is employed by a company engaged in extractive operations on the OCS. But if the employee is injured off the OCS, the employee will be covered only if his "duties contribute to operations" on the OCS and if he performs "work on the [OCS] itself that is substantial in terms of both its duration and nature." This approach is derived from our decision in *Chandris, Inc. v. Latsis* [*supra* at 189] (establishing criteria by which an employee qualifies as a "seaman" under the Jones Act), and might well have merit as legislation. But it has no basis in the text of the OCSLA as presently enacted. The "occurring as the result of operations" language in § 1333(b) plainly suggests causation. Although the Government asserts that a status-based test would be preferable to a causation-based test, we cannot ignore the language enacted by Congress.

The Third Circuit's "but for" test is nominally based on causation, but it is also incompatible with § 1333(b). Taken to its logical conclusion, the "but for" test would extend workers' compensation coverage to all employees of a business engaged in the extraction of natural resources from the OCS, no matter where those employees work or what they are doing when they are injured. This test could reasonably be interpreted to cover land-based office employees whose jobs have virtually nothing to do with extractive operations on the OCS. Because Congress extended LHWCA coverage only to injuries "occurring as the result of operations conducted on the outer Continental Shelf," we think that § 1333(b) should be interpreted in a manner that focuses on injuries that result from those "operations." * * *

Accordingly, we conclude that the Ninth Circuit's "substantial-nexus" test is more faithful to the text of § 1333(b). We understand the Ninth Circuit's test to require the injured employee to establish a significant causal link between the injury that he suffered and his employer's on-OCS operations conducted for the purpose of extracting natural resources from the OCS.

Although the Ninth Circuit's test may not be the easiest to administer, it best reflects the text of § 1333(b), which establishes neither a situs-of-injury nor a "but for" test. We are confident that ALJs and courts will be able to determine whether an injured employee has established a significant causal link between the injury he suffered and his employer's on-OCS extractive operations. Although we expect that employees injured while performing tasks on the OCS will regularly satisfy the test, whether an employee injured while performing an off-OCS task qualifies—like Valladolid, who died while tasked with onshore scrap metal consolidation—is a question that will depend on the individual circumstances of each case. The Ninth Circuit remanded the case for the Benefits Review Board to apply the "substantial-nexus" test in the first instance, and we agree with that disposition.

The judgment is affirmed, and the case is remanded to the Court of Appeals for further proceedings consistent with this opinion.

* * *

Justice SCALIA, with whom Justice Alito, concurring in part and concurring in the judgment.

I join the Court's judgment that the Ninth Circuit properly remanded this case to the Benefits Review Board, and I agree with almost all of the Court's opinion. My disagreement is limited to the last two substantive paragraphs of Part IV, which endorse the Ninth Circuit's "substantial-nexus" test for determining the scope of coverage under 43 U.S.C. § 1333(b). The Court indulges in considerable understatement when it acknowledges that this test "may not be the easiest to administer." "Substantial nexus" is novel legalese with no established meaning in the present context. I agree with the Court's rejection of some of the clearer rules proposed by the parties—which, though easier to apply, are unmoored from the text of § 1333(b). But if we must adopt an indeterminate standard (and the statute's "as the result of" language leaves us no choice) I prefer the devil we know to the devil of the Ninth Circuit's imagining. I would hold that an employee may recover under § 1333(b) if his injury was proximately caused by operations on the Outer Continental Shelf (OCS). * * *

Note

After the Supreme Court remanded *Valladolid* to the Ninth Circuit, the parties settled the case and no tribunal had the opportunity to apply the "substantial nexus" test to the facts of the case. Reviewing the prior proceedings in the Ninth Circuit, it appears that the test was not "the devil of the Ninth Circuit's imagining," as Justice Scalia described it.

The Ninth Circuit appears to have drawn the test from the Fifth Circuit's panel decision in *Mills v. Director, Office of Workers' Compensation Programs*, 846 F.2d 101 (5th Cir. 1988)—the decision that was overturned by the en banc decision discussed in *Valladolid* (a decision that was itself overruled by *Valladolid*).

After *Valladolid*, the first circuit to address the "substantial nexus" test was again the Fifth Circuit. *Baker v. Director, Office of Workers' Compensation Programs*, 834 F.3d 542, 548 (5th Cir. 2016), found no substantial nexus between extractive operations on the OCS and the employee's injury while building a housing module designed for use on a tension leg offshore oil platform that would go into service on the OCS.

E. Fatal Injury Litigation

There are two types of fatal-injury litigation. Wrongful death actions seek to compensate the decedent's family for the losses they have suffered as a result of the decedent's death. Survival actions assert the decedent's estate's right to prosecute the personal injury action that the decedent would have had but for his death. Survival damages are generally confined to those suffered by the decedent in the interval between the onset of the tort and death and will not be awardable if death was instantaneous.

Moragne v. States Marine Lines, Inc.

Supreme Court of the United States, 1970

398 U.S. 375, 90 S. Ct. 1772, 26 L. Ed. 2d 339, 1970 AMC 967

Mr. Justice HARLAN delivered the opinion of the unanimous Court.[31]

We brought this case here to consider whether *The Harrisburg*, 119 U.S. 199, in which this Court held in 1886 that maritime law does not afford a cause of action for wrongful death, should any longer be regarded as acceptable law.

The complaint sets forth that Edward Moragne, a longshoreman, was killed while working aboard the vessel *Palmetto State* on navigable waters within the State of Florida. Petitioner, as his widow and representative of his estate, brought this suit in a state court against respondent States Marine Lines, Inc., the owner of the vessel, to recover damages for wrongful death and for the pain and suffering experienced by the decedent prior to his death. The claims were predicated upon both negligence and the unseaworthiness of the vessel.

States Marine removed the case to Federal District Court for the Middle District of Florida on the basis of diversity of citizenship. * * * [States Marine then] sought dismissal of the portion of petitioner's complaint that requested damages for wrongful death on the basis of unseaworthiness, [contending] that maritime law provided no recovery for wrongful death within a State's territorial waters, and that the statutory right of action for death under Florida law [ ] did not encompass unseaworthiness as a basis of liability. The District Court dismissed the challenged portion of the complaint on this ground [ ] but made the certification necessary under 28 U.S.C. § 1292(b) to allow petitioner an interlocutory appeal to the Court of Appeals for the Fifth Circuit.

31. Editors' note: Justice Blackmun did not participate.

The Court of Appeals took advantage of a procedure furnished by state law [ ] to certify to the Florida Supreme Court the question whether the state wrongful death statute allowed recovery for unseaworthiness as that concept is understood in maritime law. After reviewing the history of the Florida Act, the state court answered this question in the negative. 211 So.2d 161 (Fla. 1968). On return of the case to the Court of Appeals, that court affirmed the District Court's order, rejecting petitioner's argument that she was entitled to reversal under federal maritime law without regard to the scope of the state statute. The court stated that its disposition was compelled by our decision in [*The Tungus v. Skovgaard*, 358 U.S. 588 (1959).] We granted certiorari and invited the United States to participate as amicus curiae to reconsider the important question of remedies under federal maritime law for tortious deaths on state territorial waters.

In *The Tungus* this Court divided on the consequences that should flow from the rule of maritime law that "in the absence of a statute there is no action for wrongful death," first announced in *The Harrisburg*. All members of the Court agreed that where a death on state territorial waters is left remediless by the general maritime law and by federal statutes, a remedy may be provided under any applicable state law giving a right of action for death by wrongful act. However, four Justices dissented from the Court's further holding that "when admiralty adopts a State's right of action for wrongful death, it must enforce the right as an integrated whole, with whatever conditions and limitations the creating State has attached." The dissenters would have held that federal maritime law could utilize the state law to "supply a remedy" for breaches of federally imposed duties, without regard to any substantive limitations contained in the state law.

The extent of the role to be played by state law under *The Tungus* has been the subject of substantial debate and uncertainty in this Court [ ], with opinions on both sides of the question acknowledging the shortcomings in the present law. On fresh consideration of the entire subject, we have concluded that the primary source of the confusion is not to be found in *The Tungus*, but in *The Harrisburg*, and that the latter decision, somewhat dubious even when rendered, is such an unjustifiable anomaly in the present maritime law that it should no longer be followed. We therefore reverse the judgment of the Court of Appeals.

I.

The Court's opinion in *Harrisburg* acknowledged that the result reached had little justification except in primitive English legal history—a history far removed from the American law of remedies for maritime deaths. That case, like this, was a suit on behalf of the family of a maritime worker for his death on the navigable waters of a State. Following several precedents in the lower federal courts, the trial court awarded damages against the ship causing the death, and the circuit court affirmed, ruling that death by maritime tort "may be complained of as an injury, and the wrong redressed under the general maritime law." This Court, in reversing, relied primarily on its then recent decision in *Insurance Co. v. Brame*, 95 U.S. 754 (1878), in which it had held that in American common law, as in English, "no civil action lies for an injury which results in ... death."[3] In *Harrisburg*, as in *Brame*, the Court did not examine the justifications for this common-law rule; rather, it simply noted that "we know of no country that has adopted a different rule on this subject for the sea from that which it maintains on the land," and concluded, despite contrary decisions of the lower federal courts both before and after *Brame*, that the rule of *Brame* should apply equally to maritime deaths.

---

3. *Brame* was decided, of course, at a time when the federal courts under *Swift v. Tyson*, 41 U.S. 1 (1842), expounded a general federal common law.

Our analysis of the history of the common-law rule indicates that it was based on a particular set of factors that had, when *Harrisburg* was decided, long since been thrown into discard even in England, and that had never existed in this country at all. Further, regardless of the viability of the rule in 1886 as applied to American land-based affairs, it is difficult to discern an adequate reason for its extension to admiralty, a system of law then already differentiated in many respects from the common law.

One would expect, upon an inquiry into the sources of the common-law rule, to find a clear and compelling justification for what seems a striking departure from the result dictated by elementary principles in the law of remedies. Where existing law imposes a primary duty, violations of which are compensable if they cause injury, nothing in ordinary notions of justice suggests that a violation should be nonactionable simply because it was serious enough to cause death. On the contrary, that rule has been criticized ever since its inception, and described in such terms as "barbarous." [ ] Because the primary duty already exists, the decision whether to allow recovery for violations causing death is entirely a remedial matter. * * * One expects, therefore, to find a persuasive, independent justification for this apparent legal anomaly.

Legal historians have concluded that the sole substantial basis for the rule at common law is a feature of the early English law that did not survive into this century—the felony-merger doctrine. [ ] According to this doctrine, the common law did not allow civil recovery for an act that constituted both a tort and a felony. The tort was treated as less important than the offense against the Crown, and was merged into, or pre-empted by, the felony. [ ] The doctrine found practical justification in the fact that the punishment for the felony was the death of the felon and the forfeiture of his property to the Crown; thus, after the crime had been punished, nothing remained of the felon or his property on which to base a civil action. Since all intentional or negligent homicide was felonious, there could be no civil suit for wrongful death.

* * *

The historical justification marshaled for the rule in England never existed in this country. * * * Nevertheless, despite some early cases in which the rule was rejected as "incapable of vindication," American courts generally adopted the English rule as the common law of this country as well. Throughout the period of this adoption, culminating in this Court's decision in *Brame,* the courts failed to produce any satisfactory justification for applying the rule in this country.

Some courts explained that their holdings were prompted by an asserted difficulty in computation of damages for wrongful death or by a "repugnance to setting a price upon human life." [ ] However, other courts have recognized that calculation of the loss sustained by dependents * * * does not present difficulties more insurmountable than assessment of damages for many nonfatal personal injuries.

* * *

The most likely reason that the English rule was adopted in this country without much question is simply that it had the blessing of age. * * * The American courts never made the inquiry whether this particular English rule, bitterly criticized in England, "was applicable to their situation," and it is difficult to imagine on what basis they might have concluded that it was.

Further, even after the decision in *Brame,* it is not apparent why the Court in *Harrisburg* concluded that there should not be a different rule for admiralty from that applied at common law. Maritime law had always, in this country as in England, been a thing apart from the common law. It was, to a large extent, administered by different courts; it owed a much greater debt to the civil law; and, from its focus on a particular subject matter, it developed general principles unknown to the common law. These principles included a special solicitude for the welfare of those men who undertook to venture upon hazardous and unpredictable sea voyages. [ ] These factors suggest that there might have been no anomaly in adoption of a different rule to govern maritime relations, and that the common-law rule, criticized as unjust in its own domain, might wisely have been rejected as incompatible with the law of the sea. This was the conclusion reached by Chief Justice Chase, prior to *The Harrisburg*, sitting on circuit in *The Sea Gull*, 21 Fed. Cas. p. 909 (No. 12,578) (C.C.Md. 1865). He there remarked that

> There are cases, indeed, in which it has been held that in a suit at law, no redress can be had by the surviving representatives for injuries occasioned by the death of one through the wrong of another; but these are all common-law cases, and the common law has its peculiar rules in relation to this subject, traceable to the feudal system and its forfeitures * * * and certainly it better becomes the humane and liberal character of proceedings in admiralty to give than to withhold the remedy, when not required to withhold it by established and inflexible rules.

* * *

II.

We need not, however, pronounce a verdict on whether *Harrisburg*, when decided, was a correct extrapolation of the principles of decisional law then in existence. A development of major significance has intervened, making clear that the rule against recovery for wrongful death is sharply out of keeping with the policies of modern American maritime law. This development is the wholesale abandonment of the rule in most of the areas where it once held sway, quite evidently prompted by the same sense of the rule's injustice that generated so much criticism of its original promulgation.

* * *

[Quite early,] the legislatures both here and in England began to evidence unanimous disapproval of the rule against recovery for wrongful death. The first statute partially abrogating the rule was Lord Campbell's Act, 9 & 10 Vict. c. 93 (1846), which granted recovery to the families of persons killed by tortious conduct, "although the Death shall have been caused under such circumstances as amount in Law to Felony."

In the United States, every State today has enacted a wrongful-death statute. [ ] The Congress has created actions for wrongful deaths of railroad employees, Federal Employers' Liability Act, 45 U.S.C. §§ 51, 59; of merchant seamen, Jones Act [46 U.S.C. § 30104]; and of persons on the high seas, Death on the High Seas Act [46 U.S.C. §§ 30301–30308]. Congress has also, in the Federal Tort Claims Act, 28 U.S.C. § 1346(b), made the United States subject to liability in certain circumstances for negligently caused wrongful death to the same extent as a private person. [ ]

These numerous and broadly applicable statutes, taken as a whole, make it clear that there is no present public policy against allowing recovery for wrongful death. The statutes evidence a wide rejection by the legislatures of whatever justifications may once have existed for a general refusal to allow such recovery. This legislative establishment of policy carries significance beyond the particular scope of each of the statutes involved. The policy thus established has become itself a part of our law, to be given its appropriate weight not only in matters of statutory construction but also in those of decisional law. * * * It has always been the duty of the common-law court to perceive the impact of major legislative innovations and to interweave the new legislative policies with the inherited body of common-law principles * * *.

The legislature does not, of course, merely enact general policies. By the terms of a statute, it also indicates its conception of the sphere within which the policy is to have effect. * * * We must, therefore, analyze with care the congressional enactments that have abrogated the common-law rule in the maritime field, to determine the impact of the fact that none applies in terms to the situation of this case. See Part III *infra.* However, it is sufficient at this point to conclude * * * that the work of the legislatures has made the allowance of recovery for wrongful death the general rule of American law, and its denial the exception. Where death is caused by the breach of a duty imposed by federal maritime law, Congress has established a policy favoring recovery in the absence of a legislative direction to except a particular class of cases.

III.

Our undertaking, therefore, is to determine whether Congress has given such a direction in its legislation granting remedies for wrongful deaths in portions of the maritime domain. We find that Congress has given no affirmative indication of an intent to preclude the judicial allowance of a remedy for wrongful death to persons in the situation of this petitioner.

From the date of *Harrisburg* until 1920, there was no remedy for death on the high seas caused by breach of one of the duties imposed by federal maritime law. For deaths within state territorial waters, the federal law accommodated the humane policies of state wrongful-death statutes by allowing recovery whenever an applicable state statute favored such recovery.[10] Congress acted in 1920 to furnish the remedy denied by the courts for deaths beyond the jurisdiction of any State, by passing [the Death on the High Seas Act and the Jones Act].

* * *

The United States, participating as *amicus curiae,* contended at oral argument that these statutes, if construed to forbid recognition of a general maritime remedy for wrongful death within territorial waters, would perpetuate three anomalies of present law. The first of these is simply the discrepancy produced whenever the rule of *Harrisburg* holds sway: Within territorial waters, identical conduct violating federal law (here the furnishing of an unseaworthy vessel) produces liability if the victim is merely injured, but frequently not if he is killed. As we have concluded, such a distinction is not compatible with the general policies of federal maritime law.

The second incongruity is that identical breaches of the duty to provide a seaworthy ship, resulting in death, produce liability outside the three-mile limit—since a claim under the Death on the High Seas Act may be founded on unseaworthiness [ ]—but not within the territorial waters of a State whose local statute excludes unseaworthiness claims. The United States argues that since the substantive duty is federal, and federal maritime jurisdiction covers navigable waters within and without the three-mile limit, no rational policy supports this distinction in the availability of a remedy.

---

10. The general understanding was that the statutes of the coastal States, which provided remedies for deaths within territorial waters, did not apply beyond state boundaries. This Court had suggested, in an early case where the plaintiff and defendant were of the same State, that the law of that State could be applied to a death on the high seas, if the State intended the law to have such scope. *The Hamilton*, 207 U.S. 398 (1907). However, probably because most state death statutes were not meant to have application to the high seas, this possibility did little to fill the vacuum.

The third, and assertedly the "strangest" anomaly is that a true seaman—that is, a member of a ship's company, covered by the Jones Act—is provided no remedy for death caused by unseaworthiness within territorial waters, while a longshoreman, to whom the duty of seaworthiness was extended only because he performs work traditionally done by seamen, does have such a remedy when allowed by a state statute.[12]

There is much force to the United States' argument that these distinctions are so lacking in any apparent justification that we should not, in the absence of compelling evidence, presume that Congress affirmatively intended to freeze them into maritime law. There should be no presumption that Congress has removed this Court's traditional responsibility to vindicate the policies of maritime law by ceding that function exclusively to the States. However, [States Marine argues] that an intent to do just that is manifested by the [the Death on the High Seas Act, which confines the federal remedy to fatal accidents "occurring on the high seas," 46 U.S.C. § 30302, states that the Act "does not affect the law of a State regulating the right to recover for death," *id.* § 30308(a), and provides that the Act "does not apply to the Great Lakes or waters within the territorial limits of a state," *id.* § 30308(b).]

The legislative history of the Act suggests that [States Marine misconceives] the thrust of the congressional concern. * * * Read in light of the state of maritime law in 1920, we believe this legislative history indicates that Congress intended to ensure the continued availability of a remedy, historically provided by the States, for deaths in territorial waters; its failure to extend the Act to cover such deaths primarily reflected the lack of necessity for coverage by a federal statute, rather than an affirmative desire to insulate such deaths from the benefits of any federal remedy that might be available independently of the Act. The void that existed in maritime law up to 1920 was the absence of any remedy for wrongful death on the high seas. Congress, in acting to fill that void, legislated only to the three-mile limit because that was the extent of the problem. The express provision that state remedies in territorial waters were not disturbed by the Act ensured that Congress' solution of one problem would not create another by inviting the courts to find that the Act pre-empted the entire field, destroying the state remedies that had previously existed.

* * *

To put it another way, the message of the Act is that it does not by its own force abrogate available state remedies; no intention appears that the Act have the effect of foreclosing any nonstatutory federal remedies that might be found appropriate to effectuate the policies of general maritime law.

* * *

We conclude that the Death on the High Seas Act was not intended to preclude the availability of a remedy for wrongful death under general maritime law in situations not covered by the Act. Because the refusal of maritime law to provide such a remedy appears to be jurisprudentially unsound and to have produced serious confusion and hardship, that refusal should cease unless there are substantial countervailing factors that dictate

12. A joint contributor to this last situation, in conjunction with the rule of *The Harrisburg*, is the decision in *Gillespie v. United States Steel Corp.*, 379 U.S. 148 (1964), where the Court held that the Jones Act * * * precludes any state remedy for wrongful death of a seaman in territorial waters. * * * [T]he remedy under general maritime law that will be made available by our overruling today of *The Harrisburg* seems to be beyond the preclusive effect of the Jones Act as interpreted in *Gillespie*. * * * [N]o question of preclusion of a *federal* remedy was before the Court in *Gillespie* or its predecessor, *Lindgren v. United States*, 281 U.S. 38 (1930), since no such remedy was thought to exist at the time those cases were decided. [ ]

adherence to *Harrisburg* simply as a matter of *stare decisis.* We now turn to a consideration of those factors.

IV.

Very weighty considerations underlie the principle that courts should not lightly overrule past decisions. Among these are the desirability that the law furnish a clear guide for the conduct of individuals, to enable them to plan their affairs with assurance against untoward surprise; the importance of furthering fair and expeditious adjudication by eliminating the need to relitigate every relevant proposition in every case; and the necessity of maintaining public faith in the judiciary as a source of impersonal and reasoned judgments. [Because the *Harrisburg* rule is both fundamentally anomalous and widely despised, all of those considerations are better served by overruling than by preserving it.]

* * *

V.

[States Marine argues] that overruling *The Harrisburg* will necessitate a long course of decisions to spell out the elements of the new "cause of action." We believe these fears are exaggerated, because our decision does not require the fashioning of a whole new body of federal law, but merely removes a bar to access to the existing general maritime law. In most respects the law applied in personal-injury cases will answer all questions that arise in death cases.

* * *

The one aspect of a claim for wrongful death that has no precise counterpart in the established law governing nonfatal injuries is the determination of the beneficiaries who are entitled to recover. General maritime law, which denied any recovery for wrongful death, found no need to specify which dependents should receive such recovery. On this question, petitioner and the United States argue that we may look for guidance to the expressions of Congress, which has spoken on this subject in the Death on the High Seas Act [and] the Jones Act. Though very similar, * * * these provisions differ slightly in the naming of dependent relatives who may recover and in the priority given to their claims.[2]

The United States contends that * * * the provision that should be borrowed for wrongful-death actions under general maritime law is that of the Death on the High Seas Act. It is the congressional enactment that deals specifically and exclusively with actions for wrongful death, and that simply provides a remedy—for deaths on the high seas—for breaches of the duties imposed by general maritime law. * * *

We do not determine this issue now, for we think its final resolution should await further sifting through the lower courts in future litigation. For present purposes we conclude only that its existence affords no sufficient reason for not coming to grips with *The Harrisburg.* If still other subsidiary issues should require resolution, such as particular questions of the measure of damages, the courts will not be without persuasive analogy for guidance. Both the Death on the High Seas Act and the numerous state wrongful-death acts have been implemented with success for decades. The experience thus built

2. Editors' note: DOHSA provides that the wrongful death remedy it creates is for the "benefit of the decedent's spouse, parent, child, or dependent relative." 46 U.S.C. § 30302. The Jones Act incorporates FELA, which sets forth a hierarchy of wrongful death beneficiaries: the decedent's spouse and children; if none, parents; if none, dependent next of kin. 45 U.S.C. § 51.

up counsels that a suit for wrongful death raises no problems unlike those that have long been grist for the judicial mill.

In sum, in contrast to the torrent of difficult litigation that has swirled about *The Harrisburg, The Tungus,* which followed upon it, and the problems of federal-state accommodation they occasioned, the recognition of a remedy for wrongful death under general maritime law can be expected to bring more placid waters. That prospect indeed makes for, and not against, the discarding of *The Harrisburg.*

We accordingly overrule *The Harrisburg,* and hold that an action does lie under general maritime law for death caused by violation of maritime duties. The judgment of the Court of Appeals is reversed, and the case is remanded to that court for further proceedings consistent with this opinion.

Notes

1. In the first sentence of the opinion Justice Harlan used an unfortunate phrase in stating that the issue was whether maritime law "afford[s] a cause of action for wrongful death." The term "cause of action" generally refers to the grounds for imposing legal responsibility upon a defendant, whereas "remedy" addresses the consequences of the defendant's legal responsibility. The rest of the opinion is correct in repeatedly characterizing the issue before the Court as the existence of a wrongful death *remedy* and in making it clear that the new remedy the Court was creating would apply to deaths caused by any "violation of maritime duties," regardless of whether the duty was to avoid unseaworthiness, Jones Act negligence, or general maritime negligence. Subsequently the Court confirmed that the *Moragne* remedy is available regardless of the particular cause of action asserted. See *Miles v. Apex Marine Corp. (infra* at 241), 498 U.S. at 27–30 (holding that the *Moragne* remedy can be invoked by a seaman's survivors asserting a cause of action for unseaworthiness); *Norfolk Shipbuilding & Drydock Corp. v. Garris*, 532 U.S. 811, 814, 820 (2001) (noting that "the wrongful-death rule of *Moragne* was not limited to any particular maritime duty" and holding that the *Moragne* remedy was available in a general maritime (*Kermarec*) negligence action for the death of a shipyard worker because "it has been clear since *Moragne* that breaches of a maritime duty are actionable when they cause death, as when they cause injury.").

2. Note that Mrs. Moragne sought both wrongful death damages for her own losses and survival damages "for the pain and suffering experienced by the decedent prior to his death." None of the opinions in the case reveal what happened to the survival claim. Probably the *Moragne* Court meant to affirm the existence of a general maritime survival remedy—it likely was using the term "wrongful death" to encompass both types of fatal-injury litigation—but as we will see in *Miles*, *infra* at 244, and *Yamaha*, *infra* at 246–48 footnotes 3 and 7, the point remains debatable.

3. The Court's seemingly offhand remark that both DOHSA and "the numerous state wrongful-death acts" were potentially useful sources on the "measure of damages" in *Moragne* actions was unsettling, because the two suggestions point in different directions. The DOHSA remedy (aside from the "commercial aviation" amendments, *infra* at 245 note 3) is confined to "pecuniary loss" (46 U.S.C. § 30303), whereas most state wrongful death statutes allow recovery for the nonpecuniary item of loss of society (companionship, consortium). In *Sea-Land Services, Inc. v. Gaudet*, 414 U.S. 573 (1974)—which involved the death of a longshoreman in state territorial waters—the Court split 5–4 on which way to look. The majority noted that "[a] clear majority of States ... permit recovery for loss of society" and held that the *Moragne* remedy should too. *Id.* at 587–88. The four

dissenters argued that the *Moragne* remedy should not include damages for loss of society because "[t]he traditional admiralty view is that such nonpecuniary damages are not recoverable under the Death on the High Seas Act and the Jones Act." *Id.* at 605.

4. *Gaudet's* holding that the *Moragne* remedy includes damages for loss of society set up a square conflict with DOHSA. In *Mobil Oil Corp. v. Higginbotham*, 436 U.S. 618 (1978), the Court split 6–2 in holding that the DOHSA "pecuniary loss" provision (46 U.S.C. § 30303) precluded the dependents of helicopter passengers who died in a high-seas crash from asserting claims under *Moragne/Gaudet* for loss of society. The Court acknowledged that *Gaudet* established a different rule for loss of society damages in cases arising from accidents in territorial waters but concluded that "a desire for uniformity cannot override the statute." *Id.* at 624. In *Offshore Logistics, Inc. v. Tallentire*, 477 U.S. 207 (1986), the Court split 5–4 in holding that the "pecuniary loss" language of DOHSA precludes victims of high-seas crashes from recovering loss-of-society damages under state law.

Miles v. Apex Marine Corp.

Supreme Court of the United States, 1990
498 U.S. 19, 111 S. Ct. 317, 112 L. Ed. 2d 275, 1991 AMC 1

Justice O'CONNOR delivered the opinion of the unanimous Court.[3]

* * *

Ludwick Torregano was a seaman aboard the vessel *M/V Archon*. On the evening of July 18, 1984, Clifford Melrose, a fellow crew member, stabbed Torregano repeatedly, killing him. At the time, the ship was docked in the harbor of Vancouver, Washington.

Mercedel Miles, Torregano's mother and administratrix of his estate, sued [the vessel's owner, charterers, and operators] (collectively "Apex") in the United States District Court for the Eastern District of Louisiana. Miles alleged negligence under the Jones Act for failure to prevent the assault on her son, and breach of the warranty of seaworthiness under general maritime law for hiring a crew member unfit to serve. She sought compensation for loss of support and services and loss of society resulting from the death of her son, * * * and compensation to the estate for Torregano's pain and suffering prior to his death and for his lost future income.[4]

[The District Court upheld Miles's claims for support, services, and Torregano's pain and suffering and dismissed the claims for loss of society and lost future income. Affirming those rulings, the Fifth Circuit held that Miles was entitled to $7,800 for loss of support and services and $140,000 for Torregano's pain and suffering. We granted Miles's petition for certiorari on the loss of society and lost future income issues] and now affirm the judgment of the Court of Appeals.

* * *

We rely primarily on *Moragne* [*supra* at 233]. * * * The central issue in *Moragne* was whether the limits of [the Jones Act and DOHSA] proscribed a more general maritime cause of action. * * * The Court found no such proscription. * * *

* * *

3. Editors' note: Justice Souter did not participate.

4. Editors' note: Miles also sought punitive damages. The courts below held that this claim must be dismissed because the evidence showed neither egregious fault nor a basis for vicarious liability against Apex. This issue did not reach the Supreme Court.

III

We have described *Moragne* at length because it exemplifies the fundamental principles that guide our decision in this case. We no longer live in an era when seamen and their loved ones must look primarily to the courts as a source of substantive legal protection from injury and death; Congress and the States have legislated extensively in these areas. In this era, an admiralty court should look primarily to these legislative enactments for policy guidance. We may supplement these statutory remedies where doing so would achieve the uniform vindication of such policies consistent with our constitutional mandate, but we must also keep strictly within the limits imposed by Congress. Congress retains superior authority in these matters, and an admiralty court must be vigilant not to overstep the well-considered boundaries imposed by federal legislation. These statutes both direct and delimit our actions. * * *

Apex asks us not to extend *Moragne* [an action for the death of a longshoreman killed by unseaworthiness] to suits for the death of true seamen. This limitation is warranted, they say, because true seamen, unlike longshoremen, are covered under the Jones Act. The Jones Act provides a cause of action against the seaman's employer for wrongful death resulting from negligence that Apex contends is preclusive of any recovery for death from unseaworthiness.

* * *

The Jones Act provides an action in negligence for the death or injury of a seaman. It thereby overruled *The Osceola* [*supra* at 148], which established that seamen could recover under general maritime law for injuries resulting from unseaworthiness, but not negligence. The Jones Act evinces no general hostility to recovery under maritime law. It does not disturb seamen's general maritime claims for injuries resulting from unseaworthiness, and it does not preclude the recovery for wrongful death due to unseaworthiness created by its companion statute, DOHSA. * * *

There is also little question that *Moragne* intended to create a general maritime wrongful death action applicable beyond the situation of longshoremen. * * * If there has been any doubt about the matter, we today make explicit that there is a general maritime cause of action for the wrongful death of a seaman, adopting the reasoning of the unanimous and carefully crafted opinion in *Moragne*.

IV.

Moragne did not set forth the scope of the damages recoverable under the maritime wrongful death action. The Court first considered that question in [*Gaudet*, *supra* at 240 note 3, in which the plaintiff] brought a general maritime action to recover for the wrongful death of her husband, a longshoreman. The Court held that a dependent plaintiff in a maritime wrongful death action could recover for the pecuniary losses of support, services, and funeral expenses, as well as for the nonpecuniary loss of society suffered as the result of the death. *Gaudet* involved the death of a longshoreman in territorial waters. Consequently, the Court had no need to consider the preclusive effect of DOHSA for deaths on the high seas or the Jones Act for deaths of true seamen.

We considered DOHSA in [*Higginbotham*, *supra* at 241 note 4]. That case involved death on the high seas and, like *Gaudet*, presented the question of loss of society damages in a maritime wrongful death action. The Court began by recognizing that *Gaudet*, although broadly written, applied only in territorial waters and therefore did not decide the precise question presented. Congress made the decision for us. DOHSA, by its terms, limits recoverable damages in wrongful death suits to ["pecuniary loss." 46 U.S.C. § 30303]. This explicit limitation forecloses recovery for non-pecuniary loss, such as loss of society, in a general maritime action.

[The *Higginbotham* plaintiffs] argued that admiralty courts have traditionally undertaken to supplement maritime statutes. The Court's answer in *Higginbotham* is fully consistent with those principles we have here derived from *Moragne*: Congress has spoken directly to the question of recoverable damages on the high seas, and "when it does speak directly to a question, the courts are not free to 'supplement' Congress' answer so thoroughly that the Act becomes meaningless." *Higginbotham*, 436 U.S. at 625. *Moragne* involved gap filling in an area left open by statute; supplementation was entirely appropriate. But in an "area covered by the statute, it would be no more appropriate to prescribe a different measure of damages than to prescribe a different statute of limitations, or a different class of beneficiaries." *Id.*

The logic of *Higginbotham* controls our decision here. The holding of *Gaudet* applies only in territorial waters, and it applies only to longshoremen. *Gaudet* did not consider the preclusive effect of the Jones Act for deaths of true seamen. We do so now.

Unlike DOHSA, the Jones Act does not explicitly limit damages to any particular form. Enacted in 1920, the Jones Act makes applicable to seamen the substantive recovery provisions of the older FELA. FELA recites only that employers shall be liable in "damages" for the injury or death of one protected under the Act. 45 U.S.C. § 51. In *Michigan Central R. Co. v. Vreeland*, 227 U.S. 59 (1913), however, the Court explained that the language of the FELA wrongful death provision is essentially identical to that of Lord Campbell's Act, 9 & 10 Vict., ch. 93 (1846), the first wrongful death statute. Lord Campbell's Act also did not limit explicitly the "damages" to be recovered, but that Act and the many state statutes that followed it consistently had been interpreted as providing recovery only for pecuniary loss. The [*Vreeland*] Court so construed FELA.

When Congress passed the Jones Act, the *Vreeland* gloss on FELA, and the hoary tradition behind it, were well established. Incorporating FELA unaltered into the Jones Act, Congress must have intended to incorporate the pecuniary limitation on damages as well. We assume that Congress is aware of existing law when it passes legislation. [ ] There is no recovery for loss of society in a Jones Act wrongful death action.

The Jones Act also precludes recovery for loss of society in this case. The Jones Act applies when a seaman has been killed as a result of negligence, and it limits recovery to pecuniary loss. The general maritime claim here alleged that Torregano had been killed as a result of the unseaworthiness of the vessel. It would be inconsistent with our place in the constitutional scheme were we to sanction more expansive remedies in a judicially created cause of action in which liability is without fault than Congress has allowed in cases of death resulting from negligence. We must conclude that there is no recovery for loss of society in a general maritime action for the wrongful death of a Jones Act seaman.

Our decision also remedies an anomaly we created in *Higginbotham*. [Plaintiffs] in that case warned that the elimination of loss of society damages for wrongful deaths on the high seas would create an unwarranted inconsistency between deaths in territorial waters, where loss of society was available under *Gaudet*, and deaths on the high seas. We recognized the value of uniformity, but concluded that a concern for consistency could not override the statute. Today we restore a uniform rule applicable to all actions for the wrongful death of a seaman, whether under DOHSA, the Jones Act, or general maritime law.

V.

We next must decide whether, in a general maritime action surviving the death of a seaman, the estate can recover decedent's lost future earnings. Under traditional maritime law, as under common law, there is no right of survival; a seaman's personal cause of action does not survive the seaman's death. [ ]

Congress and the States have changed the rule in many instances. The Jones Act, through its incorporation of FELA, provides that a seaman's right of action for injuries due to negligence survives to the seaman's personal representative. See 45 U.S.C. § 59 [ ]. Most States have survival statutes applicable to tort actions generally [ ], and admiralty courts have applied these state statutes in many instances to preserve suits for injury at sea. [ ] Where these state statutes do not apply, however, or where there is no state survival statute, there is no survival of unseaworthiness claims absent a change in the traditional maritime rule.

Several Courts of Appeals have relied on *Moragne* to hold that there is a general maritime right of survival. * * * Miles argues that we should follow [these cases] and recognize a general maritime survival right. Apex urges us to reaffirm the traditional maritime rule and overrule these decisions. We decline to address the issue, because its resolution is unnecessary to our decision on the narrow question presented: whether the income decedent would have earned but for his death is recoverable. We hold that it is not.

Recovery of lost future income in a survival suit will, in many instances, be duplicative of recovery by dependents for loss of support in a wrongful death action; the support dependents lose as a result of a seaman's death would have come from the seaman's future earnings. Perhaps for this reason, there is little legislative support for such recovery in survival. In only a few States can an estate recover in a survival action for income decedent would have received but for death. At the federal level, DOHSA contains no survival provision. The Jones Act incorporates FELA's survival provision, but, as in most States, recovery is limited to losses suffered during the decedent's lifetime. See 45 U.S.C. § 59 [ ].

This state and federal legislation hardly constitutes the kind of "wholesale" and "unanimous" policy judgment that prompted the Court to create a new cause of action in *Moragne*. To the contrary, the considered judgment of a large majority of American legislatures is that lost future income is not recoverable in a survival action. Were we to recognize a right to such recovery under maritime law, we would be adopting a distinctly minority view.

This fact alone would not necessarily deter us, if recovery of lost future income were more consistent with the general principles of maritime tort law. There are indeed strong policy arguments for allowing such recovery. See, *e.g.*, R. Posner, Economic Analysis of Law 176–181 (3d ed. 1986) (recovery of lost future income provides efficient incentives to take care by ensuring that the tortfeasor will have to bear the total cost of the victim's injury or death). Moreover, Miles reminds us that admiralty courts have always shown a special solicitude for the welfare of seamen and their families. [ ]

We are not unmindful of these principles, but they are insufficient in this case. We sail in occupied waters. Maritime tort law is now dominated by federal statute, and we are not free to expand remedies at will simply because it might work to the benefit of seamen and those dependent upon them. Congress has placed limits on recovery in survival actions that we cannot exceed. Because this case involves the death of a seaman, we must look to the Jones Act.

The Jones Act/FELA survival provision limits recovery to losses suffered during the decedent's lifetime. See 45 U.S.C. § 59. This was the established rule under FELA when

Congress passed the Jones Act, incorporating FELA [ ], and it is the rule under the Jones Act. [ ] Congress has limited the survival right for seamen's injuries resulting from negligence. As with loss of society in wrongful death actions, this forecloses more expansive remedies in a general maritime action founded on strict liability. We will not create, under our admiralty powers, a remedy that is disfavored by a clear majority of the States and that goes well beyond the limits of Congress' ordered system of recovery for seamen's injury and death. Because Torregano's estate cannot recover for his lost future income under the Jones Act, it cannot do so under general maritime law.

VI.

Cognizant of the constitutional relationship between the courts and Congress, we today act in accordance with the uniform plan of maritime tort law Congress created in DOHSA and the Jones Act. We hold that there is a general maritime cause of action for the wrongful death of a seaman, but that damages recoverable in such an action do not include loss of society. We also hold that a general maritime survival action cannot include recovery for decedent's lost future earnings. Accordingly, the judgment of the Court of Appeals is affirmed.

Notes

1. *Miles* has been a controversial decision. See, e.g., Judge Brown's strong criticism, *supra* at 109. See also Force, *The Curse of Miles v. Apex Marine Corp.: The Mischief of Seeking "Uniformity" and "Legislative Intent" in Maritime Personal Injury Cases*, 55 LA. L. REV. 745 (1995).

2. But *Miles* has also been hugely influential, leading to many changes in maritime law that go far beyond *Miles*'s direct holdings. For example, lower courts have used *Miles* to support the blanket denial of loss-of-society damages in actions by seamen's families against defendants other than shipowners and other employers of seamen. See, e.g., *Scarborough v. Clemco Industries*, 391 F.3d 660 (5th Cir. 2004). Many courts have held that the *Miles* prohibition against loss-of-society damages in wrongful death actions must apply equally to actions by spouses of nonfatally injured seamen for loss of consortium. See, e.g., *Horsley v. Mobil Oil Corp.*, 15 F.3d 200 (1st Cir. 1994). Several courts have yearned openly for the outright overruling of *Gaudet*, which *Miles* interpreted very narrowly—to allow loss-of-society damages "only" for longshoremen killed "only" in territorial waters—but did not overrule. See, e.g., *In re American River Transp. Co.*, 490 F.3d 351, 356 & n. 27 (5th Cir. 2007) (holding that plaintiffs relying on *Gaudet* cannot recover for loss of society unless they can show financial dependency on the decedent and hinting broadly that *Gaudet* should be overruled).

3. In the aftermath (and penumbra) of *Miles*, the unanimous Court in *Dooley v. Korean Air Lines Co.,* 524 U.S. 116 (1998), held that neither DOHSA nor general maritime law allows for recovery of decedents' conscious pain and suffering in fatal high-seas accidents. The intense public attention predictably drawn to air crash fatalities led Congress to amend DOHSA in 2000 to expand the survival and wrongful death remedies available for "commercial aviation accident[s]." 46 U.S.C. §§ 30307(b), 30307(c).

4. *Miles* did not involve punitive damages. But arguably the most dramatic effect of *Miles* has been its use by many courts as a springboard for the wholesale denial of punitive damages in seamen's litigation. See *infra* Section II-F.

5. The network of *Miles*-spawned restrictions on maritime injury and death rights and remedies has re-inspired plaintiffs to seek help from state law. See the next case.

Yamaha Motor Corp., U.S.A. v. Calhoun

Supreme Court of the United States, 1996
516 U.S. 199, 116 S. Ct. 619, 133 L. Ed. 2d 578, 1996 AMC 305

Justice GINSBURG delivered the opinion of the unanimous Court.

Twelve-year-old Natalie Calhoun was killed [on July 6, 1989, when she slammed a rented "Wavejammer" jet ski (manufactured by Yamaha) into a vessel anchored in the waters off the frontage of a beach-front resort hotel in Puerto Rico. Alleging that the jet ski was defectively designed or made, Natalie's parents, individually and in their capacities as administrators of their daughter's estate, sued Yamaha in the Eastern District of Pennsylvania. The Calhouns asserted several bases for recovery (including negligence, strict liability, and breach of implied warranties). Invoking Pennsylvania's wrongful-death and survival statutes, they sought damages for lost future earnings, loss of society, loss of support and services, and funeral expenses, as well as punitive damages. Yamaha moved for partial summary judgment, arguing that the federal maritime wrongful death action this Court recognized in *Moragne* [*supra* at 233] provided the exclusive basis for recovery, displacing all remedies afforded by state law. Yamaha contended that the general maritime action recognized by *Moragne* limited the Calhouns to recovery of Natalie's funeral expenses. The District Court agreed with Yamaha that *Moragne*'s maritime death action displaced state remedies; the court held, however, that loss of society and loss of support and services were compensable under *Moragne*.]

[Perceiving the types of damages allowable in *Moragne* actions as an unsettled issue, District Judge Pollak allowed an interlocutory appeal to the Third Circuit. The certifying order asked whether maritime law allowed plaintiffs to recover for loss of society, lost future earnings, and punitive damages. The Third Circuit did not answer those questions; instead it held that Judge Pollak erred in holding that *Moragne* had supplanted state law. 40 F.3d 622. We granted certiorari to consider whether the federal maritime claim for wrongful death recognized in *Moragne* supplies the exclusive remedy in cases involving the deaths of nonseafarers[2] in territorial waters.]

Traditionally, state remedies have been applied in accident cases of this order—maritime wrongful death cases in which no federal statute specifies the appropriate relief and the decedent was not a seaman, longshore worker, or person otherwise engaged in a maritime trade. We hold, in accord with the Third Circuit, that state remedies remain applicable in such cases and have not been displaced by the federal maritime wrongful death action recognized in *Moragne*.

* * *

[P]rior to *Moragne*, federal admiralty courts routinely applied state wrongful death and survival statutes in maritime accident cases.[3] The question before us is whether *Moragne* should be read to stop that practice.

Our review of maritime wrongful death law begins with *The Harrisburg* [*see supra* at 233–36], where we held that the general maritime law (a species of judge-made federal common law) did not afford a cause of action for wrongful death. * * * Federal admiralty courts tempered the harshness of *The Harrisburg*'s rule by allowing recovery under state

2. By "nonseafarers," we mean persons who are neither seamen covered by the Jones Act nor longshore workers covered by the Longshore and Harbor Workers' Compensation Act.

3. Throughout this opinion, for economy, we use the term wrongful death remedies or statutes to include survival statutes.

wrongful death statutes. * * * State wrongful-death statutes proved an adequate supplement to federal maritime law, until a series of this Court's decisions transformed the maritime doctrine of unseaworthiness into a strict liability rule. * * *

The disparity between the unseaworthiness doctrine's strict-liability standard and negligence-based state wrongful death statutes figured prominently in our landmark *Moragne* decision. [Petsonella Moragne was denied access to the unseaworthiness cause of action because the Supreme Court's 5–4 decision in *The Tungus* (*see supra* at 234) held that in wrongful death actions involving fatalities in territorial waters, state statutes provided the standard of liability as well as the remedial regime (and the Florida Supreme Court had held that Florida's wrongful death statute did not encompass unseaworthiness as a basis of liability). The *Moragne* Court determined that the root of the problem lay not so much in *Tungus* as in *The Harrisburg.*] Upon reexamining the soundness of *The Harrisburg,* [the *Moragne Court*] decided that [*The Harrisburg*'s] holding, "somewhat dubious even when rendered, is such an unjustifiable anomaly in the present maritime law that it should no longer be followed." [ ] Accordingly, the Court overruled *The Harrisburg* and held that an action "lie[s] under general maritime law for death caused by violation of maritime duties."

IV.

Yamaha argues that *Moragne*—despite its focus on "maritime duties" owed to maritime workers—covers the waters, creating a uniform federal maritime remedy for all deaths occurring in state territorial waters, and ousting all previously available state remedies. In Yamaha's view, state remedies can no longer supplement general maritime law (as they routinely did before *Moragne*), because *Moragne* launched a solitary federal scheme.[7] Yamaha's reading of *Moragne* is not without force; in several contexts, we have recognized that vindication of maritime policies demanded uniform adherence to a federal rule of decision, with no leeway for variation or supplementation by state law. [ ][8] In addition, Yamaha correctly points out that uniformity concerns informed our decision in *Moragne.*

The uniformity concerns that prompted us to overrule *The Harrisburg,* however, were of a different order than those invoked by Yamaha. *Moragne* did not reexamine the soundness of *The Harrisburg* out of concern that state damage awards in maritime wrongful death cases were excessive, or that variations in the remedies afforded by the States threatened to interfere with the harmonious operation of maritime law. Variations of this sort had long been deemed compatible with federal maritime interests. [ ] The uniformity

7. If *Moragne*'s wrongful death action did not extend to nonseafarers like Natalie, one could hardly argue that *Moragne* displaced the state law remedies the Calhouns seek. Lower courts have held that *Moragne*'s wrongful death action extends to nonseafarers. [ ] We assume, for purposes of this decision, the correctness of that position. Similarly, as in prior encounters, we assume without deciding that *Moragne* also provides a survival action. See *Miles* [*supra* at 241]. The question we confront is not what *Moragne* added to the remedial arsenal in maritime cases, but what, if anything, it removed from admiralty's stock.

8. The federal cast of admiralty law, we have observed, means that "state law must yield to the needs of a uniform federal maritime law when this Court finds inroads on a harmonious system[,] [b]ut this limitation still leaves the States a wide scope." *Romero* [*supra* at 102, 105]. Our precedent does not precisely delineate that scope. As we recently acknowledged, "[i]t would be idle to pretend that the line separating permissible from impermissible state regulation is readily discernible in our admiralty jurisprudence." [*American Dredging. supra* at 113]. We attempt no grand synthesis or reconciliation of our precedent today, but confine our inquiry to the modest question whether it was *Moragne*'s design to terminate recourse to state remedies when nonseafarers meet death in territorial waters.

concern that drove our decision in *Moragne* related, instead, to the availability of unseaworthiness as a basis of liability.

* * *

Moragne, in sum, centered on the extension of relief, not on the contraction of remedies. The decision recalled that "it better becomes the humane and liberal character of proceedings in admiralty to give than to withhold the remedy, when not required to withhold it by established and inflexible rules."

* * *

When Congress has prescribed a comprehensive tort recovery regime to be uniformly applied, there is, we have generally recognized, no cause for enlargement of the damages statutorily provided [citing *Tallentire* (*supra* at 241 note 4), *Higginbotham* (*id.*), and *Miles*]. But Congress has not prescribed remedies for the wrongful deaths of nonseafarers in territorial waters. [ ] There is, however, a relevant congressional disposition. [Section 7 of DOHSA, 46 U.S.C. § 30308(a), provides that "[t]his Act does not affect the law of a State regulating the right to recover for death."] This statement, by its terms, simply stops DOHSA from displacing state law in territorial waters. [ ] Taking into account what Congress sought to achieve, we preserve the application of state statutes to deaths within territorial waters.

For the reasons stated, we hold that the damages available for the jet ski death of Natalie Calhoun are properly governed by state law. The judgment of the Court of Appeals for the Third Circuit is accordingly affirmed.

Notes

1. In a footnote omitted from the treatment above, the *Yamaha* Court left it up to the Third Circuit on remand to determine "the source—federal or state—of the standards governing liability, as distinguished from the rules on remedies. We thus reserve for another day reconciliation of the maritime personal injury decisions [such as *Kermarec, supra* at 131, and *Pope & Talbot, supra* at 122] that rejected state substantive liability standards, and the maritime wrongful death cases [such as *Tungus*] in which state law has held sway." The Third Circuit on remand held that federal, not state, law would govern issues of liability even though under *Tungus* state law had governed that issue. The Third Circuit stated:

> We believe that *The Tungus* remains good law only with respect to its broader proposition concerning the role that state regulation may play in the admiralty arena. *The Tungus*'s remaining vitality rests only upon the limited proposition ... that state law may provide a procedure or a vehicle through which a plaintiff may institute an action to remedy death in territorial waters.

216 F.3d 338, 350 (3d. Cir. 2000). That was the gist of the *dissent* in *Tungus.*

2. The Third Circuit held that the law of Pennsylvania (decedent's domicile) would govern compensatory damages issues and that the law of Puerto Rico (the situs of the accident) would control punitive damages issues.

Eventually a jury trial on the merits was conducted. (The Calhouns had pleaded diversity jurisdiction.) The jury exonerated Yamaha. See 350 F.3d 316 (3d Cir. 2003) (affirming judgment on jury verdict for defendant).

3. For speculation on how *Yamaha* fits into the stream of Supreme Court decisions treating federal-vs.-state law issues in admiralty, see Robertson, *The Applicability of State Law in Maritime Cases After* Yamaha Motor Corp. v. Calhoun, 21 Tul. Mar. L.J. 81 (1996).

F. Punitive Damages

Exxon Shipping Co. v. Baker

Supreme Court of the United States, 2008
554 U.S. 471, 128 S. Ct. 2605, 171 L.Ed.2d 570, 2008 AMC 1521

Justice SOUTER delivered the opinion of the Court.

* * *

On March 24, 1989, the supertanker *Exxon Valdez* grounded on Bligh Reef off the Alaskan coast, fracturing its hull and spilling millions of gallons of crude oil into Prince William Sound. The owner, petitioner Exxon Shipping Co. (now SeaRiver Maritime, Inc.), and its owner, petitioner Exxon Mobil Corp. (collectively, Exxon), have settled state and federal claims for environmental damage, with payments exceeding $1 billion, and this action by respondent Baker and others, including commercial fishermen and native Alaskans, was brought for economic losses to individuals dependent on Prince William Sound for their livelihoods.

The tanker was over 900 feet long and was used by Exxon to carry crude oil from the end of the Trans-Alaska Pipeline in Valdez, Alaska, to the lower 48 States. On the night of the spill it was carrying 53 million gallons of crude oil, or over a million barrels. Its captain was one Joseph Hazelwood, who had completed a 28-day alcohol treatment program while employed by Exxon, as his superiors knew, but dropped out of a prescribed followup program and stopped going to Alcoholics Anonymous meetings. According to the District Court, "[t]here was evidence presented to the jury that after Hazelwood was released from [residential treatment], he drank in bars, parking lots, apartments, airports, airplanes, restaurants, hotels, at various ports, and aboard Exxon tankers." The jury also heard contested testimony that Hazelwood drank with Exxon officials and that members of the Exxon management knew of his relapse. Although Exxon had a clear policy prohibiting employees from serving onboard within four hours of consuming alcohol, Exxon presented no evidence that it monitored Hazelwood after his return to duty or considered giving him a shoreside assignment. Witnesses testified that before the *Valdez* left port on the night of the disaster, Hazelwood downed at least five double vodkas in the waterfront bars of Valdez, an intake of about 15 ounces of 80-proof alcohol, enough "that a non-alcoholic would have passed out."

The ship sailed at 9:12 p.m. on March 23, 1989, guided by a state-licensed pilot for the first leg out, through the Valdez Narrows. At 11:20 p.m., Hazelwood took active control and, owing to poor conditions in the outbound shipping lane, radioed the Coast Guard for permission to move east across the inbound lane to a less icy path. Under the conditions, this was a standard move, which the last outbound tanker had also taken, and the Coast Guard cleared the *Valdez* to cross the inbound lane. The tanker accordingly steered east toward clearer waters, but the move put it in the path of an underwater reef off Bligh Island, thus requiring a turn back west into the shipping lane around Busby Light, north of the reef.

Two minutes before the required turn, however, Hazelwood left the bridge and went down to his cabin in order, he said, to do paperwork. This decision was inexplicable. There was expert testimony that, even if their presence is not strictly necessary, captains simply do not quit the bridge during maneuvers like this, and no paperwork could have justified it. And in fact the evidence was that Hazelwood's presence was required, both because there should have been two officers on the bridge at all times and his departure left only one, and because he was the only person on the entire ship licensed to navigate this part of Prince William Sound. To make matters worse, before going below Hazelwood put the tanker on autopilot, speeding it up, making the turn trickier, and any mistake harder to correct.

As Hazelwood left, he instructed the remaining officer, third mate Joseph Cousins, to move the tanker back into the shipping lane once it came abeam of Busby Light. Cousins, unlicensed to navigate in those waters, was left alone with helmsman Robert Kagan, a nonofficer. For reasons that remain a mystery, they failed to make the turn at Busby Light, and a later emergency maneuver attempted by Cousins came too late. The tanker ran aground on Bligh Reef, tearing the hull open and spilling eleven million gallons of crude oil into Prince William Sound.

After Hazelwood returned to the bridge and reported the grounding to the Coast Guard, he tried but failed to rock the *Valdez* off the reef, a maneuver which could have spilled more oil and caused the ship to founder. The Coast Guard's nearly immediate response included a blood test of Hazelwood (the validity of which Exxon disputes) showing a blood-alcohol level of .061 eleven hours after the spill. Experts testified that to have this much alcohol in his bloodstream so long after the accident, Hazelwood at the time of the spill must have had a blood-alcohol level of around .241, three times the legal limit for driving in most States.

In the aftermath of the disaster, Exxon spent around $2.1 billion in cleanup efforts [and pleaded guilty to criminal violations of a number of statutes, including the Clean Water Act, 33 U.S.C. §§ 1311(a) and 1319(c)(1), occasioning fines of about $125 million.] A civil action by the United States and the State of Alaska for environmental harms ended with a consent decree for Exxon to pay at least $900 million toward restoring natural resources, and it paid another $303 million in voluntary settlements with fishermen, property owners, and other private parties.

The remaining civil cases were consolidated into this one against Exxon, Hazelwood, and others. The District Court for the District of Alaska divided the plaintiffs seeking compensatory damages into three classes: commercial fishermen, Native Alaskans, and landowners. At Exxon's behest, the court also certified a mandatory class of all plaintiffs seeking punitive damages, whose number topped 32,000. Respondents here, to whom we will refer as Baker for convenience, are members of that class.

For the purposes of the case, Exxon stipulated to its negligence in the *Valdez* disaster and its ensuing liability for compensatory damages. The court designed the trial accordingly: Phase I considered Exxon and Hazelwood's recklessness and thus their potential for punitive liability; Phase II set compensatory damages for commercial fishermen and Native Alaskans; and Phase III determined the amount of punitive damages for which Hazelwood and Exxon were each liable. (A contemplated Phase IV, setting compensation for still other plaintiffs, was obviated by settlement.)

In Phase I, the jury heard extensive testimony about Hazelwood's alcoholism and his conduct on the night of the spill, as well as conflicting testimony about Exxon officials' knowledge of Hazelwood's backslide. At the close of Phase I, the Court instructed the jury in part that

> [a] corporation is responsible for the reckless acts of those employees who are employed in a managerial capacity while acting in the scope of their employment. The reckless act or omission of a managerial officer or employee of a corporation,

> in the course and scope of the performance of his duties, is held in law to be the reckless act or omission of the corporation.

The Court went on [to say] that "[a]n employee of a corporation is employed in a managerial capacity if the employee supervises other employees and has responsibility for, and authority over, a particular aspect of the corporation's business." Exxon did not dispute that Hazelwood was a managerial employee under this definition, and the jury found both Hazelwood and Exxon reckless and thus potentially liable for punitive damages.[2]

In Phase II the jury awarded $287 million in compensatory damages to [some of the plaintiffs; others had settled their compensatory claims. The court ultimately calculated the total compensatory damages at $507.5 million.] In Phase III, the jury heard about Exxon's management's acts and omissions arguably relevant to the spill. At the close of evidence, the court instructed the jurors on the purposes of punitive damages, emphasizing that they were designed not to provide compensatory relief but to punish and deter the defendants. The court charged the jury to consider the reprehensibility of the defendants' conduct, their financial condition, the magnitude of the harm, and any mitigating facts. The jury awarded $5,000 in punitive damages against Hazelwood and $5 billion against Exxon.

On appeal, the Court of Appeals for the Ninth Circuit upheld the Phase I jury instruction on corporate liability for acts of managerial agents under Circuit precedent. [] With respect to the size of the punitive-damages award, however, the Circuit remanded twice for adjustments in light of this Court's due process cases before ultimately itself remitting the award to $2.5 billion.

We granted certiorari to consider whether maritime law allows corporate liability for punitive damages on the basis of the acts of managerial agents, whether the Clean Water Act (CWA), 33 U.S.C. § 1251 *et seq.*, forecloses the award of punitive damages in maritime spill cases, and whether the punitive damages awarded against Exxon in this case were excessive as a matter of maritime common law. We now vacate and remand.

II

On the first question, Exxon says that it was error to instruct the jury that a corporation "is responsible for the reckless acts of ... employees ... in a managerial capacity while acting in the scope of their employment." The Courts of Appeals have split on this issue, and the company relies primarily on two cases, *The Amiable Nancy,* 3 Wheat. [16 U.S.] 546 (1818), and *Lake Shore & Michigan Southern R. Co. v. Prentice,* 147 U.S. 101 (1893), to argue that this Court's precedents are clear that punitive damages are not available against a shipowner for a shipmaster's recklessness. The former was a suit in admiralty against the owners of *The Scourge,* a privateer whose officers and crew boarded and plundered a neutral ship, *The Amiable Nancy.* In upholding an award of compensatory damages, Justice Story observed that,

> if this were a suit against the original wrong-doers, it might be proper to ... visit upon them in the shape of exemplary damages, the proper punishment which belongs to such lawless misconduct. But it is to be considered, that this is a suit against the owners of the privateer, upon whom the law has, from motives of policy, devolved a responsibility for the conduct of the officers and crew employed

2. The jury was not asked to consider the possibility of any degree of fault beyond the range of reckless conduct. The record sent up to us shows that some thought was given to a trial plan that would have authorized jury findings as to greater degrees of culpability, but that plan was not adopted * * *.

> by them, and yet, from the nature of the service, they can *scarcely ever* be able to secure to themselves an adequate indemnity in cases of loss. They are innocent of the demerit of this transaction, having neither directed it, nor countenanced it, nor participated in it in the slightest degree. Under such circumstances, we are of opinion, that they are bound to repair all the real injuries and personal wrongs sustained by the libellants, but they are not bound to the extent of vindictive damages.

The Amiable Nancy, [16 U.S.] at 558–559 (emphasis in original). Exxon takes this statement as a rule barring punitive liability against shipowners for actions by underlings not "directed," "countenanced," or "participated in" by the owners.

Exxon further claims that the Court confirmed this rule in *Lake Shore, supra,* a railway case in which the Court relied on *The Amiable Nancy* to announce, as a matter of pre-*Erie* [*supra* at 119] general common law, that "[t]hough [a] principal is liable to make compensation for [intentional torts] by his agent, he is not liable to be punished by exemplary damages for an intent in which he did not participate." 147 U.S. at 110. Because maritime law remains federal common law, and because the Court has never revisited the issue, Exxon argues that *Lake Shore* endures as sound evidence of maritime law. * * *

Baker [argues that the Ninth Circuit correctly] followed the Restatement rule recognizing corporate liability in punitive damages for reckless acts of managerial employees, see Restatement (Second) of Torts § 909(c) (1977). Baker says that *The Amiable Nancy* offers nothing but dictum, because punitive damages were not at issue, and that *Lake Shore* merely rejected company liability for the acts of a railroad conductor, while saying nothing about liability for agents higher up the ladder, like ship captains. He also makes the broader point that [*Lake Shore*] was criticized for failing to reflect the majority rule of its own time, not to mention its conflict with the *respondeat superior* rule in the overwhelming share of land-based jurisdictions today. Baker argues that the maritime rule should conform to modern land-based common law, where a majority of States allow punitive damages for the conduct of any employee, and most others follow the Restatement, imposing liability for managerial agents.

The Court is equally divided on this question,[1] and "[i]f the judges are divided, the reversal cannot be had, for no order can be made." [] We therefore leave the Ninth Circuit's opinion undisturbed in this respect, though it should go without saying that the disposition here is not precedential on the derivative liability question. []

III

Exxon next says that, whatever the availability of maritime punitive damages at common law, the CWA preempts them.[2] * * * [The Ninth Circuit rejected Exxon's argument and] held that the CWA did not preempt maritime common law on punitive damages.

* * *

[We agree with the Ninth Circuit.] There are two ways to construe Exxon's argument that the CWA's penalties for water pollution, see 33 U.S.C. § 1321, preempt the common

---

1. Editors' note: Justice Alito did not participate in the decision.

2. Editors' note: Exxon's and the Court's use of the term "preemption" to treat the relationship between a federal statute and federal common law reflects an older vocabulary. More recently, there has been an effort to restrict the *preemption* label to the state-vs-federal law context and to use the term *displacement* when referring to the relationship between federal statutes and federal common law. See *supra* at 110.

law punitive-damages remedies at issue here. The company could be saying that any tort action predicated on an oil spill is preempted unless § 1321 expressly preserves it. Section 1321(b) protects "the navigable waters of the United States, adjoining shorelines, ... [and] natural resources" of the United States, subject to a saving clause reserving "obligations ... under any provision of law for damages to any publicly owned or privately owned property resulting from a discharge of any oil," § 1321(o). Exxon could be arguing that, because the [CWA] saving clause makes no mention of preserving punitive damages for economic loss, they are preempted. But so, of course, would a number of other categories of damages awards that Exxon did not claim were preempted. If Exxon were correct here, there would be preemption of provisions for compensatory damages for thwarting economic activity or, for that matter, compensatory damages for physical, personal injury from oil spills or other water pollution. But we find it too hard to conclude that a statute expressly geared to protecting "water," "shorelines," and "natural resources" was intended to eliminate *sub silentio* oil companies' common law duties to refrain from injuring the bodies and livelihoods of private individuals.

Perhaps on account of its overbreadth, Exxon disclaims taking this position, admitting that the CWA does not displace compensatory remedies for consequences of water pollution, even those for economic harms. This concession, however, leaves Exxon with the equally untenable claim that the CWA somehow preempts punitive damages, but not compensatory damages, for economic loss. But nothing in the statutory text points to fragmenting the recovery scheme this way, and we have rejected similar attempts to sever remedies from their causes of action. See *Silkwood v. Kerr-McGee Corp.*, 464 U.S. 238, 255–256 (1984). All in all, we see no clear indication of congressional intent to occupy the entire field of pollution remedies []; nor for that matter do we perceive that punitive damages for private harms will have any frustrating effect on the CWA remedial scheme, which would point to preemption.

IV

Finally, Exxon raises an issue of first impression about punitive damages in maritime law, which falls within a federal court's jurisdiction to decide in the manner of a common law court, subject to the authority of Congress to legislate otherwise if it disagrees with the judicial result. [] In addition to its resistance to derivative liability for punitive damages and its preemption claim already disposed of, Exxon challenges the size of the remaining $2.5 billion punitive-damages award. Other than its preemption argument, it does not offer a legal ground for concluding that maritime law should never award punitive damages, or that none should be awarded in this case, but it does argue that this award exceeds the bounds justified by the punitive-damages goal of deterring reckless (or worse) behavior and the consequently heightened threat of harm. The claim goes to our understanding of the place of punishment in modern civil law and reasonable standards of process in administering punitive law * * *.

* * *

[T]he consensus today is that punitives are aimed not at compensation but principally at retribution and deterring harmful conduct. This consensus informs the doctrine in most modern American jurisdictions, where juries are customarily instructed on [the] twin goals of punitive awards. * * * Under the umbrellas of punishment and its aim of deterrence, degrees of relative blameworthiness are apparent. Reckless conduct is not intentional or malicious, nor is it necessarily callous toward the risk of harming others, as opposed to unheedful of it. See, *e.g.*, Restatement (Second) of Torts § 500, Comment *a*

("Recklessness may consist of either of two different types of conduct. In one the actor knows, or has reason to know ... of facts which create a high degree of risk of ... harm to another, and deliberately proceeds to act, or to fail to act, in conscious disregard of, or indifference to, that risk. In the other the actor has such knowledge, or reason to know, of the facts, but does not realize or appreciate the high degree of risk involved, although a reasonable man in his position would do so"). Action taken or omitted in order to augment profit represents an enhanced degree of punishable culpability, as of course does willful or malicious action, taken with a purpose to injure. []

Regardless of culpability, however, heavier punitive awards have been thought to be justifiable when wrongdoing is hard to detect (increasing chances of getting away with it) * * *.

State regulation of punitive damages varies. A few States award them rarely, or not at all. * * * As for procedure, in most American jurisdictions the amount of the punitive award is generally determined by a jury in the first instance, and that "determination is then reviewed by trial and appellate courts to ensure that it is reasonable." [] Many States have gone further by imposing statutory limits on punitive awards, in the form of absolute monetary caps [], a maximum ratio of punitive to compensatory damages [], or, frequently, some combination of the two []. The States that rely on a multiplier have adopted a variety of ratios, ranging from 5:1 to 1:1.

Despite these limitations, punitive damages overall are higher and more frequent in the United States than they are anywhere else. * * *

* * *

American punitive damages have been the target of audible criticism in recent decades [], but the most recent studies tend to undercut much of it []. A survey of the literature reveals that discretion to award punitive damages has not mass-produced runaway awards, and although some studies show the dollar amounts of punitive-damages awards growing over time, even in real terms, by most accounts the median ratio of punitive to compensatory awards has remained less than 1:1. Nor do the data substantiate a marked increase in the percentage of cases with punitive awards over the past several decades.[15] The figures thus show an overall restraint and suggest that in many instances a high ratio of punitive to compensatory damages is substantially greater than necessary to punish or deter.

The real problem, it seems, is the stark unpredictability of punitive awards. Courts of law are concerned with fairness as consistency, and evidence that the median ratio of punitive to compensatory awards falls within a reasonable zone, or that punitive awards are infrequent, fails to tell us whether the spread between high and low individual awards is acceptable. The available data suggest it is not. A recent comprehensive study of punitive damages awarded by juries in state civil trials found a median ratio of punitive to compensatory awards of just 0.62:1, but a mean ratio of 2.90:1 and a standard deviation of 13.81. [] Even to those of us unsophisticated in statistics, the thrust of these figures is clear: the spread is great, and the outlier cases subject defendants to punitive damages that dwarf the corresponding compensatories. * * *

[T]hese ranges of variation might be acceptable or even desirable if they resulted from judges' and juries' refining their judgments to reach a generally accepted optimal level of

15. * * * One might posit that ill effects of punitive damages are clearest not in actual awards but in the shadow that the punitive regime casts on settlement negotiations and other litigation decisions. [] But here again the data have not established a clear correlation. []

penalty and deterrence in cases involving a wide range of circumstances, while producing fairly consistent results in cases with similar facts. [] But anecdotal evidence suggests that nothing of that sort is going on. One of our own leading cases on punitive damages, with a $4 million [punitive damages] verdict by an Alabama jury, noted that a second Alabama case with strikingly similar facts produced "a comparable amount of compensatory damages" but "no punitive damages at all." See [*BMW of North America, Inc. v. Gore,* 517 U.S. 559, 565 n. 8 (1996)]. As the Supreme Court of Alabama candidly explained, "the disparity between the two jury verdicts ... [w]as a reflection of the inherent uncertainty of the trial process." [] We are aware of no scholarly work pointing to consistency across punitive awards in cases involving similar claims and circumstances.

* * *

[This] Court's response to outlier punitive-damages awards has thus far been confined by claims at the constitutional level, and our cases have announced due process standards that every award must pass. See, *e.g., State Farm Mut. Automobile Ins. Co. v. Campbell,* 538 U.S. 408, 425 (2003); *Gore,* 517 U.S. at 574–575. Although "we have consistently rejected the notion that the constitutional line is marked by a simple mathematical formula," *id.,* at 582, we have determined that "few awards exceeding a single-digit ratio between punitive and compensatory damages, to a significant degree, will satisfy due process," *State Farm,* 538 U.S. at 425; "[w]hen compensatory damages are substantial, then a lesser ratio, perhaps only equal to compensatory damages, can reach the outermost limit of the due process guarantee."

Today's enquiry differs from due process review because the case arises under federal maritime jurisdiction, and we are reviewing a jury award for conformity with maritime law, rather than the outer limit allowed by due process; we are examining the verdict in the exercise of federal maritime common law authority, which precedes and should obviate any application of the constitutional standard. Our due process cases, on the contrary, have all involved awards subject in the first instance to state law. [] These, as state-law cases, could provide no occasion to consider a "common-law standard of excessiveness" [], and the only matter of federal law within our appellate authority was the constitutional due process issue.

Our review of punitive damages today, then, considers not their intersection with the Constitution, but the desirability of regulating them as a common law remedy for which responsibility lies with this Court as a source of judge-made law in the absence of statute. Whatever may be the constitutional significance of the unpredictability of high punitive awards, this feature of happenstance is in tension with the function of the awards as punitive, just because of the implication of unfairness that an eccentrically high punitive verdict carries in a system whose commonly held notion of law rests on a sense of fairness in dealing with one another. Thus, a penalty should be reasonably predictable in its severity * * *. Cf. *Koon v. United States,* 518 U.S. 81, 113, (1996) (noting the need "to reduce unjustified disparities" in criminal sentencing "and so reach toward the evenhandedness and neutrality that are the distinguishing marks of any principled system of justice"). The common sense of justice would surely bar penalties that reasonable people would think excessive for the harm caused in the circumstances. * * *

With that aim ourselves, we have three basic approaches to consider, one verbal and two quantitative. As mentioned before, a number of state courts have settled on criteria for judicial review of punitive-damages awards that go well beyond traditional "shock the conscience" or "passion and prejudice" tests. Maryland, for example, has set forth a nonexclusive list of nine review factors * * * that include "degree of heinousness," "the deterrence value of the award," and "whether the punitive award bears a reasonable relationship to the compensatory damages awarded." * * * These judicial review criteria are brought to bear after juries render verdicts under instructions offering, at best, guidance no more specific for reaching an appropriate penalty. * * * Examples such as these leave us skeptical that verbal formulations, superimposed on general jury instructions, are the best insurance against unpredictable outliers. Instructions can go just so far in promoting systemic consistency when awards are not tied to specifically proven items of damage (the cost of medical treatment, say), and although judges in the States that take this approach may well produce just results by dint of valiant effort, our experience with attempts to produce consistency in the analogous business of criminal sentencing leaves us doubtful that anything but a quantified approach will work.

* * *

[O]ur better judgment is that eliminating unpredictable outlying punitive awards by more rigorous standards than the constitutional limit will probably have to take the form adopted in those States that have looked to the criminal-law pattern of quantified limits. One option would be to follow the States that set a hard dollar cap on punitive damages, a course that arguably would come closest to the criminal law, rather like setting a maximum term of years. The trouble is, though, that there is no "standard" tort or contract injury, making it difficult to settle upon a particular dollar figure as appropriate across the board. And of course a judicial selection of a dollar cap would carry a serious drawback; a legislature can pick a figure, index it for inflation, and revisit its provision whenever there seems to be a need for further tinkering, but a court cannot say when an issue will show up on the docket again. []

The more promising alternative is to leave the effects of inflation to the jury or judge who assesses the value of actual loss, by pegging punitive to compensatory damages using a ratio or maximum multiple. * * * [T]his is the model many States have adopted * * * And of course the potential relevance of the ratio between compensatory and punitive damages is indisputable, being a central feature in our due process analysis. See, *e.g., State Farm,* 538 U.S. at 425; *Gore,* 517 U.S. at 580.

Still, some will murmur that this smacks too much of policy and too little of principle. [] But the answer rests on the fact that we are acting here in the position of a common law court of last review, faced with a perceived defect in a common law remedy. Traditionally, courts have accepted primary responsibility for reviewing punitive damages and thus for their evolution, and if, in the absence of legislation, judicially derived standards leave the door open to outlier punitive-damages awards, it is hard to see how the judiciary can wash its hands of a problem it created, simply by calling quantified standards legislative.

* * *

Although the legal landscape is well populated with examples of ratios and multipliers expressing policies of retribution and deterrence, most of them suffer from features that stand in the way of borrowing them as paradigms of reasonable limitations suited for application to this case. While a slim majority of the States with a ratio have adopted 3:1, others see fit to apply a lower one [e.g., 1:1, 2:1], and a few have gone higher [e.g., 5:1]. Judgments may differ about the weight to be given to the slight majority of 3:1 States, but one feature of the 3:1 schemes dissuades us from selecting it here. With a few statutory exceptions [], the States with 3:1 ratios apply them across the board (as do other States using different fixed multipliers). That is, the upper limit is not directed to cases like this one, where the tortious action was worse than negligent but less than malicious,[22] exposing the tortfeasor to certain regulatory sanctions and inevitable damages actions;[23] the 3:1 ratio in these States also applies to awards in quite different cases involving some of the most egregious conduct, including malicious behavior and dangerous activity carried on for the purpose of increasing a tortfeasor's financial gain. We confront, instead, a case of reckless action, profitless to the tortfeasor, resulting in substantial recovery for substantial injury. Thus, a legislative judgment that 3:1 is a reasonable limit overall is not a judgment that 3:1 is a reasonable limit in this particular type of case.

* * *

There is better evidence of an accepted limit of reasonable civil penalty, however, in several studies mentioned before, showing the median ratio of punitive to compensatory verdicts, reflecting what juries and judges have considered reasonable across many hundreds of punitive awards. We think it is fair to assume that the greater share of the verdicts studied in these comprehensive collections reflect reasonable judgments about the economic penalties appropriate in their particular cases.

These studies cover cases of the most as well as the least blameworthy conduct triggering punitive liability, from malice and avarice, down to recklessness, and even gross negligence in some jurisdictions. The data put the median ratio for the entire gamut of circumstances at less than 1:1, meaning that the compensatory award exceeds the punitive award in most cases. In a well-functioning system, we would expect that awards at the median or lower would roughly express jurors' sense of reasonable penalties in cases with no earmarks of exceptional blameworthiness within the punishable spectrum (cases like this one, without intentional or malicious conduct, and without behavior driven primarily by desire for gain, for example) and cases (again like this one) without the modest economic harm or odds of detection that have opened the door to higher awards. It also seems fair to suppose that most of the unpredictable outlier cases that call the fairness of the system into question are above the median; in theory a factfinder's deliberation could go awry to produce a very low ratio, but we have no basis to assume that such a case would be more than a sport, and the cases with serious constitutional issues coming to us have naturally been on the high side, see, *e.g.*, *State Farm*, 538 U.S. at 425 (ratio of 145:1); *Gore*, 517 U.S. at 582 (ratio of 500:1). On these assumptions, a median ratio of punitive to compensatory damages of about 0.65:1 probably marks the line near which cases like this one largely should be grouped. Accordingly, given the need to protect against the possibility (and the disruptive cost to the legal system) of awards that are unpredictable and unnecessary, either for deterrence or for measured retribution, we consider that a 1:1 ratio, which is above the median award, is a fair upper limit in such maritime cases.

* * * And our explanation of the constitutional upper limit confirms that the 1:1 ratio is not too low. In *State Farm*, we said that a single-digit maximum is appropriate in all but the most exceptional of cases, and "[w]hen compensatory damages are substantial,

22. Although the jury heard evidence that Exxon may have felt constrained not to give Hazelwood a shoreside assignment because of a concern that such a course might open it to liabilities in personnel litigation the employee might initiate, such a consideration, if indeed it existed, hardly constitutes action taken with a specific purpose to cause harm at the expense of an established duty.

23. We thus treat this case categorically as one of recklessness, for that was the jury's finding. But by making a point of its contrast with cases falling within categories of even greater fault we do not mean to suggest that Exxon's and Hazelwood's failings were less than reprehensible.

then a lesser ratio, perhaps only equal to compensatory damages, can reach the outermost limit of the due process guarantee." 538 U.S. at 425.[28]

V.

Applying this standard to the present case, we take for granted the District Court's calculation of the total relevant compensatory damages at $507.5 million. A punitive-to-compensatory ratio of 1:1 thus yields maximum punitive damages in that amount. We therefore vacate the judgment and remand the case for the Court of Appeals to remit the punitive-damages award accordingly.

Notes

1. Justice Alito did not participate. Justices Scalia and Thomas concurred but took the opportunity to reiterate their belief that the Court's decisions imposing constitutional limits on punitive damages were wrong.

2. Justices Stevens, Ginsburg, and Breyer dissented from the Court's imposition of the 1:1 ratio. The Stevens opinion began by quoting the statement in *Miles v. Apex Marine* that "maritime tort law is now dominated by federal statute" [*supra* at 244, 498 U.S. at 36] and went on to characterize "the many statutes governing liability under admiralty law" as "[e]vidence that Congress has affirmatively chosen *not* to restrict the availability of [the punitive damages] remedy, ... [which calls for] judicial restraint in the absence of some special justification." Justice Ginsburg wrote separately to express her agreement with the Stevens view and to argue that "the traditional common-law approach under which punitive damages are determined by a properly instructed jury, followed by trial-court, and then appellate-court review" has served fairly well to guard against abuses.

Justice Breyer agreed with the majority that a ratio-based limit is generally appropriate, but—emphasizing the view that Exxon's conduct was "highly reprehensible" and its fault "egregious"—he could not agree to impose it in this case. "The punitive damages award before us already represents a 50% reduction from the amount that the District Court strongly believed was appropriate. I would uphold it."

3. **Corporate exposure to punitive damages.** The issue that evoked the 4–4 split in *Exxon Shipping* is recurrently divisive, signaling a significant need for the Court to resolve it. In *In re Deepwater Horizon*, 21 F. Supp. 3d 657 (E.D. La. 2014), the court reported its bench-trial findings on the fault of the parties responsible for the April 2010 BP-Macondo tragedy in the Gulf of Mexico (see *infra* at 495). The court assigned 67% of the blame to BP, and it found that the conduct of BP's "senior drilling engineer" and "Well Site Leader" was "reckless, willful, and wanton." Moreover, it found that "the conduct exhibited by [those two] employees would make an award of punitive damages appropriate." But it exonerated BP from punitive damages liability, explaining:

> [T]he maritime rule in the Fifth Circuit is that operational recklessness or willful disregard [on the part of a corporation's agents and employees] is generally in-

28. The criterion of "substantial" takes into account the role of punitive damages to induce legal action when pure compensation may not be enough to encourage suit, a concern addressed by the opportunity for a class action when large numbers of potential plaintiffs are involved; in such cases, individual awards are not the touchstone, for it is the class option that facilitates suit, and a class recovery of $500 million is substantial. In this case, then, the constitutional outer limit may well be 1:1.

> sufficient to visit punitive damages upon the [corporate] employer. Rather, the [reckless or willful] conduct must emanate from corporate policy or ... a corporate official with policy-making authority [must have] participated in, approved of, or subsequently ratified the egregious conduct. * * * The Court finds that [the engineer and the well site leader] were not policy-making officials, nor did the reckless conduct emanate from corporate policy.

The *Deepwater Horizon* court went on to note that BP would have been held liable for punitive damages under the law of the First and Ninth Circuits.

4. Exxon's CWA "preemption" argument rested in significant part on reading *Miles*, *supra* at 241, to mean that legislative treatment of an area of maritime activity presumptively disables a court operating in that area from recognizing a remedy that is not provided or specifically authorized by the legislation, unless, perhaps, the remedy in question already existed when the legislation was enacted. See *Reply Brief for Petitioners,* 2008 WL 466089 at * 20–21 n. 11 (2008) (emphasizing that "[i]n the 200 years before the 1970 enactment of the CWA, [there had never been an award of punitive damages in a case] involving oil spills or purely economic loss."). The *Exxon Shipping* Court ignored this argument. It surfaces powerfully, however, in the two cases below.

Atlantic Sounding Co. v. Townsend

Supreme Court of the United States, 2009
557 U.S. 404, 129 S. Ct. 2561, 2009 AMC 1521

Justice THOMAS delivered the opinion of the Court.

The question presented by this case is whether an injured seaman may recover punitive damages for his employer's willful failure to pay maintenance and cure. Petitioners[3] argue that under *Miles v. Apex Marine Corp.,* [*supra* at 241], seamen may recover only those damages available under the Jones Act, 46 U.S.C. § 30104. We disagree. Historically, punitive damages have been available and awarded in general maritime actions, including some in maintenance and cure. We find that nothing in *Miles* or the Jones Act eliminates that availability.

I.

Respondent Edgar L. Townsend was a crew member of the Motor Tug Thomas. After falling on the steel deck of the tugboat and injuring his arm and shoulder, respondent [sued] petitioner Atlantic Sounding, the owner of the tugboat, * * * under the Jones Act and general maritime law, alleging negligence, unseaworthiness, arbitrary and willful failure to pay maintenance and cure, and wrongful termination. * * * Petitioners moved to dismiss respondent's punitive damages claim. The District Court denied the motion, holding that it was bound by the determination in *Hines v. J.A. LaPorte, Inc.,* 820 F.2d 1187, 1189 (C.A.11 1987) *(per curiam),* that punitive damages were available in an action for maintenance and cure. The court, however, agreed to certify the question for interlocutory appeal. The United States Court of Appeals for the Eleventh Circuit agreed with the District Court that *Hines* controlled and held that respondent could pursue his punitive damages claim for the willful withholding of maintenance and cure. The decision conflicted with those of other Courts of Appeals, see, *e.g., Guevara v. Maritime Overseas*

3. Editors' note: The two petitioners were the injured seaman's employer, Atlantic Sounding, Inc., and Atlantic's corporate parent, Weeks Marine, Inc. Atlantic is a wholly owned subsidiary of Weeks.

Corp., 59 F.3d 1496 (C.A.5 1995) (en banc); *Glynn v. Roy Al Boat Management Corp.*, 57 F.3d 1495 (C.A.9 1995), and we granted certiorari.

II.

Respondent claims that he is entitled to seek punitive damages as a result of petitioners' alleged breach of their "maintenance and cure" duty under general maritime law. We find no legal obstacle to his doing so.

A.

Punitive damages have long been an available remedy at common law for wanton, willful, or outrageous conduct. * * * [*See*] *Pacific Mut. Life Ins. Co. v. Haslip*, 499 U.S. 1, 25 (1991) (Scalia, J., concurring in judgment) ("[P]unitive or 'exemplary' damages have long been a part of Anglo–American law"). * * * American courts have * * * permitted punitive damages awards in appropriate cases since at least 1784. See, *e.g.*, *Genay v. Norris*, 1 S.C.L. 6, 7, 1784 WL 26 (1784) (approving award of "very exemplary damages" because spiking wine [with cantharides] represented a "very wanton outrage"); *Coryell v. Colbaugh*, 1 N.J.L. 77, 1791 WL 380 (1791) (concluding that a breach of promise of marriage was "of the most atrocious and dishonourable nature" and supported "damages for *example's* sake, to prevent such offences in future" (emphasis in original)). Although some States elected not to allow juries to make such awards, the vast majority permitted them. [] By the middle of the 19th century, "punitive damages were undoubtedly an established part of the American common law of torts [and] no particular procedures were deemed necessary to circumscribe a jury's discretion regarding the award of such damages, or their amount." *Haslip, supra*, at 26–27 (Scalia, J., concurring in judgment).

This Court has also found the award of punitive damages to be authorized as a matter of common-law doctrine. In *Day v. Woodworth*, 13 How. [54 U.S.] 363, 371 (1852), for example, the Court recognized the "well-established principle of the common law, that in actions of trespass and all actions on the case for torts, a jury may inflict what are called exemplary, punitive, or vindictive damages upon a defendant...."; see also *Philadelphia, W., & B.R. Co. v. Quigley*, 21 How. [62 U.S.] 202, 214 (1859) ("Whenever the injury complained of has been inflicted maliciously or wantonly, and with circumstances of contumely or indignity, the jury are not limited to the ascertainment of a simple compensation for the wrong committed against the aggrieved person"); *Barry v. Edmunds*, 116 U.S. 550, 562 (1886) ("[A]ccording to the settled law of this court, [a plaintiff] might show himself, by proof of the circumstances, to be entitled to exemplary damages calculated to vindicate his right and protect it against future similar invasions").

B.

The general rule that punitive damages were available at common law extended to claims arising under federal maritime law. See *Lake Shore & Michigan Southern R. Co. v. Prentice* [*supra* at 251], 147 U.S. 101, 108 (1893) ("[C]ourts of admiralty ... proceed, in cases of tort, upon the same principles as courts of common law, in allowing exemplary damages ..."). One of this Court's first cases indicating that punitive damages were available involved an action for marine trespass. See *The Amiable Nancy* [*supra* at 251], 3 Wheat. [16 U.S.] 546 (1818). In the course of deciding whether to uphold the jury's award, Justice Story, writing for the Court, recognized that punitive damages are an available maritime remedy under the proper circumstances. Although the Court found that the particular facts of the case did not warrant such an award against the named defendants, it explained that "if this were a suit against the original wrong-doers, it might be proper to ... visit upon them in the shape of exemplary damages, the proper punishment which belongs to such lawless misconduct." *Id.*, at 558; see also *Barry*, 116 U.S., at 563 ("In *The Amiable Nancy*, which was the case of a marine tort, Mr. Justice Story spoke of exemplary damages as 'the proper punishment which belongs to ... lawless misconduct'").

The lower federal courts followed suit, finding that punitive damages were available in maritime actions for tortious acts of a particularly egregious nature. * * * In short, prior to enactment of the Jones Act in 1920, "maritime jurisprudence was replete with judicial statements approving punitive damages, especially on behalf of passengers and seamen." Robertson, *Punitive Damages in American Maritime Law*, 28 J. Mar. L. & Comm. 73, 115 (1997) (hereinafter Robertson) [].

C.

Nothing in maritime law undermines the applicability of this general rule in the maintenance and cure context. See G. Gilmore & C. Black, *Law of Admiralty* §6-13, p. 312 (2d ed. 1975) (hereinafter Gilmore & Black) (explaining that a seaman denied maintenance and cure "has a free option to claim damages (including punitive damages) under a general maritime law count"); Robertson 163 (concluding that breach of maintenance and cure is one of the particular torts for which general maritime law would most likely permit the awarding of punitive damages "assuming ... the requisite level of blameworthiness"). Indeed, the legal obligation to provide maintenance and cure dates back centuries as an aspect of general maritime law, and the failure of a seaman's employers to provide him with adequate medical care was the basis for awarding punitive damages in cases decided as early as the 1800's.

The right to receive maintenance and cure was first recognized in this country in two lower court decisions authored by Justice Story. See *Harden v. Gordon* [*supra* at 147], 11 F. Cas. 480 (No. 6,047) (CC Me. 1823); *Reed v. Canfield*, 20 F. Cas. 426 (No. 11,641) (CC Mass. 1832). According to Justice Story, this common-law obligation to seamen was justified on humanitarian and economic grounds * * * This Court has since registered its agreement with these decisions. "Upon a full review ... of English and American authorities," the Court concluded that "the vessel and her owners are liable, in case a seaman falls sick, or is wounded, in the service of the ship, to the extent of his maintenance and cure, and to his wages, at least so long as the voyage is continued." *The Osceola*, [*supra* at 148], 189 U.S. at 175. * * *

In addition, the failure of a vessel owner to provide proper medical care for seamen has provided the impetus for damages awards that appear to contain at least some punitive element. For example, in *The City of Carlisle*, 39 F. 807 (DC Ore. 1889), the court added $1,000 to its damages award to compensate an apprentice seaman for "gross neglect and cruel maltreatment of the [seaman] since his injury." *Id.* at 809, 817. The court reviewed the indignities to which the apprentice had been subjected as he recovered [from his injuries] without any serious medical attention, and explained that "if owners do not wish to be mulct in damages for such misconduct, they should be careful to select men worthy to command their vessels and fit to be trusted with the safety and welfare of their crews, and particularly apprentice boys." *Id.* at 817; see also *The Troop*, 118 F. 769, 770–771, 773 (D.C. Wash. 1902) (explaining that $4,000 was a reasonable award because the captain's "failure to observe the dictates of humanity" and obtain prompt medical care for an injured seaman constituted a "monstrous wrong").[3]

3. Although these cases do not refer to "punitive" or "exemplary" damages, scholars have characterized the awards authorized by these decisions as such. See Robertson 103–105; Edelman, *Guevara v. Maritime Overseas Corp.: Opposing the Decision*, 20 Tulane Mar. L.J. 349, 351 and n. 22 (1996).

D.

The settled legal principles discussed above establish three points central to resolving this case. First, punitive damages have long been available at common law. Second, the common-law tradition of punitive damages extends to maritime claims.[4] And third, there is no evidence that claims for maintenance and cure were excluded from this general admiralty rule. Instead, the pre-Jones Act evidence indicates that punitive damages remain available for such claims under the appropriate factual circumstances. As a result, respondent is entitled to pursue punitive damages unless Congress has enacted legislation departing from this common-law understanding. As explained below, it has not.

III.

A.

The only statute that could serve as a basis for overturning the common-law rule in this case is the Jones Act, 46 U.S.C. § 30104. Congress enacted the Jones Act primarily to overrule *The Osceola, supra,* in which this Court prohibited a seaman or his family from recovering for injuries or death suffered due to his employers' negligence. * * * The Jones Act thus created a statutory cause of action for negligence, but it did not eliminate pre-existing remedies available to seamen for the separate common-law cause of action based on a seaman's right to maintenance and cure. Section 30104 bestows upon the injured seaman the right to "elect" to bring a Jones Act claim, thereby indicating a choice of actions for seamen—not an exclusive remedy. [] Because the then-accepted remedies for injured seamen arose from general maritime law, see *The Osceola,* 189 U.S., at 175, it necessarily follows that Congress was envisioning the continued availability of those common-law causes of action. See *Chandris, Inc. v. Latsis,* [*supra* at 189] 515 U.S. at 354 ("Congress enacted the Jones Act in 1920 to remove the bar to suit for negligence articulated in *The Osceola,* thereby completing the trilogy of heightened legal protections [including maintenance and cure] that seamen receive because of their exposure to the perils of the sea" (internal quotation marks omitted)). [] If the Jones Act had been the only remaining remedy available to injured seamen, there would have been no election to make.

In addition, the only statutory restrictions expressly addressing general maritime claims for maintenance and cure were enacted long after the passage of the Jones Act. They limit its availability for two discrete classes of people: foreign workers on offshore oil and mineral production facilities, see 46 U.S.C. § 30105(b), and sailing school students and instructors, 46 U.S.C. § 50504(b). These provisions indicate that "Congress knows how to" restrict the traditional remedy of maintenance and cure "when it wants to." *Omni Capital Int'l, Ltd. v. Rudolf Wolff & Co.,* 484 U.S. 97, 106 (1987). Thus, nothing in the statutory scheme for maritime recovery restricts the availability of punitive damages for maintenance and cure for those, like respondent, who are not precluded from asserting the general maritime claim.

Further supporting this interpretation of the Jones Act, this Court has consistently recognized that the Act "was remedial, for the benefit and protection of seamen who are

---

4. The dissent correctly notes that the handful of early cases involving maintenance and cure, by themselves, do not definitively resolve the question of punitive damages availability in such cases. However, it neglects to acknowledge that the general common-law rule made punitive damages available in maritime actions. Nor does the dissent explain why maintenance and cure actions should be excepted from this general rule. It is because of this rule, and the fact that these early cases support—rather than refute—its application to maintenance and cure actions that the pre-Jones Act evidence supports the conclusion that punitive damages were available at common law where the denial of maintenance and cure involved wanton, willful, or outrageous conduct.

peculiarly the wards of admiralty. Its purpose was to enlarge that protection, not to narrow it." *The Arizona v. Anelich,* 298 U.S. 110, 123 (1936); see also *American Export Lines, Inc. v. Alvez,* 446 U.S. 274, 282 (1980) (plurality opinion) (declining to "read the Jones Act as sweeping aside general maritime law remedies"); *O'Donnell v. Great Lakes Dredge & Dock Co.,* 318 U.S. 36, 43 (1943) ("It follows that the Jones Act, in extending a right of recovery to the seaman injured while in the service of his vessel by negligence, has done no more than supplement the remedy of maintenance and cure ..."); *Pacific S.S. Co. v. Peterson,* 278 U.S. 130, 134, 138–139 (1928) (holding that the Jones Act "was not intended to restrict in any way the long-established right of a seaman to maintenance, cure and wages").

Not only have our decisions repeatedly observed that the Jones Act preserves common-law causes of action such as maintenance and cure, but our case law also supports the view that punitive damages awards, in particular, remain available in maintenance and cure actions after the Act's passage. In *Vaughan v. Atkinson,* 369 U.S. 527 (1962), for example, the Court permitted the recovery of attorney's fees for the "callous" and "willful and persistent" refusal to pay maintenance and cure. In fact, even the *Vaughan* dissenters, who believed that such fees were generally unavailable, agreed that a seaman "would be entitled to exemplary damages in accord with traditional concepts of the law of damages" where a "shipowner's refusal to pay maintenance stemmed from a wanton and intentional disregard of the legal rights of the seaman." *Id.,* at 540 (opinion of Stewart, J.) [].[5]

Nothing in the text of the Jones Act or this Court's decisions issued in the wake of its enactment undermines the continued existence of the common-law cause of action providing recovery for the delayed or improper provision of maintenance and cure. Petitioners do not deny the availability of punitive damages in general maritime law, or identify any cases establishing that such damages were historically unavailable for breach of the duty of maintenance and cure. The plain language of the Jones Act, then, does not provide the punitive damages bar that petitioners seek.

B.

Petitioners nonetheless argue that the availability of punitive damages in this case is controlled by the Jones Act because of this Court's decision in *Miles.* In *Miles,* petitioners argue, the Court limited recovery in maritime cases involving death or personal injury to the remedies available under the Jones Act and the Death on the High Seas Act (DOHSA), 46 U.S.C. §§ 30301–30306.[6] Petitioners' reading of *Miles* is far too broad.

Miles does not address either maintenance and cure actions in general or the availability of punitive damages for such actions. The decision instead grapples with the entirely different question whether general maritime law should provide a cause of action for wrongful death based on unseaworthiness. By providing a remedy for wrongful death

5. In the wake of *Vaughan,* a number of lower courts expressly held that punitive damages can be recovered for the denial of maintenance and cure. See, *e.g., Hines v. J.A. LaPorte, Inc.,* 820 F.2d 1187, 1189 (C.A.11 1987) *(per curiam)* (upholding punitive damages award of $5,000 for an "arbitrary and bad faith breach of the duty to furnish maintenance and cure"); *Robinson v. Pocahontas, Inc.,* 477 F.2d 1048, 1049–1052 (C.A.1 1973) (affirming punitive damages award of $10,000 which was based, in part, on the defendant's initial withholding of maintenance and cure on the pretext that the seaman had been fired for cause).

6. DOHSA applies only to individuals killed (not merely injured) by conduct on the high seas. See 46 U.S.C. § 30302. Because this case involves injuries to a seaman, and not death on the high seas, DOHSA is not relevant.

suffered on the high seas or in territorial waters, the Jones Act and DOHSA displaced a general maritime rule that denied any recovery for wrongful death. This Court, therefore, was called upon in *Miles* to decide whether these new statutes supported an expansion of the relief available under pre-existing general maritime law to harmonize it with a cause of action created by statute.

The Court in *Miles* first concluded that the "unanimous legislative judgment behind the Jones Act, DOHSA, and the many state statutes" authorizing maritime wrongful-death actions supported the recognition of a general maritime action for wrongful death of a seaman. 498 U.S. at 24 [discussing *Moragne, supra* at 233]. Congress had chosen to limit, however, the damages available for wrongful-death actions under the Jones Act and DOHSA, such that damages were not statutorily available for loss of society or lost future earnings. *Id.* at 21, 31–32. The Court thus concluded that Congress' judgment must control the availability of remedies for wrongful-death actions brought under general maritime law. *Id.* at 32–36.

The reasoning of *Miles* remains sound. As the Court in that case explained, "[w]e no longer live in an era when seamen and their loved ones must look primarily to the courts as a source of substantive legal protection from injury and death; Congress and the States have legislated extensively in these areas." Furthermore, it was only because of congressional action that a general federal cause of action for wrongful death on the high seas and in territorial waters even existed; until then, there was no general common-law doctrine providing for such an action. As a result, to determine the remedies available under the common-law wrongful-death action, "an admiralty court should look primarily to these legislative enactments for policy guidance." It would have been illegitimate to create common-law remedies that exceeded those remedies statutorily available under the Jones Act and DOHSA. See *id.* at 36 ("We will not create, under our admiralty powers, a remedy ... that goes well beyond the limits of Congress' ordered system of recovery for seamen's injury and death").

But application of that principle here does not lead to the outcome suggested by petitioners or the dissent. Unlike the situation presented in *Miles,* both the general maritime cause of action (maintenance and cure) and the remedy (punitive damages) were well established before the passage of the Jones Act. Also unlike the facts presented by *Miles,* the Jones Act does not address maintenance and cure or its remedy. It is therefore possible to adhere to the traditional understanding of maritime actions and remedies without abridging or violating the Jones Act; unlike wrongful-death actions, this traditional understanding is not a matter to which "Congress has spoken directly." See *Miles*, 498 U.S. at 31 (citing *Higginbotham* [*supra* at 241 note 4] 436 U.S. at 26). Indeed, the *Miles* Court itself acknowledged that "[t]he Jones Act evinces no general hostility to recovery under maritime law," and noted that statutory remedy limitations "would not necessarily deter us, if recovery ... were more consistent with the general principles of maritime tort law." The availability of punitive damages for maintenance and cure actions is entirely faithful to these "general principles of maritime tort law," and no statute casts doubt on their availability under general maritime law.

Moreover, petitioners' contention that *Miles* precludes *any* action or remedy for personal injury beyond that made available under the Jones Act was directly rejected by this Court in *Norfolk Shipbuilding & Drydock Corp. v. Garris* [*supra* at 240 note 1], 532 U.S. 811, 818 (2001). That case involved the death of a harbor worker. There, the Court recognized a maritime cause of action for wrongful death attributable to negligence although neither the Jones Act (which applies only to seamen) nor DOHSA (which does not cover territorial waters) provided such a remedy. The Court acknowledged that "it will be the better course, in many cases that assert new claims beyond what those statutes have seen fit to allow, to leave further development to Congress." But the Court concluded that the cause of action at issue there was "new only in the most technical sense" because "[t]he general maritime law has recognized the tort of negligence for more than a century, and it has been clear since *Moragne* [*supra* at 233] that breaches of a maritime duty are actionable when they cause death, as when they cause injury." The [*Garris*] Court thus found that "Congress's occupation of this field is not yet so extensive as to preclude us from recognizing what is already logically compelled by our precedents."

Because *Miles* presented no barrier to [the *Garris*] endorsement of a previously unrecognized maritime cause of action for negligent wrongful death, we see no legitimate basis for a contrary conclusion in the present case. Like negligence, "[t]he general maritime law has recognized ... for more than a century" the duty of maintenance and cure and the general availability of punitive damages. [] And because respondent does not ask this Court to alter statutory text or "expand" the general principles of maritime tort law, *Miles* does not require us to eliminate the general maritime remedy of punitive damages for the willful or wanton failure to comply with the duty to pay maintenance and cure. "We assume that Congress is aware of existing law when it passes legislation," *Miles,* 498 U.S. at 32, and the available history suggests that punitive damages were an established part of the maritime law in 1920.

It remains true, of course, that "[a]dmiralty is not created in a vacuum; legislation has always served as an important source of both common law and admiralty principles." *Miles,* 498 U.S., at 24. And it also is true that the negligent denial of maintenance and cure may also be the subject of a Jones Act claim. See *Cortes v. Baltimore Insular Line, Inc.,* 287 U.S. 367 (1932). But the fact that seamen commonly seek to recover under the Jones Act for the wrongful withholding of maintenance and cure does not mean that the Jones Act provides the only remedy for maintenance and cure claims. Indeed, contrary to petitioners' view that the Jones Act replaced in their entirety the remedies available at common law for maintenance and cure, the *Cortes* decision explicitly acknowledged a seaman's right to choose among overlapping statutory and common-law remedies for injuries sustained by the denial of maintenance and cure. See 287 U.S. at 374–375 (A seaman's "cause of action for personal injury created by the statute may have overlapped his cause of action for breach of the maritime duty of maintenance and cure.... In such circumstances it was his privilege, in so far as the causes of action covered the same ground, to sue indifferently on any one of them").

As this Court has repeatedly explained, "remedies for negligence, unseaworthiness, and maintenance and cure have different origins and may on occasion call for application of slightly different principles and procedures." *Fitzgerald v. United States Lines Co.* [*supra* at 81], 374 U.S. at 18. * * * The laudable quest for uniformity in admiralty does not require the narrowing of available damages to the lowest common denominator approved by Congress for distinct causes of action. Although "Congress ... is free to say this much and no more," *Miles,* 498 U.S. at 24), we will not attribute words to Congress that it has not written.

IV.

Because punitive damages have long been an accepted remedy under general maritime law, and because nothing in the Jones Act altered this understanding, such damages for the willful and wanton disregard of the maintenance and cure obligation should remain available in the appropriate case as a matter of general maritime law.[12] Limiting recovery for maintenance and cure to whatever is permitted by the Jones Act would give greater pre-emptive effect to the Act than is required by its text, *Miles,* or any of this Court's other decisions interpreting the statute. For these reasons, we affirm the judgment of the Court of Appeals and remand the case for further proceedings consistent with this opinion.

Justice ALITO, with whom The Chief Justice, Justice Scalia, and Justice Kennedy join, dissenting.

In *Miles* this Court provided a workable framework for analyzing the relief available on claims under general maritime law. Today, the Court abruptly changes course. I would apply the analytical framework adopted in *Miles,* and I therefore respectfully dissent.

* * *

Miles * * * instructs that, in exercising our authority to develop general maritime law, we should be guided primarily by the policy choices reflected in statutes creating closely related claims. Endorsing what has been termed a principle of uniformity, *Miles* teaches that if a form of relief is not available on a statutory claim, we should be reluctant to permit such relief on a similar claim brought under general maritime law.

* * *

It is * * * reasonable to assume that only compensatory damages may be recovered under the Jones Act. [] And under *Miles*' reasoning—at least in the absence of some exceptionally strong countervailing considerations—the rule should be the same when a seaman sues under general maritime law for personal injury resulting from the denial of maintenance and cure.

* * *

[T]he search for [pre-Jones Act] maintenance and cure cases in which punitive damages were awarded yields strikingly slim results. The cases found are insufficient in number, clarity, and prominence to justify departure from the *Miles* uniformity principle.

* * *

Notes

1. The foregoing version of the dissenting opinion is radically edited; the opinion is fairly lengthy. But the dissenters did not mention *Vaughan* or *Garris,* on which the majority placed significant reliance.

2. The non-maritime Supreme Court decisions indicating that the punitive damages remedy was recognized by federal common law—*Day*, *Quigley*, *Barry*, and *Lake Shore*, treated in Parts II-A and II-B of the Court's opinion—arose during the pre-*Erie* era [see *supra* at 119]. *Day* was an action for trespass to a mill dam in Massachusetts. Quigley was a "mechanic and builder of depots, bridges, station-houses, and other structures for railroad companies" alleging defamation against one of those companies. *Barry* centered on the alleged theft of "one valuable horse, of the value of one hundred and twenty-five dollars." The defendant railroad in *Lake Shore* allegedly insulted, defamed, and falsely

12. Because we hold that *Miles* does not render the Jones Act's damages provision determinative of respondent's remedies, we do not address the dissent's argument that the Jones Act, by incorporating the provisions of the Federal Employers' Liability Act, see 46 U.S.C. § 30104(a), prohibits the recovery of punitive damages in actions under that statute.

arrested a passenger (a dignified and reputable physician from Norwalk, Ohio, on a pleasure trip to Chicago).

3. The Court's holding in *Townsend* affirmed the correctness of the Eleventh and First Circuit decisions cited in footnote 5 of the opinion. It disapproved the Fifth and Ninth Circuit decisions in *Guevara* and *Glynn* (cited at the end of Part I of the opinion). *Guevara* (1995) was a long and thorough opinion by the unanimous (17–0) Fifth Circuit, holding that seamen could not seek punitive damages in maintenance and cure cases and stating in the strongest possible dicta that seamen were precluded from seeking punitive damages in Jones Act and unseaworthiness actions as well.

4. Following *Townsend*, the Fifth Circuit directly addressed the availability of punitive damages in unseaworthiness actions. *McBride v. Estis Well Service*, 768 F.3d 382 (5th Cir. 2014) (en banc). The majority, describing the case as a conflict between *Miles* and *Townsend*, distinguished *Townsend* and followed its view of *Miles* to hold that punitive damages are categorically unavailable in unseaworthiness actions. The majority did not overtly rely on the *Guevara* dicta—indeed, it did not even cite *Guevara*—but its reasoning closely tracked the *Guevara* court's. The six dissenters argued that the *Townsend* analysis governed the issue and that punitive damages were available.

In *Tabingo v. American Triumph LLC*, 188 Wash. 2d 41, 391 P.3d 434 (2017), the Washington Supreme Court unanimously rejected the Fifth Circuit's analysis, and shortly thereafter the Ninth Circuit, in *Batterton v. Dutra Group*, 880 F.3d 1089 (9th Cir. 2018), *rev'd*, 139 S. Ct. 2275, 2019 AMC 1521 (2019), also held that punitive damages are available in an unseaworthiness case. That set the stage for the Supreme Court to resolve the conflict.

The Dutra Group v. Batterton

Supreme Court of the United States, 2019
139 S. Ct. 2275, 204 L. Ed. 2d 692, 2019 AMC 1521

Justice ALITO delivered the opinion of the Court.

By granting federal courts jurisdiction over maritime and admiralty cases, the Constitution implicitly directs federal courts sitting in admiralty to proceed "in the manner of a common law court." *Exxon Shipping Co. v. Baker* [*supra* at 249]. Thus, where Congress has not prescribed specific rules, federal courts must develop the "amalgam of traditional common-law rules, modifications of those rules, and newly created rules" that forms the general maritime law. *East River S.S. Corp. v. Transamerica Delaval Inc.* [*supra* at 140]. But maritime law is no longer solely the province of the Federal Judiciary. "Congress and the States have legislated extensively in these areas." *Miles v. Apex Marine Corp.* [*supra* at 241]. When exercising its inherent common-law authority, "an admiralty court should look primarily to these legislative enactments for policy guidance." *Ibid.* We may depart from the policies found in the statutory scheme in discrete instances based on long-established history, see, *e.g.*, *Atlantic Sounding Co. v. Townsend* [*supra* at 259], but we do so cautiously in light of Congress's persistent pursuit of "uniformity in the exercise of admiralty jurisdiction." *Miles* [*supra* at 241] (quoting *Moragne v. States Marine Lines, Inc.* [*supra* at 233]).

This case asks whether a mariner may recover punitive damages on a claim that he was injured as a result of the unseaworthy condition of the vessel. We have twice confronted similar questions in the past several decades, and our holdings in both cases were based on the particular claims involved. In *Miles*, which concerned a wrongful-death claim under the general maritime law, we held that recovery was limited to pecuniary damages, which did not include loss of society. [ ] And in *Atlantic Sounding*, after examining centuries of relevant case law, we held that punitive damages are not categorically barred as part of the award on the traditional maritime claim of maintenance and cure. [ ] Here, because there is no historical basis for allowing punitive damages in unseaworthiness actions, and in order to promote uniformity with the way courts have applied parallel statutory causes of action, we hold that punitive damages remain unavailable in unseaworthiness actions.

I

In order to determine the remedies for unseaworthiness, we must consider both the heritage of the cause of action in the common law and its place in the modern statutory framework.

A

The seaman's right to recover damages for personal injury on a claim of unseaworthiness originates in the admiralty court decisions of the 19th century. At the time, "seamen led miserable lives." D. Robertson, S. Friedell, & M. Sturley, Admiralty and Maritime Law in the United States 163 (2d ed. 2008) [see *supra* at 146]. Maritime law was largely judge-made, and seamen were viewed as "emphatically the wards of the admiralty." *Harden v. Gordon* [*supra* at 147]. In that era, the primary responsibility for protecting seamen lay in the courts, which saw mariners as "peculiarly entitled to"—and particularly in need of—judicial protection "against the effects of the superior skill and shrewdness of masters and owners of ships." [ ]

* * *

Courts used [their] power to protect seamen from injury primarily through two causes of action. The first, maintenance and cure, has its roots in the medieval and renaissance law codes that form the ancient foundation of maritime common law. [See *supra* at 156–65.]

The second claim, unseaworthiness, is a much more recent development and grew out of causes of action unrelated to personal injury. In its earliest forms, an unseaworthiness claim gave sailors under contract to sail on a ship the right to collect their wages even if they had refused to board an unsafe vessel after discovering its condition. [ ] Similarly, unseaworthiness was a defense to criminal charges against seamen who refused to obey a ship master's orders. [ ] A claim of unseaworthiness could also be asserted by a shipper to recover damages or by an insurer to deny coverage when the poor condition of the ship resulted in damage to or loss of the cargo. [ ]

Only in the latter years of the 19th century did unseaworthiness begin a long and gradual evolution toward remedying personal injury. Courts began to extend the cases about refusals to serve to allow recovery for mariners who were injured because of the unseaworthy condition of the vessel on which they had served. These early cases were sparse, and they generally allowed recovery only when a vessel's owner failed to exercise due diligence to ensure that the ship left port in a seaworthy condition. [ ]

Unseaworthiness remained a suspect basis for personal injury claims until 1903, when, in dicta, this Court concluded that "the vessel and her owner are ... liable to an indemnity for injuries received by seamen in consequence of the unseaworthiness of the ship." *The Osceola* [*supra* at 148]. * * *

B

In the early 20th century, then, under "the general maritime law ... a vessel and her owner ... were liable to an indemnity for injuries received by a seaman in consequence of the unseaworthiness of the ship and her appliances; but a seaman was not allowed to recover an indemnity for injuries sustained through the negligence of the master or any member of the crew." [ ] Because of these severe limitations on recovery, "the seaman's right to recover damages for injuries caused by unseaworthiness of the ship was an obscure and relatively little used remedy." G. Gilmore & C. Black, The Law of Admiralty § 6–38, p. 383 (2d ed. 1975) (Gilmore & Black).

Tremendous shifts in mariners' rights took place between 1920 and 1950. First, during and after the First World War, Congress enacted a series of laws regulating maritime liability culminating in [the Jones Act]. * * * In the 30 years after the Jones Act's passage, "the Act was the vehicle for almost all seamen's personal injury and death actions." Gilmore & Black § 6–20, at 327.

But the Jones Act was overtaken in the 1950s by the second fundamental change in personal injury maritime claims—and it was this Court, not Congress, that played the leading role. In a pair of decisions in the late 1940s, the Court transformed the old claim of unseaworthiness, which had demanded only due diligence by the vessel owner, into a strict-liability claim. * * * In *Mahnich v. Southern S.S. Co.* [see *supra* at 181], the Court stated that "the exercise of due diligence does not relieve the owner of his obligation" to provide a seaworthy ship and, in the same ruling, held that the fellow-servant doctrine did not provide a defense. [ ] * * * Less than two years later, we affirmed that the duty of seaworthiness was "essentially a species of liability without fault ... neither limited by conceptions of negligence nor contractual in character. It is a form of absolute duty owing to all within the range of its humanitarian policy." *Seas Shipping Co. v. Sieracki* [see *supra* at 181]. * * * As a result of *Mahnich* and *Sieracki*, between the 1950s and 1970s "the unseaworthiness count [was] the essential basis for recovery with the Jones Act count preserved merely as a jury-getting device." Gilmore & Black § 6–20, at 327–328.

The shifts in plaintiff preferences between Jones Act and unseaworthiness claims were possible because of the significant overlap between the two causes of action. See *id.*, § 6–38, at 383. One leading treatise goes so far as to describe the two claims as "alternative 'grounds' of recovery for a single cause of action." [ ] The two claims are so similar that, immediately after the Jones Act's passage, we held that plaintiffs could not submit both to a jury. [ ] We no longer require such election. [ ] But a plaintiff still cannot duplicate his recovery by collecting full damages on both claims because, "whether or not the seaman's injuries were occasioned by the unseaworthiness of the vessel or by the negligence of the master or members of the crew, ... there is but a single wrongful invasion of his primary right of bodily safety and but a single legal wrong." [ ]

* * *

III

Our resolution of this question is governed by our decisions in *Miles* and *Atlantic Sounding*. *Miles* establishes that we "should look primarily to ... legislative enactments for policy guidance," while recognizing that we "may supplement these statutory remedies where doing so would achieve the uniform vindication" of the policies served by the relevant statutes. [ ] In *Atlantic Sounding*, we allowed recovery of punitive damages, but we justified our departure from the statutory remedial scheme based on the established history of awarding punitive damages for certain maritime torts, including maintenance and cure. [ ] We were explicit that our decision represented a gloss on *Miles* rather than a departure from it. *Atlantic Sounding* [ ] ("The reasoning of *Miles* remains sound"). And we recognized the importance of viewing each claim in its proper historical context. "'[R]emedies for negligence, unseaworthiness, and maintenance and cure have different origins and may on occasion call for application of slightly different principles and procedures.'" [ ]

In accordance with these decisions, we consider here whether punitive damages have traditionally been awarded for claims of unseaworthiness and whether conformity with parallel statutory schemes would require such damages. Finally, we consider whether we are compelled on policy grounds to allow punitive damages for unseaworthiness claims.

A

For claims of unseaworthiness, the overwhelming historical evidence suggests that punitive damages are not available. Batterton principally relies on two cases to establish that punitive damages were traditionally available for breach of the duty of seaworthiness. Upon close inspection, neither supports this argument.

[The Court discussed *The Rolph*, see *supra* at 146 n.5, and *The Noddleburn*, 28 F. 855, 857–858 (Ore. 1886), the two cases on which Batterton relied, and concluded that both involved compensatory awards—with no punitive damages for unseaworthiness.]

Finally, Batterton points to two other cases [that] involve maintenance and cure claims that rest on the willful failure of the master and mate to provide proper care for wounded sailors after they were injured. [ ] Batterton characterizes these as unseaworthiness actions on the theory that the seamen *could have* pursued that claim. But, because courts award damages for the claims a plaintiff actually pleads rather than those he could have brought, these cases are irrelevant.

The lack of punitive damages in traditional maritime law cases is practically dispositive. By the time the claim of unseaworthiness evolved to remedy personal injury, punitive damages were a well-established part of the common law. [ ] American courts had awarded punitive (or exemplary) damages from the Republic's earliest days. [ ] And yet, beyond the decisions discussed above, Batterton presents no decisions from the formative years of the personal injury unseaworthiness claim in which exemplary damages were awarded. From this we conclude that, unlike maintenance and cure, unseaworthiness did not traditionally allow recovery of punitive damages.

B

In light of this overwhelming historical evidence, we cannot sanction a novel remedy here unless it is required to maintain uniformity with Congress's clearly expressed policies. Therefore, we must consider the remedies typically recognized for Jones Act claims.

The Jones Act adopts the remedial provisions of FELA, and by the time of the Jones Act's passage, this Court and others had repeatedly interpreted the scope of damages available to FELA plaintiffs. These early decisions held that "[t]he damages recoverable [under FELA] are limited ... strictly to the financial loss ... sustained." [ ] * * * And in the years since, Federal Courts of Appeals have unanimously held that punitive damages are not available under FELA. [ ]

Our early discussions of the Jones Act followed the same practices. We described the Act shortly after its passage as creating "an action for compensatory damages, on the ground of negligence." [ ] And we have more recently observed that the Jones Act "limits recovery to pecuniary loss." *Miles* [ ]. Looking to FELA and these decisions, the Federal

Courts of Appeals have uniformly held that punitive damages are not available under the Jones Act. [ ]

Batterton argues that these cases are either inapposite or wrong, but because of the absence of historical evidence to support punitive damages—evidence that was central to our decision in *Atlantic Sounding*—we need not reopen this question of statutory interpretation. It is enough for us to note the general consensus that exists in the lower courts and to observe that the position of those courts conforms with the discussion and holding in *Miles*. Adopting the rule urged by Batterton would be contrary to *Miles*'s command that federal courts should seek to promote a "uniform rule applicable to all actions" for the same injury, whether under the Jones Act or the general maritime law. [ ]

C

To the extent Batterton argues that punitive damages are justified on policy grounds or as a regulatory measure, we are unpersuaded. In contemporary maritime law, our overriding objective is to pursue the policy expressed in congressional enactments, and because unseaworthiness in its current strict-liability form is our own invention and came after passage of the Jones Act, it would exceed our current role to introduce novel remedies contradictory to those Congress has provided in similar areas. See [*Miles*] (declining to create remedy "that goes well beyond the limits of Congress' ordered system of recovery"). We are particularly loath to impose more expansive liabilities on a claim governed by strict liability than Congress has imposed for comparable claims based in negligence. [ ] And with the increased role that legislation has taken over the past century of maritime law, we think it wise to leave to the political branches the development of novel claims and remedies.

We are also wary to depart from the practice under the Jones Act because a claim of unseaworthiness—more than a claim for maintenance and cure—serves as a duplicate and substitute for a Jones Act claim. The duty of maintenance and cure requires the master to provide medical care and wages to an injured mariner in the period after the injury has occurred. [ ] By contrast, both the Jones Act and unseaworthiness claims compensate for the injury itself and for the losses resulting from the injury. [ ] In such circumstances, we are particularly mindful of the rule that requires us to promote uniformity between maritime statutory law and maritime common law. See *Miles* [ ].

Unlike a claim of maintenance and cure, which addresses a situation where the vessel owner and master have "just about every economic incentive to dump an injured seaman in a port and abandon him to his fate," in the unseaworthiness context the interests of the owner and mariner are more closely aligned. [ ] That is because there are significant economic incentives prompting owners to ensure that their vessels are seaworthy. Most obviously, an owner who puts an unseaworthy ship to sea stands to lose the ship and the cargo that it carries. And if a vessel's unseaworthiness threatens the crew or cargo, the owner risks losing the protection of his insurer (who may not cover losses incurred by the owner's negligence) and the work of the crew (who may refuse to serve on an unseaworthy vessel). In some instances, the vessel owner may even face criminal penalties. See, *e.g.*, 46 U.S.C. § 10908.

Allowing punitive damages on unseaworthiness claims would also create bizarre disparities in the law. First, due to our holding in *Miles*, which limited recovery to compensatory damages in wrongful-death actions, a mariner could make a claim for punitive damages if he was injured onboard a ship, but his estate would lose the right to seek punitive damages if he died from his injuries. Second, because unseaworthiness claims run against the owner of the vessel, the ship's owner could be liable for punitive damages while the master or operator of the ship—who has more control over onboard conditions and is best positioned to minimize potential risks—would not be liable for such damages under the Jones Act. [ ]

Finally, because "[n]oncompensatory damages are not part of the civil-code tradition and thus unavailable in such countries" [ ], allowing punitive damages would place American shippers at a significant competitive disadvantage and would discourage foreign-owned vessels from employing American seamen. [ ] This would frustrate another "fundamental interest" served by federal maritime jurisdiction: "the protection of maritime commerce." [ ]

Against this, Batterton points to the maritime doctrine that encourages special solicitude for the welfare of seamen. But that doctrine has its roots in the paternalistic approach taken toward mariners by 19th century courts. [ ] The doctrine has never been a commandment that maritime law must favor seamen whenever possible. Indeed, the doctrine's apex coincided with many of the harsh common-law limitations on recovery that were not set aside until the passage of the Jones Act. And, while sailors today face hardships not encountered by those who work on land, neither are they as isolated nor as dependent on the master as their predecessors from the age of sail. In light of these changes and of the roles now played by the Judiciary and the political branches in protecting sailors, the special solicitude to sailors has only a small role to play in contemporary maritime law. It is not sufficient to overcome the weight of authority indicating that punitive damages are unavailable.

IV

Punitive damages are not a traditional remedy for unseaworthiness. The rule of *Miles*—promoting uniformity in maritime law and deference to the policies expressed in the statutes governing maritime law—prevents us from recognizing a new entitlement to punitive damages where none previously existed. We hold that a plaintiff may not recover punitive damages on a claim of unseaworthiness.

* * *

Justice GINSBURG, with whom Justice BREYER and Justice SOTOMAYOR join, dissenting.

In *Exxon Shipping Co. v. Baker* [*supra* at 249], the Court recognized that punitive damages normally are available in maritime cases. [ ] Relying on *Miles v. Apex Marine Corp.* [*supra* at 241], the Court today holds that unseaworthiness claims are an exception to that general rule. Respondent Christopher Batterton, defending the Ninth Circuit's decision in his favor, relies on the Court's more recent decision in *Atlantic Sounding Co. v. Townsend* [*supra* at 259]. In my view, the Ninth Circuit correctly determined that *Atlantic Sounding* is the controlling precedent. [ ] * **

II

I turn now to an examination of *Miles* and *Atlantic Sounding* closer than the attention accorded those decisions by the Court.

Miles, decided in 1990, addressed this question: In a wrongful-death action premised on unseaworthiness, may a deceased seaman's parent recover damages for loss of society? [ ] * * * The *Miles* Court reasoned that loss-of-society damages were nonpecuniary, that such damages could not be recovered under DOHSA or the Jones Act, and that it would "be inconsistent with [the Court's] place in the constitutional scheme … to sanction more expansive remedies" under general maritime law. [ ]

Some 19 years after *Miles*, in *Atlantic Sounding*, this Court held that punitive damages are available in actions for maintenance and cure under general maritime law. [ ] *Atlantic Sounding*'s reasoning had four components. First, the Court observed, punitive damages had a long common-law pedigree. [ ] Second, the "general rule that punitive damages were available at common law extended to claims arising under federal maritime law." [ ] Third, "[n]othing in maritime law undermine[d] the applicability of this general rule in the maintenance and cure context," notwithstanding slim evidence that punitive damages were historically awarded in maintenance and cure actions. [ ] Finally, neither the Jones Act nor any other statute indicated that Congress sought to displace the presumption that remedies generally available under the common law are available for maritime claims. While the Jones Act armed seamen with a statutory action for negligence attributable to a vessel operator, that remedy, *Atlantic Sounding* noted, did not curtail pre-existing maritime causes of action and remedies. [ ] The *Atlantic Sounding* Court rejected as "far too broad" the argument that the remedies available under general maritime law were confined to those available under the Jones Act or DOHSA. [ ]

The *Atlantic Sounding* inquiries control this case. As in *Atlantic Sounding*, "both the general maritime cause of action"—here, unseaworthiness—"and the remedy (punitive damages) were well established before the passage of the Jones Act." [ ] And, unlike the maritime wrongful-death action at issue in *Miles*, Batterton's claim of unseaworthiness resulting in personal injury was not created to fill gaps in a statutory scheme. [ ] The damages available for Batterton's unseaworthiness claim, *Atlantic Sounding* therefore signals, need not track those available under the Jones Act. [ ]

III

Applying *Atlantic Sounding*'s test [ ], punitive damages are not categorically barred in unseaworthiness actions. *Atlantic Sounding* itself answers the first two inquiries. [ ] "Punitive damages have long been an available remedy at common law for wanton, willful, or outrageous conduct." [ ] And "[t]he general rule that punitive damages [are] available at common law extended to claims arising under federal maritime law." [ ] As next explained, the third and fourth components of *Atlantic Sounding*'s test are also satisfied.

A

Atlantic Sounding asks, third, whether anything in maritime law "undermines the applicability [to the maritime action at issue] of th[e] general rule" that punitive damages are available under general maritime law. [ ] True, there is no evidence that courts awarded punitive damages for unseaworthiness before the mid-20th century. [ ] But neither is there evidence that punitive damages were *unavailable* in unseaworthiness actions. Tr. of Oral Arg. 17.

Contrary to the Court's assertion, evidence of the availability of punitive damages for maintenance and cure was not "central to our decision in *Atlantic Sounding*." [ ] Far from it. "[A] search for cases in which punitive damages were awarded for the willful denial of maintenance and cure ... yields very little." [*Atlantic Sounding*, 557 U.S. at 430] (ALITO, J., dissenting). The Court in *Atlantic Sounding* invoked historical evidence about punitive damages in maintenance and cure actions, "strikingly slim" though it was, [ ] only to underscore this point: Without a showing that punitive damages were unavailable, the generally applicable common-law rule allowing punitive damages should not be displaced. [ ] Here, too, the absence of evidence that punitive damages were unavailable in unseaworthiness cases supports adherence to the general common-law rule permitting punitive damages.

B

Atlantic Sounding asks fourth: Has Congress "enacted legislation departing from th[e] common-law understanding" that punitive damages are generally available? [ ] Dutra contends that unseaworthiness claims and claims under the Jones Act are "simply two paths to compensation for the same injury." [ ] Positing that punitive damages are unavailable under the Jones Act,[5] Dutra concludes they are likewise unavailable in unseaworthiness suits. [ ] Dutra's argument is unavailing, for the Jones Act does not preclude the award of punitive damages in unseaworthiness cases.

As noted, the Jones Act provides a cause of action for a seaman injured by his or her employer's negligence. [ ] Congress passed the Act "primarily to overrule *The Osceola*, in which this Court prohibited a seaman or his family from recovering for injuries or death suffered due to his employers' negligence." [ ] The Jones Act was intended to "enlarge th[e] protection" afforded to seamen, "not to narrow it." [ ] Accordingly, the Jones Act did not provide an "exclusive remedy" for seamen's injuries; instead, it "preserve[d]" and supplemented "common-law causes of action." [ ] As *Miles* itself recognized, the Jones Act "d[id] not disturb seamen's general maritime claims for injuries resulting from unseaworthiness." [ ]

When the Jones Act was enacted, unseaworthiness and negligence were "discrete concepts": Unseaworthiness related "to the structure of the ship and the adequacy of [its] equipment and furnishings," while negligence concerned "the direction and control of operations aboard ship." G. Gilmore & C. Black, Law of Admiralty § 6–3, p. 277 (2d ed. 1975). Because these actions were distinct, it is improbable that, by enacting the Jones Act, Congress meant to limit the remedies available in unseaworthiness cases. Though unseaworthiness and Jones Act negligence now "significant[ly] overlap" [ ], that overlap resulted primarily from mid-20th-century judicial decisions expanding the scope of unseaworthiness liability. [ ] Those decisions do not so much as hint that Congress, in enacting the Jones Act, intended to cabin the relief available for unseaworthiness. Even today, unseaworthiness and Jones Act negligence are "not identical." [ ] The persistent differences between unseaworthiness and Jones Act claims weigh against inserting into general maritime law damages limitations that may be applicable to Jones Act suits. [ ]

The Court observes that a plaintiff may not recover twice for the same injury under the Jones Act and unseaworthiness. [ ] True enough. But the Court does not explain why a bar to double recovery of compensatory damages should affect the availability of a single award of punitive damages. Notably, punitive damages are not awarded to compensate the plaintiff; their office is to punish the defendant and deter misconduct. [ ] There is thus no tension between preventing double recovery of compensatory damages and allowing the recovery, once, of punitive damages.

IV

Finally, the Court takes up policy arguments against the availability of punitive damages in unseaworthiness actions. [ ] The Court, however, has long recognized the general availability of punitive damages under maritime law. [ ]

* * *

Dutra and the Court warn that allowing punitive damages in unseaworthiness actions could impair maritime commerce. [ ] But punitive damages have been available in

5. This Court has not decided whether punitive damages are available under the Jones Act. See [*Atlantic Sounding*, supra at 266 n.12] (reserving the question).

maintenance and cure cases in all Circuits for the last decade [ ], and in unseaworthiness cases in some Circuits for longer [ ]. No tidal wave has overwhelmed commerce in those Circuits.

Permitting punitive damages for unseaworthiness, the Court further urges, would create "bizarre disparities." [ ] I see no "bizarre disparit[y]" in allowing an injured sailor to seek remedies unavailable to survivors of deceased seamen. [ ] Nor is it "bizarre" to permit recovery of punitive damages against a shipowner "for injuries due to unseaworthiness of the vessel." [ ] Exposure to such damages helps to deter wrongdoing, particularly when malfeasance is "hard to detect." [ ] If there is any "bizarre disparit[y]," it is the one the Court today creates: Punitive damages are available for willful and wanton breach of the duty to provide maintenance and cure, but not for similarly culpable breaches of the duty to provide a seaworthy vessel.

* * *

Notes

1. The majority and the dissent characterize the Court's prior decisions in *Miles* and *Atlantic Sounding Co. v. Townsend* very differently. Which characterizations are more accurate?

2. How significant are the post-1920 developments in the unseaworthiness doctrine? If the facts of *Batterton* would have justified an award of punitive damages today, would those facts also have justified an unseaworthiness action prior to 1920?

3. A key premise in the *Batterton* majority's *Miles*-based analysis is that punitive damages are not available under the Jones Act. What is the basis for concluding that the Jones Act does not permit punitive damages? How persuasive is that analysis?

4. To what extent is the majority correct in its assertion that the Jones Act and the unseaworthiness doctrine are substantially the same? To what extent do they differ? To what extent do claims for the wrongful withholding of maintenance and cure (as in *Townsend*) overlap with Jones Act claims?

5. As a result of *Batterton*, seamen are the only maritime personal injury plaintiffs who confront a categorical exclusion from seeking punitive damages. Has the special treatment for seamen become a disadvantage rather than a benefit?

Justice Ginsburg might have mentioned another "bizarre disparit[y]": plaintiffs who suffer economic loss, even without property damage (as in *Exxon Shipping*) may recover punitive damages, but those who suffer personal injuries may not. What does this say about the interests that the Supreme Court considers worthy of protection?

Chapter III

Carriage of Goods

A. Introduction

When goods are bought and sold, they must be transported from the seller to the buyer. The most common methods of transporting goods are by sea (or other water routes), by road, by rail, and by air. Most cargo will travel by a combination of two or even three of those methods, but carriage by sea remains the most important in international trade (both in terms of volume and value). In the United States, most international trade is conducted by sea, and a significant proportion of our domestic commerce is also maritime.

There are two principal types of contract for the carriage of goods by sea—the bill of lading and the charterparty. Bills of lading are customarily used in the "liner" trades by "common carriers" that sail on fixed routes following announced schedules and that are prepared to carry "general cargoes," meaning whatever is offered for shipment that the ship is capable of carrying. Charterparties, on the other hand, are traditionally used in "tramp"[1] shipping by "private carriers" that offer the capacity of an entire ship on an *ad hoc* basis, typically for the carriage of "bulk cargoes" such as oil, grain, coal, steel, iron ore, or lumber.

The distinction between the two forms of carriage may be clearer through consideration of a more familiar land-based analogy. If an individual wishes to send a single package across the country, she may contract with a delivery company such as FedEx or UPS. The company will then pick up the package according to a posted schedule, carry it across the country along with packages from a number of other shippers, and deliver it to its destination according to the posted schedule. But if an individual wishes to relocate her entire family and needs to move the contents of a large house across the country, she will contract with a moving company such as Mayflower or United Van Lines. That company will then arrange to have an empty moving van arrive at the individual's house at an agreed time, load the house's contents, drive the loaded van across the country to the new house, and deliver the shipment as soon as possible. In these simple hypotheticals, the delivery company (FedEx or UPS) is analogous to the ocean "liner," while the moving company (Mayflower or United Van Lines) is analogous to the ocean "tramp."

---

1. Some authors have noted a similarity between vessels operating under charterparties and the "fraternity of homeless men known as tramps." Kendall & Buckley, The Business of Shipping 22 (7th ed. 2001). But in the shipping context there is no pejorative connotation to the term "tramp." See The Oxford Companion to Ships and the Sea 885 (Peter Kemp ed. 1976).

The distinction between carriage under bills of lading and carriage under charterparties is of essential importance because the legal regimes governing those two forms of transportation are completely different. In a charterparty transaction, the two parties are traditionally thought to have roughly equal bargaining power. As a result, freedom of contract has long been the governing principle. In a bill of lading transaction, on the other hand, the carrier is traditionally thought to have superior bargaining power justifying a legal regime protecting the cargo interests. The legal regime that has been enacted in the United States is the Carriage of Goods by Sea Act (COGSA), which is reprinted in the Statutory Supplement. This chapter will begin with an investigation of carriage under bills of lading, then conclude with an introductory overview of carriage under charterparties.

In liner shipments, the bill of lading is commonly said to be the contract of carriage or at least to "evidence" the contract of carriage (*i.e.*, memorialize the contractual terms that the parties concluded when booking the shipment, before the bill of lading was issued). But the bill of lading can also serve two other functions. It typically operates as a receipt for the goods, providing evidence of the carrier's having received the cargo from the shipper and some evidence of the condition of the cargo at that time. It may also operate as a document of title, enabling the shipper to sell the goods while they are in the carrier's possession by transferring the bill of lading to a subsequent holder. The focus here will be primarily on the contractual function of the bill of lading.

Traditionally, a bill of lading was issued by a carrier to cover the transportation provided by that carrier alone. Indeed, transshipment with another carrier could be regarded as a serious breach of the contract of carriage. Thus a shipment from an inland point of origin to an inland destination on a different continent would typically involve three or more bills of lading. For example, a shipment from Austin to Paris might travel by truck from Austin to Houston (under a bill of lading issued by the motor carrier), by ship from Houston to Rotterdam (under a bill of lading issued by the ocean carrier), and by train from Rotterdam to Paris (under a bill of lading issued by the railroad). In modern practice, however, it is common to have a single bill of lading for the entire journey from Austin to Paris. One of the carriers involved might issue that bill of lading, or it might be issued by someone else entirely, such as an "NVOCC" (non-vessel operating common carrier) who will in turn make the necessary arrangements with each of the performing carriers. The single bill of lading is known as a "through" bill of lading, to distinguish it from the more traditional "ocean" or "port-to-port" bill of lading.

Before the mid-nineteenth century, the parties to the contract of carriage had considerable freedom to agree on the risk allocation, subject to legal rules that were almost entirely judicial in origin.[2] Starting in the mid-nineteenth century, legislatures began to act in the field. In 1851, for example, Congress passed the Fire Statute (as part of the Limitation Act). In 1854, the British Parliament passed the Railway and Canal Traffic Act. Each of these statutes addresses specific issues but makes no effort to fully govern the subject. In 1893, Congress passed the Harter Act (see Statutory Supplement), which

2. Nineteenth-century law in both England and the United States treated the common carrier as akin to an "insurer," meaning that the carrier was liable without fault for all losses other than those arising from such irresistible causes as acts of God, acts of public enemies, etc. Both countries permitted carriers to contract out of that liability to some extent. But U.S. law differed sharply from English law in refusing to allow the carrier to escape liability for its own negligence or the negligence of its servants and agents (the master and crew).

was the world's first statute to establish generally applicable rules governing a carrier's liability for cargo loss or damage.

B. A Survey of the Leading Cargo Liability Regimes

1. The Harter Act

The Harter Act was conceived as a compromise between cargo and carrier interests.[3] The carrier's liability for the negligence of its agents and servants was at the heart of the compromise. Under sections 1 and 2 of the Act (currently recodifed at 46 U.S.C. §§ 30704 and 30705), a carrier could not escape liability for negligence in the care and custody of the cargo or for the failure to use due diligence to furnish a seaworthy vessel. But under section 3 (currently recodified at 46 U.S.C. § 30706), if the carrier had used due diligence to furnish a seaworthy vessel it would not be "responsible for damage or loss resulting from faults or errors in navigation or in management of [the] vessel." That core compromise was widely copied, and it continues (at least for now) to form the basis for cargo liability regimes in most of the world.

As you will learn in the next subsection, the Carriage of Goods by Sea Act (COGSA) largely superseded the Harter Act in 1936, but the core compromise was carried forward and many of COGSA's provisions originated in the Harter Act. The carrier's duty to use due diligence to furnish a seaworthy vessel is found in COGSA § 3(1), the carrier's responsibility for the care and custody of the cargo was enacted as part of COGSA § 3(2), and the "error in navigation or management" defense (also known as the "nautical fault" defense) was reenacted as COGSA § 4(2)(a). Judicial interpretations of the Harter Act continue to be important in understanding the corresponding provisions of COGSA, and it remains common for the courts to cite Harter Act decisions when construing comparable provision in COGSA. So long as the COGSA and Harter Act provisions are in fact comparable, there is little risk in that approach.

Although COGSA has largely superseded the Harter Act, the earlier statute remains in force in at least three situations when COGSA does not apply. Section 12 of COGSA explicitly preserves the Harter Act from implied repeal to the extent that it governs the carrier's duties prior to the time when the goods are loaded on the ship and after the time they are discharged from the ship. COGSA's legislative history demonstrates that Congress also intended the Harter Act to continue to apply to domestic carriage ("coastwise trade") and deck carriage. But even in those situations, the courts often apply COGSA. Under the "coastwise option" in COGSA § 13, the parties may stipulate for the application of COGSA in carriage between U.S. ports, in which event COGSA applies "as fully as if" directly applicable, i.e., with the full force of law. Furthermore, bills of lading often declare that COGSA shall apply to the period before loading and after discharge or to goods carried on deck. Courts regularly enforce such choices, permitting COGSA to apply as a

3. For details of the history of the Harter Act, see Sweeney, *Happy Birthday, Harter: A Reappraisal of the Harter Act on its 100th Anniversary*, 24 J. Mar. L. & Com. 1 (1993).

matter of contract. When COGSA applies with the force of law, the carrier cannot contract out of any of its provisions. When COGSA is made applicable by contract, in some circuits the carrier can add other provisions to the contract that are more favorable to it than COGSA—subject to the constraints of the Harter Act. Because COGSA and the Harter Act are so similar, however, it often makes no difference which statute applies.

2. The Hague Rules and COGSA

The Harter Act proved influential on the world stage, and was ultimately the model for an international convention popularly known as the Hague Rules. That treaty was ratified by most of the world's maritime nations, including the United States, which also enacted COGSA in substantially the same form. COGSA remains the central U.S. statute governing cargo liability in the ocean shipping context, but much of the world has moved on to new conventions, such as the Hague-Visby Rules or the Hamburg Rules. The subject today remains in a state of flux, and new developments are likely within the next few years.

The History of COGSA and the Hague Rules

22 J. Mar. L. & Com. 1 (1991)

The immediate impetus for the Hague Rules came from the British Empire. * * * In response to cargo interests' complaints on the subject, the overseas Dominions [e.g., Australia, New Zealand, and Canada] pressured the Imperial government to coordinate Harter-style legislation for the entire British Empire. * * * British opposition had long been thought to be the principal impediment to international uniform legislation on bills of lading. [As soon as] the British government was committed to enacting domestic legislation on the topic, the prospect of international agreement was much more appealing to British interests—including the powerful shipowning interests. * * *

In May 1921, the [International Law Association's] Maritime Law Committee met in London. Despite indignant protests from British shipowners that "freedom of contract" was the appropriate regime, the Committee agreed to formulate uniform model rules based on the Canadian [Water Carriage of Goods] Act [which was modeled on the Harter Act] to govern ocean bills of lading. * * * [A month later, the draft was complete. It] accepted the by-then familiar compromise between cargo and carrier interests. [T]he carrier was required to exercise due diligence to make the ship seaworthy. The carrier was also liable for "the proper and careful handling, loading, stowage, carriage, custody, care, and unloading" of the cargo. In return, the carrier was not liable for faults or errors in the navigation or management of the ship. * * *

The International Law Association ["ILA"] held its next conference at The Hague * * * to discuss the proposed draft. After [extensive] debate between cargo interests (including bankers and underwriters) and carrier interests, the [ILA adopted] the text of what became known as "the Hague Rules of 1921" * * * .

* * * The most significant topic at The Hague was the package limitation. After long debate, the parties agreed that the carrier could limit its liability to £100 (then worth almost $500) per package or unit in the absence of a declaration of higher value. In view of the limitation and agreed valuation clauses with much lower amounts that courts had previously upheld, even under Harter-type legislation, the £100 package limitation was considered a major improvement for cargo interests.

The cargo interests' other big victory at The Hague involved the time-for-suit and notice-of-claim provisions. The Harter Act and the Canadian Act had been held to permit bill of lading clauses requiring suits to be filed as soon as sixty days after delivery of the goods. [The Hague Rules] guarantee[d] cargo claimants a full year in which to bring suit.

Prior law had also sanctioned notice-of-claim provisions in bills of lading that barred all claims for cargo loss or damage unless written notice was given before removing the cargo from the carrier's custody. After the Hague Conference, this became an issue of burdens of proof. A new provision required a consignee to give the carrier written notice of a claim for loss or damage, along with the general nature of the claim, before removing the goods. Removal without such a notice would no longer bar suit completely; it would simply be prima facie evidence of proper delivery.

* * *

[After further debate and tinkering with some of the provisions under the auspices of the Comité Maritime International ("CMI"),[4] the Hague Rules of 1921 became the basis of the Brussels Convention of 1924. Great Britain and other commonwealth nations moved quickly to implement the convention.] Outside of the British Empire, however, the response to the Hague Rules was less enthusiastic. * * *

* * * [In the United States] organized opposition to COGSA came primarily from a few shippers (cargo interests) who hoped that they could do better. None of the cargo interests seriously denied that the Hague Rules were an improvement, from their point of view, over the Harter Act. The new rules effectively extended the statute of limitations for filing a claim, shifted the burden of proof in the cargo claimant's favor in most cases, and provided a much higher package limitation than was customary under the Harter Act. A few believed, however, that they could obtain a [more cargo-friendly] amendment of the Harter Act that would be even more beneficial. They were thus unwilling to accept COGSA's more modest improvement in their situation for fear that it would make it impossible to obtain more sweeping changes.

* * *

The real turning point in the battle to enact COGSA came [when the interested parties agreed to accept some limited amendments. In 1936, Congress finally passed a bill incorporating those amendments,] President Roosevelt signed the bill, and [COGSA] became law. [The United States ratified the Hague Rules the following year.]

Before the United States' enactment of COGSA and ratification of the convention, other countries had hesitated to adopt the Hague Rules. * * * With the U.S. adoption of the Hague Rules, however, the world's remaining maritime powers joined the new regime fairly quickly. * * * [By 1938], the overwhelming majority of the world's shipping was committed to the Hague Rules.

Notes

1. Original source material on the history of the Hague Rules and COGSA is reprinted in *The Legislative History of the Carriage of Goods by Sea Act and the Travaux Préparatoires of the Hague Rules* (M. Sturley ed. 1990).

---

4. Editors' note: The CMI, established in 1897 with the declared aim of unifying maritime law, is an international non-governmental organization composed of national maritime law associations in roughly fifty countries.

2. The CMI continues to be a major player in the field. Today it works closely with international organizations such as the International Maritime Organization ("IMO") and the United Nations Commission on International Trade Law ("UNCITRAL") to accomplish its goals. See *infra* at 284.

3. From 1936 to 1983, COGSA was codified at 46 U.S.C. §§ 1300-15. When Congress enacted part of title 46 as positive law, it moved the remaining provisions (including COGSA) to an appendix. Thus, COGSA was codified from 1983 to 2006 at 46 U.S.C. app. §§ 1300-15. When Congress finished recodifying title 46 in 2006 and enacting it as positive law, COGSA was not included in the recodification. It is still fully in force; Congress did not repeal it. See, e.g., Robertson & Sturley, *Developments in Admiralty and Maritime Law*, 35 TUL. MAR. L.J. 493, 566-568 (2011). But it is included in the U.S. Code only as a statutory note following the first section of the recodified Harter Act, 46 U.S.C. § 30701. As a result of the confusion, lawyers and even judges mis-cite COGSA with surprising frequency. Sometimes, they cite Harter Act provisions as though they were part of COGSA. And some have even assumed (incorrectly) that COGSA is no longer in force.

3. The Hague-Visby and Hamburg Rules

Although the United States retains its 1936 COGSA substantially unchanged, most of the world has moved forward to more modern cargo liability regimes. The Hague-Visby Rules, which currently govern most of world trade, are simply the original Hague Rules with a handful of specific amendments to address particular problems that had arisen by the late 1950s. The Hamburg Rules (formally known as the United Nations Convention on the Carriage of Goods by Sea) were a U.N. effort to replace the Hague and Hague-Visby Rules with a new regime, albeit one that retained many of the familiar principles. A few dozen nations have ratified the Hamburg Rules, but none of them are major trading nations and the convention therefore governs only a small proportion of world trade.

Transport Law for the Twenty-First Century: An Introduction to the Preparation, Philosophy, and Potential Impact of the Rotterdam Rules

14 J. INT'L MAR. L. 461 (2008)

The Hague Rules provided an internationally accepted uniform legal regime when they first achieved wide-spread acceptance, but that uniformity began to break down soon thereafter. In part, the break-down was due to changing technology, such as the "container revolution,"[5] which the draftsmen of the Hague Rules could not have anticipated. The changing world political situation was another significant factor, as former colonies became independent countries with their own agendas. National court interpretations

5. Editors' note: The "container revolution" refers to the new shipping method—first introduced in U.S. domestic carriage in 1956 and adopted in international trade starting about a decade later—whereby cargo is carried on ships in large metal boxes ("containers") measuring 8 feet by 8 feet by 20 or 40 feet. The improved efficiency of container carriage has not only revolutionized the shipping industry but has also fundamentally changed the world economy. For more information on the container revolution, see MARC LEVINSON, THE BOX: HOW THE SHIPPING CONTAINER MADE THE WORLD SMALLER AND THE WORLD ECONOMY BIGGER (2006); BRIAN J. CUDAHY, BOX BOATS: HOW CONTAINER SHIPS CHANGED THE WORLD (2006).

of the Hague Rules also produced problems that called for new solutions. And developments in the world economy produced one of the most visible problems, as rising and falling exchange rates left unit limitation values under Article 4(5) that varied among major maritime nations from US$160 to US$550 per package.

The CMI sponsored the first post-Hague effort to address some of the recognized problems. * * * At its 1963 Stockholm Conference, the CMI * * * propose[d] a draft protocol with eight specific amendments to the Hague Rules. At the end of the conference, the draft protocol was "solemn[ly] sign[ed] ... in that historic place of the old and beautiful Swedish city of Visby," thus justifying the name "Visby Amendments."

When the draft protocol came before a diplomatic conference in May 1967 and February 1968, the delegates quickly agreed on most of the issues. * * * The most controversial proposal involved unit limitation. The diplomatic conference worked out an elaborate compromise that included higher limitation amounts expressed in Poincaré francs, a weight-based limitation operating in conjunction with the package limitation, the "container clause" to clarify the identification of "packages" when goods are shipped in containers, and a provision for the loss of the right to limit liability for intentional or reckless misconduct.

* * *

The Hague Rules as amended by the Visby Protocol * * * are commonly known as the Hague-Visby Rules. That regime is now in force—in one form or another and by one method or another—in countries representing approximately two-thirds of world trade.

In sharp contrast to the Visby Protocol (which simply amended the Hague Rules on a few specific issues), the Hamburg Rules supersede the prior conventions with a completely new regime. The United Nations began its efforts in this field in 1968, when the U.N. Conference on Trade and Development (UNCTAD) requested its Committee on Shipping to create a Working Group on international shipping legislation. In 1971, the focus shifted to [the United Nations Commission on International Trade Law ("UNCITRAL")]. An UNCITRAL Working Group then spent five years preparing a draft convention, which was approved by the Commission in 1976.

After four weeks of further negotiations, a diplomatic conference in Hamburg, Germany, overwhelmingly approved the final text in March 1978. Despite the complete rewrite, the Hamburg Rules' approach was in many ways similar to that of the Hague and Hague-Visby Rules. All are fault-based systems with a reversed burden of proof, meaning that the burden is generally on the carrier to prove its absence of fault, but that the carrier can escape liability for cargo loss or damage if it meets that burden. Although the Hamburg package and weight-based limitation amounts are significantly higher than Visby's, the dual approach (with a container clause and a very high standard for breaking limitation) is essentially the same. Indeed, many of the Hamburg provisions are simply re-worded versions of the prior language in the Hague and Hague-Visby Rules.

The Hamburg Rules nevertheless introduced some innovations that proved influential in the latest negotiations. The most obvious may have been the elimination of the navigational fault exception found in Article 4(2)(a) of the Hague and Hague-Visby Rules. More significant innovations were expanding the scope to cover inbound and outbound shipments, and introducing special rules for jurisdiction and arbitration that sought to guarantee a cargo claimant's right to have claims resolved in a convenient forum. * * *

The Hamburg Rules finally entered into force (for the countries that had ratified them) in 1992. Although over 30 countries are now parties to the Hamburg Rules, they represent in the aggregate only a very small proportion of world trade.

The current situation is widely regarded as unsatisfactory. The Hague-Visby Rules provide the dominant international legal regime today, but some major commercial nations are not parties to that regime. The United States (with about a quarter of world trade) may be the most prominent example, but it is not alone. China (with about a quarter of the world's population and a growing proportion of the trade) is not a Hague-Visby country.[6] Moreover, the Hague-Visby Rules are now dated. The Hamburg Rules are only slightly more modern, and they have never achieved the wide-spread acceptance that is necessary for their success.

Notes

1. For a more detailed history of the Visby Protocol, see, e.g., Diamond, *The Hague-Visby Rules,* 1978 Lloyd's Mar. & Com. L.Q. 225. For a more detailed history of the Hamburg Rules, see Sweeney, *The UNCITRAL Draft Convention on Carriage of Goods by Sea (Part I),* 7 J. Mar. L. & Com. 69 (1975); *Part II,* 7 J. Mar. L. & Com. 327 (1976); *Part III,* 7 J. Mar. L. & Com. 487 (1976); *Part IV,* 7 J. Mar. L. & Com. 615 (1976); *Part V,* 8 J. Mar. L. & Com. 167 (1977).

2. Although the United States has not ratified the Visby Protocol, the Hague-Visby Rules have still been influential in this country. The U.S. courts, for example, have essentially adopted the Hague-Visby "container clause" as a matter of judicial interpretation of COGSA. See *infra* at 314–15. Moreover, it is not uncommon for U.S. courts to apply the Hague-Visby limitation amounts to a transaction under the clause paramount in the bill of lading. See *infra* at 315–19.

4. The Rotterdam Rules

The U.N. Convention on Contracts for the International Carriage of Goods Wholly or Partly by Sea, popularly known as the "Rotterdam Rules," creates a liability regime intended to supersede the Hague, Hague-Visby, and Hamburg Rules. (The new convention also covers a number of issues, such as electronic commerce, that are only tangentially related to liability.) Excerpts are included in the Statutory Supplement. Only a few nations have yet ratified the Rotterdam Rules, but a number of countries (including the United States) are actively considering ratification. Many are waiting to see what the United States will do, and observers therefore predict that the new convention will enter into force soon after the United States ratifies.

Transport Law for the Twenty-First Century: An Introduction to the Preparation, Philosophy, and Potential Impact of the Rotterdam Rules

14 J. Int'l Mar. L. 461 (2008)

The Hague and Hague-Visby Rules were largely CMI products. The Hamburg Rules, on the other hand, were a product of U.N. organizations with minimal CMI input. For much of the 1980s and 1990s, while advocates of the Hague-Visby and Hamburg Rules

6. Editors' note: The relevant portion of the Chinese Maritime Code contains a mix of provisions based on the Hague-Visby and Hamburg Rules along with unique domestic rules.

battled over the future of cargo liability law, many observers viewed the CMI and UNCITRAL as rivals, at least on this issue. But when UNCITRAL returned to the field near the end of the twentieth century, it was in active partnership with the CMI.

* * *

* * * [T]he UNCITRAL Secretariat invited the CMI to begin the preparatory work for a new convention. Accepting UNCITRAL's invitation, the CMI attacked its assignment with unusual speed and vigor. It first set up a Steering Committee, which considered the project and issued a report (in April 1998) outlining the work that should be undertaken. The CMI also set up an International Working Group, which met four times to complete the preliminary matters prior to the first meeting of a new International Sub-Committee. * * *

The International Sub-Committee * * * met [six times in 2000 and 2001, and the CMI discussed the project at its 2001 conference]. By the middle of December 2001, the CMI had delivered its final Draft Instrument on Transport Law to UNCITRAL.

UNCITRAL made only minor changes to convert the CMI's final Draft Instrument into its own "Preliminary Draft Instrument." which it published as an UNCITRAL document and referred to its Working Group III (Transport Law). [Working Group III] first met in April 2002, at United Nations Headquarters in New York. Generally spending two weeks in formal sessions every spring in New York and every fall at UNCITRAL Headquarters in Vienna, the Working Group during a six-year period devoted a total of twenty-five weeks of formal meetings to discussing the text that was ultimately adopted as the Rotterdam Rules.

* * *

The [U.N.] General Assembly * * * passed Resolution 63/122 on December 11, 2008. With this action, the "Draft Convention" became the "U.N. Convention on Contracts for the International Carriage of Goods Wholly or Partly by Sea." * * * The Resolution authorizes a signing ceremony in Rotterdam on September 23, 2009. At that event, the Convention will be opened for signature (and at least some countries can be expected to sign as part of the ceremony). It will then be up to the nations of the world to ratify the Rotterdam Rules. They will enter into force one year after the twentieth ratification.

Notes

1. Sixteen nations (including the United States) signed the new convention in Rotterdam on September 23, 2009. (That is a record for conventions of this type.) In 2011, Spain became the first country to ratify the Rotterdam Rules.

2. For a detailed discussion and analysis of the Rotterdam Rules, see M. Sturley, T. Fujita & G. van der Ziel, The Rotterdam Rules: The UN Convention on Contracts for the International Carriage of Goods Wholly or Partly by Sea (2d ed. 2020); The Rotterdam Rules 2008: Commentary to the United Nations Convention on Contracts for the International Carriage of Goods Wholly or Partly by Sea (A. von Ziegler, J. Schelin & S. Zunarelli eds. 2010).

3. Although the Rotterdam Rules would replace the liability regimes created by the Hague, Hague-Visby, and Hamburg Rules, the changes would be evolutionary rather than revolutionary. All four are fault-based systems with a reversed burden of proof. See *infra* at 295–300. The more significant impact of the Rotterdam Rules will be the modernization of the rules governing the carriage of goods by sea. At the moment, U.S. trade

is governed by a 1936 statute enacting a 1924 convention that was designed to give international effect to an 1893 statute that was written to address the problems of the early steam era. Most of the world has not moved far beyond that. None of the current regimes adequately address the changes in the industry as a result of the container revolution. All of the current regimes apply only to the sea carriage, even though most contracts of carriage are multimodal contracts concluded on a door-to-door basis. None of the current regimes even imagined the possibility of electronic commerce. In short, the Rotterdam Rules will bring the law into the 21st century. See generally, e.g., Sturley, *Can Commercial Law Accommodate New Technologies in International Shipping?*, in New Technologies, Artificial Intelligence and Shipping Law in the 21st Century 22 (B. Soyer & A. Tettenborn eds. 2020).

C. Delivery

The carrier's most fundamental duty under a contract of carriage is to transport the cargo and deliver it safely at its destination. COGSA neither specifies that duty explicitly nor defines what is meant by "delivery"—even though several important consequences are tied to "delivery." The following case addresses delivery under the Harter Act, but the same principles are often applied in COGSA cases.

Farrell Lines, Inc. v. Highlands Insurance Co.

United States District Court, Southern District of New York, 1982
532 F. Supp. 77, 1982 AMC 1430

EDWARD WEINFELD, District Judge.

These two consolidated admiralty actions were tried upon stipulated facts to determine the liability for damage to and loss of cargo. Farrell Lines, Inc. ("Farrell" or "carrier") received aboard its oceangoing vessel "Export Ambassador" at New York City, a shipment of 556 cartons of shoes from Jomark Textiles, Inc. for transportation by sea to the Port of Monrovia, Liberia pursuant to a bill of lading. The vessel arrived at Monrovia on March 28, 1980. The shipment was discharged between March 28 and March 30 to the stringpiece[7] by stevedores retained by Farrell. The stevedores' participation in the cargo delivery ended at the stringpiece. Farrell and the vessel lost physical custody and control of the cargo upon its discharge by the stevedores. Actual delivery of the cargo to the consignee was not made by the carrier; rather, at the stringpiece, the cargo was received by the National Port Authority of Monrovia ("NPA") which transported the goods to its warehouse and later made delivery to the consignee. NPA is a Liberian governmental entity that has exclusive authority for the regulation of the Port of Monrovia and directs and controls all activities conducted at the Port. The NPA's regulations govern the activities conducted at the Port.

At the discharge from the vessel to the stringpiece of the 556 cartons shipped, tallies conducted by the NPA listed 7 cartons short and 24 cartons damaged and pilfered, for a total loss of $5,197.50. Several weeks later, on May 6, 1980 when the goods were received into the transit warehouse at the Port of Monrovia, the NPA issued its warehouse receipt indicating receipt of 456 cartons, with exceptions for 100 non-delivered cartons and 256 cartons damaged and pilfered, for a total loss of $60,558.75.

---

7. Editors' note: The stringpiece is the portion of the pier that is directly adjacent to the ship.

Highlands Insurance Company paid the full amount of the loss to the shipper and commenced an action as subrogee against Farrell to recover the amount so paid. On the other hand, Farrell commenced an action for a declaratory judgment limiting its liability for the damage sustained to the cargo while in its physical custody or control and declaring that it is not liable for the damages to the cargo or its nondelivery subsequent to its delivery to the stringpiece when NPA took control. The dispute is over whether Farrell is liable for the pilferage and shortage that occurred after it no longer had physical control of the discharged goods and while it was in the custody of the NPA. As the parties state it, "should Highlands ... recover $5,197.50 or $60,558.75." The Court holds its recovery is limited to $5,197.50.

Upon the facts here presented, the terms of the Harter Act govern and Farrell was under a duty to effect a "proper delivery" of the cargo to the consignee. However variously stated by the parties, the basic issue is whether such "proper delivery" was made when Farrell discharged the goods to the stringpiece at the vessel's berth at the Port and physical custody and control passed to NPA.

As a general rule, proper delivery by the carrier contemplates delivery of the cargo to the consignee or designee set forth on the bill of lading, at a fit and proper wharf, with the duty upon the carrier to give reasonable notice to the consignee that the cargo has arrived, with a reasonable opportunity to pick it up, and a duty on the consignee to receive the goods at the place of outturn. But this general rule of proper delivery is subject to a well-recognized exception where custom, regulation or law of the port otherwise provide. As stated by the Supreme Court,

> No rule is better settled than that delivery must be according to the custom and usage of the port, and such delivery will discharge the carrier of his responsibility.

A host of cases have followed that doctrine.

Highland seeks to place liability upon Farrell for the total loss by relying upon Section IV-84(2) of the Monrovian port regulations which provide:

> Cargo shall only be regarded as landed when placed and safely deposited in the Transit Warehouse or at a place designated by the Port Manager, and until then delivery of the cargo shall not be considered to have been made to the Authority.

However, this self-exoneration clause from the point of delivery of the cargo until it is "safely deposited" in the warehouse would emasculate the well-established rule referred to above that where delivery is compelled according to custom and usage of the port, the carrier is discharged of its responsibility. Highlands' argument that the regulation governs the determination of when delivery occurred disregards the actual fact that Farrell, in accord with mandatory port practice, lost physical custody and control of the cargo upon its delivery to the stringpiece and that, thereupon, it was received by NPA for delivery to the consignee. Thus, Highlands would ignore local custom and practice and would substitute a local regulation in place of the Harter Act as the authority for determining when "proper delivery" occurred.

Additionally, this would go counter to the terms of the bill of lading which provided:

> It is agreed that delivery by the Carrier ... shall take place upon discharge from vessel to a safe lighter or dock and that responsibility of the Carrier ... shall altogether cease when the goods have been discharged and possession is received or taken by Customs or other authorities.... It is agreed that when possession of the goods is received or taken by the Customs or other authorities ... such authority or person shall be considered as having received delivery of the goods

> solely as agent of and on behalf of the shippers/consignee at the risk of the goods.

Highlands' fundamental error is in disregarding that the Harter Act governs and under its requirements in accord with port custom and usage, "proper delivery" was made at the stringpiece.

* * *

Highland Insurance Company is entitled to recover only the sum of $5,197.50. * * *

Notes

1. Identifying the time of "delivery" is essential for determining the carrier's period of responsibility, as in the principal case. The issue is also important in other contexts. In *Servicios-Expoarma, CA v. Industrial Maritime Carriers, Inc.*, 135 F.3d 984 (5th Cir. 1998), for example, the court needed to identify the time of "delivery" to determine if the lawsuit was timely under COGSA § 3(6).

2. In view of the importance of the subject, the Rotterdam Rules devote chapter 9 to "Delivery of the goods." See M. Sturley, T. Fujita & G. van der Ziel, The Rotterdam Rules: The UN Convention on Contracts for the International Carriage of Goods Wholly or Partly by Sea 249-283 (2d ed. 2020). Other provisions are also relevant to identifying the time of "delivery." See, e.g., articles 11, 12. Recognizing that "delivery" is the final step in the performance of a private contract, the Rotterdam Rules give the parties considerable flexibility to define when delivery will occur.

D. The Cargo Claimant's Action under COGSA

When cargo has been lost or damaged during ocean transportation, the shipper, the consignee, or another party (such as a person with a security interest in the goods) will suffer a loss. If the cargo was not insured, the injured party will typically seek compensation from the carrier under the contract of carriage (or from the person who actually damaged the cargo, such as a stevedore or terminal operator, perhaps under a tort or bailment theory).[8] If the cargo was insured, the insurer (who is subrogated to the rights of its insured) will typically seek the same sort of recovery.

Before the action proceeds, a few basic issues must be addressed. For example, is the person being sued the proper defendant? In some cases, it is necessary to determine who issued the bill of lading (which evidences the contract of carriage) in order to identify the "carrier" that is responsible under the contract of carriage. Thus in *Pacific Employers Insurance Co. v. The M/V Gloria*, 767 F.2d 229 (5th Cir. 1985), the court needed to decide whether the vessel owner, the long-term time charterer, or the voyage charterer was the "carrier." (On the *M/V Gloria* facts, the Fifth Circuit held that the vessel owner and the time charterer were carriers.)

In *The M/V Gloria*, the plaintiffs had never arrested the vessel (despite the case caption naming the vessel as a defendant), and thus the in personam liability of the other defendants

8. Whoever the nominal defendants may be, their interests are often insured, either by a traditional insurance company or by a mutual insurer known as a P&I Club. Thus cargo litigation often determines which insurance company will bear a loss. Insurance issues are explored in Chapter X, *infra* at 455.

was essential to the plaintiffs' recovery. When the plaintiff does obtain in rem jurisdiction over the vessel (and the vessel is valuable enough to provide sufficient security for the claim), identifying the defendant(s) with in personam liability is not so important.

Identifying the proper forum for bringing the action is also important. Forum selection clauses have become a prominent issue in cargo litigation since the Supreme Court's *Sky Reefer* decision, *infra* at 531. The doctrine of forum non conveniens can also be important in cargo litigation. These issues are explored in chapter XIV, *infra* at 527.

U.S. courts rarely face difficult choice-of-law issues in cargo cases. Both COGSA and the Harter Act include choice-of-law provisions calling for the application of U.S. law for shipments to or from the United States. The Supreme Court upheld the Harter Act provision for an inbound shipment in *Knott v. Botany Worsted Mills*, 179 U.S. 69, 77 (1898), and that reasoning applies with equal force in the COGSA context. Thus shipments to or from the United States are almost invariably covered as a matter of law by either COGSA or the Harter Act. When U.S. courts face cases outside the scope of COGSA and the Harter Act, a "clause paramount" in the bill of lading will almost inevitably choose the governing law, and that choice will generally be respected.

Once the parties are identified, the forum is established, and any choice-of-law issues have been resolved, it is possible to focus on the development of the case. Because most cargo litigation in the United States is subject to COGSA, that will be the focus here. The approach under the Harter Act is essentially the same. We start with the plaintiff's *prima facie* case and proceed with the allocation of burdens of proof once a *prima facie* case has been established.

1. The Plaintiff's *Prima Facie* Case

Bally, Inc. v. M/V Zim America

United States Court of Appeals, Second Circuit, 1994
22 F.3d 65, 1994 AMC 2762

MINER, Circuit Judge:

* * *

The facts of this case are largely undisputed. In August of 1990, [plaintiff-appellee Bally, Inc.] engaged Odino-Valperga Italeuropa S.p.A. ("Odino"), a large freight-forwarding agency, to consolidate several shipments of leather goods Bally had purchased from six different Italian manufacturers and arrange for their shipment to Bally's warehouse in New Rochelle, New York. The shipments were delivered to Odino's Florence, Italy warehouse in early August. Odino booked the cargo in question with [defendant-appellant Zim Israel Navigation Co., Ltd.] through Zim's agent.

Cartons containing the goods were loaded into two containers on August 23, 1990 under the supervision of Gaetano Trinca of Odino. Trinca personally noted that 301 cartons were loaded into the container in question, number ZCSU 241429/4, and that each of the shipments comprising that total and listed on Odino's waybill was loaded into the container. No problems were observed with any of the 301 cartons. The other container * * * and its contents arrived at New Rochelle in good order, and are not at issue in this case.

After it was loaded, Trinca sealed container ZCSU 241429/4 by placing a high-security steel seal, number 000013, on the latch, thereby locking the handle on the container doors. He also attached to the container an additional customs seal made of rope. The parties do not dispute that seal 000013 remained intact until it was broken at Bally's New Rochelle warehouse. The same day that the seals were affixed, both containers were transported from the Odino warehouse in Florence to the pier at Leghorn by [a] trucker hired by Zim.

At the pier, the container, the truck and the chassis were weighed, and the weight was recorded on the truck driver's delivery order * * * . By subtracting the weight of the truck, the chassis and the container from the gross weight, it was determined that the net weight of the cargo inside the container was 4,400 kilos. This weight matched almost exactly the weight Odino declared on the bill of lading, 4,396.8 kilos, which was calculated from the weights listed on the manufacturers' invoices and packing lists. After it was weighed, the container was moved about 300 yards to a container storage yard on the pier, where it was stored for six or seven days.

On August 30 or 31, 1990, the container was loaded on the [defendant vessel] *M/V Zim America*, where it was stowed above deck, with other containers above and below it. The bill of lading issued by Zim on August 30, 1990 described the container as "1X40' BOX SAID TO CONTAIN" (followed by an itemization of the goods) and was stamped "Said to Contain Shipper's Load, Stow and Count."

The *Zim America* embarked for New York on August 31, 1990, and arrived at the Maher Terminal in the Port of New York, on September 17, 1990. Maher is the stevedore for Zim in the Port of New York. Later that afternoon, the Bally containers were delivered to Maypo Trucking Corporation, which had been hired by Bally. Zim did not have the containers weighed prior to delivering them to Maypo, although there were scales available in the outbound lane at the Maher Terminal. Anthony Tricarico, a trucker employed by Maypo, arrived to pick up the containers. Tricarico inspected the seals on the containers and found seal 000013 to be intact. Observing no problems with the containers, Tricarico did not request to have them weighed at the Maher Terminal and did not bring them to any of the several commercial weigh stations nearby. Since it was late in the day, Tricarico drove directly to Ship's Side Services Inc. (known in the trade as "Port Security") to store the containers for the night. Certain precautions were taken to ensure the safety of the containers, such as placing additional seals and locks on the containers' doors.

The next morning, John Lucatuorto, another Maypo truck driver, checked the containers out of Port Security. No problems with the containers had been reported, nor were there any reported breaches of security. Lucatuorto drove to Bally's warehouse, where he was met by Hiram Quesada, Bally's receiving manager. Seal 000013 was still intact when container ZCSU 241429/4 was received. Lucatuorto and Quesada cut the seal, and the truck was taken up to the loading dock. Bally personnel then emptied the container under Quesada's supervision. Quesada testified that, when the container was opened, he noticed that it was not full. Lucatuorto and Quesada counted the cartons as warehouse personnel removed them from the container. Sixty-five of the 301 cartons originally loaded in the container were missing. Quesada notified Paul Caterina, Bally's traffic manager, that some cartons were missing. Following Caterina's instructions, the cartons were sorted by invoice and packaging list. The 236 cartons received were opened and no shortages were found inside the cartons. * * * Approximately three weeks after delivery, Bally sent Zim a claim statement dated October 10, 1990 for the amount of the loss. Zim denied liability and, accordingly, refused to pay.

Bally filed this COGSA action in August of 1991. * * * Finding that the clean bill of lading issued by Zim established that Zim had received the cargo in good order and noting that Zim had stipulated that sixty-five cartons were missing when the cargo was unloaded at Bally's warehouse, the district court concluded that Bally had established a prima facie case for recovery under COGSA. [On further concluding that the defendants did not rebut that prima facie case, the district court awarded damages to Bally for the loss of the cargo.] This appeal followed.

* * *

A plaintiff-consignee establishes a prima facie case for recovery under COGSA by demonstrating that the goods were damaged while in the defendant-carrier's custody. [ ] It is well settled that this burden can be met by proving "(1) delivery of the goods to the carrier in good condition and (2) outturn by the carrier in damaged condition." [ ] "When the consignee proves its *prima facie* case, the burden shifts to the carrier to show that the loss or damage falls within one of the COGSA exceptions set forth in [COGSA § 4(2)]." [ ]

The district court found that Bally had met the first prong of its prima facie case based on the weight and description of the cargo in the bill of lading issued by Zim. "[T]he weight listed on a bill of lading is *prima facie* proof of receipt by the carrier of that weight regardless of attempted reservations like 'said to weigh,' 'shipper's load and count,' and 'contents of packages are shipper's declaration.'" [ ] A clean bill of lading does not, however, constitute prima facie evidence of the condition of goods shipped in sealed packages where the carrier is prevented from "observing the damaged condition had it existed when the goods were loaded." [ ] Accordingly, the bill of lading in this case was prima facie proof of the weight of the cargo loaded at Leghorn. However, it was not of itself prima facie evidence of the number of cartons within the sealed containers because that aspect of the cargo was not ascertainable from any external examination of the containers. Since Bally did not weigh the cargo at outturn and seeks to prove its loss through evidence of the number of missing cartons, some other evidence was needed to establish the number of cartons loaded at Leghorn. [ ] The district court had such evidence before it.

Trinca testified that he observed 301 cartons loaded into the container prior to sealing, and the number of cartons loaded into the container was correlated with the weight of the cargo through the manufacturers' invoices and packing lists. There was an adequate evidentiary basis for the district court to find that Bally established the weight of the cargo and the number of cartons inside the container when it was delivered to Zim at Leghorn. Accordingly, the district court's finding that Bally had established the first prong of its prima facie case was not clearly erroneous.

The second prong of the prima facie case—damage at outturn—is more problematic. Based solely on the parties' stipulation that sixty-five cartons were missing when the container was inventoried at New Rochelle, the district court concluded that Bally had demonstrated a shortage of cargo at outturn. It appears that the district court incorrectly identified the point of outturn. "Outturn" occurred when Zim delivered the containers to Bally's agent, Maypo, at the Maher Terminal on September 17, 1990. [ ] It was at that location that Bally was required to establish the loss.

By proving, through a stipulation, only that the cartons were missing when the container was inventoried at its warehouse in New Rochelle, Bally did not rule out the possibility that the goods were pilfered while in Maypo's custody, while stored at Port Security, or during or after unloading of the container at the Bally warehouse. It is true that there was some evidence presented, such as the security measures taken by Port Security, which Bally contends establishes that the loss did not occur after Maypo took delivery of the goods from Zim. But there also was substantial evidence that the loss did not occur while Zim controlled the container, the most important of which is the fact that the container was sealed the entire time it was in Zim's custody. The significance of a security seal in a case such as this of course will depend on the unique facts of the case.

Delivery by a carrier of a container with an intact seal does not conclusively prove that loss did not occur while the container was in the carrier's possession. In [*Westway Coffee Corp. v. M.V. Netuno*, 675 F.2d 30 (2d Cir. 1982)], for example, a cargo of instant coffee was shipped in sealed, padlocked containers. Upon receipt by the consignee, the seals were broken and it was discovered that 419 cartons of coffee weighing about twenty tons were missing from the containers. We upheld the district court's finding that the carrier was liable based on our conclusion that the consignee had established by a preponderance of the evidence that there was a shortfall in weight at delivery. [ ] Although we did not consider the significance of the seal, the district court in that case had concluded that the unnumbered wire seals easily could have been removed and duplicated. [ ] Here, there was no evidence that the container had been tampered with, and Bally does not suggest that the high-security seal had been breached. Based on our review of the record in *this* case, we conclude that there was insufficient evidence for the district court to conclude that the cartons were missing from the sealed container when it was delivered by Zim at the Maher Terminal.

Bally argues that it was entitled to judgment because Zim had the obligation of weighing the container at the Maher Terminal to prove that there was no shortfall in the weight of the cargo. The district court apparently agreed. Relying on a footnote in our *Westway* decision, 675 F.2d at 33 n.4, the court stated that it is generally the carrier and not the consignee that has the obligation of weighing a sealed container upon delivery at the port of destination. Zim and amicus curiae Ocean Carrier Conferences assert that it is commercially impracticable for carriers to meet this burden because ocean carrier terminals, such as the Maher Terminal, generally are equipped to weigh only outbound containers. Indeed, there was evidence presented in this case that it is highly unusual for a carrier to request to have an inbound container weighed at the Maher Terminal. On the other hand, there were numerous commercial weigh stations available in the area at which Maypo could have weighed the Bally containers at a nominal cost.

We never have held that the carrier has the obligation of weighing cargo at the time of delivery, and COGSA does not impose such an obligation on either party. Our statement in *Westway* is not to the contrary. There, the consignee had proven by documentary evidence a shortfall in weight at outturn; we merely noted that had the carrier actually weighed the containers at loading and again at unloading, it might have rebutted the consignee's prima facie case. [ ] By no means did we suggest that a carrier has an obligation to weigh containers at unloading. [ ] If a sealed container is weighed both when it is delivered to the carrier and at the port of destination, unquestionably it would be easier to pinpoint where any cargo was lost from the container. In this case, Bally had the initial burden under COGSA of proving that the cargo was lost while it was in Zim's custody. Had it weighed the container while it still was sealed, and thereby demonstrated a shortfall in weight at outturn, Bally would have had a better case against Zim. Having failed to do so, and also having failed to prove by other evidence that the cargo was lost while it was in Zim's custody, Bally has not met its burden in this case.

Our holding in this case is further supported by § 3(6) of COGSA [ ]. The section provides, in relevant part:

> Unless notice of loss or damage and the general nature of such loss or damage be given in writing to the carrier or his agent at the port of discharge before or at the time of the removal of the goods into the custody of the person entitled to delivery thereof under the contract of carriage, such removal shall be prima

> facie evidence of the delivery by the carrier of the goods as described in the bill of lading. If the loss or damage is not apparent, the notice must be given within three days of the delivery.

As Zim notes, the district court did not consider the import of this section because it concluded that "it is undisputed that Plaintiff gave Defendants timely notice of the missing goods." However, Bally did not provide Zim with written notice of the missing cartons until three weeks after it discovered the loss; even oral notice, through [a] telephone call from Bally's surveyor, was not received by Zim until eight days after delivery of the containers. We thus are unable to discern the basis for the district court's conclusion that notice was timely. Accordingly, the district court erred by not properly applying § 3(6).

When the plaintiff fails to give timely notice, § 3(6) creates a presumption that the carrier delivered the cargo in good order. [ ] The presumption normally is not conclusive, and it disappears from the case once the consignee comes forward with sufficient evidence that the cargo was damaged or short prior to delivery. [ ] In this case, there was virtually no evidence that the loss occurred prior to delivery. Indeed, as the district court itself recognized, "The fate of the 65 cartons is still unknown."

There is insufficient evidence in the record to support a finding that the 65 cartons of leather goods were missing at outturn. Even if we had some doubt on this point, there certainly was insufficient evidence to overcome the presumption of good delivery created by § 3(6). Accordingly, Bally has failed to prove the second prong of its prima facie case under COGSA. [We reverse and remand with instructions to dismiss the complaint.]

Notes

1. Section 3(3) of COGSA requires a carrier to issue a bill of lading if the shipper demands one. The bill of lading must generally show three things: Under § 3(3)(a), it must show "[t]he leading marks necessary for identification of the goods." In a containerized shipment, for example, the bill of lading shows the container numbers. Section 3(3)(b) requires the bill of lading to show "[e]ither the number of packages or pieces, or the quantity or weight" of the cargo. In appropriate cases, the bill of lading customarily shows both the number of packages or pieces and the weight of the cargo. Finally, § 3(3)(c) requires the bill of lading to show "the apparent order and condition of the goods." A pre-printed bill of lading form generally satisfies that requirement by including the phrase "received in apparent good order and condition" immediately before the space for describing the goods.

A proviso to § 3(3) excuses the carrier from the obligations of § 3(3)(a) & (b) in certain circumstances. By its terms, the proviso does not apply to the obligation under § 3(3)(c) to show "the apparent order and condition of the goods." Nevertheless, courts frequently cite the proviso as though it were a proviso to § 3(3)(c)—the one part of § 3(3) to which it does not apply—presumably because it is printed in the statute immediately after § 3(3)(c).

The Rotterdam Rules specify in greater detail the information that a carrier is required to include in a "transport document" or "electronic transport record" (the modern-day equivalents in the Rotterdam Rules of the traditional bill of lading). See art. 36; M. Sturley, T. Fujita & G. van der Ziel, The Rotterdam Rules: The UN Convention on Contracts for the International Carriage of Goods Wholly or Partly by Sea 220-232 (2d ed. 2020).

2. Notwithstanding the carrier's obligation under § 3(3)(c) to show "the apparent order and condition of the goods" when issuing a bill of lading, in some contexts carriers have

managed to avoid their obligation and undermine the plaintiff's *prima facie* case with a boiler-plate bill of lading clause. In *Tokio Marine & Fire Insurance Co. v. Retla Steamship Co.*, 426 F.2d 1372 (9th Cir. 1970), the Ninth Circuit upheld a clause providing:

> THE TERM 'APPARENT GOOD ORDER AND CONDITION' WHEN USED IN THIS BILL OF LADING WITH REFERENCE TO IRON, STEEL OR METAL PRODUCTS DOES NOT MEAN THAT THE GOODS, WHEN RECEIVED, WERE FREE OF VISIBLE RUST OR MOISTURE. IF THE SHIPPER SO REQUESTS, A SUBSTITUTE BILL OF LADING WILL BE ISSUED OMITTING THE ABOVE DEFINITION AND SETTING FORTH ANY NOTATIONS AS TO RUST OR MOISTURE WHICH MAY APPEAR ON THE MATES' OR TALLY CLERKS' RECEIPTS.

The tally sheets and mate's receipts contained notations of rust and wetness but the shipper had not requested substitute bills of lading. (If the shipper had requested substitute bills of lading, the buyer would presumably have refused to pay for the cargo.) When the consignee brought suit against the carrier for the rust damage, the court held that the bills of lading provided no evidence that the carrier had received the cargo in good order:

> The rust clause in capital letters specifically recites that the "term 'apparent good order and condition' * * * does not mean that the goods, when received, were free of visible rust or moisture" and provides for a substitute bill if that information is requested. The consignee * * * could not reasonably rely upon this qualified statement as an affirmative representation that the [cargo] was free from rust or moisture when it was received by the carrier. [The carrier] was not estopped to deny liability.

Accordingly, the COGSA claim failed because the plaintiff was unable to establish the first prong of the *prima facie* case. In *GF Co. v. Pan Ocean Shipping Co.*, 23 F.3d 1498 (9th Cir. 1994), the Ninth Circuit extended the *Retla* reasoning to uphold a similar clause covering "moisture, staining, chafing and/or breakage" to wood products.

Section 3(8) of COGSA provides that a clause "relieving the carrier or the ship from liability for loss or damage to * * * the goods * * *, or lessening such liability otherwise than as provided in this Act, shall be null and void and of no effect." The Retla Rust Clause (and the Pan Ocean Wood Clause) should arguably be invalid under that provision. See Sturley, *Carriage of Goods by Sea*, 31 J. Mar. L. & Com. 241, 244–248 (2000).

The Rotterdam Rules reject the result reached in cases such as *Retla* or *GF Co.* Article 36(2)(a) requires "[a] statement of the apparent order and condition of the goods at the time the carrier or a performing party receives them for carriage," and no qualification is permitted. If the carrier fails to include the required statement, the transport document is "deemed to have stated that the goods were in apparent order and condition at the time the carrier or a performing party received them." Article 39(3). See M. Sturley, T. Fujita & G. van der Ziel, *supra* note 1, at 223–224, 234–235.

3. As a practical matter, it is usually more difficult to establish the condition of the cargo at shipment than at delivery. At the time of shipment, no one has any reason to suppose that anything will go wrong with a particular cargo, and thus there is no unusual effort to gather evidence regarding its condition. At the time of delivery, on the other hand, any relevant cargo damage will already have occurred, and the parties will be more likely to be aware of it and to be gathering relevant evidence. As *Bally* demonstrates, however, when the parties are unaware of the loss or damage at the time of delivery, the second prong of the *prima facie* case may be difficult to establish.

4. Typically, a plaintiff will seek to establish the *prima facie* case by proving both that the carrier received the cargo in good order and that it was delivered in damaged condition. In some circumstances, however, the plaintiff may be able to present direct evidence that the cargo was damaged in the carrier's custody. See, e.g., *Transatlantic Marine Claims Agency, Inc. v. M/V "OOCL Inspiration,"* 137 F.3d 94, 98–99 (2d Cir. 1998).

5. **The section 3(6) presumption.** In *Bally*, the court seemed to treat the notice-of-loss provision in § 3(6) as a secondary argument. But the courts often treat the § 3(6) presumption as dispositive. In *Pacific Employers Insurance Co. v. M/V Mini Lass*, 1983 AMC 2196 (E.D. La. 1982), *aff'd without opinion*, 721 F.2d 817 (5th Cir. 1983), the cargo plaintiff's witnesses testified that 2520 bags of rice were thoroughly wetted while aboard the carrier's ship; a damage certificate issued by the wharfinger stated that those bags came ashore "wet and crushed"; and the plaintiff showed that the bags were seized and condemned by the Jamaican Public Health Office as unfit for human consumption. But the court found for defendant, stating: "Section 3(6) is not conclusive; it simply shifts to plaintiff the burden of coming forward with evidence that the cargo was damaged prior to discharge. Plaintiffs have proven only that the bags were wet; they have not proven that the contents were damaged. The contents were never examined and there is no credible evidence of the condition of the contents." For similarly reasoned cases, see *Francosteel Corp. v. M/V Sherene*, 1993 AMC 35 (S.D.N.Y. 1992); *Insurance Co. of North America v. M/V Imperial*, 1987 AMC 1480 (E.D. La. 1987). For a case in which the plaintiff managed to overcome the presumption, see *Transatlantic Marine Claims Agency, Inc. v. M/V "OOCL Inspiration,"* 137 F.3d 949 (2d Cir. 1998).

It is difficult to understand why the § 3(6) presumption makes any difference at all. The sole consequence of the presumption, as the Second Circuit explained in the principal case, is to require the cargo claimant to "come[] forward with sufficient evidence that the cargo was damaged or short prior to delivery." But that burden is already on the cargo claimant as part of its obligation to establish its prima facie case. Although the logic of the § 3(6) presumption may be difficult to discern, it is carried forward in article 23 of the Rotterdam Rules. See M. Sturley, T. Fujita & G. van der Ziel, *supra* note 1, at 160–162.

We continue our explanation of burdens of proof in the next sub-section.

2. Burdens of Proof

Lekas & Drivas, Inc. v. Goulandris

United States Court of Appeals, Second Circuit, 1962
306 F.2d 426, 1962 AMC 2366

FRIENDLY, Circuit Judge:

Mussolini's unprovoked attack on Greece on October 28, 1940, touched off a modern Odyssey whose legal consequences have occupied the courts in this circuit for more than twenty years; hopefully, this decision may end the epic.

Having taken on cargo at Izmir, Cavalla and Salonica, principally tobacco, the *SS. Ioannis P. Goulandris* docked at Piraeus on October 26, 1940, before her intended voyage to the United States via Gibraltar, a crossing ordinarily taking 25 to 28 days. Two days later, Italy attacked. The *Ioannis* was first requisitioned by the Greek Government for a short military mission. Transit of the Mediterranean having become impracticable, she was then directed by her government to proceed to the United States via Suez and the

Cape of Good Hope. She sailed from Piraeus on November 10, 1940; she arrived in the United States in May, 1941, her cargo badly damaged during the long, hot voyage.

We have previously affirmed Chief Judge Ryan's dismissal [ ] of large claims for damage to the tobacco [ ]. The instant appeals relate to much smaller claims allowed by the judge in the same opinion [ ] for damage to a shipment of 308 cases and 7 barrels of a soft cheese known as "Kefalotyri" by libelant Lekas & Drivas, Inc. as consignor and consignee, and of 500 and 350 drums of olive oil, respectively, consigned to libelants Victor Cory Company and Pompeian Olive Oil Corporation.

The voyage took place under the difficulties expectable in wartime. The Greek Government had ordered the *Ioannis* to sail in convoy to Port Said and thereafter to follow the instructions of the British Admiralty; because these orders were confidential, the vessel was unable throughout the voyage to communicate directly with her owners, although communication by way of an intermediary in London did occur during stops in ports along the way. On December 14, the convoy the *Ioannis* had finally joined, after waiting 16 days at Port Said and three days at Great Bitter Lake, reached Aden. The *Ioannis*, drawing water uncontrollably through her stern gland and suffering severe vibrations in her tail-shaft, dropped out for repairs. Due to the needs of the British Navy, drydock facilities were unavailable, so the tail-shaft had to be drawn for inspection while the ship was afloat. To facilitate this, much cargo, including the cheese here in question, had to be removed and stored on lighters, where it was covered with tarpaulins; according to the agreed summary of the master's deposition, "There were no warehouse facilities at Aden where the cargo could be taken." By the uncontradicted deposition of the chief officer, the cheese had not begun to spoil when it was so removed. Wartime conditions caused the repairs, normally taking some three days, to require 35. The chief officer observed that, when the cheese was reloaded, it was spoiling—"it was leaking though the cases and barrels and had begun to develop a certain odor." Thereafter the *Ioannis* stopped in Durban for 13 days to take on bunkers and to make some condenser repairs; later, after a fire in the tobacco, she was at Barbados for 23 days. The *Ioannis* finally arrived at Norfolk on May 3, 1941, and in New York on May 8. A surveyor found the cheese to be "Melted with a terrible stench, and worthless"; it was subsequently sold for about a sixth of what its sound value would have been. Seventeen drums of the Cory shipment of olive oil and five of the Pompeian were cut and leaking; also, the latter was one drum short.

* * *

On April 9, 1959, Chief Judge Ryan filed a comprehensive opinion [ ] denying the tobacco owners' claims, action which we subsequently affirmed [ ], and granting those regarding the cheese and the olive oil. Respondents appeal from these awards * * * .

We find no error in the granting of the claims as to the olive oil. Under [COGSA], here applicable, a shipper makes out a prima facie case by proving that his goods were delivered to the carrier in good condition and were outturned damaged or not at all; the burden then falls upon the carrier to bring itself within an excepted cause or to prove it exercised due diligence to avoid and prevent the harm [ ]. * * *

The cheese claim presents a more difficult problem. We have concluded that as to this we must reverse.

When the cheese was loaded at Salonica, all 7 barrels and 67 of the cases were stowed in the after part of the No. 4 hold, and the other 241 cases in the poop, along with 704 other cases belonging to parties not in the present litigation. The [district] judge found [ ] that the cheese "had melted and spoiled due to the high temperatures experienced on the voyage," and [ ] that the poop was an improper place to stow cheese. The latter finding, which was the predicate of liability, was cast in terms of the poop's not being "a fit and proper place for carriage of the cheese from Greece to New York via the Mediterranean-Gibraltar route...." The reasoning was that if the voyage had been made as contemplated, the cheese would nevertheless have spoiled; that the legal cause of that spoilage would have been the stowage in the poop; and that the vessel was therefore liable for the damage which in fact occurred.

Respondents vigorously attack the judge's conclusion that the poop was an unfit place to stow the cheese. They say that if the voyage had been made via Gibraltar as contemplated, air temperatures would have ranged between 53 and 65 Fahrenheit and that, although the poop had no permanent ventilators, adequate ventilation was had through an open hatch. We find it unnecessary to pass on this challenge, for reasons that will shortly appear.

It cannot be disputed that the voyage of the *Ioannis* was affected by "restraint of princes, rulers, or people" under § 4(2)(g) of COGSA. Indeed, there was a double restraint—the threat of attack by an enemy government on the planned voyage through the Mediterranean and the order of the Greek Government to proceed via Suez and the Cape of Good Hope. "'Restraints of princes, rulers, and peoples' covers any forcible interference with the voyage or adventure at the hands of the constituted government, or ruling power of any country, whether done by it as an enemy of the State to which the ship belongs, or not." [ ] This "restraint" altered the voyage from a four week trip of 5000 miles through the Mediterranean and North Atlantic, in cool November weather, to a trip of 13,000 miles and five months around Africa, with two crossings of the Equator. Outside temperatures repeatedly hit 110 and above. Even with perfect ventilation in the poop, or with stowage elsewhere under adequate ventilation, the cheese would therefore, unless it were refrigerated, have been subject to extremely high temperatures for a period of time long enough to cause it to spoil.[1] Whether stowage of some of the cheese in the poop was improper for the Gibraltar voyage is thus immaterial; "if the accident would have happened without defendant's negligent act, then such is not the cause of it." [ ]

We could stop here were it not for the episode at Aden. As to this libelant makes two claims. One is that keeping the cheese on lighters for a month was negligent since respondents should have placed it under refrigeration. The other is that, spoilage having begun, respondents should have sold the cheese rather than reloaded it. We could remand for further consideration of these claims by the district judge who, on his view of the case, did not reach them. However, all the evidence is before us, most of it was given by deposition, and we think it best to bring this long litigation to an end.

It will be convenient first to consider the claim as to the master's duty to sell. We do not doubt that circumstances may arise when the master of a ship has not merely the authority but, under § 3(2) of COGSA, the duty to sell cargo that is at risk of further deterioration, communicating with the owner if that is feasible but still having both the authority and duty if it is not. [ ] This duty exists even if the cause of the deterioration is an excepted cause [ ]. If the spoilage had been detected early in the *Ioannis*' stay at Aden, the master would thus have been bound to endeavor to communicate with the owners via London and, failing contrary instructions, to try to sell the cheese since, even

1. During the summer it is the practice to refrigerate cheese of the sort here involved even for the Gibraltar voyage, precisely because spoilage is otherwise likely, ventilation or no ventilation. However, the bill of lading under which the cheese was shipped provides that "specially cooled stowage is not to be furnished unless contracted for at an increased freight rate." Lekas & Drivas did not so contract; indeed, the *Ioannis* was known not to have refrigeration available.

if the price at Aden were well below what had been expected at New York, it still might substantially exceed what would be realized after further spoilage. On the other hand, if the spoilage was not detected until the reloading, it would be imposing a rather heavy burden to say, "now in the peace of a quiet chamber" [ ] that the master was required further to postpone the already long postponed departure from Aden in order to achieve some possible mitigation of the damages on this relatively small part of the *Ioannis'* cargo, at the cost of perhaps enhancing the risk to the larger part. The only evidence as to the time of detection of the spoilage is the chief officer's deposition; although far from conclusive, this tends rather to the view that the spoilage was discovered only when the cheese was reloaded. Very likely the foregoing should be further qualified in the sense that the *Ioannis* was bound to maintain some surveillance while the cargo was on the lighters. As to this the evidence is simply that there were four watchmen on each lighter to see that the cargo was properly ventilated and protected from the elements; whether due diligence on their part would have detected the spoilage before the reloading, the evidence does not disclose.

Decision therefore turns, as it so often does in claims of this sort, upon the burden of proof. The classic statement, in *Clark v. Barnwell*, 53 U.S. 272, 280 (1851), is that when a carrier has discharged the burden of showing the existence of an excepting cause, "in this stage and posture of the case, the burden is upon the plaintiff to establish the negligence, as the affirmative lies upon him." From this respondents could argue that, they having shown the "cause" of the loss to be the restraint of princes, the burden of proof shifted back to the libelant. However, libelant might be expected to counter with the statement, in *Schnell v. The Vallescura*, 293 U.S. 296, 306 (1934), that "Where the state of the proof is such as to show that the damage is due either to an excepted peril or to the carrier's negligent care of the cargo, it is for him to bring himself within the exception or to show that he has not been negligent."

In fact, neither Supreme Court decision is directly in point. The respondents in *Clark v. Barnwell* had not only established a peril of the sea as a cause but had negated all others; libelants in that case not merely failed to sustain a burden, but no evidence of negligence "is found in the record" [ ]. *Schnell v. The Vallescura*, decided under the Harter Act, was a case in which the ship proved an excepted cause to have been at work and the libelant showed that negligence was also operative; the decision was that the carrier then had to show how much of the damage resulted from the excepted cause or suffer the whole liability. Here respondents proved the restraint of princes to be a cause in the important practical sense that otherwise the stop at Aden and the hot voyage around Africa would not have occurred. However, it might be argued that the possibility that diligence with respect to the cargo at Aden would have reduced the loss is sufficient to cancel recognition of the restraint as the "legal" cause unless the carrier also proves that it discharged its duty, under §3(2) of COGSA, "properly and carefully [to] load, handle, stow, carry, keep, care for, and discharge the goods carried"—in other words, that the mere raising of the issue as to the carrier's duty to sell places the burden of persuasion back where the shipper's evidence of delivery in good condition and outturn in bad had put it originally. [ ]

Such a contention gives inadequate weight to the division, made in §4(2) of COGSA, between the specifically excepted causes (a)–(p) and the "catch-all" (q), to wit, "Any other cause arising without the actual fault and privity of the carrier and without the fault or neglect of the agents or servants of the carrier, but the burden of proof shall be on the person claiming the benefit of this exception to show that neither the actual fault or privity of the carrier nor the fault or neglect of the agents or servants of the carrier contributed to the loss or damage." To hold that when a carrier has shown that the loss arose as a consequence of restraint of princes, § 4(2)(g), it still has the burden of negating any other fault or neglect of its agents or servants would be to read the qualification of (q) into (a)–(p), although Congress did not put it there. It follows that libelant had the burden of showing circumstances from which a trier of the facts could properly conclude that the master's failure to dispose of the cheese at Aden was a breach of § 3(2). Had libelant done this, we would have a parallel to *Schnell v. The Vallescura*, with one cause proved to be excepted and the other not, and the teaching of that case, which we assume to be applicable to COGSA in this respect, would then place upon respondents the burden of showing how much of the damages came from the excepted as distinguished from the unexcepted cause. However, libelant did not sustain the burden required to bring it to that stage.

The same analysis disposes of the claim with respect to failure to refrigerate during the stay at Aden, even if we were to assume in libellant's favor that this omission, since it contributed to the spoilage, could be a basis of liability when it was already inevitable that the cheese would spoil, from an excepted cause, on the hot voyage around Africa. [ ] The only evidence that refrigeration might have been obtainable was general testimony of a witness for libelant, clearly referring to normal conditions, that "they have refrigeration at Aden." Even assuming that this sufficed to raise an issue of negligence, clearly, in the face of the master's deposition that no warehouse facilities of any kind were available at Aden when the *Ioannis* was there, it did not meet a burden of proof.[2]

The decree in favor of libelants Pompeian Olive Oil Corporation and Victor Cory is affirmed; the decree in favor of libelant Lekas & Drivas, Inc. is reversed and the libel dismissed.

Notes

1. The principal case describes the burden of proof structure in COGSA cases. As the court makes clear, once the case moves past Stage One—the plaintiff's prima facie case—each stage entails a full-blown burden of producing evidence and of persuading the trier of fact.

2. **The basic burden-of-proof structure.** The Harter/COGSA burden-of-proof structure has sometimes been analogized to a ping-pong game because the burden moves back and forth between the plaintiff and the defendant. The ping-pong analogy is a useful reminder that the burden is divided, but it can be misleading, because a ping-pong ball travels back and forth in chronological order. The Harter/COGSA burden of proof does *not* shift in chronological order; the burden-of-proof structure is a conceptual grid that is superimposed upon a trial after the event rather than a description of steps taken by the parties in chronological order. (A trial is nothing like a ping-pong game; it is more like an opera.)

In *Nitram, Inc. v. Cretan Life*, 599 F.2d 1359, 1373 (5th Cir. 1979), the Court enumerated the four main burden-of-proof stages as follows:

> The plaintiff * * * must establish a prima facie case by proving both delivery of the goods to the carrier in good condition and outturn by the carrier in damaged condition. [If plaintiff does that, the carrier] bears the burden of showing that

2. No contention is now made that the stop for repairs was caused by unseaworthiness. Chief Judge Ryan found there was none, and we affirmed that finding on the [first] appeal * * * .

> the loss or damage falls within one of the COGSA exceptions set forth in § 4(2). Once that burden is satisfied, the burden shifts back to the plaintiff to show that the carrier's negligence contributed to the damage or loss. [If the plaintiff satisfies that burden], the burden then shifts to the carrier to segregate the portion of the damage due to the excepted cause from that portion resulting from its own negligence.

3. **Variations on the basic structure.** As we will see in Sections E-1 and E-3, *infra* at 303 & 307, the burden of proof scheme differs somewhat under COGSA § 4(2)(b) (the fire exception) and COGSA § 4(2)(q) (the so-called "catch-all" exception). Moreover, the explicit language of the second sentence of COGSA § 4(1) brings a potential wrinkle into the *Nitram* court's picture. In *In re Tecomar S.A.*, 765 F. Supp. 1150, 1173–74 (S.D.N.Y. 1991), the carrier's defense was "perils of the sea," COGSA § 4(2)(c); the shipper countered with an assertion that unseaworthiness caused the damage, COGSA § 4(1); and the court explained:

> Since Tecomar has conceded that it received the cargo in good order and condition, and that it failed to deliver the cargo to the owners and consignees, Claimants have met [the Stage One] burden. * * * Tecomar must [then] establish that the weather encountered by the ship constituted a peril of the sea and that the peril caused the loss. If Tecomar succeeds, the burden shifts to Claimants to establish that the vessel was unseaworthy and that the unseaworthiness was at least a concurrent cause of the loss. Even if this is proven, however, Tecomar can still avoid liability under COGSA if it shows that it exercised due diligence in attempting to make the [vessel] seaworthy.

It might be useful to think of the possibility that the shipper can prove that unseaworthiness contributed to the loss as Stage Three-A and of the possibility that the carrier can negate responsibility for unseaworthiness-caused loss by proving due diligence as Stage Three-B.

4. Article 17 of the Rotterdam Rules largely codifies the burdens of proof described in the principal case. See M. Sturley, T. Fujita & G. van der Ziel, The Rotterdam Rules: The UN Convention on Contracts for the International Carriage of Goods Wholly or Partly by Sea 101-124 (2d ed. 2020).

5. **Stage Four.** In *Schnell v. The Vallescura*, 293 U.S. 296, 306 (1934), a cargo of onions decayed as a result of inadequate ventilation. During the voyage, the ventilators and hatches were sometimes closed by necessity, due to bad weather, and were sometimes closed without justification, which constituted negligence in the care and custody of the cargo. The carrier was exempt from liability for the former cause, but not for the latter. The Second Circuit held that the burden was on the cargo claimant to prove the extent of its damage due to the carrier's negligence. The Supreme Court, reversing, held that "the carrier must bear the entire loss where it appears that the injury to cargo is due either to sea peril or negligent stowage, or both, and he fails to show what damage is attributable to sea peril." 293 U.S. at 306. Although *The Vallescura* arose under the Harter Act, the carrier is subject to the same burden under COGSA. See, e.g., *Vana Trading Co. v. S.S. Mette Skou*, 556 F.2d 100, 105 (2d Cir. 1977).

Under the Rotterdam Rules, the allocation of risk would change. Each party would bear an equal burden—the cargo claimant in showing a cause for which the carrier is responsible, and the carrier in showing a cause for which it is exempt. See art. 17(6); M. Sturley, T. Fujita & G. van der Ziel, *supra* note 4, at 124–127.

E. Excepted Perils

1. Nautical fault—COGSA § 4(2)(a)

Although the following case arose under the Harter Act (see *supra* at 279), its analysis continues to be relevant under the corresponding provisions of COGSA.

The Germanic (Oceanic Steam Navigation Co. v. Aitken)

Supreme Court of the United States, 1905
196 U.S. 589, 25 S. Ct. 317, 49 L. Ed. 610

MR. JUSTICE HOLMES delivered the opinion of the court.

This writ of certiorari brings up the record of two cases which were tried together upon libels filed by cargo owners and underwriters to recover for water damage done to goods on board the steamship Germanic. [ ] The steamer reached her pier in New York at about noon, Saturday, February 11, 1899. She was heavily coated with ice, estimated by the courts below at not less than 213 tons, and this weight was increased by a heavy fall of snow after her arrival. She was thirty-six hours late, and in order to sail at her regular time on the following Wednesday, began to discharge cargo from all of her five hatches at once. At the same time she was taking in coal from coal barges on both sides, to that end being breasted off from the dock twenty-five or thirty feet on her port side. At about 4 P.M. on Monday, February 13, she had discharged about 1370 out of her 1650 tons of cargo, including all but about 155 tons in the lower hold, the other 125 tons being on the orlop and steerage decks. She then had a starboard list of about 8°. At that moment she suddenly rolled over from starboard to port and kept a port list of 9° or more. As she rolled over the open cover of an aft coal port, about 33 inches by 22, was knocked off, leaving the bottom of the coal port about a foot above the water line. Thereupon the master, who previously had given no attention to the discharge of cargo and loading of coal, ordered that coaling should be stopped on the port side but continued on the starboard, that no more cargo should be taken from the lower hold, and that some sugar in bags should be shifted to the starboard side.

When ten tons of sugar had been shifted, at 4:45 P.M., the steamer rolled back to starboard with a list of eight degrees as before. Coaling was resumed on the port side but at 6 was stopped on the starboard side. Between 6 and 9 P.M. all her side pockets were filled with coal up to the main deck, except one on the starboard, which lacked about thirty tons of being full. Some twenty or twenty-five tons were run into her cross bunkers in the lower part of the ship, which previously were about half full. About fifty tons of goods were discharged from the orlop and steerage docks, and about sixty tons of bacon were put on board and distributed evenly in the bottom of hold. From 4:45 to 9 the starboard list was increasing constantly. At a little after 9 the steamer suddenly rolled over again to port, carrying the lower part of the open coal port below the water line. The pumps could not control the inflowing water and the ship sank before relief could be got. The damage to the goods was caused in this way.

The [carrier] argues that the danger could not have been foreseen and that there was no negligence, attributing the loss to an unusual gale and special circumstances. But the District Court and the Circuit Court of Appeals agree that the loss was due to hurried and imprudent unloading, which brought the center of gravity of the ship five or six inches above the metacenter. As usual we accept their finding. * * *

[The question] is whether the damage to the cargo was "damage or loss resulting from faults or errors in navigation or in the management of said vessel," as was set up in the answers, in which case the owner was exempted from liability by § 3 of the Harter Act, or whether it was "loss or damage arising from negligence, fault, or failure in proper loading, stowage, custody, care, or proper delivery" of merchandise under § 1 of the same, in which case he could not stipulate to be exempt. * * *

The [carrier] contends that any dealing with the ship or cargo which affects the fitness of the ship to carry her cargo is "management of the vessel," within the meaning of § 3. * * * [T]he argument is that cargo has also a function as ballast, that if, for instance, the loss is caused by the improper shifting of pigs of lead, it does not matter whether they are called ballast or cargo, but in either case, so far as the change affects the fitness of the ship as a carrier, it is management of the vessel within the act. The thing done is the same and the name of the object cannot affect the result.

Nevertheless, in a practical sense, the ship was not under management at the time, but was the inert ground or floor of activities that looked not to her, but to getting the cargo ashore. And this consideration brings to light the limitation of the section * * * to faults "primarily connected with the navigation or the management of the vessel and not with the cargo." [ ] In the case supposed the name given to the pigs of lead is not important in itself, to be sure, but may indicate a difference in the purpose and character of the change of place. If the primary purpose is to affect the ballast of the ship, the change is management of the vessel, but if, as in view of the findings we must take to have been the case here, the primary purpose is to get the cargo ashore, the fact that it also affects the trim of the vessel does not make it the less a fault of the class which the first section removes from the operation of the third. We think it plain that a case may occur which, in different aspects, falls within both sections, and if this be true, the question which section is to govern must be determined by the primary nature and object of the acts which cause the loss.

A distinction was hinted at in argument based on the fact that the damage was not to the cargo removed, but to that left behind in the ship. If the damage was attributable to negligence in unloading, it does not matter what part of the cargo is injured. The fact referred to does bring out, however, that the negligence in removing the cargo was negligence only because of its probable effect on the ship, and was negligence towards the remaining cargo, only through its effect on the ship. But, although this may be conceded, the criterion which we have given is undisturbed. That "in" which, as the statute puts it, the fault was shown was not management of the vessel, but unloading cargo; and, although it was fault only by reason of its secondary bearing, the primary object determines the class to which it belongs.

It is settled by repeated decisions that the Harter Act will be applied to foreign vessels in suits brought in the United States. *The Scotland*, 105 U.S. 24 [1882]; *The Chattahoochee*, 173 U.S. 540 [1899]. The [carrier] sets up the act and relies upon it. Under the cases it must take the burdens with the benefits, and no discussion of the terms of the bills of lading, if they might lead to a greater limitation of liability, is necessary. *Knott v. Botany Mills*, 179 U.S. 69 [1900]; *The Kensington*, 183 U.S. 263, 269 [1901]. * * *

Decree affirmed.

Notes

1. In recent years, the trend in the United States has been decidedly against carriers who seek to rely on the nautical fault exception. As *The Germanic* illustrates, a fine line

often exists between negligence in the care and custody of the cargo and negligence in the navigation or management of the vessel. A similar fine line separates the failure to exercise due diligence to furnish a seaworthy vessel (for which the carrier is responsible under the Harter Act or COGSA) from negligence in the navigation or management of the vessel. Moreover, providing a competent crew is part of the carrier's seaworthiness obligation. In other words, the carrier who argues that the crew was negligent in the navigation or management of the vessel must be careful not to show that the crew was so prone to negligence that the vessel was unseaworthy at the commencement of the voyage. If the vessel was unseaworthy as the result of an incompetent crew, the court is likely to hold the carrier liable for the failure to exercise due diligence.

A good illustration of the dilemma facing carriers (and the recent trend in U.S. decisions on the nautical fault defense) is *In re Complaint of G&G Shipping Co. Ltd. of Anguilla*, 767 F. Supp. 398, 412 (D. P.R. 1991). Two vessels collided when the helmsman of the smaller vessel inexplicably and without warning made a sudden turn into the path of an oncoming vessel that was 106 times as large. That might seem to be the very definition of an "error in navigation," but "the Court [found] that [the helmsman's] sudden turn to port was not the result of an instantaneous navigational error; rather it was a consequence of incompetence immanent in the [smaller vessel] before she ever left port. This unseaworthiness is directly attributable to [the owner]."

2. The nautical fault provision has probably been the most criticized section in COGSA, and its defenders have had difficulty formulating a convincing policy justification for retaining the defense. The Hamburg Rules (see *supra* at 282–84) and the Rotterdam Rules (see *supra* at 284–85) both eliminate the defense.

2. Fire—COGSA § 4(2)(b)

Fire is perhaps the most frightening prospect for a ship at sea (even a modern ship of predominantly metal construction), as demonstrated in such notorious disasters as the *Morro Castle*, in which a passenger liner caught fire eight miles off the coast of New Jersey in 1934 and 133 people died. Fire also causes special problems in cargo damage litigation, not only because it tends to destroy relevant evidence along with the cargo but also because the cargo itself is often the cause of the fire. The law's special treatment of fire in cargo damage cases goes back to the Fire Statute of 1851, which was section 1 of the Limitation Act and is now codified (in substantially the same terms) at 46 U.S.C. § 30504. That legislation provided that the vessel owner was not responsible for losses caused by fire on board "unless [the] fire is caused by the design or neglect of [the] owner." The same concept was adopted internationally in the Hague Rules, and thus recodified in U.S. law as COGSA § 4(2)(b). COGSA also explicitly preserves the substantially identical Fire Statute from implied repeal. See COGSA § 8.

The fire exception causes confusion under U.S. law primarily because the burden-of-proof structure is modified. As with the much-criticized "error in navigation" exception (COGSA § 4(2)(a), see *supra* at 301–03), the carrier escapes liability for cargo loss or damage caused by fire unless the carrier has "personal" responsibility for the fire (meaning that the fire was caused by the fault of senior, shore-side management rather than the negligence of the captain and crew). To further complicate matters, courts of appeals have disagreed on the proper burden-of-proof structure. Compare, e.g., *Complaint of Ta Chi Navigation (Panama) Corp.*, 677 F.2d 225, 229 (2d Cir. 1982), with *Sunkist Growers v. Adelaide Shipping Lines, Ltd.*, 603 F.2d 1327 (9th Cir. 1979). As other circuits followed *Ta*

Chi, however, and as the Ninth Circuit in *In re Damodar Bulk Carriers*, 903 F.2d 675 (9th Cir. 1990), retreated from *Sunkist*, the best statement of the current law is as follows:

> [T]he initial burden is on Cargo (shipper) to prove "good order-bad order"—that he delivered the goods to the carrier in apparent good order and condition and that, upon return, they were damaged. [ ] Once Cargo has done so, the burden shifts to the Carrier to prove that the harm was caused by one of the statutorily excepted causes. * * * Once a fire exists, the defense of fire also protects the Carrier from losses resulting from steps taken to extinguish the fire, provided there is no actual fault or privity of the owner concerning the [origin of the fire or the] firefighting efforts. [ ]
>
> Once the Carrier shows that the loss or damage was caused by fire, the burden of proof shifts back onto Cargo to prove that the fire was "caused by the design or neglect" of the shipowner. Thus, the burden is on the Cargo to identify by a preponderance of the evidence the cause of the fire, and also to establish that the cause was due to the "actual fault or privity" of the Carrier. [ ] * * * Cargo's burden is not satisfied by proving that the fire was caused by the negligence of the master or crew. "Neglect of such owner" means personal neglect of the owner, or, in case of a corporate owner, negligence of its managing officers or agents. [ ]

Westinghouse Electric Corp. v. M/V "Leslie Lykes," 734 F.2d 199, 206–07 (5th Cir. 1984).

The Hamburg Rules, which otherwise eliminate § 4(2)'s "catalogue of defenses," retain special treatment for fire. More specifically, article 5(4) allocates the burden of proof in fire cases completely differently than in all other cases. To recover, the claimant must prove the negligence of the carrier or its servants or agents in causing the fire, failing to extinguish it, or failing to mitigate its consequences. For other types of loss, the burden under the Hamburg Rules is on the carrier to prove its lack of fault.

The Rotterdam Rules eliminate the special treatment of fire. Under article 17(3)(f), fire remains an excepted peril and is treated in the same way as other excepted perils (with no special rules or burdens of proof). See M. STURLEY, T. FUJITA & G. VAN DER ZIEL, THE ROTTERDAM RULES: THE UN CONVENTION ON CONTRACTS FOR THE INTERNATIONAL CARRIAGE OF GOODS WHOLLY OR PARTLY BY SEA 114-115 (2d ed. 2020).

3. Perils of the Sea—COGSA § 4(2)(c)

Thyssen Inc. v. S/S Eurounity

United States Court of Appeals, Second Circuit, 1994
21 F.3d 533, 1994 AMC 1639

MINER, Circuit Judge:

* * *

[Plaintiffs Thyssen, Inc. and Associated Metals & Minerals Corp.] are importers of steel products. They purchased a quantity of hot rolled steel in Europe for the purpose of resale and made arrangements to ship the steel from Antwerp, Belgium to Charleston, Jacksonville, Savannah, and Houston aboard the defendant vessel *S/S Eurounity* ("Vessel"). Defendant Atlantic Lines S.A., the charterer of the Vessel, issued negotiable bills of lading for the cargo.]

On or about December 6, 1988, prior to the loading of the cargo, Atlantic Lines had entered into a charter party with [defendant Licetus Shipping, Inc.], the owner of the Vessel.

Licetus warranted that the hull, machinery and equipment were in a "thoroughly efficient state" and that, on her delivery, the Vessel was "ready to receive ... cargo with clean-swept holds and [was] tight, staunch, strong and in every way fitted for ... service." Licetus additionally "guaranteed" the Vessel's hatch covers to be "completely water-tight." * * *

During the transportation of the cargo, the Vessel encountered a severe storm on January 4, 1989. This storm was classified as an "ultra bomb" (extra-tropical cyclone) because its central pressure plummeted sixty millibars in twenty-four hours. The storm resulted in Beaufort Scale winds between Force 10 and 11,[11] waves between 10 and 11.5 meters in height and chaotic cross-seas. During the storm, the Vessel was hove to (ship's bow pointed into wind without forward motion) and her weatherdeck was awash. There is no dispute that seawater entered the cargo holds through the Vessel's cargo hatches during the storm. The Vessel's owner, Licetus, presented evidence and expert testimony to support its claim that the severe weather placed such torsional stress on the hull and hatches that seawater entry was inevitable. Thyssen, on the other hand, offered evidence and expert testimony that was intended to prove that the weather conditions did not cause the entry of the seawater. According to Thyssen, the cargo hatches and seals were not maintained properly and, as a result, were worn and unseaworthy, thereby allowing seawater to enter the cargo holds. Upon the Vessel's arrival at the designated ports, the cargo was sold to various purchasers. These purchasers demanded a discount in price due to the damaged condition of the steel caused by the seawater contamination that occurred during the voyage.

* * *

At the conclusion of trial, the district court held that the plaintiffs * * * had proved a *prima facie* case by evidence that the cargo was in good order at loading but damaged at outturn. The district court further held that defendants had failed to prove that the damage to the cargo was due to a "peril of the sea"; [and] that seawater had entered the Vessel through unseaworthy hatch covers * * * [The district court awarded damages in the amount of $336,581 to Thyssen and $19,448 to Associated. Defendants Vessel, Licetus, and Atlantic brought this appeal.]

* * *

A peril of the sea [within the meaning of COGSA § 4(2)(c)] occurs when conditions "'are of an extraordinary nature or arise from irresistible force or overwhelming power, and which cannot be guarded against by the ordinary exertions of human skill and prudence.'" [ ] The determination of whether given conditions constitute a peril of the sea is wholly dependent on the facts of each case and is not amenable to a general standard. [ ] Relevant factors that should guide a court's determination include wind strength, the nature and extent of damage to the ship and the extent of cross-seas. [ ] Courts also must be cognizant that their ultimate conclusions should turn on whether the weather conditions were foreseeable, given the location and time of the year. [ ] * * *

The Vessel's peril of the sea defense is premised on the fact that the storm encountered on January 4, 1989 was unique because of the winds and cross-seas created by the rapid decrease in pressure incident to the storm. We cannot agree, however, that the weather

11. Under the Beaufort Scale, Force 10 winds constitute a "storm"—the category above "strong gale"—and wind speeds are 48–55 knots (55–63 m.p.h.). Force 11 is a "violent storm"—the category below "hurricane," which is at the top of the scale—and wind speeds are 56–63 knots (64–73 m.p.h.).

conditions created by this storm constituted a peril of the sea. The Vessel's bridge log book, which the district court relied upon, recorded Beaufort Scale winds that did not exceed a level of 10–11 on January 4, 1989. Expert testimony at trial indicated that there were significant wave heights of between 10 and 11.5 meters. We find nothing of an extraordinary nature, nor do we find irresistible force or overwhelming power in these conditions. Indeed, the testimony of the meteorological expert witnesses for both sides revealed that, for the most part, the weather conditions experienced by the Vessel were not unusual in the North Atlantic in the wintertime. [ ] Dr. Austin Dooley, the defendants' expert, testified that Force 11 winds and significant wave heights of 10 to 11.5 meters were foreseeable. Similarly, the plaintiffs' expert, Robert Raguso, testified that the weather conditions encountered by the Vessel were foreseeable. Although the Vessel experienced strong cross-seas, perhaps stronger than usual, due to the decrease in pressure attributable to the ultra bomb of January 4, both experts indicated that cross-seas generally could have been expected. Moreover, the district court also found that "the [V]essel took waves over the hatch covers throughout the voyage, suffered strong rolling and was hove to in the winds of only 6, 7, 8 and 9 of the Beaufort Scale." Given that severe storms occur on a regular basis in the North Atlantic and that the winds, waves and cross-seas experienced by the Vessel were to be expected, we conclude that the Vessel has not proven that it is entitled to exoneration based on a peril of the sea.

* * *

Notes

1. Although the principal case represents the generally accepted view of the law in the United States, the jurisprudence is not always consistent—even within a single circuit. In *Philippine Sugar Centrals Agency v. Kokusai Kisen Kabushiki Kaisha (The Naples Maru)*, 106 F.2d 32, 34 (2d Cir. 1939), the Second Circuit (in an opinion by Judge Learned Hand) found a storm to be a peril of the sea although "it was no more than was to be expected in those waters at that time." Judge Hand further stated: "The phrase 'perils of the sea' has at times been treated as though its meaning was esoteric [but it] means nothing more ... than that the weather encountered must be too much for a well-found vessel to withstand."

2. English law is more generous to carriers in defining the "peril of the sea" under the Hague and Hague-Visby Rules. When the High Court of Australia considered whether it should follow the U.S. or English approach on the question, it opted for essentially the English interpretation. See *Great China Metal Industries Co. v. Malaysian International Shipping Corp. Berhad*, 158 A.L.R. 1, 72 Austl. L.J. Rep. 1592 (Austl. 1998).

3. The carrier's difficulty in establishing a "peril of the sea" under U.S. law does not necessarily mean that a carrier is without defenses in a situation that would constitute a "peril of the sea" under a less-demanding definition. In *Calavan Foods, Inc. v. National Shipping Corp. of the Philippines*, 1992 AMC 2692, 2695 (Cal. App. 1992), the court explained:

> The fact that the trial court apparently did not consider Typhoon Forrest to constitute a "peril of the sea," which would have made it an absolute defense, does not prevent the carrier from showing, as it did, that the typhoon was nevertheless the actual cause of the damage under the "q clause" defense.

The "catch-all" exception of the "Q" clause is considered in the following sub-section.

4. The "Q" Clause—COGSA § 4(2)(q)

Quaker Oats Co. v. M/V Torvanger

United States Court of Appeals, Fifth Circuit, 1984
734 F.2d 238, 1984 AMC 2943

TATE, Circuit Judge:

* * *

[The plaintiff, The Quaker Oats Company, purchased approximately five hundred metric tons of tetrahydrofuran, a white chemical, from Mitsubishi Corporation of Tokyo, Japan. Mitsubishi chartered the *M/V Torvanger*, a vessel owned by defendant Westfal Larsen and Company, to transport the tetrahydrofuran from Kobe, Japan to Houston, Texas.] Analysis of a composite of samples of the tetrahydrofuran taken after the cargo had been loaded on the vessel in Kobe, Japan indicated that the peroxide content was well within commercially acceptable levels. Samples taken upon the *Torvanger*'s arrival in Houston from the three tanks aboard the vessel in which the chemical was carried, however, revealed peroxide contamination in one of the tanks beyond commercially acceptable levels. Quaker Oats sued the *Torvanger* and Westfal Larsen, asserting rights under COGSA for recovery of expenses incurred in purging the peroxide from the tetrahydrofuran.

* * *

The district court in this case found that Quaker Oats had established a prima facie case by producing evidence that the tetrahydrofuran was "within purchase order specifications" upon delivery to the *Torvanger* and that "at least a portion of it was no longer in that condition when tendered to [Quaker Oats]" after shipment.

In rebuttal to that prima facie case, the carrier Westfal Larsen produced evidence by which peroxide formation could allegedly be considered an "inherent vice" of tetrahydrofuran [COGSA § 4(2)(m)], and that due diligence was exercised by Westfal Larsen to avoid any other possible causes of peroxide formation. Though finding the evidence on the "inherent vice" exception to be "nondispositive," the district court found that Westfal Larsen successfully rebutted Quaker Oats's prima facie case by producing evidence of due diligence "with respect to the preparation of the loading and storage equipment, the loading of the cargo, and the care of the cargo during voyage...," thus, "return[ing] to Quaker Oats the burden to show that the peroxide formation was caused at least in part by [Westfal Larsen's] negligence." Finding that the shipper Quaker Oats failed to carry the burden, the district court rendered judgment for Westfal Larsen, the defendant carrier.

* * *

Before explaining the error in the district court's application of the COGSA burden-shifting scheme, the nature of the chemical shipped and the reasons for its peroxide contamination should be noted.

Tetrahydrofuran ("the chemical") has a natural tendency to form peroxides, especially if exposed to oxygen, unless it is chemically inhibited. Here, before shipment, the seller had treated the chemical with an inhibitor, and in fact the two tanks fully filled with the shipped chemical arrived without contamination; only the third tank, partially filled, was found to be peroxide-contaminated upon arrival. As a further safeguard against exposure to oxygen, all tanks were injected with a "nitrogen blanket" of sufficient pressure, designed to insulate the chemical from oxygen during shipment. The vessel's officers inspected the "nitrogen blanket" periodically and with due diligence, the district court found, and a water content analysis performed upon the cargo's arrival in Texas indicated that the nitrogen blanket had been properly maintained.

We thus have the following situation: If we accept the testimony offered for the shipper Quaker Oats (as the district court did), the chemical was loaded and found after testing to be free of peroxide contamination when shipped and when the bill of lading was issued. If we accept the testimony offered for the defendant carrier, as the district court equally did, the vessel's officers performed with due diligence their duty of maintaining the protective nitrogen cover that should have made exposure to oxygen and peroxide contamination impossible during the period that the cargo was entrusted to the care of the [carrier]. Consequently, if all the evidence is true, the evidence shows no cause for the peroxide contamination. However, that contamination must have resulted either from some defect in the chemical or its processing for shipment, for which the carrier would not be responsible—which the evidence does not prove; or else that contamination must have resulted during shipment from some failure of the vessel's officers or of the vessel—which again is not proved.

* * *

The district court held that the carrier's proof of due diligence in preparation of the cargo, its loading, and its care during the voyage "was sufficient to return to the Plaintiff the burden to show that the peroxide formation was caused at least in part by the Defendant's negligence." None of the specific excepting causes (including the "inherent defect" exception) [COGSA § 4(2)(a)–(p)], were proved by the carrier, so the burden did not shift back to the shipper to prove that carrier negligence contributed to the damage. Under COGSA, the carrier's proof of the remaining general catch-all exception to liability relied upon, § 4(2)(q), is not shown by its simple and to be expected evidence that its crew did all it was supposed to do (although here, however, somewhat corroborated as to the nitrogen blanket by testing on arrival). The statute provides, more stringently, that the carrier shall prove that its fault did not contribute to the accident: "The burden of proof shall be on the person claiming the exception to show that neither the actual fault or privity of the carrier nor the fault or neglect of the agents or servants of the carrier contributed to the loss or damage." [COGSA § 4(2)(q)].

For purposes of this catch-all no-fault exception to liability [COGSA § 4(2)(q)], the presumption of fault—resulting from the arrival of cargo, damage free when shipped under bill of lading, but contaminated on arrival—is thus not rebutted by simple proof of the carrier's own due diligence, evidence peculiarly within its knowledge and control during the period of the shipment of the cargo entrusted to its care. For the § 4(2)(q) exception to come into play, the carrier must first prove what that "other cause" was. [ ] But the district court found that "no one knows what caused the cargo to form peroxide in the way it did" and indeed concluded that the cause of the damage was a "mystery."

To rebut the presumption of fault when relying upon its own reasonable care, the carrier must further prove that the damage was caused by something other than its own negligence. [ ] Once the shipper establishes a prima facie case, under "the policy of the law" the carrier must "explain what took place or suffer the consequences." [ ] "[T]he law casts upon [the carrier] the burden of the loss which he cannot explain or, explaining, bring within the exceptional case in which he is relieved from liability." *The Vallescura*, 293 U.S. 296, 303 (1934).

Here, contrary to the policy of the statute, the trial court placed the burden upon the shipper, not the carrier, to explain the unexplained or unexplainable loss. Its judgment must therefore be reversed, and the case remanded for entry of judgment awarding the plaintiff the damages sustained.

* * *

Notes

1. By its terms, the "Q" clause requires the carrier to prove only that neither its negligence nor the negligence of its agents or servants caused the loss. But as the principal case illustrates, it is difficult to imagine how a carrier can carry the burden of proving a negative without showing what *did* cause the loss, and that the proven cause was unrelated to the negligence of the carrier or its agents and servants. When a cargo container arrives with seals intact but contents missing, as in *Bally*, *supra* at 289, proving what happened to the cargo will sometimes be impossible. But see *Roco Carriers, Ltd. v. M/V Dusseldorf Express*, 1989 AMC 2527 (S.D.N.Y. 1989), *aff'd*, 899 F.2d 1292 (2d Cir. 1990), in which the carrier succeeded under the "Q" clause because the evidence showed that the theft probably occurred while the goods were in the custody of a trucker engaged by the shipper.

2. Under article 17(2) of the Rotterdam Rules, the substance of the "Q" clause remains a central part of the risk allocation, but the presentation is completely new. See M. Sturley, T. Fujita & G. van der Ziel, The Rotterdam Rules: The UN Convention on Contracts for the International Carriage of Goods Wholly or Partly by Sea 109-111 (2d ed. 2020).

F. The Package Limitation

If at the end of the day—when the burden of proof has finished all of its shifts from the cargo claimant to the defendant carrier and back again—the court concludes that the carrier is liable for the cargo damage, the case is still not over. Once liability is established, it is still necessary to calculate damages. That is often a major issue in its own right. Indeed, in many cases the carrier concedes liability and the sole contentious issue is the measure of damages.

Sometimes, the measure of damages issues hearken back to basic contracts principles. More frequently, the contentious issue is whether the package limitation will apply and, if so, how it will apply. Under § 4(5) of COGSA, the carrier is generally entitled to limit liability to $500 "per package ... or in case of goods not shipped in packages, per customary freight unit." Unfortunately, the statute does not define either "package" or "customary freight unit."

Fishman & Tobin, Inc. v. Tropical Shipping & Construction Co.

United States District Court, Southern District of Florida, 1999
1999 AMC 1051, *aff'd*, 240 F.3d 956, 2001 AMC 1663 (11th Cir. 2001)

GRAHAM, District Judge:

* * *

Plaintiffs are the owners and insurers of cargo lost in ocean transport from the Dominican Republic to West Palm Beach, Florida. Plaintiffs sue Tropical Shipping (or the "carrier") for damages relating to the lost cargo.

While Tropical Shipping admits liability, it asserts that [§ 4(5)] of [COGSA] limits its liability to $500 *per package.* The parties differ as to what constitutes the applicable package in each shipment.

The MacClenny Products Cargo.

Plaintiff MacClenny Products was the owner of the lost cargo that consisted of 5000 men's jackets. X-Cell Fashions Corporation assembled the jackets for MacClenny Products at its factory in the Dominican Republic. After X-Cell constructed the jackets, it placed each jacket on a hanger, wrapped the jacket in plastic, then hung the jacket inside a 40 foot container that Tropical Shipping supplied to it.

Tropical Shipping picked up the loaded container from X-Cell's factory, and delivered it to the Dominican Republic port from which it would travel to Florida. Along with the container, X-Cell provided the carrier with a customs document called a reembarque and a commercial invoice. Both of these documents listed the package as "1 [container]", and described the shipment as 5000 units of men's jackets.

Based on the information in the reembarque and commercial invoice, Tropical Shipping issued a bill of lading. The bill of lading described the shipment as *one forty foot container said to contain 5000 units of men's jackets.* The container with the 5000 jackets was lost overboard in transit from the Dominican Republic to Florida.

MacClenny Products asserts that each individually wrapped jacket is a package, and that Tropical Shipping is liable to it in the amount of $231,557.96. Tropical Shipping, on the other hand, argues that the one forty foot container holding the jackets is the COGSA package, and that its liability to MacClenny Products is therefore limited to $500. * * *

The Fishman & Tobin Cargo.

Plaintiff Fishman & Tobin owned the cargo that consisted of 27,908 pairs of boys' pants. Minikin Togs assembled the pants for Fishman & Tobin at its factory in the Dominican Republic. According to Fishman & Tobin, Minikin Togs sorted the pants into bundles. Each bundle "was not to exceed a dozen" pairs of pants, and was held together by a three inch wide paper band. After banding the pants, Minikin Togs packaged them into 39 cartons called big packs. It then placed the big packs into one 40 foot container that Tropical Shipping supplied to it.

Tropical Shipping picked up the loaded container from the Minikin Togs factory, and transported it to the port. It also picked up a reembarque and commercial invoice prepared by Minikin Togs. The reembarque listed the packages as big packs and described the shipment as dozens of boys' pants. The shipper entered the numbers of big packs under the "packages" column of the commercial invoice. Under the "quantity" column of the invoice, the shipper listed the numbers of dozens of boys' pants. Based on the information in these two documents, Tropical Shipping issued a bill of lading that described the shipment as *one 40 foot container said to contain 39 big packs containing 27,908 units of boys' pants.*[2]

Fishman & Tobin argues that each paper bundle containing not more than one dozen boys' pants constitutes a package, and that Tropical Shipping is liable to it in the amount of $190,600.60. Tropical Shipping argues that each big pack containing the boys' pants is

2. A big pack is a fully enclosed carton with skids on the bottom and top to facilitate movement by forklifts and stacking, if desired.

a package and that its liability to Fishman & Tobin is therefore limited to $19,500, or $500 per lost big pack.

* * *

The Carriage of Goods by Sea Act and its Limitation of Liability Provision.

* * *

[COGSA § 4(5)] limits a carrier's liability to $500 *per package,* unless the shipper explicitly declares a higher value. Congress enacted the section to curtail the greater bargaining power of carriers, and to set a reasonable amount below which a carrier could not reasonably limit its liability. [ ] This congressional purpose requires courts to look not at the larger unit of transport into which goods are consolidated, but at the smaller unit, or package, into which goods are prepared.

While COGSA does not define "package," courts have construed the term to mean, "the result of some 'preparation' [of the cargo item] for transportation ... which facilitates handling, but which does not necessarily conceal or enclose the goods." *Hayes-Leger Associates, Inc. v. M/V Oriental Knight,* 765 F.2d 1076, 1080 (11th Cir. 1985) (quoting *Binladen BSB Landscaping v. M.V. "Nedlloyd Rotterdam,"* 759 F.2d 1006, 1012 (2d Cir. 1985)) [ ].

The MacClenny Products "Packages."

MacClenny Products contends that each jacket is a package, since each was placed on a separate hanger and individually enclosed in plastic wrap. Tropical Shipping relies primarily on the terms of the bill of lading, and argues that the one container holding the jackets is the single package.

The leading Eleventh Circuit case concerning containers and the COGSA limitation provision is *Hayes-Leger* [*supra*]. In that case, the court determined that the term "piece" in a bill of lading was insufficient to connote a package. In *Hayes-Leger,* the Eleventh Circuit adopted the Second Circuit's rules governing the application of COGSA's liability limitations to containerized shipping:

> (1) when a bill of lading discloses the number of COGSA packages in a container, the liability limitation of § 4(5) applies to those packages; but (2) when a bill of lading lists the number of containers as the number of packages, and fails to disclose the number of COGSA packages within each container, the liability limitation of § 4(5) applies to the containers themselves.

Hayes-Leger, 765 F.2d at 1080, citing *Binladen,* 759 F.2d at 1013–16 (holding that where bill of lading described the quantity of packages as "1" and the goods as one 40 foot container said to contain "7,990 live plants," plants were not separate packages, even if some of the plants might have been prepared in ways entitling them to treatment as packages).

In formulating these rules, the *Binladen* court decided that the terms of a bill of lading should govern, "notwithstanding [the] traditional reluctance to treat a container as a COGSA package." [ ] The *Binladen* court's goal, apparently, was to create a standard that incorporated the "virtue of certainty." [ ]

With the predictability that the *Binladen* standard bestows, shippers are better prepared to determine whether they should place the risk of loss on a carrier or third-party insurer, rather than gamble on COGSA's liability limitation. [ ]

The Act itself provides a vehicle through which a shipper can place the risk of loss on a carrier. COGSA limits a carrier's liability to $500 per package, "unless the nature and value of such goods have been declared by the shipper before shipment and inserted on the bill of lading." COGSA § 4(5) [ ]. Therefore, the shipper—which is in the best position to assess the value of its cargo—can opt out of the Act's limitation by declaring the nature and value of its shipment on the bill of lading. This option, of course, comes with a price. If a shipper declares a higher value for its goods on the bill of lading, it will necessarily pay a higher rate for shipment of the goods. [ ]

In addition to placing the risk on the carrier, a shipper has a second option. It may elect to insure its goods with a third-party insurer.[13] If the shipper, however, is reluctant to either shift the risk to the carrier and pay a higher rate, or insure the goods, and instead chooses to gamble on safe delivery, the shipper should not later be allowed to argue before a court that the statute is inequitable. [ ] Moreover, it is important to recognize that only Congress, and not the courts, can cure any "unfairness" in the Act. [ ]

An important aspect of the *Binladen* approach is that a court must consider the bill of lading as the touchstone of its COGSA package evaluation. [ ] As to the shipment of jackets, Tropical Shipping drafted the MacClenny Products cargo bill of lading based on the information included in the commercial invoice and reembarque, both of which the shipper prepared. * * *

The MacClenny Products customs and shipping documents in this case—the bill of lading, commercial invoice and reembarque—all list the number of packages as "1 [container]", and describe the cargo as 5000 units of men's jackets. MacClenny Products asks this Court to look beyond these documents, and conclude that each unit consisting of a man's jacket is a package. But since the Court sees no ambiguity in the documents, it declines to stray from the *Binladen* standard which considers the bill of lading the "touchstone" of the COGSA limitation of liability analysis.

Based on the pertinent evidence before it and applicable case law, the Court finds that the term "unit" does not connote preparation in any way for transportation, and, accordingly, each unit consisting of a man's jacket is not a package under COGSA. Thus, the MacClenny Products shipment falls into the second *Binladen* rule: when the bill of lading lists the number of containers as the number of packages, and fails to disclose the number of "COGSA packages" within each container, the $500 liability limitation applies to the container itself. * * *

Based on the above analysis, the Court grants summary judgment in favor of Tropical Shipping and against MacClenny Products, and finds that Tropical Shipping is liable to MacClenny Products, its parent company and its insurer in the amount of $500.

The Fishman & Tobin "Packages."

Fishman & Tobin contends that each individually wrapped "bundle" of not more than a dozen pants is the applicable COGSA package. Tropical Shipping posits that the big packs into which the banded pants were placed are the packages.

As to the Fishman & Tobin cargo, the bill of lading that Tropical Shipping drafted did not conform to the description of goods that the shipper provided in the commercial invoice and reembarque. While the shipper described the goods as "dozens" in the commercial documents, Tropical Shipping described the goods as "units" on the bill of

13. Editors' note: In practice, third-party insurance is the option that virtually every shipper chooses. Cargo insurance premiums are generally much lower than the "ad valorem" rates that carriers charge when shippers declare a higher value for the cargo. Cargo insurance also offers broader coverage and faster claims handling.

lading. COGSA mandates that a carrier describe goods on the bill of lading as the shipper describes them in the shipping documents.[14] [ ] The Court finds that the Act required [Tropical] to describe the pants on the bill of lading in terms of dozens. Accordingly, the Court will construe the Fishman & Tobin bill of lading as having described the shipment as "dozens" and not "units" of pants. [ ]

In support of its position that each dozen pair of pants is the appropriate package, Fishman & Tobin cites several cases where courts have held that the smaller package as listed on the bill of lading, rather than the container or pallet, is the COGSA package. See, e.g., *Sony Magnetics Products, Inc. v. Merivienti O/Y.*, 863 F.2d 1537, 1543 (11th Cir. 1989) (holding that liability limitation applied to cartons rather than pallets or containers); *Vegas v. Compania Anonima Venezolana*, 720 F.2d 629, 631 (11th Cir. 1983) (finding that cartons, rather than wooden pallets, were the appropriate packages); *Monica Textile Corp. v. S/S Tana*, 952 F.2d 636, 643 (2d Cir. 1991) (holding that bales, rather than the shipping containers, were the COGSA packages); *Smythgreyhound v. M/V "Eurygenes"*, 666 F.2d 746, 753 (2d Cir. 1981) (holding that each carton, and not the container, was a COGSA package).

In those cases, however, there was and could be no dispute that the smaller unit was indeed some type of COGSA package, i.e., prepared in a way that facilitates handling, "such as 'bundles,' 'cartons,' or the like." [ ] Here, in contrast, Tropical Shipping challenges Fishman & Tobin's characterization that each dozen constitutes a package. Tropical Shipping argues that "dozen" refers to the quantity of pants and not to the manner of packaging. In support of its position, the carrier points to the commercial invoice that the shipper provided to it, and which the bill of lading specifically incorporated. On that invoice, the shipper entered the description of dozens of pants under the column labeled "quantity." Under the "packages" column of that same invoice, the shipper listed the number of big packs. * * *

Fishman & Tobin now claims that "dozen" connotes a form of preparation for transportation—arguing that the Court should view the dozens as bundles. Nowhere in the commercial documents, however, does the shipper describe the cargo as bundles of boys' pants. If it had, the Court's decision would be simpler because the term bundle connotes some form of preparation for transportation. In fact, bundle is a term that courts have used when providing examples of COGSA package. [ ] In contrast to bundle, the term dozen, standing alone in the shipping documents, does not connote that it was prepared in a manner to facilitate handling in transportation.

* * *

Accordingly, the Court grants summary judgment in favor of Tropical Shipping and against Fishman & Tobin, and finds that Tropical Shipping is liable to Fishman & Tobin and its insurer in the amount of $19,500.

Notes

1. **The per-package amount.** At the Hague Conference in 1921, the stated rationale for the package limitation was that the cargo claimant should be able to obtain a full recovery in most cases but the carrier should be protected from the risk of being responsible for unusually high-value packages when it had no idea of their contents.

14. Editors' note: COGSA § 3(3) provides in pertinent part that "[a]fter receiving the goods into his charge, the carrier ... shall, on demand of the shipper, issue to the shipper a bill of lading showing among other things—* * * (b) Either the number of packages or pieces, or the quantity or weight, as the case may be, *as furnished in writing by the shipper*" (emphasis added).

In the United States, inflation since 1936 has completely changed the real value of the package limitation: $500 in 1936 dollars is equivalent to over $9400 in 2020 dollars (based on the Consumer Price Index). In some countries, the changes have been even more striking.

Despite the inflation since 1936, most cargo carried by sea is still worth less than the COGSA limitation amount. During the negotiation of the Rotterdam Rules, the U.S. delegation (with the assistance of other government agencies) estimated that about two-thirds of U.S. imports and exports are worth less than $500 per package. The explanation is found in the tremendous changes in the shipping industry since 1936. The so-called "container revolution" (see *supra* at 282 n.5) made it economical to transport much less valuable cargo and to load fairly small "packages" into a shipping container. That combination of smaller packages and less valuable cargo means that a higher proportion of shipments fall below the package limitation amount.

The Visby Amendments provide for a package limitation of 666.67 SDRs per package. (The "SDR," or Special Drawing Right, is a creation of the International Monetary Fund. Its value is defined by a market-basket of currencies, and it fluctuates to some extent against every currency.) At 1 SDR=$1.40, the Hague-Visby package limitation is equivalent to approximately $935 in U.S. currency. The Hamburg Rules also use the SDR, but raise the package limitation amount to 835 SDRs. At 1 SDR=$1.40, the Hamburg Rules package limitation is equivalent to approximately $1170 in U.S. currency. Under the Rotterdam Rules, the amount will increase to 875 SDRs per package ($1225 at 1 SDR=$1.40). See Rotterdam Rules art. 59(1); M. Sturley, T. Fujita & G. van der Ziel, The Rotterdam Rules: The UN Convention on Contracts for the International Carriage of Goods Wholly or Partly by Sea 172-174 (2d ed. 2020).

2. **Weight-based limitation.** One proposal made in the negotiations leading to the Visby Amendments would have eliminated the package limitation completely, replacing it with a weight-based limitation. (Other international transport-law conventions, such as the Warsaw Convention governing air carriage, use only a weight-based limitation regime.) That proposal was rejected in favor of a "mixed" system, whereby the cargo claimant could recover either the package limitation amount (666.67 SDRs per package) or a weight-based limitation amount (2 SDRs per kilo, a little less than $1.30 per pound at 1 SDR=$1.40), whichever was higher in the context of the case. As a result, the package limitation applies to all packages weighing less than 333.33 kilos (approximately 735 pounds) and the weight-based limitation applies to all heavier packages.

The Hamburg Rules adopted essentially the same mixed system but raised the limitation amounts. The weight-based limitation amount rose to 2.5 SDRs per kilo (a little over $1.50 per pound at 1 SDR=$1.40). Under the Rotterdam Rules, the weight-based limitation amount increases to 3 SDRs per kilo (just over $1.90 per pound at 1 SDR=$1.40). See art. 59(1); M. Sturley, T. Fujita & G. van der Ziel, *supra* note 1, at 172-176.

Part of the rationale for the weight-based limitation was that difficult questions of the "package" definition would become essentially irrelevant because most "packages" weigh more than 735 pounds. But the Visby Amendments also included the "container clause," which provides:

> Where a container, pallet or similar article of transport is used to consolidate goods, the number of packages or units enumerated in the bill of lading as packed in such article of transport shall be deemed the number of packages or units for the purpose of [calculating the limitation amount]. Except as aforesaid such article of transport shall be considered the package or unit.

(Hamburg Rules art. 6(2)(a) and Rotterdam Rules art. 59(2) are similar.) The container clause—by treating the individual items inside the container, which are often relatively small, as "packages" for limitation purposes—defeated the expectation that the "package" definition would become essentially irrelevant.

During the negotiation of the Rotterdam Rules, the U.S. delegation estimated that about 90% of U.S. imports and exports are worth less than the Hague-Visby limitation amount. Most of the increased coverage under the Hague-Visby Rules (as compared to COGSA) is attributed to the availability of the weight-based limitation amount for particularly heavy cargo that cannot be placed in small packages, such as machinery, heavy equipment, steel coils, and the like. *Norfolk Southern Railway Co. v. James N. Kirby, Pty Ltd.* (*supra* at 60, *supra* at 127, *infra* at 320) provides a good example of the sort of cargo that would benefit from a weight-based limitation system.

3. **The customary freight unit.** The Hague Rules provided for a £100 limitation "per package or unit." When Congress enacted COGSA, it sought to clarify that "unit" meant "customary freight unit." Although there was no intention to change the meaning of the Hague Rules, it is not clear that the amendment was in fact a clarification. Indeed, foreign courts have rejected the intended clarification and ruled that the Hague Rules' "unit" is a physical unit of goods, which is legally distinct from COGSA's customary freight unit. See *Falconbridge Nickel Mines, Ltd. v. Chimo Shipping Ltd.*, 1974 S.C.R. 933, 946–947, 37 D.L.R.3d 545, 555, [1973] 2 Lloyd's Rep. 469, 475 (Can. 1973); *Vinnlustodin HF v. Sea Tank Shipping AS ("The Aqasia")*, [2016] EWHC 2514, at ¶ 59, 2016 AMC 2415, 2442 (Eng. Comm.).

U.S. courts have interpreted "customary freight unit" to refer to "the actual freight unit used by the parties to calculate freight for the shipment at issue." *FMC Corp. v. S.S. Marjorie Lykes*, 851 F.2d 78, 80 (2d Cir. 1988). When freight for a shipment is charged on a "lump sum" basis, that can mean that the entire shipment is treated as a single customary freight unit. See, e.g., *Craddock International Inc. v. W.K.P. Wilson & Son*, 116 F.3d 1095, 1108–10 (5th Cir. 1997). Recent decisions look solely to the "unit" identified in the tariff or bill of lading as the basis for the freight, even when it is clear that the freight was actually calculated on a different basis. See generally 2A Benedict on Admiralty § 168.

The Rotterdam Rules reject the customary freight unit, specifying that the 875 SDR limit applies "per package or other shipping unit." Article 59(1). See M. Sturley, T. Fujita & G. van der Ziel, *supra* note 1, at 169.

4. **Avoiding the COGSA package limitation.** Because the package limitation provision can effectively deprive a cargo owner of any meaningful remedy, many cases involve attempts to avoid COGSA's $500 per package limitation. The next case illustrates one possible approach.

Associated Metals & Minerals Corp. v. M/V Arktis Sky

United States District Court, Southern District of New York, 1991
1991 AMC 1499

John S. Martin, Jr., D.J.:

This is an admiralty and maritime action commenced pursuant to Rule 9(h) of the Federal Rules of Civil Procedure for damages arising out of a shipment of galvanized steel sheets in coils aboard the *M/V Arktis Sky* from Bilbao, Spain to Newark, New Jersey in May of 1988.

* * * [A]s their fourth affirmative defense, defendants contend that their liability, if any, for damages in this case is limited to the sum of $500 per package pursuant to the Bill of Lading and [COGSA § 4(5)]. * * * The matter is now before the Court on plaintiff's motion, pursuant to Rule 12(f), to strike the defendants' fourth * * * affirmative defense [ ]. * * * [T]he Court grants plaintiff's motion to strike defendants' fourth affirmative defense * * * .

* * *

Applicability of Hague-Visby Rules

With respect to the fourth affirmative defense, defendants, as previously noted, attempt to limit their liability to $500 per package in accordance with [COGSA § 4(5)]. COGSA applies to all bills of lading which cover the transportation of goods to or from the United States ports. [ ] COGSA, however, permits shippers and carriers to agree by contract to raise their liability to an amount exceeding $500 per package. [ ] The dispute in the present case focuses on whether the language of the subject bill of lading evidences the parties' intent to apply COGSA's limitation or a rate in excess of COGSA.

This bill of lading, issued by the defendants, provides in relevant part:

> (2) *General Paramount Clause.* The [Hague Rules] as enacted in the country of shipment shall apply to this contract. When no such enactment is in force in the country of shipment, the corresponding legislation of the country of destination shall apply, but in respect of shipments to which no such enactments are compulsorily applicable, the terms of the said Convention [the Hague Rules] shall apply.
>
> *Trades where Hague-Visby Rules apply.* In trades where the [Hague-Visby Rules] apply compulsorily, the provisions of the respective legislation shall be considered incorporated in this Bill of Lading. * * *"

At the outset, it must be made clear that the International Convention of 1924 (the "Hague Rules") referred to in the Bill of Lading provides for a package limitation of 100 pounds sterling. The Hague Rules were ratified in 1937 in the United States, here the country of destination, as COGSA with its modified $500 per package limitation. [ ]

The 1968 Protocol mentioned in the Bill of Lading paragraph entitled "Trades where Hague-Visby Rules apply" (the "Visby Paragraph") refers to the "Protocol to Amend the Hague Rules of 1924," commonly known as and referred to herein as the Visby Amendments. These amendments, drafted in 1968 and not adopted in the United States, raised the per unit limitation of liability using a limitation based on gold, to 30 francs Poincaré[1] per kilogram or 10,000 francs Poincaré per package, whichever is higher. An additional protocol to the Visby Amendments, the 1979 Protocol, changed the applicable standard to the Special Drawing Right used by the International Monetary Fund, a fluctuating unit of account. [ ] Plaintiff provides evidence, not disputed by defendants, that Spain, here the country of shipment, adopted the 1979 Protocol on February 11, 1984 and that this modification is compulsorily applicable to all bills of lading issued in Spain for carriage to the United States of America.

---

1. Editors' note: The Poincaré franc is a unit of account whose value is defined by reference to the price of gold. U.S. courts convert Poincaré francs to dollars using the last official price of gold. See *TWA v. Franklin Mint Corp.*, 466 U.S. 243 (1984). By that method, the original Visby limits were $800 per package or $2.40 per kilogram (approximately $1.09 per pound).

Relying upon the General Paramount Clause's references to the application of the Hague Rules, defendants argue that COGSA, the United States' local adoption of the Hague Rules, determines the package limitation for damages to the shipment in question, and, thus, defendants' maximum liability to plaintiff is limited to $500 per package. Defendants argue, without much explanation, that the Visby Amendments are not applicable to the present case despite the Visby Paragraph because the "U.S. is not, as the second clause reads, a 'trade'" where the Visby Amendments apply. In essence, defendants argue that any shipment to or from the United States renders COGSA compulsory. This argument, however, ignores the fact that the statute explicitly permits shippers and carriers to raise the carrier's liability above the $500 per package limitation. [ ]

Defendants also appear to argue that the present case involves a United States' "trade" because plaintiff selected a United States forum in which to litigate. However, the phrase in the Bill of Lading "trades where the Hague-Visby Rules apply compulsorily" most logically refers back to the preceding paragraph. That paragraph calls for the application of the Hague Rules if they are compulsorily applicable in the country of shipment. Since in this case the Hague Rules are compulsorily applicable in Spain, the country of shipment, and Spain has also adopted the Visby Amendments, this action involves "trades" where the Visby Amendments apply.

The next question the Court must decide is whether the Bill of Lading and, more specifically, the Visby Paragraph, should be interpreted to include the 1979 Protocol or simply the Visby Amendments.

The Bill of Lading provides that, in "trades where the Hague-Visby Rules apply compulsorily," "the provisions of the respective legislation shall be considered incorporated in this Bill of Lading." This phrase does not clearly say that the Visby Amendments in their original version are the only ones potentially paramount in construing and applying the Bill of Lading. On the other hand, the phrase does not clearly say that the Visby Amendments, including amendments thereto, in force in the country of shipment at the time the bill of lading is signed apply. [ ] The Court, however, finds that the phrase "the provisions of the respective legislation" accords more closely to an interpretation which would include whatever version of the Visby Amendments is in force in the country of shipment.

* * *

Thus, the Court concludes that the Bill of Lading not only forms the requisite contractual agreement to raise the per package limitation above COGSA's $500 per package limitation, but that it should be interpreted to adopt both the Visby Amendments and the Protocol. Accordingly, plaintiff's motion to strike defendants' fourth affirmative defense is granted.

* * *

Notes

1. In view of the court's *Arktis Sky* decision, what limitation amount would the court have applied instead of the COGSA $500 per package limitation?

2. In the *Arktis Sky,* the parties agreed to apply a foreign cargo liability regime with a higher limitation amount. In the context of the case, the limitation amount was the only relevant provision of the foreign regime. Suppose that the bill of lading had provided for the application of a foreign regime with a *lower* limitation amount, or that the carrier had sought to rely on a provision of the Hague-Visby Rules that was more favorable to carriers than the corresponding provision of COGSA. Would that have been permissible?

Because COGSA applies with the force of law to bill of lading shipments by sea *to or from* the United States, in most cases U.S. courts are required to apply COGSA even if a foreign court would be required to apply the Hague-Visby Rules to the same shipment. (In the *Arktis Sky*, for example, a Spanish court would have been required to apply the Hague-Visby Rules because they are compulsorily applicable under Spanish law for shipments from Spain.) Applying the Hague-Visby Rules was permissible in the *Arktis Sky* not as a choice of governing law—under U.S. law, COGSA was compulsorily applicable because it was a shipment to the United States—but as a voluntary increase in the carrier's liability (which COGSA expressly permits).

3. Other courts have followed the *Arktis Sky* reasoning to apply the Hague-Visby limitation provisions in cases involving similar clauses paramount. See generally 2A Benedict on Admiralty § 46.

4. **Breaking the package limitation.** In the *Arktis Sky*, the cargo claimant was able to avoid the COGSA package limitation and obtain a higher recovery under the Hague-Visby Rules. The U.S. courts recognize other doctrines that allow cargo claimants to "break" the package limitation entirely and recover full damages, without limitation. The most prominent are the "deviation" and "fair opportunity" doctrines.

The deviation doctrine originated in English law and was once widely recognized throughout the common-law world. Prior to COGSA, a carrier was fully liable for all cargo damage that occurred after a "deviation"—a departure from the contractual voyage—and could not claim the benefit of any defenses or limitations of liability in the bill of lading. In addition to the classic "geographic deviation," the doctrine grew to include a range of other breaches of contract, called "quasi-deviations," such as the unauthorized deck carriage of cargo, that the courts considered serious enough to justify the harsh consequences associated with deviation. For a discussion of the origins and development of the judicial doctrine, see Friedell, *The Deviating Ship*, 32 Hastings L.J. 1535 (1981).

Most common-law countries no longer apply the deviation doctrine, and U.S. courts in recent years have generally applied it less harshly. See 2A Benedict on Admiralty §§ 121–29. Article 24 of the Rotterdam Rules declares that a deviation is nothing more than a breach of the contract of carriage, and it does not affect a carrier's defenses or limitations. See M. Sturley, T. Fujita & G. van der Ziel, The Rotterdam Rules: The UN Convention on Contracts for the International Carriage of Goods Wholly or Partly by Sea 181-182 (2d ed. 2020).

The fair opportunity doctrine is a unique creation of the U.S. courts. Under the doctrine, the carrier loses the benefit of the package limitation if it does not offer the shipper at the time of shipment a "fair opportunity" to declare a higher value for the cargo so that it can be listed on the bill of lading. The precise definition of what constitutes a fair opportunity varies somewhat among the circuits that apply the doctrine, but those requirements have generally become more relaxed since the Ninth Circuit's decision in *Carman Tool & Abrasives, Inc. v. Evergreen Lines*, 871 F.2d 897 (9th Cir. 1989). The Third Circuit has expressly rejected the doctrine. See *Ferrostaal, Inc. v. M/V Sea Phoenix*, 447 F.3d 212, 219–28 (3d Cir. 2006). And the First Circuit has seriously questioned it. See *Henley Drilling Co. v. McGee*, 36 F.3d 143 (1st Cir. 1994). But sometimes a court still relies on the doctrine to break the package limitation. See, e.g., *Krystal Inc. v. China United Transport, Inc.*, 2018 AMC 2365 (C.D. Cal. 2017). For a critique of the doctrine, see Sturley, *The Fair Opportunity Requirement Under COGSA Section 4(5): A Case Study in the Misinterpretation of the Carriage of Goods by Sea Act (Part I)*, 19 J. Mar. L. & Com. 1 (1988). For a more current summary, see 2A Benedict on Admiralty § 166[c].

Under the Hague-Visby, Hamburg, and Rotterdam Rules, a carrier loses the benefit of the limitation provisions only for intentional or reckless misconduct related to the loss. See, e.g., Rotterdam Rules art. 61(1); M. STURLEY, T. FUJITA & G. VAN DER ZIEL, *supra*, at 178-180.

G. Negligent Third Parties

COGSA § 4(5) extends the benefit of the package limitation to "the carrier" and "the ship." Similarly, COGSA § 3(6) protects "the carrier" and "the ship" from suits filed more than one year after the "delivery" of the goods. The terms "carrier" and "ship," however, are not limited. In particular, COGSA § 1(a) says only that the term carrier "*includes* the owner of the vessel or the charterer who enters into a contract of carriage with a shipper." The Act is ambiguous, therefore, as to whether exculpatory provisions (such as the package limitation and the time-for-suit provision) protect, or can be extended to protect, anyone other than the vessel owner or charterer.

The issue is particularly important when an independent contractor is involved in a transaction. Most carriers contract with independent stevedores to load and unload vessels. Thus a third party often performs the carrier's duties during operations when cargo is most likely to be damaged. Similarly, with the growth of multimodal transport, the contracting carrier may perform only part of the transportation. An independent contractor typically performs the road or rail segment of an international carriage that goes primarily by sea. And when the shipper contracts with a non-vessel operating common carrier (NVOCC) for the carriage of its goods, thus making the NVOCC the "carrier," even the ocean carrier is simply the carrier's sub-contractor (having no contractual relationship with the shipper).

If the cargo is damaged at the hands of an independent contractor, the carrier that issued the bill of lading may well be liable for the loss. But its liability is generally subject to the package limitation and the time-for-suit provision. Can a cargo claimant avoid COGSA § 4(5) or § 3(6) by bringing suit directly against the negligent stevedore or railroad that in fact caused the damage? Or is the independent contractor entitled to claim the same rights as the carrier, thus making the third-party action pointless in many cases? This section addresses these issues.

The first U.S. courts explicitly to address the issue of third-party liability held that third parties performing a carrier's duties were automatically entitled to the benefit of the carrier's exculpatory rights. In *A.M. Collins & Co. v. Panama R. Co.*, 197 F.2d 893 (5th Cir. 1952), for example, the Fifth Circuit decided that the carrier's bill of lading governed every step of the transportation, including unloading, whether the carrier or its independent contractor performed a particular service. Because the carrier itself would have been entitled to the benefit of the package limitation if it had damaged cargo during unloading, the stevedore who actually unloaded the cargo for the carrier was also entitled to the benefit of the package limitation.

In *Robert C. Herd & Co. v. Krawill Machinery Corp.*, 359 U.S. 297 (1959), the Supreme Court rejected the *Collins* analysis and held that Congress had not intended the benefits of COGSA § 4(5) to extend to the negligent stevedore that had dropped part of the cargo into Baltimore Harbor. Although the *Herd* Court decided every issue against the defendant stevedore, the decision ultimately favored third parties such as stevedores because it suggested that a properly drawn bill of lading could limit an agent's liability. Carriers therefore responded to the decision by including what came to be known as a "Himalaya clause"[15] in their bills of lading to protect their employees, agents, and independent contractors.

The *Herd* Court also offered some guidance for future cases, explaining how exculpatory clauses should be construed:

> [C]ontracts purporting to grant immunity from, or limitation of, liability must be strictly construed and limited to intended beneficiaries, for they are not to be applied to alter familiar rules visiting liability upon a tortfeasor for the consequences of his negligence, unless the clarity of the language used expresses such to be the understanding of the contracting parties.

Herd, 359 U.S. at 305. That passage became the touchstone for Himalaya clause analysis for the next forty-five years. Literally hundreds of cases addressed whether particular Himalaya clauses expressed with sufficient clarity the parties' intent to protect the particular defendants claiming the benefits of those provisions.

When the Supreme Court returned to the subject forty-five years later, it purported to follow *Herd*. As you read the following case, consider the extent to which the Court remained faithful to *Herd*'s spirit.

Norfolk Southern Railway Co. v. James N. Kirby, Pty Ltd.

Supreme Court of the United States, 2004

543 U.S. 14, 125 S. Ct. 385, 160 L. Ed. 2d 283, 2004 AMC 2705

Justice O'Connor delivered the opinion of the Court.

[The facts, the rulings of the lower courts, and the Supreme Court's reasoning on the admiralty jurisdiction issue are set forth *supra* at 60. Having determined that the contract at issue was maritime, and that the general maritime law governed, see *supra* at 127, the Court then turned to the substantive issues.]

III.

A.

Turning to the merits, we begin with the ICC bill of lading, the first of the contracts at issue. Kirby and ICC made a contract for the carriage of machinery from Sydney to Huntsville, and agreed to limit the liability of ICC and other parties who would participate in transporting the machinery. The bill's Himalaya Clause states:

> These conditions [for limitations on liability] apply whenever claims relating to the performance of the contract evidenced by this [bill of lading] are made against *any servant, agent or other person (including any independent contractor) whose services have been used in order to perform the contract.*

The question presented is whether the liability limitation in Kirby's and ICC's contract extends to Norfolk, which is ICC's sub-subcontractor. The Circuits have split in answering this question. Compare, *e.g., Akiyama Corp. of America v. M.V. Hanjin Marseilles*, 162

15. The "Himalaya clause" is named for an English case popularly known as *The Himalaya* (*Adler v. Dickson*, [1955] 1 Q.B. 158 (C.A. 1954)). The plaintiff was injured while she was a passenger on *The Himalaya*. Because the carrier was contractually exempt from liability, she sued the negligent master and boatswain. Because the contract did not have a "Himalaya clause," she succeeded. The case accordingly demonstrated to carriers (or at least to carriers who indemnify their agents and employees) why a Himalaya clause was desirable.

F.3d 571, 574 (9th Cir. 1998) (privity of contract is not required in order to benefit from a Himalaya Clause), with *Mikinberg v. Baltic Steamship Co.*, 988 F.2d 327, 332 (2d Cir. 1993) (a contractual relationship is required).

This is a simple question of contract interpretation. It turns only on whether the Eleventh Circuit correctly applied this Court's decision in [*Herd*]. We conclude that it did not. In *Herd*, the bill of lading between a cargo owner and carrier said that, consistent with COGSA, " 'the Carrier's liability, if any, shall be determined on the basis of $500 per package.' " [ ] The carrier then hired a stevedoring company to load the cargo onto the ship, and the stevedoring company damaged the goods. The Court held that the stevedoring company was not a beneficiary of the bill's liability limitation. Because it found no evidence in COGSA or its legislative history that Congress meant COGSA's liability limitation to extend automatically to a carrier's agents, like stevedores, the Court looked to the language of the bill of lading itself. It reasoned that a clause limiting " 'the Carrier's liability' " did not "indicate that the contracting parties intended to limit the liability of stevedores or other agents.... If such had been a purpose of the contracting parties it must be presumed that they would in some way have expressed it in the contract." [ ] The Court added that liability limitations must be "strictly construed and limited to intended beneficiaries." [ ]

The Eleventh Circuit, like respondents, made much of the *Herd* decision. Deriving a principle of narrow construction from *Herd*, the Court of Appeals concluded that the language of the ICC bill's Himalaya Clause is too vague to clearly include Norfolk. Moreover, the lower court interpreted *Herd* to require privity between the carrier and the party seeking shelter under a Himalaya Clause. But nothing in *Herd* requires the linguistic specificity or privity rules that the Eleventh Circuit attributes to it. The decision simply says that contracts for carriage of goods by sea must be construed like any other contracts: by their terms and consistent with the intent of the parties. If anything, *Herd* stands for the proposition that there is no special rule for Himalaya Clauses.

The Court of Appeals' ruling is not true to the contract language or to the intent of the parties. The plain language of the Himalaya Clause indicates an intent to extend the liability limitation broadly—to "*any* servant, agent or other person (including *any* independent contractor)" whose services contribute to performing the contract. "Read naturally, the word 'any' has an expansive meaning, that is, 'one or some indiscriminately of whatever kind.' " *United States* v. *Gonzales*, 520 U.S. 1, 5 (1997) (quoting Webster's Third New International Dictionary 97 (1976)). There is no reason to contravene the clause's obvious meaning. [ ] The expansive contract language corresponds to the fact that various modes of transportation would be involved in performing the contract. Kirby and ICC contracted for the transportation of machinery from Australia to Huntsville, Alabama, and, as the crow flies, Huntsville is some 366 miles inland from the port of discharge. [ ] Thus, the parties must have anticipated that a land carrier's services would be necessary for the contract's performance. It is clear to us that a railroad like Norfolk was an intended beneficiary of the ICC bill's broadly written Himalaya Clause. Accordingly, Norfolk's liability is limited by the terms of that clause.

B.

The question arising from the Hamburg Süd bill of lading is more difficult.[16] It requires us to set an efficient default rule for certain shipping contracts, a task that has been a

16. Editors' note: The Hamburg Süd "Himalaya Clause extend[ed] the benefit of its liability limitation to 'all agents ... (including inland carriers) ... and all independent contractors whatsoever.' " 543 U.S. at 21.

challenge for courts for centuries. See, *e.g., Hadley v. Baxendale*, 9 Exch. 341, 156 Eng. Rep. 145 (1854). ICC and Hamburg Süd agreed that Hamburg Süd would transport the machinery from Sydney to Huntsville, and agreed to the COGSA "package limitation" on the liability of Hamburg Süd, its agents, and its independent contractors. The second question presented is whether that liability limitation, which ICC negotiated, prevents Kirby from suing Norfolk (Hamburg Süd's independent contractor) for more. As we have explained, the liability limitation in the ICC bill, the first contract, sets liability for a land accident higher than this bill does. [ ] Because Norfolk's liability will be lower if it is protected by the Hamburg Süd bill too, we must reach this second question in order to give Norfolk the full relief for which it petitioned.

To interpret the Hamburg Süd bill, we turn to a rule drawn from our precedent about common carriage: When an intermediary contracts with a carrier to transport goods, the cargo owner's recovery against the carrier is limited by the liability limitation to which the intermediary and carrier agreed. The intermediary is certainly not automatically empowered to be the cargo owner's agent in every sense. That would be unsustainable. But when it comes to liability limitations for negligence resulting in damage, an intermediary can negotiate reliable and enforceable agreements with the carriers it engages.

We derive this rule from our decision about common carriage in *Great Northern R. Co. v. O'Connor*, 232 U.S. 508 (1914). In *Great Northern*, an owner hired a transfer company to arrange for the shipment of her goods. Without the owner's express authority, the transfer company arranged for rail transport at a tariff rate that limited the railroad's liability to less than the true value of the goods. The goods were lost en route, and the owner sued the railroad. The Court held that the railroad must be able to rely on the liability limitation in its tariff agreement with the transfer company. The railroad "had the right to assume that the Transfer Company could agree upon the terms of the shipment"; it could not be expected to know if the transfer company had any outstanding, conflicting obligation to another party. [ ] The owner's remedy, if necessary, was against the transfer company. [ ]

Respondents object to our reading of *Great Northern*, and argue that this Court should fashion the federal rule of decision from general agency law principles. Like the Eleventh Circuit, respondents reason that Kirby cannot be bound by the bill of lading that ICC negotiated with Hamburg Süd unless ICC was then acting as Kirby's agent. Other Courts of Appeals have also applied agency law to cases similar to this one. [ ]

We think reliance on agency law is misplaced here. It is undeniable that the traditional indicia of agency, a fiduciary relationship and effective control by the principal, did not exist between Kirby and ICC. [ ] But that is of no moment. The principle derived from *Great Northern* does not require treating ICC as Kirby's agent in the classic sense. It only requires treating ICC as Kirby's agent for a *single, limited* purpose: when ICC contracts with subsequent carriers for limitation on liability. In holding that an intermediary binds a cargo owner to the liability limitations it negotiates with downstream carriers, we do not infringe on traditional agency principles. We merely ensure the reliability of downstream contracts for liability limitations. In *Great Northern*, because the intermediary had been "entrusted with goods to be shipped by railway, and, nothing to the contrary appearing, the carrier had the right to assume that [the intermediary] could agree upon the terms of the shipment." [ ] Likewise, here we hold that intermediaries, entrusted with goods, are "agents" only in their ability to contract for liability limitations with carriers downstream.

Respondents also contend that any decision binding Kirby to the Hamburg Süd bill's liability limitation will be disastrous for the international shipping industry. Various participants in the industry have weighed in as *amici* on both sides in this case, and we must make a close call. It would be idle to pretend that the industry can easily be characterized, or that efficient default rules can easily be discerned. In the final balance, however, we disagree with respondents for three reasons.

First, we believe that a limited agency rule tracks industry practices. In intercontinental ocean shipping, carriers may not know if they are dealing with an intermediary, rather than with a cargo owner. Even if knowingly dealing with an intermediary, they may not know how many other intermediaries came before, or what obligations may be outstanding among them. If the Eleventh Circuit's rule were the law, carriers would have to seek out more information before contracting, so as to assure themselves that their contractual liability limitations provide true protection. That task of information gathering might be very costly or even impossible, given that goods often change hands many times in the course of intermodal transportation. [ ]

Second, if liability limitations negotiated with cargo owners were reliable while limitations negotiated with intermediaries were not, carriers would likely want to charge the latter higher rates. A rule prompting downstream carriers to distinguish between cargo owners and intermediary shippers might interfere with statutory and decisional law promoting nondiscrimination in common carriage. [ ] It would also, as we have intimated, undermine COGSA's liability regime.

Finally, as in *Great Northern,* our decision produces an equitable result. [ ] Kirby retains the option to sue ICC, the carrier, for any loss that exceeds the liability limitation to which they agreed. And indeed, Kirby *has* sued ICC in an Australian court for damages arising from the Norfolk derailment. It seems logical that ICC—the only party that definitely knew about and was party to both of the bills of lading at issue here—should bear responsibility for any gap between the liability limitations in the bills. Meanwhile, Norfolk enjoys the benefit of the Hamburg Süd bill's liability limitation.

IV.

We hold that Norfolk is entitled to the protection of the liability limitations in the two bills of lading. Having undertaken this analysis, we recognize that our decision does no more than provide a legal backdrop against which future bills of lading will be negotiated. It is not, of course, this Court's task to structure the international shipping industry. Future parties remain free to adapt their contracts to the rules set forth here, only now with the benefit of greater predictability concerning the rules for which their contracts might compensate. * * *

Notes

1. Is it sensible policy to permit a plaintiff to avoid a principal's reliance on an exculpatory provision by allowing a direct action against a negligent agent? (Is your answer to this question influenced by whether you think it is sensible policy to permit the principal itself to rely on the exculpatory provision?) Section 347(2) of the Restatement (Second) of Agency provides:

> Where, because of his relation to a third person, a master owes no duty, or a diminished duty, of care, a servant in the performance of his master's work owes no greater duty, unless there has been reliance by the master or by a third person upon a greater undertaking by the servant.

The *Herd* Court declined to apply the *Restatement.* What impact would § 347(2) have if the courts applied it in the Himalaya clause context?

2. Article 4(1) of the Rotterdam Rules automatically extends a carrier's limitations and defenses to every "maritime performing party," which is broadly defined to include all those who perform any of the carrier's duties at sea or in the ports but does not include inland carriers such as railroads. See M. Sturley, T. Fujita & G. van der Ziel, The Rotterdam Rules: The UN Convention on Contracts for the International Carriage of Goods Wholly or Partly by Sea 154-157 (2d ed. 2020). Although there is little policy justification for treating maritime and non-maritime performing parties differently, the powerful U.S. and European railroads were adamant that they did not want to be included in the new convention.

3. The *Kirby* Court gives three policy reasons to justify its new "limited agency" rule, announced in part III-B of the opinion. How persuasive are those reasons? Would the policies identified by the Court have been better served if each inland carrier were instead permitted to rely on the limitations and defenses established by the contract of carriage to which it was a party? The contract for rail carriage between Norfolk Southern and Hamburg Süd limited the railroad's liability to $250,000 per container.

4. The Court describes its new agency rule as "an efficient default rule" and declares that "[f]uture parties remain free" to contract around it. How could a future party in Kirby's position contract around the Court's default rule to achieve a different result?

5. The U.S. courts have recently begun to enforce "covenants not to sue," which English courts have enforced for many years. An effective covenant protects a negligent third party from litigation entirely (rather than simply limiting the third party's exposure to match the carrier's, as does a traditional Himalaya clause). See *Sompo Japan Insurance Co. of America v. Norfolk Southern Railway*, 762 F.3d 165 (2d Cir. 2014); *Federal Insurance Co. v. Union Pacific Railroad Co.*, 651 F.3d 1175 (9th Cir. 2011).

H. Introduction to Charterparties

A charterparty (often shortened to "charter") is simply a contract (typically in writing) under which the "charterer" is entitled to use the vessel belonging to the "owner." Although charters are an essential tool of the shipping industry, very few U.S. judicial decisions address the issue. Almost every charter contains an arbitration clause, so charter disputes are typically resolved by expert arbitrators in commercial centers such as New York or London, and rarely go to court. *CITGO Asphalt Refining Co. v. Frescati Shipping Co.*, 140 S. Ct. 1081 (2020), in which the Supreme Court held that the "safe berth" clause in a charterparty creates a strict warranty, is a rare exception.

Because the owner and the charterer have almost complete freedom to enter into any contract they wish, it is possible in theory that every charter would be unique. In practice, charters are regularly concluded on standard forms that have been developed and promulgated by the affected commercial interests.[17] Contracting parties, acting through

17. For convenience, standard charter forms are often given highly abbreviated names. Thus the Tanker Voyage Charter Party issued by the Association of Ship Brokers and Agents (USA) Inc. the charterparty at issue in *CITGO Asphalt Refining Co. v. Frescati Shipping Co.*, has the code word "ASBATANKVOY." In similar fashion, "AMWELSH" is the Americanized Welsh Coal Charter, "NORGRAIN" is the North American Grain Charterparty, and "NYPE 93" is the 1993 revision of the New York Produce Exchange's popular Time Charter. Dozens of other forms exist, some for general usage and some for very specific trades.

brokers, typically start with one of those standard forms, delete clauses or phrases that do not apply, and add whatever extra clauses they feel are necessary. Because different charterparties serve a number of different functions, they can be classified according to their function. Traditionally, a charterparty fell into one of three categories: the "demise" or "bareboat" charter, the "voyage" charter, or the "time" charter. More recently, the "slot" or "space" charter has also become important.

1. The Demise or Bareboat Charter

The "demise" or "bareboat" charter is conceptually the easiest to understand. The charterer takes possession and operates the ship during the period of the charter as though the vessel belonged to the charterer. The bareboat charterer is thus analogous to the driver who leases a car for a specified period or a tenant who rents a house for a term of years. The charterer provides the vessel's master and crew (much as the lessee-driver personally drives the car) and pays the operating expenses (much as the lessee-driver buys the gasoline). In *Reed v. The Yaka*, 373 U.S. 410, 412 (1963), the Supreme Court summarized the arrangement as follows:

> Under [a bareboat charter] full possession and control of the vessel are delivered up to the charterer for a period of time. The ship is then directed by [the charterer's] Master and manned by his crew; it makes his voyages and carries the cargo he chooses. Services performed on board the ship are primarily for his benefit. It has long been recognized in the law of admiralty that for many, if not most, purposes the bareboat charterer is to be treated as the owner, generally called owner *pro hac vice*.

The bareboat charter can serve many functions. It permits a shipping company to supplement its fleet, perhaps on a temporary basis. For example, a company may require between ten and fifteen vessels, depending on market conditions, to operate a liner service. It may therefore choose to purchase ten vessels and charter up to five additional vessels, depending on its needs at a particular time. The bareboat charter also permits a company in effect to acquire a vessel without incurring the full rights and obligations of legal ownership. For example, the bank that provides the financing may become the registered owner of a new vessel while the carrier for whom the vessel was built becomes the long-term bareboat charterer.

The subject of bareboat charters is relevant primarily in a discussion of ship construction and finance; it has little direct relevance to the carriage of goods by sea. Voyage and time charters, in contrast, form an important part of the subject of the carriage of goods by sea, and thus they will be the focus of further attention here.

2. Voyage and Time Charters

"Voyage" and "time" charters are conceptually very different from bareboat charters. The voyage or time charterer obtains the use of the ship in a more limited sense, while the owner continues to operate the vessel. More specifically, the owner provides the vessel's master and crew and (depending on the circumstances) pays the normal operating expenses, while the charterer obtains the commercial benefit of having its cargo carried. Continuing the analogies suggested above, "voyage" and "time" charters are more like taxis or limousine services or hotels than they are like typical leases. Just as a limousine passenger is carried to the agreed destination, while the limousine's owner furnishes the driver and pays for maintenance (but not necessarily for the passenger's alcoholic drinks), so the voyage or time charterer's cargo is carried to the agreed destination, while the vessel's owner furnishes the crew and pays for the vessel's normal operating expenses (but not necessarily for the special expenses associated with a particular cargo).

The fundamental difference between voyage and time charters is how the "freight" or "charter hire"—the money paid for the use of the vessel—is calculated. A voyage charterparty specifies the amount due for carrying a specified cargo on a specified voyage (or series of voyages), regardless of how long a particular voyage takes. A time charterparty specifies the amount due for each day that the vessel is "on hire," regardless of how many voyages are completed. Returning once again to the limousine analogy, a voyage charter resembles the situation in which the passenger agrees to pay a fixed fare for a specified journey (and the limousine company bears the risk that heavy traffic will slow the trip, or that road construction or an accident will require a detour). For example, limousine service between an airport and cities in the region is generally offered on a basis similar to a voyage charter. A time charter, on the other hand, resembles the situation in which a limousine is hired for the evening at an hourly rate (and the passenger bears the risks of heavy traffic and detours). For example, students going to their prom might engage a limousine on a basis similar to a time charter.

At any particular time, a vessel may be subject to multiple charterparties. For example, the registered owner of a vessel (perhaps a financial institution) may turn the ship over to Carrier A under a bareboat charter. Carrier A (as "owner") may agree to operate the vessel on behalf of Carrier B under a time charter, thus dividing responsibility for the navigational and commercial operations. Carrier A would be responsible for running the vessel, while Carrier B is responsible for finding the cargo for her to carry. Carrier B, in turn, may find a shipper who wishes to transport a shipload of a bulk commodity, and thus Carrier B (as "owner") enters into a voyage charter with the shipper. As a result, Carrier A, Carrier B, and the shipper are all "charterers," each under a different charterparty. Such arrangements are very common, and far more complicated arrangements are not unusual. In *Cactus Pipe & Supply Co. v. M/V Montmartre*, 756 F.2d 1103, 1105–06 (5th Cir. 1985), for example, the Fifth Circuit described one arrangement as follows:

> [The vessel owner] bareboat chartered the *Montmartre* to Eternity Navigation Co., S.A. (Eternity), in September, 1976. Eternity, as bareboat charter owner, time chartered the vessel to Iino Kaiun Kaisha, Ltd. (Iino). Iino in turn time chartered the *Montmartre* to Canadian Forest Navigation Co., Ltd. (Canadian) in June, 1979. In July, 1979, Canadian voyage chartered the *Montmartre* to Seanav International Co. (Seanav). Seanav in turn voyage chartered the vessel to [the plaintiff shipper].

The existence of a charterparty (or charterparties) does not make bills of lading irrelevant, despite the very different legal regimes that govern the two forms of carriage. Indeed, it is common for bills of lading to be issued even when cargo is carried under one or more charterparties. (In *Cactus Pipe*, bills of lading were issued in addition to the five charterparties that applied.) Typically the shipper, who owns the cargo and wishes to sell it, has chartered the vessel to transport an entire shipload of goods. The goods, however, will be sold in smaller quantities. Thus the charterer will need bills of lading, each representing only a fraction of the total cargo, so that a document of title can be negotiated to each buyer for the amount of cargo that the particular buyer is purchasing. So long as the charterer retains control of the bills of lading, they are simply receipts for the goods and documents of title. COGSA, by its terms, does not apply. See COGSA § 5. But when a bill of lading is negotiated to a third party, relations between the carrier and the holder of the bill of lading are governed by the bill of lading—not the charterparty—and COGSA provides the governing legal framework (assuming that it would otherwise apply). See COGSA §§ 1(b), 5.

The potential existence of bills of lading highlights a common problem in the charterparty context. When bills of lading are issued, they will customarily be prepared by a freight forwarder who acted on behalf of the shipper in arranging the carriage. The same freight forwarder, however, may be the carrier's agent for purpose of preparing the necessary documents. If the freight forwarder signs the bills of lading "as agent" when the ship is operating under several charters, it may be unclear on whose behalf the bills of lading were issued. Depending on the circumstances, a bareboat charterer, a time charterer, and a voyage charterer may all be plausible candidates for carrier status under the bill of lading.

3. The Voyage Charter

In a typical voyage charter, the "owner" (which might itself be a charterer) agrees to carry a specified cargo by a named ship on a single voyage from one specified port or range of ports to another specified port or range of ports. For example, the charter might specify a voyage on the *M.V. Lollipop* carrying chemicals from Houston to Antwerp, or from Houston to "a safe port between Bordeaux and Hamburg." In this latter case, the charterer would be required to nominate a port of discharge (such as Antwerp) in timely fashion (typically when the cargo is loaded). The freight charged will typically be based on the amount of cargo actually loaded on the vessel, with a penalty (known as "deadfreight") for failing to load a full cargo. If the charterparty lists a range of ports, it may provide for different freight rates, depending on the ports selected.

The owner may agree that the vessel will be available for loading at the port of shipment at a particular time or within a specified range of dates, or that the vessel will proceed from its present position (specified in the charter) as quickly as is reasonably possible. The vessel's normal operational costs are paid by the owner. Costs relating to the particular cargo, however, will be divided between the owner and the charterer as agreed in the charterparty. In particular, the charter typically will specify who pays the costs of loading and discharge. For example, a FIOS ("free in and out, stowed") clause imposes the costs of loading, stowing, and discharge on the charterer, while under "liner terms" those costs are paid by the owner.

Because the owner is paid the same amount for the voyage regardless of how long it may take, the owner has an incentive to ensure that every aspect of the operation proceeds expeditiously. The actual sailing, of course, is within the owner's control, and thus a voyage charter need not address those issues in great detail. But loading and unloading the cargo are often within the charterer's control. At the very least, the charterer will be in a position to influence how quickly loading and unloading take place. Thus a voyage charter almost inevitably contains provisions for "demurrage" to create an incentive for charterers to load and unload the vessel as quickly as possible.

Demurrage is the most commonly litigated or arbitrated issue arising under a voyage charter. The basic concept is that a charterer is permitted a certain amount of time, known as "laytime," for loading and unloading the vessel. If those operations exceed the allowed time, then the charterer must pay the owner "demurrage," at a rate established in the charterparty, as a form of liquidated damages for the delay. (Some charterparties also require the owner to pay "dispatch" to the charterer if loading and unloading are completed before the expiration of the laytime.)

The charterparty must define the demurrage rate (and the dispatch rate, if appropriate) and set the number of lay days that are allowed for loading and unloading. Sometimes there will be a single allowance for loading and unloading, so that time saved on loading may be used for unloading. Sometimes separate laytime will be allowed for each operation. The number of lay days may be set explicitly (for example, "five days for loading, four days for discharging") or by a formula referring to the amount of the cargo (for example, "loading at a rate of 500 metric tons per day" or "loading at a rate of 100 metric tons per working hatch per day"). A formula has the obvious benefit of allowing more time when more cargo needs to be loaded or discharged. Once the relevant values are known, the actual number of lay days can be calculated arithmetically.

Other factors make the subject more confusing. The charterparty must also define when laytime begins. For example, it may be when the ship arrives in port, or when it arrives at its berth, or when it is actually prepared to begin loading or unloading. Particular forms of notice from the owner to the charterer may also be required. Having defined when laytime begins, it is then necessary to determine which days count as lay days. For example, it may be "running days," meaning that every day counts, or it may be "working days," meaning that the days (such as Sundays and holidays) on which work is not performed in the port do not count, or it may be "weather working days," which also excludes the days that work is not performed due to bad weather.

The discussion in the previous four paragraphs merely hints at the complexity of the issues. It is no exaggeration to say that entire books have been written on the narrow subject. See, e.g., Simon Baughen, Summerskill on Laytime (6th ed. 2017); John Schofield, Laytime and Demurrage (7th ed. 2016); Hugo Tiberg, The Law of Demurrage (5th ed. 2013). For more detail on the full range of issues that arise under voyage charters, the standard reference is Julian Cooke et al., Voyage Charters (4th ed. 2014).

4. The Time Charter

In a typical time charter, the "owner" (which might itself be a demise or time charterer) agrees to employ a named ship as directed by the charterer for the number of voyages that can be completed within a specified time period, with charter hire paid at a specified daily rate. The charterparty may specify the geographic area in which the voyages will occur, or it may be on a world-wide basis. The charterer pays a defined "charter hire" for each day that it has use of the vessel. Typically the time charterer is also liable for the costs directly connected with the use of the vessel, including bunker fuel, port charges, and the costs of loading and unloading the cargo.

The time charterer may be a cargo owner with an ongoing need for transportation. For example, an oil or chemical company may time charter a vessel to transport its products so that it will have commercial control of the vessel without assuming the obligations of ownership. In this case, the time charter serves a similar function to the typical voyage charter or even to shipment under a bill of lading. It is simply another alternative for arranging the carriage of goods by sea. The time charterer may instead be another carrier who wishes to enlarge its fleet on a temporary basis without assuming the obligations of operating a vessel that it does not own. In this case, the time charter becomes a device for dividing responsibility for the vessel's navigational and commercial operations. The owner operates the vessel while the time charterer decides where she will sail and finds the cargo to fill her. Other justifications for time chartering are also possible.

For example, a speculator who believes that the freight market is about to rise may time charter a vessel to profit from that expectation.

Because the owner is paid for the time that the charterer has the vessel regardless of how many voyages are completed, it is in the charterer's interest to ensure that every aspect of the operation proceeds expeditiously. Thus concepts like demurrage are irrelevant in the time charter context, but the charterparty will typically contain a great deal more information about the vessel—particularly about how fast she can sail, and how quickly she can load and unload the cargo. Statements about the vessel in the charterparty are typically treated as the owner's warranties. It is also in the charterer's interest to ensure that the vessel remains in operation during the charter period. Otherwise the charterer would be paying for time that the owner would not be delivering. Thus the typical time charter will include a "cesser of hire" clause specifying the circumstances under which the vessel will be considered "off hire," and payment to the owner will not be due.

Another issue that arises in the time charter context is the problem of "overlap" and "underlap." As noted above, the charterer is essentially buying the number of voyages that can be completed within a specified time period. For example, in a two-year time charter the owner will be required to complete as many voyages as the charterer can schedule during the two-year period. Suppose that the vessel is now in the port of redelivery, having just completed a voyage; that fifteen days are left in the charter period; and that it would take thirty days to complete another round-trip voyage. In other words, the charterer could redeliver the vessel fifteen days early (an "underlap") or fifteen days late (an "overlap"). (It is theoretically possible that the vessel could sit idle for fifteen days, and that the charterer could then effect redelivery on the precise date contemplated by the charterparty. That is neither commercially reasonable nor legally required.) The parties' preferences will be driven by market conditions. If the freight market has gone up, and the owner will thus be able to charter the vessel at a higher rate when the current charter ends, the owner will be eager to have an early redelivery (thus getting the higher rate fifteen days sooner) while the charterer will be eager to have a late redelivery (thus getting the benefit of the lower rate fifteen days longer). If the freight market has gone down, on the other hand, their preferences will be reversed. The "final voyage doctrine" addresses the problem.

5. The "Slot" or "Space" Charter

Traditionally, both voyage and time charters were for the entire capacity of the vessel. In 1975, Professors Gilmore and Black wrote, "Actually, a charter of less than the entire ship is possible, but occurs quite infrequently. It is not unknown, however, even in modern times." GILMORE & BLACK, THE LAW OF ADMIRALTY §4-1, at 193 (2d ed. 1975). The practice has since become so common that in 1993 BIMCO (the Baltic and International Maritime Conference), one of the leading sources of standard charter forms, issued a standard document called "SLOTHIRE" to enable a charterer to obtain a specific number of "slots" on a container vessel (each slot being the space to carry a 20-foot container). Under SLOTHIRE, freight is based on the capacity booked per voyage. Freight could also be based on the capacity actually used or on a time basis.

Slot charters (and vessel sharing agreements) have become increasingly popular in the container trades, as they enable two or more carriers to combine their capacities and offer more frequent service on their routes. If three carriers all serve the New York to Rotterdam route, for example, and each devotes one vessel to the route every three weeks, they can implicitly (with slot charters) or explicitly (with a vessel sharing agreement) join forces and each offer weekly service. The first carrier would sail from New York to Rotterdam itself the first week, carrying whatever cargo its traffic department has been able to obtain and, under slot charters, cargo that had been booked by the other two carriers. In the second and third weeks, the first carrier would send its cargo, under slot charters, on the other two carriers' vessels. The carrier booking the cargo will issue its own bill of lading and, so far as the shipper is concerned, be treated as the contracting carrier. Slot charters also permit an NVOCC (non-vessel operating common carrier) to operate what is essentially a liner service without owning, operating, or (in the traditional sense) chartering any vessels. The cargo at issue in *Norfolk Southern Railway Co. v. James N. Kirby, Pty Ltd.* (*supra* at 60, *supra* at 127, *supra* at 320) was almost certainly carried under either a slot charter or a vessel sharing agreement. Although Hamburg Süd issued a bill of lading, the carrying vessel was owned by Blue Star (North America) Ltd., a different shipping line.

Although slot charters are particularly popular in the container trades, the same concept can be found in other trades (where it is more likely to be called a space charter). The charterer simply hires a part of the owner's vessel, such as a specified hold or deck, or a specified part of the vessel's carrying capacity (defined by weight, volume, or other appropriate measure). The arrangement may permit the sort of cooperative venture described above for container lines, or it may allow a time charterer (such as an oil or chemical company) to sell the excess capacity that it does not need on a particular voyage.

Chapter IV

Collision

Rules of navigation cover most conduct that might result in a collision. Included are rules governing the need for proper lookout, speed, radar, action to avoid collision, lights, sounds, and signals. For collisions on the high seas, the current applicable rules are known as COLREGS. See Statutory Supplement. Very similar rules, known as the Inland Navigation Rules, cover navigation in U.S. waters not covered by COLREGS. They are set out in 33 C.F.R. part 83. COLREGS, adopted in 1977, and the domestic rules for inland waters, which were adopted four years later, replaced a more complicated scheme under which the United States had four sets of navigation rules applicable to different waters.[1] In most countries COLREGS govern both international and inland navigation. The case below arose long before COLREGS were adopted, but it vividly illustrates the significance of violating a rule of navigation.

The Pennsylvania

Supreme Court of the United States, 1874
86 U.S. (19 Wall.) 125, 22 L. Ed. 148, 1998 AMC 1506

Mr. Justice STRONG delivered the opinion of the Court.

[An act of Congress for preventing collisions at sea (Act of April 29, 1864, 13 Stat. 61, art. 10) provides as follows:

Rules Governing Fog Signals

Whenever there is a fog, whether by day or night, the fog signals described below shall be carried and used:

- Steamships under way shall use a steam whistle.
- Sailing ships under way shall use a foghorn.
- Steamships and sailing ships when not under way shall use a bell.

Britain has essentially the same statute, Merchants' Shipping Act of 1862.] This statute being in force, the *Mary Troop*, a British bark, was bound from Androssan, in Scotland, to New York, with a cargo of iron, and at ten o'clock on a morning of June, 1869, found herself still on the high seas, about two hundred miles from Sandy Hook. A dense fog

1. For a detailed discussion of COLREGS and the domestic rules, see Healy & Sweeney, The Law of Marine Collision 71–239 (1998). The treatise remains highly relevant despite its date because the substance of the rules has remained very stable over time.

was prevailing at the time, so thick that a large vessel could hardly be seen at the distance of fifty feet. * * * The bark was under way, * * * moving [about] a mile an hour * * *. She had a bell, * * * and this bell was rung by a lanyard tied to the tongue of the bell, from fifteen to twenty times a minute. She also had a good foghorn. This horn had been used the day before, but was not used on the morning of which we are speaking.

The whistle of a steamer was heard through the fog off the port side. The second mate, who had just at that moment reached the deck, called to the captain and mate, "Do you hear that foghorn?" The mate replied, "It is a whistle," and he and the captain at once ran aft. As they got on the quarter deck, the bows of a large steamer appeared through the fog heading rapidly for the bark, and but a short distance off. The steamer * * * struck the bark stem on, on the port side of the bark by the forerigging. The blow cut the bark in two and she sank instantly. The captain, the second mate, and four of the crew were drowned. The only persons saved were the mate, the cook, and two men who were in the watch below.

The steamer proved to be the British steam propeller *Pennsylvania*, a vessel of 300 horsepower, 2388 tons, and 341 feet long. Her speed at the time when she thus appeared to the bark and coming down upon her, was seven knots an hour.

There was nothing in the evidence beyond the evidence of her speed * * * to show any want of efficiency, vigilance, or precaution in the navigation and management of the steamer up to the first intimation of the bark's proximity. She had two lookouts at their stations, "keeping their eyes and ears open for anything that might come in the way." They heard the bell of the bark, and reported, "Ship ahead, a little on the starboard bow." Order was given to the engineer, "Full speed astern," and the order was executed as soon as practicable. The helm was ported;[2] then a call to "starboard" was heard from some quarter, and she starboarded; then again ported, but in less than half a minute after the report of "ship ahead" was made, and before the steamer had run her own length, she went head on into the bark with the deplorable result already stated.

* * *

[When the steamer reached port, the owners of the bark libelled her in the District Court for the Southern District of New York, which condemned the steamer for the whole loss. The Second Circuit Court of Appeals affirmed.]

It may be that when the bark was discovered by those on board the steamer it was too late to avoid a collision. The two vessels were then not more than three or four hundred feet apart, and the steamer had the bark almost across her bow. Yet it is possible that if her helm had been put to starboard instead of to port when the lookout announced, "Bell on the starboard bow," and had been kept starboarded, the collision might either have been avoided or have been much less disastrous. By porting her helm she was turned toward the point where the bell indicated the bark was, and this apparently increased the danger of a collision.

But if this is not to be attributed to her as a fault, there is no excuse to be found in the evidence for the high rate of speed at which she was sailing during so dense a fog as prevailed when the vessels came together. The concurrent testimony of witnesses is that objects could not be seen at any considerable distance, probably not farther than the length of the steamer,

2. Editors' note: To "port the helm" meant to move the tiller to port (left), which would turn the vessel to starboard (right).

and yet she was sailing at the rate of at least seven knots an hour, thus precipitating herself into a position where avoidance of a collision with the bark was difficult, if not impossible, and would have been, even if the bark had been stationary. * * *

It is next to be considered whether any fault of the bark contributed to the collision. That she was in fault is beyond controversy. She was in plain violation of the rules of navigation, which required her to blow a foghorn. Both our own and the British shipping acts enact that sailing ships, when under way, shall use a foghorn, and, when not under way, shall use a bell. The British merchants' shipping acts expressly declare that owners and masters of ships shall use no other fog signals than such as are required by the regulations, and that if in any case of collision it appears to the court * * * that such collision was occasioned by the non-observance of any regulation, * * * the ship by which the regulation has been infringed shall be deemed to be in fault, unless it is shown to the satisfaction of the court that the circumstances of the case made a departure from the regulation necessary. Our own statute does not contain this provision expressed, but its meaning is the same. The bark in this case was under way * * *. She was constantly changing her position. It was her duty, therefore, to blow a foghorn, and not to ring a bell. By ringing a bell, as she did, she gave a false signal, and, so far as she could, assured all approaching vessels that she was not under way. There is some evidence that a bell can be heard as far as can a foghorn, and some that it can be heard farther. On the other hand there is evidence that a foghorn can be heard farthest. However this may be, the bark had no right to substitute any equivalent for the signal required by the navigation rules. * * * In addition to this it may be remarked that a bell can never be an equivalent for a foghorn. It gives different information. Both may notify an approaching vessel that the signalling ship is in the neighborhood, but the one gives notice that the ship is moving, and the other that the ship is stationary.

Concluding then, as we must, that the bark was in fault, it still remains to inquire whether the fault contributed to the collision, whether in any degree it was the cause of the vessels' coming into a dangerous position. It must be conceded that if it clearly appears the fault could have had nothing to do with the disaster, it may be dismissed from consideration. The liability for damages is upon the ship or ships whose fault caused the injury. But when, as in this case, a ship at the time of a collision is in actual violation of a statutory rule intended to prevent collisions, it is no more than a reasonable presumption that the fault, if not the sole cause, was at least a contributory cause of the disaster. In such a case the burden rests upon the ship of showing not merely that her fault might not have been one of the causes, or that it probably was not, but that it could not have been. * * * In some cases it is possible to show this with entire certainty. In others it cannot be. The evidence in the present case leaves it uncertain whether if a foghorn had been blown on the bark, it would not have been heard sooner than the bell was heard, and thus earlier warning have been given to the steamer * * *. If it be said this is speculation, it may be admitted, but it is speculation rendered necessary by a certain fault of the bark. * * * The truth is, the case is one in which, while the presumption is that the failure to blow a foghorn was a contributory cause of the collision, and while the burden of showing that it was in no degree occasioned by that failure rests upon the bark, it is impossible to rebut the presumption. It is a well-known fact that in some states of the atmosphere a foghorn can be heard at much greater distances than in others. How far it could have been heard when this collision occurred can never be known. Nor can it be known what precautions the steamer would have adopted if the true and proper signal had been given her. Hence, it appears to us the bark has not proved that her failure to obey the shipping regulations was not a concurrent cause of the injury she received; and, consequently, as both vessels were in fault, the damages, according to the admiralty rule, should be divided.

* * *

Decree reversed, and the cause remanded with instructions to enter a decree in accordance with this opinion.

Notes

1. In many states, statutory violations can constitute negligence *per se*. See, e.g., *Martin v. Herzog*, 228 N.Y. 164 (1920) (Cardozo, J.). The Court in *The Pennsylvania* discussed admiralty's similar rule, see *supra* at 333, but the rule for which the case stands—the so-called "Pennsylvania rule"—is something different. That rule, articulated in the next paragraph of the opinion, creates a strong presumption that the statutory violation was a *cause in fact* of the accident. See generally HEALY & SWEENEY, THE LAW OF MARINE COLLISION 46 (1998).

2. How strong is the *Pennsylvania* presumption? Will it suffice that there is any possibility, however far-fetched, that the statutory violation contributed to the loss? Consider *Seaboard Tug & Barge, Inc. v. Rederi AB/DISA*, 213 F.2d 772, 775 (1st Cir. 1954):

> We cannot believe that the Supreme Court in *The Pennsylvania* intended to establish as a hard and fast rule that every vessel guilty of a statutory fault has the burden of establishing that its fault could not by any stretch of the imagination have had any causal relation to the collision no matter how speculative, improbable or remote. * * * Notwithstanding the dictum in *The Martello*, 153 U.S. 64, 75 (1894), that the offending ship has the burden of showing that its statutory fault "could not by any possibility have contributed" to the collision, we nevertheless feel that in applying the rule of *The Pennsylvania* "we are limited to the reasonable probabilities."

In *Poulis-Minott v. Smith*, 388 F.3d 354, 365 (1st Cir. 2004), the First Circuit considerably extended that approach, holding that the plaintiff could not use the *Pennsylvania* presumption without first proving "that under the circumstances there was a reasonable possibility that compliance with the regulatory standard would have prevented the accident." Does that mean that the only plaintiffs who can use the *Pennsylvania* rule are those who do not need it?

3. Over the years the jurisprudence has broadened the sphere of application of the *Pennsylvania* rule so that generally any vessel operator who violates a statutory rule aimed at preventing the type of injury incurred by the plaintiff—whether by collision or by some other manner of operating a ship—falls under the presumption. The lower courts are divided, however, on whether a Jones Act plaintiff may assert the *Pennsylvania* presumption. Compare, e.g., *Reyes v. Vantage Steamship Co.*, 609 F.2d 140 (5th Cir. 1980) (applying the *Pennsylvania* rule), with, e.g., *Wills v. Amerada Hess Corp.*, 379 F.3d 32 (2d Cir. 2004) (rejecting the application of the *Pennsylvania* rule).

4. **The *Oregon* and *Louisiana* rules.** The *Pennsylvania* rule is just one of the presumptions that may be relevant in a collision case. Under the "*Oregon* rule," see *The Oregon*, 158 U.S. 186 (1895), a vessel under power that strikes a stationary object is presumed to be negligent. The courts often cite the presumption when it seems unnecessary (because the vessel's fault is otherwise clear). See, e.g., *Puerto Rico Ports Authority v. M/V Manhattan Prince*, 897 F.2d 1 (1st Cir. 1990). But sometimes the presumption is pivotal. See, e.g.,

Mount Washington Tanker Co. v. Wahyuen Shipping, Inc., 833 F.2d 1541 (11th Cir. 1987) (per curiam) (using the presumption to impose in personam liability on the owner of a vessel that caused damage while under the command of a compulsory pilot who was specifically found to have been free of fault in the circumstances); *Bunge Corp. v. M/V Furness Bridge*, 558 F.2d 790, 795 (5th Cir.1977) ("This presumption requires the moving vessel to show that it was without fault or that the collision was occasioned by fault of the stationary object or was the result of an inevitable accident.").

What if the stationary object is submerged? See *Pelican Marine Carriers, Inc. v. City of Tampa*, 791 F. Supp. 845 (M.D. Fla. 1992), *aff'd*, 4 F.3d 999 (11th Cir. 1993) (no presumption). What if the stationary object was itself at fault? See *I & M Rail Link v. Northstar Navigation*, 198 F.3d 1012 (7th Cir. 1999), *on reh'g*, 202 F.3d 333 (7th Cir. 2000) (indicating that the presumption should not apply on behalf of a bridge that the Coast Guard had determined was an unreasonable obstruction to navigation).

The "*Louisiana* rule" is a presumption of fault against a vessel that drifts into a stationary object. See *The Louisiana*, 70 U.S. 164 (1865); *Bunge Corp. v. Freeport Marine Repair, Inc.*, 240 F.3d 919 (11th Cir. 2001).

5. **The *in extremis* rule.** One possibility for a vessel to avoid a presumption of fault is the "*in extremis*" rule. The leading case is *The Bywell Castle*, L.R. 4 P.D. 219 (C.A. 1879). Two vessels, the *Bywell Castle* and the *Princess Alice*, were passing to the port of each other at a short distance when the *Princess Alice* made a turn to port. The *Bywell Castle* had up to that point acted with due care. But she "in the very agony, just at the time when the two ships were close together," made a turn to starboard, which the Trinity Masters and the trial judge concluded was the wrong maneuver. It was nevertheless forgiven. You may recognize the similarity of the rule to the emergency doctrine in torts.

Although courts are lenient in judging a vessel's behavior when it is placed in a sudden danger, they will not excuse conduct that they view as plainly unreasonable even under the exigent circumstances. When one vessel took a hard-a-port wheel to a red light on his starboard bow—an action that "all the instincts of good seamanship told him not to do"—the conduct was not excused. *The Testbank*, 72 L.L.R. 6 (C.A. 1942). See Marsden on Collisions at Sea 68 (12th ed. 1998).

The *in extremis* rule is broadly similar to Rule 2(b) of COLREGS, which is reprinted in the Statutory Supplement.

The *in extremis* rule has survived the Supreme Court's adoption of pure comparative fault in *Reliable Transfer*, just below. See Healy & Sweeney, The Law of Marine Collision 41 (1998). But will courts be less likely to invoke the *in extremis* rule now that they can freely apportion fault?

United States v. Reliable Transfer Co.

Supreme Court of the United States, 1975
421 U.S. 397, 95 S. Ct. 1708, 44 L. Ed. 2d 251, 1975 AMC 541

Mr. Justice STEWART delivered the opinion of the unanimous Court.

More than a century ago, in *The Schooner Catharine v. Dickinson*, 58 U.S. 170 (1855), this Court established in our admiralty law the rule of divided damages. That rule, most commonly applied in cases of collision between two vessels, requires the equal division of property damage whenever both parties are found to be guilty of contributing fault, whatever the relative degree of their fault may have been. The courts of every major maritime nation except ours have long since abandoned that rule, and now assess damages in such cases on the basis of proportionate fault when such an allocation can reasonably be made. In the present case we are called upon to decide whether this country's admiralty rule of divided damages should be replaced by a rule requiring, when possible, the allocation of liability for damages in proportion to the relative fault of each party.

I.

On a clear but windy December night in 1968, the *Mary A. Whalen*, a coastal tanker owned by the respondent Reliable Transfer Co., embarked from Constable Hook, N.J., for Island Park, N.Y., with a load of fuel oil. The voyage ended, instead, with the vessel stranded on a sand bar off Rockaway Point outside New York Harbor.

The *Whalen*'s course led across the mouth of Rockaway Inlet, a narrow body of water that lies between a breakwater to the southeast and the shoreline of Coney Island to the northwest. The breakwater is ordinarily marked at its southernmost point by a flashing light maintained by the Coast Guard. As, however, the *Whalen*'s captain and a deckhand observed while the vessel was proceeding southwardly across the inlet, the light was not operating that night. As the *Whalen* approached Rockaway Point about half an hour later, her captain attempted to pass a tug with a barge in tow ahead, but, after determining that he could not overtake them, decided to make a 180 turn to pass astern of the barge. At this time the tide was at flood, and the waves, whipped by northwest winds of gale force, were eight to ten feet high. After making the 180 turn and passing astern of the barge, the captain headed the *Whalen* eastwardly, believing that the vessel was then south of the breakwater and that he was heading her for the open sea. He was wrong. About a minute later the light structure on the southern point of the breakwater came into view. Turning to avoid rocks visible ahead, the *Whalen* ran aground in the sand.

The respondent brought this action against the United States in [the Eastern District of New York seeking to recover for damages to the *Whalen* caused by the stranding. The district court found that "[t]he fault of the vessel was more egregious than the fault of the Coast Guard" and assessed the parties' fault as 25% to the Coast Guard and 75% to the *Whalen*. But the court held that, under the settled admiralty rule of divided damages, the United States was liable for one-half of the damages to the vessel. The Second Circuit affirmed.] * * * We granted certiorari to consider the continued validity of the divided damages rule.

II.

The precise origins of the divided damages rule are shrouded in the mists of history. In any event it was not until early in the 19th century that the divided damages rule as we know it emerged clearly in British admiralty law. * * * It was against this background that in 1855 this Court adopted the rule of equal division of damages in *The Schooner Catharine* [ ]. The rule was adopted because it was then the prevailing rule in England, because it had become the majority rule in the lower federal courts, and because it seemed the "most just and equitable, and ... best [tended] to induce care and vigilance on both sides, in ... navigation." [ ] There can be no question that subsequent history and experience have conspicuously eroded the rule's foundations.

It was true at the time of *The Catharine* that the divided damages rule was well entrenched in English law. The rule was an ancient form of rough justice, a means of apportioning damages where it was difficult to measure which party was more at fault. [ ] But England has long since abandoned the rule and now follows the Brussels Collision Liability Convention of 1910 [see Statutory Supplement] that provides for the apportionment of damages on the basis of "degree" of fault whenever it is possible to do so.[6] Indeed, the United States is now virtually alone among the world's major maritime nations in not adhering to the Convention with its rule of proportional fault—a fact that encourages transoceanic forum shopping. See GILMORE & BLACK, THE LAW OF ADMIRALTY 529 (2d ed. 1975).

While the lower federal courts originally adhered to the divided damages rule, they have more recently followed it only grudgingly * * *. Judge Learned Hand was a particularly stern critic of the rule. * * *

It is no longer apparent, if it ever was, that this Solomonic division of damages serves to achieve even rough justice.[11] An equal division of damages is a reasonably satisfactory result only where each vessel's fault is approximately equal and each vessel thus assumes a share of the collision damages in proportion to its share of the blame, or where proportionate degrees of fault cannot be measured and determined on a rational basis. The rule produces palpably unfair results in every other case. * * *

And the potential unfairness of the division is magnified by the application of the rule of *The Pennsylvania* [*supra* at 331], whereby a ship's relatively minor statutory violation will require her to bear half the collision damage unless she can satisfy the heavy burden of showing "not merely that her fault might not have been one of the causes, or that it probably was not, but that it *could not have been*."

The Court has long implicitly recognized the patent harshness of an equal division of damages in the face of disparate blame by applying the "major-minor" fault doctrine to find a grossly negligent party solely at fault. But this escape valve, in addition to being inherently unreliable, simply replaces one unfairness with another. That a vessel is primarily negligent does not justify its shouldering all responsibility, nor excuse the slightly negligent vessel from bearing any liability at all. * * *

The divided damages rule has been said to be justified by the difficulty of determining comparative degrees of negligence when both parties are concededly guilty of contributing fault. [ ] Although there is some force in this argument, it cannot justify an equal division of damages in every case of collision based on mutual fault. When it is impossible fairly to allocate degrees of fault, the division of damages equally between wrongdoing parties is an equitable solution. But the rule is unnecessarily crude and inequitable in a case like this one where an allocation of disparate proportional fault has been made. Potential problems of proof in some cases hardly require adherence to an archaic and unfair rule in all cases. Every other major maritime nation has evidently been able to apply a rule of comparative negligence without serious problems [ ], and in our own admiralty law a

6. Article 4 of the Convention provides in part: "If two or more vessels are in fault the liability of each vessel shall be in proportion to the degree of the faults respectively committed. Provided that if, having regard to the circumstances, it is not possible to establish the degree of the respective faults, or if it appears that the faults are equal, the liability shall be apportioned equally."

11. It is difficult to imagine any manner in which the divided damages rule would be more likely to "induce care and vigilance" than a comparative negligence rule that also penalizes wrongdoing, but in proportion to measure of fault. A rule that divides damages by degree of fault would seem better designed to induce care than the rule of equally divided damages, because it imposes the strongest deterrent upon the wrongful behavior that is most likely to harm others.

rule of comparative negligence has long been applied with no untoward difficulties in personal injury actions. See, e.g., *Pope & Talbot* [*supra* at 122].

The argument has also been made that the divided damages rule promotes out-of-court settlements, because when it becomes apparent that both vessels are at fault, both parties can readily agree to divide the damages—thus avoiding the expense and delay of prolonged litigation and the concomitant burden on the courts. It would be far more difficult, it is argued, for the parties to agree on who was more at fault and to apportion damages accordingly. But the argument is hardly persuasive. For if the fault of the two parties is markedly disproportionate, it is in the interest of the slightly negligent party to litigate the controversy in the hope that the major-minor fault rule may eventually persuade a court to absolve it of all liability. And if, on the other hand, it appears after a realistic assessment of the situation that the fault of both parties is roughly equal, then there is no reason why a rule that apportions damages would be any less likely to induce a settlement than a rule that always divides damages equally. Experience with comparative negligence in the personal injury area teaches that a rule of fairness in court will produce fair out-of-court settlements.[13] But even if this argument were more persuasive than it is, it could hardly be accepted. For, at bottom, it asks us to continue the operation of an archaic rule because its facile application out of court yields quick, though inequitable, settlements, and relieves the courts of some litigation. Congestion in the courts cannot justify a legal rule that produces unjust results in litigation simply to encourage speedy out-of-court accommodations.

Finally, the respondent suggests that the creation of a new rule of damages in maritime collision cases is a task for Congress and not for this Court.[14] But the Judiciary has traditionally taken the lead in formulating flexible and fair remedies in the law maritime, and "Congress had largely left to this Court the responsibility for fashioning the controlling rules of admiralty law."[2] [ ] No statutory or judicial precept precludes a change in the rule of divided damages, and indeed a proportional fault rule would simply bring recovery for property damage in maritime collision cases into line with the rule of admiralty law long since established by Congress for personal injury cases. * * *

The rule of divided damages in admiralty has continued to prevail in this country by sheer inertia rather than by reason of any intrinsic merit. The reasons that originally led to the Court's adoption of the rule have long since disappeared. The rule has been repeatedly criticized by experienced federal judges who have correctly pointed out that the result it works has too often been precisely the opposite of what the Court sought to achieve in *The Schooner Catharine*—the "just and equitable" allocation of damages. And worldwide

---

13. The rule of comparative negligence applicable to personal injury actions in our maritime law * * * does not appear to discourage the negotiation of settlements in such litigation. It has been reported, for example, that of the marine personal injury cases involving a federal question that were terminated in fiscal year 1974, only 9.6% ever reached trial. 1974 *Proceedings of the Judicial Conference of the United States and Annual Report of the Director of the Administrative Office of the United States Courts*, Table C4, p. 416.

14. The respondent also relies on the fact that the Senate has twice failed to ratify the Brussels Convention with its proportional fault rule. It is urged that this inaction indicates "grave doubt" in Congress that rejection of the divided damages rule will further justice. But * * * it appears that the Senate took no action with respect to the Convention, not because of opposition to a proportional fault rule, but because of the Convention's poor translation and the opposition of cargo interests to the provision which would prevent cargo from recovering in full from the non-carrying vessel by eliminating joint and several liability of vessels for cargo damage. [ ]

2. Editors' note: But cf. *Miles*, *supra* at 244 ("Maritime tort law is now dominated by federal statute...").

experience has taught that that goal can be more nearly realized by a standard that allocates liability for damages according to comparative fault whenever possible.

We hold that when two or more parties have contributed by their fault to cause property damage in a maritime collision or stranding, liability for such damage is to be allocated among the parties proportionately to the comparative degree of their fault, and that liability for such damages is to be allocated equally only when the parties are equally at fault or when it is not possible fairly to measure the comparative degree of their fault.

Accordingly, the judgment before us is vacated and the case is remanded for further proceedings consistent with this opinion.

Notes

1. In the 1970s, states began to abolish the doctrine of contributory negligence, replacing it with some form of comparative negligence. They had to confront a number of problems. What effect would comparative negligence have on the doctrines of last clear chance and other doctrines that ameliorated the harsh effects of contributory negligence? In the wake of *Reliable Transfer*, maritime courts have had to confront similar issues. For example, they have held that *Reliable Transfer* abolished the major-minor fault doctrine but not the *in extremis* rule.

2. The *Pennsylvania* rule was of course not an ameliorative doctrine, but it has occasionally been argued that *Reliable Transfer* may have abolished or weakened it. We do not see the basis for that argument.

3. Footnote 14 of *Reliable Transfer* is an oblique indication that *Reliable* did not change the long-standing maritime rule of joint and several liability. *McDermott, Inc. v. AmClyde*, 511 U.S. 202 (1994), makes that clear. One application of joint and several liability is the rule that innocent cargo damaged in a collision caused by the COGSA-exempt negligence of the carrying vessel and the negligence of a noncarrying vessel can recover in full from the noncarrying vessel. See *Allied Chemical Corp. v. Hess Tankship Co.*, 661 F.2d 1044 (5th Cir. 1981). In that situation, can the noncarrying vessel seek contribution from the COGSA-exempt carrying vessel? If so, can the carrying vessel then in turn seek indemnity or contribution from the cargo? See the next case.

United States v. Atlantic Mutual Insurance Co.

Supreme Court of the United States, 1952
343 U.S. 236, 72 S. Ct. 666, 96 L. Ed. 907, 1952 AMC 659

Mr. Justice BLACK delivered the opinion of the Court.

Respondents are cargo owners who shipped goods on the steamship *Nathaniel Bacon* owned by petitioner, the United States, and operated as a common carrier of goods for hire. It collided with the *Esso Belgium* and respondents' cargo was damaged. The ships were also damaged. This litigation was brought in the District Court to determine liability for the damages suffered by the cargo owners and for the physical damage caused the ships. It was agreed in the District Court that:

> (a) The collision was due to negligent navigation by employees of both ships. The cargo owners were in no way at fault.
>
> (b) The *Belgium*, as one of two joint tortfeasors, must pay 100% of damages suffered by the *Bacon*'s cargo owners.

(c) Because of § 3 of the Harter Act [ ], and § 4(2) of the Carriage of Goods by Sea Act [ ], the cargo owners are barred from directly suing the *Bacon* for cargo damages.[3]

(d) Since the two ships were mutually at fault, the aggregate of all damages to both should be shared by both.

(e) In computing the aggregate damages caused both ships, account should be taken of the cargo damages recovered from the *Belgium* by the cargo owners.

(f) The bill of lading issued by the *Bacon* to the cargo owners contained a "Both-to-Blame" clause.[5] This clause, if valid, requires the cargo owners to indemnify the carrier *Bacon* for any amounts the *Bacon* loses because damages recovered by the cargo owners from the *Belgium* are included in the aggregate damages divided between the two ships.

The only question presented to us is whether the "Both-to-Blame" clause is valid. * * * The District Court held the clause valid. The Court of Appeals reversed. * * *

There is a general rule of law that common carriers cannot stipulate for immunity from their own or their agents' negligence. While this general rule was fashioned by the courts, it has been continuously accepted as a guide to common-carrier relationships for more than a century and has acquired the force and precision of a legislative enactment. Considering the relationship of the rule to the Harter Act, this Court said in 1901 that "in view of the well-settled nature of the general rule at the time the statute was adopted, it must result that legislative approval was by clear implication given to the general rule as then existing in all cases where it was not changed." [ ] Our question therefore is whether the language of the Harter Act, substantially reenacted in the Carriage of Goods by Sea Act, has carved out a special statutory exception to the general rule so as to permit a carrier to deprive its cargo owners of a part of the fruits of any judgment they obtain in a direct action against a noncarrying vessel that contributes to a collision.

Prior to the passage of the Harter Act in 1893 [ ] cargo damages incurred in a both-to-blame collision could be recovered in full from either ship. [ ] The Harter Act, under some circumstances, took away the right of the cargo owner to sue his own carrier for cargo damages caused by the negligent navigation of the carrier's servants or agents. It did not deprive the cargo owner of his tort action against the noncarrying ship. *The Chattahoochee*, 173 U.S. 540 (1899). * * *. [Nor did it] exonerate the carrier from its obligation to share with the noncarrier one-half the damages paid by the noncarrier to the cargo owners. *The Chattahoochee*, 173 U.S. at 551–552 [ ].

Apparently it was not until about forty years after the passage of the Harter Act that shipowners first attempted by stipulation to deprive cargo owners of a part of their recovery against noncarrying ships. [ ] The present effort of shipowners appears to date from 1937

3. Editors' note: The parties' agreement was based on the "nautical fault" defense. See *supra* at 279.

5. The clause reads as follows: "If the ship comes into collision with another ship as a result of the negligence of the other ship and any act, neglect or default of the Master, mariner, pilot or the servants of the Carrier in the navigation or in the management of the ship, the owners of the goods carried hereunder will indemnify the Carrier against all loss or liability to the other or non-carrying ship or her owners insofar as such loss or liability represents loss of, or damage to, or any claim whatsoever of the owners of said goods, paid or payable by the other or non-carrying ship or her owners to the owners of said goods and set off, recouped or recovered by the other or non-carrying ship or her owners as part of their claim against the carrying ship or Carrier."

when the North Atlantic Freight Conference adopted the "Both-to-Blame" clause. So far as appears, this is the first test of the legality of the clause that has appeared in the courts. When Congress passed the Carriage of Goods by Sea Act in 1936 [ ] it indicated no purpose to bring about a change in the long-existing relationships and obligations between carriers and shippers which would be relevant to the validity of the "Both-to-Blame" clause. At that time all interested groups such as cargo owners, shipowners, and the representatives of interested insurance companies were before the congressional committees. Although petitioner and respondents both appear to find comfort in the language and the hearings of the 1936 Act, nothing in either persuades us that Congress intended to alter the Harter Act in any respect material to this controversy.

Petitioner argues that the clause does nothing more than remove an "anomaly" which arises from this Court's construction of the Harter Act. It is said to be "anomalous" to hold a carrier not liable at all if it alone is guilty of negligent navigation but at the same time to hold it indirectly liable for one-half the cargo damages if another ship is jointly negligent with it. Assuming for the moment that all rules of law must be symmetrical, we think it would be "anomalous" to hold that a cargo owner, who has an unquestioned right under the law to recover full damages from a noncarrying vessel, can be compelled to give up a portion of that recovery to his carrier because of a stipulation exacted in a bill of lading. Moreover, there is no indication that either the Harter Act or the Carriage of Goods by Sea Act was designed to alter the long-established rule that the full burden of the losses sustained by both ships in a both-to-blame collision is to be shared equally. Yet the very purpose of exacting this bill of lading stipulation is to enable one ship to escape its equal share of such losses by shifting a part of its burden to its cargo owners.

Here, once more, "we think that legislative consideration and action can best bring about a fair accommodation of the diverse but related interests" of the varied groups who would be affected by permitting carriers to deviate from the controlling rule that without congressional authority they cannot stipulate against their own negligence or that of their agents or servants. If that rule is to be changed, the Congress, not the shipowners, should change it.[10]

Affirmed.

[Justices Frankfurter and Burton dissented.]

Notes

1. Should the Court reconsider the case in light of the comparative fault rule of *Reliable Transfer*? Under COGSA if the carrying vessel was 100% at fault in causing a collision it would pay nothing to its cargo claimants. If the carrying vessel is 90% at fault, is it fair that it should pay 90% of the damage to its cargo? Might the Court conclude that it is

10. We have not overlooked the argument that this bill of lading stipulation should be upheld because of this Court's holding and opinion in *The Jason*, 225 U.S. 32 (1912) [*infra* at 378]. The *Jason* case upheld a stipulation that both shipowner and cargo owner should contribute in general average on account of sacrifices and expenses necessarily incurred by the master of the ship in order to preserve the cargo as a whole. Moreover, this general average clause "was sustained because it admitted the shipowner to share in general average only in circumstances where by the Harter Act he was relieved from responsibility." [ ] Here the shipowner attempted to relieve itself from responsibility for negligence of its employees in connection with damages inflicted on another ship—"circumstances where by the Harter Act he was [not] relieved from responsibility."

fair—because negligent parties are generally made to pay for the damage they cause? Or is such a judgment improper in light of Congress's determination in COGSA?

2. Is it fair for the Court to refer the issue to Congress? What if Congress never acts to change the law? Reconsider *Reliable Transfer*, text following footnote 14.

3. Should the Court have given more weight to the goal of international uniformity? As was pointed out in footnote 6 of *Reliable Transfer*, under article 4 of the 1910 Collision Convention, each vessel at fault is responsible for only a proportion of the damage.

Otal Investments Ltd. v. M.V. Clary

United States Court of Appeals, Second Circuit, 2007
494 F.3d 40, 2007 AMC 1817

HALL, Circuit Judge:

The owner of the vessel the *M/V Kariba*, and owners of cargo on the *M/V Tricolor*, appeal from a judgment of the United States District Court for the Southern District of New York [which] found the *M/V Kariba* solely liable for a collision off the coast of Dunkerque, France. We reverse and remand.

I. Background

A. The Collision

Before dawn on December 14, 2002, three vessels [the *Kariba*, the *Tricolor*, and the *Clary*] were navigating a Traffic Separation Scheme ("TSS") [in the English Channel]. At the relevant point of the TSS, two branches intersect at approximately right angles, one branch cutting roughly North-South, the other roughly East-West. On the night in question, the fog was thick and visibility was low. The *Kariba* was proceeding westward at about 16 knots. The *Tricolor* was also proceeding westward at 17.9 knots, one-half mile to the starboard aft of the *Kariba*, and in the process of gradually overtaking her. At the same time, the *Clary* was moving northward, along the intersecting branch of the TSS, at 13 knots, on a collision course with the *Kariba*.

Noticing that it was on a collision course, the *Clary* planned to turn starboard and steer astern of the *Kariba*. Before the *Clary* began to turn, however, the *Kariba* initiated its own evasive maneuver. The *Kariba*, seeking to avoid a collision with the *Clary*—and perhaps unaware of the proximity of the *Tricolor*—made an abrupt turn to starboard. The *Kariba* struck the port side of the *Tricolor*, rending the *Tricolor*'s hull below its bridge. The *Tricolor* along with its cargo then sank. There were no human casualties.

In the quarter-hour leading up to the collision, none of the vessels sounded its foghorn or communicated with any other vessel via radio.

B. The Collision from the Perspective of the Three Different Ships

1. Onboard the Kariba

The *Kariba* is a 175.75 meters-long Bahamian flagged container ship, built in 1982, with a carrying capacity of about 1200 standard containers. Having left port in Antwerp, Belgium, the *Kariba* was bound for Le Havre, France, and traveling westward in the East-West Branch of the TSS. There were three men present on the bridge at the time of the collision: Captain Kamola, making his first restricted-visibility voyage as a Master; Second Officer Szymanski; and Able-Bodied Seaman Ignacio. The bridge featured an Automatic Radar Plotting Aid ("ARPA"), described as a computer system that "automatically tracks and plots target vessels and calculates their courses and speeds," thus predicting the "closest point of approach" of other vessels.

Captain Kamola first noticed the *Clary* on his radar at 1:55 a.m. At 2:00 a.m., upon making a planned adjustment to his course by rounding a point called the Fairy South Buoy, Captain Kamola noticed he might be headed for a collision with the *Clary*. Captain Kamola did not act, however, because he expected the *Clary* to steer astern of him. At 2:04 a.m., when his ARPA would have shown he was approximately 3.5 miles and eight minutes away from colliding with the *Clary*, Captain Kamola asked Szymanski to go onto the port wing of the ship and to check for the *Clary*'s lights. After looking for approximately two minutes, Szymanski did not see anything. At this point, the *Kariba* was 2.8 miles away from a collision with the *Clary*.

By 2:09 a.m., Captain Kamola's radar still indicated the *Clary* had not changed course. Concerned about a collision, and now only 2.0 miles away from a collision with the *Clary*, Captain Kamola ordered a 10 degree turn to starboard (registered on the Dunkerque radar at 2:09:45 a.m.). Fifteen or 20 seconds later, Captain Kamola ordered another 20 degree turn to starboard. Seconds later, Captain Kamola saw the lights of the *Tricolor* and ordered the rudder full to starboard. It was too late, however; Kamola exclaimed, "Oh my God, we will hit them." Within the next minute or so, the *Kariba*'s bow struck the *Tricolor* broadside. The *Tricolor* listed hard, capsized and sank.

2. Onboard the Tricolor

Built in 1987, the *Tricolor* was a 190 meters-long roll-on roll-off Norwegian flagged carrier, with a capacity to carry over 3,000 cars. On the day of the collision, the *Tricolor* was on a voyage from Zeebrugge, Belgium, to Southampton, England, and headed westward in the East-West branch of the TSS. There were three men on the bridge of the *Tricolor*: Captain Knutsen, Second Officer Cabanda and Able-Bodied Seaman Matel.

After 2:00 a.m., Captain Knutsen was aware of the *Kariba*, as well as two other ships, ahead of him. At 2:12 a.m., Captain Knutsen noticed he was beginning to overtake the *Kariba*—and indeed, could see her lights. Knutsen was also aware of the *Clary* and its being on a collision course with the *Kariba*. Then suddenly, Captain Knutsen noticed the *Kariba* had abruptly and without warning turned to starboard, and was heading straight for him. In the moments leading up to the collision, Captain Knutsen had the *Tricolor* on autopilot. Seeking to avoid the collision, Captain Knutsen and Cabanda simultaneously converged on the wheel, hurriedly disengaged the autopilot and sent the vessel hard to starboard. Despite their efforts, the *Kariba* struck the *Tricolor*, which listed hard, capsized and sank.

3. Onboard the Clary

The *Clary*, a 138.5 meters-long Singaporean flagged bulk carrier, was built in 1979. On the day of the collision, the *Clary* had been on a voyage from Savannah, Georgia, to the Netherlands. In the moments leading up to the collision, there was only one man on the bridge: Second Officer Toncic. While the *Clary*'s bridge did not include an ARPA system, it did have a device that calculated closest points of approach, but only for vessels selected by Toncic.

By 2:00 a.m., Second Officer Toncic noticed the *Tricolor* and the *Kariba* on his radar. By 2:02 a.m., if Toncic had plotted the point of possible collision, he would have noticed that only 3.1 miles separated the *Clary* from the point of collision with the *Kariba*. At 2:11:15 a.m., Toncic decided it was time to make his starboard turn in order to pass astern the *Kariba* and the *Tricolor*, as suggested by basic navigational rules. According to the findings of the district court, Toncic then "moved away from his radar, plotted his position on the chart table," then disengaged his autopilot and made a "dramatic" turn to starboard. In making his turn "dramatic," Toncic had sought to ensure the maneuver would register on the radars of other ships. In their brief and at oral argument, counsel for the *Clary* stated an appropriately dramatic turn would be 50 or 55 degrees in magnitude. By the time the *Clary* turned to starboard, had the *Kariba* been able to maintain its westward course, the two ships would have been only about two miles apart while both were on a collision course. Two minutes later, Toncic heard "collision, collision, collision" on his VHF radio. Realizing the blips representing the *Kariba* and the *Tricolor* had coalesced and ceased to move, Toncic readjusted his course to sail northward, west of the collided ships. Toncic did not answer the distress call.

Toncic later explained he thought the ships had only "kissed." After passing through the area of the collision, Toncic erased his chart. At trial, Toncic admitted that "someone" had altered the *Clary*'s logbook pages so as to reflect that conditions were clear, and that there were two other men on deck at the time of the collision—an Able Bodied Seaman at the wheel, and a lookout.

C. The Procedural Posture

In June 2003, Otal Investments, Ltd., the owner of the *Kariba* (hereinafter, Otal and the *Kariba* together will be called the "*Kariba*"), filed a complaint in the [district court] "seeking Exoneration from or Limitation of Liability." See [ ] 46 U.S.C. § 30505, et seq. and Fed. R. Civ. P. Supplemental Admiralty Rule F. In response to this complaint, numerous claimants filed claims against the *Kariba* * * * .

* * * After a bench trial, the [district] court ruled in favor of the *Clary* and the *Tricolor*, finding the *Kariba* to have been the sole cause of the collision. * * *

II. Discussion

A. The Applicability of the Rule in *The Pennsylvania*

All parties agree the substantive law governing this case derives from treaties ratified by the vessels' flag states. Specifically, the navigational duties are contained in [COLREGS]. In addition, the parties have stipulated their claims should be adjudicated "in accordance with" [the 1910 Collision Convention]. [ ] Of course, while these treaties govern the substantive law, the law of the forum—federal maritime law—governs procedural law. [ ]

Appellants * * * argue this procedural law includes the rule in *The Pennsylvania.* * * * [T]he rule operates in a manner reminiscent of negligence per se; it establishes a presumption based on a statutory duty of care. Unlike negligence per se, however, the rule in *The Pennsylvania* creates a presumption only as to causation, and not as to "fault" or negligence. [ ] Originally, the rule in *The Pennsylvania* stated quite a harsh presumption, requiring the party against whom the presumption operated to show their wrongdoing "could not have been" the cause. [ ] But since then, our Circuit has interpreted the presumption more permissively; now, a party must prove its wrongdoing "could not have been" the cause within the bounds of "reasonable probability." [ ] Widely criticized, the rule in *The Pennsylvania* appears to be, today, rejected by all maritime states other than the United States. [ ]

The district court found the rule in *The Pennsylvania* did not apply in this case. "Generally," the court held, "United States courts will apply the 1910 Collision Convention when a collision occurs in international waters between vessels that fly flags of signatory states." Article 6 of that Convention states "[a]ll legal presumptions of fault in regard to liability for collision are abolished." If the rule in *The Pennsylvania* is substantive, the court noted, Article 6 of the Convention would override it. * * * [T]he district court held that because the rule in *The Pennsylvania* "is outcome determinative," it must be substantive. [ ] Because it is substantive, the rule cannot apply in a case where the 1910 Collision Convention governs. [ ]

We agree * * *.

B. Violation of the COLREGS

Having concluded the district court correctly declined to apply the rule in *The Pennsylvania*, we now must consider whether the district court erred in finding the "collision was the sole and exclusive fault of the *Kariba*." [ ] The relevant navigational duties are contained in the COLREGS, a treaty ratified by the flag states of all vessels-parties. We affirm the district court's findings to the extent they determine that the *Kariba* was responsible for the collision. We reverse, however, the findings that determined that the *Kariba* was *solely* responsible, as well as the finding that the *Tricolor* and the *Clary* bore no responsibility for the collision.

1. The Kariba

We begin by noting that the *Kariba* concedes it was at fault, but maintains that its fault was not the sole cause of the collision. We agree with both contentions....

a. Cautious Navigation

COLREG 19(e) requires vessels in conditions of restricted visibility to slow down or "take all her way off and in any event navigate with extreme caution until danger of collision is over." [ ] Instead of turning abruptly to starboard, the *Kariba* should have slowed down until the danger of collision had passed. [ ] * * *

b. Avoiding Action

The district court also determined the *Kariba* violated COLREG 19(d)(ii), which states: "[I]f a close-quarters situation is developing and/or a risk of collision exists," then a vessel must avoid the collision, taking care not to steer "toward a vessel abeam or abaft the beam."[2] [ ] The district court found the *Kariba* had steered directly into a vessel abaft its beam in violation of COLREG 19(d). * * *

c. Special Circumstances

At trial, the *Kariba* attempted to justify its otherwise illegal abaft-the-beam turn by appealing to COLREG 2(b) on "special circumstances." * * *. The district court rejected the *Kariba*'s defense, noting it is not at all unusual or "special" for three ships to pass the juncture of a TSS simultaneously. Moreover, the danger was not "immediate" insofar as several minutes separated the Kariba from the expected collision. The district court did not err * * *.

* * *

2. Editors' note: An object is "abeam" a ship when it lies on an imaginary line running through the middle of the ship at a right angle to the direction the ship is pointing. An object is "abaft the beam" when it lies behind that imaginary line.

e. Conclusion

We affirm the district court in its findings of liability with respect to the *Kariba*.

2. The Tricolor

We conclude the district court misinterpreted COLREGS 13 and 16 on overtaking, and COLREG 6 on safe speed. We clarify those rules and hold that, as a matter of law, the *Tricolor* violated the rules on both overtaking and safe speed.

a. Overtaking and Overtaken Vessels

COLREG 13 states: "[A]ny vessel overtaking any other shall keep out of the way of the vessel being overtaken." A related rule, COLREG 16, states: "Every vessel which is directed to keep out of the way of another vessel shall, so far as possible, take early and substantial action to keep well clear." As the district court acknowledged, an overtaken vessel may "make predictable adjustments in course and speed necessary for safe navigation."

Some courts have suggested that the overtaking vessel not only must avoid [the overtaken vessel's] predictable adjustments, but all [its] adjustments, predictable or not. A district court in the Fifth Circuit typified the latter absolutist approach when it held that a "leading vessel is under no obligation to keep out of the way." [ ] Indeed, that court continued, "[t]he overtaking vessel takes the risk of necessary alteration of course or checking of speed by the leading vessel to avoid a third vessel or stopping to let another vessel pass." [ ] We reject this absolutist approach. Under COLREGS 13 and 16, an overtaking vessel has a duty to maintain such a distance from the overtaken vessel so as to allow the overtaken vessel to conduct reasonably predictable adjustments. [ ]

We note further that Rule 13 does not govern only the conduct of vessels in an overtaking situation. It also governs the very choice to overtake. Specifically, Rule 13 obliges an overtaking vessel to select a safe place to overtake another vessel in the first instance. [ ] Whether or not it is safe to attempt to overtake under COLREG 13 depends on contextual factors, including visibility, sea conditions, the space that confines the overtaking and overtaken vessels, the vessels' speed and the vessels' capabilities.

In this case, the district court found the *Tricolor* did not violate COLREGS 13 and 16 in overtaking the *Kariba* when positioned ".4 to .5 miles" off its starboard quarter. In analyzing the overtaking situation, the district court determined the overtaking vessel only needed to keep clear of the overtaken vessel's predictable adjustments. To this extent, the district court correctly interpreted COLREGS 13 and 16. The district court erred, however, in failing to consider whether the *Tricolor* breached its COLREGS 13 and 16 duties in attempting to overtake the *Kariba* in the first place or at least, in not adjusting its speed and course as it proceeded with the overtaking. Here, the *Tricolor* first became aware of the *Kariba* at 2:00 a.m. and at 2:12 a.m. the *Tricolor*'s Captain noticed he was beginning to overtake her. At this point, the *Tricolor* did not slow down but instead attempted to overtake the *Kariba* in a fog, at 17.9 knots, in a heavily trafficked TSS, with the knowledge the *Kariba* was on a collision course with a northbound vessel, the *Clary*. We deem this a strikingly precarious situation: attempting to overtake without slowing or altering course in anticipation of adjustments that the overtaken vessel reasonably could be expected to make in response to a third approaching vessel. We hold that as a matter of law, the *Tricolor* violated COLREGS 13 and 16 in attempting to overtake under these conditions.

b. Safe Speed

* * * Traveling at a safe speed is not just the fiat of COLREGS 6 and 19(b); it is also a matter of good seamanship. [ ]

Whether a speed is "safe" depends on the circumstances. In determining safe speed, a vessel must take into account various factors, including "visibility," 6(a)(i), and "traffic density," 6(a)(ii), as well as vessels' capabilities, 6(a)(iii), sea conditions, 6(a)(v), and draught relative to total depth, 6(a)(vi). Among other things, vessels with radar must consider "the number, location and movement of vessels detected by radar." 6(b)(v). Traditionally, courts often analyzed the question of speed largely as a function of stopping distance. [ ] * * * Ultimately, however, a court also must consider the full range of other factors, including visibility, sea conditions, traffic and the vessels' capabilities * * *.

* * * [W]e hold that as a matter of law, the *Tricolor*'s speed under these conditions constituted a violation of COLREGS 6 and 19(b).

d. Conclusion

The district court erred in its determination of the *Tricolor*'s liability. The *Tricolor* violated COLREGS 13 and 16 on overtaking, and COLREGS 6 and 19(b) on safe speed.

3. The Clary

We affirm the district court's determination that the *Clary* violated COLREG 5 on proper lookout. The district court erred, however, in its interpretation and application of COLREG 19(d) on avoiding action. Further, the district court erred in failing to apply an important presumption regarding the unexplained alteration of logbooks.

a. Proper Lookout

COLREG 5 states: "Every vessel shall at all times maintain a proper look-out by sight and hearing as well as by all available means appropriate in the prevailing circumstances and conditions so as to make a full appraisal of the situation and of the risk of collision." COLREG 2(a), concerning the "ordinary practice of seamen" encompasses this same command. * * * [T]he *Clary* violated both of these COLREGS in staffing its bridge with a lone mariner. * * *

b. Avoiding Action

COLREG 19(d) requires a vessel not in sight of another, upon entering "close-quarters" or realizing a "risk of collision," to "take avoiding action in ample time...." [ ] The Ninth Circuit has held that for "large, ocean going vessels, objective estimates" of close-quarters "range from two miles ... to almost five miles." [ ]

The district court sought to distinguish these cases: "[T]hese cases describe ships on the high seas where it is reasonable to expect vessels to remain further away from each other..., but the West Hinder TSS is a different story." The West Hinder TSS is "heavily trafficked and despite the late hour there were quite a few other vessels in the area. It would be naive to assume that a vessel was obligated to maneuver when it was ten or more minutes away from collision, because to avoid one collision could serve only to put it on a collision course with another."

We reject this reasoning. Most important, it contains a faulty premise; it was not the case that if the *Clary* turned ten minutes before the collision such "could serve only to put it on a collision course" with another vessel. To the contrary, the record discloses a number of alternative routes—encompassed by starboard turns of various degrees and reduction of speed—none of which would have entailed colliding with another vessel. Moreover, in focusing on the term "close-quarters," the district court failed to interpret correctly COLREG 19(d). COLREG 19(d) functions to prevent collisions by urging action at an early stage, requiring vessels to "take avoiding action *in ample time*" whenever a "*risk* of collision" exists or a "close-quarters situation *is developing*" (emphases added). In this case, the risk of collision arose when the *Kariba* steadied on its westward course after rounding the Fairy South Buoy. At this point—approximately ten minutes before the *Kariba* decided to make its fateful turn—the *Clary* had a COLREG 19(d) duty to take avoiding action.

The avoiding action under COLREG 19(d) could have taken either one of two basic forms. First, the *Clary* could have slowed. Second, the *Clary* could have made a starboard turn astern the *Kariba* and the *Tricolor*. The *Clary* argues it made its starboard turn at the earliest possible moment because it was limited by its desire to make a "dramatic" 50 or 55 degree turn so that its change of course would register on other vessels' radar. At the same time, asserts the *Clary*, the COLREGS prohibited it from crossing outside the bounds of the TSS. The point at which it actually turned, the *Clary* notes, was the earliest point at which it could make a "dramatic" turn while staying within the bounds of the TSS.

This argument is unpersuasive. Certainly, the avowed custom of making a "dramatic" 50 or 55 degree turn is wise. But nothing in the COLREGS mandates a turn of this magnitude; the COLREGS only mandate avoidance. Thus it makes no sense for a vessel to try to reach the magical 55 degree angle, all while increasing the risk of collision ahead. Further, the COLREGS do not prohibit turns that lead a vessel to cross out of a TSS. According to COLREG 10, vessels must "so far as practicable keep clear of a traffic separation line or separation zone." "[N]ormally," a vessel should "join or leave a traffic lane at the termination of the lane...." 10(b)(iii). The conspicuous qualifying language—"normally," "so far as practicable"—demonstrates the relative flexibility of COLREG 10. COLREG 10 even includes guidance for those obliged to cross out of a TSS; those who "do so shall cross on a heading as nearly as practicable at right angles to the general direction of traffic flow." 10(c). In other words, the text of COLREG 10 specifically anticipates that vessels sometimes must cross out of the TSS. It is clear from the record the *Clary* faced no particular risks in crossing out of the TSS; while there was traffic in the TSS, no vessels were proceeding on the North-South branch near the *Clary*. Meanwhile, the *Clary* encountered great risk in continuing on its collision course with the *Kariba*—a risk that contributed to the collision in this case.

We hold, therefore, that the *Clary* violated COLREG 19(d) in failing to take avoiding action promptly. * * *

c. Unexplained Alterations of Ships' Records

[The court was very critical of the *Clary*'s unexplained alteration of logbooks, which gives rise to a presumption the logbook contained adverse entries. Here the presumption was not relevant because the true facts were known, but the court concluded that the alteration should still have a bearing on the allocation of damages.]

d. Conclusion

The district court correctly determined the *Clary* violated COLREG 5 on proper lookout. The district court erred in its interpretation and application of COLREG 19(d) on avoiding action; as a matter of law, the *Clary* violated COLREG 19(d). The *Clary*'s alteration of its logbook will have some bearing on the ultimate issue of allocating liability for damages and the district court must take it under consideration.

C. Causation

There remains the question whether these violations of COLREGS caused the collision. Put another way, we still must determine whether the violations of the COLREGS constitute causative fault. * * *

1. The Proper Standard of Causation

The standard of causation under COLREGS and the Collision Convention mirrors the standard of causation under American maritime tort law. [ ] To show causation, a plaintiff must demonstrate the defendant's act was a factual or but-for cause of a harm and the defendant's act proximately caused the harm. [ ]

* * *

2. The Causative Impact of the Kariba

* * * [T]he *Kariba*'s turn was a factual cause of the collision. [It was also a proximate cause because the turn resulted in the damage that the COLREGS intended to prevent in prohibiting such turns.]

3. The Causative Impact of the Tricolor

As for the *Tricolor*, the district court erred in failing to find its violations to have caused the collision. If the *Tricolor* had not chosen to overtake in an unsafe place and in an unsafe manner, the collision would not have occurred; the *Kariba* would have passed across the *Tricolor*'s bow. The *Tricolor*'s decision to overtake and the manner of overtaking was thus a factual cause of the collision.

As noted above, the *Tricolor* violated the COLREGS in choosing to overtake the *Kariba* at an unsafe place and time and in an unsafe manner. This choice to overtake created a risk that other vessels, particularly the *Kariba*, would have less space, and less time, to avoid navigational exigency leading to a collision—the very same risk as makes inopportune overtaking a violation of the COLREGS. The *Kariba* and the *Clary* themselves might have increased the risk of collision to which the *Tricolor* contributed, but these actions were not "extraordinary." Rather, these actions or similar actions intended to avoid a collision were foreseeable under the circumstances, and thus did not supercede the *Tricolor*'s causative impulse. Commonsense and reasonable judgment dictate the *Tricolor* was both a factual and proximate cause of the collision. We thus hold, as a matter of law, the *Tricolor*'s overtaking was a cause of the collision.

It is possible the *Tricolor* also caused the collision through its violation of the COLREG on safe speed. Here, however, a distinction must be made. True, the *Tricolor*'s violation of the COLREG on safe speed was a but-for cause of the collision; if the *Tricolor* had been travelling slower, the *Kariba* would have turned safely in front of its bow. * * * [W]e nevertheless cannot consider the factor of the *Tricolor*'s speed, when taken in isolation, to have "caused" the collision. As we have consistently reaffirmed * * *, "the issue ... is whether, even after the event, we can say that the risk of such an accident was increased by the defendant's behavior." [ ] In this case, the *Tricolor*'s unsafe speed, taken in isolation, is not the kind of transgression that leads a vessel to find itself in close proximity to another, abruptly turning vessel. In this sense, the *Tricolor*'s unsafe speed alone did not stand as a cause of the collision.

Yet * * * the *Tricolor*'s unsafe speed still might have been a cause of the collision. This question hinges entirely on whether the *Tricolor*, had it not been proceeding at an unsafe speed, would have been able to stop soon enough to avert or mitigate the harm of the collision. In other words, the question hinges not on the factor of the *Tricolor*'s speed in isolation, but whether that speed reflected an inability to stop, or slow, in time to avoid the *Kariba*'s abrupt abaft-the-beam turn. As the record does not reveal the answer to this question, we must remand for further findings.

4. The Causative Impact of the Clary

[The *Clary* also caused the collision. If it had taken prompt avoiding action, the collision would not have occurred. The failure to keep a proper lookout created a risk it could not respond to a navigational exigency and avoid a collision—the same risk as makes the failure a COLREGS violation. The failure to take avoiding action constrained the space and time in which the *Kariba* and the *Tricolor* could maneuver, thus creating the same risk of harm as makes that failure a COLREGS violation.]

5. Conclusion

The district court correctly held the *Kariba*'s violations of the COLREGS to have been a cause of the collision. The district court erred, however, in determining the *Tricolor*'s and the *Clary*'s violations of the COLREGS did not cause the collision. In reversing, we conclude all three vessels committed violations of the COLREGS that caused the collision. It is unclear whether the *Tricolor*'s unsafe speed was a cause of the collision; to the extent the answer to that question requires further findings, the district court must make those findings as part of its inquiries into allocation of liability for damages, an issue to which we now turn.

D. Allocation of Liability for Damages

Since we have ruled that all three vessels were at fault and that, at least to some extent, their respective fault caused the collision, the issue remains for the district court on remand to allocate liability for damages among the three vessels. In *United States v. Reliable Transfer Co.* [*supra* at 335], the Supreme Court replaced the admiralty rule of equally divided damages with a rule that "when two or more parties have contributed by their fault to cause property damage in a maritime collision or stranding, liability for such damage is to be allocated among the parties proportionately to the comparative degree of their fault," unless such measurement is not possible. [ ] The phrase "degree of their fault" created an ambiguity as to whether the Court meant the comparative degree of their culpability or blameworthiness, *i.e.*, how extensively each ship departed from a proper standard of care, or the comparative causative effect of each ship's conduct, *i.e.*, the extent to which each ship's culpable conduct contributed to causing the collision. American courts have understood *Reliable Transfer* to mean liability "according to relative culpability of the parties' actions rather than their respective degrees of physical causation." [ ]

However, * * * Article 4 of the 1910 Collision Convention, which allocates liability "in proportion to the degree of the faults respectively committed," has been understood by the courts of Great Britain to assess comparative fault on the basis of both relative culpability and relative causative effect of each party's acts. [ ] Courts in France, Germany, and Italy have done the same. [ ] We * * * interpret the Convention, which applies in the pending case, to require consideration of both culpability and causative effect.

Thus, on remand the district court will have to consider the relative culpability of each vessel and the relative extent to which the culpability of each caused the collision. In making the culpability comparison, the district court should include in its consideration of the fault of the *Clary* the fact that its logbook was altered. We hasten to add, however, that allocation of liability for damages, requiring consideration of matters not readily amenable to precise analysis, does not oblige an admiralty judge to do more than provide ultimate percentages of allocation, accompanied only by sufficient explanation to provide a reviewing court with some general understanding of the basis for the decision. [ ] * * *

III. Conclusion

The district court did not err in declining to apply the rule in *The Pennsylvania.* The *Kariba*, the *Tricolor* and the *Clary* all committed violations of the COLREGS. Moreover, each vessel committed at least one violation that constituted a cause of the collision. * * *

[Judge Newman, joined by the other two members of the panel, filed a concurring opinion "to urge the development of some form of sea traffic control system for crowded sea lanes to lessen the risk of a ship collision of the sort illustrated by this appeal." He argued that "the lack of even a rudimentary nautical counterpart to the systems that monitor and control crowded air spaces cries out for a remedy."]

Notes

1. The court applied the 1910 Collision Convention because The Bahamas, Norway, and Singapore (the three flag states) are all parties to the convention. Indeed, 85 countries are parties, including many of the world's major maritime powers. Should the United States ratify it? In view of the size of the U.S.-flag fleet, how significant is the United States' failure to ratify?

2. Whether a U.S. court applies the 1910 Collision Convention in a particular case will depend on the court's choice-of-law analysis. The flags of the vessels involved is an important factor that the court may consider (as in *Otal Investments*), particularly when the collision takes place on the high seas, but it is not the only possible factor. In *The Mandu*, 102 F.2d 459 (2d Cir. 1939), for example, the place of the collision was the most important factor in the court's decision to apply the convention to a collision between two vessels in Brazilian territorial waters (although both vessels were also from convention countries). See also, e.g., *Man Ferrostaal v. M/V Vertigo*, 447 F. Supp. 2d 316 (S.D.N.Y. 2006) (examining the factors identified in *Lauritzen v. Larsen*, 345 U.S. 571 (1953) [*infra* at 550], but ultimately applying the convention based on the place of the collision).

3. On remand, the district court held that the *Kariba* was 63% liable for the collision, the *Clary* was 20% liable, and the *Tricolor* was 17% liable. The Second Circuit affirmed that holding. The district court reached its figures by first finding that the *Kariba* was 40% culpable, the *Clary* 36% culpable, and the *Tricolor* 24% culpable. Those percentages referred to the "relative blameworthiness" of each vessel (considered in the abstract). The court then assigned "relative causation" percentages, which referred to the causal connection between each ship's culpable conduct and the collision. These percentages were 86% for the *Kariba*, 10% for the *Tricolor*, and 4% for the *Clary*. The final liability percentages were the averages of the culpability and causation percentages. Do those percentages seem appropriate in light of each ship's actions? Does that method of calculating each ship's overall liability seem appropriate?

Chapter V

Towage and Pilotage

A. Towage

"The supplying of power by a vessel ... to tow or draw another is towage. Many vessels, such as barges and canal boats, have no power of their own and are built with a view to receiving their propelling force from other sources. And vessels having motive power often employ auxiliary power to assist them in moving about harbors and docks." *Stevens v. The White City*, 283 U.S. 195, 201 (1932). The vessel supplying the motive power is generally called the *tug* or *towboat*. The vessel being moved or assisted in moving is the *tow*. The arrangement between tug and tow is properly called towage regardless of whether the tug pulls the tow (on a hawser or wire rope) or pushes it from behind.

"Just as there are many types of tugs and barges, there are many contractual relationships between the players in the towage industry. * * * [T]he two simplest classifications of towage contractual relationships are towage [the subject of this Chapter] and carriage [treated *supra* Chapter III]."[1] The law of carriage of goods is potentially relevant whenever the tow is transporting cargo. In the simplest type of situation—for example, *The T.J. Hooper*, 60 F.2d 737 (2d Cir. 1932), in which two coal-laden barges being towed from Norfolk to New York were lost in a storm—the "cargo owners sued the barges under the contracts of carriage, [and] the owner of the barges sued the tugs under the towing contract." In other situations, the cargo may have a carriage-based relationship with the tug. *See, e.g., Sacramento Navigation Co. v. Salz*, 273 U.S. 326, 327 (1927) (treating the tug propelling a cargo-carrying barge as part of the "vessel transporting merchandise" for purposes of the Harter Act exemption from liability for negligent navigation). The carriage-vs.-towage inquiry can become complex. One analyst has offered this summary:

> When there are three parties (tug, tow, and cargo) and two contracts (one for carriage and one for towage), the carriage contract should govern the relationship [of] both the tug and the barge with the cargo. The towing contract will control the rights between tug and tow.[2]

The cases below show that the "rights between tug and tow" turn in significant part on the general maritime law of negligence, with this proviso: Both the tug and tow are

1. Davey, *The Tug and Tow Relationship in the United States*, 70 Tul. L. Rev. 475, 479 (1995).
2. *Id.* at 486.

deemed to warrant the initial seaworthiness (reasonable fitness for the contemplated journey) of their vessels.

In re Denet Towing Services, Inc.

United States Court of Appeals, Fifth Circuit, 2006
178 Fed. Appx. 427, 2006 AMC 1517

PER CURIAM:

This case arises from an accident on the Mississippi River Gulf Outlet ("MRGO") in New Orleans wherein a barge, owned by Halliburton and being towed [pushed] by a Denet Towing tug boat, suddenly listed to port. The port bow of the barge submerged and seven of eight large cargo tanks mounted to the deck of the barge broke free and fell overboard. [The tanks contained a heavy metal called barite in its bulk dry form and were later recovered from thirty feet of water in the middle of the MRGO channel.] The barge "sprang back on the boat," and Captain Denet, the captain of the tug, then maneuvered the barge to shore. Halliburton sued Denet Towing and various insurers for damages under general maritime tort, contract, and cargo damage law, and for cost of recovery and contribution under [the Comprehensive Environmental Response, Compensation and Liability Act (CERCLA), 42 U.S.C. §§9601 et seq.]. Halliburton alleged that Captain Denet, through negligent operation of the tug, lost control of the barge and caused the tanks to break loose or, alternatively, that Captain Denet negligently took the unseaworthy barge under tow. Denet Towing argues that Halliburton tendered an unseaworthy vessel for tow, and that the unseaworthiness was caused by cracks and holes in the barge near the waterline that were not apparent when the Denet Towing crew conducted its visual inspection before leaving dock. The case was heard before a judge sitting without a jury in a bifurcated trial. The district court found for Denet Towing. Given the clear error standard of review, we see no reason to overturn the district court's factual determination.

Captain Denet and his crew testified that they inspected the barge before departing from the Halliburton facility where it was loaded, noticing only a slight list to port bow. Captain Denet testified that at the time of the accident the tug and barge were in the middle of the MRGO and did not hit anything, but that the barge just suddenly listed to port and the tanks slid off the deck as the barge "sprang back" on the tug.

Two Halliburton experts and two Denet Towing experts all testified that the barge had cracks and wasted holes in the hull which predated the accident. Denet Towing's experts testified that the cracks would not have been apparent upon normal inspection. The Denet Towing experts, as well as both Halliburton experts, differed in opinion as to what caused the accident. One Halliburton expert noticed two recently incurred scrapes on the bottom of the vessel and opined that the barge ran around. Another Halliburton expert opined that the vessel hit debris as the barge drifted toward shallow water, but could not have run aground because it would have become stuck. The Denet experts opined that the cracks and wasted holes allowed water to flow into two of the barge's compartments, causing the barge to lose stability. Both Denet Towing experts testified about the shoreline of the MRGO in the vicinity of the accident, which is solid rock extending approximately thirty feet from the shoreline into the channel to a depth of nine feet. Thus, both testified, if the barge had run aground, the bottom of the barge would have sustained significant damage; one expert testified that the barge would have sunk on the spot. Both Denet Towing experts also agreed that given the post-accident location of the extremely heavy cargo tanks, the accident must have occurred in the middle of the MRGO channel.

The district court found the testimony of the Denet Towing experts more credible. The district court also found that the cause of the accident was the unseaworthiness of the barge before it left the dock and that Captain Denet was not negligent either in taking the vessel under tow, or in piloting the vessel down the MRGO in a manner that caused the accident. We find no clear error in these findings of fact.

In a towage contract, the towing vessel owes a duty to exercise such reasonable care and maritime skill that prudent navigators employ in performing similar services. [ ] The *Pennsylvania* rule [*supra* at 331] is "a presumption in admiralty law that a statutory violation by a party to a collision is a cause of the damage unless it is established that the violation could not have caused or contributed to the collision." [ ] Halliburton argues that the district court misapplied the *Pennsylvania* rule. We disagree.

At the time of the accident Captain Denet had been captain for eighteen and one-half hours in the relevant twenty-four hour period, six hours longer than allowed by regulation. [46 C.F.R. § 15.705]. Denet also committed other regulatory violations, including failing to have a second licensed operator on board when a tug is operating more than twelve hours in a twenty-four hour period. [ ]

The district court found that the statutory violations were unrelated to the cause of the accident, *viz.*, the unseaworthiness of the barge, and so the *Pennsylvania* burden shifting rule did not apply. "As we have explained, the Supreme Court in *The Pennsylvania* "did not intend to establish a hard and fast rule that every vessel guilty of a statutory fault has the burden of establishing that its fault could not by any stretch of the imagination have had any causal relation to the collision, no matter how speculative, improbable or remote." [ ] We find no error in the trial court's view of the relationship between the *Pennsylvania* Rule and this case. Affirmed.

Lone Star Industries, Inc. v. Mays Towing Co.

United States Court of Appeals, Eighth Circuit, 1991
927 F.2d 1453, 1991 AMC 1540

BEAM, Circuit Judge:

* * *

Lone Star [Industries] produces cement in Cape Girardeau [Mo.] and ships some of it by barge to its Memphis facility. For this purpose, Lone Star maintains a fleet of double-raked, self-unloading cement barges, a rare commodity among inland river barges. The cement barge [the sinking of which gave rise to this litigation], the *LS 1501*, was manufactured in 1949, and by the testimony of several experts at trial, was, in December of 1983, at or near the end of its useful life. Mays Towing, which itself owns no barges, regularly transported cement barges for Lone Star between Cape Girardeau and Memphis. It used two of its tug boats, the *M/V Sherry K. Mays* and the *M/V Peggy Mays*, to tow the *LS 1501*.

The district court found that the barge was undamaged when received by the *Sherry K. Mays* on the evening of December 23, 1983, at Cape Girardeau. The *LS 1501*, loaded with approximately 1,400 tons of cement, was placed in tow together with the *LS 1502* and *LS 1503* for the trip to Memphis on an icy Mississippi River. From Cape Girardeau almost to Memphis, the *LS 1502* was the lead barge, with the *LS 1503* to the port side of the *LS 1501*, behind the *LS 1502*. At Cairo, Illinois, the *Peggy Mays* joined the tow; the *Sherry K. Mays* faced up to the stern of the *LS 1501* and the *Peggy Mays* to the *LS 1503*.

At Columbus, Kentucky, the *Sherry K. Mays* left the tow, and the *Peggy Mays* moved over, facing up to the stern of the *LS 1501*, where the *Sherry K. Mays* had been. The barges remained in the same configuration until they reached Island 39, fifteen miles above Memphis. There the *Peggy Mays* turned the entire tow around, so that the *1501*, stern first, was at the front of the tow. The barges reached Memphis in the early afternoon on December 25, 1983. All crew members testified that nothing unusual occurred en route.

Unloading was the responsibility of Lone Star employees, so the *Peggy Mays* left the barges moored at the dock while it remained nearby, as it was required to do until the barges were unloaded. The *LS 1501* sat at the dock without listing, in normal trim, covered with ice and snow (up to ten or twelve inches on its stern), until December 27. On that day, Lone Star employees attempted to conduct a standard pre-unloading inspection, which normally involved opening all the hatches and entering the void compartments to look for water or hull damage. Because the barge is unloaded bow to stern, so that part of the stern necessarily submerges during unloading, an inspection of the stern compartments is especially critical. While they did open the forward hatches, as a result of accumulated ice, which they attempted to chip away from the hatches with sledgehammers, Lone Star employees were unable to open the stern hatches. They waited until the next day, December 28, but the weather did not relent, and they were still unable to inspect the stern compartments. Under some financial pressure to unload the barges, and knowing that the *LS 1502* had been unloaded without incident, Lone Star took, by its own admission, a calculated risk, and decided to unload the *LS 1501* without inspection of the stern compartments.

Unloading began at mid-afternoon on December 28 with one employee present, as was Lone Star's practice. That employee worked inside the pump room of the barge, located at the bow and from which location he could not see the stern during unloading. Testimony at trial suggested that other cement companies used two or three people to supervise unloading, and one expert called Lone Star's practice of unloading with only one person "ludicrous." By 8:00 p.m., Lone Star was aware that the barge was taking on water at the stern, and by 10:00 p.m., water was covering the stern deck, something that should never happen. The cold, icy conditions hampered rescue efforts, and the barge sank. The *LS 1503* was not unloaded until the ice on its stern melted, on January 5, 1984.

Later, when the *LS 1501* was raised, marine surveyors found a vertical crack in its stern log—the heavy steel at the stern of the barge to which tugboats face up. The crack was eight or ten inches above the waterline, but, because the barge is unloaded bow to stern, it became submerged during unloading. No one disputes that the barge sank because water entered the stern compartments through the crack.

Because the barge was undamaged when picked up by the *Sherry K. Mays*, the district court concluded "that the negligence of Mays Towing Company caused the damage to the *LS 1501*, resulting in the loss of the barge and its cargo." The district court also held that Lone Star was negligent in failing to inspect the stern compartments prior to unloading and in employing only one person during unloading. Thus, the district court determined the fault of Mays Towing to be sixty percent, and that of Lone Star to be forty percent. The court valued the barge at $35,000, its cargo at $55,000, and awarded an additional $180,394.15 in necessary expenses. Total damages were then reduced by the comparative fault of Lone Star. Both parties appeal.

* * * The district court opinion does not * * * recite any instances of negligent conduct by Mays Towing, nor does it suggest any actions that may have caused the fracture. * * * From its premise that the damage to the barge must have occurred en route to Memphis,

the district court moved to a conclusion that the elements of res ipsa loquitur were met: the barge was in the exclusive control of Mays Towing, Lone Star could not have caused the damage en route, and "the damage to the *LS 1501* is of a type that ordinarily does not occur in the absence of negligence." The court held that Mays Towing did not rebut the inference of negligence.

* * *

In *Stevens v. The White City,* 285 U.S. 195 (1932), the Supreme Court made it clear that a tug is not a bailee of a vessel in its tow. [A bailee is subject to a presumption of negligence whenever goods in its care and custody are damaged.] For liability to attach to the tug, plaintiff must show something more than "receipt of a tow in good order and delivery in damaged condition." Plaintiff must show breach of the duty to exercise "such reasonable care and maritime skill as prudent navigators employ for the performance of similar service." In *The White City,* the vessel in tow arrived at its destination damaged, but there was no evidence to explain when, how, or where the damage occurred. The Supreme Court found insufficient evidence from which to conclude that the tug had been negligent. "There is nothing about the injury itself to warrant any inference that it resulted from fault or negligence."

This circuit has read *The White City* to allow an inference of negligence upon [appropriate] facts. [We have held that] *The White City* preclude[s] an inference of negligence only on facts which reveal "nothing about the injury itself to warrant" an inference of negligence. [On the other hand, when it is possible to conclude from the character of the damage sustained that there was more of a basis for attributing the damage to some kind of incident that likely would not have occurred without negligence than merely damage to the good while in defendant's custody, an inference of negligence is permissible.]

[As the district court indicated, res ipsa loquitur] applies when "(1) the injured party was without fault; (2) the instrumentality causing the injury was under the exclusive control of the defendant; and (3) the mishap is of a type that ordinarily does not occur in the absence of negligence." [ ] Given that only Mays Towing had control of the barge between Cape Girardeau and Memphis, the first and second elements are easily satisfied. The third element, however, whether the damage is of a sort that does not ordinarily occur absent negligence, is more troublesome. * * * On this point the district court opinion is sketchy. It does not describe the fracture in any detail, but refers to it only as "the rupture in the stern log." The record, however, is more clear. The fracture was on the port side of the stern log, approximately three feet from the corner, eight or ten inches above the water line. The hull indentation containing the fracture was ten or twelve inches wide, twenty-three inches long, and ran vertically. The fracture inside the indentation had a maximum opening of three-fourths of an inch. At its deepest, the indentation was two and one-half inches deep. One witness testified that the indentation, except for the fracture, was similar to others on the barge.

The district court did not make a finding as to the cause of the indentation. The record, however, suggests that it was most likely made by the corner of another boat or barge. It was probably not caused by the tow knee of a tug, which would not have been high enough for the necessary contact to have occurred. Thus, the record makes clear only that the indentation was likely caused by contact with another vessel.

* * * [T]he critical inquiry is whether the fracture would probably not have occurred from normal or safe contact with another vessel. For an inference of negligence to apply,

the fracture must be of such a character that it is more probably than not the result of negligence. [ ] While the district court's opinion contains only a legal conclusion that "the damage to the *LS 1501* is of a type that ordinarily does not occur in the absence of negligence," we are satisfied that the facts do not preclude an inference of negligence. Viewing the evidence in the light most favorable to the appellee, [ ] the record contains some evidence to support the district court's conclusion. John G. Stickling, Jr., a marine surveyor and Lone Star's expert witness, testified that in his opinion it would have taken a substantial impact to cause the fracture. Moreover, Stickling testified that the fracture was not the result of normal wear and tear, and required contact inconsistent with safe handling of the barge. Given the testimony by Mays Towing's experts to the contrary, that such an indentation could be caused by normal contact with another vessel, consistent with safe handling, and that the indentation probably cracked because the barge was old and its steel fatigued and brittle due to the ice and cold, we are not certain that we would have reached the same conclusion as the district court. We cannot, however, say that the district court's determination was clearly erroneous.

[The court went on to conclude that Lone Star's negligence in the manner and timing of unloading the *LS 1501* was so egregious and unforeseeable as to constitute a superseding cause of the sinking, relieving Mays Towing of any liability. Judge Gibson vigorously dissented.]

Notes

1. By definition, towage is always conducted under oral or written contract, but *Denet* and *Lone Star* illustrate that damages litigation between tug and tow is predominantly governed by normal maritime negligence law. While courts sometimes say that towage contracts include an implied "warranty" that the towage operation will be conducted with reasonable skill and diligence, *Denet* and *Lone Star* show that the so-called warranty is simply another way of referring to the general negligence law's requirement of reasonable care under the circumstances.

2. As the *Lone Star* opinion sought to emphasize, towage law does not hold the tug to the high standard of conduct demanded of a bailee. For applications of the higher bailee standard in other contexts, see *Agrico Chemical Co. v. M/V Ben W. Martin*, 664 F.2d 85, 90 (5th Cir. 1981) (invoking the reasoning of *Sacramento* [*supra* at 353] and stating that "when a tug is engaged to do more than merely tow another's vessel, the contract is considered one for the movement of the tow and its contents, a contract of affreightment, subject to the more exacting duties applicable to those who undertake as carriers to transport cargo"); *United Barge Co. v. Notre Dame Fleeting & Towing Serv., Inc.*, 568 F.2d 599, 602 & n.5 (8th Cir. 1978) (holding that when a barge was damaged while stored at defendant's fleeting facility, the defendant was liable as a bailee unless it could "come[] forward with evidence that the damage resulted from causes or circumstances other than ... its own negligence").

3. Cases indicating that the towage contract subjects the tug to an implied "warranty of workmanlike performance" are irreconcilable with the weight of the jurisprudence. See Parks & Cattell, Law of Tug, Tow and Pilotage 356 (3d ed. 1994). Most of the cases seem to end up equating "workmanlike performance" with reasonable care under the circumstances, so that perhaps little harm is done by the aberrant terminology.

4. As *Denet* shows, the owner of the tow is obligated to deliver it to the tug in seaworthy condition and can be held responsible for damages to the tug, tow, or cargo resulting

from the tow's unseaworthiness. But if the tug is negligent in accepting an unseaworthy tow or in continuing to move a tow that exhibits unseaworthiness, sole responsibility may be imposed upon it. See, e.g., *Ryan Walsh Stevedoring Co. v. James Martin Service, Inc.*, 557 F. Supp. 457 (E.D. La. 1983), *aff'd*, 729 F.2d 1457 (5th Cir. 1984) (holding tug solely liable to a bridge that was damaged by too-tall crane on towed barge); *Houma Well Service, Inc. v. Tug Capt. O'Brien*, 312 F. Supp. 257 (E.D. La. 1970) (holding tug solely liable to tow and cargo for continuing to try to move the tow after it became unstable).

Dillingham Tug & Barge Corp. v. Collier Carbon & Chemical Corp.

United States Court of Appeals, Ninth Circuit, 1983
707 F.2d 1086, 1984 AMC 1990

KENYON, District Judge [sitting by designation]:

* * *

[In the spring of 1976, Collier Carbon & Chemical Corporation, a division of the Union Oil Company, bought the barge *Columbia*. The barge needed to be towed from Galveston to Portland, Oregon. It had been built as an inland barge and Union meant to use it as an inland barge, but it had to be modified so that it could survive the ocean tow. Union retained a naval architect, who initially recommended the construction of an expensive hopper cover. When Union objected to the expense, the architect agreed that the barge could be safely towed if its tie-down straps were strengthened, which was accomplished.]

[Union's underwriters required the barge to be surveyed by a designated surveyor. The surveyor determined that the barge was seaworthy for the proposed tow, but he issued several recommendations, including restricting the maximum speed to eight knots, checking the barge periodically to insure that it was not taking on water, and promptly pumping out any water found. Union hired Dillingham Tug & Barge Corporation to perform the tow. The towing contract required Dillingham to give "due regard" to the surveyor's recommendations.]

* * *

The tow commenced on January 29, 1977. By the time the barge reached the Panama Canal, several feet of water had accumulated in the barge's hopper, but the towing crew did not pump it out. After leaving the Canal, the tow consistently exceeded the recommended speed of eight knots. On February 25, the tow encountered heavy seas; speed was reduced at this time, but the barge continued to take on water. After some time, and several speed reductions, the captain of the tug decided to head for Bahia Ballenas to pump out the barge. Bahia Ballenas was over one hundred miles away at this point, and the tug had to head into the northwesterly seas to reach it, while the port of Bahia Santa Maria was only about twenty miles away, and was due east of the tug and tow. Eventually the captain changed course for Bahia Santa Maria, but it was too late; the straps on the barge gave way, the cargo tanks broke off the barge, and the barge was lost.

[The towing contract provided that "neither [Dillingham] nor the tug shall be responsible for the loss of ... the barge ... arising from act, neglect, or fault of the master ... or the servants of [Dillingham] in the navigation or in the management of the tug, tow or towing equipment...." Moreover, under the terms of the contract Union agreed to pay Dillingham $125,000 for the towage service to "be deemed earned by [Dillingham] upon the commencement of the towage service even though at any stage of the venture thereafter the barge be lost." Relying on these clauses, Dillingham sued Union for its towing fees in the

District Court for the Northern District of California. Union counterclaimed, alleging that Dillingham's negligence caused the loss of the barge.

[The trial court correctly held that the exculpatory provision was void under the rule of *Bisso v. Inland Waterways Corp.*, 349 U.S. 85 (1955), in which the Court invalidated as against public policy a towage contract clause placing the sole risk on the barge. The trial court also correctly held that the broad policy of *Bisso* meant that Dillingham could not recover its towage fees. "If it is against public policy to contract against your own negligence, it is against public policy to profit from your own negligence which in this case would be collecting the towage."]

[Determining the effect of other provisions in the towing contract is more difficult. The towing contract required Union to maintain hull and machinery insurance on the barge to its full value naming Dillingham as an additional assured with loss payable to Union. It further required a waiver of subrogation against Dillingham, and stated that Union would look only to the insurance for any loss or damage to the barge. The *Columbia* was placed on Union's fleet hull and machinery policy, with the required waiver of subrogation against Dillingham.]

[Union argues that the benefit-of-insurance provision, like the directly exculpatory provision, is invalid under *Bisso*, reasoning] that the insurance provision in this contract is merely an indirect exculpatory clause, since it effectively seeks to shield Dillingham from any liability for the loss of the barge.

The Supreme Court's holding in *Bisso* was based on two public policy factors. The Court wished to discourage negligence by making wrongdoers pay for damage they cause, and the Court also wished to protect those in need of goods and services from being overreached by others who have the power to drive hard bargains. *Bisso* dealt with a pure exculpatory clause. That is not the case herein, though, and the public policy factors key to the holding in *Bisso* do not carry the same weight in the case of an insurance provision like the one at hand. In fact, there are public policy considerations in favor of such provisions.

The Fifth Circuit has previously considered this issue in several cases. [Its decisions in *Fluor Western, Inc. v. G & H Offshore Towing Co.*, 447 F.2d 35 (5th Cir. 1971), *Twenty Grand Offshore, Inc. v. West India Carriers, Inc.*, 492 F.2d 679 (5th Cir. 1974), and *BASF Wyandotte Corp. v. Tug Leander, Jr.*, 590 F.2d 96 (5th Cir. 1979), set forth a strong basis for upholding benefit-of-insurance provisions like the one in this case.]

We believe that the reasoning of the Fifth Circuit is sound, and that it is not against public policy to enforce an insurance provision in a towage contract. Furthermore, it is economically efficient to allow the enforcement of such provisions. The parties to a towage contract with such a provision are effectively insuring themselves under one policy against any loss due to the fault of either one of them, instead of each obtaining separate policies for this purpose. A single policy can be obtained cheaper than two individual policies. In the event of a loss, the same insurance company pays for the loss, despite who is at fault.

Union argues that even if such provisions are not invalid per se, this one should be held invalid because Union produced uncontradicted evidence of overreaching in the towing industry regarding such provisions. The trial judge found that there was no monopoly in the towing industry, and that there had been no overreaching by Dillingham. The evidence to which Union refers was testimony by an employee of Dillingham that he couldn't recall ever negotiating a contract without such a provision, and that other major towing companies also used such provisions. Union also relies on the testimony by a Union employee that Dillingham refused to delete the provision from the contract.

[This evidence does not justify a finding that the provision was so coercive as to be unenforceable. The judgment should provide that Dillingham is not liable for the loss of the barge, and that Union must look solely to its insurer for recovery.]

Notes

1. *Bisso* is at odds with most of the commercial maritime law, under which exculpatory clauses (sometimes called "red letter" clauses) are generally effective. See *Royal Ins. Co. v. Southwest Marine*, 194 F.3d 1009 (9th Cir. 1999); *La Esperanza de P.R., Inc. v. Perez & Cia. De P.R., Inc.*, 124 F.3d 10 (1st Cir. 1997). See generally Bauer, *Making Sense of Maritime Exculpation Clause Jurisprudence*, 22 T.M. Cooley L. Rev. 309 (2005).

2. The Supreme Court weakened the *Bisso* rule in *Southwestern Sugar & Molasses Co. v. River Terminals Corp.*, 360 U.S. 411 (1959), upholding an exculpation clause that was part of a tariff filed with the Interstate Commerce Commission. It further weakened *Bisso* in *The Bremen v. Zapata Offshore Co.*, 407 U.S. 1 (1972) (*infra* at 529–30), holding that the *Bisso* rule was inapplicable to an international towage contract. Moreover, as illustrated by *Dillingham*, the lower courts have approved a variety of contractual devices amounting to end runs around *Bisso*. As was stated in *Metal Processing, Inc. v. Humm*, 56 F. Supp. 2d 455, 462 (D. N.J. 1999), "[t]he *Bisso* rule now has so many exceptions that its viability as a bright line rule must be questioned." See generally Donovan, *Exculpatory and Benefit of Insurance Clauses in Towage and Pilotage*, 70 Tul. L. Rev. 605 (1995).

B. Pilotage

The China

Supreme Court of the United States, 1868
74 U.S. (7 Wall.) 53, 19 L. Ed. 67, 2002 AMC 1504

Mr. Justice SWAYNE delivered the opinion of the Court.

This is a case arising out of a collision between the steamship *China*, a British vessel, then leaving the port of New York for Liverpool, and the brig *Kentucky*, then on a voyage from Cardenas to New York. [The district court held the *China* liable in rem to the owners of the *Kentucky*, and the circuit court affirmed. The case is here on appeal.] The collision occurred on the 15th of July, 1863, a short distance outside of Sandy Hook. The brig was sunk. The steamship was wholly in fault. It was not alleged, in the argument here for the appellants, that there was either fault or error on the part of the brig. The case turns upon the effect to be given to the statute of New York, of the 3d of April, 1857. At the time of the collision the steamship was within the pilot waters of the port of New York, and was in charge of a pilot, licensed under this act, and taken by the master pursuant to its provisions. The pilot's orders were obeyed, and the catastrophe was entirely the result of his gross and culpable mismanagement. No question was made in the argument, upon the subject; the evidence is too clear to admit of any. * * *

It is insisted by the appellants that the statute referred to compelled the master of the steamship to take the pilot, and that they are therefore not liable for the results of his misconduct. [The New York statute is indeed compulsory; it states that the master "shall take a licensed pilot" and provides that in case of refusal, pilotage must be paid to the first licensed pilot offering his services.] [I]t seems to us clear * * * that the pilot was taken by the steamship upon compulsion.

This brings us to the examination of the second proposition. Does the fact that the law compelled the master to take the pilot, exonerate the vessel from liability?

* * *

The argument for the appellants proceeds upon the general legal principle that one shall not be liable for the tort of another imposed upon him by the law, and who is, therefore, not his servant or agent. The reasoning by which the application of this principle to the case before us is attempted to be maintained, is specious rather than solid. It is necessary that both outward and inward bound vessels, of the classes designated in the statute, should have pilots possessing full knowledge of the pilot grounds over which they are to be conducted. The statute seeks to supply this want, and to prevent, as far as possible, the evils likely to follow from ignorance or mistake as to the qualifications of those to be employed by providing a body of trained and skillful seamen, at all times ready for the service, holding out to them sufficient inducements to prepare themselves for the discharge of their duties, and to pursue a business attended with so much of peril and hardship. The services of the pilot are as much for the benefit of the vessel and cargo as those of the captain and crew. His compensation comes from the same source as theirs. Like them he serves the owner and is paid by the owner. If there be any default on his part, the owner has the same remedies against him as against other delinquents on board. The difference between his relations and those of the master is one rather of form than substance. It is the duty of the master to interfere in cases of the pilot's intoxication or manifest incapacity, in cases of danger which he does not foresee, and in all cases of great necessity. The master has the same power to displace the pilot that he has to remove any subordinate officer of the vessel. He may exercise it or not, according to his discretion.

The maritime law as to the position and powers of the master, and the responsibility of the vessel, is not derived from the civil law of master and servant, nor from the common law. It had its source in the commercial usages and jurisprudence of the middle ages. Originally, the primary liability was upon the vessel, and that of the owner was not personal, but merely incidental to his ownership, from which he was discharged either by the loss of the vessel or by abandoning it to the creditors. But while the law limited the creditor to this part of the owner's property, it gave him a lien or privilege against it in preference to other creditors.

The maxim of the civil law—*sic utere tuo ut non laedas alienum* [so use your own property as not to injure that of another]—may, however, be fitly applied in such cases as the one before us. The remedy of the damaged vessel, if confined to the culpable pilot, would frequently be a mere delusion. He would often be unable to respond by payment—especially if the amount recovered were large. Thus, where the injury was the greatest, there would be the greatest danger of a failure of justice. According to the admiralty law, the collision impresses upon the wrongdoing vessel a maritime lien. This the vessel carries with it into whosesoever hands it may come. It is inchoate at the moment of the wrong, and must be perfected by subsequent proceedings. Unlike a common-law lien, possession is not necessary to its validity. It is rather in the nature of the hypothecation of the civil law. It is not indelible, but may be lost by laches or other circumstances. The proposition of the appellants would blot out this important feature of the maritime code, and greatly impair the efficacy of the system. The appellees are seeking the fruit of their lien.

All port regulations are compulsory. The provisions of the statute of New York are a part of the series within that category. A damaging vessel is no more excused because she was compelled to obey one than another. The only question in all such cases is, was she in fault? The appellants were bound to know the law. They cannot plead ignorance. [Even though the immunity of the wrongdoing vessel when the pilot is in charge and alone in fault is now well settled in English jurisprudence, such is not the law of the United States.] This ship was brought voluntarily within the sphere of [operation of United States law, and the appellants] cannot complain because [United States law] throws the loss upon them rather than upon the owners of the innocent vessel. We think the rule which works this result is a wise and salutary one, and we feel no disposition to disturb it.

The steamship is a foreign vessel. We have, therefore, considered the learned and able argument of the counsel for the appellants with more care than we should otherwise have deemed necessary. Maritime jurisprudence is a part of the law of nations. We have been impressed with the importance of its right administration in this case.

Affirmed.

Notes

1. In *Homer Ramsdell Transportation Co. v. La Compagnie Generale Transatlantique*, 182 U.S. 406, 416–17 (1901), the Court held that a shipowner is not vicariously liable in personam for the results of the fault of a compulsory pilot. The Court indicated that when a shipowner engages a pilot in noncompulsory circumstances, the shipowner is vicariously liable for the pilot's fault.

2. *The Framlington Court*, 69 F.2d 300 (5th Cir. 1934), held that a ship's master's refusal of a local pilot's services in departing the port of Corner Brook, Newfoundland, violated the Harter Act obligation to "exercise due diligence to make the vessel seaworthy." 46 U.S.C. § 30705(a))(1) [see *supra* at 279]. "However capable the master may have been to navigate his ship from port to port in open water, he was utterly incompetent to guide her through that particular part of the voyage from Corner Brook to sea."

3. Congress has left the regulation of pilotage primarily to the states. 46 U.S.C. § 8502 requires vessels engaged in the coastwise trade to engage federally licensed pilots. But otherwise the matter is left to the states. 46 U.S.C. § 8501(a) provides generally that "pilots in the bays, rivers, harbors, and ports of the United States shall be regulated only in conformity with the laws of the States." *Cooley v. Board of Wardens*, 53 U.S. 299 (1851), held that there is no constitutional impediment to Congress's decision to defer to the states.

4. Louisiana's complex and colorful system of regulating lower Mississippi River pilots is described in *Kotch v. Board of River Pilot Commissioners*, 330 U.S. 552 (1947) (holding that the Fourteenth Amendment's equal protection clause does not impede Louisiana's approval of the pilot associations' reliance on nepotism and personal friendships in selecting future pilots), and in *Coleman v. New Orleans and Baton Rouge S.S. Pilots' Ass'n*, 437 F.3d 471 (5th Cir. 2006) (holding that the pilot associations are not "employers," "employment agencies," or "labor organizations" and are therefore not subject to the Age Discrimination in Employment Act, 29 U.S.C. § 621 et seq.). See also *Gillis v. Louisiana*, 294 F.3d 755 (5th Cir. 2002) (holding that nothing in federal law impedes Louisiana's right to regulate pilotage in the Calcasieu Ship Channel all the way out to its end about 33 miles off the Louisiana coastline).

5. *Guy v. Donald*, 203 U.S. 399 (1906), held that pilots are not employed by the pilots' associations, which precluded imposing vicarious liability on the association for a pilot's fault.

6. *Evans v. United Arab Shipping Co.*, 4 F.3d 207 (3d Cir. 1993), held that river and harbor pilots are not employees of the vessels they serve—instead, they are independent contractors—and hence have no Jones Act rights. *Bach v. Trident Steamship Co.*, 947 F.2d 1290 (5th Cir. 1991), held that they are not Jones Act seamen because they lack the required substantial-in-duration connection with any particular vessel or fleet (see *supra* at 200 note 6(c)). The *Bach* court indicated without deciding that pilots might still be able to sue for unseaworthiness by virtue of being "*Sieracki* seamen" who are not covered by the LHWCA. See *supra* at 189 note 1.

United States v. Nielson

Supreme Court of the United States, 1955
349 U.S. 129, 75 S. Ct. 654, 99 L. Ed. 939, 1955 AMC 935

Mr. Justice BLACK delivered the opinion of the Court.

The respondent, Dauntless Towing Line, contracted to use two of its tugs in assisting the United States, petitioner here, [to] move its steamship *Christopher Gale* from Hoboken to a Brooklyn pier. The *Gale* was to move under its own propelling power under guidance of one of respondent's tugboat captains or some other licensed pilot. The contract further provided that a tugboat captain or pilot going on board would become the "servant of the owners of the vessel assisted in respect to the giving of orders to any of the tugs furnished to or engaged in the assisting service and in respect to the handling of such vessel, and neither those furnishing the tugs and/or pilot nor the tugs, their owners, agents, or charterers shall be liable for any damage resulting therefrom." One of the respondent's tug captains went aboard the government vessel to pilot it in connection with the moving operation. The two tugs of respondent were at the time fastened to the *Gale* by lines to help guide its movements. One of the tugs was crushed between the *Gale* and a pier while attempting to carry out a maneuver under orders of the tug captain piloting the *Gale*.

The respondent brought this suit in admiralty to recover damages from the United States alleging that damages to the tug were caused by negligent pilotage orders of the tug captain while temporarily acting as "servant" of the *Gale*. After hearings the District Court found that the damages were caused by the pilot's negligence "in persisting in his attempt to enter the slip after he knew or should have known that he could not overcome the force of the wind and tide and keep the *Christopher Gale* from sagging down on Pier 1." On this finding the District Court entered a decree requiring the United States to pay respondent for damages brought about by this negligence. This decree was entered over the Government's contention that the contract was invalid if construed as exempting respondent from liability for its own servant's negligence. [ ] Agreeing with the District Court's reasoning and decree, the Court of Appeals affirmed. We granted certiorari to consider the meaning and validity of the pilotage clause * * * .

Sun Oil Co. v. Dalzell Towing Co., 287 U.S. 291 (1932), involved the meaning and validity of a pilotage contract substantially the same as the one here. One of Dalzell's tug captains negligently piloted Sun Oil's vessel causing the boat to ground and suffer damages. Sun Oil sued Dalzell. The contract exempting Dalzell from liability for pilotage was pleaded as a defense. This Court held that the tug company could validly contract against being "liable for any damage" caused by the negligence of one of its captains in piloting Sun

Oil's vessel and construed the contract there as having that effect. The question in this case, however, is whether the agreement of the ship being piloted to release the tug company from being "liable for any damages resulting" from negligent pilotage not only relieves the tug company from liability for damage, but allows it affirmatively to collect damages for injury to its own tug due to negligent pilotage by one of its tug captains.

An agreement that one shall not be liable for negligence of a third person cannot easily be read as an agreement that one is entitled to collect damages for negligence of that third person. And there is no reason to stretch contractual language to force payment of damages under circumstances like these. A person supplying his own employees for use by another in a common undertaking cannot usually collect damages because of negligent work by the employee supplied. Clear contractual language might justify imposition of such liability. But the contractual language here does not meet such a test and we do not construe it as authorizing respondent to recover damages from petitioner.

Reversed.

[Justices Reed and Burton dissented. Justice Harlan did not participate.]

Notes

1. *Nielson* was handed down the same day as *Bisso*, *supra* at 360.

2. Justice Black authored both *Nielson* and *Bisso* (in which Justices Frankfurter, Reed, and Burton dissented). Here is his explanation in the *Bisso* opinion, 349 U.S. at 93–94, of the Court's distinction between pilotage exculpatory clauses and towage exculpatory clauses:

> There are distinctions between a pilotage and a towage exemption clause which make it entirely reasonable to hold one valid and the other invalid. A pilotage clause exempts for the negligence of pilots only; a towage clause exempts from all negligence of all towage employees. Pilots hold a unique position in the maritime world and have been regulated extensively by both the States and Federal Government. Some state laws make them public officers, chiefly responsible to the State, not to any private employer. Under law and custom they have an independence wholly incompatible with the general obligations of obedience normally owed by an employee to his employer. Their fees are fixed by law and their charges must not be discriminatory. As a rule no employer, no person can tell them how to perform their pilotage duties. When the law does not prescribe their duties, pilots are usually free to act on their own best judgment while engaged in piloting a vessel. Because of these differences between pilots and towage employees generally, contracts stipulating against a pilot's negligence cannot be likened to contracts stipulating against towers' negligence. It is one thing to permit a company to exempt itself from liability for the negligence of a licensed pilot navigating another company's vessel on that vessel's own power. That was the *Sun Oil* case. It is quite a different thing, however, to permit a towing company to exempt itself by contract from all liability for its own employees' negligent towage of a vessel. Thus, holding the pilotage contract valid in the *Sun Oil* case in no way conflicts with the rule against permitting towers by contract wholly to escape liability for their own negligent towing.

Chapter VI

General Average

A. Historical Background

Digest of Justinian

XIV.2.1

The Rhodian law provides that if cargo has been jettisoned in order to lighten a ship, the sacrifice for the common good must be made good by common contribution.

The Laws of Oleron

30 Fed. Cas. 1171

Article VIII

If a vessel be laden to sail from Bordeaux to Caen, or any other place, and it happens that a storm overtakes her at sea, so violent, that she cannot escape without casting some of the cargo overboard for lightening the vessel, and preserving the rest of the lading, as well as the vessel itself; then the master ought to say, *Gentlemen, We must throw part of the goods overboard;* and, if there are no merchants to answer him, or if those that are there approve of what he says by their silence, then the master may do as he thinks fit; and if the merchants are not pleased with his throwing over any part of the merchandize, and forbid him, yet the master ought not to forbear casting out so many of the goods as he shall see to be for the common good and safety; he and the third part of his mariners making oath on the Holy Evangelists, when they arrive at their port of discharge, that he did it only for the preservation of the vessel, and the rest of the lading that remains yet in her. And the wines, or other goods, that were cast overboard, ought to be valued or prized according to the just value of the other goods that arrive in safety. And when these shall be sold, the price or value thereof ought to be divided livre a livre among the merchants. * * *

Article IX

If it happen, that by reason of much foul weather the master is like to be constrained to cut his masts, he ought first to call the merchants, if there be any aboard the ship, and such as have goods and merchandize in the vessel, and to consult them, saying, *Sirs, it is requisite to cut down the mast to save the ship and lading, it being in this case my duty.* And frequently they also cut their mooring cables, leaving behind them their cables and anchors to save the ship and her lading; all which things are reckoned and computed *livre* by *livre*, as the goods are that were cast overboard. * * *

Notes

1. The laws of Oleron take their name from the Isle of Oleron, which lies off the southwestern coast of France. Their origin is uncertain. They have been claimed to be of English and of French origin and may date back to the time of Richard I, who reigned 1189–1199.

2. For another early statement of general average, which is probably over 1800 years old, see Babylonian Talmud, Bava Kamma 116b (applying a similar rule to vessels and to caravans).

3. The word "average" in this context means the "expense or loss to owners, arising from damage at sea to the ship or cargo." 1 Oxford English Dictionary 817 (2d ed. 1989). The word's derivation is much debated, but it may be related to the Arabic *awariyah*. A general average is one borne proportionately by all property interests in the voyage. By contrast, a "particular average" is borne solely by the owner of the property that has suffered a loss. That usage is also important in the closely related marine insurance context. See *infra* at 455.

B. Introduction to the Current Doctrine

The current general average doctrine—as it is applied in the context of modern shipping transactions—is fundamentally the same as the concept expressed in the Rhodian law and the laws of Oleron. The U.S. general maritime law has recognized essentially the current doctrine since the earliest days of the republic, and the courts established the basic U.S. principles during the nineteenth century. The core idea was well expressed in *The Star of Hope*, 76 U.S. 203, 228 (1870):

> Common justice dictates that where two or more parties are engaged in the same sea risk, and one of them, in a moment of imminent peril, makes a sacrifice to avoid the impending danger or incurs extraordinary expenses to promote the general safety, the loss or expenses so incurred shall be assessed upon all in proportion to the share of each in the adventure.

General average is, in short, perhaps the most ancient doctrine of modern maritime law, not only in its underlying principles but also in the applicable doctrine.

Although the doctrine is part of the general maritime law, the parties to a maritime transaction have considerable freedom to specify by contract how general average will be handled in a particular case. As with most aspects of commercial maritime law, however, the industry benefits from having uniform rules that give effect to shared expectations. Beginning with a conference in Glasgow in 1860, international maritime interests have created private rules to govern general average. For well over a century, bills of lading and charterparties have incorporated a version of these uniform rules. The York Rules of 1864 were amended at a conference in Antwerp to produce the York-Antwerp Rules of 1877. Subsequent revisions—generally occurring every 25 years or so, but more frequent in recent years—continued to be known as the York-Antwerp Rules, regardless of where they were negotiated. The current version is known as "the York-Antwerp Rules 2016." Since World War II, the rules have been maintained under the auspices of the Comité Maritime International (CMI). Cf. *supra* at 282 note 2. The York-Antwerp Rules have never been adopted by treaty or statute, but courts nevertheless give effect to them (as contractually agreed by the parties) even when they conflict with the general maritime law.

It is important to understand the limited scope of general average. The owner of property that has been sacrificed is not made whole. Instead, the owners of the property that has been saved contribute so that each property owner suffers the same percentage of loss. (The problem below illustrates the principle.) Not every loss is compensated. In *Barnard v. Adams*, *infra* at 370, the Supreme Court explained the three essential requirements that must be satisfied to bring a case within the doctrine. In brief, there must be a "peril," a common danger that threatens the entire common adventure; there must be a voluntary "sacrifice" for the common benefit that falls more heavily on some participants than on others; and the sacrifice must be successful (at least in part) to avoid the peril. The next two sections will explore the "sacrifice" and "peril" requirements in greater detail.

An actual general average adjustment is typically complex and time-consuming. In theory it is the master's duty to calculate the amount of each party's contribution and to make payment to the owner whose property has been sacrificed. In practice, when a master of a vessel determines that a general average event has occurred, the vessel owner hires an average adjuster to determine the amount that the vessel owner and each cargo owner must contribute. The vessel has a possessory lien on cargo for the payment of general average. The master will release the cargo upon receiving a guarantee of an insurer or some other acceptable security to pay any contribution that is ultimately found to be due.

It will help you to understand the doctrine and the cases applying it if you carefully work through the simplified problem here. Keep in mind that the goal of the adjustment is to ensure that each participant in the common adventure bears a proportionate share of the general average expenses. In other words, if one shipper has cargo on the vessel worth twice as much as another shipper's cargo, then the first shipper should bear twice as much of the total loss when the vessel's owner declares a general average. Each owner's share will consist of the value of the property that it has lost and the amount of the contribution that it must make under the adjustment. The proportionate shares are based on each participant's stake in the enterprise. Just as the shippers have put their cargo "at risk," the shipowner also participates in the common adventure, putting at risk both the ship and any freight that is due on the completion of the voyage.

Problem

Suppose that a shipowner operates a vessel worth $25 million. On the fateful voyage, all of the cargo belongs to three shippers. The first shipper's cargo is worth $10 million and the freight on that cargo totals $500,000. The second shipper's cargo is worth $15 million and the freight on that cargo totals $1 million. The third shipper's cargo is worth $20 million and the freight on that cargo totals $1.5 million. (All of the freight is earned on the completion of the voyage.) Facing a covered peril, the shipowner incurs general average expenses of $3 million and also sacrifices 10% of the third shipper's cargo (i.e., cargo worth $2 million). In the general average adjustment, what sums should be paid, by whom, and to whom?

In analyzing this problem, you should first calculate how much each party has at risk. For the shipowner, remember to include both the value of the ship and the pending freight. Then you can calculate the total amount at risk for all the parties. Next, you should calculate how much each party lost. For the shipowner, remember to include both the general average expenses and any lost freight. (The sacrifice of 10% of the third shipper's cargo entailed a corresponding loss of pending freight for that cargo.) Then you can calculate the total amount of the losses. Finally, you can calculate each party's proportionate share of the loss and the adjustments that need to be made so that each party suffers only its proportionate share.

Notes

1. The vessel owner pays the adjuster's costs, which are partially recoverable as a general average expense from the other property interests. Even if it is ultimately determined that no other general average is due, the costs of the adjuster are recoverable unless the vessel owner acted unreasonably in proceeding with the average adjustment.

2. General average adjustments are rarely litigated. When litigation does occur, the case is more likely to ask whether general average was appropriate at all than to challenge the details of the adjustment.

3. A vessel owner generally declares general average with the goal of recovering from the cargo interests a portion of its expenses in dealing with a peril. (That is one reason general average tends to be less popular with cargo interests.) But cargo interests sometimes benefit from a general average adjustment, as in the classic case when "cargo has been jettisoned in order to lighten a ship," see *supra* at 367. And cargo interests may assert the right to general average. In *American African Export Co. v. S.S. Export Champion*, 442 F. Supp. 715 (S.D.N.Y 1977), the successful plaintiffs were the owners of cargo that was damaged as the result of efforts to prevent the spread of a fire in the hold. The owners of the cargo burned by the fire could not recover in general average.[1] That damage was caused not by a voluntary sacrifice to save the venture from the peril but by the peril itself. It was a "particular average." See *supra* at 368 note 3. But the court held that the owners of cargo that had been damaged by efforts to prevent the spread of the fire were permitted to recover in general average. As a practical matter, how should the cargo interests' damages be calculated when no general average adjustment took place?

C. The Sacrifice

Barnard v. Adams

Supreme Court of the United States, 1850
51 U.S. (10 How.) 270, 13 L. Ed. 417, 2004 AMC 899

Mr. Justice GRIER delivered the opinion of the Court.

The plaintiffs below, Joseph Adams and others, brought this action against Charles Barnard and others, in the Circuit Court of New York, to recover contribution in general average for the loss of their vessel called the *Brutus*, on board of which certain goods were

1. Under the Fire Statute and COGSA § 4(2)(b), see *supra* at 303–04, the owners of the burned cargo were also unable to recover from the carrier.

shipped, and consigned to [the defendants], and delivered to them on their promise to pay, provided contribution were justly due.

On the 8th of October, 1843, the ship *Brutus* was lying at anchor, at the usual place of mooring vessels in the outer roads at Buenos Ayres, about seven miles from the shore. The width of the river at that place, between Buenos Ayres and Colonia on the opposite shore, is about fifteen miles. The *Brutus* had taken her cargo on board for New York, consisting of nutria skins, dry hides, horns, and jerked beef. The master was on shore, and [the ship] was in charge of the first mate, with a crew consisting of twelve persons in all. On the 7th, a gale had commenced, which on the 8th had become dangerous. About four o'clock next morning the ship began to drag her anchors, and the small bower anchor was let go. About nine o'clock in the evening, the gale increasing, the best bower anchor parted with a loud report. About ten o'clock, the small bower parted, and the ship commenced drifting broadside with the wind and waves.

* * * The chains were then slipped, and the vessel got before the wind. Two men were put to the wheel, and one to the lead, and it was determined "to run the ship ashore for the preservation of the cargo and the lives of the crew." It was now about eleven o'clock at night when the ship was got before the wind and under command of the helm. The shore next to Buenos Ayres, towards which the ship had been drifting, had banks and shallows extending out some three or four miles. If the vessel had been driven on these by the tempest, she would have been wrecked and lost, together with the cargo and crew. On the Colonia side of the river were sunken rocks several miles from the shore. "For the purpose of saving the cargo and crew anyhow, and possibly the ship," she was steered up the river, inclining a little towards the Buenos Ayres side, with the intention of running her on shore at a convenient place. After they had proceeded up the river about ten miles, the mate discovered from the flashes of lightning that the vessel was approaching a point called St. Isidro, off which he perceived something black which he supposed to be rocks, and "being afraid," or "thinking it impossible to get by" this point without being wrecked and lost, he directed the course of the vessel to be changed towards the shore, where he had seen what he supposed to be a house, but which turned out to be a large tree. About midnight the vessel struck the beach and the rudder was knocked away. * * *

The place where she was stranded was a level beach about two hundred yards above ordinary low-water-mark. The ship was not wrecked, or broken up, though somewhat damaged, and the cargo was not injured. The master chartered the bark *Serene*, and transferred the cargo to her. But it was found that, with the means to be obtained in that vicinity, it would have cost more than the ship was worth to get her off the beach. She was therefore sold. The *Serene* afterwards arrived safely at New York, under command of Captain Adams, former master of the *Brutus*. * * *

On these facts the court instructed the jury as follows:

> The evidence on the subject of the stranding consists in the uncontradicted and unimpeached testimony of a single witness. He was the acting master of the vessel at the time of the loss in question. He states that when the vessel was without any means of resisting the storm, and her going ashore upon a rocky and more dangerous part of the shore was, in his opinion, inevitable, he did intentionally and for the better security of the property and persons engaged in the adventure, give her a direction to what he supposed to be, and what proved to be, a part of the shore where she could lie more safely. These facts, if credited by you, constitute in judgment of law a voluntary sacrifice of the vessel, and for such sacrifice the plaintiffs are entitled to recover in general average.

This instruction * * * raises the most important question in the case. [Defendants argue that the instruction was legally erroneous. The essence of their argument is that if the loss of the vessel by the storm was "inevitable," then the stranding cannot have been "voluntary."]

* * *

The law of general average has its foundation in equity. The principle, that "what is given for the general benefit of all shall be made good by the contribution of all," is recommended, not only by its equity, but also by its policy, because it encourages the owner to throw away his property without hesitation in time of need. In order to constitute a case for general average, three things must concur:

> 1st. A common danger; a danger in which ship, cargo, and crew all participate; a danger imminent and apparently "inevitable," except by voluntarily incurring the loss of a portion of the whole to save the remainder.
>
> 2d. There must be a voluntary jettison ... or casting away of some portion of the joint concern for the purpose of avoiding this imminent peril ... or, in other words, a transfer of the peril from the whole to a particular portion of the whole.
>
> 3d. This attempt to avoid the imminent common peril must be successful.

It is evident from these propositions, that the assertion so much relied on in the argument, namely, "that if the peril be inevitable there can be no contribution," is a mere truism, as the hypothesis of the case requires that the common peril, though imminent, shall be successfully avoided. Those who urge it must therefore mean something else. And it seems, when more carefully stated, to be this, "that if the common peril was of such a nature that the ... thing cast away to save the rest would have perished anyhow, or perished 'inevitably,' even if it had not been selected to suffer in place of the whole, there can be no contribution."

If this be the meaning of this proposition * * *, it is a denial of the whole doctrine upon which the claim for general average has its foundation. For the master of the ship would not be justified in casting a part of the cargo into the sea, or slipping his anchor, or cutting away his masts, or stranding his vessel, unless compelled to it by the necessity of the case, in order to save both ship and cargo, or one of them, from an imminent peril which threatened their common destruction. The necessity of the case must compel him to choose between the loss of the whole and part; but, however metaphysicians may stumble at the assertion, it is this forced choice which is necessary to justify the master in making a sacrifice (as it is called) of any part for the whole. * * *

But the right to contribution is not made to depend on any real or presumed intention to destroy the thing cast away, but on the fact that it had been selected to suffer the peril in place of the whole, that the remainder may be saved. * * *

There is therefore no error in the instruction given by the court below on this point. * * * The judgment of the Circuit Court is therefore affirmed.

Mr. Justice DANIEL dissenting.

* * * Mr. Phillips, in his work on Insurance (Vol. I., p. 338), and in a note to STEVENS ON AVERAGE (p. 81), lays down the law, both in England and in the United States, to be this: that "the voluntary stranding of the ship is general average; but not the mere steering her to a less dangerous place for stranding, when she is inevitably drifting to the shore." * * *

Note

It was long debated whether a voluntary stranding ought to constitute a general average act. Out of concern that a liberal rule might promote fraud on the part of the master, the early versions of the York-Antwerp Rules narrowly restricted the right to recover general average in cases of voluntary stranding. Over time, the York-Antwerp Rules liberalized the treatment of the subject to the point that it is now similar to *Barnard v. Adams*. Under the current version of the York-Antwerp Rules, Rule V extends general average to cases in which "a ship is intentionally run on shore for the common safety."

Ralli v. Troop

Supreme Court of the United States, 1895
157 U.S. 386, 15 S. Ct. 657, 39 L. Ed. 742, 2004 AMC 1484

Mr. Justice GRAY delivered the opinion of the Court.

* * *

[The British bark *J.W. Parker* was moored in the port of Calcutta, fully loaded and preparing to depart for Boston, when a fire broke out in a cargo hold.] [A]s soon as the mate sounded the alarm of fire, "from sixty to seventy men from the crews of the neighboring vessels" came to his assistance, bringing their buckets with them, as well as a force pump "from a ship near by,"' and poured water into the hold. Afterwards the port authorities came with fire engines, and took the direction of the vessel, and were found by the master, when he returned on board, in charge of her. The port authorities pumped steam and water from their engines into the hold, and moved the vessel from her moorings, and put her aground. The master does not appear to have objected to their taking charge of and moving the ship, and any objection on his part would have been futile, for it was clearly within their powers as conservators of the port. The master successfully removed part of the cargo, and desired, and believed it to be prudent and feasible, to remove more. But the port authorities forbade and prevented his doing so, because of the danger of increasing the fire, and, acting upon their own judgment, extinguished the fire by scuttling the vessel, whereby she became a wreck, not worth repairing. The master, being then permitted by the port authorities to resume charge of the vessel, saved the rest of the cargo in a damaged condition. [Subsequently the bark's owners claimed general average contributions from the cargo that was saved. The circuit court allowed the claim. We reverse.]

* * *

The circuit court * * * has found as facts that "the measures taken by the mate before the port authorities took charge of the ship, and those subsequently taken by the port authorities, were the best available to extinguish the fire, and to save greater loss upon the cargo." But it is not found whether the motive and purpose of the port authorities was to save this vessel and her cargo, or to save other vessels and property in the port; whereas, in order to constitute a general average, the sole object of the sacrifice must appear to have been to save this vessel and cargo.

* * *

[Moreover, as] the sacrifice must be for the benefit of the common adventure, and of that adventure only, so it must be made by some one specially charged with the control and the safety of that adventure, and not be caused by the compulsory act of others, whether private persons or public authorities. * * * A sacrifice of vessel or cargo by the act of a stranger to the adventure, although authorized by the municipal law to make the sacrifice for the protection of his own interests or of those of the public, gives no right of contribution, either for or against those outside interests, or even as between the parties to the common adventure.

The port authorities are strangers to the maritime adventure, and to all the interests included therein. They are in no sense the agents or representatives of the parties to that adventure, either by reason of any implied contract between those parties or of any power conferred by law over the adventure as such. They have no special authority or special duty in regard to the preservation or the destruction of any vessel and her cargo, as distinct from the general authority and the general duty appertaining to them as guardians of the port, and of all the property, on land or water, within their jurisdiction. * * * Their sole office and paramount duty, and, it must be presumed, their motive and purpose, in destroying ship or cargo, in order to put out a fire, are not to save the rest of a single maritime adventure, or to benefit private individuals engaged in that adventure, but to protect and preserve all the shipping and property in the port, for the benefit of the public. In the execution of this office and in the performance of this duty they act under their official responsibility to the public, and are not subject to be controlled by the owners of the adventure, or by the master of the vessel as their representative.

In fine, the destruction of the *J. W. Parker* by the act of the municipal authorities of the port of Calcutta was not a voluntary sacrifice of part of a maritime adventure for the safety of the rest of that adventure, made, according to the maritime law, by the owners of vessel or cargo, or by the master as the agent and representative of both. But it was a compulsory sacrifice, made by the paramount authority of public officers deriving their powers from the municipal law, and the municipal law only; and therefore neither gave any right of action nor of contribution against the owners of property benefited by the sacrifice, but not included in the maritime adventure, nor yet any right of contribution as between the owners of the different interests included in that adventure.

* * *

Mr. Justice BROWN [joined by Mr. Justice Harlan], dissenting.

* * * I find myself unable to escape the conviction that a person who has lawful possession of a vessel, and exercises the authority of a master over it, either by appointment or consent of the owner or by operation of law, is to be considered the master *pro hac vice*, and competent to bind the vessel or her cargo by all acts without the scope of his apparent authority.

There is in this case a failure to find an important fact, namely, whether the action of the port authorities was taken in the interest of the ship and cargo alone, or in the interest of other neighboring property, exposed to the conflagration. * * * [T]the case should have been remanded for a further finding upon this point * * *.

* * *

The opinion of the court tends, in every such emergency, to put the master and local authorities in antagonism, to give rise to unseemly conflicts between them, and to prevent the master from availing himself of their superior facilities for extinguishing fires. It seems to me there is no distinction in principle between a sacrifice made by a master and one made by authority of law, provided the common safety of the ship and cargo be the object of their action.

Notes

1. **The purpose of the "sacrifice."** In *Dabney v. New England Mutual Marine Insurance Co.*, 96 Mass. 300 (1867), the *Freedonia* took on board over 300 people from another vessel which was sinking. To make room for them, the master of the *Freedonia* ordered that a large amount of fruit be jettisoned. The court held that the jettison was not a general average act because the motive was to save the passengers, not to preserve the *Freedonia* from peril.

Similar reasoning was used in *The John Perkins*, 13 Fed. Cas. 702 (C.C.D. Mass. 1857) (No. 7,360), in which a vessel's crew cut its cable and anchor to avoid a collision with another vessel that was headed toward her. The second vessel was not required to contribute in general average toward the loss of the cable and anchor.

2. **Who ordered the sacrifice?** When the master or one acting on his authority summons the fire department to put out a fire, the owners of property sacrificed in the effort to put out the fire are entitled to general average. *The Northern No. 30*, 24 F.2d 975 (E.D.N.C. 1928). The opinion suggested that it would also constitute general average if the fire company had not been summoned by the vessel but had acted solely for the benefit of the vessel and cargo. A similar case is *The Beatrice*, 36 F.2d 99 (S.D.N.Y. 1924).

D. The Peril

Navigazione Generale Italiana v. Spencer Kellogg & Sons, Inc.

United States Court of Appeals, Second Circuit, 1937
92 F.2d 41, 1937 AMC 1506

AUGUSTUS N. HAND, Circuit Judge:

* * *

The *Mincio*, a steel single screw steamer of from 7,000 to 8,000 tons, was overhauled at Genoa [in August, 1926], where she had received the highest classification from the Italian Lloyds. She left Rosario in the Argentine on October 7, 1926, having at that port taken on board a partial cargo of 232,947 bushels (or 5963 tons) of linseed in bulk belonging to the respondent [Spencer Kellogg & Sons]. She was in charge of a local compulsory pilot and was bound for Buenos Aires, where she was to complete her cargo of linseed in bulk by loading about 1,000 tons additional. She was to carry the cargo of linseed in bulk to New York under a charter party * * * [which] provided that "average if any" should be "payable according to York-Antwerp Rules of 1924."

[The] *Mincio*, with a draft of 22 feet, 6 inches, * * * proceeded down the Parana river [until] the water was running too low in the channel for safe navigation. [When informed] that the water in the channel had reached a depth of 22 feet, 8 inches, she weighed anchor by order of her pilot and resumed her voyage down the river. About 10:15 a.m., as she was nearing buoy K-93 just above the entrance of Nuevo Channel, she stranded on the muddy, sandy bottom of the river. The river there is approximately 14 miles wide and the distance from the Uruguayan coast from 2 to 2½ miles. The width of the navigable channel at the point of stranding is about 150 feet, and the depth of water according to the soundings taken by the first officer, accompanied by the second officer, shortly after grounding, was 22 feet, 1 to 2 inches, at the bow and stern, and 23 feet at the center of the vessel. As soon as the vessel grounded, she lay on the bottom of mud and sand a little to the left side of the channel. Her engines were at once stopped and her anchors run out, including a kedge anchor run to the "starboard aft" in order to prevent the wash of any vessel passing on the starboard from pushing her stern "against the nearby bank." The place where the stranding occurred was within the zone of the Pamperos or South American hurricanes. There was evidence that such a hurricane, coming as it ordinarily does from the southwest, would tend further to lower the depth of the water. In any event it would rock, pound, and strain the vessel. The master of the *Mincio* testified that there was "danger of opening up seams in the plating of the steamer," though he said "the vessel was resting on an even keel with a slight list to starboard." The second officer testified that the ship was resting on the bottom at the bow and at the stern but not in the center, that, as the cargo was in the center, the ship would be strained, and, if the wind increased in velocity, might be pushed further into the bank of the channel so that, in order to proceed, she would have to be lightened and the cargo discharged. The master thought that the danger was not "immediate," but the second officer stated that it was imminent. If a serious leak developed by reason of the opening of the seams, the linseed would have been damaged and would tend to swell and choke the pumps and perhaps burst the ship's plating.

After the *Mincio* had stranded, the master notified the ship's agent at Buenos Aires that she had stopped at buoy K-93 "for insufficiency of water" and the agents sent a tug with an official on board from the harbor master's office. The steamer attempted to get off the strand by running her engines full speed astern from 11:30 a.m. to 11:45 a.m. This was done because it was thought that the water had risen sufficiently so that she could be floated, but the attempt met with no success. On October 10, according to the engine log, the engines were again run from 11:30 to 11:45, also from 12 noon until 4 p.m., and again from 7:30 p.m. to 10:30 p.m., when the vessel got free from the bar. * * *

After being released from the strand, the *Mincio* proceeded to Buenos Aires, a survey of her engines and the rudder transmission lines was held, and slight repairs to them were made. After she reached New York and discharged her cargo she was dry-docked. It was then found that seventeen plates forward on the port side of the bottom of the ship were more or less badly set up or indented and the rivets and landings were leaking. Approximately 5,000 rivets scattered through the bottom plating were leaking, the cement in the double bottom on the port and starboard side was broken and disturbed from forward to aft of amidships, the frames, the floors and intercostals in the way of the damaged plating on the port side were more or less started and buckled and rivets were broken off. Rivets were leaking in No. 1 and No. 2 tank margins and there was also substantial damage to the ship's engine and steering machinery.

On the discharge of the cargo at New York, the owner of the *Mincio* asserted a general average lien, and in consideration of the surrender of that lien [Spencer Kellogg] agreed in writing that, if Johnson & Higgins were appointed adjusters * * *, it would pay to the owners of the vessel or Johnson & Higgins according to its ratable proportion so much of the losses and expenses as upon an adjustment of the same to be stated by Johnson & Higgins might be shown by the statement to be a charge upon the cargo. [Johnson & Higgins reported that the total damage as a result of the stranding was $50,554.43, that $40,503.33 thereof was particular average chargeable to the owner of the vessel alone, and that of the balance amounting to $10,049.10 cargo's ratable portion was $6,451.16. Spencer Kellogg refused to pay. The owner of the *Mincio* libelled Spencer Kellogg in the District Court for the Southern District of New York. The district court dismissed the libel.]

The errors assigned by the appellant are that the District Court erred (1) in holding that there was no danger threatening the vessel sufficient to constitute a case in general average and (2) in not enforcing the agreement to pay whatever the average adjusters should find to be due to the shipowner.

There must be fair reason to regard a vessel in peril in order to require a contribution in general average. While the courts in some cases have used expressions indicating that both in general average and in salvage cases it is essential that the property at risk be subject to an immediately impending danger, we think the "imminency" of the peril is not the critical test. If the danger be real and substantial, a sacrifice or expenditure made in good faith for the common interest is justified, even though the advent of any catastrophe may be distant or indeed unlikely. In pointing out the broad discretion which must be allowed in such cases to the master of the vessel, Judge Hough said in *Willcox, Peck & Hughes v. American Smelting & Refining Co.*, 210 F. 89, 91 (S.D.N.Y. 1913): "If he finds danger in a land-locked harbor, in shallows, at anchor, or moored to a wharf, it should be no answer to register a landsman's opinion as to the necessary absence of danger at such a place."

As Curtis, J., said in *Lawrence v. Minturn*, 58 U.S. 100, 109 (1854), where the necessity of a jettison of cargo was questioned: "It is true, that when it was actually made, the sea was smooth, and the ship in no immediate danger. But it satisfactorily appears, that these boilers and chimneys could not be thrown overboard, without the greatest risk, when there was any considerable sea. To require delay until a storm, would be, in effect, to prohibit the sacrifice."

It is argued on behalf of the cargo that there was no real risk. The master is quoted as testifying that "there was no immediate danger to ship or cargo," but he qualified this by saying that there was a danger "of opening up seams in the plating of the steamer"—a prognosis which the survey showed was actually realized. Indeed, when a vessel is stranded she and her cargo are practically always in a substantial peril. * * *

In the present case we think the elements requisite to a general average act were established. There was the danger that the seams of the steamer's plating would open as was proved by the testimony of both the master and the mate and likewise by the heavy bottom damage actually sustained. There was the realization of that peril acknowledged in the master's testimony and manifested by the care with which he watched for rising water in the steamer's bilges. There was the intentional extraordinary use of the steamer's engine machinery to drive her over the bar into the deeper water and thereby at the earliest opportunity to free her from her position of peril, regardless of the risk of damage which such extraordinary use necessarily involved. These things constituted the general average act and rendered the respondent liable to contribute its proportion of expenditures incurred for the common benefit of ship and cargo.

The claim of the respondent that large vessels were constantly stranding in the river, though readily released without damage or risk, is disputed, and seems to us without sufficient foundation. The notice to the Argentine government of the stranding of the *Mincio* resulted in an official investigation and the dispatching of an official from the harbor master's office. Such attention would hardly be given to an ordinary incident of frequent occurrence and no importance.

Inasmuch as a case for general average was established, the agreement to pay whatever the average adjusters found due to the shipowner ought to be enforced. * * *

Note

If there is a peril, but the master is mistaken as to its degree and takes more drastic action than necessary, general average can still be allowed. *The Wordsworth*, 88 F. 313 (S.D.N.Y. 1898). As the Supreme Court said in *The Star of Hope*, 76 U.S. 203, 230 (1870):

> Masters are often compelled, in the performance of their duties, to choose between the probable consequences of imminent perils threatening the loss of the ship, cargo, and all on board, and a sacrifice of some portion of the associated interests in their custody and under their control, as the only means of averting the dangers of the impending peril in their power to employ. They must elect in such an emergency, and if they, in the exercise of their best skill and judgment, decide that it is their duty to lighten the ship, cut away the masts, or to strand the vessel, courts of justice are not inclined to overrule their determinations.

But general average has been disallowed when the master was mistaken as to the existence of peril. In one case the master thought that there was a fire in a hold carrying cotton, but it turned out that there was no fire. The heat from the hold had been caused by a broken steam pipe. *Ravenscroft v. United States*, 1936 AMC 696, *aff'd*, 88 F.2d 418 (2d Cir. 1937).

E. Vessel Fault

The Jason

Supreme Court of the United States, 1912
225 U.S. 32, 32 S. Ct. 560, 56 L. Ed. 969

Mr. Justice PITNEY delivered the opinion of the Court.

* * *

On July 30, 1904, the Norwegian Steamship *Jason*, while bound on a voyage from Cienfuegos, Cuba, to New York, with general cargo, including 12,000 bags of sugar consigned to Arbuckle Brothers, * * * stranded off the south coast of Cuba, through the negligence of her navigators. * * *

The vessel was relieved from the strand on August 9 as the result of sacrifices by jettison of 2,042 bags of sugar (1,657 bags being the property of Arbuckle Brothers), of sacrifices and extraordinary expenditures voluntarily made or incurred by the shipowner through the master, and of the services of salvors specially employed. Said sacrifices and expenditures were necessary to relieve ship, cargo, and freight from common peril. She then completed her voyage, and made delivery of the remainder of her cargo to the several consignees at New York on their executing an average bond * * *.

[Johnson & Higgins, adjusters, determined that Arbuckle Brothers owed a general average contribution of $5060.24. Arbuckle refused to pay on the ground that the stranding resulted from the ship's negligence. The *Jason*'s owners libelled Arbuckle in the Southern District of New York. The district court dismissed the libel. On appeal to the Second Circuit, the court initially affirmed. Thereafter it granted a rehearing and certified the below-discussed question to the Supreme Court.]

The bills of lading for all of the *Jason*'s cargo contained the following provision:

* * *

> If the owner of the ship shall have exercised due diligence to make said ship in all respects seaworthy and properly manned, equipped, and supplied, it is hereby agreed that in case of danger, damage, or disaster resulting from fault or negligence of the pilot, master, or crew, in the navigation or management of the ship, or from latent or other defects, or unseaworthiness of the ship, whether existing at time of shipment or at beginning of the voyage, but not discoverable by due diligence, the consignees or owners of the cargo shall not be exempted from liability for contribution in general average, or for any special charges incurred, but, with the shipowner, shall contribute in general average, and shall pay such special charges, as if such danger, damage, or disaster had not resulted from such fault, negligence, latent or other defect or unseaworthiness.

* * *

That the facts present a case of general average within the meaning of the clause embodied in the bills of lading is entirely clear. There was a common, imminent peril involving ship and cargo, followed by a voluntary and extraordinary sacrifice of property (including extraordinary expenses), necessarily made to avert the peril, and a resulting common benefit to the adventure. * * *

The principal controversy is upon the question of the validity of the agreement that if the shipowner "shall have exercised due diligence to make said ship in all respects seaworthy, and properly manned, equipped, and supplied," then, in case of danger, damage, or disaster resulting from (inter alia) negligent navigation, the cargo owners shall not be exempted from liability for contribution in general average, but, with the shipper, shall contribute as if such danger, damage, or disaster, had not resulted from negligent navigation. The facts show that the shipowner had fulfilled the condition imposed upon him by this clause; that is, he had "exercised due diligence to make said ship in all respects seaworthy and properly manned, equipped, and supplied." The question presented for solution turns upon the effect of [§ 3 of the Harter Act] * * * .

Prior to the Harter Act it was established that a common carrier by sea could not, by any agreement in the bill of lading, exempt himself from responding to the owner of cargo for damages arising from the negligence of the master or crew of the vessel. [ ] But of course the responsibilities of the carrier were subject to modification by law, and with respect to vessels transporting merchandise from or between ports of the United States and foreign ports they were substantially modified by the Harter Act.

* * *

In the case now before us it is argued in behalf of the shipowner that since by the 3d section of the Harter Act he is absolved from responsibility for the negligence of his master and crew under the circumstances existing, there is nothing in the policy of the law to debar him from bargaining with the owners of cargo for a participation in the general average contribution. In behalf of the cargo owners it is insisted that the construction placed upon the legislation in question by this court in *The Irrawaddy* [171 U.S. 187 (1898)] leaves the shipowner still disabled from making an agreement with the cargo owners for a participation with them in general average contributions resulting from negligent navigation or management of the ship by its master and crew.

* * *

The point of the decision in *The Irrawaddy* (and as an authority the case goes no further) is, that while the Harter Act relieved the shipowner from liability for his servant's negligence, it did not of its own force entitle him to share in a general average rendered necessary by such negligence.

It is, however, further insisted in behalf of the cargo owners that the agreement in question is contrary to public policy in another respect; namely, in that it attempts to relieve the shipowner from one of the essential duties arising out of the relation of carrier and shipper, and from which the Harter Act has not relieved him. The argument is that although that act exempts him from the consequences of the negligent stranding, it leaves him still under the duty and obligation of caring for and preserving the cargo, after the stranding; that whenever the safety of the property intrusted to the shipowner is menaced, whether the peril be occasioned by vis major or by fault, and whether such fault be or be not of such character as to fall within the 3d section of the Harter Act, "the master is nevertheless bound to exert every effort to save the property, and if he fail in his duty, his owners are liable to the cargo for the resulting loss." If by "every effort" is meant every reasonable effort, we see no occasion to question the soundness of the reasoning. But it is further insisted that the duty of the master to save the imperiled property extends so far as to call for a sacrifice of a part of the owner's property if necessary to save the cargo. In our opinion the master's duty as agent of the owner is not so extensive. If it were, there would be an end at once of all contribution in general average for ship's sacrifices, for such sacrifices could not be deemed voluntary and extraordinary, if made in performance of the owner's general duty to his cargo.

* * *

In our opinion, so far as the Harter Act has relieved the shipowner from responsibility for the negligence of his master and crew, it is no longer against the policy of the law for him to contract with the cargo owners for a participation in general average contribution growing out of such negligence; and since the clause contained in the bills of lading of the *Jason*'s cargo admits the shipowner to share in the general average only under circumstances where by the act he is relieved from responsibility, the provision in question is valid, and entitles him to contribution under the circumstances stated.

* * *

Note

Modern bills of lading generally contain a "new Jason clause." A typical version reads as follows:

> In the event of accident, danger, damage or disaster before or after commencement of the voyage, resulting from any cause whatsoever whether due to negligence or not, for which or for the consequence of which, the Carrier is not responsible by statute, contract, or otherwise, the goods, shippers, consignees or owners of the goods shall contribute with the Carrier in general average to the payment of any sacrifices, losses or expenses of a general average nature that may be made or incurred, and shall pay salvage and special charges incurred in respect of the goods.

The clause is designed to apply should the bill of lading be governed by COGSA or another statute, or should the shipment be governed by a charterparty.

F. The Future of the Doctrine

Does the law of general average continue to make sense in today's commercial world? When the second edition of their classic treatise was published in 1975, Gilmore and Black added a new section questioning whether general average is "a necessary or useful institution." GILMORE & BLACK, THE LAW OF ADMIRALTY 270–271 (2d ed. 1975). Such criticism is not new. Over a century earlier, the Committee of Lloyd's had criticized the general average system in connection with the proposal that subsequently became the York Rules of 1864. Indeed, the marine insurance industry has been a regular critic of general average to this day.

The principal argument against general average is that the adjustment process is frequently expensive and complicated, and that the benefits achieved do not justify the high cost. Because vessel and cargo owners are typically insured (and inevitably have the option of obtaining insurance), the practical result of an adjustment today is merely to transfer funds from one insurer to another. Abolishing general average would save the high costs and allow insurers to adjust their premiums accordingly. In its origins, the doctrine spread the risks of a voyage among all the participants on that voyage, thus providing a primitive form of insurance. Today, a sophisticated marine insurance industry spreads those risks more broadly and more efficiently.

The strongest argument for retaining the doctrine has generally been that it gives a master of a vessel the freedom to deal with a crisis in the manner that will preserve life and property to the greatest extent possible, secure in the knowledge that the losses will be paid by the same parties in the same proportions regardless of whose property is sacrificed. In the absence of general average, the master's decisions might be constrained by the financial interests of the vessel's owner or by a fear of after-the-fact second-guessing from those who would argue that those interests (rather than the overall interest of the common adventure) drove the master's decisions. The doctrine's defenders also point to the practical difficulties in changing an existing regime that many still support.

The editors of a previous edition of the leading treatise on this specialized subject included an appendix detailing the arguments for and against the abolition of general average. See WILSON & COOKE, LOWNDES AND RUDOLF: THE LAW OF GENERAL AVERAGE AND THE YORK-ANTWERP RULES, app. 5 (12th ed. 1997).

Despite the criticisms, in 2016 the CMI completed a multi-year project to revise the York-Antwerp Rules. In conjunction with that revision, the CMI also produced non-binding "CMI Guidelines Relating to General Average," which are designed "to assist commercial interests with general average matters." Ultimately, it will be up to the industry to decide whether to incorporate the latest version of the Rules into its contracts.

Chapter VII

Salvage

Markakis v. S/S Volendam

United States District Court, S.D. New York, 1980
486 F. Supp. 1103, 1980 AMC 915

WEINFELD, District Judge:

[Plaintiff, master of the vessel *S.S. Monarch Sun*, commenced this suit on behalf of himself and the crew members of the *Sun* to recover a salvage award for services allegedly rendered to the *S.S. Monarch Star* between January 10 and 11, 1977.[1] The *Sun* and the *Star* were Panamanian-flag vessels engaged in passenger cruise voyages from Miami to various points in the Caribbean and return. Both vessels were owned by Monarch Cruise Lines, N.V., and operated by Technical Marine Planning ("TMP") of Miami.]

[At 14:35 hours on January 10, 1977, the *Star*, which was carrying 368 passengers and a crew of an almost equal number, sustained an engine failure while sailing off the northern coast of Cuba. A few hours later, her emergency generator also failed. Thus, the ship was left without power or lights and with only batteries to operate its radio. Throughout this time, the *Star* was having difficulty communicating with the head office in Miami.]

[During this same period the *Sun* was en route from Florida to Puerto Rico. At 21:15 hours on January 10, TMP radio-telephoned the *Sun* that the *Star* was disabled and instructed Markakis to change course and render assistance to the *Star*.] The *Sun* thereupon altered course and headed toward the northern coast of Cuba, where the *Star* lay disabled off the Cuban coast at various distances estimated from between twelve to fifteen miles. The ships rendezvoused on January 11 at 11:00 hours. The two captains agreed on procedures for transferring the passengers, some of the crew, baggage, and provisions of the crippled ship to the *Sun*. The transfer operation, carried out on tenders sent from the *Sun* and manned by the *Sun*'s crew, began at noon on January 11, and was completed five hours later. One crewman was slightly injured in the operation when he fell off one of the tenders. After it was completed, Captain Avdelas and other members of his crew remained on board the *Star*. Thereafter, at Captain Avdelas' request, TMP ordered Markakis to tow the *Star* farther away from the coast of Cuba and into the Old Bahama Channel, a deep and well-traveled shipping route. Avdelas himself acknowledged that the purpose

1. The *Sun* is now known as the *S.S. Volendam*. The other defendant, the *S.S. Veendam*, was formerly known as the *Monarch Star*. At trial plaintiff abandoned any claim against his own vessel, the *Volendam*.

of the tow was to bring the ship "to a safer place" until a tugboat sent from Miami by the *Star*'s owners arrived and finished the job.

Towing of the *Star* commenced at 18:05 and lasted about four hours. The *Sun*, with passengers from both vessels aboard, towed the *Star* a distance of approximately 13 miles in a generally northeasterly direction and away from the coast of Cuba. At 22:00 the tow lines were released at the request of Captain Avdelas. The *Sun* resumed its journey, embarking at destinations on its own route as well as those that would have been on the *Star*'s itinerary. The *Star* was left in the Old Bahama Channel to await its appointed rendezvous with the tug *Curb*, which arrived on January 12 at about 13:00 and which eventually towed the *Star* 324 miles back to Miami.

From the time that its engines first failed until the time of its rendezvous with the *Curb*, the *Star* remained close to the coast of Cuba and in constant motion. When its engines first stopped, the *Star* was located 12 miles off the coast. The Captain reported that he could see lights from the land and two Cuban gunboats were visible on the horizon. Immediately thereafter, the ship began to drift with the currents; first it was carried slightly south toward Cuba, and thereafter, on a steady line to the northwest along the Channel, running roughly parallel to the coast, although gradually moving away from it. * * * By the time of its rendezvous with the *Sun*, the *Star* had drifted 34.4 miles northwest from the point of its breakdown; when the *Sun* began to tow the *Star* it was then 23.3 miles off the coast of Cuba. It was towed 13.8 miles directly east, which brought it six more miles away from the coast. After the *Sun* had released its tow ropes, the wind picked up from the east, carrying the *Star* across the water currents and directly toward the Cuban coast. By the time of the arrival of the *Curb*, on January 12 at 13:00 hours, the *Star* had drifted 23 miles back toward Cuba and was only 17 miles from its coast. * * *

In order to prevail upon a claim for a salvage award, the plaintiff must prove three essential elements: "1. A marine peril. 2. Service voluntarily rendered when not required as an existing duty or from a special contract. 3. Success in whole or in part, or that the service rendered contributed to such success." There is no dispute that the third element has been satisfied. * * * However, the defendant disputes both of the other elements. * * *

Marine Peril

In determining whether there exists a marine peril sufficient to justify a salvage award, the Court must decide "not whether the peril is imminent, but rather whether it is 'reasonably to be apprehended.'" In order to prevail, the plaintiff need only establish that "'at the time the assistance [was] rendered, the ship [had] encountered any damage or misfortune which might expose her to destruction if the service were not rendered.'"

A variety of services, many of which seem more mundane than daring, qualify for salvage awards. [According to GILMORE & BLACK, THE LAW OF ADMIRALTY 536–537 (2d ed. 1975)]:

> The prototypical act [of salvage] is rescuing a ship in peril at sea and towing her to a place of safety.... In deciding [whether to make an award] ... courts look to the situation that existed at the time the ship was taken in tow: If she was not under command, unable to navigate or to reach port unaided, the service will be considered salvage even though the ship was not in imminent danger of destruction and even though the towage itself was calm and uneventful.... The act of salvage need not be so dramatic and need not even consist in rendering physical assistance: standing by or escorting a distressed ship in a position to give aid if it becomes necessary, giving information on the channel to follow ... to avoid running

> aground, carrying a message as a result of which necessary aid and equipment are forthcoming have all qualified. So long as the ship is in peril, any voluntary act which contributes to her ultimate safety may rank as an act of salvage.

The most frequent instances of salvage awards involve situations in which the salvor renders assistance to a vessel lodged in a sandbar or run aground on a reef. In such situations, the courts often justify the award by citing the possibility that storms could arise and further injure the stranded vessel, which is incapable of dislodging itself under its own power. * * *

Just as a stranded ship is imperiled, so too, one adrift without power may be equally endangered. Salvage awards have long been accorded to those who tow disabled and imperiled vessels from the open sea into port. * * *

The facts of the instant case clearly support the conclusion that on January 10 and 11, 1977, the *Star* was exposed to peril "'reasonably to be apprehended.'" Not only was the ship unable to "pursue her intended voyage or deal effectively with any emergency" that might have arisen, she was left to drift, at times in total darkness and without adequate power to communicate by radio. * * * Between the time of the *Sun*'s departure and the *Curb*'s arrival, the *Star* drifted 23 miles back toward the coast of Cuba. Had that drift occurred before the *Sun* had towed her, the *Star* might well have been dashed against the reefs lining the northern coast of Cuba.

In addition, it is noted that at the time of the breakdown, the *Star* was about 12 miles off the shore of Cuba, or at the edge of the territorial waters claimed by that country; and that it was in sight of at least two Cuban warships. Had it drifted closer to the shore, it faced a real possibility of interception or even reprisal.[17] * * * Though the danger to the *Star* was less than compelling and the rescue operation short of heroic, the ship was sufficiently imperiled to justify a salvage award.

Voluntary Act

The [defendant] also contends that the *Sun*'s crew acted under compulsion, rather than voluntarily, in that they were ordered by the owners to [go to the *Star*'s aid]. Initially, the [defendant] argues that the vessels' joint ownership by Monarch Lines precludes a salvage award. In essence, the [defendant] seeks to analogize this situation to those cases in which courts have refused to permit awards to crews that perform salvage services to their own vessels. The principles of those cases, however, are not apt here. At least since 1912, when Congress codified the trend of the common law, the fact of common ownership of the salvor and salved vessels has played no part in the grant of salvage awards.[20]

The [defendant] also contends that the *Sun*'s crew were, in effect, under a duty to obey the orders of their owner, and that they had no choice in the matter. Although there are instances in which a would-be salvor's pre-existing duty to act defeats his claim, those

---

17. On December 28, 1977, the United States Coast Guard issued an "Advisory Notice" to inform the United States maritime community that the Cuban government was enforcing its claim to a 12-mile territorial sea by stopping, and at times detaining, vessels approaching within 30 miles of the north coast of Cuba.

20. 46 U.S.C. § 80107(b) (effective August 1, 1912) provides: "The right to remuneration for aid or salvage services is not affected by common ownership of the vessels giving and receiving the aid or salvage services." * * *

cases are rare.[21] Where an individual performs a salvage service outside the normal scope of his employment, the rule is that "nothing short of a contract [between the owners of the salved vessel and the salvors] to pay a given sum for the services to be rendered, or a binding agreement to pay at all events, whether successful or unsuccessful, in the enterprise, will operate as a bar to a meritorious claim for salvage." Indeed, even if the master, the owner or the charterer of the salvor vessel is found expressly to have waived his rights, the crew is not bound by the waiver.

* * *

In the instant case there is not even a suggestion that the articles of employment of the *Sun*'s crew contemplate salvage service. * * * If their claim could be defeated merely because their employer had ordered them to perform salvage service, Congress' purpose of fostering salvage service by eliminating common ownership as an impediment to an award would likewise be defeated: the owner of a vessel in distress could always order other, commonly-owned vessels to the rescue, without the requirement of a salvage contract and without being required to pay any salvage award. Plainly such a result is contrary to the Congressional purpose. We hold that Captain Markakis and the crew of the *Sun* performed voluntary salvage service on January 10 and 11, 1977, when they rescued baggage and provisions of the *Star* and towed the vessel to safety.[28]

* * *

The Court holds the owners of the *Star* liable to the captain and crew of the Sun for salvage services performed. The matter will be referred, pursuant to the parties' stipulation, to a special master for a computation of the award.

Notes

1. **The Salvage Act (1912).** Most of the law of salvage is court-made. The Salvage Act, 46 U.S.C. § 80107 (formerly 46 U.S.C. app. §§ 727–731), merely codifies a few general principles, some of which came from the 1910 Salvage Treaty, 37 Stat. 1658, TS 576. Note that the Salvage Act includes a two-year statute of limitations. 46 U.S.C. § 80107(c).

2. **Jurisdiction.** The Salvage Act contains no provision directed to judicial jurisdiction. Under the general principles treated in Section I-F, *supra*, there is no legitimate basis for concluding that salvage litigation is exclusively for the federal admiralty courts. Yet there is a fairly strong current of authority that salvage cases may be maintained only in federal admiralty court. See, e.g., *Phillips v. Sea Tow*, 578 S.E.2d 846 (Ga. 2003). That viewpoint evidently traces to *Houseman v. The North Carolina*, 40 U.S. 40, 48 (1841), in which Chief Justice Taney's opinion for the Court included this dictum: "The admiralty is the only court where such a question can be tried; for what other court, but a court of admiralty, has jurisdiction to try a question of salvage?" The quoted dictum was correct as to *Houseman*, because it was an in rem action. Almost all of the authority for the view that salvage litigation is confined to the admiralty court come from dicta in in rem actions,

---

21. Firemen who aid in extinguishing blazes upon ships are precluded from obtaining salvage awards [ ], as are pilots acting within the scope of their employment duties [ ]. * * *

28. There are no grounds upon which to grant a life salvage award in the instant case. Although such an award is sometimes appropriate [see *Peninsular & Oriental*, *infra* at 404; see also 46 U.S.C. § 80107(a)], it can be granted only to those who have foregone the opportunity to engage in the more profitable work of property salvage. * * *

and indeed, most salvage litigation is in rem. All maritime in rem litigation is exclusively for the admiralty court under the general principles treated in Chapter IF. But as to in personam salvage litigation, the better view is that admiralty jurisdiction is not exclusive.

Even when brought in federal court there are limits on the court's subject matter jurisdiction to hear salvage claims. One court upheld the dismissal of a salvage claim of a partially submerged house that was being towed across the frozen surface of Lake Superior, saying that the action lacked a "nexus with traditional maritime activities." *Provost v. Huber*, 594 F.2d 717 (8th Cir. 1979). Another court held that it lacked jurisdiction over a salvage claim of an aircraft that had crashed into a landlocked lake. *Historic Aircraft Recovery Corp. v. Wrecked and Abandoned Voight F4U-1 Corsair Aircraft*, 294 F. Supp. 2d 132 (D. Me. 2003).

3. **Maritime Peril.** In *Fine v. Rockwood*, 895 F. Supp. 306, 1995 AMC 2048 (S.D. Fla. 1995), a vessel struck a rock and began taking on water. The captain managed to bring the vessel to a marina where it was secured to the dock as its engines flooded and it began to settle toward the bottom. The plaintiffs were two scuba divers who took underwater photographs of the vessel and began to patch the hull. The court granted them quantum meruit but denied them salvage, finding that the vessel was not exposed to loss or destruction.

Some courts employ a strict standard for determining whether a maritime peril existed. In *Girard v. M/V "Blacksheep,"* 840 F.3d 1351 (11th Cir. 2016), the Eleventh Circuit overruled an earlier decision that required that in order to show peril the salvor must show that the property "could not have been rescued without the salvor's assistance." The court held that the requirement was inconsistent with precedent and the policy of encouraging rescue. The earlier holding was based on Gilmore and Black's treatise.

4. **Salvage of one's own ship.** As the *Markakis* court noted, seamen are generally not entitled to salvage of their own vessel. It is said that crew members have a pre-existing duty to save their own ship. Another explanation for the rule disallowing salvage by a crew member of his own vessel is to discourage fraud. The rule has some exceptions, which were summarized in *The C.P. Minch*, 73 F. 859, 865 (2d Cir. 1896) as follows:

> [I]t is apparent that, in every case where compensation in the nature of salvage has been awarded to seamen, the voyage has terminated by the shipwreck of the vessel, which has either gone to the bottom or left her bones on the shore, or she has been abandoned by all, or by all except the salvors, under circumstances which show conclusively that the abandonment was absolute, without hope or expectation of recovery, or the seaman has been by the master unmistakably discharged from the service of the shipowner.

5. **Coast Guard.** It remains an open question whether the Coast Guard can claim salvage for its routine rescue efforts. The Fifth Circuit ruled that the Coast Guard could not recover for services performed in responding to a threatened oil spill because the Federal Water Pollution Control Act, 33 U.S.C. § 1321, required those services. *United States v. Ex-USS Cabot/Dedalo*, 297 F.3d 378 (5th Cir. 2002).

6. **No cure-no pay.** Under the general rule (sometimes called the "no cure-no pay" rule), there can be no reward if nothing is saved. But as mentioned by the principal case, partial success suffices.

7. **What services count?** The salvor need only contribute to the saving of the property to be entitled to salvage. Salvage efforts frequently involve more than one set of salvors. As the court's quotation from Gilmore & Black states, merely standing by a vessel in

distress can be a salvage act. *The Pendragon Castle*, 5 F.2d 56 (2d Cir. 1924). So can radioing for help. *In re Ta Chi Navigation (Panama) Corp. S.A.*, 583 F. Supp. 1322 (S.D.N.Y. 1984).

But when a putative salvor played heavy streams of water on a burning pier where the fire threatened a vessel docked at the next pier, *Merritt & Chapman Derrick & Wrecking Co. v. United States*, 274 U.S. 611 (1927), held that no salvage was due from the vessel owner. The Court stated:

> [Plaintiff's] fireboats did not put water upon [defendant's ship]. The fires that started on her were put out by other means. All effort of plaintiff ... was put forth directly for the purpose of extinguishing fire at and about Pier 5, and to save property not at all related to the *Leviathan*. The elimination of that fire contributed mediately to her safety. But, whatever the aid or benefit resulting to her, it was incidental and indirect for which, in the absence of request for or acceptance of the service, a claim for salvage cannot be sustained.

In *Sunglory Maritime Ltd. v. PHI, Inc.*, 212 F. Supp. 3d 618 (E.D. La. 2016), a district court awarded salvage when a helicopter landed on a vessel as a precaution to avoid "real but uncertain risk of danger to the property or passengers." The helicopter pilots had not contacted anyone on board the vessel, nor did they receive permission to land. But once the helicopter had safely landed, the vessel transported it (and its passengers) six miles to the port. In a lengthy opinion discussing many aspects of salvage law, the court applied the 1989 Salvage Convention and the general maritime law.

8. **Crew members' share.** The principal case notes that a waiver by the salving vessel's owner or master would not necessarily defeat the crew members' rights. It is common for the salving master or owner to sue on behalf of the crew. Such representative suits are not subject to the class action rules of the Federal Rules of Civil Procedure. *St. Paul Marine Transp. Corp. v. Cerro Sales Corp.*, 505 F.2d 1115 (9th Cir. 1974).

9. **How much?** The next case demonstrates how the amount of salvage is calculated.

Margate Shipping Co. v. M/V JA Orgeron

United States Court of Appeals, Fifth Circuit, 1998
143 F.3d 976, 1998 AMC 2383

JOLLY, Circuit Judge:

This appeal arises from the grant of what appears to be the largest maritime salvage award in recorded history. During a severe tropical storm off the Florida coast, the *M/V Cherry Valley*, an oil tanker belonging to Margate Shipping Co., rescued a barge containing a valuable external fuel tank ["ET-70"] for NASA's space shuttle. The district court awarded Margate approximately $6.4 million in salvage. The United States appeals only as to the amount of the award. Based on the district court's mistaken valuation of the fuel tank, we reduce the award to $4.125 million and render.

I.

'Twas a dark and very stormy night, November 14–15, 1994, and the situation looked bleak for the barge *Poseidon*. Caught in the clutches of Tropical Storm Gordon, *Poseidon* and her escort, the *J.A. Orgeron*, were without power and adrift. Driven on the gales of the tempest, the flotilla was swiftly approaching the Bethel Shoal; if they ran aground, the ships were sure to founder and be lost. Acutely aware of the danger, *Orgeron*'s captain radioed for help. Alas, the Coast Guard was not in a position to mount a rescue. In despair, the captain made plans to release *Poseidon* and her valuable cargo, an external fuel tank for the space shuttle. Although this action would result in the certain loss of *Poseidon* and the tank, the captain hoped thereby to save *Orgeron* and her crew.

* * *

At approximately 2:00 a.m. on November 15, *Orgeron* lost the effective use of both her engines. At the time, the flotilla was between ten and eighteen miles off Florida's Atlantic coast, somewhere between Fort Pierce and Cape Canaveral. Without *Orgeron*'s engines, the tug and barge were left adrift, and began to be blown west towards shore. *Orgeron* immediately notified the Coast Guard of her predicament, and requested assistance. Because of the storm's ferocity, however, the Coast Guard was unable to help.

* * *

Orgeron's distress call had been picked up by the *M/V Cherry Valley*. *Cherry Valley* was a 688-foot oil tanker owned by Margate with a crew of 25 and a value of $7.5 million. On November 15, the ship was fully laden with nine million gallons of heavy fuel oil and had a draft of about 35 feet. * * * Although under no obligation to assist, *Cherry Valley*'s master, the suitably named Captain Strong, immediately altered course to rendezvous with the tug. In so doing, he took his relatively unmaneuverable craft into perilous shoal waters in direct violation of standing orders.

Cherry Valley arrived on the scene shortly after 4:00 a.m., whereupon Captain Strong decided to try to pass a line to *Orgeron* and tow the flotilla to safety. To do this, however, he would need to maneuver clumsy *Cherry Valley* directly alongside *Orgeron* in the churning seas. Time was short, as the vessels were rapidly approaching the Bethel Shoal; the Shoal had depths of six to seven fathoms in places, far too shallow for *Cherry Valley*, which required at least ten fathoms for safe operation in heavy seas. The flotilla had almost reached this depth when *Cherry Valley* arrived.

Captain Strong's plan was to pass close enough to *Orgeron* to send over a messenger line on a line-throwing rocket. This line could then be used to transfer larger mooring lines capable of sustaining the tow. Captain Strong ordered several crewmen onto deck to conduct the line-passing operation. Throughout the salvage operation, *Cherry Valley*'s deck would be awash with green seas and extremely dangerous, even for experienced seamen.

On *Cherry Valley*'s first pass, the messenger line fell short, and Captain Strong was forced to bring the ship about for another attempt. This time, he passed even closer to *Orgeron*, and the messenger line was successfully transferred. It parted, however, before the deck crew was able to transfer a mooring line, and Captain Strong was compelled to bring *Cherry Valley* about once more.

Time was becoming increasingly critical. The vessels were now less than one mile from the Shoal, and the water was becoming quite shallow. If *Cherry Valley* ran aground in the storm, she would likely break up and cause a massive oil spill. * * *

Fortunately, the third effort was successful. *Cherry Valley*'s deck crew managed to pass two hawsers to *Orgeron*, which were quickly made fast. * * *

At 6:20 a.m., *Cherry Valley* finally was able to take the flotilla in tow. By this time, her propeller was churning mud and the fathometer indicated that there were less than ten feet between her keel and the bottom.

With *Orgeron* and *Poseidon* in tow, *Cherry Valley* steamed slowly southeast, back into deep water. The tow put great strain on the hawsers and chocks, however, which required constant attention in the form of "slushing" [lubrication]. In addition to the inherent dangers of being on deck in the storm, slushing put *Cherry Valley*'s deck crew in constant danger of being struck by a parting line; a hawser that parts under great strain can snap like a giant rubber band, causing severe injury to all nearby.

* * *

[By afternoon], the storm began to overcome even *Cherry Valley*. As the storm worsened, she was pushed westward, back into the shallows. Out of options, Captain Strong decided to anchor and ride out the rest of the storm. Although this operation exposed the deck crew to additional risks, it was accomplished without incident at 5:00 p.m.

While [the vessels were] anchored, one of the mooring lines parted. *Cherry Valley*'s deck crew was able to replace and supplement it, and the flotilla remained intact.

The vessels remained at anchor throughout the night of November 15 and the following day, with *Cherry Valley*'s deck crew constantly tending the lines. * * *

By midmorning of November 17, the storm had finally passed and [the tug] *Dorothy Moran* and another tug were able to relieve *Cherry Valley*. * * * ET-70 was delivered intact and completely unharmed, and was later used in a successful space shuttle launch.

* * *

II.

On December 12, 1994, Margate filed an action for salvage against the *J.A. Orgeron* in the Federal District Court for the Eastern District of Louisiana. [Montco Offshore, Inc., the *Orgeron*'s operator] answered, and then filed its own claim for limitation of liability. The United States, fearing an eventual salvage action against itself, filed a claim in the limitation action seeking indemnification from Montco. Margate then filed a cross-claim for salvage against the United States. Eventually, everything was settled except for Margate's cross-claim against the United States, which went to trial in July 1996 before District Judge Stanwood Duval.

On July 9, after a brief bench trial, Judge Duval * * * found that, based on the entirety of the evidence, Margate was entitled to a salvage award equal to 12.5% of the value of the salved property, *Poseidon* and ET-70.

In reaching this figure, Judge Duval relied on the six traditional salvage factors first announced[8] in *The Blackwall*, 77 U.S. 1 (1869). He determined that the facts of the case pointed to the highest possible award under each of the factors, and chose what he considered to be a high percentage of a high salved value to reflect this circumstance. * * *

With regard to ET-70, Judge Duval determined that it was specialized property without a market value, and therefore most appropriately appraised at its "replacement cost." This value, he found, was the production cost of ET-71, $51,387,000, because ET-71 was the likely "replacement" of ET-70. * * *

Combining this $51 million value for ET-70 with the $2 million stipulated value of *Poseidon*, Judge Duval declared a total award of $6,406,440 based on the 12.5% figure. He noted in the alternative that, even if the value of ET-70 were only $19 million as the United States claimed, the award would be the same as he would adjust the percentage accordingly. On July 12, final judgment was entered for Margate in the amount of $6,406,440. The United States appeals the amount of this award.

---

8. And, interestingly, last announced as well. *The Blackwall* contains the most recent bit of guidance that the Supreme Court has deigned to give on the subject of the calculation of salvage awards.

III.

Because of the fact-specific nature of the calculation of a salvage award, "the amount allowed is to be decided by the district court in its sound discretion." [ ] "[A]n award will be altered only if it was based upon incorrect principles of law or misapprehension of the facts or it is either so excessive or so inadequate as to indicate an abuse of discretion." * * *

IV.

* * *

The district court traditionally determines the amount of a salvage award according to the six *Blackwall* factors.[9] * * * In this case, the district court made the following findings under the factors, listed here in order of the court's assessment of their importance to the calculation of an award:

1. [*Blackwall* 6.[1]] *Poseidon* and ET-70 were in imminent danger of complete loss.
2. [*Blackwall* 5.] The combined value of *Poseidon* and ET-70 was $53,387,000.
3. [*Blackwall* 4.] The salvors incurred extremely high risk in securing *Poseidon* and ET-70, both as to loss of their ship and lives and as to the creation of substantial environmental liability in the event of an oil spill.
4. [*Blackwall* 2.] The salvors displayed extremely high promptitude, skill, and energy in rescuing *Poseidon* and ET-70 by virtue of their daring and successful seamanship under very difficult conditions.
5. [*Blackwall* 3.] The value of *Cherry Valley* was $7.5 million.
6. [*Blackwall* 1.] The salvors expended two and one-third days of labor in rendering the salvage service.

* * *

The United States makes three basic challenges to the district court's analysis. First, it argues that the court erred in its general application of the *Blackwall* factors, by giving too much weight to the value of the salved property, by counting the potential for environmental liability as risk to the salvors, and by using a percentage of the salved value ultimately to fix the award. Second, even assuming that the district court made a correct legal interpretation of the factors, the United States argues that the district court clearly erred in its valuation of ET-70. Finally, even assuming that the district court made a correct legal interpretation of the *Blackwall* factors and properly valued ET-70, the United States argues that the court nonetheless abused its discretion in picking such a high percentage and generally making such a large award in this case. We address each argument in turn.

A.

* * * As many commentators have noted, the sense and contours of the [*Blackwall*] factors are less than plainly engraved upon their face.[10] In this case, however, the United

9. At least in theory. Some commentators have said that the district court traditionally "pull[s] an arbitrary figure out of the air." GILMORE & BLACK, THE LAW OF ADMIRALTY 563 (2d ed.1975).

1. Editors' note: These numbers show the order in which each factor was listed in the *Blackwall* opinion.

10. See, e.g., GILMORE & BLACK at 559 (noting that the traditional "recitation of Justice Clifford's six 'ingredients' [really just] serves the useful purpose of indicating that the variables are so many and so incapable of exact measurement that it will probably be fruitless for either party to take an appeal merely on the ground that the award was incorrectly computed"). As we shall see, we ultimately take a somewhat more sanguine view of the rationality of the factors as a legal rule.

States squarely asks us to decide whether the particular interpretation and application adopted by the district court comports with the factors' essential meaning. In order for us to answer this question, we must first ascertain what purpose the factors serve.

* * *

Fortunately, the principles underlying the *Blackwall* factors have not escaped the attention of our most prominent modern scholars. See Landes & Posner, *Salvors, Finders, Good Samaritans, and Other Rescuers: An Economic Study of Law and Altruism*, 7 J. Leg. Stud. 83 (1978). Beginning with our first principle that the law of salvage seeks to preserve society's resources, they explain that "the purpose of [court-granted] salvage awards is to encourage rescues in settings of high transaction costs by simulating the conditions and outcomes of a competitive market." In an ideal world, every meeting of salvor and salvee would result in a freely negotiated contract for salvage services priced at a competitive level. In the real world, however, most meetings of salvor and salvee cannot be resolved in this fashion.

To accommodate this reality, the law of salvage aims to create a post-hoc solution that will induce the parties to save the ship without first agreeing on terms. * * * In order properly to induce the salvor (and salvee) to act * * *, the law must provide for a proper and reasonable salvage award, one that gives neither the salvor too little incentive to do the salvage properly, nor the salvee too little reason to care if his property is saved. [ ] By definition, this "efficient" fee is the one that would have been reached by the parties through voluntary negotiation in an open and competitive market, and its value will depend on a number of factual considerations. By far the most important of these considerations, however, will be the cost to potential salvors of performing the service and the benefit to the salvee of it being performed; obviously, no voluntary salvor would be willing to perform a salvage for less than it would cost him to do it, just as no salvee would agree to pay more for a salvage than the loss he could thereby avoid. * * *

With this background in mind, it becomes immediately apparent that the *Blackwall* factors represent an explicit guide for the court to use in measuring these two most significant considerations for voluntary negotiation in the salvage context. Labor expended by the salvors (1), their promptitude and skill (2), value of the salving property (3), risk to the salvors (4), and risk to the salved property (6) are all direct or indirect measures of the actual cost to the salvor of performing the salvage in question, which should in turn be at least indicative of the costs that would have prevailed. Correspondingly, value of the salved property (5) and risk to the salved property (6) are measures of the benefit that the salvage has conferred on the salvee. * * *

* * *

The United States * * * complains that the district court gave too much weight to the fifth factor—value of the salved property—by ranking it second in its assessment of the considerations bearing upon an award. In the light of our just-concluded explication of the function of that factor, this contention is readily seen to be wholly lacking in merit.

As the principal measure of the benefit of the salvage to the salvee, the fifth is clearly one of the most important of the *Blackwall* factors * * *. The general economic reality is simply that, the greater the value of the threatened property, the greater the potential loss, and, consequently, the more the salvee would be willing to pay to save that property from destruction.

* * *

The United States next argues that the district court erred by counting the risk of environmental liability as risk to the salvors under the fourth factor, when it should more properly have counted against them in some way. There is no merit to this contention either.

As just discussed, the fourth factor is intended to provide a direct measure of some of the salvor's actual salvage costs. In this context, there is no principled reason to distinguish between the costs imposed by the risk of injury or death, and those costs imposed by the risk of negligence liability or strict environmental damage liability. All are actual costs to the salvor, and he would presumably be unwilling to perform the salvage service without their recompense. For this reason, the risk of environmental liability was properly counted under the rubric of the fourth factor.[17]

* * *

Finally, and most significantly, the United States also complains that the district court erred by using a percentage of the salved value in its ultimate calculation of the salvage award. There is no merit to this contention either.

* * * [A]s we just stated above, our analysis of the economic foundations of the *Blackwall* rule indicates that the value of the salved property is one of the most important of the factors. The most natural way to effectuate its salient character is simply to make the award a function of that value. * * * [And we] see no reason why the district court may not use the other five factors to set a customized percentage to be applied to the salved value for purposes of calculating an award in the case before it. * * *

* * *

Although none of the United States' own arguments with regard to interpretation of the factors bears any fruit, we feel compelled to raise one additional concern that has been fairly implicated, even if not squarely addressed.

* * * After determining that the salved value was $53 million, * * * the court also noted that, even if the value were actually lower, as the United States argued, the dollar amount of the award would remain the same, as the court would adjust the percentage accordingly.

Based on our above interpretation of the *Blackwall* factors, we cannot approve this alternate holding. * * * To the extent that the district court attempted to evade the fifth factor by tying the percentage to a fixed dollar amount, we reverse that portion of its ruling. For the remainder of this opinion, we may therefore restrict our discussion to the district court's primary holding that an award of 12.5% of the salved value was appropriate, and that this figure was approximately $6.4 million.

To determine whether that holding may be allowed to stand, we must consider the United States' two remaining major complaints, i.e., that the value assigned to ET-70 was

17. To the extent the United States is actually arguing that maritime law be altered to reduce the incentive for overeager salvors to wreck environmental havoc in pursuit of their prize, we note that there is no need for such a change in the law. As the United States itself admits, applicable law already made Margate strictly and completely liable for any oil spill that might have resulted from the salvage operation. See, e.g., 33 U.S.C. § 2702(a) ("Notwithstanding any other provision or rule of law . . . , each responsible party for a vessel or a facility from which oil is discharged . . . into or upon the navigable waters or adjoining shorelines . . . is liable for the removal costs and damages . . . that result from such incident."); see also 33 U.S.C. § 2718(c). As such, the environment was and is adequately protected, and there is no need to conscript admiralty law for that purpose. Putting this concern to one side, Margate was entitled to the benefit of all the calculated risks it ran in the determination of its award. This is not to say, of course, that any amount of environmental risk could justify an award for more than the value of the salved property. The maximum limitations and general principles of salvage apply regardless.

a clear error, and that the overall award was excessive both as to percentage and total dollar value. We address each in turn.

B.

* * *

Generally, the value of property for salvage purposes is its market value as salved. * * * In the case of a unique good like a space shuttle fuel tank, however, this measure is clearly inapposite; as there is no market of any kind for space shuttle fuel tanks, there can be no market value.

In this situation, and bearing in mind that ET-70 remained in perfect condition despite the trials of the storm, the parties now agree that the most appropriate measure of value is "replacement cost." * * * The question becomes how replacement cost is to be determined. [The production cost of ET-70 was $53,834,000. The production cost of ET-71, ET-70's likely replacement, was $51,387,000. But the trial judge was wrong to use the latter figure to arrive at a replacement cost for ET-70, because the record shows that Martin Marietta, the manufacturer, had offered the government four additional tanks to be produced 36 months in the future at a cost of about $19 million per tank. Thus, we think the proper method of arriving at a figure for the replacement cost of ET-70 is to start with the $19 million option for a replacement and then add to that the estimated value of avoiding a three-year wait for its delivery, which we set at $12 million.[2]] We therefore hold that the district court was clearly in error in valuing ET-70 at $51,387,000, and that the correct value was $31 million. Adding the $2 million stipulated value of *Poseidon*, this leaves a total value for the salved property of $33 million. Applying the district court's 12.5% salvage percentage, * * * we are left with a new salvage award of $4.125 million.

C.

* * * [Finally,] the United States argues that, even assuming a correct and error-free assessment of the *Blackwall* factors, any award in excess of either $2.5 million or 10% of the salved value constitutes an abuse of discretion in this case. * * * For the reasons that follow, we hold that a $4.125 million/12.5% award is not so excessive as to constitute an abuse of discretion in the context of this case.

* * * Where, as here, the district court has applied the *Blackwall* factors in an appropriate way with a correct understanding of their underlying purpose, the only useful review that this court can conduct of the ultimate award is a general comparison to similar decisions. Indeed, even this limited type of review has been criticized by some courts [ ], and we will conduct it in only the most deferential and general way.

* * * [W]e have compiled a list of the nine largest federal salvage awards in comparable high-value, high-order[3] cases since the advent of the *Blackwall* rule. [Here the opinion sets forth a tabular summary of nine cases decided between 1880 and 1941 with the salvage awards shown as adjusted to 1994 dollars on the basis of the relevant U.S. Consumer Price Index deflator. These awards ranged from $750,000 to $3.5 million.] In the context of these past awards, it is difficult to say that the reduced $4.125 million/12.5% award here is wrong, much less an abuse of discretion. The range of percentages [award of value of salved property] appears to run from about 4% to 25%, and the percentage here is

2. Editors' note: The court's method of arriving at $12 million was complex and case-specific.

3. Editors' note: A "high order" salvage situation is one "involving extraordinary efforts or extreme risks to the salvors." H.R.M., Inc. v. S/V Venture VII, 972 F. Supp. 92, 99 (D. R.I. 1997).

smack in the middle of that range. Furthermore, as the district court noted, it is rare that a salvage action would involve such high ratings on each of the factors [skill, risk, and value of salving property] as was the case here. * * * Although the dollar amount of the award in this case would still appear to be the highest ever * * *, in the light of all its factors, it simply does not look out of place in the context of high-value, high-order salvage cases. For this reason, it is not so excessive as to constitute an abuse of discretion.

* * *

For the stated reasons, we reduce Margate's salvage award from $6,406,440 to $4,125,000 and direct that judgment be entered in that amount.

Notes

1. **The Blackwall factors.** Prior to *The Blackwall*, some judges discussed only three factors: (1) the service rendered, (2) the risk of the party rendering the service, and (3) the value of the property saved. *Taylor v. Twenty-five Thousand Dollars*, 23 Fed. Cas. 806 (D. S.C. 1801). The *Blackwall* factors seem to be a further elaboration of those factors. The value of the property saved sets an upper limit on the amount of salvage. The value of the service sets a bottom limit. The degree of risk would determine how much to multiply the value of the service.

Another common formulation was:

> First, enterprise in the sailors in rendering assistance in tempestuous weather, and at risk of life. Secondly, the degree of danger and distress from which the property is rescued. Thirdly, the degree of labour and skill displayed by the sailors, and the time they are occupied. And fourthly, the value of the property saved.

Robson v. The Huntress, 20 Fed. Cas. 1060, 1062 (C.C.E.D. Pa. 1851). Does the *Margate* court's economic analysis of the *Blackwall* factors improve on *Blackwall*? For another economic analysis of the salvage factors, see Note, *Calculating and Allocating Salvage Liability*, 99 Harv. L. Rev. 1896 (1986).

2. **Additional factors.** The 1989 Convention on Salvage, which became effective in the United States in 1996, sets out a non-hierarchical list of ten factors.[4] In reality, no list of factors is likely to exhaust the considerations that may become relevant. For example, the salvor's success in averting liability of the owner of the property saved can be significant. See *Allseas Maritime, S.A. v. M/V Mimosa*, 812 F.2d 243 (5th Cir. 1987); Friedell, *Salvage and the Public Interest*, 4 Cardozo L. Rev. 431 (1983). In other contexts, it is easy to see the potential importance of the degree to which the salvors worked to protect the historical and archaeological value of the wreck and the items salved. *Columbus-America Discovery Group v. Atlantic Mutual Ins. Co.*, 974 F.2d 450 (4th Cir. 1992).

---

4. See 6 Benedict on Admiralty, Doc. 4-2A at 4–13. The factors are:
(a) the salved value of the vessel and other property;
(b) the skill and efforts of the salvors in preventing or minimizing damage to the environment;
(c) the measure of success obtained by the salvor;
(d) the nature and degree of the danger;
(e) the skill and efforts of the salvors in salving the vessel, other property and life;
(f) the time used and expenses and losses incurred by the salvors;
(g) the risk of liability and other risks run by the salvors or their equipment;
(h) the promptness of the services rendered;
(i) the availability and use of vessels or other equipment intended for salvage operations;
(j) the state of readiness and efficiency of the salvor's equipment and the value thereof.

3. **Environmental risks.** As the principal case discusses, the risk of environmental liability is one of the salvor's risks that the court considers in rendering its award. One district court added a seventh factor to the *Blackwall* list: "skill and effort of the salvors in preventing and minimizing damage to the environment." *Trico Marine Operators, Inc. v. Dow Chemical Co.*, 809 F. Supp. 440, 443 (E.D. La. 1992). (In an edited-out portion of the *Margate* opinion, the court expressed some doubt about the wisdom of *Trico*.) The *Trico* opinion was influenced by the 1989 Convention on Salvage, *supra* note 2.

The "no cure-no pay" rule (requiring at least partial success) has been modified in response to some well-publicized disasters of vessels carrying oil that polluted the shoreline. Article 14 of the 1989 convention gives the salvor a right to recover his expenses if he renders service to a vessel which itself or through its cargo threatened damage to the environment. If the salvor has prevented or minimized damage to the environment, he may receive up to twice his expenses. Those provisions are applicable under the standard form contract used for salvage services, the Lloyd's Open Form-2000, section C.[5]

4. **Misconduct, Negligence or Damage.** A salvor's misconduct may reduce or eliminate an award. Looting is an obvious type of misconduct, but courts allow salvors to make reasonable use of items found on board the salved vessel. See 3A Norris, Benedict on Admiralty § 98 et seq. (7th rev. ed. 2007).

A salvor's negligence will reduce the award. But salvors are often given wide latitude. The reasonable care requirement is adjusted in light of the emergency, and some courts have shown additional leniency. In one case the would-be salvor collided with the vessel in an effort to board her, leaving a 33-foot hole near her bow. The salvor's efforts to tow the vessel were fruitless, but the salvor did manage to advise the owners of the distressed vessel of her condition and location. For that service it was awarded $8,000. *In re Ta Chi Navigation (Panama) Corp. S.A.*, 583 F. Supp. 1322 (S.D.N.Y. 1984).

Making an extravagant claim counts as a form of salvor misconduct that can reduce or even potentially eliminate the reward.

When the salvor has wrongfully caused the peril it cannot claim salvage for its services. In *The Clarita*, 90 U.S. 1, 2003 AMC 901 (1875) a tug that was towing a burning ferry-boat away from a dock wrongfully caused it to collide with a schooner and set it ablaze. The tug extinguished the flames on the schooner but was denied salvage for saving it.

5. **Distribution of the award.** Ordinarily the salvage award will be divided between the owners and the crew of the salving vessel, the relative amounts being within the discretion of the court. Typically the owner will receive approximately two-thirds of the award. *E.g.*, *St. Paul Marine Transp. Corp. v. Cerro Sales Corp.*, 505 F.2d 1115 (9th Cir. 1974). In a high-order case the crew might receive a higher share; in low-order cases the crew will likely receive less. See *Bartholomew v. Crowley Marine Serv.*, 337 F.3d 1083 (9th Cir. 2003) (owner's share has ranged from as low as one-fifth to as much as nine-tenths). In *Markakis* [*supra* at 383] the captain of the salving vessel received the largest award, $7,500, equivalent to three month's salary; other crew members who actively participated in the salvage operations received 1 1/2 months of salary; all other crew members received $50 each. *Markakis v. S/S Veendam (ex S/S Monarch Star)*, 1981 AMC 2275 (S.D.N.Y. 1981) (Special Master's recommendation). In *Margate Shipping* the crew and owner agreed that the owner would be compensated for some expenses and receive 63% of the remainder of the award. The crew members agreed to binding arbitration to divide among themselves

5. See *id.*, Doc. 4-7 at 4–13.

their share of the award. Captain Strong received 16.42% of the crew members' share. *See* Strong & Braden, In Peril 244–45 (2003). The book, co-authored by Captain Strong, provides a detailed account of the case.

In *In re Dorothy J v. City of New York*, 749 F. Supp. 2d 50, 2010 AMC 2409 (E.D.N.Y. 2010), a ferry allided with a pier, resulting in several deaths and injuries. A tug, the *Dorothy J*, arrived alongside, providing comfort to the crew and passengers of the stricken ferry. The court apportioned 1/3 to the tug's owner and 2/3 to the crew. The court noted that the *Dorothy J* was ill-equipped to perform salvage services and that the policy behind generously rewarding owners is to prevent that from happening. The tug's captain and another crew member declined to seek a share of the award, and their shares inured to the owner of the ferry.

6. **Property subject to salvage.** As we saw in Section I-C, *supra* at 23, *Cope v. Vallette Dry Dock Co.*, 119 U.S. 625, 629 (1887), held that a drydock permanently moored in the Mississippi River was not subject to salvage, stating:

> There has been some conflict of decision with respect to claims for salvage services in rescuing goods lost at sea, and found floating on the surface or cast upon the shore. When they have belonged to a ship or vessel as part of its furniture or cargo, they clearly come under the head of wreck, flotsam, jetsam, ligan, or derelict, and salvage may be claimed upon them. But when they have no connection with a ship or vessel, some authorities are against the claim, and others are in favor of it.

A house being transported across the frozen surface of Lake Superior that broke through the ice was not a subject of salvage. *Provost v. Huber*, 594 F.2d 717 (8th Cir. 1979). But a seaplane is subject to salvage. *Lambros Seaplane Base v. The Batory*, 215 F.2d 228 (2d Cir. 1954). Floating fish frames are also subject to salvage. *Colby v. Todd Packing Co.*, 77 F. Supp. 956 (D. Alaska 1948). The 1989 salvage convention sweeps very broadly, defining *salvage operation* as "any act or activity undertaken to assist a vessel or any other property in danger in navigable waters or in any other waters whatsoever" and *property* as "any property not permanently and intentionally attached to the shoreline and includes freight at risk."[6]

7. **The right to refuse salvage. A** vessel can "decline the assistance of others so long as only the owner's property interests are at stake." But salvage may be awarded if the owner acquiesces to the rescue efforts. *International Aircraft Recovery, L.L.C. v. Unidentified, Wrecked & Abandoned Aircraft*, 218 F.3d 1255 (11th Cir. 2000). The operation of those principles was well illustrated in *Hamburg-American Line v. United States*, 168 F.2d 47, 56 (1st Cir. 1948). In November 1941, shortly before the United States entered the war, a German merchant vessel that had been trying to run the British blockade by flying a U.S. flag was sighted by a U.S. naval vessel on neutrality patrol. The German ship's officers and crew tried to scuttle her, but the Americans managed to save her. In upholding a salvage award to the United States, the court of appeals stated:

> When the salvage party approached the *Odenwald*, the master and crew had taken to the life boats, having finally abandoned the ship in the confident belief that she had received her mortal wound. They had waved good-by to her and consigned her to her expected doom, having displayed on her the flag signal "I am sinking, send boats for passengers and crew." To the surprise of her former

6. *Id.*, Doc. 4-2A, Articles, 1a and 1c.

> crew, the salvors by skill and daring kept the derelict afloat and brought her to a safe harbor.
>
> We think it is immaterial that the master had done his best, or his worst, to scuttle the ship * * * Assuming that the owner wanted at one time to destroy his ship, he cannot later change his mind and claim his ship back except in subordination [to] the lien of the salvors without whose exertions she would not have been preserved for future use. This proposition is founded on the plainest dictates of equity.
>
> It is urged that salvage services may not be forced on the unwilling. [ ] There are cases cited in this connection which go to the extent of holding that salvage services are not compensable when forced upon a vessel after an offer of assistance has been expressly rejected, the crew remaining on board capable of meeting the peril. [ ] Indeed, in some of these cases the view seems to have been that the libelants had not rendered any real service at all because of the ability of the libeled ship to take care of herself. The case at bar is quite a different one....

The district court in *Hamburg-American* had offered a different rationale:

> It may be that the Hamburg Line and through it the Government of the German Reich authorized the scuttling of the *Odenwald* * * *. However, the Master was not by that authorization entitled to sink her, ignoring thus, the rights of the intervenor, a Swiss mortgagee, and the rights of the unknown owners of her cargo. [71 F. Supp. 314, 316–317 (D.P.R. 1947).]

Sea Hunt, Inc. v. Unidentified Shipwrecked Vessel

United States Court of Appeals, Fourth Circuit, 2000
221 F.3d 634, 2000 AMC 2113

WILKINSON, Chief Judge:

* * *

[The Abandoned Shipwreck Act of 1987 ("ASA"), 43 U.S.C. §§2101–2106, asserts the United States' title to any shipwreck that is abandoned and embedded in the submerged lands of a state and then in the same provision transfers that title to the state. *Id.* §2105. Pursuant to the ASA, the Virginia Marine Resources Commission issued permits to Sea Hunt, Inc., a marine salvage company based in the Eastern Shore of Virginia, to explore for shipwrecks off the Virginia coast and conduct salvage operations. Sea Hunt began to explore for shipwrecks within its permit areas and has spent about a million dollars in conducting remote sensing, survey, diving, and identification operations. It claims to have found the two shipwrecks described below.]

La Galga ("*The Greyhound*") was a fifty-gun frigate commissioned into the Spanish Navy in 1732. *La Galga* left Havana on its last voyage on August 18, 1750, in order to escort a convoy of merchant ships to Spain. It carried the Second Company of the Sixth Battalion of Spanish Marines, Spanish Royal property, and English military prisoners. On August 25, 1750, the convoy encountered a hurricane near Bermuda that scattered the ships and forced them westward toward the American coast. *La Galga* eventually sank off the coast of the Maryland/Virginia border. Most of the crew and passengers reached land safely. When Captain Daniel Houny attempted to salvage items from the wreck, he found that local residents had already begun looting the vessel. He secured the assistance of Governor Ogle of Maryland, but any further salvage efforts ended when a second storm came and broke up what was left of the ship. *La Galga* remained undisturbed until the recent salvage efforts by Sea Hunt.

The *Juno*, a thirty-four gun frigate, entered the service of the Spanish Navy in 1790. On January 15, 1802, *Juno* set sail from Veracruz bound for Spain. On board *Juno* were the soldiers of the Third Battalion of the Regiment of Africa, their families, and various civilian officials. The *Juno* was beset by a ferocious storm and began taking on water. It encountered the American schooner *La Favorita.* The two ships sailed together trying to reach an American port before *Juno* succumbed to her leaks. As *Juno* continued to take on water, the Captain ordered his passengers and crew to begin transferring to *La Favorita.* But only seven persons were able to transfer before the storm picked up and *Juno* was lost in a heavy fog. *La Favorita* could come close enough only to hear the anguished cries for help as *Juno* went under. At least 413 sailors, soldiers, and civilians perished in the sinking of *Juno*. Spanish authorities ordered an investigation into the sinking, but the location of the wreck was not discovered until Sea Hunt's recent efforts.

[When Sea Hunt found what it believes are the two wrecks, it brought artifacts assertedly from each before the United States District Court for the Eastern District of Virginia and] initiated an in rem admiralty action against the two wrecks [seeking] a declaratory judgment that the shipwrecked vessels "have never been subject to the sovereign prerogative of the Kingdom of Spain and [are] subject to admiralty's laws of abandonment and the law of finds," that "the Commonwealth of Virginia be adjudged the true, sole and exclusive owner of the Shipwrecked Vessel(s)," and that any items salvaged therefrom by Sea Hunt be distributed pursuant to the permits issued by Virginia. In the alternative, Sea Hunt sought a liberal salvage award for its efforts. [The State of Virginia intervened, asserting an ownership interest in the two wrecks.] On March 12, 1998, the district court issued an order directing the arrest of the shipwrecked vessels and granting Sea Hunt exclusive rights of salvage until further notice. The court also directed Sea Hunt to send specific notice of the action to both the United States and to Spain.

In response, the United States moved to intervene and filed a verified claim [to the vessels] on behalf of Spain. [It did so because Article X of the 1902 Treaty of Friendship and General Relations between the United States and Spain (33 Stat. 2105) provides that "in cases of shipwreck, damages at sea, or forced putting in, each party shall afford to the vessels of the other ... the same immunities which would have been granted to its own vessels in similar cases." United States vessels may only be abandoned by an express, unambiguous, and affirmative act. (This follows from Article IV § 3 cl. 2 of the Constitution, which provides that the property of the United States cannot be disposed of except by an act of Congress.) The State Department reasoned that the treaty required the same treatment of Spanish vessels.] The district court found that the United States lacked authority to appear on behalf of Spain and granted Spain 90 days to refile a verified claim. Spain's verified claim stated that the Kingdom of Spain "was and still is the true and bona fide owner of the vessels *Juno* and *La Galga* ... and that title and ownership interest in said vessels has never been abandoned or relinquished or transferred by the Kingdom of Spain." * * *

[Ultimately the district court found that Spain had abandoned its claim to the *La Galga* but not to the *Juno*. This left Sea Hunt free to pursue its "finder's" claim to *La Galga* with the Virginia authorities. Re the *Juno*, the district court held that] Sea Hunt could not rightfully claim a salvage award because Spain, as the acknowledged owner of *Juno*, had expressly refused salvage services. The Kingdom of Spain now appeals the judgment concerning *La Galga*. The Commonwealth and Sea Hunt note a cross-appeal with regard to *Juno* and the denial of a salvage award.

II.

In order for Virginia to acquire title to the shipwrecks and to issue salvage permits to Sea Hunt, these vessels must have been abandoned by Spain. Sea Hunt and the Commonwealth argue that the Abandoned Shipwreck Act requires application of an implied abandonment standard for shipwrecks in coastal waters, and that Spain has abandoned *La Galga* and *Juno*. Because Spain has asserted an ownership claim to the shipwrecks, however, express abandonment is the governing standard. [ ] To adopt a lesser standard would not only go beyond what the ASA requires. It would also abrogate America's obligations to Spain under the 1902 Treaty of Friendship and General Relations.

The ASA does not define the critical term "abandoned." Nothing in the Act indicates, however, that implied abandonment should be the standard in a case such as this where a sovereign asserts ownership to its vessels. The Act states in its findings that "abandoned shipwrecks" are those "to which the owner has relinquished ownership rights with no retention." 43 U.S.C. § 2101(b). The statute thus provides that a shipwreck is abandoned only where the owner has relinquished ownership rights. When an owner comes before the court to assert his rights, relinquishment would be hard, if not impossible, to show. Requiring express abandonment where an owner makes a claim thus accords with the statutory text. Further, although the legislative history states that abandonment may be implied, it may be implied "as by an owner never asserting any control over or otherwise indicating his claim of possession." [ ] An owner who comes forward has definitely indicated his claim of possession, and in such a case abandonment cannot be implied.

[Moreover, the] legislative history of the ASA suggests that sovereign vessels must be treated differently from privately owned ones. The House Report incorporates a State Department letter, which states, "the U.S. only abandons its sovereignty over, and title to, sunken U.S. warships by affirmative act; mere passage of time or lack of positive assertions of right are insufficient to establish such abandonment. [ ] The implications of this for other sovereign vessels is also underscored." * * * Under the ASA, then, an implied abandonment standard would seem least defensible where, as here, a nation has stepped forward to assert ownership over its sovereign shipwrecks.

* * *

Further, courts have held that the ASA "did not affect the meaning of 'abandoned,' which serves as a precondition for the invocation of the ASA's provisions." [ ] According to the Supreme Court, "the meaning of 'abandoned' under the ASA conforms with its meaning under admiralty law." *California v. Deep Sea Research, Inc.*, 523 U.S. 491, 508 (1998). * * *

Under admiralty law, where an owner comes forward to assert ownership in a shipwreck, abandonment must be shown by express acts.

* * *

Finally, the express abandonment standard is required by Article X of the 1902 Treaty of Friendship and General Relations between the United States and Spain.

* * *

III.

We now address whether there has been an express abandonment of *La Galga*. [Sea Hunt and Virginia must demonstrate express abandonment by "clear and convincing evidence."] The district court found that Spain had expressly abandoned *La Galga* in Article XX of the [1763 Definitive Treaty of Peace between France, Great Britain, and Spain (*Consol. T.S.* 279, 331–332).] * * * Article XX of the 1763 Treaty provides:

> [H]is Catholick Majesty cedes and guaranties, in full right, to his Brittanic Majesty, Florida, with Fort St. Augustin, and the Bay of Pensacola, as well as all that Spain possesses on the continent of North America, to the East or to the South East of the river Mississippi. And, in general, every thing that depends on said countries and lands, with the sovereignty, property, possession, and all rights, acquired by treaties or otherwise.... [S]o that the Catholick King cedes and makes over the whole to the said King and to the Crown of Great Britain, and that in the most ample manner and form.... It is moreover stipulated, that his Catholick Majesty shall have power to cause all the effects that may belong to him, to be brought away, whether it be artillery or other things.

* * *

* * * Article XX does not contain "clear and convincing" evidence of express abandonment. While the language of Article XX encompasses a great deal of land and property, it does not mention vessels or shipwrecks, nor does Article XX refer to Spanish property in the sea or on the seabed. Such general treaty language does not come close to an "express declaration abandoning title" [ ], and therefore cannot amount to clear and convincing evidence of an express abandonment.

* * *

IV.

We reverse the judgment of the district court that the Kingdom of Spain abandoned the vessel *La Galga*. We affirm the judgment of the district court as to *Juno*. [We agree that no express abandonment of the *Juno* can be found in the 1819 Treaty of Amity, Settlement and Limits (8 Stat. 252) which ended the War of 1812. We further] affirm the district court's denial of a salvage award [re *Juno*]. The district court found, "it is the right of the owner of any vessel to refuse unwanted salvage. Sea Hunt knew before bringing this action that the *Juno* was a Spanish ship and that Spain might make a claim of ownership and decline salvage.... Because Sea Hunt had prior knowledge of Spain's ownership interests and had reason to expect Spain's ownership claim and refusal to agree to salvage activity on *Juno*, Sea Hunt can not be entitled to any salvage award." [We agree.]

* * *

Notes

1. Congress has codified the holding in the principal case with respect to military craft owned by a government when it sank. Sunken Military Craft Act, P.L. 108-375, Div. A, Title XIV, §§ 1401–08, 118 Stat. 2094 (Oct. 28, 2004). reprinted as a note to 10 U.S.C. § 113.

As the principal case indicates, when an abandoned shipwreck is embedded in a state's submerged land the Abandoned Shipwreck Act ("ASA") vests title in the state and displaces the law of salvage and finds. In the case of property that was privately owned and is embedded in a state's land, abandonment can be shown by circumstantial evidence but must be proven by clear and convincing evidence. *Northeast Research, LLC v. One Shipwrecked Vessel*, 729 F.3d 197 (2d Cir. 2013).

2. **Salvage law versus law of finds.** When the abandoned property is not governed by the ASA, the law of finds rather than the law of salvage applies. In *Columbus-America Discovery Group v. Atlantic Mutual Ins. Co.*, 974 F.2d 450 (4th Cir. 1992), the court held

that insurance underwriters had not abandoned their claim to gold more than 130 years after its loss at sea.

What law, salvage or finds, makes more sense in the context of historical wrecks? It has been suggested that the law of salvage is more likely to encourage honesty and cooperation with possible owners and other potential rescuers. *Hener v. United States*, 525 F. Supp. 350 (S.D.N.Y. 1981). A court will not allow a salvor-in-possession of an historic wreck to convert its status to that of a finder. *R.M.S. Titanic, Inc. v. The Wrecked and Abandoned Vessel*, 435 F.3d 521 (4th Cir. 2006). Historical wrecks frequently involve difficult conflicts between various interest groups, including historians, recreational divers, entrepreneurs, and those who simply want the wrecks to be left undisturbed.

In one case the law of finds was applied where the plaintiff rescued an abandoned vessel that had been used in a criminal activity. *Sea Services of The Keys, Inc. v. The Abandoned 20-Foot Midnight Express Vessel*, 16 F. Supp. 2d 1369 (S.D. Fla. 1998). Quite naturally the owner chose not to appear in court to assert ownership. The State of Florida maintained that the vessel was not abandoned because it was tied to another person's lobster trap and was therefore constructively possessed by that person. The court disagreed, holding that constructive possession can only be established when a person has the power to possess the vessel and the intention to exercise dominion over it. The court concluded:

> The State of Florida, for over a year and a half and at taxpayer expense, has fought to retain possession of this twenty-nine foot vessel, which it never undertook efforts to salvage, tow, or restore. Plaintiff, at its own personal risk, battled the elements to return the Defendant vessel to a condition useful to society, only to later find itself having to wage another battle with the state to retain the fruits of its labor.

3. The Eleventh Amendment prevents suit against a state in federal court. See generally Section XIII-B, *infra* at 517. The prohibition applies to claims in admiralty. *Ex parte New York*, 256 U.S. 490 (1921). That places a salvage claimant in a difficult position when a state has claims to an historical wreck, since a salvage claim in rem can be brought only in federal court. The Supreme Court cast doubt on the ability of a salvor to obtain adequate relief in such circumstances. *Florida Dept. of State v. Treasure Salvors, Inc.*, 458 U.S. 670 (1982). But in *California v. Deep Sea Research, Inc.*, 523 U.S. 491(1998), the Court held that the Eleventh Amendment does not bar a salvor from asserting rights when the *res* is not in the possession of a state.

4. As indicated in the principal case, the United States cannot abandon property absent an act of Congress. For a robust application of that rule, see *International Aircraft Recovery, L.L.C. v. Unidentified, Wrecked & Abandoned Aircraft*, 218 F.3d 1255 (11th Cir. 2000) (involving the salvage of a World War II navy plane).

5. Does a federal court have jurisdiction to hear claims of rival salvors to vessels lying deep in international waters where no part of the vessel or cargo has been raised? If not, who does? See *R.M.S. Titanic, Inc. v. Haver*, 171 F.3d 943 (4th Cir. 1999) (using "constructive in rem jurisdiction" to legally declare but not finally enforce salvage rights).

Note on Contract Salvage

It often happens that a salvor will contract with a vessel owner before saving the vessel. Although those contracts can provide for compensation at a certain sum or rate, it is common for the contract to leave the amount of compensation open to later determination by arbitration. One of the most commonly used form contracts, a Lloyd's Standard Form of Salvage Agreement (usually called the "Lloyd's Open Form" or "LOF"), provides for arbitration in London. Several courts have held that the contract is unenforceable in a purely domestic context, i.e., when a U.S. vessel is salvaged by a U.S. salvor in U.S. waters. *Jones v. Sea Tow Services Freeport NY Inc.*, 30 F.3d 360 (2d Cir. 1994); *Reinholtz v. Retriever Marine Towing & Salvage*, 1994 AMC 2981 (S.D. Fla. 1993); *Brier v. Northstar Marine, Inc.*, 1993 AMC 1194 (D. N.J. 1992). The reasoning in each case was similar: (a) The enforceability of such agreements is controlled by the Convention on the Recognition and Enforcement of Foreign Arbitral Awards, June 10, 1958, 330 U.N.T.S. 38 (1970), as implemented by 9 U.S.C. §§ 201–208. (b) Under 9 U.S.C. § 202, "[a]n agreement ... which is entirely between citizens of the United States shall be deemed not to fall under the Convention unless the relationship involves property located abroad, envisages performance or enforcement abroad, or has some other reasonable relationship with one or more foreign states."

The salvage contract context is often "a cautionary tale for the owners of small vessels in distress." *Jones, supra*, 30 F.3d at 361. The salvors in *Jones* sought over $15,000—based on a percentage of the "salved" vessel's value—for towing an essentially undamaged yacht six miles. The yacht owners had come ashore on a cold and rainy night. After the Coast Guard determined that they were not seriously hurt, it contacted the salvor, who met them and talked with them in his land vehicle. It was alleged that the yacht owners did not comprehend the six-page salvage contract and were told that it merely authorized the salvor to tow the vessel back to port. They were also told that they would be stranded on the beach if they did not sign, but were given a ride home after signing. The salvor maintained that he provided the owners with a "Miranda" warning for salvage. As described in *Brier, supra*, 1993 AMC at 1196 n.4, the standard such warning runs as follows:

> The Lloyds of London Salvage Agreement is a no cure, no pay agreement which permits us to assist you immediately without lengthy negotiations. After we have completed the job, if we are successful in salving your boat, we will make a salvage claim based upon the value of what we have saved. If we are not successful we will claim nothing. If you or your insurer believe that our claim is too high, you may request Lloyd's to appoint an arbitrator to determine how much we should be paid. Whatever amount the arbitrator awards us, we will accept. This agreement is published and approved by Lloyd's of London for use in salvage situations. Do you accept?

The *Jones* court relieved the owners of the London-arbitration feature of the contract but not necessarily the rest of it.

The Society of Maritime Arbitrators has adopted a "U.S. Open Form Salvage Agreement" that provides for arbitration in New York. It allows the parties to check whether payment is to be based on either no cure-no pay, no cure-no pay with a fixed fee, a scheduled rate based on time and materials, or such other agreement as the parties make.

If a salvage contract stipulates a certain price and the work turns out to be easier than originally expected, should the court set the contract aside? In *The Elfrida*, 172 U.S. 186, 197 (1898), the Supreme Court said the following:

> We do not say that to impugn a salvage contract such duress must be shown as would require a court of law to set aside an ordinary contract; but, where no such circumstances exist as amount to a moral compulsion, the contract should not be held bad simply because the price agreed to be paid turned out to be much greater than the services were actually worth. The presumptions are in

> favor of the validity of the contract [ ], although in passing upon the question of compulsion the fact that the contract was made at sea, or under circumstances demanding immediate action, is an important consideration. If when the contract is made the price agreed to be paid appears to be just and reasonable, in view of the value of the property at stake, the danger from which it is to be rescued, the risk to the salvors and the salving property, the time and labor probably necessary to effect the salvage, and the contingency of losing all in case of failure, this sum ought not to be reduced by an unexpected success in accomplishing the work, unless the compensation for the work actually done be grossly exorbitant.

The two-year statute of limitations provided in the Salvage Act applies also to contract salvage. See *Ormerod v. Hedger Transp. Co.*, 1932 AMC 933 (W.D.N.Y. 1932).

Salvage vs. towage. On the distinction between salvage and towage, consider the following summary in *Evanow v. M/V Neptune*, 163 F.3d 1108 (9th Cir. 1998):

> Whether a contract is one for towage or for salvage has several consequences. If the fee is not agreed to, salvage service commands a larger award. [ ] Under a salvage contract, not only is the vessel liable for payment, but the cargo is as well. [ ] A salvage contract also creates a "preferred" maritime lien, which has a higher priority than the maritime lien created by a towage contract. Compare 46 U.S.C. § 31301(5) with § 31342(a). Finally, the crew of the salving vessel has additional rights under a salvage contract. [ ]

The character of the service rendered determines whether a contract is one for salvage. *The Camanche*, 75 U.S. 448, 477 (1869):

> There is a marked and clear distinction between a towage and a salvage service. When a tug is called or taken by a sound vessel as a mere means of saving time, or from considerations of convenience, the service is classed as towage; but if the vessel is disabled, and in need of assistance, it is a salvage service. * * *

Peninsular & Oriental Steam Navigation Co. v. Overseas Oil Carriers, Inc.

United States Court of Appeals, Second Circuit, 1977
553 F.2d 830, 1977 AMC 283

KAUFMAN, Chief Judge:

* * *

I.

[On July 4, 1973, the *S.T. Overseas Progress*, an American flag tanker of approximately 13,030 gross tons and a maximum speed of about 13.8 knots (15.9 mph),] was traveling in the mid-Atlantic Ocean, en route from Haifa, Israel to Baltimore. Suddenly, the ship's fireman, William Turpin, was stricken with severe chest pains. The *Overseas Progress* did not have a doctor aboard. Her officers, suspecting that the 63-year-old seaman had suffered a heart attack, aided Turpin as best they could. Guided by the ship's medical books and radio advice from the Public Health Service, they administered several morphine injections to relieve Turpin's severe pain and gave him glycerin nitrate tablets. Nonetheless, Turpin's condition did not improve. During the evening of July 5, 1973, he suffered another attack, again accompanied by severe chest pains.

Realizing that his vessel's resources were inadequate to deal with Turpin's increasingly serious condition, the Captain of the *Overseas Progress*, W. J. Lidwin, sent out a radio message calling for responses from all ships in the vicinity with doctors aboard. Three vessels answered the call. The nearest was the *S.S. Canberra*, a British flag passenger vessel. The *Canberra*, with a maximum speed of 25 knots (approx. 28.8 mph) was considerably faster than the *Overseas Progress*, and was consequently able to convey Turpin more quickly to shore facilities. Moreover, the *Canberra* itself carried a hospital with a fully equipped operating room and medical personnel able to provide Turpin with immediate attention. At the time she received the *Overseas Progress*'s call, the *Canberra* was en route to New York from Dakar, Senegal, traveling at 23 knots.

* * * [T]he *Overseas Progress* directed a second radio message to the British liner, explaining that one of her crew members was in critical condition after suffering an apparent heart attack. The *Canberra* was requested to rendezvous with the *Overseas Progress* and provide treatment for the ailing seaman. In response to the distress call, the *Canberra* changed course and increased her speed to 25 knots. * * *

At that time the *Overseas Progress* was 740 miles from the nearest shore hospital, at St. John's, Newfoundland. It would have taken the tanker, traveling at close to maximum speed, 57 hours to reach that destination. By contrast, the meeting of the *Canberra* and the *Overseas Progress* was achieved in 6 1/2 hours.

In the course of their radio communications, the masters of the *Canberra* and the *Overseas Progress* briefly considered the allocation of the rescue effort's costs. Captain Snowden of the *Canberra* informed Captain Lidwin that the *Canberra*'s owner, the Peninsular & Oriental Steam Navigation Co. (P & O), "may look" to the owner of the *Overseas Progress* for "reimbursement of diversion costs, medical and out of pocket expenses." Captain Lidwin did not in any way indicate that such compensation would be refused. When the two ships met, Captain Snowden presented a letter reiterating the likelihood that P & O would seek reimbursement. This letter was then countersigned by Captain Lidwin. * * *

Upon encountering the *Overseas Progress*, the *Canberra* lowered one of her lifeboats and transferred William Turpin aboard. He was examined by the *Canberra*'s surgeon, who diagnosed his illness as a myocardial infarction, a form of heart attack that results in the partial destruction of the central heart muscle. After taking Turpin aboard, the *Canberra* resumed her course to New York at maximum speed, 25 knots. * * * Turpin was rushed by ambulance to the United States Public Health Hospital on Staten Island. Eventually, he recovered and was discharged.

Overseas Oil Carriers, the owner of the *Overseas Progress*, promptly paid $248 to the *Canberra*'s surgeon for medical expenses rendered to Turpin. But it was far less generous in responding to P & O's request for reimbursement. In response to P & O's letter of September 26, 1973, seeking $12,108.95 for Turpin's accommodation and nursing while on the *Canberra* and, principally, for the additional fuel consumed by the liner * * *, Overseas Oil Carriers's agent, in a letter dated October 3, declined to pay any part of this amount. Although the agent wrote, "we are extremely grateful for the kind assistance you have rendered Mr. Turpin", he continued to assert that payment of the claim would be out of keeping with the "traditional concept of rescue at sea."

On April 26, 1974, P & O filed a complaint in the Southern District of New York, seeking recovery of the $12,108.95 it had requested previously. The parties each moved for summary judgment on stipulated facts. In an opinion dated August 20, 1976, Judge Goettel granted recovery of $500 for nursing services but denied any reimbursement for the *Canberra*'s additional fuel expenses. He noted that under traditional admiralty doctrines of "salvage", there could be no reward for "pure life salvage", i.e. a rescue at sea where men's lives are saved but property is not simultaneously recovered. Judge Goettel also rejected any claim based on "quasi-contract" because he failed to find "misconduct or fault" by Overseas Oil Carriers. He did, however, grant recovery for nursing services since Overseas would have been obliged to pay such costs if Turpin had been placed in a shore hospital. * * *

II.

When Turpin fell ill, the Captain of the *S.T. Overseas Progress* became obligated to make reasonable efforts to provide him with swift medical care, pursuant to the ship's responsibility for "maintenance and cure." * * *

On vessels that do not carry a surgical staff, the ship's master has a duty, in the sound exercise of his judgment and depending on the circumstances, to have the seaman taken speedily to a hospital or the nearest port where surgical care may be obtained. [ ] Without the assistance of the *S.S. Canberra*, or a vessel with similar facilities, performance of this duty would have required the *Overseas Progress* to travel to the shore hospital at St. John's, Newfoundland, entailing a considerable expenditure of time and additional fuel. The *Canberra*, by agreeing to rendezvous, provided Turpin with swifter medical attention and saved the *Overseas Progress* considerable costs. * * * In such circumstances, the principles of "quasi-contract" require recovery.

Although the law ordinarily frowns on the claims of a "mere volunteer", there is a class of cases where it is imperative that a duty be performed swiftly and efficiently for the protection of the public or an innocent third party, in which a "good Samaritan" who voluntarily intervenes to perform the duty may receive restitution for his services. This rule has become crystallized in the doctrine that performance of another's duty to a third person, if rendered by one qualified to provide such services with intent to charge for them, is a ground for recovery in quasi-contract. This principle is limited to cases where the services are immediately necessary to prevent injury or suffering. [ ] Restatement of Restitution § 114. [ ]

The circumstances of this case compel application of the rule. The *Overseas Progress* had a manifest duty to provide Turpin with speedy medical attention. Her captain, in the exercise of his reasonable discretion, asked the *Canberra* to perform that duty in her stead. It is undisputed that the *Canberra*, with her fully equipped hospital and greater speed, was a proper party to provide such services, and the countersigned letter from the *Canberra*'s captain suffices to demonstrate the liner's intent to charge.

Moreover, this is not a case in which a "good Samaritan" volunteered his services without the knowledge or consent of the person whose duty was discharged. * * *

III.

Overseas contends that the principles of quasi-contract, though presumably reflecting our sense of fair and orderly arrangement of affairs on terra firma, should not be applied to occurrences on the sea. We fail to perceive any reason for this distinction. Although it is true that the fortuitousness of jurisdiction in eighteenth century English courts long left the application of restitutionary principles to admiralty in doubt, today the law is clear that quasi-contractual claims may be considered by the federal courts in admiralty * * *, see *Archawski v. Hanioti*, 350 U.S. 532 (1956) [*supra* at 50]. * * *

Overseas urges that quasi-contractual recovery under these circumstances would, in effect, subvert the long-established rule in admiralty that prohibits recovery for "pure life salvage." In admiralty, a person who rescues property at sea may obtain an award based not merely on the costs he incurs but on the value of the property saved and the degree of danger encountered. * * * Yet it seems to have been admiralty law that rescuing lives at sea, rather than property, merited moral approbation, but no pecuniary reward.[7]

Overseas bids us to ignore the sound reasons that warrant recovery in this case, and to defer instead to this hoary, and almost universally condemned, rule of the sea. But, we do not find the rule on pure life salvage, regardless of its dubious vitality, relevant to the facts. P & O is not seeking a reward; it merely requests reimbursement for its expenses. And, we do not confront a daring "rescue at sea", but the transfer of an ailing seaman from one seaworthy vessel to another. Under these circumstances we do not believe the questionable doctrine of "pure life salvage" bars recovery.

Finally, Overseas contends that the rule we announce today will disrupt traditional maritime practices, making assistance to an ailing seaman a matter of negotiation rather than moral duty. On the contrary, we believe this rule will encourage seamen aboard large vessels to perform their moral obligation to their brethren on smaller ships without fear their benevolence will result in unreasonable expenses to their ship's owners.

Overseas also predicts that masters of small ships will be reluctant to call for aid, knowing their actions may result in the imposition of sizable fuel costs. But, masters are already under a legal obligation to make reasonable efforts to secure medical care for their stricken crewmen. In determining the proper course of action, they must consider the seriousness of the seaman's illness, the availability and adequacy of medical facilities and the costs that will be incurred in securing aid. Once it is established that the fuel expenses of a ship rendering assistance is one of these costs, it will simply become another factor to be considered in the master's calculation. With radio-telegraphy, it is a simple matter for him to ascertain the size and location of ships in the vicinity, just as the *Overseas Progress* did, and to determine which vessel can be reached with minimum expense and delay. Thus, we believe the rule we announce today will result both in greater willingness of large vessels to render assistance and in the utilization of the medical facilities of those vessels in the most efficient and productive manner.

* * *

Notes

1. 46 U.S.C. § 2304 makes it a crime for an individual in charge of a vessel to fail to render assistance to a person in danger at sea if that can be done without serious danger. There have been no reports of any prosecutions. But what about civil suits? In *Warshauer v. Lloyd Saboudo S.A.*, 71 F.2d 146 (2d Cir. 1934), the court held that the shipowner was not liable for a master's dereliction. It relied on Article 11 of the 1910 salvage treaty that provided, "The owner of the vessel incurs no liability by reason of the contravention of

7. This rule was modified by the enactment of 46 U.S.C. § 729 in 1912 [since recodified at 46 U.S.C. § 80107(a)]. That statute allowed life salvors to receive a fair share of a property salvage award arising out of the same maritime accident. It was intended to remove the disincentive to life salvage that resulted from the traditional rule, which encouraged sailors to rescue property rather than aid fellow seamen in jeopardy. The irrationality of providing rewards for property salvage but not requiring payment for rescuing lives has been under attack for many years. Jarett, *The Life Salvor Problem in Admiralty*, 63 Yale L.J. 779 (1954). Under British statutory law, a person who saves a life on a British vessel anywhere in the world, or on a foreign vessel in British waters, may claim a life salvage award. [ ]

the [provision requiring masters to save life at sea]." The case was distinguished in *Caminiti v. Tomlinson Fleet & American S.S. Co.*, 1981 AMC 201 (N.D. Ohio 1979), holding that the treaty did not apply when both parties were from the United States, and that the employer was vicariously liable. The 1989 salvage treaty applies even when all interested parties are from the same State.

2. The early English practice was to deny a life salvage award, but if the life salvors also saved property, the court was willing to award a liberal amount of salvage. The English practice was substantially changed by a series of statutes beginning in the 1840s and culminating in the Merchant Shipping Act of 1894, 57–58 Vict., ch. 60, §§ 544–545. Under that legislation, which has been copied in part by many countries that were part of the Commonwealth or were under British control, a life salvor has a right to salvage against the vessel and cargo that have been saved. The life salvor's lien outranks even the property salvor's lien. If no property has been saved, or if insufficient property has been saved to satisfy the life salvor's claim, then the claim is to be paid out of public funds.

3. The nineteenth and early twentieth century U.S. practice paralleled in most respects the early English practice. Liberal awards were made when a salvor saved life and property, even if the salvor's original intention had been only to save life. A few courts made specific awards for saving life to those who also saved property. And courts awarded salvage for saving the lives of slaves in those states that had slave markets. See *United States v. The Amistad*, 40 U.S. 58 (1841).

In *The Mulhouse*, 17 F. Cas. 962 (S.D. Fla. 1859) (No. 9910), the court awarded life salvage to some who saved lives when others saved property. Life salvage awards were paid out of all of the property saved, it being in the interest of shipowners and cargo owners to encourage people to engage in salvage activities.

4. The 1910 salvage treaty contained several provisions bearing on life salvage. Article 8 listed the danger run by the salved vessel's passengers and crew as a factor to be considered in determining the amount of salvage. Article 9 provided that people saved are not liable for salvage, unless national laws provided otherwise. That article further provided:

> Salvors of human life, who have taken part in the services rendered on the occasion of the accident giving rise to salvage or assistance, are entitled to a fair share of the remuneration awarded to the salvors of the vessel, her cargo, and accessories.

Under Articles 8 and 9, the life salvor is to paid by the property salvor who has received an award that took into account the peril to life.

In the 1912 Salvage Act, Article 8 of the treaty was not enacted, presumably because it restated U.S. law. The Act also did not provide that saved persons would not owe salvage because that, too, was assumed to be part of U.S. law. *See* S. Rep. No. 477, 62d Cong., 2d Sess. 2 (1912). The Act gave effect to the other aspect of Article 9 of the treaty. In its current form, 46 U.S.C. § 80107(a), the Salvage Act provides:

> A salvor of human life, who gave aid following an accident giving rise to salvage, is entitled to a fair share of the payment awarded to the salvor for salvaging the vessel or other property or preventing or minimizing damage to the environment.[8]

The United Kingdom did not change its life salvage provisions to conform to the 1910 treaty. It apparently relied on a report of the treaty's drafting committee that "each nation

8. The environmental damage provision was added in 1991.

remains free to give life salvors greater or more specific rights." *Procès-verbaux du Conférence Maritime* 102 (1910).

5. Even though the 1910 treaty was most likely intended to set a floor on life salvage awards, U.S. courts have in effect treated it as setting a ceiling and have ignored the 19th century cases that provided more liberal awards. Courts have also read several limitations into the 1912 statute. In *The Eastland,* 262 F. 535 (N.D. Ill. 1919), *aff'd without opinion sub nom. Mattocks v. Great Lakes Towing Co.* (7th Cir. 1920), an excursion boat capsized and sank at its dock in Chicago killing 835 people. Many lives were saved "through magnificent and heroic efforts." A towing company contracted for a set price to raise the vessel, and did so two months later. The court denied the life salvor's claims against the towing company. It held that the Salvage Act provides a right only to those who render service "at the time that the property was saved," even though the services were rendered "on the occasion that the accident" that gave rise to salvage. It further held that the statute did not apply when the property was saved by salvors acting under a contract. Finally it held that life salvors only have a right to a reward if they had a choice between saving life and saving property. Later courts have echoed *The Eastland.*

Some courts have read the Salvage Act to deny an enhanced reward to those who save life and property. See, e.g., *Markakis, supra* at 386 n.28. Those courts read the statute as the sole basis for any life salvage claim. We think that those courts have misinterpreted the Salvage Act, and that the Second Circuit in *P & O* reached a sound result.

6. Many feel that since there is a natural incentive to save life at sea—and since it is a crime not to—a monetary award should not be necessary. Others take the position that even if the amount of an award for life salvage is small, it still has an important symbolic value. See generally Friedell, *Compensation and Reward for Saving Life at Sea*, 77 MICH. L. REV. 1218 (1979).

Chapter VIII

Maritime Liens and Ship Mortgages

If a party has a maritime lien, it means that the party can sue the vessel in rem. See *The Rock Island Bridge, supra* at 67–68. In U.S. admiralty terminology, an action in rem to enforce a maritime lien results in the admiralty court's *arrest* of the vessel. Other judicial seizures of vessels are generally called *attachments* or simply seizures. See *supra* at 68.

This chapter considers the nature of the maritime lien, the kinds of claims that give rise to a maritime lien, the order of priority among competing lien claimants, the effect of the Ship Mortgage Act on maritime liens, and some of the complications that arise when a vessel owner is in bankruptcy.

A. The Personification Theory

Harmer v. Bell (The Bold Buccleugh)

Judicial Committee of the Privy Council, 1852
7 Moore P.C. 267, 13 Eng. Rep. 884

Sir John JERVIS:

[A Scottish steamship, the *Bold Buccleugh*, ran down and sank the *William* in the Humber River in England. A suit in rem was brought in England, but the *Bold Buccleugh* left for Scotland before process could be served on it. The *William*'s owners then sued the owner of the *Bold Buccleugh* in the Scottish Court of Sessions. The steamer was attached in Scotland and was released on bail. She was then sold to Daniel Harmer. When the vessel returned to England (with the Scottish action against its former owners still pending), it was arrested under authority of the High Court of Admiralty. Harmer appeared under protest and contested the power of the admiralty court to entertain the second suit. The parties disagreed about whether Harmer had notice of the collision claims when he bought the vessel. The admiralty judge, Dr. Lushington, ruled that the Admiralty Court had jurisdiction and that the sale of the vessel had not released it from responsibility for the collision. Harmer appealed. After hearing argument, the court directed the parties to reargue the question "whether the *bona fide* sale of the vessel after the damage, without notice to the purchaser, discharged the vessel from liability."]

[In the Privy Council decision handed down after the reargument, the Council dealt first with the argument that an arrest of a vessel in an in rem proceeding is only a means of compelling the owners to appear, and that since the owner (Harmer) had appeared in the English admiralty proceeding, the only question for the court was to determine that party's interests and responsibilities. The court refuted this argument by pointing out several differences between a proceeding in rem and a suit in personam.]

[It is argued] that the damage confers no lien upon the ship. * * *

A maritime lien does not include or require possession. The word [*lien*] is used in Maritime Law not in the strict legal sense in which we understand it in Courts of Common Law, in which case there could be no lien where there was no possession, actual or constructive; but to express, as if by analogy, the nature of claims which neither presuppose nor originate in possession. This was well understood in the Civil Law, by which there might be a pledge with possession, and a hypothecation without possession, and by which in either case the right travelled with the thing into whosesoever possession it came. Having its origin in this rule of the Civil Law, a maritime lien is well defined by Lord Tenterden, to mean a claim or privilege upon a thing to be carried into effect by legal process; and Mr. Justice Story [in *The Nestor,* 18 F. Cas. 9, 11 (C.C.D. Me. 1831) (No. 10,126)] explains that process to be a proceeding in rem, and adds, that wherever a lien or claim is given upon the thing, then the Admiralty enforces it by a proceeding in rem, and indeed is the only Court competent to enforce it.

A maritime lien is the foundation of the proceeding in rem, a process to make perfect a right inchoate from the moment the lien attaches; and whilst it must be admitted that where such a lien exists, a proceeding in rem may be had, it will be found to be equally true, that in all cases where a proceeding in rem is the proper course, there a maritime lien exists, which gives a privilege or claim upon the thing, to be carried into effect by legal process. This claim or privilege travels with the thing, into whosesoever possession it may come. It is inchoate from the moment the claim or privilege attaches, and when carried into effect by legal process, by a proceeding in rem, relates back to the period when it first attached.

* * *

This rule, which is simple and intelligible, is, in our opinion applicable to all cases. [W]here reasonable diligence is used, and the proceedings are had in good faith, the lien may be enforced, into whosesoever possession the thing may come.

The remaining point may be disposed of in a few words. The pleadings show that the proceedings in Scotland were commenced by process against the persons of the Defendants, and that the seizure of the vessel was collateral to that proceeding, for the mere purpose of securing the debt. We have already explained that, in our judgment, a proceeding in rem differs from one in personam, and it follows, that the two suits being in their nature different, the pendency of the one cannot be pleaded in suspension of the other.

For these reasons, we are of opinion, that the judgment of the Court below must be affirmed, with costs.

Notes

1. As the remainder of this chapter will make clear, U.S. courts have accepted the personification theory of *The Bold Buccleugh*. See also *supra* at 100. By contrast, modern English practice has rejected this theory. In England today, the arrest of a vessel resembles our maritime attachment. See generally TETLEY, MARITIME LIENS AND CLAIMS 1029–41

(2d ed. 1998). Several treaties have attempted to unify the law of maritime arrest, but the United States has not ratified any of them.

2. The maritime lien differs radically from a mechanic's lien or a lien under article 9 of the Uniform Commercial Code. Those liens are created by statute and are perfected either by possession of the article on which the lien is claimed or by publicly recording the lien. If more than one claimant has a lien against an item, the usual rule for establishing priority is "first in time, first in right." By contrast, most maritime liens are based on judge-made law. Except for ship mortgages, they need not be recorded. The order of priority of liens of the same type generally follows a so-called "inverse order" rule of "last in time, first in right." For further discussion of the differences between maritime liens and land liens, see GILMORE & BLACK, THE LAW OF ADMIRALTY 586–589 (2d ed. 1975).

3. The defining characteristic of the maritime lien is that it provides the successful claimant with the ability to have the arrested vessel sold free and clear of all liens, even those not before the court. By contrast, when a court orders the sale of a vessel pursuant to an attachment in an in personam proceeding, the buyer acquires only the interest of the defendant, subject to all other interests and liens. That means that a judicial sale following an admiralty in rem proceeding will generally bring a considerably higher price than would a normal judicial sale. Having a maritime lien can be crucial when the value of the vessel will not suffice to pay all claims. Those who have a maritime lien will prevail over those claimants who do not. See generally GILMORE & BLACK, THE LAW OF ADMIRALTY 622 (2d ed. 1975).

4. The maritime lien attaches to the vessel and includes all of the components, accessories, and appurtenances. For example, a winch on a fishing ship or a refrigerator on a vessel is part of the vessel and is subject to a maritime lien. Even a fishing vessel's fishing permits are appurtenances. *Gowen, Inc. v. F/V Quality One*, 244 F.3d 64 (1st Cir. 2001). The lien can be imposed on appurtenances even if they are owned by someone other than the shipowner if they are deemed to be an integral part of the vessel's operation. See generally 1 SCHOENBAUM, ADMIRALTY AND MARITIME LAW § 9:1, at 780–781 (6th Practitioner ed. 2018); Smith, *Ship Mortgages*, 47 TUL. L. REV. 608, 618 (1973). See also *Oil Shipping (Bunkering) B.V. v. Sonmez Denizcilik Ve Ticaret A.S.*, 10 F.3d 176 (3d Cir. 1993) (a ship mortgage extends to the fuel on board).

5. As the principal case illustrates, a maritime lien may provide a plaintiff with a claim against a vessel even though the plaintiff has no in personam claim against the current vessel owner. That can happen when a vessel is involved in a collision caused solely by the negligence of a compulsory pilot. In such an event, the plaintiff will have a lien against the vessel and can therefore sue it in rem, but the vessel owner would not be liable for the pilot's negligence. *The China*, *supra* at 361. For another application of the personification theory, see the following case.

Cavcar Co. v. M/V Suzdal

United States Court of Appeals, Third Circuit, 1983
723 F.2d 1096, 1984 AMC 609

POLLAK, District Judge, sitting by designation:

This appeal raises the question whether a vessel may be liable in rem for breach of the contract of carriage by the operator of the vessel when the vessel's owner is not liable in personam for the breach. The district court held that there can be no in rem liability in such circumstances. For the reasons stated below, we reverse.

I.

* * * In 1975, appellant, Sherkate Sahami Khass Auto Pars ("Auto Pars") ordered 200 Ford Bronco trucks from Ford Export Corporation. This purchase was financed by two letters of credit issued by Iranian banks. At the port of Philadelphia, forty-nine of these vehicles were loaded on the *M/V Finn Amer* ("*Finn Amer*"), the appellee.

The *Finn Amer* is registered in Finland and is owned by Amer Sea O/Y ("Amer Sea") a Finnish company. When this controversy arose, the *Finn Amer* was time-chartered to Gloucester Shipping Corporation which is not a party to these proceedings. Although the master of the *Finn Amer* was employed by Amer Sea, the vessel was operated by Marine Transport Services (MTS), a New Jersey corporation. The district court found that "MTS provided the operational infrastructure, arranged the stevedoring, solicited cargo, processed all documents and established an agency network in overseas points with respect to the *Finn Amer*. It did not charter that vessel."

When the forty-nine Broncos were loaded on the vessel, MTS issued a negotiable bill of lading. The bill of lading specified Bandar Shahpour, a port of Iran, as the destination. * * * Amer Sea was not a party to the bill of lading and the master of the *Finn Amer* never saw the bill of lading.

The *Finn Amer* arrived at Bandar Shahpour on January 23, 1976. Auto Pars was notified of the vessel's arrival and was requested by MTS to "preclear" the Broncos. Preclearance is a procedure by which the customs duty on the cargo is paid in advance of discharge and the consignee takes direct delivery from the side of the vessel. The district court found that there was no legal requirement of preclearance and that consignees generally resisted the preclearance system.

The *Finn Amer* was granted berth on February 19, 1976. It discharged all of its cargo other than the forty-nine Broncos. The Broncos were the only cargo which was not precleared. While the vessel was at Bandar Shahpour no bill of lading was presented for these vehicles. * * *

On February 23, without giving notice to Auto Pars, MTS ordered the *Finn Amer* to depart from Bandar Shahpour with the Broncos. It did so and returned the vehicles to Philadelphia as directed by MTS. The Broncos were impounded and eventually sold by United States Customs.

[T]he action presently before us [is] a suit for damages for nondelivery of the Broncos which was filed in 1977 by Auto Pars against the *Finn Amer* and Amer Sea. After a bench trial, the district court * * * found that neither Amer Sea nor the *Finn Amer* were parties to the bill of lading and the master of the ship had taken all relevant actions solely under the direction of MTS. The court concluded that Amer Sea, the owner of the *Finn Amer*, was not liable for the nondelivery of the cargo and that Auto Pars had failed to establish any basis for the imposition of in rem liability.

Auto Pars has appealed the district court's decision solely with respect to the finding on in rem liability. It does not dispute the lower court's finding that Amer Sea is not personally liable for the nondelivery. The primary issue before us is whether in rem liability exists when the charterer or operator of the vessel has breached the contract of carriage but the shipowner is not personally liable for the breach.

II.

In arguing to the district court that the Finn Amer was liable in rem, Auto Pars relied on the Supreme Court's venerable decision in *The Barnstable,* 181 U.S. 464 (1901). In that case the libeled vessel was the British steamship *Barnstable* which had collided off Cape Cod with the schooner *Fortuna*—"a collision resulting from the negligence of the officers and crew, who are appointed and paid by the charterers." The question before the Court was whether, under the terms of the charter party governing the negligently operated *Barnstable*, ultimate liability lay with the charterers or the owners. En route to resolving this issue [by imposing ultimate responsibility on the charterers], Justice Brown, speaking for a unanimous Court, observed that, "[w]hatever may be the English rule with respect to the liability of a vessel for damages occasioned by the neglect of the charterer, as to which there appears to be some doubt ... the law in this country is entirely well-settled that the ship itself is to be treated in some sense as a principal, and as personally liable for the negligence of anyone who is lawfully in possession of her, whether as owner or charterer." [ ]

* * * [T]he district court in the instant case concluded that *The Barnstable* was of little avail to Auto Pars, [stating that] since Auto Pars' "claim sounded in contract and not negligence, *The Barnstable* did not, even remotely, support imposition of liability under the facts of this case."

Auto Pars may not be able to derive any comfort from the Court's decision in *The Barnstable*, or from what the Court held or said in *Reed v. The Yaka*, 373 U.S. 410 (1963), an in rem proceeding of more recent vintage.[1] Neither of those suits involved the type of claim presented here—an action by a shipper of goods against a vessel in rem for breach of the contract of carriage. On the other hand, nothing in those Supreme Court holdings or opinions forecloses the transposition of that in rem analysis to a situation involving a breach of the contract of carriage.

Within the Second Circuit, at both the trial and appellate levels, there has developed over the past six decades a corpus of authority which strongly supports the imposition on the *Finn Amer* of in rem liability for failure to fulfill the various obligations contained in the bill of lading. * * * In 1921, Judge Learned Hand, then a District Judge, considered a claim which was in important respects closely analogous to the present action. *The Poznan*, 276 F. 418 (S.D.N.Y.). That suit involved claims by numerous shippers against the ship in rem and the shipowner and charterer in personam for failure to deliver their goods in Havana, the ship having returned to New York with its cargo after waiting for a berth in Havana for almost two months. * * * [T]he shipowner was not a party to the contract of carriage. Judge Hand nonetheless held that "[b]eing once laden she was bound for right delivery though the charterers sign.... Indeed, the cargo would have a 'privilege' against the ship for right delivery even without any bill of lading." * * *

Soon thereafter, Judge Hand considered a similar in rem claim arising from a ship's deviation from the course established by the bill of lading and again found liability in rem although the shipowner had no personal liability under the bill of lading. *The Blandon*, 287 F. 722 (S.D.N.Y. 1922). The charterer had signed the bill of lading and the master had not, but the court found "that the master must be held to ratify all bills of lading once he sets sail. * * * Whatever ... may be the rule before the ship breaks ground, it seems to me clear that thereafter the bill of lading, though signed by the charterer only, is the measure of the ship's duty and the cargo's 'privilege.'"

* * *

---

1. Editors' note: *Reed* was a successful tort action by an injured longshoreman against a ship under bareboat charter to the longshoreman's employer. See the discussion of *Reed* in *Jones & Laughlin*, *supra* at 217.

[I]n *United Nations Children's Fund v. S/S Nordstern,* 251 F. Supp. 833 (S.D.N.Y. 1965), * * * [t]he vessel was held liable in rem [for nondelivery of cargo] despite the fact that, as in the present action, the master had not signed the bill of lading and the charterer was solely responsible for the decision to bypass the designated port. Judge Levet reviewed the cases discussed above and found that "in this court's opinion, those decisions make good sense. Once the voyage has begun, the goods are beyond the shipper's control. It seems eminently reasonable to hold that the ship has a duty to deliver them to the destination provided in the bill of lading.... Indeed, the maritime lien and the proceeding against the ship itself do seem 'the best and surest pledge for the compensation and indemnity to the injured party.'"

In 1972, the Court of Appeals for the Second Circuit gave its full imprimatur to the ratification principle. *Demsey & Associates, Inc. v. S.S. Sea Star*, 461 F.2d 1009 (1972). Judge Medina, speaking for the court, found that "[a]lthough the Master did not sign the bills of lading, the sailing of the *Sea Star* with the coils aboard constituted a ratification of the bills of lading." [ ] Thus, the ship was held liable despite the absence of in personam liability of the shipowner.

The consistent trial and appellate court holdings in the Second Circuit * * * find impressive support in GILMORE & BLACK, THE LAW OF ADMIRALTY §§4–17, 9-18a (2d ed. 1975), [which] points out that such a result is proper as a matter of public policy in that it provides security to those who suffer a wrong through the instrumentality of the ship by creating limited shipowner liability for the actions of third parties to whom they have entrusted control.

We find the foregoing analysis doctrinally persuasive and dispositive of the present appeal. Although the master of the *Finn Amer* did not sign the bill of lading for the forty-nine Broncos, the departure of the ship from Philadelphia with the cargo on board effected an implied ratification of the bill of lading, binding the ship to the obligations therein, including the duty to deliver the goods at the designated port. Therefore, the vessel is liable in rem even though Amer Sea is not personally liable in contract for the breach. Our decision does not address the *Finn Amer*'s possible right to indemnification from the party primarily responsible for the injury. * * *

Accordingly, the judgment below will be reversed and the case remanded for proceedings consistent with this opinion.

Notes

1. Courts have not carried the personification theory to its logical extreme of regarding the vessel as a separate person for all purposes. For example, under general maritime law a vessel is not liable in rem if the damage is caused by someone who misappropriates the vessel. See *Churchill v. F/V Fjord*, 892 F.2d 763 (9th Cir. 1988). Similarly, under the Commercial Instruments and Federal Maritime Lien Act "a person tortiously or unlawfully in possession or charge of a vessel has no authority to procure necessaries for the vessel." 46 U.S.C. §31341(b).

2. There are other limitations on the personification theory. The dismissal or settlement of an in rem claim will bar relitigation in an in personam action on the grounds of res judicata. *Burns Bros. v. Central R.R. of N.J.*, 202 F.2d 910 (2d Cir. 1953).

3. An instructive case on the personification theory's limits is *The Western Maid*, 257 U.S. 419 (1922). In that case vessels caused damage while they were owned or chartered

by the United States during or shortly after World War I. The vessels were sued in rem after they were returned to their non-governmental owners. The case arose before passage of the Public Vessels Act so that United States enjoyed immunity from suit. (See *infra* Chapter XIII.) The Supreme Court, in an opinion by Justice Holmes, ruled that the vessels could not be sued. He wrote:

> It may be said that the person who actually did the act complained of may or might be sued and that the ship for this purpose is regarded as a person. But that is a fiction not a fact and as a fiction is the creation of the law. It would be a strange thing if the law created a fiction to accomplish the result supposed. It is totally immaterial that in dealing with private wrongs the fiction, however originated, is in force. [ ] The personality of a public vessel is merged in that of the sovereign.

4. In rem actions can be transferred pursuant to 28 U.S.C. § 1404(a) despite the fact that the vessel could not be arrested in the transferee district. *Continental Grain Co. v. The FBL-585,* 364 U.S. 19 (1960). On similar reasoning, the personification theory does not prevent dismissing in rem actions for forum non conveniens provided adequate substitute security can be furnished.

5. Section 8 of the Federal Arbitration Act, 9 U.S.C. § 8, provides that an in rem action may be stayed pending an arbitration. The statute "does not contemplate [the vessel] as being [a] party to the arbitration agreement." *Marine Transit Corp. v. Dreyfus,* 284 U.S. 263, 275 (1932). Thus, the arbitrators cannot issue any orders directly against the vessel. But the admiralty court can use in rem process to enforce an arbitral award against the vessel's owner.

6. For an explanation of the personification theory in the carriage of goods context (as well as a more detailed discussion of the theory), see Davies, *In Defense of Unpopular Virtues: Personification and Ratification,* 75 Tul. L. Rev. 337 (2000).

B. Claims that Give Rise to Maritime Liens

Osaka Shosen Kaisha v. Pacific Export Lumber Co. (The Saigon Maru)

Supreme Court of the United States, 1923

260 U.S. 490, 43 S. Ct. 172, 67 L.Ed. 364, 1923 AMC 55

Mr. Justice McREYNOLDS delivered the opinion of the unanimous Court.

March 19, 1917, through its agent at Tacoma, Wash., [petitioner] Osaka Shosen Kaisha, incorporated under the laws of Japan and owner of the Japanese steamer *Saigon Maru,* then at Singapore, chartered the whole of that vessel, including her deck, to respondent Lumber Company to carry a full cargo of lumber from the Columbia or Willamette River to Bombay. In May, 1917, the vessel began to load at Portland, Or. Having taken on a full under-deck cargo and 241,559 feet upon the deck, the captain refused to accept more. After insisting that the vessel was not loaded to capacity and ineffectively demanding that she receive an additional 508,441 feet, respondent libeled her, setting up the charter party and the captain's refusal, and claimed substantial damages. The owner gave bond; the vessel departed and safely delivered her cargo.

* * *

Petitioner excepted to the libel upon the ground that the facts alleged showed no lien or right to proceed in rem. The trial court ruled otherwise and awarded damages upon the evidence. The Circuit Court of Appeals approved this action.

* * *

Both courts below acted upon the view that while the ship is not liable in rem for breaches of an affreightment contract so long as it remains wholly executory, she becomes liable therefor whenever she partly executes it, as by taking on board some part of the cargo. * * * We think the argument is unsound.

* * *

In *The Yankee Blade*, 60 U.S. 82 (1857), Mr. Justice Grier, speaking for the Court, declared:

> The maritime "privilege" or lien is adopted from the civil law, and imports a tacit hypothecation of the subject of it. It is a "*jus in re*," without actual possession or any right of possession. It accompanies the property into the hands of a bona fide purchaser. It can be executed and divested only by a proceeding in rem.... But this privilege or lien, though adhering to the vessel, is a secret one; it may operate to the prejudice of general creditors and purchasers without notice; it is therefore "*stricti juris*," and cannot be extended by construction, analogy, or inference....
>
> * * *
>
> [Under a contract of affreightment, the] duty of the vessel, to the performance of which the law binds her by hypothecation, is to deliver the cargo at the time and place stipulated in the bill of lading or charter party, without injury or deterioration. If the cargo be not placed on board, it is not bound to the vessel, and the vessel cannot be in default for the nondelivery, in good order, of goods never received on board. Consequently, if the master or owner refuses to perform his contract, or for any other reason the ship does not receive cargo and depart on her voyage according to contract, the charterer has no privilege or maritime lien on the ship for such breach of the contract by the owners, but must resort to his personal action for damages, as in other cases.

* * *

The contract of affreightment itself creates no lien, and this court has consistently declared that the obligation between ship and cargo is mutual and reciprocal and does not attach until the cargo is on board or in the master's custody. We think the lien created by the law must be mutual and reciprocal; the lien of the cargo owner upon the ship is limited by the corresponding and reciprocal rights of the shipowner upon the cargo.

The theory that partial acceptance of the designated cargo under a contract of affreightment creates a privilege of lien upon the ship for damages resulting from failure to take all, is inconsistent with the opinions of this court and, we think, without support of adequate authority. In *The S.L. Watson*, 118 F. 945, 952 (1st Cir. 1902), the court well said:

> The rule of admiralty, as always stated, is that the cargo is bound to the ship and the ship to the cargo. Whatever cases may have been decided otherwise disregarded the universal fact that no lien arises in admiralty except in connection with some visible occurrence relating to the vessel or cargo or to a person injured. This is

necessary in order that innocent parties dealing with vessels may not be the losers by secret liens....

* * *

Reversed.

Notes

1. The Court's statement that the cargo's lien on the ship and the ship's lien on the cargo "must be mutual and reciprocal" is not entirely accurate. The vessel's lien on cargo for unpaid freight (or for any other claim) is lost once the cargo is unconditionally released, *4,885 Bags of Linseed*, 66 U.S. 108 (1861), whereas cargo's lien on the ship is entirely non-possessory. See *Kraus Bros., infra.*

2. The rule that no lien attaches to an executory contract is not limited to contracts of affreightment. It applies to all contracts. A contract ceases to be "executory" at the point at which performance is deemed to have begun. That point must be defined for each type of contract.

(a) Passengers do not have a lien until they board the vessel. *Acker v. City of Athens*, 177 F.2d 961 (4th Cir. 1949).

(b) For contracts of affreightment, the goods need not actually be placed on board. It is enough that they have been delivered to the custody of the master or to someone authorized by him to receive them. *The Keokuk*, 76 U.S. 517 (1869). Hence, a lien will arise if the goods are placed on lighters or delivered alongside the vessel and are under the master's control. See Gilmore & Black, The Law of Admiralty 637–638 (2d ed. 1975).

(c) A time charterer "must begin his performance well before cargo is ... loaded on the vessel—by paying hire, appointing and funding a port agent, and arranging and paying for pilotage, tug assistance and line handlers and all else necessary to berth the vessel in order to load cargo." *Navieros Inter-Americanos, S.A. v. M/V Vailia Express*, 120 F.3d 304, 314 (1st Cir. 1997). In *Navieros* the charterer—who had boarded the vessel several times, changed instructions as to its destination, ordered fuel for the vessel, confirmed its reservation of berth space, and issued a check to pay a customs fee—had a lien on the ship although no cargo was ever loaded or placed alongside the ship.

3. In the principal case, did the Court's opposition to extending the concept of maritime liens by analogy mean that no new types of maritime liens would be recognized? See the next case.

Krauss Brothers Lumber Co. v. Dimon Steamship Corp. (The Pacific Cedar)

Supreme Court of the United States, 1933
290 U.S. 117, 54 S. Ct. 105, 78 L. Ed. 216, 1933 AMC 1578

Mr. Justice STONE delivered the opinion of the Court.

This suit in admiralty was brought by petitioner in the District Court for Western Washington to recover an alleged overpayment of freight and to establish a lien on the vessel for the amount of the overpayment. The libel alleges a contract by petitioner with the owner, by which the latter agreed to receive for loading on the *Pacific Cedar*, on or about January 18, 1930, at named Pacific Coast ports, a quantity of lumber, and to transport it to Philadelphia and New York at the rate of $10 per thousand feet, but with a provision that in the event "a regular intercoastal carrier moves similar cargo at a lower rate," such lower rate should be applied. * * * [T]he lumber was shipped and transported, and between March 1st and 20th was delivered, all under the provisions of the contract, and * * * at the conclusion of the voyage and while the vessel was discharging her cargo, respondents, at destination, demanded and received payment of freight at the $10 rate, although in January, 1930, a regular intercoastal carrier had carried a similar cargo from Seattle to Baltimore at $8.50 per thousand feet.

The lien asserted is for the difference between the freight paid and the freight earned at the agreed lower rate. * * * [Taking an anachronistically narrow view of the criteria for classifying contracts as maritime, the district court dismissed petitioner's in personam and in rem actions.] The Court of Appeals for the Ninth Circuit reversed the decree dismissing the libel in personam, but affirmed so much of it as dismissed the libel in rem. * * * The only question presented here is whether the petitioner is entitled to a lien on the vessel for the overpaid freight.

While there has been a lack of unanimity in the decisions as to the precise limits of the lien in favor of the cargo, see *Osaka Shosen* [*supra* at 417], the cases are agreed that the right to the lien has its source in the contract of affreightment and that the lien itself is justified as a means by which the vessel, treated as a personality or as impliedly hypothecated to secure the performance of the contract, is made answerable for nonperformance. * * *

It is not questioned here that the union of ship and cargo, once established, gives rise to the right of the vessel to a lien on the cargo for the freight money and of the cargo on the vessel for failure to carry safely and deliver rightly. The breach now alleged is only that the freight demanded on discharge of the cargo was in excess of that stipulated by the contract, and respondent insists that the liens in favor of cargo growing out of the contract of affreightment are restricted to those claims founded on breach of the obligation to carry and deliver. But the undertaking to charge the agreed freight and no more is an inseparable incident to every contract of affreightment, as essential to it and as properly a subject of admiralty jurisdiction as is the obligation of the cargo to pay freight when earned, or of the vessel to carry safely. [ ] It is unlike an agreement to pay a commission to the broker procuring the charter party [ ] or a provision for storing cargo in the vessel at the end of the voyage [ ] which, though embodied in the contract of carriage for hire, are no necessary part of it.

It is not denied and the cases hold that there is a lien for excessive freight knowingly exacted as a condition of delivery of the cargo, [ ] but it is argued that in that case the generating source of the right is the failure to perform the transportation contract by refusal to deliver the cargo. The fact that the breach of one term of the contract, the agreement to charge only the stipulated freight, coincides with the breach of another to make delivery, does not obscure the fact that both terms are broken and that the substance of the right to recover is for the freight collected in excess of that agreed upon, not damages for failure to make delivery. Nor does the fact that there is breach of both afford any basis for saying that the breach of either term alone could not give rise to the lien.

* * *

We see no distinction, either in principle or with respect to the practical operation or convenience of maritime commerce, between the lien asserted here for overpayment of freight by mistake and those for overpayments similarly made but induced by other means.

Here, as there, the overpayment, made as the cargo was unloaded, occurred while the union of ship and cargo continued, and the liability asserted was determined by events contemporaneous with that union. The circumstances which called the lien into being do not differ in point of notoriety from those giving rise to other affreightment liens upon the vessel. While it is true that the maritime lien is secret, hence is *stricti juris* and not to be extended by implication, this does not mean that the right to the lien is not to be recognized and upheld, when within accepted supporting principles, merely because the circumstances which call for its recognition are unusual or infrequent.

The suggestion made on the argument that the lien asserted here, after the cargo is discharged, is affected by application of the often stated rule that the liens on ship and cargo are mutual and reciprocal, is without basis. It is only the obligations of ship and cargo under the contract of affreightment which are to be characterized as mutual and reciprocal, not the liens which result from the breach of those obligations. The one lien may come into existence without the other and the lien on the ship in favor of cargo, not being possessory, [ ] may survive the lien of ship on cargo which is terminated by unconditional delivery. [ ]

* * *

Reversed.

Mr. Justice McREYNOLDS, Mr. Justice Sutherland, Mr. Justice Butler, and Mr. Justice Roberts are of opinion that the challenged judgment should be affirmed.

Secret liens are not favored, they should not be extended by construction, analogy, or inference, or to circumstances where there is ground for serious doubt. *Osaka Shosen* [*supra* at 417].

Notes

1. In general, claims for maritime torts give rise to maritime liens. Seamen have liens for claims for wages, maintenance and cure, and injuries caused by unseaworthiness. But claims under the Jones Act do not give rise to maritime liens and can be brought only in personam. *Plamals v. The Pinar Del Rio, supra* at 167 n. 19.

2. A cargo owner with a general average claim has a maritime lien against the vessel. Likewise, a vessel's general average claim gives rise to a (possessory) lien against the cargo.

3. After a vessel is seized and is in a federal court's custody, services provided to the vessel do not give rise to maritime liens. But a court will give claims for necessary services provided to a vessel *in custodia legis* priority over maritime liens. *New York Dock Co. v. The Poznan*, 274 U.S. 117 (1927). That is based on the equitable power of the court administering the *res*. To qualify, the services must be necessary to preserve the *res*. In *Oil Shipping (Bunkering) B.V. v. Sonmez Denizcilik Ve Ticaret A.S.*, 10 F.3d 176 (3d Cir. 1993), the court denied a claim for bunkers supplied to a vessel when it was in the custody of the court because the vessel already had substantial bunkers on board. Adding to the supplier's woes, after it supplied the bunkers a bank intervened in the proceedings to assert an in rem claim based on its ship mortgage. The court held that the mortgage attached also to the bunkers supplied by the plaintiff.

In *Dresdner Bank AG v. M/V Olympia Voyager*, 465 F.3d 1267 (11th Cir. 2006), the court held that an insurance company's provision of post-arrest insurance did not entitle it to equitable prioritization because it did not first seek or receive permission from the district court to provide such insurance.

C. The Commercial Instruments and Federal Maritime Lien Act (CIMLA)

In 1819 the Supreme Court decided that supplies and repairs to a vessel in its home port did not qualify for maritime liens under the general maritime law. *The General Smith*, 17 U.S. 438 (1819). Gilmore and Black characterized that case as one of the two "most ill-advised admiralty decision[s] ever handed down by the Supreme Court." GILMORE & BLACK, THE LAW OF ADMIRALTY 642 (2d ed. 1975) (the other was *Jensen*, *supra* at 116). To fill the gap, state statutes created home-port supplier/repair liens. The Supreme Court ultimately held that they could not be enforced in state court, but that federal admiralty courts would enforce them provided they did not conflict with liens under the general maritime law. See *The Hine v. Trevor*, *supra* at 67. The states *were* able to create liens—enforceable in state court—on non-maritime claims. See *The Robert W. Parsons*, 191 U.S. 17 (1903). That scheme of overlapping and potentially conflicting rules on liens led to confusion.

In response, in 1910 Congress passed the Federal Maritime Lien Act (FMLA), 36 Stat. 604. Among other things, the statute abolished the home-port lien doctrine. FMLA was incorporated in the Ship Mortgage Act of 1920, 41 Stat. 1005. The two statutes have been recodified as Commercial Instruments and Federal Maritime Lien Act (CIMLA) in 46 U.S.C. §§ 31301–31343. (The Ship Mortgage Act is treated in Section E, *infra* at 434.)

Parts of CIMLA are set out in the Statutory Supplement. It is not a comprehensive code of maritime lien law. But it codifies the key concepts. Under 46 U.S.C. § 31342(a):

> [A] person providing[1] necessaries to a vessel on the order of the owner or person authorized by the owner—
>
> (1) has a maritime lien on the vessel;
>
> (2) may bring a civil action in rem to enforce the lien; and
>
> (3) is not required to allege or prove in the action that credit was given to the vessel.

46 U.S.C. § 31341(a) provides:

> The following persons are presumed to have authority to procure necessaries for a vessel:
>
> (1) the owner;
>
> (2) the master;
>
> (3) a person entrusted with the management of the vessel at the port of supply; or
>
> (4) an officer or agent appointed by—
>
> (A) the owner;
>
> (B) the charterer;
>
> (C) an owner *pro hac vice*; or

1. Earlier versions of FMLA had used the phrase "furnishing ... necessaries to any vessel." 46 U.S.C. § 971 (1982). The change in language was not intended to be substantive. See H.R. Rep. No. 100-918, 110th Cong., 2d Sess. 48 (1988).

(D) an agreed buyer in possession of the vessel.

These provisions have been the subject of substantial litigation as the following cases and notes will illustrate.

1. Providing Necessaries to a Vessel

Silver Star Enterprises, Inc. v. Saramacca MV

United States Court of Appeals, Fifth Circuit, 1996
82 F.3d 666, 1996 AMC 1715

JONES, Circuit Judge:

Plaintiff Silver Star Enterprises, Inc. (Silver Star), appeals the judgment of the district court granting Trans Ocean Ltd. (Trans Ocean), a lessor of cargo containers to a shipping company, a maritime lien in the vessel *M/V Saramacca*. * * *

Scheepvaart Maatschappij Suriname N.V. (SMS) * * * operated a shipping container service from Suriname to the United States, particularly Houston and New Orleans, and Rotterdam. SMS owned or chartered eight different vessels, including the *M/V Saramacca*, on which appellant Silver Star held two preferred ship mortgages [securing a debt of about $1.2 million].

Beginning in May 1991, Appellee Trans Ocean began furnishing up to one hundred twenty-two cargo containers to the SMS fleet pursuant to a Master Container Lease. * * * The lease did not "earmark" particular containers for service on particular SMS vessels and indeed left needed flexibility with SMS to deploy the containers. The lease did not prevent intermodal use of the containers in land or even air transport.

Barely a year later, Silver Star commenced an in rem action * * * to enforce its preferred ship mortgages against the *M/V Saramacca*. Trans-Ocean [came into the action and] claimed maritime lien rights arising from the lease of containers, including those used aboard the *M/V Saramacca*. Ultimately, the *M/V Saramacca* was seized and sold at auction [for $1,420,000]; her proceeds were deposited in the registry of the district court awaiting division among SMS, Trans-Ocean and other claimants.

Trans Ocean * * * conduct[ed] discovery of cargo manifests and other documents to determine what portion of its leased containers had actually been used aboard the *M/V Saramacca*, [eventually demonstrating] that sixty-four containers were used at least once aboard the *M/V Saramacca* on voyages between the United States and Suriname, and ten of those had been used exclusively aboard the seized vessel.

The district court granted partial summary judgment in favor of Trans Ocean, acknowledging a maritime lien for past due rentals, repair costs, and depreciated replacement values for the ten containers used exclusively aboard the *M/V Saramacca*, and for prorated rentals, repair costs, and depreciated replacement values for the other fifty-four containers. In reaching this conclusion, the court held that for purposes of establishing a maritime lien, it was not necessary that the containers be earmarked for use aboard a particular vessel.

Judgment was entered in favor of Trans Ocean for a maritime lien of $73,352.00. When the court transferred and attached the lien to the proceeds of the vessel's sale, it limited the lien to $36,698.86, representing rentals, costs, and replacement values for containers provided in the United States. Upon ranking the creditors' competing claims, the court ruled that Trans Ocean outranked Silver Star in the amount of $36,698.86. Silver Star [has] timely appealed the Rule 54(b) judgment.[2]

* * *

The Federal Maritime Lien Act, 46 U.S.C. §§ 31341-43 (FMLA) establishes a maritime lien for "providing necessaries to a vessel on the order of the owner or a person authorized by the owner." 46 U.S.C. § 31342. "Necessaries" include "repairs, supplies, towage, and the use of a dry dock or marine railway." 46 U.S.C. § 31301(4).

Three of our sister circuits have recently held that maritime lien rights do not attach for the benefit of bulk lessors of containers to owners or charterers of multiple vessels. [ ] *Foss Launch & Tug Co. v. Char Ching Shipping U.S.A., Ltd.*, 808 F.2d 697 (9th Cir. 1987), the earliest of these cases, rests persuasively on the language of the maritime lien law and its interpretation by the Supreme Court. * * * *Foss Launch* held that although the containers were "necessaries" within the meaning of the Act, they had not been furnished "to" the vessels as is statutorily required. [ ] The court also felt bound by the seminal Supreme Court case, *Piedmont & Georges' Creek Coal Co. v. Seaboard Fisheries Co.*, 254 U.S. 1 (1920). In *Piedmont*, a coal company agreed to provide the entire supply of coal for a company that owned both a fish factory and a fleet of vessels. Despite the fact that the quantity of coal delivered to each vessel could be established after the fact, the Court held that the coal company did not have a maritime lien in the vessels. [ ] The Court stated that although the use of the coal aboard the vessels had been contemplated, "the fact that such a use had been contemplated does not render the subsequent appropriation by the owner a furnishing *by the coal dealer to the several vessels*" (emphasis added). *Piedmont* has been repeatedly construed as preventing the creation of a maritime lien where it is not the supplier but the fleet user of the "necessaries" that determines to which vessel or vessels they will be furnished. [ ]

Although the district court considered *Foss Launch* [and the similar holdings of the Second and Fourth Circuits], he declined to follow them because of this court's decision in *Equilease Corp. v. M/V Sampson*, 793 F.2d 598 (5th Cir. 1986) (en banc). * * * *Equilease* * * * considered whether an FMLA lien could arise in favor of a provider of insurance to a vessel. This court decided that insurance is a "necessary", but that actual physical delivery of "necessaries" is not the sole means to satisfy the "furnishing" requirement of the Act. [ ] *Equilease* expansively decries "layering technicalities onto [the Act]," [ ] but there is no factual similarity between that case and the present one. In *Equilease*, the charterer "purchased insurance for each vessel," [ ] an act strongly suggesting earmarking of the insurance to each vessel. *Equilease* is inapposite to interpreting the statute to cover cargo containers that, leased in bulk, were not only not earmarked but could be used intermodally on land as well as on numerous vessels.

* * *

We find the reasoning of our sister circuits dispositive on this issue. In this case, [Trans Ocean] furnished containers to SMS, not to the SMS vessels, and it was SMS which ultimately dictated upon which vessel the containers were placed. Neither party knew aboard which ship a particular container would be placed at any given time. [Trans Ocean] has therefore failed to demonstrate that necessaries were provided to a vessel as required by the FMLA.

* * *

2. Editors' note: Fed. R. Civ. P. 54(b) provides that in a multi-claim or multi-party action, the court can enter a final judgment "as to one or more but fewer than all of the claims or parties." Such a judgment is then appealable although the remainder of the action is pending in the trial court.

For the foregoing reasons, the district court erred in holding that Trans Ocean is the beneficiary of a lien for providing necessaries—cargo containers—that were leased in bulk and not earmarked for use on board the *M/V Saramacca.* The judgment is reversed and remanded for further proceedings consistent herewith.

Notes

1. As the principal case exemplifies, many of the disputes about maritime liens are litigated between competing lienors. When the value of the vessel is insufficient to pay all lien claims, each lienor has an interest in knocking out the competitors. When the competing lienors have valid liens, the court will need to establish the priority of the liens. See Section D, *infra* at 427–33.

2. Nothing in CIMLA requires that the "necessary" have been provided to the vessel in the United States. When the trial judge cut Trans Ocean's lien down from ca. $73,000 to the ca. $36,000 that represented containers provided in the United States, he did so in the exercise of the discretion that is inherent in the prioritization process. See 1994 U.S. Dist. LEXIS 15343 at *3–4 & n.1, 1994 WL 590272 at *2 & n.1 (E.D. La. 1994) (stating that the reduction was done for "ranking" purposes). Prioritization is treated *infra* in Section D.

3. What are necessaries? As *Silver Star* explains, CIMLA provides that "'necessaries' includes repairs, supplies, towage, and the use of a dry dock or marine railway." 46 U.S.C. § 31301(4). The list is not exclusive. As the Fifth Circuit said in *Equilease*, 793 F.2d at 603: "The term 'necessary' under the FMLA includes most goods or services that are useful to the vessel, keep her out of danger, and enable her to perform her particular function." As the principal case indicates, the issue in *Equilease* was whether insurance purchased for a vessel was a necessary. Overruling a 97 year-old precedent, the court held that it was. The court said, "We therefore hold that because insurance is essential to keep a vessel in commerce, insurance is a 'necessary'... and unpaid insurance premiums [do] give rise to a maritime lien under the FMLA." Despite the characterization of insurance as "essential," many cases allow liens for items that are merely useful. In an earlier case the Fifth Circuit had said, "[T]he term 'necessary' under the Maritime Lien Act has been held to include expenditures that are not absolutely indispensable. It includes most goods or services that are convenient or useful to the vessel ..." *Ajubita v. S/S Peik*, 428 F.2d 1345, 1346 (5th Cir. 1970). Some of the more nontraditional services that have qualified have been services of an advertising agency for a cruise ship, printing supplies, supplying cigarettes or liquor to a pleasure yacht, uniforms for a yacht crew, fumigation of passenger's baggage, and the master's travel expenses as he attempted to obtain funds from the owners to pay the crew and prevent the vessel's arrest. See *Payne v. SS Tropic Breeze*, 423 F.2d 236, 240–41 (1st Cir. 1970).

4. The Fifth Circuit held that a law firm does not have a maritime lien for its services in releasing a vessel from seizure. *Gulf Marine & Industrial Supplies, Inc. v. Golden Prince M/V*, 230 F.3d 178 (5th Cir. 2000). The court acknowledged that the law firm's claim had some merit since the firm's services enabled the vessel to perform her function and "were useful to her." It applied a strict test, however, saying that the legal services were not "essential to keep a vessel in commerce." The court also had policy considerations in mind:

> Despite its superficial similarities to other goods and services that have been deemed necessaries, a maritime lien for attorney fees would conflict with the purposes of the FMLA. The FMLA "was intended to encourage private investment in the maritime industry." [ ] A judgment for [the law firm] securing attorney fees would encourage ship owners and attorneys to spare no expense defending

> owner financial interests. Such a lien would prefer ship owners to the claimants for necessaries, whose attorneys' fees are unsecured by the FMLA.[3] [ ] If [the law firm's] position were the law, an owner could quickly dissipate a supplier's claim for necessaries simply by hiring attorneys and encouraging them to run up fees that would offset the claimant's lien. Even the threat of such an action would tend to force suppliers to settle, undermining the very protection the law aimed for. Ultimately, maritime industry investment would be discouraged.

If it were applied generally, do you think withholding lien status for all but "essential" services would encourage investment in the maritime industry?

2. On the Order of the Owner

Until its 2014 bankruptcy, O.W. Bunker was the world's largest supplier of bunker fuel. In a typical transaction, a shipowner would contract with O.W. Bunker (or an affiliated company) to purchase bunker fuel; O.W. Bunker would sub-contract with a local supplier to furnish the fuel to the ship; and the local supplier would deliver the fuel directly to the ship. When all went well, the shipowner paid the contractually agreed price to O.W. Bunker, which then paid the local supplier. When O.W. Bunker declared bankruptcy, many unpaid local suppliers asserted maritime liens against the ships to which they had delivered fuel. Under U.S. law, a supplier can claim a lien for providing bunker fuel (a necessary), but only if it acted "on the order of the owner or person authorized by the owner." 46 U.S.C. § 31342(a). Most courts have denied liens to the local suppliers on these typical facts, concluding that they acted not "on the order of the owner or person authorized by the owner" but on O.W. Bunker's order. See, e.g., *NuStar Energy Services, Inc. v. M/V COSCO Auckland*, 760 Fed. App'x 245 (5th Cir. 2019); *Clearlake Shipping Pte Ltd. v. NuStar Energy Services, Inc.*, 911 F.3d 646, 2019 AMC 385 (2d Cir. 2018) (Kearse, J.).; *Valero Marketing & Supply Co. v. M/V Almi Sun*, 893 F.3d 290 (5th Cir. 2018); *ING Bank N.V. v. M/V Temara*, 892 F.3d 511, 2019 AMC 1521 (2d Cir. 2018).

3. On the Credit of the Vessel

Despite the statute's provision that a lienor "is not required to allege or prove in the action that credit was given to the vessel," it is clear that the statute creates only a rebuttable presumption that the one who provides necessaries to a vessel extended credit to the vessel. "[T]he party attacking this presumption has the burden of establishing that the personal credit of the owner or charterer was solely relied upon." *Equilease*, *supra* at 424. In *Equilease* the presumption was overcome by uncontradicted testimony that the insurance broker was relying only on the credit of the vessel owner or charterer. See also *Racal Survey U.S.A. Inc. v. M/V Count Fleet*, 231 F.3d 183 (5th Cir. 2000) (finding that the presumption was overcome by a showing that the creditor looked solely to the credit of the charterer which was its customer). But merely billing the vessel's agent rather than the vessel owner will not overcome the presumption. *Navieros Inter-Americanos, S.A. v. M/V Vailia Express*, 120 F.3d 304 (1st Cir. 1997).

---

3. Editors' note: For this proposition, the court cited *Bradford Marine v. M/V Sea Falcon*, 64 F.3d 585, 589 (11th Cir. 1995), which explained that neither the legal fees a ship repairer incurred in pursuing a claim against the ship nor the legal services those fees represented were provided to the ship, nor were they (in any suitably immediate sense) useful to the ship.

4. Presumed Authority

46 U.S.C. § 31341(a), *supra* at 422, lists several persons as having presumed authority to procure necessaries; that presumption, too, can be rebutted. See *Epstein v. Corporation Peruana de Vapores*, 325 F. Supp. 535 (S.D.N.Y. 1971) (master was without express, implied, or apparent authority to buy large quantities of cigarettes and liquor which he may have been using in a smuggling scheme).

Recall that 46 U.S.C. § 31341(a) includes among those with presumed authority "an officer or agent appointed by ... the charterer." Owners of vessels under charter have frequently tried to protect themselves by inserting a "no lien" or "prohibition of lien" clause in the charterparty. Prior to 1971, the provider of necessaries was denied a lien if it "knew or by the exercise of reasonable diligence could have ascertained, that because of the terms of a charter party, ... the person ordering the repairs, supplies, or other necessaries was without authority to bind the vessel." 46 U.S.C. § 973. A 1971 amendment dropped the quoted language. The current statute does not give materialmen the complete protection that they had hoped for. See Gilmore & Black, The Law of Admiralty 670 (2d ed. 1975). Under the current view, the materialman has no duty to inquire into the charterer's authority to bind the vessel—there is no more need for "reasonable diligence" in that regard—but he will not be able to assert a lien on the vessel if it is shown that he knew that the person ordering the services lacked the authority to bind the vessel. *Ferromet Resources, Inc. v. Chemoil Corp.*, 5 F.3d 902 (5th Cir. 1993); *Belcher Oil Co. v. M/V Gardenia*, 766 F.2d 1508 (11th Cir. 1985).

Although prohibition-of-lien clauses are not usually effective against materialmen, such clauses will generally be fully effective against liens asserted by would-be charterers and subcharterers. As explained in *Cardinal Shipping Corp. v. M/S Seisho Maru*, 744 F.2d 461, 470–471 (5th Cir. 1984):

> A would-be charterer, by contrast [to a materialman], is under much less time pressure and has earlier notice of his need to obtain a vessel. Consequently, he has greater freedom to conduct an adequate inquiry. Furthermore, the corporations that typically charter vessels are more sophisticated and have greater resources to devote to an investigation than has the local materialman. [ ] As between a shipowner, charterer and subcharterer, it is not so obvious that the owner should bear all risks. Permitting a contractual allocation of risks between these parties is much more equitable than in the case of shipowner and materialman.

D. Priority among Maritime Liens

The John G. Stevens

Supreme Court of the United States, 1898

170 U.S. 113, 18 S. Ct. 544, 42 L.Ed. 969, 2005 AMC 2389

Mr. Justice GRAY delivered the opinion of the unanimous Court.

The question presented by this record is whether a lien upon a tug, for damages to her tow by negligent towage bringing the tow into collision with a third vessel, is to be preferred, in admiralty, to a statutory lien for supplies furnished to the tug in her home port before the collision.

This question may be conveniently divided, in its consideration by the court, as it was in the arguments at the bar, into two parts: First. Is a claim in tort for damages by a collision entitled to priority over a claim in contract for previous supplies? Second. Is a claim by a tow against her tug, for damages from coming into collision with a third vessel by reason of negligent towage, a claim in tort?

[I.]

* * *

[A] claim for damages by collision and a claim for supplies are both maritime liens. The question of their comparative rank is now for the first time presented to this court for adjudication, and it has been the subject of conflicting decisions in other courts of the United States, and especially in those held within the state of New York.

* * *

The case at bar * * * presents no question of the comparative rank of seamen's wages, which may depend upon peculiar considerations, and which, according to the favorite saying of Lord Stowell and of Mr. Justice Story, are sacred liens, and, as long as a plank of the ship remains, the sailor is entitled, against all other persons, to the proceeds as a security for his wages. [ ]

Nor does this case present any question as between successive liens for repairs or supplies, the general rule as to which is that they are to be paid in inverse order, because it is for the benefit of all the interests in the ship that she should be kept in condition to be navigated. [ ]

Nor does it present a question of precedence between two claims for distinct and successive collisions, as to which there has been a difference of opinion in the Southern district of New York; Judge Choate, in the district court, giving the preference to the later claim upon the ground that the interest created in the vessel by the first collision was subject, like all other proprietary interests in her, to the ordinary marine perils, including the second collision; and Mr. Justice Blatchford, in the circuit court, reversing the decree, because the vessel libeled had not been benefited, but had been injured, by the second collision. *The Frank G. Fowler*, 8 Fed. 331 [S.D.N.Y. 1881], 17 Fed. 653 [C.C.S.D.N.Y. 1883].

Nor yet does it present the question whether a lien for repairs made after the collision, so far as they increase the value of the vessel, may be preferred to the lien for the damages by the collision, in accordance with the English cases * * *.

But the question we have to deal with is whether the lien for damages by the collision is to be preferred to the lien for supplies furnished before the collision.

* * *

The collision, as soon as it takes place, creates, as security for the damages, a maritime lien or privilege, *jus in re*, a proprietary interest in the offending ship, and which, when enforced by admiralty process in rem, relates back to the time of the collision. The offending ship is considered as herself the wrongdoer, and as herself bound to make compensation for the wrong done. The owner of the injured vessel is entitled to proceed in rem against the offender, without regard to the question who may be her owners, or to the division, the nature, or the extent of their interests in her. With the relations of the owners of those interests, as among themselves, the owner of the injured vessel has no concern. All the interests, existing at the time of the collision, in the offending vessel, whether by way of part ownership, of mortgage, of bottomry bond, or of other maritime lien for repairs or supplies, arising out of contract with the owners or agents of the vessel, are parts of the vessel herself, and as such are bound by and responsible for her wrongful acts. Any one who had furnished necessary supplies to the vessel before the collision, and had thereby acquired, under our law, a maritime lien or privilege in the vessel herself, was, as was said in *The Bold Buccleugh* [*supra* at 411] of the holder of an earlier bottomry bond, under the law of England, "so to speak, a part owner in interest at the date of the collision, and the ship in which he and others were interested was liable to its value at that date for the injury done, without reference to his claim." [ ]

[II.]

We are, then, brought to the question whether a claim by a tow against her tug, for damages from coming into collision with a third vessel because of negligent towage, is a claim in tort, standing upon the same ground as a claim of the third vessel for damages against the tug.

Upon this question, again, there have been conflicting opinions in the district courts of the United States. * * * [But] the decisions of this court are in accordance with the [tort] view, and are inconsistent with any other. [See also *supra* at 358 note 1.] * * *

The result of applying to the case at bar the principles of the maritime law of the United States, as heretofore declared by this court, is that the lien for the damages occasioned by the negligent towage must be preferred to the previous lien for supplies.

* * *

Notes

1. *The John G. Stevens* has been the Supreme Court's last word on the issue of lien priority. As the case indicates, there was substantial variety among the lower courts, and that has continued. One court said: "[I]t is scarcely too much to say that each court is a law unto itself." *The City of Tawas*, 3 F. 170, 172 (E.D. Mich. 1880). According to Professor Schoenbaum, "[T]he business of priorities is largely judge-made law based on equitable considerations and the traditions of admiralty law.... [I]nevitably there are disagreements and inconsistencies; nevertheless, widespread consensus exists as to the applicable rules." 1 Schoenbaum, Admiralty and Maritime Law § 9:6, at 808 (6th Practitioner ed. 2018). With the exception of the court's treatment of expenses of the vessel while in the United States marshal, the next case sets forth the priorities that are often followed and demonstrates the kind of equitable factors that courts consider.

2. One writer has noted two theories, often at odds with one another, that may be at work. "The 'beneficial service' rule theorizes that some services contribute more than others to the preservation of the vessel and its continuing operation and consequently are entitled to a superior position in the hierarchy of liens.... Under the 'proprietary interest' rule a maritime lienor becomes a part-owner and takes the risk that it will incur other expenses and liabilities." Varian, *Rank and Priority of Maritime Liens*, 47 Tul. L. Rev. 751 (1973).

The "beneficial service" theory helps to explain why salvage claims generally outrank all but seamen's wage claims: The salvor has preserved the vessel so that it is available for other claimants.

3. A good-sized portion of the *John G. Stevens* opinion (here edited out) demonstrated that the U.S. jurisprudence has differed from that of other countries, both on whether particular claims are entitled to lien status and on lien priorities.

The William Leishear

United States District Court, District of Maryland, 1927
21 F.2d 862, 1927 AMC 1770

COLEMAN, District Judge:

The schooner William Leishear was sold under admiralty process as a result of various libels, and this proceeding is to determine the rights, if any, of the libelants to share according to their respective priorities in the net proceeds of the sale amounting to $1,011.17. The claims are as follows:

(1) For salvage under a written contract dated July 22, 1926, $850.

(2) For labor and materials furnished between September 1 and November 20, 1926, $4,132.90.

(3) For transporting the sails of the vessel on or about October 1, 1926, $45.

(4) For wages of crew during October and November, 1926, $640.

(5) For wharfage from November 10, 1926, to March 26, 1927, $126.

(6) For watchman from January 19, 1927, to March 26, 1927, $198.

It is obvious that the proceeds will be grossly insufficient to pay all demands. Therefore the fund must go to those entitled to priority as far as possible, and the unsatisfied claimants must seek elsewhere for payment. [ ]

The question of priority of maritime liens is filled with confusion. The rules conflict. Tort liens generally rank contract liens. *The John G. Stevens* [*supra* at 427.] Seamen's wage liens are especially favored under the ancient doctrine * * * that seamen are in effect wards of the admiralty. So also of salvage, since the law wishes to encourage persons in saving maritime property from destruction. [ ] All maritime claims rank all nonmaritime. [ ]

There is the general rule that maritime liens rank in an order inverse to the order of their creation, a principle contrary to what is common in other branches of the law. * * * Generally speaking, the law of maritime liens may be said to be made up of exceptions to the [inverse-order doctrine], so that to-day it is possible to deduce, from the decisions, the following order of priority, existing irrespective of time, which represents the weight of authority: (1) Seamen's wages; (2) salvage; (3) tort and collision liens; (4) repairs, supplies, towage, wharfage, pilotage, and other necessaries; (5) bottomry bonds * * *; (6) nonmaritime claims. This, however, is no more than a very general statement, since any summary is subject to further exceptions of more or less narrow application. With this general background, we may now take up the various claims involved in the present case.

1.

The wage claims amounting to $640, are made by five sailors, claiming to have had contracts to ship as crew on board the schooner for the oyster dredging season at a fixed rate per month, and that, whereas, because the schooner was laid up, undergoing repairs, they never actually shipped aboard her, they nevertheless, during part of the period, did various kinds of work aboard her, from carpentering to cooking, and that they are thus entitled to be paid their stipulated wages, just as if the vessel had been in commission. It appears that they did make some effort to obtain other employment after they learned the schooner would not be in commission, but were unsuccessful.

In view of the special consideration universally accorded wage claims by the admiralty courts, it seems not unreasonable to hold upon these facts that the seamen are entitled to a lien for their wages, where, through no fault of their own, they are prevented from earning them aboard the vessel while in navigation. * * * A lien is therefore allowed to each of these libelants for the respective amounts claimed, aggregating $640. Such are entitled to first priority. The weight of authority seems clear to this effect, especially in view of the fact that the services were performed subsequent to the salvage. [ ] It has even been held that claims, such as for penalties and repatriation expenses, are to be classed as wages and entitled to the priority generally accorded to them. [ ]

* * *

2.

As to the claim in the nature of salvage for floating and delivering the schooner at the shipyard, the evidence is that the vessel, being hard aground in one of the small tributaries of Chesapeake Bay as the result of a storm, and there not being sufficient rise of the tide to float her, the intervening libelant, pursuant to a contract to salvage her, dug a ditch some 300 or 400 feet long, 5 feet deep and 20 feet wide, thereby floating her. While this work was done in the month of July, no claim appears to have been made until the intervening libel was filed, some seven months later. The salvor was the son of the managing owner of the vessel, with whom he contracted, and the only written evidence of the claim is a certificate, signed by the managing owner. In spite of some doubt in the mind of the court as to the entire good faith of this claim as actually made, by reason of its size and the rather peculiar surrounding circumstances, the court believes that a salvage service was performed. [ ]

* * * It is within the discretion of the court to cut down the award, as required by the peculiar circumstances of the case. [ ] Therefore a quantum meruit claim in this case would appear to be justified, and the court feels that $350 is reasonable and proper. This lien is entitled to second priority, because it ranks supply and repair liens, [ ] and also wharfage. [ ]

3.

As to the claim for labor and materials, which amounts to $4,132.90, there is no evidence that any of the items comprising this bill are unreasonable. It appears that the shipbuilding company, which did the work, received instructions to put her in first-class condition for the approaching oyster season, and that it was found necessary to make very extensive repairs. Hence the large bill. The labor and materials so used created a maritime lien under the Merchant Marine Act of 1920. [ ] This lien is third in order of priority. It ranks evenly with all like liens of even date. [ ]

4.

Next is the claim for wharfage. There seems no doubt but that a lien exists for this service even as to a domestic vessel, since this is a necessary maritime service during the course of repairs. [ ] But after the filing of the libel the vessel was withdrawn from navigation, and no further lien for wharfage accrues. *The Poznan*, 9 F.2d 838, 846 (2d Cir. 1925). The claim is therefore allowed from and including November 20, 1926, to and including January 19, 1927, or 61 days, which, at $1 per day, amounts to $61. Since the wharfage service was performed about the same time that the materials and supplies were furnished, this claim ranks equally with the claim for the latter. [ ]

5.

The claim for services of the watchman covers the period from January 19, 1927, the date of the filing of the libel, to March 26, 1927, the date when the vessel was sold. The vessel being under custody of the marshal during this period, the watchman's services cannot be regarded as maritime. This claim is therefore not allowed.

6.

Likewise the claim for transporting sails is not allowed. No part of the service seems to have been rendered upon the vessel. From the libel it appears that nothing was done, other than to haul the sails overland from Crisfield, Md., to the shipyard at White Haven, Md., where the vessel was being rebuilt. This cannot be regarded as a maritime service, and falls in the class of contracts only incidentally maritime. [ ]

Summarizing the situation with respect to the allowed claims, it is as follows: First, wage claims, $640; second, salvage claim, $350; third, materials, supplies, and wharfage, aggregating $4,193.90. Since the first two allowances will consume all but $21.17 of the total fund in the registry of the court, there is nothing left for the claims of the third group, which rank equally, except a pro rata share of this small residue.

Notes

1. In denying the claims for wharfage and watchman services that occurred while the ship was *in custodia legis*, the court cites the Second Circuit's decision in *The Poznan*. About five months earlier, that decision had been reversed by the Supreme Court in *New York Dock Co. v. The Poznan* (*supra* at 421 note 3). Under the Supreme Court decision, those claims would have ranked first.

2. In *Todd Shipyards Corp. v. The City of Athens*, 83 F. Supp. 67 (D. Md. 1949), the claims against the *res* (a trans-Atlantic passenger-cargo ship) aggregated over $775,000. The judicial sale of the ship yielded $400,000, and the trial judge appointed a seasoned Baltimore admiralty lawyer to serve as Commissioner to sort it all out. For two months the Commissioner took evidence and heard argument on matters ranging across almost the full spectrum of maritime law, including the merits of an injured seaman's claim to have been injured by unseaworthiness, transnational choice-of-law issues engendered by the seaman's injury claim, seamen's wage claims, maintenance and cure claims, penalty wages claims, seamen's claims for repatriation costs, cargo-damage claims, claims by passengers who had been preparing to embark at New York on the ship's next voyage to Europe,[1] an array of claims by materialmen, repairmen, and suppliers of necessaries, and claims arising from the Immigration and Naturalization Service's attempt to detain for deportation a portion of the crew. The Commissioner's eventual report—which after full adversary hearing was approved in full by the court—recommended paying his fee (a modest $10,000) first and then following the general scheme of *William Leishear* whereby the claims whose lien status had survived the Commissioner's scrutiny would be prioritized first by class and then, within each class, according to the inverse-order approach.

Under the Commissioner's approach, a large number of the claims for repairs, supplies, and other necessaries fell into a class that could not be paid in full, and the way in which the inverse-order principle should operate became one of the most hotly-contested issues. The court used a "voyage rule," which it described and explained as follows:

> The rule originally developed in admiralty law and still the basic rule is that maritime liens of the same class are entitled to priority of payment in the inverse order of the time of accrual and that therefore liens arising in connection with the last voyage of the ship have priority of payment over liens accruing on a prior

1. As you will have surmised from note 2(a), *supra* at 419, these claims did not survive. Many individual claims were also denied lien status for particular fact-specific reasons.

> voyage.... The voyage rule contemplates that at the end of each voyage liens that have arisen during its course should be promptly enforced before the ship departs on another voyage, if there is opportunity to the claimant to so enforce it by libel.
>
> * * *
>
> My conclusion ... is that the voyage rule still prevails despite greater rapidity of transportation and communication. The reasons which originally gave rise to the voyage rule still exist even though their importance in some respects may have been lessened. Many ocean voyages are still of several months' duration and there is still at times the most imperative need that a ship in a port far distant from the owner should have the ability to obtain repairs and supplies on the credit of the ship itself. This ability to obtain such credit would obviously be much impaired if a long-prior claim originating in connection with a previous voyage, as in this case, and amounting to a sum much larger than the sale value of the ship, were to rate equally with the supplies or repairs on the last voyage, imperatively needed to keep the ship a "going concern," and to enable it to return to its home.

The court also gave a useful discussion of some analogous approaches:

> [T]he application of the voyage rule presupposes that the voyages are separated "by an appreciable length of time." While this is necessarily still true with respect to transatlantic or other similar ocean voyages, it is obviously not so with respect to the much shorter and more frequent voyages of harbor craft and merely coastwise vessels or other comparatively local transportation. To meet the necessities of such particular local conditions and to accord with the customary business practice locally prevailing it has been found necessary to substitute a rule of priorities other than the voyage rule, and the tendency seems to have been to adopt, as the period allowed prior to the filing of the libel for preferential claims arising therein, a period which can be regarded as a reasonable time for the extension of credit. Thus for New York harbor craft, that period has been fixed at 40 days, and in Puget Sound at 90 days; while on the Great Lakes, where the rigor of winter generally interrupts navigation, the period has been fixed as the navigating season, and thus claims arising during such a particular season are preferred over those of a prior season.

3. In *Fredelos v. Merritt-Chapman & Scott*, 447 F.2d 435 (5th Cir. 1971), the trial court and the appellate panel on original hearing followed a rule of thumb whereby the claims in suit were ranked (1) seamen's wage claims, (2) a claim for contract salvage, and (3) seamen's personal injury and maintenance and cure claims. On rehearing, the appellate panel decided that the maintenance and cure claims should be promoted to the first rank, stating: "[T]he ship may be the only security the seaman has ... and no other interest or rule of law should be allowed to deprive him of the assurance that he will thereby be sustained."

In another case the court held that a catering firm's employees who lived aboard ship were entitled to a lien for "crew's wages." Since the catering company paid those wages, it was subrogated to the crew's "sacred lien" against the vessel, thereby outranking a preferred ship mortgage. *International Paint Co. v. M/V Mission Viking*, 637 F.2d 382 (5th Cir. 1981).

4. Given the importance of the issue of priority among maritime liens, the small number of reported cases is odd. Gilmore and Black summed up the situation as follows: "Any branch of the law that is administered at the trial level, with infrequent appellate review, is apt to become highly flexible and the law of lien priorities is no exception.... Nine times out of ten, what seems fair to the trial judge will be the law of the case for all time." Gilmore & Black, The Law of Admiralty 736 (2d ed. 1975).

E. Ship Mortgages

Prior to 1920, ship mortgages were a matter of state concern. Because they were deemed to be nonmaritime contracts, those mortgages were unenforceable in in rem actions. *Bogart v. The John Jay*, 58 U.S. 399 (1854). That gave mortgagees inadequate security, as their claims were subordinated to all maritime liens, even those arising after the creation of the mortgage. In 1920 Congress passed the Ship Mortgage Act, which gave maritime lien status to certain ship mortgages. The Supreme Court upheld the statute's constitutionality in *The Thomas Barlum*, 293 U.S. 21 (1934). As we have seen, the Ship Mortgage Act and FMLA together are recodified at 46 U.S.C. §§ 31301–31343.

In order to have lien status, a ship mortgage must qualify as a "preferred ship mortgage." 46 U.S.C. § 31322(a) spells out three basic requirements for a preferred ship mortgage: (1) It must include the whole of the vessel. (2) It must be filed with the Coast Guard "in substantial compliance" with the requirements of § 31321. (3) It must cover a documented vessel or a vessel for which a properly formulated application for documentation has been filed.[1]

Priority Among Maritime Liens and Ship Mortgages

The Ship Mortgage Act introduces complexities into the lien-prioritization process. Whereas with ordinary maritime liens the usual rule is inverse-order preference, with ship mortgages the order of priority is reversed. The first recorded mortgage will have priority over subsequent mortgages. *Westinghouse Credit Corp. v. O/S Dorothy Claire*, 732 F. Supp. 59 (E.D. Tex. 1989).

How are priorities worked out in cases involving both preferred ship mortgages and other types of maritime liens? The statute addresses that problem in §§ 31326(b)(1) and 31301(5). Under 46 U.S.C. § 31326(b)(1), the preferred ship mortgage lien "has priority over all claims against the vessel (except for expenses and fees allowed by the court, costs imposed by the court, and preferred maritime liens)." Section 31301(5) in turn states:

Preferred maritime lien means a maritime lien on a vessel—

(A) arising before a preferred mortgage was filed [with the Coast Guard];

(B) for damage arising out of maritime tort;

(C) for wages of a stevedore when employed by a person listed in section 31341 [as having presumptive authority to procure necessaries for a vessel];

(D) for wages of the crew of the vessel;

(E) for general average; or

(F) for salvage, including contract salvage.

Read together, the two provisions say on their face that the preferred ship mortgage will be outranked by virtually any general maritime lien except a later-arising contract lien.

The Ship Mortgage Act will sometimes alter the ranking among general maritime liens. Suppose that Repairman A furnishes necessaries to the vessel; the vessel then gets a loan

1. The documentation requirements are spelled out in 46 U.S.C. §§ 12101–12112. A vessel can be mortgaged before its construction is completed if the vessel is documented and the mortgage is properly recorded. *United States v. Trident Crusader*, 366 F.3d 391 (5th Cir. 2004).

that is secured by a preferred ship mortgage; and thereafter Repairman B furnishes necessaries to the vessel. Under the general maritime law, Repairman B would outrank Repairman A. But under the ranking scheme of the Ship Mortgage Act, Repairman A will come first, then the mortgage, then Repairman B.

In cases not subject to the ranking scheme of the Ship Mortgage Act, tort claims will generally outrank contract claims. In cases that do fall under the Act's ranking scheme, tort claims will virtually always be preferred. So naturally, cargo-damage plaintiffs struggle to have their claims classified as tort-based rather than contract-based. Gilmore and Black disapprove, arguing that cargo claims ought to be viewed as contractual in nature principally because they are virtually always insured (whereas the materialmen, repairers, and suppliers the subrogated cargo insurer would be prevailing over by capturing the "tort" flag typically are uninsured). GILMORE & BLACK, THE LAW OF ADMIRALTY 741 (2d ed. 1975). But the recent cases seem to be favoring the cargo side of the argument. See *Associated Metals & Minerals Corp. v. The Alexander's Unity*, 41 F.3d 1007 (5th Cir. 1995); *All Alaskan Seafoods, Inc. v. M/V Sea Producer*, 882 F.2d 425 (9th Cir. 1989); *Oriente Commercial, Inc. v. M/V Floridian*, 529 F.2d 221 (4th Cir. 1975).

Governor & Company of Bank of Scotland v. Maria S.J. M/V

United States District Court, Eastern District of Louisiana, 1998
1999 AMC 774, *aff'd*, 211 F.3d 261 (5th Cir. 2000)

FALLON, District Judge:

* * *

[When the Bank of Scotland libeled the *M/V Maria S.J.* in rem in this Court, seeking to enforce a preferred ship mortgage lien in an amount exceeding $15 million, former crew members of the vessel intervened, alleging that Golden Lines Shipping, Inc. ("Golden Lines") owned the vessel and had failed to pay wages pursuant to a settlement agreement between Golden Lines and the union for the crewmembers. The former crew members assert] claims for unpaid wages, delay [penalty] wages pursuant to 46 U.S.C. § 10313, attorneys' fees, and costs. The 102 crewmembers involved allege that they are still owed a total of $292,635.00 in overdue wages. Apparently, only forty-eight of the seamen seek the statutory delay wage payment.

On July 2, 1998, the Bank purchased the *M/V Maria S.J.* at an auction conducted by the marshal for $3.7 million, using the outstanding amount of the mortgage, which exceeded $15 million, in a credit bid in lieu of cash payment. On July 7, 1998, on motion of the Bank and by Order of this Court, the Bank posted a letter of undertaking for the amount of the purchase "to pay any final judgment in relation to any claim[s] against the vessel filed prior to July 2, 1998, in the above-referenced action that are held to have priority over Bank of Scotland's claims against the vessel."

On October 13, 1998 the Bank filed [the present] motion for summary judgment, asking the Court to dismiss the claims filed by the former crewmembers. The Bank cites [two main] grounds upon which it urges the Court to grant the motion. First, the Bank argues that only the owner or master of the vessel is liable for delay or penalty wages under [46 U.S.C. § 10313], so that such awards are not recoverable from the proceeds of sale of a vessel where, as here, the balance owed by the owner far exceeds the amount of proceeds. To tap the sale proceeds for penalty wages would effectively penalize parties other than the owner or master, who possesses no interest in such proceeds. According to the Bank, such a result is contrary to * * * 46 U.S.C. § 10313. Second, the Bank contends that wage claimants do not enjoy a preferred maritime lien for *penalty* wages. * * *

* * *

[I.]

A preferred ship mortgage enjoys priority over all claims against a vessel, with the exception of expenses and preferred maritime liens. [ ] Wages of the crew fall within the category of preferred maritime liens. Indeed, it is axiomatic that claims for seamen's wages "have the highest priority among maritime liens," and courts treat these as "sacred liens" [ ].

When seamen are not paid the wages due them, "the master or owner shall pay to the seaman 2 days' wages for each day payment is delayed." 46 U.S.C. § 10313. The Bank asserts that payments under this provision are penalty wages, thus deserving the priority assigned to other penalties or fines rather than that accorded wages. [But this court has held that the] "seamen's lien for penalty wages is accorded the same sacred priority as the lien for wages, and attaches to proceeds from both the sale of the vessel and the earned 'freight.'" *Peterson v. S.S. Wahcondah*, 235 F. Supp. 698, 700 (E.D. La. 1964). Although the court in *Peterson* was construing 46 U.S.C. § 596, the predecessor to § 10313, this Court has located no case law which persuasively suggests that Congress intended the two provisions to be read differently with regard to the priority of penalty wage claims. Accordingly, the Court adopts the rule stated in *Peterson* and holds that claims for penalty wages under § 10313 enjoy the same sacred priority accorded claims for seamen's wages.

The case law is clear that claims for seamen's wages enjoy priority status over a preferred ship mortgage. Claims for penalty wages are afforded equal ranking. The Bank cannot sustain its position that these two liens merit different priority.

* * *

[II.]

Although the jurisprudence affords wage claims and penalty wage claims equal priority, the availability of penalty wages is nevertheless narrower than that of unpaid wages in general. The language of the penalty wage statute commands this result, since it clearly states that "the *master or owner* shall pay the seaman 2 days' wages for each day payment is delayed." 46 U.S.C. § 10313 (emphasis added). Courts interpreting § 596 have refused to assess penalty wages against parties who were neither owner nor master of the vessel in question. * * *

The issue in this case is whether the proceeds from the sale of the *M/V Maria S.J.* constitute an interest of the owner or master such that the crewmembers may claim against [the sale proceeds] for penalty wages. * * * If the owner or master possess no interest in the proceeds of sale, permitting a penalty wage claim against the proceeds is the functional equivalent of allowing the claim against a party other than the owner or master, a result clearly at odds with the jurisprudence. * * *.

In the present case, Golden Lines's outstanding indebtedness to the Bank approximates $15 million. Sale of the *M/V Maria S.J.* has yielded $3.7 million. Under these facts, the Bank asserts, and the Court agrees, that the owners lack any real interest in the proceeds of sale. Consequently, permitting a penalty wage claim against the proceeds would essentially penalize a party other than the owner or master, be it the Bank or some other creditor. This result violates the language and spirit of * * * § 10313.

The foregoing analysis dictates that the proceeds from the sale of the *M/V Maria S.J.* are available to pay the crewmembers' claims for unpaid wages. Although the law accords the same priority to claims for penalty wages under § 10313, the Court finds that, in this case, penalty wages are not payable out of the proceeds from the sale of the vessel. [The Bank's motion for summary judgment is denied as it relates to claims for unpaid wages. It is granted as it relates to the penalty wages claims, which are hereby dismissed.]

Notes

1. The Fifth Circuit's affirmance, 211 F.3d 261, was by a divided panel. The majority opinion—while far longer and more elaborate than the district court's—was ultimately based on the same reasoning. Dissenting at 211 F.3d 276–80, Judge Dennis made three main points: (a) In *Collie v. Ferguson*, 281 U.S. 52, 54 (1930), the Supreme Court stated that "[t]he claim for double [penalty] wages ... [is] embraced in the seaman's lien for wages, with priority over other liens, and governed by the procedure applicable to suits for the recovery of seamen's wages." (b) Under well-settled jurisprudence, a maritime lien "arises when the debt arises [and thereafter] adheres to the vessel wherever it may go." It has become the vessel's debt, regardless of the original debtor's continuing interest in the vessel, and indeed "has been held to follow the vessel even after it is sold to an innocent purchaser" (quoting *Equilease Corp. v. M/V Sampson*, 793 F.2d 598, 602–03 (5th Cir. 1986)). (c) "By furnishing their labor and personal services to the *M/V Maria*, the seamen were entitled to a maritime lien which was created by operation of law when their wages were due and payable. That lien followed the vessel even after it was sold to the Bank of Scotland. Based upon the plain language of the Ship Mortgage Act, the seaman's penalty wage lien attached to the proceeds of the sale as a preferred maritime lien with priority over the Bank of Scotland's preferred ship mortgage. See 46 U.S.C. § 31326(b)(1)." 211 F.3d at 278. Judge Dennis's reasoning did not persuade his colleagues to grant rehearing en banc, and certiorari was denied.

2. A seaman's claim under a union-negotiated contract calling for additional compensation upon dismissal gives rise to a maritime lien. *Gayner v. The New Orleans*, 54 F. Supp. 25 (N.D. Cal. 1944).

3. Can a shipowner transfer title to a wholly-owned and undercapitalized subsidiary, take a preferred ship mortgage equal in value to the vessel, and thereby establish priority over all subsequent suppliers? In *Custom Fuel Services, Inc. v. Lombas Industries, Inc.*, 805 F.2d 561 (5th Cir. 1986), the court used principles of equitable subordination to refuse to give priority to the mortgage, which it found to be a sham. The "debtor" borrowed the entire purchase price from the parent and made no regular payments on the note. The circumstance indicated that "the advance was not intended to be repaid in the ordinary course of the [subsidiary's] business, but rather was expected to remain outstanding as a permanent part of the [subsidiary's] financial structure."

4. In prioritizing mortgages and liens, the crucial question is often when does a maritime lien arise? For a scholarly opinion on that point, see *Bank One, Louisiana N.A. v. Mr. Dean MV*, 293 F.3d 830 (5th Cir. 2002). Offshore Supply Ships, the owner of a towboat, executed a time charter with BargeCarib, a rice exporter, which began using the vessel. Offshore then sold the vessel to Global Towing, which received a line of credit from a bank and gave the bank in return a preferred ship mortgage. Global then breached its charter with BargeCarib and defaulted on its loan. Reversing the district court, the Fifth Circuit held that the BargeCarib's maritime lien had priority over the preferred ship mortgage. "[T]he maritime lien attaches at the commencement of the undertaking and any subsequent breach perfecting the lien relates back to that time."

F. Bankruptcy

Introductory Note

Article I, § 8, cl. 4 of the Constitution provides that "Congress shall have power to ... establish ... uniform laws on the subject of bankruptcies throughout the United States." 28 U.S.C. § 1334(a) grants the federal district courts exclusive jurisdiction over bankruptcy proceedings. That jurisdiction is handled in the specialized way provided in various sections of titles 11 and 28 of the U.S. Code.

Bankruptcy judges are not Article III judges. They are appointed by the courts of appeals for fourteen-year terms. 28 U.S.C. § 152. They are paid 92% of a district judge's salary. 28 U.S.C. § 153. Their decisions are appealable to the district courts. 28 U.S.C. § 158. Before the Bankruptcy code was amended in 1984, there was much doubt and conflict about the many ways in which the law of maritime liens (and exclusive admiralty jurisdiction) can collide with bankruptcy law. Under the amended code:

(a) Bankruptcy courts "may rule on the validity and the priorities of maritime liens." 1 Schoenbaum, Admiralty and Maritime Law § 9:9, at 831 (6th Practitioner ed. 2018).

(b) "Uncertainty exists whether a bankruptcy court has jurisdiction to *execute* a maritime lien—to issue a final order selling a vessel or other maritime property free and clear of all liens." *Id.* at 832.

(c) Once the bankruptcy petition is filed, in rem actions against the debtor's property must cease. The "automatic stay" of 11 U.S.C. § 362 kicks in, and the bankruptcy court acquires exclusive jurisdiction over the *res. In re Modern Boats, Inc.*, 775 F.2d 619, 620 (5th Cir. 1985) ("the petition for reorganization withdrew jurisdiction from the admiralty court and lodged it exclusively in the [bankruptcy] court"). *In re Louisiana Ship Management, Inc.*, 761 F.2d 1025 (5th Cir. 1985), is a dramatic demonstration of the effects of the automatic stay. The admiralty court in an in rem action had already ordered the ship judicially sold when the shipowner filed for bankruptcy. Thereafter the sale took place. Acting before the sale had been confirmed, the Court of Appeals determined that the district court had to set aside the sale as "null and void."

In *In re Millenium Seacarriers, Inc.*, 419 F.3d 83, 2005 AMC 87 (2d Cir. 2005), in an opinion by then-judge Sotomayor, the court decided that a bankruptcy court can adjudicate maritime liens where the lienors voluntarily submit their lien claims to its jurisdiction. It left unaddressed the "murky question" of whether the bankruptcy court could have expunged those liens "had it not had jurisdiction over the lienors." *Id.* at 102–03.

There is unfortunately still some dispute as to whether a bankruptcy court sale of a vessel free and clear of all maritime liens violates Article III of the Constitution. The Fifth Circuit did not reach that issue in *In re Modern Boats, supra,* because the issue was raised for the first time on appeal. *See* Stewart F. Peck, *Navigating the Murky Waters of Admiralty and Bankruptcy Law*, 87 Tul. L. Rev. 955 (2013).

There is good reason to insist that in rem proceedings respecting the debtor's property must yield. "[T]he goal of bankruptcy law ... is to ensure a fair distribution of the debtor's assets. If an admiralty court proceeds with an in rem action after a petition for liquidation has been filed, the rights of the debtor's creditors may not be adequately represented in the admiralty action. Indeed, if a vessel were sold in the admiralty action, the plaintiff could potentially recover a greater proportion—perhaps even 100 percent—of his claim against the debtor than could other secured or unsecured creditors. Holders of claims cognizable in admiralty would effectively be granted a priority in the liquidation of the debtor superior even to that of the holders of other secured claims." *United States v. LaBouf Bros. Towing Co.*, 45 B.R. 887, 889–90 (E.D. La. 1985). For these reasons—and under the terms of 11 U.S.C. § 362 and its legislative history—"the automatic stay appl[ies] to all actions automatically." *Id.* at 890.

Should the authority of a bankruptcy court to sell a vessel free and clear of all prior interests, including maritime liens, be seen as a startling exception to the fundamental rule to which Section I-F, *supra* at 64, is devoted: that only a federal admiralty court can accomplish that feat? There is no reason to think so. It should be recalled that the federal district court's exclusive jurisdiction over in rem procedures is based on an interpretation of 28 U.S.C. § 1333(1) and is not clearly required by the Constitution. One could say that the federal admiralty court has been directed by Congress to delegate its in rem jurisdiction in those limited circumstances to the bankruptcy court.[1] More straightforwardly, one could regard that situation as a statutory exception to the general rule, analogous to the law-enforcement exception stemming from *C.J. Hendry Co. v. Moore*, *supra* at 74 note 3. (The bankruptcy exception seems less troublesome than the law-enforcement one, because it confines the lien-stripping authority to federal courts.)

But courts are not always comfortable with ceding quintessential maritime matters such as the "sacred" wage of lien of seamen to bankruptcy courts. See the next case.

United States v. The Chandon

United States Court of Appeals, Ninth Circuit, 1989
889 F.2d 233, 1990 AMC 316

ALARCON, Circuit Judge:

The plaintiff-intervenors (the crew members) appeal from [an] order granting summary judgment to the United States on all claims for seamen's wages filed by the crew members. * * * The district court concluded that the automatic stay provisions of 11 U.S.C. § 362(a)(4) precluded the creation of a lien for seamen's wages earned after the filing of a petition for reorganization under Chapter 11 of the Bankruptcy Act. [ ]

We must decide whether a claim for seamen's wages earned after the filing of a petition for reorganization under Chapter 11 has priority over a preferred ship mortgage. We reverse because we have concluded that in enacting the Bankruptcy Act, Congress did not intend to repeal or invalidate *sub silentio* the priority rules of maritime law.

I.

On October 1, 1981, Tractug Associates, a California Limited Partnership, obtained a loan from the Federal Maritime Administration (MARAD) to finance the construction of three vessels, the *ZP Chandon*, the *ZP Chalone*, and the *ZP Montelena*. Tractug executed

1. Two nonmaritime cases illustrate that the delegation idea has constitutional limits. In *Northern Pipeline Constr. Co. v. Marathon Pipe Line Co.*, 458 U.S. 50 (1982), the divided Court struck down portions of the Bankruptcy Reform Act of 1978 for giving what the majority perceived to be too much jurisdiction to the bankruptcy judges, stating that "the judicial power of the United States must be exercised by judges who have the attributes of life tenure and protection against salary diminution specified by Art. III." In *Stern v. Marshall*, 131 S. Ct. 2594, 2618–19 (2011), another divided Court struck down a provision of the Bankruptcy Act that authorized bankruptcy courts to try compulsory counterclaims arising under state law that are independent of the bankruptcy law, and said that bankruptcy courts are not adjuncts of the district courts.

United States Government guaranteed ship financing notes in the amount of $17,320,000. These notes were secured by a first preferred fleet mortgage which was supplemented to include each ship as construction was completed.

On September 30, 1983, Tractug defaulted in making the payments required by the notes. Upon Tractug's failure to remedy the default within 30 days, MARAD had the right to foreclose on its first preferred fleet mortgage. [It did so on December 12, libeling the vessels in the United States District Court for the Northern District of California.]

* * *

On December 13, 1983, Tractug filed a voluntary petition for reorganization under Chapter 11 of the Bankruptcy Act in the Northern District of California. The vessels were released from arrest due to the automatic stay provision of 11 U.S.C. § 362(a)(4).

The United States sought relief from the automatic stay in the bankruptcy court for the purpose of prosecuting its pending admiralty foreclosure action. After six weeks of hearings, the bankruptcy court denied the motion for relief from the automatic stay.

The bankruptcy court approved a wage deferral agreement entered into on October 24, 1984, by the International Organization of Masters, Mates and Pilots (MMP) and the owners of the vessels * * * which permitted the vessels to continue to operate around San Francisco, California, and Seattle, Washington. The wage deferral agreement provided that Tractug would pay $165 per day to each Master (tugboat captain), $132 per day to each mate, and $100 per day (base wages) to each deckhand for one year commencing October 24, 1984. * * *

On November 21, 1985, the United States Bankruptcy Court for the Northern District of California granted the renewed motion of the United States for relief from the automatic stay. [About three weeks later it] issued an order granting relief from the automatic stay to MMP and each of its members to allow them to intervene in any foreclosure action.

[The] vessels sailed from San Francisco to Puget Sound during the pendency of the automatic stay. The United States brought this admiralty foreclosure action in rem against [them] in the United States District Court for the Western District of Washington in Seattle to foreclose on its first preferred fleet mortgage.

The crew members [intervened in the Seattle action, seeking] to enforce maritime liens totaling $665,244.77 arising from wages earned prior to the automatic stay [and] wages deferred pursuant to the agreement approved by the bankruptcy court * * *. Pursuant to the request of the parties * * *, the district court in Seattle consolidated the admiralty action before it [ ] with the admiralty action initially brought in the United States District Court for the Northern District of California [ ].

On May 23, 1986, the [Seattle court] issued an order for the sale of the vessels * * *. The court ordered that "all properly filed and perfected maritime liens and other interests permitted by law in accordance with orders of this Court related thereto, shall attach to the net proceeds of the sales of the individual defendant vessels, insofar as any said liens or interests have already attached to any of the individual in rem defendants at the time of the sales ordered herein." [This order contemplated that if the United States were the successful bidder at the judicial sale, it would be liable for the payment of all valid maritime liens having priority over its mortgage interests.]

[The United States then moved for summary judgment against plaintiffs-in-intervention, arguing that the filing of the bankruptcy petition on December 13, 1983, invalidated the crew members' claims for post-petition wages. The district court granted the United States' motion and held that the crew members had no claim against the vessels or the proceeds of the judicial sale for their unpaid wages earned after December 13, 1983, the date the automatic stay went into effect. The crew members filed a timely notice of appeal.]

II.

* * *

The issue before us involves a conflict between the rights of a seaman under admiralty law and the protection accorded debtors under our bankruptcy laws. The crew members argue that under maritime law a seaman's claim for wages is entitled to the proceeds of the sale of a ship over all persons. The United States argues with equal force that the automatic stay provisions of the Bankruptcy Act make the seamen's maritime liens unenforceable as to wages earned after the date a petition for reorganization is filed. We must decide whether the enactment of the Bankruptcy Act and the Congressional grant of jurisdiction to the bankruptcy courts restricts the district court's jurisdiction in admiralty or maritime cases.

* * *

Section 362(a)(4) [11 U.S.C. § 362(a)(4)] does not expressly refer to *maritime* liens. * * * The United States argues that in applying the automatic stay to "any lien" in § 362(a)(4), Congress intended to include a maritime lien for seamen's wages. The United States' reliance on *In re Alberto,* 823 F.2d 712, 722 (3d Cir. 1987), for this proposition is misplaced. *In re Alberto* does not involve a maritime lien for wages. The Third Circuit held in *In re Alberto* that a preferred ship mortgage would not be entitled to priority if it was not perfected until after the filing of the petition in bankruptcy. A maritime lien for wages is not subject to any filing or recording requirements. [ ]

We decline to speculate that Congress *may* have intended to include maritime liens for seamen's wages within the words "any liens" in § 362(a)(4) of the Bankruptcy Act. Maritime liens for seamen wages have priority over a preferred ship mortgage, and are "sacred liens" entitled to protection "as long as a plank of the ship remains." *The John Stevens* [*supra* at 427]. * * * [I]t is unlikely that the drafters of the Bankruptcy Act would have casually neglected to express [their] intention to rewrite a "sacred" principle of maritime law. We construe Congress' omission of any reference to maritime law in § 362(a)(4) as evidence of its intention to limit the reach of that statute to land-based transactions where (1) a recording of a lien interest is required and (2) the creditor first in time is entitled to priority. The district court erred in holding that the automatic stay provisions of the Bankruptcy Act apply to seamen's wages.

* * *

* * * The district court must distribute the funds received from the foreclosure sale according to the priorities established under maritime law. The mere fact that crew members continued to work during the period of time allowed to the debtor to attempt to reorganize his business affairs under a contract calling for additional pay does not demonstrate inequitable conduct justifying an extinction of their maritime lien priority.

Notes

1. There is no available information on the reasoning of the bankruptcy court, so we cannot say why—after having first denied the Government's motion for relief from the automatic stay—the court then granted that motion. But note that 11 U.S.C. § 362(b)(12)

provides a basis for the relief: this was a special kind of Government-backed preferred ship mortgage that is expressly given an escape from the automatic stay.

2. The crew members had no corresponding statutory dispensation in subsection (b)—the exceptions subsection—of § 362. So the only way to keep the seamen's wages lien from being wholly destroyed by the Government's foreclosure action was to find a basis for excluding their lien from the expansive language of subsection (a). The Ninth Circuit did that by refusing to read the word "lien" in § 362(a)(4) to include maritime liens. That was strange reasoning, because the pertinent definitions provision, 11 U.S.C. § 101(36), defines "lien" in broad terms to include any "charge against or interest in property to secure payment of a debt or performance of an obligation." In edited-out portions of the opinion the Court seems to have looked instead to 11 U.S.C. § 101(53), which defines a "statutory lien" as one "arising solely by force of a statute on specified terms or conditions...." Clearly general maritime liens do not fall under the narrow "statutory lien" definition, but that fact does not seem a tenable basis for excluding them from the facial meaning of the term "lien" in § 362(a)(4).

3. Rutherglen, *Admiralty and Bankruptcy Revisited: Effects of the Bankruptcy Reform Act of 1978*, 65 Tul. L. Rev. 503 (1991), demonstrates that *ZP Chandon* got a good result on poor reasoning. Professor Rutherglen points out that on the court's view—that "lien" in § 362(a)(4) means "statutory lien" as defined in § 101(53)—the only maritime liens that would be subject to the stay would be "preferred ship mortgages and liens for supplies and services to the vessel, which are [already] explicitly authorized by statute." *Id.* at 508.

Providing the *Chandon* seamen with some limited protection without doing violence to the language of the Bankruptcy Act might have been achieved by looking to subsection (d) of § 362, which allows for "relief from the stay ... for cause, including the lack of adequate protection of an interest in property." Once the Government had invoked its statutory exception to the stay—putting it in a position to destroy a "sacred" lien that clearly outranked its security interest—the application of subsection (d) seems appealing.

But using § 362(d) to allow the seamen to escape the stay would only have allowed them to assert their lien claim for wages earned before the bankruptcy filing. To be protected respecting their post-petition wage claims, they would have needed to invoke 11 U.S.C. § 364(d), which provides:

> (1) The [bankruptcy] court, after notice and a hearing, may authorize the obtaining of credit or the incurring of debt secured by a senior or equal lien on property of the estate that is subject to a lien only if—
>
> > (A) the trustee is unable to obtain such credit otherwise; and
> >
> > (B) there is adequate protection of the interest of the holder of the lien on the property of the estate on which such senior or equal lien is proposed to be granted.
>
> (2) In any hearing under this subsection, the trustee has the burden of proof on the issue of adequate protection.

That does not look like an impossible road: Re subsection 1(A): Ships can not run without seamen, so maybe the trustee could not "obtain such credit otherwise" than by helping the seamen preserve their wage lien status. Re subsection 1(B): Perhaps some courts would be inclined to a lenient view of the meaning of "adequate protection" in a situation involving Government versus hardworking seamen. But obviously it would have been a tough road, which may explain the *Chandon* court's different tack.

Chapter IX

Limitation of Liability

This chapter presents an overview of the body of law emanating from the 1851 Limitation of Liability Act, 46 U.S.C. §§ 30501–30512, and Supplemental Rule F of the Federal Rules of Civil Procedure, which implements the Act. Both the Act and Rule F are set out in the Statutory Supplement. The cases presented below sketch out the background, general structure, and normal operation of the Act. The notes accompanying the cases identify a number of areas in which the courts disagree, sometimes without any apparent awareness that disagreement exists. Many who are critical of United States limitation law believe that the 1976 Convention on Limitation of Liability for Maritime Claims (LLMC Convention)[1] sets out a more rational approach. This convention came into force on December 1, 1986, but it has not been accepted in the United States.

Two areas of disagreement among U.S. courts that are not implicated in the cases and notes that follow should be briefly identified here. First, many believe strongly that pleasure boat owners should not be entitled to the benefits of the Act.[2] The great weight of authority, exemplified by *Kroemer v. Guglielmo*, 897 F.2d 58 (2d Cir. 1990), is to the contrary. See also *In re Keys Jet Ski, Inc.*, 893 F.2d 1225 (11th Cir. 1990) (holding that the owner of an aquatic scooter is entitled to the protection of the Limitation Act). On the face of the Act, the majority viewpoint—however unwise as a matter of policy—seems virtually unavoidable. 46 U.S.C. §§ 30502 and 30505 grant the right to limitation to owners of all kinds of seagoing vessels and inland vessels, and § 30506(a) indicates that "pleasure yachts" are included except when explicitly excluded. Even before *Stewart v. Dutra* [*supra* at 21] announced that the broad definition of *vessel* in 1 U.S.C. § 3 is the default definition of the term throughout the U.S. Code, courts assumed that the Limitation Act takes its definition of *vessel* from 1 U.S.C. § 3. See, e.g., *In re Mobro Marine, Inc.*, 2005 AMC 527, 561 (M.D. Fla. 2004).

The second dispute involves the situation in which a shipowner elects not to take advantage of 46 U.S.C. § 30511 and Supplemental Rule F—which authorize the shipowner to invoke the mandatory federal-court concursus proceeding discussed in the cases below—but instead waits to be sued and then pleads the substantive right granted by 46 U.S.C.

1. International Convention for the Unification of Certain Rules Relating to the Limitation of Liability of Owners of Seagoing Ships, reprinted in 6 Benedict on Admiralty Doc. No. 5–4 (7th rev. ed. 2000).

2. Reluctance to afford a pleasure boat owner the protections of the Limitation Act may explain the no-jurisdiction ruling of the district court and Seventh Circuit in *Sisson v. Ruby*, *supra* at 32. See Robertson & Sturley, *The Admiralty Extension Act Solution*, 34 J. Mar. L. & Com. 209, 217–18 (2009).

§ 30505 of the Act as an affirmative defense. It is clear that only an admiralty court can entertain a shipowner's petition for limitation of liability and preside over the kind of concursus envisaged by § 30511 and Rule F. *Norwich Co. v. Wright*, 80 U.S. 104 (1871). But there is no good reason for thinking that state courts lack jurisdiction to apply the § 30505 defense. See *Mapco Petroleum, Inc. v. Memphis Barge Line*, 849 S.W. 2d 312 (Tenn. 1993). Scattered rulings to the contrary should be regarded as outliers.

Empresa Lineas Maritimas Argentinas S.A. v. United States

United States Court of Appeals, Fourth Circuit, 1984
730 F.2d 153, 1984 AMC 1698

BUTZNER, Senior Circuit Judge:

* * *

This suit arises out of a collision between the United States Coast Guard Cutter *Cuyahoga* and the Argentinian freighter *Santa Cruz II.* How the collision occurred is undisputed. On a clear night in October 1978, the *Cuyahoga,* under the command of Chief Warrant Officer Donald K. Robinson, was northbound in the Chesapeake Bay on an officer candidate training cruise from its base at the Coast Guard Reserve Training Center (RTC) in Yorktown, Virginia. The *Santa Cruz II,* a freighter loaded with coal, was southbound in the Bay from Baltimore, Maryland.

While standing watch on the *Cuyahoga,* Captain Robinson and several officer candidates noticed the lights of a vessel, which turned out to be the *Santa Cruz II,* off the port bow. Captain Robinson checked the radar and determined that the vessel was about eight miles away and had a left-bearing drift. From the configuration of the lights, Captain Robinson, despite many years of experience, guessed erroneously that the *Santa Cruz II* was a small vessel traveling in the same direction as the *Cuyahoga.* When the vessels were about a mile apart, Captain Robinson ordered a change of course, turning left to take the *Cuyahoga* into the mouth of the Potomac River to moor for the night. Having erroneously concluded that the *Cuyahoga* and the *Santa Cruz* were traveling in the same direction, Captain Robinson thought that by turning left the *Cuyahoga* would cross astern of the *Santa Cruz.* In fact, the left turn caused the *Cuyahoga* to cross the bow of the *Santa Cruz II.* When the *Cuyahoga* crossed its path, the *Santa Cruz II* sounded its warning signals. Captain Robinson did not realize that his vessel was in the path of the *Santa Cruz* until it was too late. The bow of the *Santa Cruz* struck the *Cuyahoga.* The *Cuyahoga* sank in two to three minutes. Eleven of her crew died. The *Santa Cruz II* sustained substantial injury to her bow.

Empresa Lineas Maritimas Argentinas, S.A. (ELMA), the owner of the *Santa Cruz II,* filed a complaint against the United States seeking recovery for damages to the *Santa Cruz II* * * *. The United States denied liability but asserted that, in the event that it was found liable, its liability should be limited under [46 U.S.C. § 30505] to the value of the *Cuyahoga,* which is nothing.

In a memorandum opinion, Judge Blair found that the multiple errors of judgment and perception made by Captain Robinson were the sole cause of the collision. Consequently, the United States was 100% liable. The court also held that the government was entitled to limit its liability [under § 30505] because the United States did not have privity or knowledge of the cause of the collision.

Before judgment was entered, Judge Blair died. The case was reassigned to Judge Thomsen. Upon motion of ELMA, which the government opposed, Judge Thomsen reopened the case and held another trial at which additional evidence was received and new witnesses heard. Judge Thomsen agreed with Judge Blair's conclusion that the *Cuyahoga* was solely responsible for the collision. Judge Thomsen, however, held that the United States could not limit its liability [under § 30505] because "one or more persons in the chain of command over Robinson had knowledge or were charged with knowledge of the existence of Robinson's physical problems and loss of sleep, which were responsible for his bad judgment, the cause of the collision." It is from this judgment that the United States appeals.

Under [46 U.S.C. § 30505] the liability of a shipowner for any loss, damage, or injury by collision may not exceed the amount or value of the interest of the owner in the vessel if the loss is occasioned without the privity or knowledge of the owner. Determining whether a shipowner may limit liability under this section is a two-step process. First, the court must consider what acts of negligence or conditions of unseaworthiness caused the accident. Here, the United States does not appeal the district court's finding that Captain Robinson's errors of judgment due to his physical condition caused the collision. Consequently, we must address only the second question, whether the shipowner had knowledge of the events which caused the loss.

To preclude limitation [under § 30505], the shipowner's knowledge need not be actual. The shipowner is chargeable with knowledge of acts or events or conditions of unseaworthiness that could have been discovered through reasonable diligence. [ ] Thus, the inquiry here is whether the United States had sufficient knowledge of Robinson's medical condition, which the district court found caused his errors in judgment, so that limitation of liability should be denied.

The same standards are applicable to the United States when it seeks a limitation of liability because it lacked privity or knowledge of the cause of the loss as when a private corporation seeks the same benefit. [ ] In both instances, liability may not be limited [under § 30505] where the negligence is that of an executive officer, manager, or superintendent, whose scope of authority includes supervision over the phase of the business out of which the injury occurred. [ ] Here, the record shows that three officers were above Captain Robinson in the chain of command at Yorktown. The authority of the commanding officer of the Reserve Training Center in Yorktown included the operational control of the *Cuyahoga*. Below him in the chain of command was the executive officer. Finally, Captain Robinson's reporting officer was the chief of the training division at Yorktown. As head of the training division, he had operational and administrative control of the *Cuyahoga*. Each of these officers had sufficient authority over the operation of the *Cuyahoga* to impute to the United States his knowledge of the events that caused the accident. [ ]

The United States argues that it cannot be charged with privity or knowledge of Robinson's errors of navigation and seamanship when the vessel is underway. [ ] Nonetheless, the United States may not absolve itself if through the use of reasonable diligence it could have taken action while the vessel was in port and under its authority and control that would have prevented Robinson's negligent acts at sea. [ ] We turn then to consider whether Robinson's superiors exercised reasonable diligence to ascertain the effect Robinson's medical condition might have on his performance as commanding officer of the *Cuyahoga*.

Robinson first visited the medical clinic at the RTC in Yorktown in April 1978 complaining of wheezing, coughing, and shortness of breath. Initially, he was treated by corpsmen at the medical clinic who apparently diagnosed his condition as a sinus infection and prescribed antihistamines and a cough expectorant. Robinson returned to the medical clinic several times over the next few months because his symptoms persisted. Sometimes he was seen by a doctor, at others by a physician's associate or corpsman. From July to September he visited the clinic frequently, going two to three times a week for treatment. During this period he was treated by a doctor who had diagnosed Robinson's illness as bronchial asthma. Robinson repeatedly complained to the doctor that his coughing and difficulty in breathing were affecting his sleep. Some nights he said he slept only two to three hours. * * *

Robinson's condition did not improve materially, so in September the doctor sent him to the allergy clinic at Walter Reed Hospital. Robinson visited the allergy clinic at Walter Reed three times between September 14 and October 20, 1978. * * * His last visit to Walter Reed was the day before the collision, at which time he still complained of coughing, wheezing, chest congestion, and sleeplessness. Because Robinson's condition had not improved, his physician at the allergy clinic arranged for him to go to the pulmonary clinic for further testing. Robinson's illness was not correctly diagnosed as aspergillosis until after the accident, in December 1978.

The medical clinic at Yorktown documented most visits on a daily medical report that was circulated to the commanding and executive officers. It listed patients seen at the clinic, their diagnosis, and a fitness-for-duty determination made by medical personnel. The district court found that, although Robinson's superiors knew his name was appearing frequently on this list, they took no reasonably adequate steps to determine whether his medical condition affected his ability to perform his duties as the commanding officer of the training vessel *Cuyahoga*. * * *

The United States argues that to require Robinson's superiors to conclude that he should not perform his duties as commanding officer when the doctors at Yorktown and Walter Reed had not recommended that he be removed from duty is to hold the United States to a standard of omniscience. The government relies on the doctor's testimony that, had he thought Robinson was too ill for duty, he would have insisted that Robinson stay home in a not-fit-for-duty status.

Conflicting evidence undermines the government's reliance on the doctor's testimony. Medical personnel at the RTC generally did not place senior officers like Robinson on limited or not-fit-for-duty status because senior officers could determine their own duty status. Consequently, a senior officer often would not be put on not-fit-for-duty status under circumstances where an enlisted man would be. Indeed, the doctor testified at Robinson's court martial that he would have put Robinson on not-fit-for-duty status on several occasions had Robinson been an enlisted man on the *Cuyahoga*.

Robinson, however, did not know that he could declare himself non-fit-for-duty for medical reasons, nor did he feel that he was incapable of performing his duties. He was confident that if he were unfit, the medical officers would tell him. Robinson believed that because his superiors received the daily medical report and thus were aware of his condition, they would relieve him of his duty if they thought it was necessary. Unfortunately, Robinson's superiors considered senior officers listed on the daily medical report fit-for-duty unless medical personnel or the individual recommended otherwise. Consequently, they did not suggest independently that Robinson may not be fit-for-duty.

That the policy was unclear for declaring senior officers not-fit-for-duty does not absolve the United States. Knowledge within the context [of § 30505] includes both actual knowledge and the knowledge of conditions likely to produce or contribute to loss which the owner or superintendent could have discovered through reasonable diligence. "The measure in such cases is not what the owner knows, but what he is charged with finding out." [ ] The executive officer's limited questioning of the doctor did not meet this standard. The Coast Guard officers whose authority included the operational command of the *Cuyahoga* had a duty to conduct a more probing inquiry to determine whether Robinson's condition might affect his ability to perform as the commanding officer on training missions on the *Cuyahoga.* Failing in this duty, the United States may not limit its liability [under § 30505]. [ ]

* * *

The judgment of the district court is affirmed.

Notes

1. **Admiralty jurisdiction.** No one challenged the district court's subject matter jurisdiction in *Empresa.* This was because admiralty jurisdiction under *Grubart* (and/or the Admiralty Extension Act) was obvious. But recall that the Limitation Act is not itself a basis for admiralty jurisdiction. See *supra* at 50 note 3. Thus, for example, while the language of the Limitation Act might cover a vessel-involved incident on a landlocked intrastate lake, the Act could not apply because the incident would fail the navigable waters criterion for admiralty jurisdiction.

2. **The limitation fund.** As the court indicates, even though the fault of the U.S. was solely responsible for the collision, if it had succeeded with its limited-liability argument it would have owed nothing. This illustrates the peculiar United States rule whereby the main measure of the limitation fund is the value of the ship at the end of the voyage on which the incident occurred. *Norwich Co. v. Wright*, 80 U.S. 104, 120–22 (1871). "Thus if the ship is lost, the value is zero." Gilmore & Black, The Law of Admiralty 907 (2d ed. 1975). Section 30505(a) provides that the limitation fund includes the value of the vessel "and pending freight," but the *Cuyahoga* earned no freight. ("Pending freight" means money earned by the vessel for carrying goods on the voyage in question.)

When personal injury or death claims are made against the owner of the vessel seeking limitation, 46 U.S.C. § 30506 may raise the limitation fund ceiling to $420 times the tonnage of the vessel. (This provision was not directly involved in *Empresa*, but it might have become relevant in related litigation against the owners of the *Santa Cruz* on behalf of the Coast Guard crewmen who were injured and killed in the collision.)

When multiple claimants end up having to share in a limitation fund that is inadequate to satisfy their claims, Supplemental Rule F(8) comes into play; it provides that the fund "shall be divided pro rata, subject to all relevant provisions of law, among the several claimants in proportion to the amounts of their respective claims, duly proved, saving, however, to all parties any priority to which they may be legally entitled." As a practical matter, this leaves the distribution of the fund largely to the district judge's discretion. Cf. Section VIII-D, *supra* at 427–33.

3. **Seamen's claims.** While Jones Act and unseaworthiness claims by seamen are subject to limitation of liability, certain other types of seamen's claims are not. 46 U.S.C. § 30505(c) provides that seamen's wage claims are not subject to limitation. And many courts have held that "a shipowner cannot limit its liability for maintenance and cure." *Brister v. A.W.I., Inc.*, 946 F.2d 350, 361 (5th Cir. 1991); *In re RJF Int'l Corp.*, 354 F.3d 104, 107 (1st Cir. 2004).

4. **The personal contracts doctrine.** A more general exclusion from the purview of the limitation act is implicit in an "amorphous 'personal contracts' doctrine [whereby] the

shipowner may not limit his liability for those contracts which are deemed 'personal.'" MARAIST, GALLIGAN & MARAIST, ADMIRALTY IN A NUTSHELL 381 (6th ed. 2010). Most authorities have found this doctrine puzzling. After exploring the personal contracts doctrine at some length, the Fifth Circuit concluded that it is probably restricted to "situations in which the breach, as well as the execution, of the contract, could be said to be 'personal' to the vessel owner." *Signal Oil & Gas Co. v. Barge W-701*, 654 F.2d 1164, 1169 (5th Cir. 1981). So restricted, the doctrine does not seem to add much if anything to the "privity or knowledge" exception; presumably a "personal" breach of contract by a vessel owner would *ipso facto* fall within the owner's privity or knowledge.

5. **Whose "privity or knowledge"?** The *Empresa* court's view that "privity or knowledge" of a corporate shipowner generally means "negligence of an executive officer, manager, or superintendent, whose scope of authority includes supervision over the phase of the business out of which the injury occurred" has often been expressed. Under this view, a ship's captain or master is ordinarily not high-ranking enough; the majority position is that a master's fault does not normally amount to "privity or knowledge" on the part of the shipowner/employer. See, e.g., *Waterman Steamship Corp. v. Gay Cottons*, 414 F.2d 724, 734–35 (9th Cir. 1969). This view is reinforced by the negative implication flowing from 46 U.S.C. § 30506(e), which imputes the master's privity or knowledge "at or before the beginning of [the] voyage" to the shipowner in the limited context of wrongful death and personal injury actions. But see the apparently contrary ruling in *Potomac Transport, Inc. v. Ogden Marine, Inc.*, 909 F.2d 42, 46 (2d Cir. 1990): "The failure of a ship's master to exercise diligence in selecting, training, or supervising crew members whose navigational faults contribute to an accident is proper grounds to deny limitation of liability."

6. **First-party insurance.** Any first-party insurance the owner might have on the destroyed vessel is his to keep: "The law does not compel the shipowner to surrender his insurance in order to have the benefit of limited liability." *Place v. Norwich & New York Transp. Co.*, 118 U.S. 468, 504 (1886).

7. **Third-party insurance.** Shipowners' liability insurers (protection and indemnity insurers) are indirectly protected by the Act. The courts have upheld the validity of insurance policy provisions that tie the insurer's obligation to the insured's ultimate (post-limitation) liability. See *Crown Zellerbach Corp. v. Ingram Industries, Inc.*, 783 F.2d 1296 (5th Cir. 1986).

Lewis v. Lewis & Clark Marine, Inc.

Supreme Court of the United States, 2001

531 U.S. 438, 121 S. Ct. 993, 148 L. Ed. 2d 931, 2001 AMC 913

Justice O'CONNOR delivered the opinion of the unanimous Court.

* * *

Petitioner, James F. Lewis, worked as a deckhand aboard the M/V *Karen Michelle*, owned by respondent, Lewis & Clark Marine, Inc. Petitioner claims that on March 17, 1998, he was injured aboard the *Karen Michelle* when he tripped over a wire and hurt his back. In April 1998, petitioner sued respondent in the Circuit Court of Madison County, Illinois. Petitioner claimed negligence under the Jones Act, unseaworthiness, and maintenance and cure. * * * Petitioner did not demand a jury trial in state court.

In anticipation of petitioner's suit, respondent had filed a complaint for exoneration from, or limitation of, liability in the United States District Court for the Eastern District of Missouri pursuant to the Limitation of Liability Act. The District Court followed the procedure for a limitation action provided in Supplemental Admiralty and Maritime Claims Rule F. The court entered an order approving a surety bond of $450,000, representing respondent's interest in the vessel. The court ordered that any person with a claim for the events of March 17, 1998, file a claim with the court within a specified period. The court then enjoined the filing or prosecution of any suits against respondent related to the incident on March 17, 1998.

Petitioner filed an answer to respondent's complaint, a claim for damages for injury, and a motion to dissolve the restraining order. Petitioner averred that he was the sole claimant concerning the events of March 17, 1998. He waived any claim of res judicata concerning limited liability based on a state court judgment; he stipulated that respondent could relitigate issues relating to the limitation of liability in District Court. Petitioner later stipulated that the value of his claim was less than the value of the limitation fund, recanting his earlier allegation that his claim exceeded the vessel's value.

The District Court dissolved the restraining order that prevented petitioner from proceeding with his cause of action in state court. The court recognized that federal courts have exclusive jurisdiction to determine whether a vessel owner is entitled to limited liability. The court also noted, however, that the statute that confers exclusive jurisdiction over admiralty and maritime claims to federal courts contains a clause that saves to suitors "all other remedies to which they are otherwise entitled." 28 U.S.C. § 1333(1). The court reasoned that "a tension exists between the exclusive jurisdiction vested in the admiralty courts to determine a vessel owner's right to limited liability and the saving to suitors clause."

The District Court found two exceptions to exclusive federal jurisdiction under which a claimant is allowed to litigate his claim in state court. The first is where the value of the limitation fund exceeds the total value of all claims asserted against the vessel owner. The second is where a single claimant brings an action against the vessel owner seeking damages in excess of the value of the vessel. The court concluded that it should dissolve the injunction in this case because petitioner met the limited fund exception and probably met the single claimant exception as well. The court decided to retain jurisdiction over the limitation action to protect the vessel owner's right to limitation in the event that the state proceedings necessitated further proceedings in federal court.

The Eighth Circuit Court of Appeals held that the District Court abused its discretion in dissolving the injunction. The Court of Appeals, like the District Court, recognized potential tension between the saving to suitors clause in the jurisdictional statute and the Limitation Act. The Court of Appeals, however, perceived no conflict between those provisions in the instant case. The Court of Appeals * * * concluded that respondent had a right to seek exoneration from liability, not merely limitation of liability, in federal court. The court also concluded that because petitioner did not request a trial by jury, he had not sought a saved remedy in state court. * * * For these reasons, the court held that there was no basis for dissolving the injunction.

We granted certiorari to resolve a conflict between the Eighth Circuit's decision and the decisions of other Courts of Appeals. [ ]

* * *

* * * [The Limitation] Act allows a vessel owner to limit liability for damage or injury, occasioned without the owner's privity or knowledge, to the value of the vessel or the owner's interest in the vessel. * * * Congress passed the Limitation Act in 1851 "to encourage ship-building and to induce capitalists to invest money in this branch of industry." [ ]

The Act also had the purpose of "putting American shipping upon an equality with that of other maritime nations" that had their own limitation acts. [ ]

* * *

* * *Supplemental Admiralty and Maritime Claims Rule F * * * sets forth the process for filing a complaint seeking exoneration from, or limitation of, liability. The district court secures the value of the vessel or owner's interest, marshals claims, and enjoins the prosecution of other actions with respect to the claims. In these proceedings, the court, sitting without a jury, adjudicates the claims. The court determines whether the vessel owner is liable and whether the owner may limit liability. The court then determines the validity of the claims, and if liability is limited, distributes the limited fund among the claimants.

Some tension exists between the saving to suitors clause and the Limitation Act. One statute gives suitors the right to a choice of remedies, and the other statute gives vessel owners the right to seek limitation of liability in federal court. We confronted this tension in *Langnes v. Green*, 282 U.S. 531 (1931). The respondent in *Langnes* was employed on the petitioner's vessel. The employee sued the vessel owner in state court for $25,000 for personal injuries suffered aboard the vessel. The vessel owner later filed a petition for limitation of liability in Federal District Court. The District Court enjoined any further proceedings in state court and issued a notice that all claimants appear. The employee filed his claim in District Court. The parties stipulated that the vessel was worth no more than $5,000.

The employee sought dissolution of the injunction. He argued that the state court had jurisdiction over his claim, that he was the only possible claimant, that there was only one vessel owner, and therefore the vessel owner could claim the benefit of the Limitation Act by proper pleading in state court. The District Court denied the motion * * *. On review, this Court concluded that [the District Court] erred in failing to recognize that the state court was competent to hear the employee's personal injury claim and the vessel owner's claim for limitation. In our view, the choice before the District Court was whether it should retain the limitation action and preserve the right of the vessel owner but destroy the right of the employee in state court to a common law remedy, or allow the action in state court to proceed and preserve the rights of both parties. We concluded that the latter course was just. We decided that the District Court should have dissolved the injunction and allowed the employee to proceed with his claim in state court, and retained jurisdiction over the petition for limitation of liability in the event that the state proceedings necessitated further proceedings in federal court. We explained that the District Court's decision is "one of discretion in every case" * * *.

* * *

We have also considered the conflict between the saving to suitors clause and the Limitation Act in a case where several claimants attempted to sue a vessel owner in state court. *Lake Tankers Corp. v. Henn*, 354 U.S. 147 (1957). A pleasure yacht, the *Blackstone*, capsized after a collision with a tug that was push-towing a barge, injuring several persons and killing one. Claimants sued the owner of the tug and barge in state court actions. The owner filed a petition for exoneration from, or limitation of, liability in federal court. The owner also filed a bond for the tug in the amount of approximately $119,000 and a bond for the barge in the amount of $165,000. The District Court enjoined other proceedings concerning the collision. Thereafter, the claimants made their demands for damages; the total claims were less than the amount of the two bonds. All claimants relinquished any right to damages in excess of that set forth in their claims. They further waived any claim of res judicata relating to the issue of the vessel owner's ability to limit liability. The District Court decided to dissolve the injunction because the total limitation fund exceeded the amount of the claims. The Court of Appeals affirmed.

We affirmed the Court of Appeals' decision. In examining the Limitation Act and its history, we found it "crystal clear that the operation of the Act is directed at misfortunes at sea where the losses incurred exceed the value of the vessel and the pending freight." Where the value of the vessel and the pending freight exceed the claims, however, there is no necessity for the maintenance of the action in federal court. The stipulations, in addition to other restrictions on the state court proceedings, ensured "beyond doubt that [the owner's] right of limitation under the Act was fully protected." We explained that to expand the scope of exclusive jurisdiction to prevent the state court actions

> would transform the Act from a protective instrument to an offensive weapon by which the shipowner could deprive suitors of their common-law rights, even where the limitation fund is known to be more than adequate to satisfy all demands upon it. The shipowner's right to limit liability is not so boundless. The Act is not one of immunity from liability but of limitation of it and we read no other privilege for the shipowner into its language over and above that granting him limited liability. In fact, the Congress not only created the limitation procedure for the primary purpose of apportioning the limitation fund among the claimants where that fund was inadequate to pay the claims in full, but it reserved to such suitors their common-law remedies.

Since these decisions, the Courts of Appeals have generally permitted claimants to proceed with their claims in state court where there is only a single claimant, as in *Langnes*, or where the total claims do not exceed the value of the limitation fund, as in *Lake Tankers*. [ ] See also *Kreta Shipping S.A. v. Preussag International Steel Corp.*, 192 F.3d 41 (2d Cir. 1999) (foreign forum).

In the instant case, we believe that the District Court properly exercised its discretion in dissolving the injunction that prevented petitioner from pursuing his claims in state court. The District Court, guided by our prior cases, attempted to reconcile petitioner's right to his remedy under the saving to suitors clause with respondent's right to seek limited liability under the Limitation Act. The court dissolved the injunction against the state court proceedings after it concluded that respondent's right to seek limitation of liability would be adequately protected. Respondent's rights were protected by petitioner's stipulation that his claim did not exceed the limitation fund, petitioner's waiver of any defense of res judicata with respect to limitation of liability, and the District Court's decision to stay the Limitation Act proceedings pending state court proceedings.

The Eighth Circuit held that the District Court should not have dissolved the injunction without first "finding ... actual statutory conflict between the Limitation Act and the saving to suitors clause in the case at bar." The Court of Appeals concluded that there was no conflict here because respondent had a right to seek exoneration from liability in federal court, and petitioner did not have a saved remedy under the saving to suitors clause. That reasoning misapprehends this Court's prior decisions.

* * *

In deciding that the case should proceed in federal court, the Court of Appeals relied on two flawed premises: that the Limitation Act grants vessel owners a right to obtain exoneration from liability in federal court where limitation of liability is not at issue, and that the saving to suitors clause reserves to claimants only the right to receive a jury trial.

By its own terms, the Limitation Act protects the right of vessel owners to limit their liability to the value of the vessel, provided that the events or circumstances giving rise to the damage occurred without the vessel owner's privity or knowledge. The Act was designed to encourage investment and protect vessel owners from unlimited exposure to liability. We have also made clear, however, that the scope of exclusive federal jurisdiction is proportional to the federal interest in protecting the vessel owner's right to seek limitation of liability. See *Lake Tankers*, 354 U.S. at 153. We have explained that "[t]he Act is not one of immunity from liability but of limitation of it." 354 U.S. at 152. We see no reason to revisit that conclusion and decline respondent's invitation to expand the scope of the Act.

In construing the Limitation Act, this Court long ago determined that vessel owners may contest liability in the process of seeking limited liability, and we promulgated rules to that effect * * *. Supplemental Admiralty and Maritime Claims Rule F(2). Thus, we agree with respondent that a vessel owner need not confess liability in order to seek limitation under the Act. The Act and the rules of practice, however, do not create a free-standing right to exoneration from liability in circumstances where limitation of liability is not at issue. In this case, petitioner stipulated that his claim for damages would not exceed the value of the vessel and waived any claim of res judicata from the state court action concerning issues bearing on the limitation of liability. The District Court concluded that these stipulations would protect the vessel owner's right to seek limited liability in federal court. Then, out of an "abundance of caution," the court stayed the limitation proceedings so that it could act if the state court proceedings jeopardized the vessel owner's rights under the Limitation Act. We believe nothing more was required to protect respondent's right to seek a limitation of liability.

The district courts have jurisdiction over actions arising under the Limitation Act, and they have discretion to stay or dismiss Limitation Act proceedings to allow a suitor to pursue his claims in state court. If the district court concludes that the vessel owner's right to limitation will not be adequately protected—where for example a group of claimants cannot agree on appropriate stipulations or there is uncertainty concerning the adequacy of the fund or the number of claims—the court may proceed to adjudicate the merits, deciding the issues of liability and limitation. [ ] But where, as here, the District Court satisfies itself that a vessel owner's right to seek limitation will be protected, the decision to dissolve the injunction is well within the court's discretion.

The Court of Appeals reasoned that the District Court also erred in dissolving the injunction because petitioner had no saved remedy in state court. The Court of Appeals apparently treated as dispositive petitioner's failure to demand a jury trial in state court. The jurisdictional statute, however, reserves to suitors "all other remedies to which they are otherwise entitled." 28 U.S.C. § 1333(1). * * * Trial by jury is an obvious, but not exclusive, example of the remedies available to suitors. [ ]

* * *

In sum, this Court's case law makes clear that state courts, with all of their remedies, may adjudicate claims like petitioner's against vessel owners so long as the vessel owner's right to seek limitation of liability is protected. Respondent seeks to invert that rule, making run-of-the-mill personal injury actions involving vessels a matter of exclusive federal jurisdiction except where the claimant happens to seek a jury trial. We reject that proposal and hold that the Court of Appeals erred in reversing the District Court's decision to dissolve the injunction. The judgment of the United States Court of Appeals for the Eighth Circuit is therefore reversed, and the case is remanded for further proceedings consistent with this opinion.

Notes

1. Both 46 U.S.C. §30511(c) and Rule F(3) provide that when the shipowner files a timely and procedurally proper petition for limitation of liability, all related actions against the shipowner in other forums "shall cease." In light of that facially mandatory language, it is not surprising that under pre-*Lewis & Clark* law some of the lower courts had developed fairly demanding (and sometimes complex) criteria for the stipulations required of claimants seeking to litigate outside a limitation proceeding. See Landrieu, *Stipulations: Sidestepping the Limitation of Shipowners' Liability Act*, 23 TUL. MAR. L.J. 429 (1999). *Lewis and Clark* seems to bring needed clarification and leniency. See, e.g., *In re Tetra Applied Technologies*, 362 F.3d 338 (5th Cir. 2004) (holding that it is now clear that a claimant need not stipulate that the issue of exoneration is for the exclusive determination of the admiralty court). See also *In re Offshore Marine Towing, Inc.*, 333 F. Supp. 2d 1286, 1292 (S.D. Fla. 2004)—a case with fascinating facts—in which the court held that the following stipulation was adequate:

> Duncan has stipulated to [the vessel owner's right to litigate its claim to limited liability exclusively in federal admiralty court], and she has agreed not to seek a determination of the liability limitation issue nor the amount of any limitations fund in any other forum. Duncan has also stipulated to waive any res judicata or issue preclusion effect the decisions of any other forum might have on these issues. Finally, Duncan has stipulated not to enforce any state court judgment until the [federal admiralty court] has adjudicated the [vessel owner's] right to limit that liability * * *.

2. **No transnational effect.** "Limitation judgments do not have extraterritorial effect and claimants who abstain from filing damage claims in courts of the United States are free to pursue actions in foreign tribunals." *In re Bowoon Sangsa Co.*, 720 F.2d 595, 599 (9th Cir. 1983). *In re Bethlehem Steel Corp.*, 631 F.2d 441, 1980 AMC 2122 (6th Cir. 1980), is illustrative. A Bethlehem-owned steamship's allision with a highway bridge caused the closure of the Welland Canal (connecting Lakes Erie and Ontario) and disrupted vessel traffic on both sides of the U.S.-Canada border. Multiple lawsuits were filed against Bethlehem in both countries. Bethlehem's pursuit of limited-liability protection required it to institute limitation-of-liability proceedings in both countries and post a separate limitation-fund bond in each.

3. **Is U.S. law out of step?** In *Bethlehem*, the Canadian admiralty court applied Canada law to set the amount of the required bond at $692,000 (U.S.). The U.S. admiralty court applied U.S. law to set the bond at about $850,000. Bethlehem's appeal of the latter ruling, arguing that the U.S. court should have followed Canadian law, was rejected.

In the recurrent fight in U.S. courts over whether the measure of the limitation fund should come from forum law or foreign law, the shipowner is sometimes on one side and sometimes on the other. As we have seen, U.S. law measures the fund by the value of the vessel after the accident. (In Learned Hand's phrase, our limitation-of-liability law "subjects the sufferer to the gamble of the offending ship's survival." *Kloeckner Reederei Und Kohlenhandel, G.M.B.H. v. A/S Hakedal (The Western Farmer)*, 210 F.2d 754, 757 (2d Cir. 1954).) But most maritime countries—and the 1976 LLMC Convention—measure the fund by the vessel's tonnage rather than its post-accident value. That difference means that the U.S. limit will often be higher than the competing foreign limit if the ship was not much damaged in the accident and lower when the ship has been seriously damaged or lost. Transnational forum-shopping on a fairly large scale is thus inevitable.

Chapter X

Marine Insurance

Elementary Taxonomy

First-party insurance protects the insured against harms and losses to itself and its property. Mundane examples are health and accident insurance, fire insurance, and automobile collision and comprehensive insurance. *Third-party insurance* protects the insured against potential liabilities to others. Mundane examples are automobile liability insurance, professionals' errors and omissions insurance, and comprehensive general liability insurance.

An insurance *policy* is the formal manifestation of the contract between insured and insurer. (The contract is typically formed when the insured's *application* is accepted by the insurer to become a *binder*; the formal policy is issued some time later.) The same insurance policy may include both first- and third-party protection. This is true of many automobile policies and of most homeowners' policies.

In the complex world of marine insurance, the principal types of policies are *hull insurance*, which provides vessel owners with first-party protection against some harms to the ship and includes some third-party protection; *cargo insurance*, which affords first-party protection (and sometimes third-party protection) to shippers and buyers of goods; and *protection and indemnity (P&I) insurance*, which is third-party insurance protecting the insured marine operator against some of its potential liabilities. (Third-party policies usually also afford the insured a defense in any litigation asserting a liability allegedly covered by the policy.) See generally Hayden & Balick, *Marine Insurance Varieties, Combinations, and Coverages*, 66 Tul. L. Rev. 311 (1991).

Two Troublesome Terms

In the fields of insurance and general average (see *supra* at 368 note 3), the term *average* usually lacks all of its normal connotations. It simply means *loss*. Thus, a "particular average" is a partial loss to a single interest; a "general average" is a loss to the whole venture. The term may come from an Arabic word (*awariyah*) that simply meant *damaged goods*. The term made its way into Old Italian and then into Old French, where it took on the meaning of *goods damaged in shipping*. It then made its way through the maritime law of general average (where it probably acquired its present-day connotation of distribution or adjustment) and into modern English.

Warranty has many meanings. In the marine insurance field, at least three distinctly different usages can be identified. (a) In the strictest sense, a warranty is a promise that, if broken, voids the entire contract. For example, the insured under a voyage hull insurance policy impliedly warrants that the vessel is seaworthy when it breaks ground (unless the contract clearly provides to the contrary). If that warranty is breached—if the vessel sails in an unseaworthy condition—there is no coverage under the policy, regardless of whether the loss being claimed has anything to do with the unseaworthy condition. The same strict treatment is often applied to breaches of express warranties. (b) In a more relaxed sense, a warranty is a promise to try one's best. For example, some cases say that under "the American Rule" the insured under a time hull policy (covering multiple voyages) owes a strict warranty of seaworthiness at the point when the insurance attaches and thereafter a watered-down "warranty" to use due diligence to correct unseaworthy conditions as they arise. A breach of that watered-down "warranty" will not oust the policy, but it will defeat coverage for any loss flowing from an unseaworthy condition that the insured should have corrected. (c) The word "warranty" is also used (confusingly) to signal particular exclusions from coverage. A typical example would be a clause providing that an identified type of cargo is "warranted free of particular average." This simply means that the insurer will not pay for partial losses to that type of cargo.

A Little History

For centuries shipowners have found it advantageous if not essential to spread and share the risks of their ventures. An *underwriter* is an individual who has agreed to bear some portion of the loss if a shipping venture fails. In London in the late 1600s, underwriters often gathered at the coffee house of Edward Lloyd to discuss their affairs. The house eventually became the center of the business, and "Lloyd's" remains to this day an association of individual underwriters. (In the United States, the insurance business is conducted almost exclusively by corporations.)

The London underwriters developed what they called the *Lloyd's S.G. (Ship and Goods) Policy*, the core of which was as follows:

> Touching the adventures and perils which we the assurers are contented to bear and do take upon us in this voyage: they are of the seas, men of war, fire, enemies, pirates, rovers, thieves, jettisons, letters of mart and countermart, surprisals, takings at sea, arrests, restraints, and detainments of all kings, princes, and people, of what nation, condition, or quality soever, barratry of the master and mariners, and of all other perils, losses, and misfortunes, that have or shall come to the hurt, detriment, or damage of the said goods and merchandises, and ship, & c., or any part thereof. And in case of any loss or misfortune it shall be lawful to the assured, their factors, servants and assigns, to sue, labour, and travel for, in and about the defence, safeguards, and recovery of the said goods and merchandises, and ship, & c., or any part thereof, without prejudice to this insurance; to the charges whereof we, the assurers, will contribute each one according to the rate and quantity of his sum herein assured. And it is especially declared and agreed that no acts of the insurer or insured in recovering, saving, or preserving the property insured shall be considered as a waiver, or acceptance of abandonment. And it is agreed by us, the insurers, that this writing or policy of assurance shall be of as much force and effect as the surest writing or policy of assurance heretofore made in Lombard Street, or in the Royal Exchange, or elsewhere in London. And so we, the assurers, are contented, and do hereby promise and bind ourselves, each one for his own part....

The policy was in general use for over two hundred years, and much of its language still appears in modern policies.

Note that the Lloyd's S.G. Policy is worded broadly enough to afford third-party protection. But *DeVaux v. Salvador*, 111 Eng. Rep. 845, 849–50 (K.B. 1836), held that "the sum of money which [an insured shipowner had to pay] in consequence of some proceedings commenced in the Court of Admiralty at Calcutta, in consequence of an accidental collision with another vessel in the Hoogly River" was not covered by the S.G. Policy:

> [This loss] is neither a necessary nor a proximate effect of the perils of the sea; it grows out of an arbitrary provision in the law of nations from views of general expediency, not as dictated by natural justice, nor (possibly) quite consistent with it; and can no more be charged on the underwriters than a penalty incurred by contravention of the Revenue laws of any particular State, which was rendered inevitable by perils insured against.

Shipowners responded to *DeVaux* by prevailing on the London underwriters to add collision liability—in the form of a "Running Down Clause"—to the basic S.G. Policy's coverage. But—evidently fearing that full coverage might lead to laxity on the part of ships' masters—the underwriters were unwilling to take on more than three-fourths of the collision liability risk. Shipowners formed Protection and Indemnity Clubs to cover the remaining fourth. Gradually the coverage of the resultant P&I policy was broadened to include other third-party risks and other risks not covered by hull policies. Today the P&I policy is the basic third-party coverage for marine operators. But the modern cases still frequently reflect the view that P&I coverage is derivative of and supplementary to the more basic hull coverage.

Standard Oil Co. v. United States

Supreme Court of the United States, 1950
340 U.S. 54, 71 S. Ct. 135, 95 L.Ed. 68, 1951 AMC 1

Mr. Justice BLACK delivered the opinion of the Court.

These are admiralty proceedings involving the Government's liability on a policy of war risk insurance by which it insured petitioner's steam tanker *John Worthington* against "all consequences of hostilities or warlike operations."[1] Stipulated facts show that on December 16, 1942, there was a collision between the *Worthington* and the *YMS-12*, one of three United States Navy minesweepers clearing the channel approaches to New York harbor. Both vessels were at fault in failing "to comply with the applicable rules" of good seamanship "under the circumstances."

* * * [We] are asked only to determine whether as a matter of law the provision insuring against "all consequences of ... warlike operations" covered the loss resulting from collision between the *Worthington* and the minesweeper. Of course, the intention of the contracting parties would control this decision, but as is so often the case, that intention is not readily

1. The quoted language comes from the "F.C. & S. Clause" ("Free from Capture and Seizure") and is incorporated by reference in the war risk policy. War risk insurance is written in the following manner: The marine policy, which covers common perils of the sea, generally contains an "F.C. & S. Clause" eliminating from coverage certain named war risks, one of which is "all consequences of hostilities or warlike operations." The excepted risks are insured against either by adding a rider to the original marine policy, or by buying coverage from another underwriter—here the Government—who insures the perils excluded by [the] "F.C. & S. Clause." * * *

ascertainable. Losses from collisions are prima facie perils of the sea covered by standard marine risk policies. To take such a loss out of the marine policy and to bring it within the coverage of the provision insuring against "all consequences of" warlike operations, common sense dictates that there must be some causal relationship between the warlike operation and the collision. * * * [T]he existence or non-existence of causal connection between the peril insured against and the loss [is] determined by looking to the factual situation in each case and applying the concept of "proximate cause." Proximate cause in the insurance field has been variously defined. It has been said that proximate cause referred to the "cause nearest to the loss." Again, courts have properly stated that proximate cause "does not necessarily refer to the cause nearest in point of time to the loss. But the true meaning of that maxim is, that it refers to that cause which is most nearly and essentially connected with the loss as its efficient cause."

In view of the foregoing, can it be said that the Court of Appeals erred in failing to hold as a matter of law that the mine-sweeping, a warlike operation, was the "predominate and determining" cause of the collision? * * * [R]easonable triers of fact considering all of the circumstances of this collision might differ as to whether the loss was predominately or proximately caused by usual navigational hazards (and therefore an ordinary marine insurance risk) or whether it was caused by extraordinary perils stemming from the minesweeping (and therefore a war insurance risk). Indeed, the District Court and the Court of Appeals did differ on this factual determination. Since certiorari was not granted to consider that divergence in the findings of fact, we need go no further than to hold that the courts below properly considered the case as depending on the resolution of factual questions.

Petitioner nevertheless contends that (1) we are bound by certain decisions in the House of Lords and (2) these opinions have announced a rule-of-thumb construction of the phrase "all consequences of ... warlike operations" under which the facts in this case result in war risk liability as a matter of law. We cannot accept these arguments. It is true that we and other American courts have emphasized the desirability of uniformity in decisions here and in England in interpretation and enforcement of marine insurance contracts. Especially is uniformity desirable where, as here, the particular form of words employed originated in England. But this does not mean that American courts must follow House of Lords' decisions automatically. Actually our practice is no more than to accord respect to established doctrines of English maritime law.

The difficulties inherent in the rigid conformity rule urged by petitioner are obvious to those familiar with the search for state decisional law under the *Erie-Tompkins* doctrine. In this very case, we, like the Court of Appeals, cannot be sure what conclusion the House of Lords would reach were this case presented to it. Some of their decisions indicate that they would have held as a matter of law that the collision was the "consequence" of the warlike operation; other cases cannot easily be reconciled with such a result. * * *

The proximate cause method of determining on the facts of each case whether a loss was the "consequence" of warlike operations may fall short of achieving perfect results. For those insured and those insuring cannot predict with certainty what a trier of fact might decide is the predominant cause of loss. But neither could they predict with certainty what particular state of facts might cause a court to discover liability "as a matter of law." Long experience with the proximate cause method in American and English courts has at least proven it adaptable and useful in marine and other insurance cases. There is no reason to believe that its application in this case will disappoint the just expectations of insurer or insured.

The judgment of the Court of Appeals is affirmed.

Mr. Justice FRANKFURTER, joined by Mr. Justice Jackson, dissenting.

* * *

The only question before the Court is whether the collision was a "consequence" of the warlike operation, or, in the jargon of insurance cases, whether the warlike operation was the "proximate cause" of the collision. "Proximate cause," as a requirement of liability under an insurance policy, is not a technical legal conception but a convenient tag for the law's response to good sense. It is shorthand for saying that there must be such a nexus between the policy term under which insurance money is claimed and the events giving rise to the loss that it can be fairly declared that the loss was within the risk assumed. The case is one of "common-sense accommodation of judgment to kaleidoscopic situations." [ ]

Unlike obligations flowing from duties imposed upon people willy-nilly, an insurance policy is a voluntary undertaking by which obligations are voluntarily assumed. Therefore the subtleties and sophistries of tort liability for negligence are not to be applied in construing the covenants of a policy. It is one thing for the law to impose liability by its own notions of responsibility, and quite another to construe the scope of engagements bought and paid for. The law of marine insurance is concerned with and reflects the practicalities of commercial dealings. The law does not play an unreal metaphysical game of trying to find a single isolatable factor as the sole responsibility to which is to be attributed a loss against which insurance has been bought. As a matter of experience and reason such losses are invariably the resultant of a combination of factors. The scope of the undertaking to cover for such losses is partly the law's confirmation of the settled understanding of those whose business is shipping—their understanding of what contingencies the undertaking covered. It is partly the law's endeavor, in view of the inevitable treacheries of language, to shield the insurer from liability for a loss on the basis of a factor too remote, and therefore too tenuous, in the combination of elements that converged toward the loss.

* * *

The collision occurred between 5 and 6 a.m. on December 16, 1942, in the swept channel in the approaches to New York harbor. The *YMS-12* was proceeding seaward with her mine-sweeping gear streamed. She was the starboard vessel in a formation of three mine sweepers engaged in sweeping the buoyed channel. In the words of the District Judge, who questioned counsel closely on the way in which mine sweeping was carried on:

> * * * The *YMS-12* and the two accompanying vessels, in mine sweeping formation, proceeding with mine sweeping gear streamed and trailing paravanes,[2] presented an unusual and unexpected obstacle to navigation. *YMS-105* was the guide ship of the formation, the *YMS-12* was stationed several hundred yards on the starboard beam of the *YMS-105* and the third vessel in the formation, the *AMC-95*, was echelon to the right of the guide ship, in a position approximately a half mile astern and midway between the *YMS-105* and the *YMS-12*. From the time of the encounter until actual collision the vessels continued in their mine sweeping operations with their paravanes trailing; in all her manoeuvres and in her navigation the *YMS-12* was necessarily restricted and impeded. This unusual formation, of which the *YMS-12* was a part, closed to the *S. S. John Worthington* lanes of

2. Editors' note: A paravane is a device equipped with sharp teeth and towed alongside a ship to cut the mooring cables of submerged mines.

navigation affording possible escape which would ordinarily have been open to her.

* * *

Whether the Court of Appeals reached its decision by application of an erroneous rule of law [or] by the erroneous application of the proper rule of law * * * is not clear. In [either] case, it should be reversed. If the matter is viewed simply—according to the fair judgment of men of commerce and clear of beclouding abstractions—one can hardly escape the conclusion of the District Court. The fact that the English courts have reached the same conclusion in similar cases does not weaken its force.

* * *

Mr. Justice DOUGLAS, dissenting.

We have here a question not of tort liability but of the determination of insurance coverage. The accidents which had been held to be covered by this insurance clause prior to 1942, when this contract was made, would therefore seem to be the reliable standards for interpretation. *Board of Trade v. Hain S.S. Co.*, [1929] A.C. 534, and *Attorney General v. Adelaide S.S. Co.*, [1923] A.C. 292, dealt with this precise situation and held that where a ship engaged in a warlike operation collided with another vessel partly or wholly due to faulty navigation on its part the war insurer was liable. Adherence to British precedents in this field was early admonished. *Queen Insurance Co. v. Globe Insurance Co.*, 263 U.S. 487 (1924). The rule of the foregoing English cases is for me the most authentic standard for interpreting the present contract. * * *

Notes

1. **Deference to England.** While English law is not binding in U.S. courts, it is often an excellent guide. The British Marine Insurance Act of 1906 (6 Edw. 7, c. 41) is an important codification that has been widely copied in the common-law world. Justice Holmes's opinion for the Court in *Queen Insurance Co.* stated that "[t]here are special reasons for keeping in harmony with the marine insurance laws of England, the great field of the business." 263 U.S. at 493. Two such reasons are England's longer and deeper expertise and the interdependency of the British and U.S. insurance markets: The same ship may well have part of its coverage in London and part in New York.

2. **Proximate cause "analysis" in other "kaleidoscopic situations."**(a) In *Lanasa Fruit Steamship & Importing Co. v. Universal Insurance Co.*, 302 U.S. 556, 562 (1938), a cargo policy covered losses resulting from stranding but not from decay. Plaintiff's bananas rotted while the ship was stranded. The court held that "the stranding should be regarded as the proximate cause of the loss." (b) The cargo policy in *Kimta A/S v. Royal Insurance Co.*, 9 P.3d 239, 242 (Wash. App. 2000), covered harms resulting from the master's negligent management of the ship but excluded harms resulting from "seizure." When the master of the ship negligently refused an order to return to port, the Russian authorities confiscated the cargo. The court held that the "dominant or 'efficient'" cause of the loss was the seizure. (c) In *Tillery v. Hull & Co.*, 876 F.2d 1517, 1520 (11th Cir. 1989), a hull policy on a fishing boat called the *Texas Pride* covered losses resulting from barratry (deliberate misconduct by master or crew) but excluded losses resulting from "seizure." The master took the *Texas Pride* from its fishing grounds to Jamaica for marijuana, where it was seized and damaged by the authorities. The court held that "the ultimate cause" of the loss was seizure, not barratry. (d) When four armed crew members identifying

themselves as Sandinistas took over the ship and diverted it to Cuba, the "real efficient cause" of the resultant losses was the Nicaraguan civil war (an excluded peril) rather than barratry (a covered peril). *Ope Shipping, Ltd. v. Allstate Insurance Co.*, 687 F.2d 639, 641 (2d Cir. 1982). (e) When the crews of several Nationalist Chinese ships defected (with the ships) to the Chinese Communist government, the resulting losses were ascribed to barratry (a covered peril) rather than to "capture and seizure." *National Union Fire Insurance Co. v. Republic of China*, 254 F.2d 177, 187 (4th Cir. 1958). (f) *Continental Insurance Co. v. Lone Eagle Shipping Ltd.*, 134 F.3d 103 (2d Cir. 1998), exonerated a hull insurer on concluding that the proximate cause of the damage in suit was the ship's poor condition, not perils of the sea in the form of heavy winds and high swells.

3. **Marine insurance cases in the Supreme Court**. From 1800 through 1954, the Court decided hundreds of marine insurance cases, many of them involving seemingly routine, even minuscule, substantive points. Then it handed down its infamous *Wilburn Boat* decision. Since *Wilburn Boat*, the Court has lapsed into virtual silence on marine insurance law. In dozens of subsequent marine insurance cases, it has routinely denied certiorari.

Wilburn Boat Co. v. Fireman's Fund Insurance Co.

Supreme Court of the United States, 1955
348 U.S. 310, 75 S. Ct. 368, 99 L. Ed. 337, 1955 AMC 467

Mr. Justice BLACK delivered the opinion of the Court.

This case raises questions concerning the power of States to regulate the terms and conditions of marine insurance contracts.

Glenn, Frank and Henry Wilburn, merchants in Denison, Texas, bought a small houseboat to use for commercial carriage of passengers on nearby Lake Texoma, an artificial inland lake between Texas and Oklahoma. The respondent Firemen's Fund Insurance Company insured the boat against loss from fire and other perils. While moored on the lake the boat was destroyed by fire. Following respondent's refusal to pay for the loss, this suit was brought in a Texas state court by the Wilburns and by their wholly owned corporation, the Wilburn Boat Company, to which the boat's legal title had been transferred. After removal of the case to the United States District Court because of diversity, respondent answered, admitting issuance of the policy, payment of premiums and destruction of the boat. Liability was denied, however, because of alleged breaches of printed policy terms or "warranties," providing that, without written consent of the company, the boat could not be sold, transferred, assigned, pledged, hired or chartered, and must be used solely for private pleasure purposes. The case was submitted on stipulated facts supplemented by oral testimony. Contending that the evidence showed the policy contract to have been made and delivered in Texas, petitioners urged that all questions concerning alleged policy breaches were controlled by Texas law. If Texas law does govern, the policy provision against pledging may be wholly invalid. Furthermore, no breach by the insured of the provisions of a fire insurance policy is a defense to any suit under Texas law unless the breach contributes to the loss. Without finding whether the policy had been made and delivered in Texas, the court refused to give that State's law any effect at all, holding that since a marine policy is a maritime contract, federal admiralty law—not state law—governed. The court went on to hold that there is an established admiralty rule which requires literal fulfillment of every policy warranty so that any breach bars recovery, even though a loss would have happened had the warranty been carried out to the letter. Finding that the Wilburns had breached policy provisions against transfer, pledge and use of the boat, the District Court entered judgment for the insurance company. Approving the District Court's actions in all respects, the Court of Appeals affirmed, saying that "It is the settled doctrine that a marine contract of insurance is 'derived from,' is 'governed by,' and is a 'part of' the general maritime law of the world." Importance of the questions involved prompted us to grant certiorari.[6]

Since the insurance policy here sued on is a maritime contract the Admiralty Clause of the Constitution brings it within federal jurisdiction. *Insurance Co. v. Dunham* [*supra* at 51]. But it does not follow, as the courts below seemed to think, that every term in every maritime contract can only be controlled by some federally defined admiralty rule. In the field of maritime contracts as in that of maritime torts, the National Government has left much regulatory power in the States. As later discussed in more detail, this state regulatory power, exercised with federal consent or acquiescence, has always been particularly broad in relation to insurance companies and the contracts they make.

Congress has not taken over the regulation of marine insurance contracts and has not dealt with the effect of marine insurance warranties at all; hence there is no possible question here of conflict between state law and any federal statute. But this does not answer the questions presented, since in the absence of controlling Acts of Congress this Court has fashioned a large part of the existing rules that govern admiralty. And States can no more override such judicial rules validly fashioned than they can override Acts of Congress. [ ] Consequently the crucial questions in this case narrow down to these: (1) Is there a judicially established federal admiralty rule governing these warranties? (2) If not, should we fashion one?

The only decision of this Court relied on by the Court of Appeals to support its holding that there is an established admiralty rule requiring strict fulfillment of marine insurance warranties was *Imperial Fire Insurance Co. v. Coos County*, 151 U.S. 452 [1894]. There, because of a breach of warranty, an insurance company was relieved of liability for loss of a courthouse by fire, and this Court said it was immaterial whether the breach contributed to the loss. But no question of marine insurance was remotely involved nor was there any reliance on a marine insurance rule. Writing its own "general commercial law," as was the custom in diversity cases prior to *Erie R. Co. v. Tompkins* [*supra* at 119], this Court in the *Coos County* case simply followed a general doctrine commonly applied to warranties in all types of insurance. A mere cursory examination of the cases, state and federal, will disclose that through the years this common-law doctrine, when accepted, has been treated not as an admiralty rule but as a general warranty rule applicable to many types of contracts including marine and other insurance. There are very few federal cases on marine insurance in which the strict breach of warranty rule has even been considered. And only two circuits appear to have thought of the rule as a part of the general admiralty law. On the contrary, other circuit court decisions, including the ones relied on in those few cases holding the rule to be one of federal admiralty, seem to indicate state law was followed in applying the rule or that the question was decided as one of "general commercial law," a uniform practice during the era of *Swift v. Tyson*, [41 U.S. (16 Pet.) 1 (1842)]. This Court did say in one marine insurance case that warranties "must be strictly and literally performed." [ ] But there is not the slightest indication that this statement referred to a

6. The Court of Appeals assumed that if any state law applied it was that of Texas. The question of the appropriate state law is not before us, however, and we express no opinion on that aspect of the case. * * *

federal admiralty rule and the Court in fact expressly followed and applied Massachusetts law to decide another question in that very case. Whatever the origin of the "literal performance" rule may be, we think it plain that it has not been judicially established as part of the body of federal admiralty law in this country. Therefore, the scope and validity of the policy provisions here involved and the consequences of breaching them can only be determined by state law unless we are now prepared to fashion controlling federal rules.

The whole judicial and legislative history of insurance regulation in the United States warns us against the judicial creation of admiralty rules to govern marine policy terms and warranties. The control of all types of insurance companies and contracts has been primarily a state function since the States came into being. * * *

Not only courts, but Congress, insurance companies, and those insured have all acted on the assumption that States can regulate marine insurance. * * * [The] McCarran Act [of 1945, 15 U.S.C. §§ 1011–15] was designed to assure that existing state power to regulate insurance would continue. Accordingly, the Act contains a broad declaration of congressional policy that the continued regulation of insurance by the States is in the public interest, and that silence on the part of Congress should not be construed to impose any barrier to continued regulation of insurance by the States.

The hearings on the McCarran Act reveal the complexities and difficulties of an attempt to unify insurance law on a nationwide basis, even by Congress. Courts would find such a task far more difficult. Congress in passing laws is not limited to the narrow factual situation of a particular controversy as courts are in deciding lawsuits. And Congress could replace the presently functioning State regulations of marine insurance by one comprehensive Act. Courts, however, could only do it piecemeal, on a case-by-case basis. Such a creeping approach would result in leaving marine insurance largely unregulated for years to come.

In this very case, should we attempt to fashion an admiralty rule governing policy provisions, we would at once be faced with the difficulty of determining what should be the consequences of breaches. We could adopt the old common-law doctrine of forfeiting all right of recovery in the absence of strict and literal performance of warranties, but that is a harsh rule. Most States, deeming the old rule a breeder of wrong and injustice, have abandoned it in whole or in part. But that has left open the question of what kind of new rule could be substituted that would be fair both to insurance companies and policy holders. Out of their abundant broad experience in regulating the insurance business, some state legislatures have adopted one kind of new rule and some another. Some States for example have denied companies the right to forfeit policies in the absence of an insured's bad faith or fraud. Other States have thought this kind of rule inadequate to stamp out forfeiture practices deemed evil. The result, as this Court has pointed out, has been state statutes like that of Texas which "go to the root of the evil" and forbid forfeiture for an insured's breach of policy terms unless the breach actually contributes to bring about the loss insured against. [ ] Thus there are a number of other possible rules from which this Court could fashion one for admiralty. But such a choice involves varied policy considerations and is obviously one which Congress is peculiarly suited to make. And we decline to undertake the task. [ ]

Under our present system of diverse state regulations, which is as old as the Union, the insurance business has become one of the great enterprises of the Nation. Congress has been exceedingly cautious about disturbing this system, even as to marine insurance where congressional power is undoubted. We, like Congress, leave the regulation of marine insurance where it has been—with the States.

The judgments of the Court of Appeals and the District Court are reversed and the cause is remanded to the District Court for a trial under appropriate state law.

Mr. Justice FRANKFURTER, concurring in the result.

* * * [T]he only question now to be decided is whether the demands of uniformity relevant to maritime law require that marine insurance on a houseboat yacht brought to Lake Texoma for private recreation should be subject to the same rules of law as marine insurance on a houseboat yacht "confined," after arrival, to the waters of Lake Tahoe or Lake Champlain. The provision of the policy whereby the insured warranted "that the vessel will be confined to Lake Texoma" conveys the emphasis of the situation—the essentially localized incidence of the transaction * * *. It is reasonable to conclude that the interests concerned with shipping in its national and international aspects are substantially unconcerned with the rules of law to be applied to such limited situations. I join in a result restricted within this compass.

Unfortunately, for reasons that I do not appreciate, the Court's opinion goes beyond the needs of the problem before it. Unless I wholly misconceive that opinion, its language would be invoked when cases so decisively different in degree as to be different in kind come before this Court. It seems directed with equal force to ocean-going vessels in international maritime trade, as well as coastal, intercoastal and river commerce. Is it to be assumed that were the *Queen Mary*, on a world pleasure cruise, to touch at New York City, New Orleans and Galveston, a Lloyd's policy covering the voyage would be subjected to the varying insurance laws of New York, Louisiana and Texas? Such an assumption, I am confident, would not prevail were decision necessary. The business of marine insurance often may be so related to the success of many manifestations of commercial maritime endeavor as to demand application of a uniform rule of law designed to eliminate the vagaries of state law and to keep harmony with the marine insurance laws of other great maritime powers. See *Queen Ins. Co. of America v. Globe Ins. Co.*, 263 U.S. 487, 493 [1924]; *Calmar Steamship Corp. v. Scott*, 345 U.S. 427, 442–443 [1953]. It cannot be that by this decision the Court means suddenly to jettison the whole past of the admiralty provision of Article III and to renounce requirements for nationwide maritime uniformity, except insofar as Congress has specifically enacted them, in the field of marine insurance.

* * *

[Justice Reed, joined by Justice Burton, dissented.]

Notes

1. Like Justice Frankfurter, the Fifth Circuit had trouble believing Justice Black really meant what he had seemed to say. On remand in *Wilburn Boat*, the trial judge applied Texas law to hold that the insured's breaches of express warranties did not defeat coverage under the hull policy. Reversing and ordering judgment for the insurance company, the Fifth Circuit held that the insured's conduct in using the boat to carry passengers for hire was not only a breach of warranty but also entailed a misrepresentation. From the time the Wilburns applied for the insurance policy, they knew that they meant to use the boat commercially; at no time did they disclose that intention and use to the insurer. Under a well-established principle often called *uberrimae fidei* (which translates as "utmost good faith"), an insured owes the insurer a demanding duty to reveal anything that a prudent underwriter might consider to be material to the decision whether to undertake the risk and what premium to charge. The Fifth Circuit held that the principle applied:

> Nothing is better established in the law of *marine* insurance than that "a mistake or commission material to a marine risk, whether it be wilful or accidental, or result from mistake, negligence or voluntary ignorance, avoids the policy." * * * Although we have found no Texas case expressly applying this rule, there is no indication that the Texas courts have departed from this firmly established principle of marine insurance.

Fireman's Fund Insurance Co. v. Wilburn Boat Co., 300 F.2d 631, 646–47 (5th Cir. 1962). On the choice-of-law question, the court of appeals suggested that federal maritime law should properly apply, but that the result would be the same:

> We are merely assuming here that Texas law is applicable to a defense of concealment raised in connection with a marine insurance policy. There is good reason behind appellant's argument that federal maritime law, rather than state law, governs that issue. Appellant contends, and we agree, that [the Supreme Court's decision] merely held that state law is to be applied in the field of marine insurance only where "entrenched federal precedent is lacking" with respect to a specific issue. * * * Since the [*uberrimae fidei* doctrine] is solidly entrenched in our body of federal maritime law [ ], it would seem that this rule should apply in the instant case. Because, however, we believe the same rule obtains in Texas, this point is of minimal significance to a decision here.

Id. at 647 n.12. The Supreme Court declined to review that decision; Justice Black's was the only recorded vote for certiorari.

2. For many informed observers, *Wilburn Boat* is the Supreme Court's most disappointing maritime-law decision. In a detailed article, Professor Joel Goldstein demolishes the opinion's reasoning and demonstrates the difficulties that lower courts have experienced in determining the content, if any, of the federal maritime law of marine insurance and in deciding when to resort to state law in marine insurance cases (and which state's law to apply when necessary). Goldstein, *The Lives and Times of Wilburn Boat: A Critical Guide*, 28 J. Mar. L. & Com. 395, 555 (1997). The case inspired calls for a federal statute patterned after the British Marine Insurance Act of 1906, see, e.g., Cattell, *An American Marine Insurance Act: An Idea Whose Time Has Come*, 20 Tul. Mar. L.J. 1 (1995), and an unsuccessful effort to persuade the American Law Institute to promulgate a Restatement of Marine Insurance Law, see Sturley, *Restating the Law of Marine Insurance: A Workable Solution to the Wilburn Boat Problem*, 29 J. Mar. L. & Com. 41 (1998). A distinguished practitioner argues that *Wilburn Boat* has been implicitly overruled. *See* Staring, *Wilburn Boat Is A Dead Letter: R.I.P.*, 42 J. Mar. L. & Com. 465 (2011).

3. The following case illustrates some of the difficulties that lower courts have experienced in applying *Wilburn Boat.*

Albany Insurance Co. v. Anh Thi Kieu

United States Court of Appeals, Fifth Circuit, 1991
927 F.2d 882, 1991 AMC 2211

JOHNSON, Circuit Judge:

Oblivious to the tangled mess it has left the practitioner to decipher, this Court has extended numerous—and often seemingly inconsistent—explanations of the appropriate choice of law in marine insurance disputes. Our task in the instant appeal is to untie the Gordian knot. Albany Insurance Company ("Albany") challenges the district court's declaration that appellee Anh Thi Kieu recover some $90,405 in damages and "sue and labor" charges under a marine insurance contract. The district court determined that Texas insurance law, and not federal maritime or Louisiana insurance law, governed the parties' rights and obligations. Unable to conclude that the district court committed reversible error, this Court affirms the judgment of the district court.

I. FACTS AND PROCEDURAL HISTORY

In February 1988, Anh Thi Kieu, a Vietnamese immigrant who resides in Texas, attempted to secure marine hull insurance coverage on the *F/V Stacy Marie*, a sixty-five foot shrimping vessel. An independent agent, the Edgar Coco Agency, Inc., of Marksville, Louisiana, submitted to Anh Thi Kieu an application for insurance coverage from Albany Insurance Company. Although it was printed in English, Anh Thi Kieu completed the application. The Edgar Coco Agency forwarded the application to Albany's general agent, G & M Insurance Company. On March 1, 1988, Albany approved coverage of the *Stacy Marie* and forwarded a policy to Anh Thi Kieu.

It is undisputed that Anh Thi Kieu's application for insurance coverage contained several inaccurate statements. Among other things, Anh Thi Kieu recited (1) that she regularly operated the *Stacy Marie* as captain, (2) that the vessel had sustained no damages in the last five years, and (3) that she had purchased the vessel for $110,000. In truth, Anh Thi Kieu purchased the *Stacy Marie* in 1984 for $30,000 and assembled an independent crew to guide the vessel in fishing and shrimping operations off the coast of Port Arthur, Texas. Late in 1984, the *Stacy Marie* collided with an offshore repair boat and suffered minor damage that was repaired by a marine shipyard in Freeport, Texas. Albany Insurance Company had ample opportunity to discover these facts and cancel coverage. Instead, Albany continued to receive premiums from Anh Thi Kieu and to extend coverage on the *Stacy Marie*.

On November 3, 1988, the *Stacy Marie* allided with an unmarked offshore Department of Energy platform. The allision damaged the hull planking on the vessel and opened a gaping hole on its port bow. Assisted by the Coast Guard and another shrimp boat, the crew of the *Stacy Marie* successfully floated the vessel to Sabine Pass, Texas. There, Sabine Offshore Services, Inc. ("Sabine Offshore"), agreed to place the *Stacy Marie* in dry storage in its dock yard. Anh Thi Kieu apparently secured these dry storage arrangements with Sabine Offshore in an effort to "save and preserve" the *Stacy Marie*.

After learning from Anh Thi Kieu that the vessel had suffered an allision, Albany investigators surveyed the damage. The investigators recommended that Albany deny any liability under the marine hull insurance policy. Subsequently, Albany filed a declaratory judgment action in federal district court requesting a declaration of Anh Thi Kieu's rights in the policy. The district court entered findings of fact and conclusions of law [declaring] that Anh Thi Kieu should recover the insured value of the *Stacy Marie* ($90,000) minus the salvage value of the vessel's hull ($15,000)—a total of $75,000 in damages. In addition, the court ordered that Anh Thi Kieu recover $15,405 in "sue and labor" charges—an amount intended to cover the storage fees at Sabine Offshore.

II. DISCUSSION

Albany raises a number of arguments on appeal. The most significant of these arguments attack the district court's application of Texas insurance law. Albany argues that the district court erroneously applied Texas insurance law and instead should have applied the federal law of *uberrimae fidei*. In the alternative, Albany argues that the district court should have applied Louisiana insurance law instead of Texas insurance law. * * *

A. *Maritime Preemption*

Albany contends that the federal law of *uberrimae fidei*, which invalidates marine insurance contracts on evidence of the assured's material misrepresentations to the underwriter, supports its denial of liability on the policy covering the *Stacy Marie*. Anh Thi Kieu responds that relevant provisions of the Texas Insurance Code preclude Albany's denial of coverage. The issue is simply stated, but the law is complex: does federal maritime law or state insurance regulation determine the effect of an assured's misrepresentations? * * *

In *Wilburn Boat Co. v. Fireman's Fund Insurance Co.* [*supra* at 461], the United States Supreme Court concluded that the regulation of marine insurance is, in most instances, properly left with the states. [ ] Following the direction of the Court in *Wilburn Boat*, the Fifth Circuit has ruled that "the interpretation of a contract of marine insurance is—in the absence of a specific and controlling federal rule—to be determined by reference to appropriate state law." [ ] This presumption of state law is, by now, "axiomatic." [ ] State law, therefore, governs the interpretation of marine insurance policies unless an available federal maritime rule controls the disputed issue. This Circuit has identified three factors that a court should consider in determining if a federal maritime rule controls the disputed issue: (1) whether the federal maritime rule constitutes "entrenched federal precedent" [ ]; (2) whether the state has a substantial and legitimate interest in the application of its law [ ]; (3) whether the state's rule is materially different from the federal maritime rule [ ]. These factors are merely instructive and not dispositive. We address them in reverse order.

State insurance law generally should not govern marine insurance disputes if it is materially different from federal maritime law. The application of state law inconsistent with the core principles of maritime law "would defeat the reasonably settled expectations of maritime actors." [ ] While there is no requirement that state insurance regulations precisely mirror parallel federal regulations, state law should not be applied unless it bears a reasonable similarity to the federal maritime practice. We find a reasonable similarity between the applicable federal and state laws in the instant case. Under the *uberrimae fidei* doctrine, an assured's material misrepresentations invalidate the policy of insurance *ab initio*. [ ] Under Texas law, an assured's misrepresentations may invalidate the policy of insurance, but only if the insured intended to deceive the insurer. [ ] Texas law, unlike federal law, imposes an appropriate limitation that relatively minor misstatements which the insured did not intend to make do not afford the insurer an excuse to refuse payment. The fundamental nature of both laws, however, is the same. Texas insurance law shares the concern of federal maritime law that an assured should not profit from her material misrepresentations to the underwriter.

State insurance law generally should not govern marine insurance disputes if the state does not have a substantial and legitimate interest in the application of its law. Federal maritime law properly controls any maritime dispute in the absence of a substantial and legitimate state interest. Stated conversely, state law should not be applied unless the local state interest materially exceeds the comparative maritime concerns in the controversy. [ ] It is evident in the instant case that the local state interest is substantial and legitimate. Regulation of insurance relationships, including marine insurance relationships, has historically been a matter of state concern. [ ] From their experience, states are far better equipped to balance the risks that each party to an insurance contract endures. The State of Texas has concluded that the burden of unintentional misrepresentations should fall on the insurance underwriter. Texas has a material interest in ensuring that marine insurance underwriters do not invalidate the insurance protection of Texas citizens on the basis of misrepresentations that were neither willfully [nor] intentionally asserted.

State insurance law generally should not govern marine insurance disputes if an existing federal maritime rule constitutes "entrenched federal precedent." Maritime law, as federal common law, supersedes state law if the maritime law specifically governs the conduct in question and consistently has been invoked to control such conduct. In the absence of preexisting entrenched federal maritime law, this Court will refuse to impose unfamiliar federal common law maritime requirements on the parties to a marine insurance contract. [ ] The application of unfamiliar federal maritime rules engenders undesirable uncertainty among maritime actors; this Court can easily avoid such uncertainty by the application of "already well-developed state laws." [ ]

The question whether the *uberrimae fidei* doctrine is entrenched federal precedent is troublesome. Repeated references to the doctrine appear in early United States Supreme Court opinions. [ ] The Supreme Court applied the *uberrimae fidei* doctrine as a "traditional" aspect of insurance law in general. [ ] As mentioned, though, insurance law is typically a matter of state concern. Over the years most states abandoned the strict *uberrimae fidei* articulation. Today, the sole remaining substantial vestige of the doctrine is in maritime insurance law. [ ]

Even under maritime law, the federal courts have rarely invoked the *uberrimae fidei* doctrine. Despite the long history of the doctrine in the Supreme Court, only three cases—two of which date from the 1960s—have examined the availability of the doctrine in this Circuit. Each of these cases has confidently asserted that the doctrine is "well recognized" in federal law. Indeed, in *Fireman's Fund Insurance Co. v. Wilburn Boat Co.* [ ], the Court expressly declared that the *uberrimae fidei* doctrine "is solidly entrenched in our body of federal maritime law." [ ].[4] * * * [But] the Court assumed, without formally deciding, that the *uberrimae fidei* doctrine was controlling federal precedent. The Court nonetheless resolved [the] case on state law grounds, concluding that state insurance law would not permit the [plaintiff] to recover. * * * [T]he Court remarked that, because Texas law would not afford relief anyway, the applicability of the *uberrimae fidei* doctrine was "of minimal significance." [ ] * * * [In all three cases, the] expression of the significance of the doctrine was mere dicta.

It is the accepted practice of this Court that one panel cannot overturn the decisions of another. [ ] None of the opinions of this Court which have cited the *uberrimae fidei* doctrine *authoritatively* conclude, however, that the doctrine applies to the exclusion of state law. For that matter, no opinion of this Court has ever explicitly authorized the application of the *uberrimae fidei* doctrine to invalidate a marine insurance policy. The *uberrimae fidei* doctrine, in sum, is a rule which this Court has recognized, *but never applied.* We therefore conclude, albeit with some hesitation, that the *uberrimae fidei* doctrine is not "entrenched federal precedent."

* * *

* * * Perhaps the doctrine was [once] "entrenched federal precedent" * * * but its spotty application in recent years—even in other circuits[6]—suggests that the *uberrimae fidei* doctrine is entrenched no more.

---

4. The Court's opinion in *Fireman's Fund Insurance Co.* was rendered on remand from the Supreme Court's reversal of this Circuit's original conclusion that a marine insurance contract should be interpreted under general maritime law requiring literal performance of warranties. [ ] [See *supra* at 464–65 note 1.]

6. We recognize that our sister circuit, the Eleventh Circuit, has concluded that the *uberrimae fidei* doctrine is well settled and "as a clear rule of maritime law it is the controlling federal rule even in the face of contrary state authority." *Steelmet, Inc. v. Caribe Towing Corp.*, 747 F.2d 689, 695 (11th

Concluding, as we do, that all three factors a court should consider in the marine insurance preemption analysis favor the application of state law, we therefore must examine the relevant state law to determine the viability of Anh Thi Kieu's request for compensation. * * *

B. *Choice of State Law*

After concluding that federal maritime law does not govern the assured's right to payment on the marine insurance policy, we next must determine whether Texas or Louisiana insurance law applies. Albany argues that, even if federal maritime law does not apply, the district court should have applied a similarly strict Louisiana law. Although a federal court customarily applies the choice of law rules of the forum in which it is located [ ], the court in maritime cases must apply general federal maritime choice of law rules. [ ] In this case, we must consider the choice of law rules which specifically govern marine insurance disputes.

The decisions of this Court that attempt to explain the proper choice of state insurance law governing the interpretation of marine insurance policies are seemingly in conflict. This Court has held that "the law of the state in which the [insurance] contract was formed" determines the parties' rights. [ ] It has held that "the law of the state where the marine insurance contract was issued and delivered is the governing law." [ ] It has held that "[i]n identifying the appropriate state law to apply, we look to the state having the greatest interest in the resolution of the issues." [ ] Considered separately under the circumstances of this particular appeal, these choice of law rules point the Court in entirely different directions: the contract was countersigned and therefore likely formed in Louisiana; it was issued in Louisiana but delivered in Texas; and Texas appears to have the greatest interest in the application of its law.

Nonetheless, we believe that we can reconcile these seemingly inconsistent choice of law rules. Modern choice of law analysis, whether maritime or not, generally requires the application of the law of the state with the "most significant relationship" to the substantive issue in question. *See* Restatement (Second) of Conflict of Laws § 6 (1980). In contract cases, courts must consider such factors as the place of formation of the contract and the place of negotiation of the contract to determine which states have sufficient contact with the transaction and the parties to support the application of their law. *Id.* § 188 (1971). However, the application of the most significant relationship approach does not simply turn on the number of contacts each state has with the controversy. The most significant relationship approach instead examines the relative interests of *all* of the states which share a sufficient relationship with the transaction and the parties. *Id.* § 6.

We conclude that the first two choice of law rules this Court has applied in marine insurance disputes * * * identify only the states which have sufficient contact with the policy and the parties that their laws *can* be applied. The third choice of law rule—requiring the application of the law of the state with the greatest interest—identifies the state law that *should* be applied. A federal court in a marine insurance dispute must apply the first two rules to isolate the "eligible" states; of these states, the court then must determine which state has "the greatest interest in the resolution of the issues." [ ]

Cir. 1984). However, the Eleventh Circuit itself has retreated from this broad view and held that state law may in at least some circumstances control to the exclusion of the *uberrimae fidei* doctrine. *See King v. Allstate Ins. Co.*, 906 F.2d 1537, 1540 (11th Cir. 1990) (parties to a marine insurance policy may agree to the application of state law).

A review of the first two choice of law rules reveals that both Texas and Louisiana have sufficient contact with the marine insurance policy and the parties to support the application of their insurance laws. Of these two states, Texas has a considerably greater interest in the application of its insurance code. Texas has a strong interest in the protection of its citizens, including Anh Thi Kieu, against the overbearing tactics of insurance underwriters. Louisiana's interest in the protection of citizens of foreign states is less significant. The insurance laws of Texas should have been applied, and appropriately, the district court so applied them. Albany's argument that Louisiana insurance law governs its dispute with Anh Thi Kieu lacks merit.

C. *Application of Texas Insurance Law*

[Applying Texas insurance law, the court (1) rejected Albany's misrepresentation defense because Albany failed to fulfill its burden of proof and (2) rejected Albany's warranty defenses because the breaches neither caused nor contributed to the destruction of the insured property.]

* * *

F. *Calculation of "Sue and Labor" Charges*

The district court awarded Anh Thi Kieu "sue and labor" charges in the amount of $15,405, some $8,000 short of the $23,000 requested. Even so, Albany contends that the district court's award is excessive as a matter of law. Sue and labor expenses are sums spent by the assured in an effort to mitigate damages and loss. "The purpose of the sue and labor clause [in an insurance contract] is to reimburse the insured for those expenditures which are made primarily for the benefit of the insurer to reduce or eliminate a covered loss." [ ]

* * * Testimony at trial suggested that the safest place for the *Stacy Marie* in light of its extensive damage was dry storage. If the vessel had not been stored, it likely might have capsized or sunk. Accordingly, Anh Thi Kieu, in an effort to mitigate potential damages, placed the *Stacy Marie* in the dry dock at Sabine Offshore. Anh Thi Kieu was entitled to reimbursement for these storage expenses; the court's award of $15,405 finds support in the evidence.

* * *

III. CONCLUSION

Upon consideration of the relevant choice of law principles, this Court concludes that Texas insurance law, rather than federal maritime law or Louisiana insurance law, properly governs the instant marine hull insurance dispute. The provisions of the Texas Insurance Code require that Albany compensate Anh Thi Kieu for the losses incurred by the insured vessel. Finding no reversible error in the district court's actions, this Court affirms.

Notes

1. The *Anh Thi Kieu* court's avoidance of the *uberrimae fidei* doctrine is at odds with dozens of other cases, including appellate cases in several other circuits. The Ninth Circuit, for example, explained the law as follows:

> *Uberrimae fidei* is a "long-standing federal maritime doctrine" that "applies to marine insurance contracts." [ ] *Uberrimae fidei* "imposes a duty of utmost

> good faith," [ ] so "an applicant for a marine insurance policy is bound to reveal every fact within his knowledge that is *material* to the risk." [ ] If an insured fails to do so, the insurer may rescind the policy, even if the material misrepresentation wasn't intentional. * * * *Uberrimae fidei* is a well-entrenched doctrine that protects not merely the insurer but also the integrity of the risk pool. * * *

New Hampshire Insurance Co. v. C'Est Moi, Inc., 519 F.3d 937, 938, 939 (9th Cir. 2008); see also, e.g., *Fireman's Fund Insurance Co. v. Great American Insurance Co.*, 822 F.3d 620, 633 (2d Cir. 2016); *Catlin (Syndicate 2003) at Lloyd's v. San Juan Towing & Marine Services, Inc.*, 778 F.3d 69, 80 (1st Cir. 2015); *New York Marine & General Insurance Co. v. Continental Cement Co.*, 761 F.3d 830, 839–40 (8th Cir. 2014); *AGF Marine Aviation & Transport v. Cassin*, 544 F.3d 255, 262–63 (3d Cir. 2008); *HIH Marine Services, Inc. v. Fraser*, 211 F.3d 1359, 1362–63 (11th Cir. 2000).

2. *Uberrimae fidei* is not the only marine insurance doctrine that lower federal courts have held to be sufficiently established in federal maritime law to satisfy the *Wilburn Boat* requirements. See, e.g., *Galilea, LLC v. AGCS Marine Insurance Co.*, 879 F.3d 1052, 1058 (9th Cir. 2018) (finding a settled rule on enforcing arbitration clauses); *American National Fire Insurance Co. v. Kenealy*, 72 F.3d 264, 270–271 (2d Cir. 1995) (finding a settled rule on the award of attorney's fees). Somewhat surprisingly, *Travelers Property Casualty Co. of America v. Ocean Reef Charters, LLC*, 396 F. Supp. 3d 1170, 1176 (S.D. Fla. 2019), concluded that there is "an entrenched federal rule" that "express warranties in maritime insurance contracts *must* be strictly construed in the absence of some limiting provision in the contract." Although that result seems directly contrary to *Wilburn Boat*, the court reasoned that the rule had become entrenched in the years since *Wilburn Boat*.

3. Recall that the *Wilburn Boat* Court posed two "crucial" questions. The second was whether in the absence of an established federal rule a court should fashion a new rule of marine insurance law. See *supra* at 462. Did the Fifth Circuit address that second question in *Anh Thi Kieu*? In contrast with the Fifth Circuit, the Sixth Circuit in *Aasma v. American Steamship Owners Mutual Protection & Indemnity Association*, 95 F.3d 400, 403–05 (6th Cir. 1996), fashioned a new maritime-law rule upholding the P & I Clubs' "pay to be paid"[7] clause in the face of a direct action[8] by personal injury plaintiffs with judgments against a bankrupt member. Most other circuits, however, have generally followed the same approach as the Fifth Circuit. See, e.g., *Acadia Insurance Co. v. McNeil*, 116 F.3d 599, 603 (1st Cir. 1997) (reading *Wilburn Boat* as discouraging the creation of new federal law and favoring the application of existing state law).

4. *Wilburn Boat* requires a court to determine whether a particular rule is sufficiently "established," but the Supreme Court gave very little guidance on what is required to "establish" a federal rule. The number of decisions applying the rule could logically be viewed as a relevant factor, but if a marine insurance doctrine is so firmly established that no litigant is willing to challenge it for many years, then no judicial decision can reaffirm it. Can a doctrine be so "entrenched" that as a result it becomes "entrenched no more"?

7. Under a "pay to be paid" clause, a P & I Club agrees to reimburse a member (the equivalent of a typical insurance company's policy-holder) only after the member has first paid the underlying obligation.

8. A "direct action" permits a plaintiff with a claim against an insured party to proceed directly against the liability insurer.

5. Once a court decides to apply state law in a marine insurance dispute, it may find that there is no state law on point. *5801 Associates, Ltd. v. Continental Insurance Co.*, 983 F.2d 662, 666 n.10 (5th Cir. 1993) (per curiam), for example, involved the sinking of a barge in the open seas off the coast of South Carolina. The Fifth Circuit applied Missouri law, but finding no marine insurance decision on point, it followed an automobile insurance decision.

6. There is no doubt that the Supreme Court's *Wilburn Boat* abdication and the broad call for state law have caused the lower courts many problems. But the worst problems arise in controversial areas (such as warranties or the doctrine of *uberrimae fidei*) in which state law is more likely to diverge from the traditional approaches of marine insurance. Most cases are controlled by broadly accepted general insurance principles that do not generate significant disagreement. Consider the role that state law plays in the following case.

Shaver Transportation Co. v. Travelers Indemnity Co.

United States District Court, District of Oregon, 1979
481 F. Supp. 892, 1980 AMC 393

SKOPIL, Circuit Judge, sitting by designation:

* * *

[Plaintiffs Shaver Transportation Company, a barge company, and Weyerhaeuser Company, a producer of caustic soda, entered into a contract for Shaver to transport soda from Weyerhaeuser's plant to the soda's buyer, GATX. Shaver and Weyerhaeuser arranged for marine cargo insurance with defendant, The Travelers Indemnity Company. The policy had a standard perils clause supplemented with "specially to cover" clauses.]

Shaver loaded the first shipment of caustic soda on one of its barges and transported it to the consignee, GATX. GATX refused delivery. The soda had been contaminated with tallow. It was unfit for GATX's purposes. The parties agree that contamination occurred as Shaver was loading the caustic soda aboard the barge. The barge had previously carried a load of tallow, and Shaver had not thoroughly cleaned the barge input lines.

The barge was returned to Shaver's dock. The cargo was heated to prevent the caustic soda from solidifying. A report of the contaminated cargo was made to the defendant through its insurance brokers, Johnson and Higgins (J & H). Shortly thereafter J & H notified Shaver that the contamination did not represent a recoverable loss under the defendant's marine open cargo policy.

Shaver continued to store the soda on board the barge. Shaver investigated possible on-shore storage facilities and finally contracted with a chemical salvage company for removal of the liquid. Because of the caustic nature of the cargo, Shaver incurred expenses in storage, including the cost of heating the soda and repairs to corroded boilers and pipes. Weyerhaeuser lost the value of the shipment, offset partly by the salvage value. Shaver and Weyerhaeuser notified Travelers that they claimed under the marine cargo insurance policy and tendered abandonment of the cargo to Travelers. Travelers refused the tender and denied liability under the policy.

* * *

Plaintiffs have meticulously examined the policy and argue for recovery under several theories.

* * *

I. Recovery under Perils of the Sea clause and Free from Particular Average clause

The Perils clause,[1] almost identical to ancient perils provisions dating back several hundred years [see the Lloyd's S.G. Policy *supra* at 456], defines the risks protected by the policy. [ ] In addition to a long list of "perils of the sea", the clause concludes with "and all other perils, losses, and misfortunes, that have or shall, come to the hurt, detriment, or damage to the said goods and merchandise." Plaintiff argues that the "forced" disposition of the caustic soda was like jettison (an enumerated peril) and is covered by the concluding language of the clause. That language has been interpreted to include only perils that are similar to the enumerated perils. [ ]

Whether or not I conclude the forced disposition was a type of jettison, plaintiffs are unable to show an insurable loss due to jettison. The loss—contamination of the cargo—occurred at the time of loading. The disposition of the cargo caused no loss to plaintiffs but rather an offset against previous losses. Plaintiffs cannot recover under the Perils clause of the policy.

The term "jettison" also appears in the Free from Particular Average clause.[2] * * * However, I find that a jettison did not occur in this instance. Jettison is the act of throwing overboard from a vessel a part of the cargo, in case of extreme danger, to lighten the ship. The orderly unloading and sale of the cargo to a chemical salvage company is not "jettison." Plaintiff cannot recover under the Free from Particular Average clause.

II. Recovery under Warehouse-to-Warehouse clause; Marine Extension clause; Shore Coverage clause

These clauses augment the Perils clause by defining the scope of the coverage intended. However, with the exception of the shore coverage, these clauses do not define the nature of the risks covered by the policy but merely define where physically the coverage extends.

* * *

The shore coverage clause[6] provides coverage for enumerated risks occurring on shore. Plaintiffs argue that contamination while loading is a shore accident. However, since the contamination occurred within the barge's intake lines, the incident arose "on board."

---

1. (Clause 39) "Touching the adventures and perils which the said Assurers are contented to bear, and take upon themselves, they are of the seas and inland waters, man [sic] of war, fires, enemies, pirates, rovers, assailing thieves, jettisons, letters of mart and countermart, reprisals, taking at sea, arrests, restraints and detainments of all kings, princes of [or?] people of what nation, condition or quality soever, barratry of the master and mariners, and all other perils, losses and misfortunes, that have or shall come to the hurt, detriment or damage to the said goods and merchandise, or any part thereof."

2. (Clause 12B) "Other shipments covered hereunder are insured: Free of Particular Average unless caused by the vessel and/or interest insured being stranded, sunk, burst, on fire or in collision with another ship or vessel or with ice or with any substance other than water, but liable for jettison and/or washing overboard, irrespective of percentage." [This is a typical "warranted free of particular average" clause. See the introductory note on *Two Troublesome Terms*, *supra* at 455–56.]

6. (Clause 13) "Including while on docks, wharves or elsewhere on shore and/or during land transportation, risks of collision, derailment, fire, lightning, sprinkler leakage, cyclones, hurricanes, earthquakes, floods, the rising of navigable waters, or any accident to the conveyance and/or collapse and/or subsidence of docks and/or structures, and to pay loss or damage caused thereby, even though the insurance be otherwise F.P.A."

Therefore shore coverage does not apply. Even if it were to apply, contamination of cargo is not within the enumerated risks covered by the shore coverage clause.

III. Recovery of Extraordinary Expenses under Landing and Warehousing clause; Extra Expenses clause; Sue and Labor clause

Under these provisions the insured is entitled to recover expenses associated with losses incurred as a result of an insured peril. [ ] For reasons outlined in Paragraph I, I find that the losses suffered by plaintiffs were not caused by a peril covered by the policy. Recovery under these provisions is therefore precluded.

IV. Recovery under Inchmaree clause[7]

The purpose of the Inchmaree clause[10] is to expand the coverage of the policy beyond the perils provision. [ ] Federal law—[§ 3 of the Harter Act and § 4(2)(a) of the Carriage of Goods by Sea Act]—allows a vessel owner to become exempt from liability for fault or error in navigation or management of the ship.[2] In contrast, the shipowner must retain liability for negligence in the care and custody of the cargo. [ ] The Inchmaree clause is intended to provide coverage to a cargo owner when a loss is due to error in navigation or management of the vessel since the carrier is exempt from liability. [ ] Plaintiffs argue the contamination was the result of an error in management and therefore covered under the Inchmaree clause. Defendant naturally urges the court to find the loss caused by fault in the care and custody of the cargo.

The United States Supreme Court has addressed the distinction between error in management and error in care of cargo but has not articulated a clear test. [ ] The Ninth Circuit, noting that no precise definitions exist, advocates a case-by-case determination using the following test:

> If the act in question has the primary purpose of affecting the ship, it is "in navigation or in management"; but if the primary purpose is to affect the cargo, it is not "in navigation or in management". [ ]

Using this test, I find that the contamination of the cargo in this case was caused by fault in the care, custody, and control of the cargo. [ ] The Inchmaree clause will not provide coverage for plaintiffs' losses under the facts of this case.

---

7. Editors' note: Inchmaree clauses are named for "the vessel in *Thames & Mersey Marine Insurance Co. v. Hamilton, Fraser & Co.*, 12 A.C. 484 (H.L. 1887), where the House of Lords restrictively read [the perils clause in a Lloyd's S.G. Policy of time hull insurance] in the then new age of steam vessels not to include damage from a pump clogged through valve failure." *Northwestern Mutual Life Insurance Co. v. Linard*, 498 F.2d 556, 560 (2d Cir. 1974). Their Lordships reasoned that the strange new type of harm was not "a peril *ejusdem generis* with those specified" in the old S.G. perils clause. 12 A.C. at 494. Shipowners and cargo interests responded by persuading underwriters to include clauses along the lines of the one quoted in footnote 10 of the *Shaver* opinion. Modern Inchmaree clauses are generally somewhat broader in terms than the one in *Shaver*.

10. (Clause 24) "This insurance is also specially to cover any loss of or damage to the interest insured hereunder, through the bursting of boilers, breakage of shafts or through any latent defect in the machinery, hull or appurtenances, or from faults or errors in the navigation and/or management of the vessel by the Master, Mariners, Mates, Engineers or Pilots; provided, however, that this clause shall not be construed as covering loss arising out of delay, deterioration or loss of market, unless otherwise provided elsewhere herein."

2. Editors' note: The "error in navigation" (or "navigational fault") exception is discussed in Chapter III. See generally *supra* at 301–03.

V. Recovery under Negligence clause

The Negligence clause[11] provides coverage against losses due to enumerated perils caused by the unseaworthiness of the vessel. To recover under this clause plaintiffs must show that the barge was unseaworthy. This unseaworthiness must then cause a loss through one of the enumerated perils : "sinking, stranding, fire, explosion, contact with seawater, or by any other cause of the nature of any of the risks assumed in the policy."

"Seaworthiness" depends on such factors as the type of vessel, character of the voyage, reasonable weather, navigational conditions, and type of cargo. [ ] A vessel is unseaworthy if she is not reasonably fit to carry cargo she has undertaken to transport. [ ] I find Shaver's barge unseaworthy as a result of improper loading of cargo. [ ]

Plaintiffs must demonstrate that the unseaworthiness of the barge caused a loss to cargo by one or more of the enumerated perils. Since contamination is not an enumerated peril, plaintiff urges coverage under the doctrine of *ejusdem generis*[12] by suggesting the barge was in imminent danger of sinking. Although there is evidence that the caustic soda would have eventually corroded through the barge and caused it to sink, the process would have taken three to five years. This possibility is too far removed to find coverage under a provision providing for loss due to sinking. No recovery is possible under the Negligence clause of this policy.

* * *

Plaintiffs [have suggested] a number of theories of recovery under the marine cargo insurance policy. None is suited to this case. I am aided in my construction of this policy by one additional fact. Shaver *rejected* insurance coverage costing more but expressly covering the risks of contamination of cargo. I conclude that the plaintiffs did not believe contamination was covered under the policy. Plaintiffs' present attempt to include this type of loss within the coverage of the policy is an afterthought.

Judgment shall be entered for the defendant.

Notes

1. **The warranty of seaworthiness in cargo policies.** Traditional marine insurance law implied a warranty of seaworthiness in all voyage policies, including cargo policies. But obviously the ordinary cargo insured is in no position to control or perhaps even to know about the vessel's condition. For that reason, cargo policies usually waive the warranty, as was done in Clause 21 (note 11) of the *Shaver* policy.

---

11. (Clause 21) "The Assured are not to be prejudiced by the presence of the negligence clause and/or latent defect clause in the bills of lading and/or charter party and/or contract of affreightment. The seaworthiness of the vessel and/or craft as between the Assured and Assurers is hereby admitted, and the Assurers agree that in the event unseaworthiness or a wrongful act or misconduct of shipowner, charterer, their agents or servants, shall, directly or indirectly, cause loss or damage to the cargo insured by sinking, stranding, fire, explosion, contact with seawater, or by any other cause of the nature of any of the risks assumed in the policy, the Assurers will (subject to the terms of average and other conditions of the policy) pay to an innocent Assured the resulting loss. With leave to sail with or without pilots, and to tow and assist vessels or craft in all situations and to be towed."

12. *Ejusdem generis* is a rule of construction. Where general words are used in a contract after specific terms, they are to be confined to things of the same kind or class as the things previously specified.

2. **Ejusdem generis.** The concept—that general language at the end of an enumeration is limited in scope by the types of things enumerated—has wide application throughout the law. Its influence—often unremarked—is especially pervasive in marine insurance law. The *Shaver* court, for example, mentioned *ejusdem generis* only in connection with the negligence clause (note 11); but it had already implicitly used the approach to restrict the meaning of the phrase "all other perils, losses, and misfortunes" in the perils clause (note 1) and of the phrase "any accident to the conveyance" in the shore coverage clause (note 6).

3. **Return of premium.** When an insurer resists payment on policy-coverage grounds, the theory of its case is that the insured got the protection it paid for and is simply trying to finagle some additional coverage into the policy. In that situation, there is no good argument for insisting that the insurer return the unused portion of the premium. But when the insurer's theory is that the policy was voided by a misrepresentation or breach of warranty, the insurer must return the unused premium.

4. **"Enumerated perils" policies; "all risks" policies.** The policy in dispute in the principal case was an "enumerated perils" policy, so the assured had to show the court a clause expressing coverage. In disputes involving "all risks" policies, the insurer has to point to a clause excluding coverage.

Chapter XI

Piracy and Drug Smuggling

Title 18 of the U.S. Code, the federal penal code, contains many provisions that pertain to activities aboard vessels within the admiralty jurisdiction. From assault and arson to video voyeurism, crimes committed within the "special maritime and territorial jurisdiction of the United States" as defined in 18 U.S.C. § 7 are subject to federal prosecution. Numerous other maritime crimes are treated in Title 46 and other titles of the U.S. Code. This chapter will focus on two types of crimes that have attracted attention in recent years, piracy and drug smuggling.

United States v. Shibin

United States Court of Appeals, Fourth Circuit, 2013
722 F.3d 233, 2013 AMC 1817

NIEMEYER, Circuit Judge:

On May 8, 2010, Somali pirates seized the German merchant ship the *Marida Marguerite* on the high seas, took hostages, pillaged the ship, looted and tortured its crew, and extorted a $5-million ransom from its owners. Mohammad Saaili Shibin, while not among the pirates who attacked the ship, boarded it after it was taken into Somali waters and conducted the negotiations for the ransom and participated in the torture of the merchant ship's crew as part of the process.

On February 18, 2011, Somali pirates seized the American sailing ship the *Quest* on the high seas. A U.S. Navy ship communicated with the pirates on board in an effort to negotiate the rescue of the ship and its crew of four Americans, but the pirates referred the Navy personnel to Shibin as their negotiator. When the Navy ship thereafter sought to bar the pirates from taking the *Quest* into Somali waters, the pirates killed the four Americans.

Shibin was later located and arrested in Somalia and turned over to the FBI, which flew him to Virginia to stand trial for his participation in the two piracies. A jury convicted him on 15 counts, and he was sentenced to multiple terms of life imprisonment.

On appeal, Shibin contends that the district court erred by refusing (1) to dismiss the piracy charges on the ground that Shibin himself did not act on the high seas and therefore the court lacked subject-matter jurisdiction over those charges; ... [and] (3) to dismiss the non-piracy counts involving the *Marida Marguerite* because "universal jurisdiction" did not extend to justify the U.S. government's prosecution of those crimes ...

We conclude that the district court did not err in refusing to dismiss the various counts of the indictment ... Accordingly, we affirm.

I

The Piracy of the Marida Marguerite

As the *Marida Marguerite* was making way in the Indian Ocean on a trip from India to Antwerp and preparing to join a protected convoy to transit the Gulf of Aden, she was attacked by Somali pirates in a small, high-speed boat. The *Marida Marguerite* was manned by a crew of 22 from Bangladesh, India, and Ukraine, and was carrying a shipment of benzene and castor oil. As the *Marida Marguerite* attempted evasive maneuvers, the pirates fired two rocket-propelled grenades at the ship, prompting the ship's captain to surrender. After taking control of the ship in international waters, the pirates, armed with AK-47s, forced the crew to head for Somali waters. While in route, they looted the ship, including the personal valuables of crew members.

The *Marida Marguerite* arrived first at an anchorage near Hafun on the east coast of Somalia, where "a multitude" of other hijacked ships were anchored. At that location, additional pirates boarded the ship with more weapons, including assault weapons, rocket-propelled grenades, and two large stationary machine guns. The ship was then moved to an anchorage off Garaad, a town controlled by pirates, where Shibin boarded the ship. It was ultimately moved to Hobyo, on the southeast coast of Somalia. Shibin remained on board for over 7 months (except for a vacation of 10 to 12 days during the summer) until the ransom was received.

During the period that the ship was held captive, Shibin, who had a high position among the pirates, served principally as the negotiator, using tactics that included the psychological and physical torture of the crew. Ultimately, Shibin was able to extort a $5 million ransom from the ship's owners, and the money was air-dropped at the ship. After the money was confirmed, the pirates released the ship to a waiting U.S. frigate, which escorted it to safety. Shibin was among the last of the pirates to disembark.

* * *

The Piracy of the Quest

Several months later, on February 18, 2011, as a U.S. sailing vessel, the *Quest*, was making way from India to Oman as part of an international yacht rally, a group of Somali pirates hijacked the ship. The ship was manned by four Americans—its owners Scott and Jean Adams, and their friends Phyllis Macay and Robert Riggle. The pirates, carrying automatic weapons and a rocket-propelled grenade launcher, boarded the *Quest* in the Arabian Sea, roughly 400 miles from Oman and 900 miles from Somalia. The pirates planned to take the ship back to Somalia, where their colleague Shibin would negotiate a ransom.

The U.S. Navy learned of the *Quest's* seizure, and several Navy ships began shadowing it. After Navy personnel were able to establish bridge-to-bridge radio communications with the pirates, the pirates told the Navy that they lacked the authority to negotiate and that their job was to capture vessels and hostages and return them to Somalia where their English-speaking negotiator would arrange a ransom. As the pirates and the *Quest* continued towards Somali territorial waters, the Navy asked the pirates for the name and contact information of their negotiator. The pirates told the Navy that the person to contact was Shibin, and they provided the Navy with Shibin's cell phone number. The Navy did not, however, then attempt to call him, for strategic reasons.

By the morning of February 22, 2011, as the *Quest* was nearing Somali waters, Navy personnel advised the pirates that they had to stop. When the pirates did not comply, the Navy attempted to position one of its ships to block the pirates, prompting the pirates to fire a rocket-propelled grenade at the Navy. As the Navy continued to close in, but before it reached the *Quest*, the pirates shot and killed all four Americans on board.

Shibin's Capture

... [During the FBI's investigation of the *Quest* piracy it learned of Shibin's possible involvement in the hijacking of the *Marida Marguerite*. "Host Nation Defense Forces" acting in cooperation with the FBI arrested Shibin in Somalia, and he was eventually placed in the FBI's custody.] The FBI placed Shibin under arrest for charges related to the *Quest* piracy and transported him to the Oceana Naval Air Station in Virginia Beach, Virginia.

Prosecution

Shibin was initially charged in a three-count indictment for his alleged role in the piracy of the *Quest*. A later superseding indictment, returned on August 17, 2011, added charges relating to the piracy of the *Marida Marguerite*, as well as additional charges relating to the piracy of the *Quest*. Counts 1 through 6, arising from the piracy of the *Marida Marguerite*, charged the following crimes:

1. Piracy under the law of nations, in violation of 18 U.S.C. §§ 1651 and 2;
2. Conspiracy to commit hostage taking, in violation of 18 U.S.C. § 1203(a);
3. Hostage taking, in violation of 18 U.S.C. §§ 1203(a) and 2;
4. Conspiracy to commit violence against maritime navigation, in violation of 18 U.S.C. § 2280(a)(1)(H);
5. Violence against maritime navigation, in violation of 18 U.S.C. §§ 2280(a)(1)(A) and 2; and
6. Use of a firearm during a crime of violence, in violation of 18 U.S.C. §§ 924(c) and 2.

Counts 7 through 15, arising from the piracy of the *Quest*, charged the following crimes:

7. Piracy under the law of nations, in violation of 18 U.S.C. §§ 1651 and 2;
8. Conspiracy to commit hostage taking, in violation of 18 U.S.C. § 1203(a);
9. Hostage taking, in violation of 18 U.S.C. §§ 1203(a) and 2;
10. Conspiracy to commit kidnapping, in violation of 18 U.S.C. § 1201(c);
11. Kidnapping, in violation of 18 U.S.C. §§ 1201(a)(2) and 2;
12. Conspiracy to commit violence against maritime navigation, in violation of 18 U.S.C. § 2280(a)(1)(H);
13. Violence against maritime navigation, in violation of 18 U.S.C. §§ 2280(a)(1)(A) and 2;
14. Use of a firearm during a crime of violence, in violation of 18 U.S.C. §§ 924(c) and 2; and
15. Use of a firearm during a crime of violence, in violation of 18 U.S.C. §§ 924(c) and 2.

Shibin filed multiple pretrial motions, including a motion to dismiss the piracy charges in Counts 1 and 7, because the government did not allege that Shibin himself acted on the high seas, and a motion to dismiss all charges for lack of jurisdiction. The district court deferred ruling on the motion to dismiss the piracy charges until hearing evidence at trial and denied the other motions. Shibin renewed all motions to dismiss at the close of the government's case and again prior to sentencing, all of which the court denied.

* * *

The jury convicted Shibin on all counts, and the district court sentenced him to 12 terms of life imprisonment, two of which were to be served consecutively; a consecutive 120-month term of imprisonment; and several concurrent 240-month terms.

This appeal followed.

II

Shibin contends first that he did not "commit the crime of piracy," as charged in Counts 1 and 7, because, "according to statutory text, legislative history, and international law, [he] could only be convicted of aiding and abetting piracy if the government proved that he was on the high seas, and while on the high seas, facilitated piratical acts."

The government observes that there is no dispute that the piracies in this case occurred on the high seas beyond the territorial waters of Somalia, which are generally defined as the waters within 12 nautical miles of the coast. It contends that Shibin is liable as a principal in those piracies, even though he did not personally venture into international waters, because he "intentionally facilitated" and thereby aided and abetted the piracies. The government argues that liability for aiding and abetting piracy is not limited to conduct on the high seas, explaining:

> That no such limitation is imposed is sensible. Once members of a joint criminal enterprise trigger the universal jurisdiction that applies to piracy on the high seas, both international and domestic law prudently include in the scope of the crime all those persons that worked together to commit it, including those leaders like Shibin who facilitate the crime and without which the crime itself would not be possible.

In Counts 1 and 7, Shibin was charged with committing and aiding and abetting the crime of piracy, in violation of 18 U.S.C. §§ 1651 and 2. Section 1651 provides:

> Whoever, on the high seas, commits the crime of piracy as defined by the law of nations, and is afterwards brought into or found in the United States, shall be imprisoned for life.

18 U.S.C. § 1651. And § 2 provides:

> Whoever commits an offense against the United States or aids, abets, counsels, commands, induces or procures its commission, is punishable as a principal.

18 U.S.C. § 2(a).

The district court's jurisdiction over these crimes arises from "universal jurisdiction." Universal jurisdiction is an international law doctrine that recognizes a "narrow and unique exception" to the general requirement that nations have a jurisdictional nexus before punishing extraterritorial conduct committed by non-nationals [ ]; *United States v. Dire*, 680 F.3d 446 (4th Cir. 2012). It allows any nation "jurisdiction to define and prescribe punishment for certain offenses recognized by the community of nations as a universal concern." Restatement (Third) of Foreign Relations Law § 404 (1987). Universal jurisdiction requires "not only substantive agreement as to certain universally condemned behavior but also procedural agreement that universal jurisdiction exists to prosecute a subset of that behavior." [ ] The parties agree that piracy is subject to universal jurisdiction, as pirates are considered *hostis humani generis*, the enemies of all humankind. [ ]

... The issue ... reduces to a question of whether the conduct of aiding and abetting § 1651 piracy must itself take place on the high seas.

Section 1651 punishes piracy as that crime is defined by the law of nations *at the time of the piracy*. See *Dire*, 680 F.3d at 469 (noting that "§ 1651 incorporates a definition of piracy that changes with advancements in the law of nations"). In *Dire*, we held that Article 101 of the United Nations Convention on the Law of the Sea ("UNCLOS") accurately articulates the modern international law definition of piracy. Id. at 459, 469.*

Article 101 of UNCLOS provides:

> Piracy consists of any of the following acts:
>
> (a) any illegal acts of violence or detention, or any act of depredation, committed for private ends by the crew or the passengers of a private ship or a private aircraft, and *directed*:
>
> > (i) *on the high seas, against another ship* or aircraft, or against *persons or property on board such ship* or aircraft;
> >
> > (ii) against a ship, aircraft, persons or property in a place outside the jurisdiction of any State;
>
> (b) any act of voluntary participation in the operation of a ship or of an aircraft with knowledge of facts making it a pirate ship or aircraft;
>
> (c) any *act* of inciting or *of intentionally facilitating an act described in subparagraph (a)* or (b).

UNCLOS art. 101, Dec. 10, 1982, 1833 U.N.T.S. 397, 436 (emphasis added). Thus, as relevant here, Article 101(a) defines piracy to include specified acts "directed on the high seas against another ship ... or against persons or property on board such ship," and Article 101(c) defines piracy to include any act that "intentionally facilitat[es]" any act described in Article 101(a). The parties agree that the facilitating conduct of Article 101(c) is "functionally equivalent" to aiding and abetting criminal conduct, as proscribed in 18 U.S.C. § 2.

While Shibin's conduct unquestionably amounted to acts that intentionally facilitated Article 101(a) piracies on the high seas, he claims that in order for his facilitating conduct to amount to piracy, his conduct must also have been carried out on the high seas. The text, however, hardly provides support for this argument. To the contrary, the better reading suggests that Articles 101(a) and 101(c) address distinct acts that are defined in their respective sections.

Article 101(a), which covers piracies on the high seas, explicitly requires that the specified acts be directed *at ships on the high seas*. But Article 101(c), which defines different piratical acts, independent of the acts described in Article 101(a), is linked to Article 101(a) only to the extent that the acts must *facilitate* Article 101(a) acts. Article 101(c) does not limit the facilitating acts to conduct on the high seas. Moreover, there is no conceptual reason why acts facilitating high-seas acts must themselves be carried out

* Although over 160 nations are parties to UNCLOS, making up an "overwhelming majority of the world," the United States has not signed or ratified the Convention because "of its disagreement with the deep seabed regime set out in Part XI of the Convention." [*United States v. Hasan*, 747 F. Supp. 2d 599, 619 (E.D. Va. 2010), *aff'd sub nom United States v. Dire*, 680 F.3d 446 (4th Cir. 2012)] (citing 1 Thomas J. Schoenbaum, Admiralty and Maritime Law § 2-2 (4th ed. 2004)).

on the high seas. The text of Article 101 describes one class of acts involving violence, detention, and depredation of ships on the high seas and another class of acts that facilitate those acts. In this way, Article 101 reaches all the piratical conduct, wherever carried out, so long as the acts specified in Article 101(a) are carried out on the high seas.

We thus hold that conduct violating Article 101(c) does not have to be carried out on the high seas, but it must incite or intentionally facilitate acts committed against ships, persons, and property on the high seas. See also *United States v. Ali*, 718 F.3d 929, 937, 941, (D.C. Cir. 2013) (similarly interpreting Article 101(c) in the course of holding that the liability of an aider and abettor of a § 1651 piracy "is not contingent on his having facilitated these acts while in international waters himself").

Citing UNCLOS Article 86, Shibin argues that we should read a "high-seas" requirement into the definition of the facilitating acts described in Article 101(c). Article 86 provides: "The provisions of this Part [Part VII, "High Seas," which includes Article 101] apply to all parts of the sea that are not included in the exclusive economic zone, in the territorial sea or in the internal waters of a State, or in the archipelagic waters of an archipelagic State." UNCLOS art. 86, 1833 U.N.T.S. at 432.

Our reading of Article 101, however, is not inconsistent with Article 86, as Article 101(a) does indeed identify piratical acts as acts against ships *on the high seas*. The subordinated acts of Article 101(c) are also acts of piracy because they facilitate Article 101(a) acts. Moreover, Article 86 serves only as a general introduction, providing context to the provisions that follow. It does not purport to limit the more specific structure and texts contained in Article 101. See *RadLAX Gateway Hotel, LLC v. Amalgamated Bank*, [566 U.S. 639, 645] (2012) ("[I]t is a commonplace of statutory construction that the specific governs the general"....).

Additionally, Shibin's argument is inconsistent with the interpretation of Article 101 given by various international authorities, including the United Nations Security Council.... In 2011, the Security Council adopted Resolution 1976, which reaffirmed that "international law, as reflected in ... [UNCLOS], in particular its articles 100, 101 and 105, sets out the legal framework applicable to combating piracy and armed robbery at sea." [ ] Importantly, the Resolution stressed "the need to investigate and prosecute those who illicitly *finance, plan, organize, or unlawfully profit* from pirate attacks off the coast of Somalia, recognizing that individuals and entities who incite or *intentionally facilitate* an act of piracy are themselves engaging in piracy as defined under international law." [ ] (emphasis added). Clearly, those who "finance, plan, organize, or unlawfully profit" from piracy do not do so on the high seas.

* * *

Shibin makes a similar argument that he made with respect to UNCLOS to the domestic law provisions of 18 U.S.C. §§ 1651 and 2. Thus, he argues that the "on the high seas" requirement contained in § 1651 means that even those who are charged under § 2 for aiding and abetting a § 1651 piracy must act on the high seas. As he did with Article 101, Shibin seeks to import the high seas locational component of § 1651 into § 2. We believe that this argument fairs no better.

To violate § 1651, a principal must carry out an act of piracy, as defined by the law of nations, *on the high seas*. But Shibin was not prosecuted as a principal; he was prosecuted as an aider and abettor under § 2. Section 2 does not include any locational limitation, just as Article 101(c) of UNCLOS does not contain a locational limitation. Section 2 more broadly punishes conduct that "aids, abets, counsels, commands, induces or procures" commission of "an offense against the United States," including conduct punished in § 1651. [ ] And nothing in § 1651 suggests that an aider and abettor must satisfy its locational requirement.

It is common in aiding-and-abetting cases for the facilitator to be geographically away from the scene of the crime. For example, to be convicted of aiding and abetting a bank robbery, one need not be inside the bank. * * * Similarly, "[o]ne need not be present physically at the time to be guilty as an aider and abettor in an embezzlement." [ ]

Nonetheless, Shibin relies on *United States v. Ali*, 885 F. Supp. 2d 17 (D.D.C. 2012), *rev'd in relevant part*, 718 F.3d at 947, to contend that we should read a locational limitation into § 2 based on the Supreme Court's interpretation of the predecessor statute. In *United States v. Palmer*, 16 U.S. (3 Wheat.) 610, 633–34 (1818), the Supreme Court concluded that the piracy provisions of the Crimes Act of 1790 did not reach conduct committed by foreign vessels traversing the high seas. To reverse that ruling, Congress revised the offense of general piracy. But in doing so, it did not alter § 10 of the Crimes Act of 1790, which is § 2's predecessor. From this history, Shibin argues that § 2 is therefore a municipal statute, applying only to piracy within United States territory. But the tie between *Palmer* and § 2 is not strong enough to validate Shibin's argument. First, the Supreme Court's comments in *Palmer* on § 2's predecessor are dicta. See *Palmer*, 16 U.S. at 629–30. But more importantly, § 2's predecessor was tied to the crimes proscribed by the Crimes Act of 1790 and was narrower than today's § 2. Thus, Palmer did not construe the modern aiding-and-abetting liability. We are satisfied to give § 2, in its present form, its natural reading.

Accordingly, we affirm Shibin's piracy convictions in Counts 1 and 7, based on his intentionally facilitating two piracies on the high seas, even though his facilitating conduct took place in Somalia and its territorial waters.

* * *

IV

Shibin next contends that the non-piracy counts related to the *Marida Marguerite*, Counts 2 through 6, must be dismissed because "the universal jurisdiction doctrine did not provide the [district] court with jurisdiction" over those counts.[1] [As noted above, Counts 2 through 6 charge Shibin with offenses related to "hostage taking," "violence against maritime navigation," and "use of a firearm during a crime of violence."] Shibin argues that these crimes do not fit within the small set of crimes that are universally cognizable and therefore subject to prosecution under universal jurisdiction.

The government contends that universal jurisdiction was not invoked for the prosecution of Counts 2 through 6. Rather, "the criminal statutes [themselves] are clear in the extraterritorial scope, and in each case Congress acted pursuant to a constitutional grant of lawmaking power" to extend U.S. jurisdiction over those offenses.

At the outset, we agree that Counts 2 through 6 do not depend on universal jurisdiction. Rather, they rely on the jurisdiction provided by the statutes themselves. [And it] is well-established that Congress may criminalize extraterritorial conduct. * * * To be sure, statutes extend extraterritorially only if Congress clearly so provides. See *Morrison v. Nat'l Australia Bank Ltd.*, [561 U.S. 247, 255, 265] (2010); see also *Kiobel v. Royal Dutch*

1. Editors' note: Evidently Shibin did not appeal the non-piracy convictions related to the *Quest*.

Petroleum Co., [569 U.S. 108, 115–117] (2013) (applying the presumption against extraterritoriality). But when Congress provides a clear indication of extraterritoriality, U.S. jurisdiction is not limited to offenses criminalized under international law nor dependent on universal jurisdiction. * * *

In this case, the substantive statutes on which Counts 2 through 6 rest clearly manifest Congress' intent to criminalize conduct that takes place outside the municipal jurisdiction of the United States.[18 U.S.C. § 1203], on which Counts 2 and 3 are based, criminalizes hostage taking and provides:

> (a) Except as provided in subsection (b) of this section, whoever, whether *inside or outside the United State*s, [takes hostages], shall be punished by imprisonment for any term of years or for life and, if the death of any person results, shall be punished by death or life imprisonment.
>
> (b)(1) It is not an offense under this section if the conduct required for the offense occurred outside the United States unless—
>
> > (A) the offender or the person seized or detained is a national of the United States;
> >
> > (B) *the offender is found in the United States*; or
> >
> > (C) the governmental organization sought to be compelled is the Government of the United States.

18 U.S.C. § 1203 (emphasis added). This statute explicitly reaches hostage taking anywhere in the world, so long as the offender ends up in the United States. In this case, Shibin was involved in hostage taking on the *Marida Marguerite* and was later found in Virginia, where he was prosecuted.

[On similar reasoning the court upheld the convictions under Counts 4 and 5 criminalizing maritime violence and the conviction under Count 6 criminalizing the use or possession of a firearm in connection with a crime of violence.]

Congress' power to enact statutes that extend extraterritorially is derived generally from the Define and Punish Clause, U.S. Const. art. I, § 8, cl. 10; the Treaty Power, U.S. Const. art. II, § 2, cl. 2; and the Necessary and Proper Clause, U.S. Const. art. I, § 8, cl. 18.

Thus, § 1203, the hostage-taking statute, is constitutionally valid as the implementation of the International Convention Against the Taking of Hostages, December 17, 1979. [ ]

Similarly, § 2280, punishing maritime violence, is constitutionally valid as the implementation of the Convention for the Suppression of Unlawful Acts Against the Safety of Maritime Navigation arts. 7, 11, March 10, 1988. [ ]

Finally, § 924(c), criminalizing gun use in connection with any crime of violence that can be prosecuted in the United States, is constitutionally valid under the Necessary and Proper Clause in connection with other statutes' implementation of treaties. [ ]

At bottom, we reject Shibin's argument that the district court did not have jurisdiction under "universal jurisdiction" over the non-piracy counts related to the *Marida Marguerite*, Counts 2 through 6. Universal jurisdiction was irrelevant to the prosecution of those counts, and, we conclude, each of those counts is based on a statute that Congress validly applied to extraterritorial conduct, including Shibin's conduct.

* * *

For the foregoing reasons, we affirm Shibin's judgments of conviction.

Notes

1. **Conspiracy and attempt.** *United States v. Ali*, 718 F.3d 929, 2013 AMC 1843 (D.C. Cir. 2013) used similar reasoning to allow prosecution for aiding and abetting piracy and hostage taking even though the defendant's criminal acts occurred in territorial waters. But the court held that Ali could not be prosecuted for conspiracy to commit piracy because international law does not recognize the crime and Congress did not clearly indicate that the conspiracy statute was intended to have extraterritorial effect.

The Fourth Circuit has ruled that failed attempts are included in the crime of piracy even though they would not have been considered piracy at the time of the statute's enactment in 1819. *United States v. Dire*, 680 F.3d 446, 2012 AMC 1217 (4th Cir. 2012). The court concluded that because the statute defines piracy by reference to the law of nations, Congress meant to incorporate an evolving definition. Piracy is not limited to robbery but under UNCLOS includes "illegal acts of violence ... committed for private ends by the crew or passengers of a private ship ... and directed on the high seas against another ship ..."

In *Dire* the defendants were swiftly apprehended after they launched an attack on a United States Navy frigate in the mistaken belief that it was a merchant vessel. Convicted of piracy and other criminal offenses each defendant was sentenced to life plus eighty years imprisonment.

2. **Piracy as a tort.** Piracy can give rise to a tort claim. The Alien Tort Statute, 28 U.S.C. § 1350, which was first adopted as part of the Judiciary Act of 1789, provides, "The district courts shall have original jurisdiction of any civil action by an alien for a tort only, committed in violation of the law of nations or a treaty of the United States." The statute is a grant of jurisdiction "enacted on the understanding that the common law would recognize a cause of action for the modest number of international law violations with a potential for personal liability at the time." *Sosa v. Alvarez-Machain*, 542 U.S. 692, 724 (2004). Piracy was one of those violations. Id. at 719; *Kiobel v. Royal Dutch Petroleum Co.*, [569 U.S. 108, 119-121] (2013). In *Institute of Cetacean Research v. Sea Shepherd Conservation Society*, 725 F.3d 940, 2013 AMC 1695 (9th Cir. 2013), the court held that Japanese researchers who hunt whales in the Southern Ocean under Japanese permits stated a cause of action seeking an injunction and declaratory relief against defendants who allegedly engaged in various acts of violence against the plaintiffs' vessels. The court held that the defendant's alleged acts fell within the definition of piracy because the defendants' acts of violence were for "private ends," a term that includes "those pursued on personal, moral or philosophical grounds, such as Sea Shepherd's professed environmental goals. That the perpetrators believe themselves to be serving the public good does not render their ends public." 725 F.3d at 944.

In March 2014 the International Court of Justice held that Japan was in violation of a treaty, the International Convention for the Regulation of Whaling, under which Japan issued the whaling permits. *Whaling In The Antarctic (Australia v. Japan: New Zealand Intervening)*, http://www.icj-cij.org/docket/files/148/18136.pdf.

Environmentalist protests can also result in criminal prosecution. In 2013 Russia arrested 30 Greenpeace activists for piracy for attempting to board a Russian oil platform in the Arctic Ocean. Amidst some international pressure, the charges were first reduced to hooliganism, for which the defendants faced up to seven years imprisonment, and after spending two months in Russian jails the protestors were granted amnesty.

3. **The Define and Punish Clause.** Congress's authority to adopt the legislation that was considered in the principal case derives from the Constitution's Art. I § 8 cl. 10: "To

define and punish Piracies and Felonies committed on the high Seas, and Offences against the Law of Nations." Courts have said that the clause authorizes Congress to proscribe, and prescribe punishments for, three distinct sets of offenses (1) "Piracies ... committed on the high Seas," (2) "Felonies committed on the high Seas," and (3) "Offenses against the Law of Nations." E.g., *United States v. Hasan*, 747 F. Supp. 2d 599, 603–04, 2010 AMC 2705, 2712 (E.D.Va. 2010). *See generally* Eugene Kontorovich, *The "Define and Punish" Clause and the Limits of Universal Jurisdiction*, 103 Nw. U.L. Rev. 149 (2009). The District Court in *Ali* held that the hostage taking statute was within the Necessary and Proper Clause "because it fulfills U.S. obligations under a valid treaty". 885 F. Supp. 2d 17, 39 (D.D.C. 2012).

4. **High Seas.** The term "high seas" as used in the Define and Punish Clause means international waters belonging to no sovereign. *E.g., United States v. Romero-Galue*, 757 F.2d 1147 (11th Cir. 1985). The term's meaning here is narrower than it is under the Death on the High Seas Act, which extends to territorial waters of foreign states. *See Howard v. Crystal Cruises, Inc.*, 41 F.3d 527 (9th Cir. 1994).

5. **Extraterritorial effect.** The presumption against extraterritorial application of U.S. law is a strong one. Even reference in a statute to foreign commerce is not enough to overcome the presumption. E.g., *New York Central R. Co. v. Chisholm*, 268 U.S. 29 (1925) (F.E.L.A. does not apply to fatal injuries to a U.S. worker on a train owned by a company that occurred in Canada even though the statute applied to common carriers by railroad engaged in "interstate or foreign commerce"). As explained in *Kiobel, supra*, "The presumption ... helps ensure that the Judiciary does not erroneously adopt an interpretation of U.S. law that carries foreign policy consequences not clearly intended by the political branches." [569 U.S. at 116]. The Court in *Kiobel* went on to explain that even though it "has generally treated the high seas the same as foreign soil for purposes of the presumption against extraterritorial application ... [a]pplying U.S. law to pirates, ... does not typically impose the sovereign will of the United States onto conduct occurring within the territorial jurisdiction of another sovereign and therefore carries less direct foreign policy consequences. Pirates were fair game wherever found, by any nation, because they generally did not operate within any jurisdiction." Id. at 1667.

6. **Sovereign immunity.** In *Wu v. United States*, 777 F.3d 175 (4th Cir. 2015), a Taiwanese citizen sued the United States for the wrongful death of her husband and the intentional destruction of his fishing vessel. Somali pirates had captured the fishing vessel and used it as a base of operations. They held Mr. Wu, who was its owner and captain, as hostage. More than a year later, acting under orders of a Dutch NATO commander, a U.S. Naval vessel fired shots at Wu's vessel, including its central compartments, for about an hour. That shooting apparently killed Wu. A day after the pirates surrendered, the U.S. Navy, again under orders from the Dutch commander, intentionally sank the fishing vessel with Mr. Wu's body still on board. The court held that the political question doctrine precluded the district court from having subject matter jurisdiction to hear the claims, and that even if there were subject matter jurisdiction, the discretionary function doctrine would preclude liability. Wu's widow characterized the NATO operation as an oceanic traffic stop or police action on the high seas. The court rejected that view, stating "American military forces typically do not take part in simple law enforcement." Id. at 182. Instead the court thought that courts must not be involved in "a sensitive multinational counter-piracy operation" nor "second-guess the conduct of a military engagement." Id. at 179. Nonetheless, it said that "in all kindness" recompense was due through diplomatic channels and noted that the United States had paid something to the Wu family.

7. **The Maritime Drug Law Enforcement Act.** Does Congress have authority under the Define and Punish Clause to punish all crimes on the high seas? Which crimes committed within another country's territorial waters are "offenses against the law of nations"? Those questions arise frequently in prosecutions of foreigners accused of drug smuggling under the Maritime Drug Law Enforcement Act, 46 U.S.C. §§46 U.S.C. §70501 et seq., ("The MDLEA") as the next case demonstrates. The MDLEA has several unusual features. It purports to apply to vessels without nationality, and to vessels in another country's territorial waters if that nation consents to United States enforcement of United States law (46 U.S.C. §70502). A "vessel without nationality" is defined broadly to include:

> (A) a vessel aboard which the master or individual in charge makes a claim of registry that is denied by the nation whose registry is claimed;
>
> (B) a vessel aboard which the master or individual in charge fails, on request of an officer of the United States authorized to enforce applicable provisions of United States law, to make a claim of nationality or registry for that vessel; and
>
> (C) a vessel aboard which the master or individual in charge makes a claim of registry and for which the claimed nation of registry does not affirmatively and unequivocally assert that the vessel is of its nationality.

46 U.S.C. §70502(d)(1). In addition, the statute provides that the federal government can conclusively prove the foreign nation's response under (A) or (C) "by certification of the Secretary of State or the Secretary's designee." 46 U.S.C. §70502(d)(2). Moreover, a person charged with violation of the statute "does not have standing to raise a claim of failure to comply with international law as a basis for a defense." 46 U.S.C. §70505. That section further provides, "A claim of failure to comply with international law in the enforcement of this chapter may be made only by a foreign nation. A failure to comply with international law does not divest a court of jurisdiction and is not a defense to a proceeding under this chapter." Id.

8. Although 46 U.S.C. §70502 makes it relatively easy for the government to conclusively prove that a vessel is without nationality, failure by the Coast Guard to comply with its technicalities can result in dismissal of the indictment. In *United States v. Prado*, 933 F.3d 121 (2d Cir. 2019), Coast Guard officers stopped a go-fast vessel carrying large amounts of cocaine. They found no registration documents and none of the three defendants aboard the vessel claimed to be the master or individual in charge. The Coast Guard officers did not inquire as to the nationality or registration of the vessel. All three of the defendants claimed that they were Ecuadorians and the vessel had an image of the Ecuadorian flag printed on its side, but the Coast Guard officers did not communicate with the registry of Ecuador or any other nation to determine whether the vessel was registered. The Coast Guard sank the vessel. Although the defendants pled guilty, the convictions were set aside on appeal. The Second Circuit held that the vessel was outside the reach of the MDLEA because it was not "without nationality" under the statute. No master or individual in charge failed "upon request" to make a claim of registry as required by §70502(d)(1)(B), and no effort was made to seek verification from Ecuador as required by §70502(d)(1)(C). Although the district court concluded that the flag on the side of the vessel was too small to constitute a claim of Ecuadorian nationality, the Second Circuit held that even absence of a claim of registry does not establish that the vessel is without nationality. To establish statelessness, the officer must request the master or person in charge for a claim of registry. One judge on the panel concurred in the judgment on the grounds that the Coast Guard's failure to comply with the statutory requirements deprived the district court of subject-matter jurisdiction.

United States v. Bellaizac-Hurtado

United States Court of Appeals, Eleventh Circuit, 2012
700 F.3d 1245

PRYOR, Circuit Judge:

This appeal presents a novel issue about the scope of congressional power to proscribe conduct abroad: whether the Maritime Drug Law Enforcement Act, 46 U.S.C. §§70503(a), 70506, exceeds the power of Congress to "define and punish ... Offences against the Law of Nations," U.S. Const. Art. I, §8, cl. 10, as applied to the drug-trafficking activities of Yimmi Bellaizac-Hurtado, Pedro Felipe Angulo-Rodallega, Albeiro Gonzalez-Valois, and Luis Carlos Riascos-Hurtado in the territorial waters of Panama. Because we conclude that drug trafficking is not an "Offence[] against the Law of Nations" and that Congress cannot constitutionally proscribe the defendants' conduct under the Offences Clause, we vacate their convictions.

I. BACKGROUND

During a routine patrol of Panamanian waters in 2010, the United States Coast Guard observed a wooden fishing vessel operating without lights and without a flag. The Coast Guard informed the Panamanian National Aero-Naval Service of the vessel. The Panamanian Navy pursued the vessel until its occupants abandoned the vessel and fled into a jungle. When members of the Panamanian Navy searched the vessel the next morning, they discovered approximately 760 kilograms of cocaine. The Panamanian National Frontier Service searched on land for the occupants of the abandoned vessel and arrested Bellaizac-Hurtado, Angulo-Rodallega, Gonzalez-Valois, and Riascos-Hurtado in various locations on the beach and in the jungle. After an exchange of diplomatic notes, the Foreign Ministry of the Republic of Panama consented to the prosecution of the four suspects in the United States.

A federal grand jury indicted [the four] for conspiracy to possess with intent to distribute five kilograms or more of cocaine, and for actual possession with intent to distribute five kilograms or more of cocaine, on board a vessel subject to the jurisdiction of the United States. See 46 U.S.C. §§70503(a), 70506; 21 U.S.C. §960(b)(1)(B). The defendants moved to dismiss the indictment "based upon the lack of jurisdiction and the unconstitutionality of the Maritime Drug Law Enforcement Act as applied to [their] conduct." A magistrate judge recommended that the motion be denied. The magistrate judge reasoned that the district court had jurisdiction because the defendants were operating a stateless vessel and that the Act was constitutional as applied because Congress and several courts had determined that drug trafficking was "universally condemned" by various nations with "reasonably developed" legal systems. The district court adopted the magistrate judge's report. The district court also explained that section 70505 of the Act "limits the actors that have standing to challenge the validity of an MDLEA prosecution on international law grounds."

The defendants conditionally[2] pleaded guilty to the conspiracy charge. The district court sentenced each of them to a term of imprisonment (ranging from 90 months down to 25

2. Editors' note: Rule 11(a)(2) of the Federal Rules of Criminal Procedure provides, "With the consent of the court and the government, a defendant may enter a conditional plea of guilty or nolo contendere, reserving in writing the right to have an appellate court review an adverse determination of a specified pretrial motion. A defendant who prevails on appeal may then withdraw the plea." It appears that the defendants' pleas were conditioned on the appellate court determining that Congress acted within its power under the Constitution.

months), supervised release (ranging from five years to two years) and a $100 fine.] The defendants appealed their convictions on the ground that the Act, as applied, exceeded the power of Congress under Article I, Section 8, Clause 10. We consolidated their appeals.

II. STANDARD OF REVIEW

"We review de novo the legal question of whether a statute is constitutional." [ ]

III. DISCUSSION

The United States argues that the Maritime Drug Law Enforcement Act, as applied to the defendants, is a constitutional exercise of the power granted to Congress "[t]o define and punish Piracies and Felonies committed on the high Seas, and Offences against the Law of Nations." [ ] The Supreme Court has interpreted that Clause to contain three distinct grants of power: the power to define and punish piracies, the power to define and punish felonies committed on the high seas, and the power to define and punish offenses against the law of nations. See *United States v. Smith*, 18 U.S. (5 Wheat.) 153, 158–59 (1820). The first two grants of power are not implicated here: piracy is, by definition, robbery on the high seas, *United States v. Furlong*, 18 U.S. (5 Wheat.) 184, 198 (1820), and the Felonies Clause is textually limited to conduct on the high seas, see U.S. Const., Art. I, § 8, cl. 10. The United States relies instead on the third grant—the Offences Clause—as the source of congressional power to proscribe the defendants' drug trafficking in the territorial waters of Panama. The question whether Congress has the power under the Offences Clause to proscribe drug trafficking in the territorial waters of another nation is an issue of first impression in our Court.

We divide our discussion in two parts. First, we explain why the power of Congress to define and punish conduct under the Offences Clause is limited by customary international law. Second, we explain why drug trafficking is not a violation of customary international law and, as a result, falls outside of the power of Congress under the Offences Clause.

A. Customary International Law Limits the Power of Congress to Define and Punish Crimes Under the Offences Clause.

The power granted to Congress in the Offences Clause is limited by customary international law for two reasons. First, the related Supreme Court precedent and the text, history, and structure of the Constitution confirm that the power to "define" is limited by the law of nations. Second, the phrase "Offences against the Law of Nations" is understood today to mean violations of customary international law.

1. The Power of Congress to Define "Offences against the Law of Nations" Is Limited to Established Offenses Against the Law of Nations.

The power to "define" offenses against the law of nations does not grant Congress the authority to punish conduct that is not a violation of the law of nations. The Supreme Court has explained that the power to "define" in Article I, Section 8, Clause 10, is limited by the three specific subjects of the Clause. For example, the Supreme Court has explained that Congress may not define murder as "piracy" to punish it under the Piracies Clause:

> Nor is it any objection to this opinion, that the law declares murder to be *piracy*. These are things so essentially different in their nature, that not even the omnipotence of legislative power can confound or identify them. Had Congress, in this instance, declared *piracy* to be murder, the absurdity would have been

> felt and acknowledged; yet, with a view to the exercise of jurisdiction, it would have been more defensible than the reverse, for, in one case it would restrict the acknowledged scope of its legitimate powers, in the other extend it. If by calling murder *piracy*, it might assert a jurisdiction over that offence committed by a foreigner in a foreign vessel, what offence might not be brought within their power by the same device? The most offensive interference with the governments of other nations might be defended on the precedent. Upon the whole, I am satisfied that Congress neither intended to punish murder in cases with which they had no right to interfere, nor leave unpunished the crime of piracy in any cases in which they might punish it....

Furlong, 18 U.S. (5 Wheat.) at 198. And, on the issue whether Congress must declare the conduct to be an offense against the law of nations to exercise its power under the Offences Clause, the Supreme Court has explained that "[w]hether the offense as defined is an offense against the law of nations depends on the thing done, not on any declaration to that effect by Congress." *United States v. Arjona*, 120 U.S. 479, 488, (1887).

This precedent is consistent with the original understanding of the word "define." During the Founding period, the word "define" meant "[t]o give the definition; to explain a thing by its qualities" and "[t]o circumscribe; to mark limits." Samuel Johnson, *A Dictionary of the English Language*, at DEF, DEF (10th ed. 1792); see also Thomas Sheridan, *A General Dictionary of the English Language*, at DEF, DEF (1780) ("To Define.... To give the definition, to explain a thing by its qualities; to circumscribe, to mark the limit."). These definitions reveal that the word "define" would not have been understood to grant Congress the power to create or declare offenses against the law of nations, but instead to codify and explain offenses that had already been understood as offenses against the law of nations.

The records of the debates at the Constitutional Convention confirm that the Framers also understood the word "define" to be limited by international law. *** The insertion of the power to "define" enabled Congress to provide notice to the people through codification; it did not enable Congress to create offenses that were not recognized by the law of nations.

The structure of the Constitution also confirms the limited power of Congress under the Offences Clause. If Congress could define any conduct as "piracy" or a "felony" [as] an "offence against the law of nations," its power would be limitless and contrary to our constitutional structure. * * * For these reasons, we look to international law to ascertain the scope of power granted to Congress under the Offences Clause.

2. The Phrase "Offences Against the Law of Nations"
Is Synonymous With Violations of Customary International Law.

We and our sister circuits agree that the eighteenth-century phrase, the "law of nations," in contemporary terms, means customary international law. * * * Five of our sister circuits [the Fourth, Sixth, Seventh, Ninth, and D.C. Circuits] have adopted the definition in the Restatement (Third) of Foreign Relations, which provides that customary international law is the "general and consistent practice of states followed by them from a sense of legal obligation." [ ]

* * *

Private criminal activity will rarely be considered a violation of customary international law because private conduct is unlikely to be a matter of mutual legal concern:

> Matters of "mutual" concern between States are those involving States' actions performed ... towards or with regard to the other—matters that, as Judge

> Friendly aptly noted, concern the dealings of States "inter se." Matters of "several" concern among States are matters in which States are separately and independently interested. Even if certain conduct is universally proscribed by States in their domestic law, that fact is not necessarily significant or relevant for purposes of customary international law.... Therefore, for example, murder of one private party by another, universally proscribed by the domestic law of all countries (subject to varying definitions), is not actionable ... as a violation of customary international law because the nations of the world have not demonstrated that this wrong is of mutual, and not merely several, concern. [ ]

* * *

B. Because Drug Trafficking Is Not a Violation of Customary International Law, Congress Lacks the Power to Proscribe Drug Trafficking Under the Offences Clause.

The text of the Offences Clause does not resolve the question whether it limits the power of Congress to define and punish only those violations of customary international law that were established at the Founding or whether the power granted under the Clause expands and contracts with changes in customary international law. The Supreme Court has not resolved the issue * * * Scholars have long debated whether the Offences Clause is affected by the later development of customary international law. * * *

We need not decide whether the power granted to Congress under the Offences Clause changes with the evolution of customary international law because, under either approach, the result is the same. Drug trafficking was not a violation of customary international law at the time of the Founding, and drug trafficking is not a violation of customary international law today.

1. Drug Trafficking Was Not a Violation of the Law of Nations During the Founding Period.

When the Constitution was ratified, the range of conduct that could be viewed as a violation of customary international law was even more limited than it is today. In his Commentaries on the Laws of England, William Blackstone explained that, because offenses against the law of nations are "principally incident to whole states or nations," they "can rarely be the object of the criminal law of any particular state." [ ] As a result, "[t]he principal offences against the law of nations [that could be committed by private individuals and punished criminally] ... [we]re of three kinds: 1. Violation of safe conducts; 2. Infringement of the rights of ambassadors; and, 3. Piracy." [ ] Although the Supreme Court added counterfeiting of foreign currency and violations of the laws of war to this list in *Arjona* and *Ex Parte Quirin*, [317 U.S. 1 (1942)], respectively, those norms were also discussed in Vattel's influential treatise on the law of nations from that period. * * *

Drug trafficking was not a matter of international concern in 1789, let alone a violation of customary international law. Vattel's Law of Nations contains no references to narcotics, opium, or drug trafficking. And the international community did not even begin its efforts to limit the drug trade until the turn of the twentieth century. * * *

2. Drug Trafficking Is Not a Violation of Customary International Law Today.

Drug trafficking is also not a violation of contemporary customary international law. Although a number of specially affected States—States that benefit financially from the drug trade—have ratified treaties that address drug trafficking, they have failed to comply with the requirements of those treaties, and the international community has not treated drug trafficking as a violation of contemporary customary international law. Scholars also agree that drug trafficking is not a violation of contemporary customary international law.

The United States argues that the widespread ratification of the 1988 United Nations Convention Against Illicit Traffic in Narcotic Drugs and Psychotropic Substances establishes that drug trafficking violates a norm of customary international law, but we disagree. Treaties may constitute evidence of customary international law, but "will only constitute sufficient proof of a norm of customary international law if an overwhelming majority of States have ratified the treaty, and those States uniformly and consistently act in accordance with its principles." [ ] "Of course, States need not be universally successful in implementing the principle in order for a rule of international law to arise.... But the principle must be more than merely professed or aspirational." [ ] And as the International Court of Justice has explained, a customary international law norm will not form if specially affected States have not consented to its development through state practice consistent with the proposed norm. [ ]

The 1988 Convention was ratified by an overwhelming majority of States and currently has 188 States Parties, [ ] but the drug trade continues to flourish in many specially affected States despite their ratification of the Convention. In 2011, the President of the United States designated 21 of these States Parties as "major drug transit or major illicit drug producing countries." [ ] And the President described Bolivia, Burma, and Venezuela "as countries that have failed demonstrably during the previous 12 months to make substantial efforts to adhere to their obligations under international counternarcotics agreements." [ ] The International Narcotic Control Board—the independent, quasi-judicial body established by the United Nations to monitor compliance with international drug treaties—has reported that drug-related corruption "has increasingly weakened the criminal justice systems in Central America and the Caribbean." [ ] The 2011 Report of the Board found that "[c]orruption and limited law enforcement capacity in Central America and the Caribbean have facilitated the use of smuggling channels and drug trafficking activities." [ ]The Board also has expressed concern about corruption and lack of progress in reducing illicit opium poppy cultivation in Afghanistan. [ ]

The practice of these specially affected States evidences that drug trafficking is not yet considered a violation of customary international law. Governments corrupted by the interests of drug traffickers are not simply unable to prosecute drug traffickers, but are often unwilling to do so because their economies are dependent upon the drug trade. * * *

Because drug trafficking is not a violation of customary international law, we hold that Congress exceeded its power, under the Offences Clause, when it proscribed the defendants' conduct in the territorial waters of Panama. And the United States has not offered us any alternative ground upon which the Act could be sustained as constitutional. As applied to these defendants, the Act is unconstitutional, and we must vacate their convictions.

IV. CONCLUSION

We **VACATE** the defendants' convictions.

BARKETT, Circuit Judge, specially concurring:

I concur in the majority's conclusion that drug trafficking does not constitute an "Offence[] against the Law of Nations" and agree with much of the majority's opinion. However, my conclusion is based on my view that when conduct has no connection to the United States, such as the conduct at issue here, it can only be punished as an "Offence[] against the Law of Nations" if it is subject to universal jurisdiction. * * *

Notes

1. Several circuits have upheld the constitutionality of applying the MDLEA to the transportation of illegal drugs on the high seas even if there is no nexus between the criminal conduct and the United States. E.g., *United States v. Saac*, 632 F.3d 1203 (11th Cir. 2011); *United States v. Martinez-Hidalgo*, 993 F.2d 1052, (3d Cir.1993). See also *United States v. Carvajal*, 924 F. Supp. 2d 219 (D.D.C. 2013). The Ninth Circuit held that due process requires a "sufficient nexus" between the defendant and the United States so that application of the statute would not be arbitrary or fundamentally unfair. *United States v. Davis*, 905 F.2d 245, 1990 AMC 2289 (9th Cir. 1990). A later case limits that holding to conduct on board foreign flag vessels and requires no nexus when a stateless vessel is involved. *United States v. Caicedo*, 47 F.3d 370, 1995 AMC 1085 (9th Cir. 1995). But see *United States v. Cardales-Luna*, 632 F.3d 731, 738 (1st Cir. 2011) (Torruella, J., dissenting) (arguing that Congress has exceeded its power because the Felonies Clause does not apply to felonies on the high seas that lack a nexus with the United States). Judge Torruella relied on the analysis in Kontorovich, *Beyond the Article I Horizon: Congress's Enumerated Powers and Universal Jurisdiction over Drug Crimes*, 93 MINN. L. REV. 1191 (2009).

2. Disagreeing with *Bellaizac-Hurtado*, a district court ruled that the Offenses Clause is not limited to empowering Congress to punish crimes under customary international law. Rather, it also authorizes Congress to punish criminal offenses that treaties require the United States to prevent. *United States v. Balbuena-Peguero*, 2017 WL 1399696, 2017 U.S. Dist. LEXIS 59114 (D.P.R. Apr. 18, 2017). The court upheld the validity of an indictment charging the defendants with various drug offenses on board a stateless vessel in international waters. It did not base its decision on the Felonies Clause. The court relied heavily on Sarah H. Cleveland & William S. Dodge, *Defining and Punishing Offenses Under Treaties*, 124 YALE L.J. 2202 (2015).

3. In a case involving international sex trafficking, the Eleventh Circuit suggested that it might have reached a different result in *Bellaizac-Hurtado* had the government invoked the Foreign Commerce Clause. *United States v. Baston*, 818 F.3d 651, 666-667 (11th Cir. 2016).

4. Might Article III's grant of admiralty and maritime jurisdiction, combined with the Necessary and Proper Clause, provide Congress with sufficient power to reach the conduct described in *Bellaizac-Hurtado*? Consider *United States v. Flores*, 289 U.S. 137, 1933 AMC 649 (1933), in which a U.S. seaman was charged with murder of another U.S. citizen aboard a U.S. vessel while at anchor in the Belgian Congo, 250 miles inland from the mouth of the Congo River and thus not on the high seas for purposes of the Define and Punish Clause. The United States Code made it a crime to commit murder "within the admiralty and maritime jurisdiction of the United States and out of the jurisdiction of any particular State of the United States on board any vessel belonging in whole or in part to the United States" or any of its nationals. The Supreme Court held that the statute was constitutional since the grant of admiralty jurisdiction was an independent basis of jurisdiction that was not confined to the limits applicable to the Define and Punish Clause. Although that reasoning suggests that a carefully drawn criminal statute could apply to any matter within the admiralty jurisdiction, the issue before the Court was only whether the admiralty grant authorized the punishment of crimes committed on U.S. vessels. The Court supported its conclusion by noting the English practice of extending jurisdiction to crimes committed aboard English vessels in foreign waters.

Chapter XII

Admiralty and Oil Pollution

Pollution of the earth's air, soil, and water by marine and maritime activities is a dauntingly enormous arena of human, industrial, and governmental concern. We can only hint here at the complex of state, national, and international laws addressing those problems. The materials below present a thin slice, using the 1989 *Exxon Valdez* disaster, involving an oil spill of about 11 million gallons, and the 2010 *Deepwater Horizon* tragedy—a spill of ca. 168 million gallons—as observational standpoints.[1]

The *Exxon Shipping* Case

The *Exxon Valdez* grounding and immediate aftermath are described in *Exxon Shipping Co. v. Baker*, *supra* at 249. The wide-ranging consequences of the resulting oil spill are evoked by the Court's enumeration of the federal statutes implicated. Those included "the Clean Water Act, [CWA[2]], 33 U.S.C. §§1311(a) and 1391(c)(1); the Refuse Act of 1899, 33 U.S.C. §§407 and 411; the Migratory Bird Treaty Act, 16 U.S.C. §§703 and 707(a); the Ports and Waterways Safety Act, 33 U.S.C. §1232(b)(1); and the Dangerous Cargo Act, 46 U.S.C. §3718(b)." 554 U.S. at 479. Courts in related litigation applied provisions of the Trans-Alaska Pipeline Authorization Act, 43 U.S.C. §§1651–1656. And, of course, disasters like *Exxon Valdez* also implicate state statutory and common law, as well as the federal general maritime law.

In re Oil Spill By the Oil Rig "Deepwater Horizon" In the Gulf of Mexico on April 20, 2010

United States District Court for the Eastern District of Louisiana, 2014
21 F. Supp. 3d 657, 2014 AMC 2113

BARBIER, District Judge:

* * *

On the evening of April 20, 2010, a blowout, explosions, and fire occurred aboard the MODU ["Mobile Offshore Drilling Unit"] *Deepwater Horizon* as it was in the process of temporarily abandoning a well, known as Macondo, it had drilled on the Outer Continental

1. For an accessible overview of international perspectives, see Soyer & Tettenborn, Pollution at Sea: Law and Liability (2012).
2. "Clean Water Act" is another name for the Federal Water Pollution Control Act, 33 U.S.C. §§1251–1377.

Shelf off the coast of Louisiana.[3] [The *Deepwater Horizon* was owned and operated by Transocean Offshore Deepwater Drilling Inc. and affiliated entities. The Macondo well was owned by BP Exploration & Production Inc. and affiliates.] Eleven men died tragically in the incident * * *. At least seventeen others were injured. The survivors evacuated to the *M/V Damon Bankston,* a supply vessel that was near the *Horizon* when the explosions occurred.

The explosions and/or fire should have triggered the automatic function on the *Horizon*'s BOP ["blowout preventer," located on the ocean floor at the top of the 13,360-foot-deep well], but that function either failed to activate the BOP or the BOP otherwise failed to shut in the well. Subsequent attempts to operate the BOP with remotely operated vehicles also failed to stop the blowout.

Several vessels responded to the distress calls and attempted to extinguish the fire with their monitors (water cannon). Despite these efforts, the *Horizon* burned continuously until mid-morning on April 22, when it capsized and sank into the Gulf of Mexico. As the rig descended, the marine riser—the approximately 5,000 feet of pipe that connected the rig to the BOP—collapsed and broke. Millions of gallons of oil discharged into the Gulf of Mexico over the next 87 days.[4] After multiple unsuccessful attempts, the well was finally capped and the discharge halted on July 15, 2010. In mid-September, a relief well intercepted the Macondo well and permanently sealed it with cement.

It was not long after the initial explosions that the first lawsuits were filed. Since that time, approximately 3,000 cases, with over 100,000 named claimants, have been filed in federal and state courts across the nation. These suits asserted a wide array of claims including wrongful death and personal injury due to the explosion and fire,[5] post-incident personal injury resulting from exposure to oil and/or the chemical dispersants used during the oil spill response, damage to property or natural resources, and economic losses resulting from the oil spill. On August 10, 2010, the United States Judicial Panel on Multidistrict Litigation transferred most federal cases to this Court as Multidistrict Litigation no. 2179 ("MDL 2179").

This Court adopted a phased trial proceeding that ultimately focused on two cases within MDL 2179: [Transocean's action for Limitation of Liability and the United States' action against BP for CWA penalties.] Both cases are before the Court for all purposes,[7] and both are proceedings in admiralty under 28 U.S.C. § 1333(1) and Fed. R. Civ. P. 9(h). Consequently, these cases may be tried to this Court without a jury. * * *

---

3. Editors' note: For an excellent diagram of the MODU and well, see 21 F. Supp. 3d 666.

4. Editors' note: The court subsequently quantified the spill at four million barrels (ca. 168 million gallons), explaining: "There is no way to know with precision how much oil discharged into the Gulf of Mexico. There was no meter counting off each barrel of oil as it exited the well. The experts used a variety of methods to estimate the cumulative discharge. None of these were perfect. * * * After weighing all of the evidence and considering all the arguments, the Court finds that 4.0 million barrels of oil released from the reservoir. After deducting the Collected Oil from this amount per the parties' stipulation, the Court finds for purposes of calculating the maximum possible civil penalty under the CWA that 3.19 million barrels of oil discharged into the Gulf of Mexico." 77 F. Supp. 3d 500, 523, 525 (E.D. La. 2015). In a follow-up opinion, the court held that "the maximum per-barrel civil penalty that may be imposed under the [CWA] is $4,300 per barrel of oil discharged." 2015 WL 729701 (E.D. La. Feb. 19, 2015).

5. Editors' note: These cases have been settled.

7. This is in contrast to cases that were transferred to this Court pursuant to the MDL statute, 28 U.S.C. § 1407, which are here for pretrial purposes only.

The "Phase One" trial commenced on February 25, 2013, and concluded on April 17, 2013. * * * It addressed fault determinations relating to the loss of well control, the ensuing explosion and fire, the sinking of the *Deepwater Horizon*, and the initiation of the release of oil from the well. Phase One also considered issues related to Transocean's limitation defense, as well as the various cross-, counter-, and third-party-claims between the several defendants. * * * The Court's conclusions relative to the Phase One trial are summarized below:

[1] BP Exploration & Production, Inc. ("BPXP") is subject to enhanced civil penalties under the Clean Water Act ("CWA"), 33 U.S.C. § 1321(b)(7)(D), as the discharge of oil was the result of BPXP's gross negligence and BPXP's willful misconduct.

[2] BP (meaning BPXP and BP America Production Company, but not BP p.l.c.), Transocean (meaning Transocean Holdings L.L.C., Transocean Deepwater Inc., and Transocean Offshore Deepwater Drilling Inc., but not Transocean Ltd. or Triton Asset Leasing GmbH), and Halliburton (meaning Halliburton Energy Service Inc. and Halliburton's Sperry division) are each liable under general maritime law for the blowout, explosion, and oil spill. BP's conduct was reckless. Transocean's conduct was negligent. Halliburton's conduct was negligent. Fault is apportioned as follows:

BP: 67%

Transocean: 30%

Halliburton; 3%[6]

[3] Although BPs conduct warrants the imposition [of] punitive damages under general maritime law, BP cannot be held liable for such damages under Fifth Circuit precedent.[300] * * *

[4] [Transocean is] not entitled to limitation of liability [because it had privity and knowledge of multiple acts of negligence and unseaworthy conditions that were proximate causes of the explosion, fire, and oil spill.] * * *

[5] Transocean * * * was an "operator" of an "Outer Continental Shelf facility" under the Oil Pollution Act of 1990, 33 U.S.C. § 2704(c). Consequently, Transocean is liable to the United States for removal costs.

Note

The foregoing findings and conclusions resulted from the "Phase One" trial, a 29-day bench trial conducted in early 2013. That trial focused on the relevant events leading up to and immediately surrounding the collapse of the riser and onset of the spill. The above is a heavily edited version of the court's opinion, which is very detailed and thorough in its presentation of the facts.

---

6. Editors' note: Halliburton was the cement contractor on the job. The Court explained the low fault assignment as follows: "As to Halliburton, it had two failures; one concerned cement and the other concerned well monitoring. With respect to the former, Halliburton's conduct [was] egregious. * * * Nevertheless, because the Court ultimately finds that the unstable foamed cement was not a cause of the blowout, no legal fault is attributable to Halliburton for these failures. Halliburton's failure concerning well monitoring was relatively small when compared to others' failures, and it was a failure shared by Transocean's drill crew."

300. To the extent the standards of the First Circuit or Ninth Circuit would apply to a particular claim, the Court finds that BP would be liable for punitive damages under those rules. [See *supra* at 251–52, 258 note 3.]

The "Phase Two" bench trial was conducted in the fall of 2013. Its focus was "Source Control"—issues pertaining to the efforts to stop or control the discharge of oil—and "Quantification"—addressing the amount of oil actually released into the Gulf of Mexico. The court's findings and conclusions are reported at 77 F. Supp. 3d 500 (E.D. La. 2015) and 2015 WL 729701 (E.D. La. Feb. 19, 2015).

Further trials are contemplated. For example, the court recently ruled that the State of Alabama is entitled to a jury trial on its claims against BP for removal costs and damages under OPA, 33 U.S.C. §§ 2702(b)(1), 2702(b)(2)(B), 2702(b)(2)(D), and 2702(b)(2)(F). MDL Doc. 14347, 3/30/15.

In re Deepwater Horizon: United States v. B.P. Exploration & Production, Inc.

United States Court of Appeals for the Fifth Circuit, 2014
753 F.3d 570, 2014 AMC 1521

BENAVIDES, Circuit Judge:

Before the Court is the federal government's civil enforcement action for Clean Water Act violations associated with the 2010 *Deepwater Horizon* oil spill in the Gulf of Mexico. Defendants BP Exploration & Production Inc. and Anadarko Petroleum Corporation appeal summary judgment in favor of the government on the question of their liability for civil penalties under 33 U.S.C. § 1321(b)(7)(A), which imposes mandatory penalties upon the owners of facilities "from which oil or a hazardous substance is discharged." The district court held that discharge is the point where "uncontrolled movement" begins. Applying this standard, the court concluded that oil flowing from the well through the *Deepwater Horizon*'s riser was a discharge from the well. The court then entered summary judgment on the issue of BP's and Anadarko's liability as co-owners of that well. Because we agree that there is no dispute of material fact regarding the discharge of oil from the well, we affirm.

I.

The Macondo Well was an exploratory well located about fifty miles off the Louisiana coast in the Gulf of Mexico. Anadarko and BP were co-owners of the well and co-lessees of the continental shelf block in which the well was located. The well itself was drilled by the *Deepwater Horizon,* a mobile offshore drilling vessel owned and operated by several Transocean entities. [Transocean, an original defendant in this action, has settled with the government.] The *Deepwater Horizon* was connected to the well by a [5,000-foot-long] riser. At the junction of the well and the riser was a blowout preventer that could be used automatically or manually to interrupt an impending blowout. Both the blowout preventer and riser were appurtenances of the *Deepwater Horizon.*

The blowout occurred on April 20, 2010, while the *Deepwater Horizon* was preparing to depart from the site in anticipation of the permanent extraction operation. As part of this preparation, the well had been lined and sealed with cement. Before the *Deepwater Horizon* departed, this cement failed, resulting in the high-pressure release of gas, oil, and other fluids. The blowout preventer also failed, thus allowing these fluids to burst from the well, flowing up through the riser and onto the deck of the *Deepwater Horizon.* The oil and gas subsequently caught fire, and the ensuing blaze capsized the *Deepwater Horizon,* which was still connected to the well via the riser. The strain from the sinking vessel severed the riser, and for nearly three months oil flowed continuously through the broken riser and into the Gulf of Mexico. Authorities eventually installed a cap over what remained of the riser, and oil continued to leak for two days, with the well finally sealed on July 15, 2010.

Following the incident, the federal government filed the present action, seeking civil penalties under § 311 of the Clean Water Act, 33 U.S.C. § 1321(b)(7)(A), which mandates the assessment of fines on the owners or operators of any vessel or facility "from which oil or a hazardous substance is discharged." The government then moved for summary judgment on several issues, including the well owners' civil-penalty liability for any "sub-surface" discharge of oil. Anadarko filed a cross-motion for summary judgment on the same issue, arguing that the subsurface discharge emanated from the riser owned by Transocean, and thus that the oil was not discharged from any facility owned or operated by Anadarko or BP. Holding that discharge is the point where "uncontrolled movement" begins, the [district] court concluded that the oil released from the well via the third party's broken riser was a discharge from the well. Because Anadarko and BP did not contest their ownership of the well, the district court then entered summary judgment in favor of the Government. Anadarko and BP filed a timely appeal.

* * *

III.

The Clean Water Act is "not a model of clarity." In its current form, the Act is the result of over a century of successive statutory schemes and amendments. Yet it is, in some respects, not overly complex. The legislation attempts to eliminate the introduction of any kind of pollutant—everything from paint and pesticides to rocks and dirt—into the waters of the United States. 33 U.S.C. §§ 1251(a), 1362(6). The Act does so by creating a regulatory framework and then prohibiting any discharge in violation of the regulations. [ ] Because of the heightened potential for "environmental disaster" resulting from the release of oil or hazardous waste, 33 U.S.C. § 1321 establishes increased fines for the discharge of these pollutants. [ ]

Specifically, the section prohibits the "discharge of oil or hazardous substances (i) into or upon the navigable waters of the United States, adjoining shorelines, or into or upon the waters of the contiguous zone ... in such quantities as may be harmful," except under circumstances not implicated by the present case. 33 U.S.C. § 1321(b)(3). The section further provides that:

> Any person who is the owner, operator, or person in charge of any vessel, onshore facility, or offshore facility from which oil or a hazardous substance is discharged in violation of [33 U.S.C. § 1321(b)(3)] shall be subject to a civil penalty in an amount up to $25,000 per day of violation or an amount up to $1,000 per barrel of oil or unit of reportable quantity of hazardous substances discharged.

[ ] In the instant case, no one denies that there has been a discharge of harmful quantities of oil into navigable waters. Anadarko and BP further stipulate that the well is an offshore facility, and that they are the owners of that facility. The only question, then, is whether it is beyond factual dispute that the well is a facility "from which" the harmful quantity of oil was discharged. We find no dispute as to the question.

Discharge is not defined for the purposes of this section, but is instead illustrated by a list of examples. Discharge "includes, but is not limited to, any spilling, leaking, pumping, pouring, emitting, emptying or dumping[.]" 33 U.S.C. § 1321(a)(2). Each of these statutory examples denotes the loss of controlled confinement. Similarly, the ordinary use of "discharge" refers to a fluid "flow[ing] out from where it has been confined" [citing several online dictionaries]. Accordingly, a vessel or facility is a point "from which oil or a hazardous substance is discharged" if it is a point at which controlled confinement is lost. Turning to the facts, we find no dispute as to whether the well is such a facility. The parties stipulate that cement had been deposited at the well. There is no genuine dispute that controlled confinement was lost when this cement failed—the defendants do not contest the cement's failure, and they concede that oil then "escaped" and "flowed freely" from the well and ultimately into navigable waters. And although the defendants argue that the blowout preventer should have engaged and prevented the progression of the blowout, the need for this intervention only underscores the extent to which the oil was already unconfined and flowing freely. Accordingly, we find that the well is a facility from which oil was discharged in violation of 33 U.S.C. § 1321(b)(3).

It is immaterial that the oil flowed through parts of the vessel before entering the Gulf of Mexico. Anadarko argues that discharge is the point at which oil "enters the marine environment." Yet Anadarko provides no relevant legal authority in support of the proffered interpretation. Nor does our research reveal any. On the contrary, it seems well settled that the section proscribes any discharge of oil that ultimately flows "into or upon ... navigable waters," irrespective of the path traversed by the discharged oil. For example, a discharge of oil violates the section even where the oil flows over a rail yard or hillside before reaching water. [ ] Similarly, the Environmental Protection Agency fined a factory owner for oil that spilled from a boiler gasket, into an industrial drain, through a conduit, and eventually into a creek. *See generally Pepperell Assocs. v. United States, EPA*, 246 F.3d 15 (1st Cir. 2001). The First Circuit ultimately denied review of the case, finding the agency's decision reasonable. *Id.* So oil need not flow from a facility directly into navigable waters to give rise to civil-penalty liability under 33 U.S.C. § 1321.

Nor is liability precluded by the fact that the property traversed by the oil was owned by a third party. The *Pepperell* factory owner was held liable for his facility's discharge even though the oil had traveled through a third party's conduit before reaching water. * * *. Indeed, we are aware of no case in which a court or administrative agency exempted a defendant from liability on account of the path traversed by discharged oil. The well owners' liability is thus unaffected by the fact that the oil traversed part of Transocean's vessel before entering the Gulf of Mexico.

We recognize that the aforementioned incidents involved blameless third parties, whereas here the owner or operator of the *Deepwater Horizon* might have contributed to the discharge. By all accounts, if the vessel's blowout preventer had functioned properly, the oil would not have entered navigable waters in violation of the Clean Water Act. The defendants therefore reason that liability is properly imposed upon the owner or operator of the *Deepwater Horizon.* Yet it is well established that this section of the Clean Water Act leaves no room for civil-penalty defendants to shift liability via allegations of third-party fault. * * * In fact, courts have consistently rejected attempts to shift liability on the basis of shared fault, instead choosing to consider any contributing cause as a mitigating factor at penalty calculation. This Court, in particular, recognizes the section as "an absolute liability system with limited exceptions, which are to be narrowly construed." *United States v. W. of Eng. Ship Owner's Mut. Prot. & Indem.*, 872 F.2d 1192, 1196 (5th Cir. 1989). And although 33 U.S.C. § 1321 includes a third-party-fault exception for removal cost liability, it includes no such exception for civil-penalty liability. That being the case, any culpability on the part of the *Deepwater Horizon* 's operators does not exempt the well owners from the liability at issue here.

* * *

Note

BP's and Anadarko's petitions for rehearing en banc were denied, with six judges dissenting. 775 F.3d 741. A petition for certiorari was filed on March 24, 2015. While the rehearing petitions were pending, the panel issued a supplementary *per curiam* opinion "address[ing] some of the arguments raised in the petitions for rehearing en banc." 772 F.3d 350, 352. The supplementary opinion clarified what the panel had done:

> BP suggests that the panel "realized" that "only one instrumentality can bear [CWA] liability for a discharge of a given quantum of oil," and that the opinion's "logic suggests that Transocean could not be held liable at all." Although [BP] would perhaps have preferred that the court adopt its "single instrumentality" theory, we did no such thing. * * * Because the Transocean entities settled, we did not need to consider whether the oil discharged from the well might also have constituted a "discharge" from the *Deepwater Horizon.* Nor did we need to decide for purposes of other hypothetical scenarios not at issue here precisely under what circumstances civil penalty liability attaches for the owners and operators of vessels or facilities "upstream" and "downstream" from the facility or vessel at which controlled confinement was lost.

Id. at 354–55.

In re Deepwater Horizon (Louisiana Parishes)

United States Court of Appeals, Fifth Circuit, 2014
745 F.3d 157, 2014 AMC 2600

JONES, Circuit Judge:

[Eleven Louisiana coastal parishes filed suits against BP and other defendants involved in the *Deepwater Horizon* oil spill to recover penalties under the Louisiana Wildlife Protection Statute for the pollution-related loss of aquatic life and wildlife.] Suits filed originally in state court were removed to federal court, which denied the Parishes' motions to remand and then dismissed all of the Parishes' claims as preempted by federal law. Both decisions are challenged in the Parishes' appeal. We concur with the district court that the state law claims were removable pursuant to the jurisdictional provision of the Outer Continental Shelf Lands Act ("OCSLA"). We also affirm their dismissal as preempted by federal law.

Background

The Macondo well, which was being drilled by the mobile offshore drilling rig *Deepwater Horizon*, experienced a catastrophic blowout and explosion in April 2010 and caused hydrocarbon, mineral, and other contaminant pollution all along the shores and estuaries of the Gulf Coast states, inflicting billions of dollars in property and environmental damage and spawning a litigation frenzy. Among the thousands of cases transferred for consolidated management by the Judicial Panel on Multidistrict Litigation to the Eastern District of Louisiana were the Parishes' lawsuits, some of which had been removed from state court. * * * [Predicating federal court jurisdiction on § 23(b)(1) of the Outer Continental Shelf Lands Act, 43 U.S.C. § 1349(b)(1), the district court upheld its removal jurisdiction notwithstanding that the cases alleged only penalties accruing under state law for pollution damage that occurred in state waters or along the coastline. The court subsequently held that the Parishes' claim for penalties under the Wildlife Statute were preempted by the Clean Water Act (CWA), 33 U.S.C. §§ 1251 *et seq.*]

Removal Jurisdiction

The Appellees principally rely on OCSLA's broad jurisdictional grant in petitioning for federal court removal jurisdiction. Defendants may generally remove a case from state court if the federal court would have had original jurisdiction over it. [The removal statute, 28 U.S.C. § 1441(a), states:

> Except as otherwise expressly provided by Act of Congress, any civil action brought in a State court of which the district courts have original jurisdiction, may be removed by the defendant or defendants, to the district court of the United States for the district and division embracing the place where such action is pending.]

The pertinent [original jurisdiction] provision, OCSLA § 23(b)(1), 43 U.S.C. § 1349(b), states:

> [T]he district courts of the United States shall have jurisdiction of cases and controversies arising out of, or in connection with ... any operation conducted on the outer Continental Shelf which involves exploration, development, or production of the minerals, of the subsoil and seabed of the outer Continental Shelf, or which involves rights to such minerals....

The Fifth Circuit has interpreted [the language of § 1349(b)] as straightforward and broad. * * * Courts typically assess jurisdiction under this provision in terms of whether (1) the activities that caused the injury constituted an "operation" "conducted on the outer Continental Shelf" that involved the exploration and production of minerals, and (2) the case "arises out of, or in connection with" the operation. [ ] As the district court noted, the fact that the oil spill occurred because of the Appellees' "operations" in exploring for and producing oil on the Outer Continental Shelf ("OCS") cannot be contested.

The Parishes do not concede, however, that, under the second half of the inquiry, their statutory wildlife claims arose out of or in connection with the oil production operation. Following the migration of contaminants from the well, the injury to wildlife and aquatic life was wholly situated in state territorial waters and on land. The statutory wildlife claims, they assert, have no effect on the "efficient exploitation of resources from the OCS," nor do they "threaten the total recovery of federally-owned resources." [ ] "Mere connection" to activities on the OCS, in other words, is insufficient to meet the jurisdictional test.

This argument, however, cannot be squared with applicable Fifth Circuit law or the facts before us. Even though one can hypothesize a "mere connection" between the cause of action and the OCS operation too remote to establish federal jurisdiction, this court deems § 1349 to require only a "but-for" connection. [ ] The but-for test does not include a purposive element as the Parishes advocate. It is undeniable that "the oil and other contaminants would not have entered into the State of Louisiana's territorial waters 'but for' [Appellees'] drilling and exploration operation." [ ] This is not, in short, a challenging case for asserting original federal jurisdiction, and therefore removal jurisdiction, under OCSLA.

* * *

Choice of Law

The more difficult question in this appeal is whether the Wildlife Statute's penalties can be applied against the Appellees. The Parishes' arguments are easily summarized. [They] acknowledge that the * * * *Deepwater Horizon* is a vessel. [ ] [They] assert that for this reason, the OCSLA choice of law provisions [43 U.S.C. §§ 1333(a)(1) and

1333(a)(2)(A)] cannot apply to their claims. ("Since * * * OCSLA situs is lacking, OCSLA cannot apply.") The Parishes thus foreswear any reliance on § 1333(a)(2)(A), which borrows state law as surrogate federal law to regulate certain OCSLA activity. As Orleans Parish puts it, '[i]t is not the adoption of state law as federal surrogate law that allows for penalties under [the Wildlife Statute], but the fact that the harm to wildlife ... occurred exclusively within Louisiana state waters, and Louisiana has the right to exercise its traditional police power ... by pursuing penalty claims under Louisiana state law."[8] * * * [But analysis of federal law] inevitably precedes the Parishes' simplistic *lex loci delicti* theory. [Under] OCSLA, "[a]ll law applicable to the outer Continental Shelf is federal law," and all cases "involving events occurring on the Shelf [are] governed by federal law...." *Gulf Offshore Co. v. Mobil Oil Corp.*, 453 U.S. 473, 480–81 (1981). [ ] Federal law governs injuries arising from activity on an OCSLA situs even if the injury occurs elsewhere. *See Alleman v. Omni Energy Servs. Corp.*, 580 F.3d 280, 286 (5th Cir. 2009) (OCSLA applies to helicopter accident although victims fell into the sea after the helicopter crashed into an offshore platform). * * * [The OCSLA § 1333(a)(1) regime] includes the federal statutes regulating water pollution and oil pollution, to which we now turn.

[*CWA*]

The Federal Water Pollution Control Act (*aka* Clean Water Act, "CWA"), 33 U.S.C. §§ 1251–1376, and its implementing regulations comprehensively govern oil exploration and development on the OCS. * * * Under the regulations, states like Louisiana that might be affected by offshore pollutant discharges may offer comments before permits are issued, but they have no other express regulatory role. * * *

[*International Paper Co. v. Ouellette,* 479 U.S. 481, 494 (1987) held that the "CWA precludes a court from applying the law of an affected State against an out-of-state source." Thus, Vermont law could not be applied to water pollution that spread to Vermont from a point source in New York.] The Court stated:

> After examining the CWA as a whole, its purposes and its history, we are convinced that if affected States were allowed to impose separate discharge standards on a single point source, the inevitable result would be a serious interference with the achievement of the "full purposes and objectives of Congress." * * *

[It added that it] "would be extraordinary for Congress, after devising an elaborate permit system that sets clear standards, to tolerate common-law suits that have the potential to undermine this regulatory structure." *Id.* at 497. * * *

The Parishes contend that *Ouellette* is distinguishable. First, [they argue that] it applies only to the CWA's permitting provision (33 U.S.C. § 1342), not to the oil discharge prohibition (33 U.S.C. § 1321(o)). * * * Second, [they argue that] since *Ouellette* considered only interstate water pollution, the decision has no bearing on discharges from the OCS. We find these distinctions unpersuasive. * * *

* * *

8. The crux of the Parishes' argument is this analogy: "If someone commits murder on the navigable waters within the State of Louisiana, admiralty law might apply to any civil claim arising from that death, but Louisiana would undoubtedly be able to prosecute the murder under Louisiana law." It is a bad analogy because it assumes the murder was committed in Louisiana waters, unlike the pollution that simply migrated into state waters. It is also an inapt basis for considering federal preemption, a subject that demands close textual analysis of case law and statutes.

[*OPA*]

Because the CWA was inadequate to provide complete remedies for the Valdez, Alaska oil spill catastrophe, Congress passed the Oil Pollution Act ("OPA") in 1990. 33 U.S.C. §§ 2701–62. Congress intended that the OPA would "build [ ] upon section 311 of the Clean Water Act [33 U.S.C. § 1321] to create a single Federal law providing cleanup authority, penalties, and liability for oil pollution." S.Rep. No. 101–94, at 9 (1989) [ ]. The OPA prescribes a supplemental, comprehensive federal plan for handling oil spill responses, allocating responsibility among participants and prescribing reimbursement for cleanup costs and injuries to third parties. The remedial efforts for the Macondo well blowout occurred under the auspices of both the CWA, 33 U.S.C. § 1321(b)(1) (the CWA applies to oil discharges in connection with activities above the OCS), and the OPA, 33 U.S.C. § 2701(32)(C) (extending the OPA to offshore facilities above the OCS).

Effect of Savings Clauses

With *Ouellette* as the controlling law, there are no state remedies to "save." The OPA applies as the law of the OCSLA point source and, along with the CWA penalties, furnishes a comprehensive remedial regime for affected states' governmental and private claims. Just because the Parishes are located in the most closely adjacent state, they fare no better than the "down-current" states of Texas, Mississippi, Alabama, and Florida. The CWA and the OPA "savings" clauses preserve but do not create state law claims. [ ]

* * * [E]ach savings clause is powerless to "save" the Parishes' claims under the Wildlife Statute. In general, the savings clauses must be read with particularity and, as *Ouellette* demonstrates, a savings clause does not disrupt the ordinary operation of conflict preemption. * * * Most closely on point in the CWA is Section 1321(o)(2), which provides that, "[n]othing in this Section shall [preempt any state or local] requirement or liability with respect to the discharge of oil ... into any waters within such state...." The provision only saves state laws imposing liability or additional requirements with respect to the "discharge" of oil "into any waters within such State." The provision does not save a state's laws where the discharge did not occur "within" the state. The Parishes contend that the term "discharge" should be read to include "any means by which oil enters state waters." According to the statute, however, "discharge" "includes, but is not limited to, any spilling, leaking, pumping, pouring, emitting, emptying or dumping...." 33 U.S.C. § 1321(a)(2). These gerunds connote active conduct or movement from a point source to a place within the state rather than the mere passive migration or floating of oil into state waters. Contrary to the Parishes' view, the word "emitting" does not change this analysis. "Emit" means to send out or release. *Webster's Third New International Dictionary* 742 (3d ed.1986). The principle of *noscitur a sociis*, that words grouped in a list should be given related meaning, reinforces our interpretation because, taken in context with the other gerunds, "emitting" must take on an active cast. [ ][13] * * *

The Parishes place the most emphasis on [the] savings clause from the OPA, [33 U.S.C. § 2718(c)]. The section states that "[n]othing in this Act [OPA] ... shall in any way affect ... the authority of the United States or any State [or locality] ... to impose ... any fine or penalty ..." relating to an oil discharge. First, they assert, the OPA was enacted to supplement the older CWA apparatus for redressing the consequences of oil pollution. Second, the Parishes urge that the OPA, being specific with regard to oil pollution, controls over the

13. *Askew v. Am. Waterways Operators, Inc.*, 411 U.S. 325 (1973), does not support the Parishes' interpretation of Section 1321 as preserving state law regulation of oil pollution that originated outside state waters. The spill in that case occurred adjacent to Florida's shore.

more general requirements of the CWA, which applies to both illegal oil and hazardous substance discharges into navigable waters. Third, the exact language of Section 2718(c) differs critically from the CWA's Section 1321(o) because it lacks the narrowing reference to state waters. * * * On balance, however, we conclude that the Parishes place more weight on this savings provision than it can bear.

To begin, the canon of construction that mandates application of a specific over a general statutory provision is not easily adapted to this statutory scheme. As all parties acknowledge, the CWA, the fountainhead of clean water regulation, contains the provisions that prohibit oil discharges and set penalties for illegal discharges. [ ] These provisions led the district court to declare the CWA's savings provision more specific than those in the OPA. The Parishes, in contrast, characterize Section 2718(c) as plainly more specific both because it resides in the OPA and it preserves state penalty actions. We do not, however, perceive the applicability of these provisions to be an either/or proposition. Instead, each requires interpretation within a statutory framework in which the OPA was designed to complement, not compete with the CWA. That the OPA was enacted more recently than the CWA means little where there is no fundamental conflict with provisions of the CWA. The statutes, in other words, must be construed, as the district court noted, in *pari materia.*

Moving to the specific language of Section 2718(c), the provision more precisely states, "Nothing in this Act, the Act of March 3, 1851 [i.e., the Limitation of Liability Act] or § 9509 of Title 26[7] [shall affect] the authority of the United States or any State or political subdivision thereof. . . ." Statutory construction begins with the language of the statute [ ], and, in the absence of ambiguity, often ends there. Two features of this prefatory language are notable. The savings provision does not apply beyond the OPA itself and two other laws. Further, Congress did not refer to the CWA. Courts are not at liberty to expand the language chosen by Congress, and the omission here is telling. Thus, while Section 2718(c) saves from the OPA's diminution the ability of the United States or state entities to impose requirements relating to oil discharges, it does not save those powers from the effects of the CWA or any other non-identified federal law. * * *

Other principles of statutory construction are relevant because of the prefatory language here. If Section 2718(c) were interpreted, as the Parishes contend, to "supersede" the CWA and *Ouellette* by allowing all affected states to layer their unique penalty and regulatory laws on top of those governing this OCSLA blowout, the result would be an implied repeal of CWA preemption. Implied repeals, however, are disfavored. [ ] * * *

It is also possible to understand why Section 2718(c) omits a reference to waters within the affected state. Simply, the provision saves remedies available to the United States as well as the states, rendering a geographic limitation to state waters meaningless. Viewed in light of Congress' presumed awareness of *Ouellette* when the OPA was passed, and Congress' failure to change the scope of CWA preemption despite its intent generally to broaden remedies against oil pollution, this omission cannot be controlling on the scope of this savings provision.

* * *

Conclusion

For the reasons stated above, the district court had removal jurisdiction over the Parishes' Wildlife Statute claims. Further, it correctly concluded that the claims are preempted by the CWA as interpreted in *Ouellette*, and that Congress did not reject that

7. Editors' note: 26 U.S.C. § 9509 sets up the Oil Spill Liability Trust Fund.

interpretation explicitly or by negative implication in the CWA or when it passed the OPA. The judgment of the court dismissing the Parishes' claims is affirmed.

Note

Note the opinion's careful delineation between the application of state law via 43 U.S.C. § 1333(a)(2)(A) and the application of state law of its own force. As the court noted, the Parishes eschewed reliance on § 1333(a)(2)(A). The Fifth Circuit went on to indicate that reliance on that provision would in any event have been futile, because the provision explicitly limits its coverage to "artificial islands and fixed structures erected [on the seabed of the OCS]," whereas the *Deepwater Horizon* was a vessel. 745 F.3d at 166 & n. 10.

In re Deepwater Horizon: OPA Damages

United States District Court for the Eastern District of Louisiana, 2012
902 F. Supp. 2d 808

BARBIER, District Judge:

* * *

This matter arises from the April 20, 2010 blowout, explosion, and fire aboard the *Deepwater Horizon* semi-submersible drilling rig as it was engaged in oil exploration on the Outer Continental Shelf, and the subsequent discharge of millions of gallons of oil into the Gulf of Mexico. After cases were consolidated in a multidistrict litigation ("MDL") proceeding, the Court created various pleading bundles to manage the numerous and varied claims asserted. Relevant here is the "B1 Bundle," which concerns non-governmental claims for economic loss and property damage.

Pursuant to the Court's instruction, the Plaintiffs' Steering Committee ("PSC") filed a Master B1 Complaint [asserting] claims under the Oil Pollution Act of 1990 ("OPA"), 33 U.S.C. § 2701, *et seq.*, general maritime law, and state law. Many defendants moved to dismiss the B1 Master Complaint. On August 26, 2011, the Court issued an Order and Reasons granting in part and denying in part these motions ("B1 Order"). The B1 Order held, *inter alia*, that the *Deepwater Horizon* was a vessel, the claims in the B1 Master Complaint fall within the Court's admiralty jurisdiction, and that general maritime law is not entirely displaced by OPA. However, to the extent maritime law supplements OPA, traditional limitations such as the *Robins Dry Dock* rule [*supra* at 111, 144 note 6] remain in effect. The B1 Order also held that state law was preempted by maritime law, notwithstanding OPA's state-law savings clause, 33 U.S.C. § 2718. * * *

On May 2, 2012, the Court preliminarily approved a proposed class-action settlement regarding many, but not all, claims by private parties for economic loss and property damage resulting from the oil spill. [Subsequently the Court gave final approval to the settlement, the Fifth Circuit affirmed, 739 F.3d 790 (Jan. 10, 2014), and the Supreme Court denied certiorari, 574 U.S. 1054 (Dec. 8, 2014).] In the interim, the Court directed the parties to file motions addressing the viability of three types of claims outside the proposed settlement: the "Pure Stigma," "BP Dealer," and "Recreation Claims." [Defendants] moved to dismiss these claims under Fed. R. Civ. P. 12(b)(6). * * *

Pure Stigma Claims

* * * "Pure Stigma Claims" means claims alleging a reduction in the value of real property caused by the oil spill or other contaminant even though (1) the property was

not physically touched by oil and (2) the property was not sold. * * * [For illustrative purposes, the following [two] Short-Form Joinders[3] reflect Pure Stigma Claims. The Short-Form Joinder of Linda Hall, states:

> Mrs. Linda Hall ("Plaintiff") owns a condominium at the Phoenix VIII located ... in Orange Beach, Alabama (residential). Plaintiff has experienced a diminution on the value of her property because of the oil spill. No known physical damage at this time.

The Short-Form Joiner of Philip Michael Reid states:

> My claim is for loss of value of my residence ... in Orange Beach, Al. No damage occurred to the property as a result of the spill. I had my property appraised in December 2005 @ $975,000. Another appraisal in December 2010 resulted in $470,000.]

* * * [U]nder the Court's previous rulings the Pure Stigma Claims are not viable under general maritime law or state law. The PSC argues that the Pure Stigma Claims are recoverable under two of OPA's damages provisions, 33 U.S.C. §§ 2702(b)(2)(B) & E. * * * Section 2702(a) contains OPA's general liability provision:

> Notwithstanding any other provision or rule of law, and subject to the provisions of this Act, each responsible party for a vessel or a facility from which oil is discharged ... into or upon the navigable waters or adjoining shorelines or the exclusive economic zone is liable for the removal costs and damages specified in subsection (b) of this section that result from such incident.

33 U.S.C. § 2702(a). Section 2702(b)(2) then enumerates six [recoverable] categories of damage, Subsections (A) through (F). Plaintiffs urge that the Pure Stigma Claims are cognizable under two categories, Subsection (B) and Subsection (E). The Court considers Subsection (E) first. It states:

> (E) Profits and earning capacity
>
> Damages equal to the loss of profits or impairment of earning capacity due to the injury, destruction, or loss of real property, personal property, or natural resources, which shall be recoverable by any claimant.

Id. § 2702(b)(2)(E). This Court previously recognized that Congress intended OPA to allow a broader class of claimants to recover economic losses than allowed under general maritime law. Consistent with this intention, Subsection (E) does not require the plaintiff to be the owner of the property or natural resources injured, destroyed, or lost in order to recover under that Section. Thus, the *Robins Dry Dock* rule [*supra* at 111, 144 note 6] does not apply to a claim pursued under Subsection (E) of OPA.

Nevertheless, OPA is not without limits. Notably, Subsection (E) only allows recovery for "loss of profits" or "impairment of earning capacity." As explained above, the Pure Stigma Claims concern property that was not sold; they are claims for ***unrealized*** diminution of real property value. Such claims concern neither a "loss of profits" nor "impairment of earning capacity." Before real property is sold, there can be no "profits" to be lost. Likewise, unrealized diminution of property value usually is not an "impairment [of] earning capacity." Furthermore, until property is sold and a loss realized, damages are

---

3. Short-Form Joinders permitted Plaintiffs/Claimants to file an answer and claim in Transocean's Limitation Action and intervene in one or more of the Master Complaints without paying a filing fee. * * *

speculative—it is possible that the value of real property eventually may meet or exceed its pre-spill amount. For these reasons, the Pure Stigma Claims are not viable under Subsection (E). * * *

Turning to Subsection (B), that provision states:

> (B) Real or personal property
>
> Damages for injury to, or economic losses resulting from destruction of, real or personal property, which shall be recoverable by a claimant who owns or leases that property.

Id. § 2702(b)(2)(B). In order to be viable under Subsection (B), a claim must concern "injury to" or "destruction of" one's property. Pure Stigma Claims do not involve cases where oil contacted property; thus, they do not involve "destruction of" property. Nor do these claims involve "injury to" property, because Subsection (B) is interpreted as requiring ***physical*** injury to the property. * * * Because the Pure Stigma Claims concern property that was not physically injured or destroyed, the Pure Stigma Claims are not viable under Subsection (B). * * *

BP Dealer Claims

The Order directing the parties to file the instant motions described the "BP Dealer Claims" as "claims by or on behalf of entities marketing BP-branded fuels that they have suffered damages, including loss of business, income, and profits, as a result of the loss of value to the 'BP' brand or name." After considering the parties' briefs, the Court narrows the definition of "BP Dealer Claims" to mean only those plaintiffs whose claims for economic loss are based ***solely*** on consumers' decisions not to purchase fuel or goods from BP fuel stations and convenience stores following the explosion and oil spill; i.e., claims solely based on consumer animosity toward BP. For clarity, a BP Dealer Claim is distinguished from, for example, a hypothetical claim by a BP franchisee whose gas station is located near the Gulf Coast (or located along a highway frequently traveled by tourist heading to the Gulf Coast) alleging lost profits for reasons other than or in addition to consumer animosity toward BP, such as an area-wide decline in tourism. Again, the "BP Dealer Claims" concern only those plaintiffs/claimants whose claims are based ***solely*** on consumer animosity toward BP and the BP brand.

The Short-Form Joinder of Chmaysam Maher/East Main Getty is illustrative of a BP Dealer Claim:

> In 2009 BP converted nearly 250 Getty fuel stations in the New England area to the BP brand. All remaining Getty fuel stations remained Getty branded, however, each station purchased its fuel from BP. The oil spill in the Gulf of Mexico received world-wide attention. As a protest against BP and all things associated with BP thousands of drivers chose not to fill their vehicles at BP or BP associated fuel/service stations. As a result, my business [East Main Getty in Webster, Mass.] saw a dramatic decline in profits from which it has yet to recover.

[Under this Court's previous rulings the BP Dealer Claims are not viable under general maritime law or state law.] The PSC contends that the BP Dealer Claims are recoverable under Subsection (B) of OPA (quoted above). * * * [The PSC argues] that the "injured property" for purposes of Subsection (B) is the "BP brand" leased by the BP Dealers. However, as explained in the context [of] the Pure Stigma Claims, a claim under Subsection (B) requires a physical injury to the property leased or owned by the Plaintiff; e.g., a boat or real estate that is oiled. Because the "BP brand" is intangible property, it is not susceptible to physical injury. Therefore, the BP Dealer Claims are not compensable under Subsection (B).

Although the PSC does not urge that the BP Dealer Claims are viable under Subsection (E), the Court takes note of Professor David Robertson's article, cited by BP, which concluded that BP Dealer Claims likely would not be viable under Subsection (E).[11] * * *

Recreation Claims

The Order directing the parties to file the instant motions described the "Recreation Claims" as "claims by or on behalf of recreational fishermen, recreational divers, beachgoers, recreational boaters, etc., that they have suffered damages that include loss of enjoyment of life from the inability to use portions of the Gulf of Mexico for recreation and amusement purposes." The B1 Master Complaint provides an example of a Recreation Claim when it alleged:

> As a direct and proximate result of the Petitioners' negligence, the Recreation Claimants have suffered damages including, *inter alia*, loss of deposits for vacation rentals, loss of enjoyment of life from the inability to use the Gulf of Mexico for recreation and amusement purposes.

The Short-Form Joinder of Emily Wisniewski similarly states:

> Emily Wisniewksi owns a 2009 19 foot Tahoe QSI recreational boat stored ... in Fort Morgan, Alabama.... Due to the presence of oil in the Gulf of Mexico and Mobile Bay, boat traffic was restricted and waters were closed. Ms. Wisniewski was denied use of her boat for seven weeks (June 7, 2010 to July 26, 2010) due to the oil spill. During this period, she paid for the upkeep and maintenance of the boat.

BP interprets the B1 Master Complaint as advancing two types of Recreational Claims: (1) "Loss of Enjoyment" claims, which allege a loss of enjoyment from the plaintiffs' inability to engage in preferred recreational activities (e.g., fishing, diving, boating, or beachgoing), and (2) "Loss of Deposit" claims, which allege that plaintiffs wasted money spent in preparation for such recreational activities. * * * [N]either are recoverable here.

* * *

With respect to OPA and the "Loss of Enjoyment" Recreation Claims, although no party appears to urge that these claims are compensable under OPA, the Court notes that these are not claims for "loss of profits" or "impairment of earning capacity," and, thus, would not be recoverable under Subsection (E). The "Loss of Enjoyment" claims that do not arise from a physical injury or destruction to property owned or leased by the plaintiff also are not recoverable under Subsection (B). To the extent a "Loss of Enjoyment" claim actually involved physical injury or destruction to one's property (e.g., where a pleasure boat was oiled), Subsection (B) does not compensate this type of emotional, non-pecuniary damage. [ ]

---

11. David W. Robertson, *The Oil Pollution Act's Provisions on Damages for Economic Loss*, 30 Miss. C.L.Rev. 157, 172–173 (2011) ("G owns a gas station in Boise, Idaho that sells Oil Co.-brand gasoline. Although G owns and operates the station as an independent franchise, his station becomes the target of a boycott by a local environmental group demanding greater corporate accountability. G claims lost income resulting from the boycott.... It seems unlikely that the existence of 'injury, destruction, or loss' of resources or property played any causal role in producing these damages.... [T]he boycott ... would probably have occurred as a result of the reputational effects of the spill, regardless of whether the spill had actually produced any 'injury, destruction, or loss' of anything physical").

As to the "Loss of Deposit" Recreation Claims, those claims are not available under Subsection (E) for the reasons just stated. "Loss of Deposit" claims are also not available under Subsection (B), because they do not involve "injury to" or "destruction of" real or personal property owned or leased by the Recreation Claimants as contemplated by Subsection (B). Although a monetary payment may qualify as "property" in some legal contexts, it does not qualify as property under Subsection (B) given that it is not capable of being "injured" or "destroyed" by oil pollution. * * *

* * *

Note

The BP Dealer Claims dramatize a particularly difficult issue: the scope of causation contemplated by OPA's provision specifying oil spillers' liability for pure economic loss, 33 U.S.C. § 2702(b)(2)(E). The case law is surprisingly thin, but the academic debate has been fierce. A number of the relevant law review articles are treated in Robertson, *Criteria for Recovery of Economic Loss Under the Oil Pollution Act of 1990*, 7 TEX. J. OIL, GAS & ENERGY L. 241 (2012). See also Note, *In re Oil Spill by the Oil Rig "Deepwater Horizon,"* 36 HARV. ENVTL. L. REV. 533 (2012).

Chapter XIII

Sovereign Immunity

A. Federal Governmental Immunity

For the first hundred years of its existence, the United States was immune from suit except so far as it consented to be sued.[1] During that era, virtually the only avenue to relief for one harmed by federal government action was a private bill in Congress.

Eventually Congress enacted a number of general statutes waiving various aspects of federal governmental immunity. The presently important statutes are the 1887 Tucker Act, 28 U.S.C. §§ 1346(a)(2) and 1491(a)(1); the 1920 Suits in Admiralty Act (SAA), 46 U.S.C. §§ 30901–18; the 1925 Public Vessels Act (PVA), 46 U.S.C.§§ 31101–13; the 1946 Federal Tort Claims Act (FTCA), 28 U.S.C. §§ 1346(b), 1402(b), 2401(b), 2402, 2412, 2671–80; and the 1978 Contract Disputes Act, 41 U.S.C. §§ 7101–09.

This section focuses primarily on the SAA and PVA. It should be borne in mind throughout the following discussions of federal governmental liability in contract and tort cases that government ships are not subject to in rem liability. See 46 U.S.C. §§ 30903(a), 31112. "No government will allow its warships to be subject to arrest." Rutherglen, *The Future of Maritime Law in the Federal Courts: Sovereign Immunity*, 31 J. Mar. L. & Com. 317, 317 (2000).

1. Government Contracts

The Tucker Act applies generally to nonmaritime contracts and contemplates litigation in the Court of Federal Claims. The SAA and PVA apply generally to maritime contracts and contemplate in personam litigation in admiralty.

The Contracts Disputes Act requires both maritime and nonmaritime contract claims against the U.S. to be first submitted to the involved federal agency for its review. A non-maritime contract claimant who is dissatisfied with the result of that process has a choice: it can take an administrative appeal to an agency board of contract appeals or it can sue in the Court of Federal Claims. Appeals from the agency boards of contract appeals and from the Court of Federal Claims lie in the Federal Circuit.

1. "[The constitution] created one partial exception to the general immunity by providing that government [ ] could not take private property for public use without just compensation. See U.S. Const. Amend. V (just compensation required)." Dobbs, The Law of Torts 693 (2000).

Respecting most maritime contracts,[2] the Contracts Disputes Act provides that the dissatisfied claimant—rather than taking the administrative appeal or Court of Federal Claims route—must sue the U.S. under either the PVA or the SAA. 41 U.S.C. § 7102(d). The PVA covers claims for "compensation for towage and salvage services, including contract salvage, rendered to a public vessel of the United States," 46 U.S.C. § 31102(a)(2), and the SAA covers other maritime-contract claims against the government, 46 U.S.C. § 30903(a).

2. Government Torts

The SAA and PVA waive governmental immunity from suits in tort—*maritime* tort—as well as in contract. Up to the end of World War II, relief in nonmaritime tort situations continued to be confined to the private-bill route. In 1946, Congress passed a comprehensive waiver of tort liability in the FTCA. The FTCA does not cover "[a]ny claim for which a remedy is provided" by the SAA or the PVA. 28 U.S.C. § 2680(d). The meaning of § 2680(d) was confused for a time, but it seems to have become settled that the SAA/PVA regime for governmental maritime torts and the FTCA regime for governmental nonmaritime torts are mutually exclusive; "an admiralty claim cannot be brought under the.... FTCA."[3]

Some governmental maritime torts will fall under the coverage provisions of both the SAA and PVA. In such situations, the PVA controls. As was stated in *Marine Coatings of Alabama v. United States*, 71 F.3d 1558, 1561 n.3 (11th Cir. 1996) (omissions not signaled):

> Generally, it makes no difference which of the two acts applies, since the same substantive law governs and since the PVA incorporates most of the procedural provisions of the SAA. There are a few differences, however. [The PVA disallows] pre-judgment interest on money damages. [It also] has a more liberal venue provision, restricts subpoenas against officers and crews without the permission of certain authorities, [and] requires reciprocity in order for an alien to bring suit under the act.[4]

The courts treat governmental immunity as "jurisdictional," meaning that there is a working assumption of immunity and that the requirements the waiver statutes place upon potential plaintiffs are generally treated as rigid and unforgiving. When a plaintiff who should have proceeded under the SAA and/or PVA mistakenly takes the FTCA route, a typical result is that the two-year statute of limitations of the SAA/PVA (46 U.S.C. §§ 30905, 31103) will expire before the mistake is corrected. A plaintiff who makes the mistake in reverse—invoking the SAA and/or PVA when the right statute was the FTCA—will often find that the case has died because of failure to comply with administrative notice and other procedural requirements in the FTCA. The only safe thing for plaintiffs to do in all situations in which there is any doubt about coverage is to comply with both the SAA/PVA and the FTCA limitations periods and procedures. Note also that the Admiralty Extension Act (AEA), 46 U.S.C. § 30101(c)(2), contains an additional procedural

---

2. *United States v. United Continental Tuna Corp.*, 425 U.S. 164, 179 n.18 (1976), seems to take government-employed seamen's wage claims out of the PVA/SAA system, stating that "wage claims exceeding $10,000 by Government employees working aboard Government vessels are still cognizable exclusively in the Court of [Federal] Claims, where wage claims by Government employees have traditionally been cognizable."

3. Schoenbaum, Admiralty and Maritime Law 1034 (4th [hornbook] ed. 2004). See also *id.* at note 8 (arguing that contrary holdings are erroneous).

4. Recall that the PVA's "reciprocity" requirement was in play in *Taghadomi*, *supra* at 41.

pitfall. As noted in *Anderson v. United States*, 317 F.3d 1235, 1239 (11th Cir. 2003), for cases in which a government vessel on navigable water has caused injury or damage on land, the AEA effectively "reduces the two-year statute of limitations to eighteen months."

The FTCA sets out a large number of exceptions, i.e., situations in which the government's immunity from tort liability is retained. The most important is the "discretionary function" exception, 28 U.S.C. § 2680(a), which precludes suit on "[a]ny claim ... based upon the exercise or performance or the failure to exercise or perform a discretionary function or duty on the part of a federal agency or an employee of the Government, whether or not the discretion involved be abused." The SAA and PVA contain nothing comparable, but the courts have read the discretionary function exception into the SAA and PVA. See *McMellon v. United States*, 387 F.3d 329, 338 (4th Cir. 2004) (en banc): "[E]very circuit to consider the question [has] concluded that an implied discretionary function exception should be read into the [SAA and PVA]."

Moreover, the courts have created other exceptions to the statutory waivers of immunity, the best-known of which is the doctrine that takes its name from *Feres v. United States*, 340 U.S. 135 (1950), holding that members of the Armed Forces cannot bring torts suits against the U.S. The operation of the *Feres* doctrine in maritime tort cases is potentially complex. Compare *Hillier v. Southern Towing Co.*, 714 F.2d 714 (7th Cir. 1983) (holding that *Feres* precluded private shipowners sued by the widow of a Coast Guard marine safety inspector from seeking tort indemnity from the U.S.) with *Ionian Glow Marine v. United States*, 670 F.2d 462 (4th Cir. 1982) (holding that *Feres* did not keep a private shipowner who had settled tort claims brought against it by U.S. Navy sailors from recovering tort contribution from the U.S.).

B & F Trawlers, Inc. v. United States

United States Court of Appeals, Fifth Circuit, 1988
841 F.2d 626, 1988 AMC 1577

JONES, Circuit Judge:

* * *

On February 23, 1985, the Coast Guard cutter *Dallas* inspected the *F/V Star Trek* in the Gulf of Mexico and discovered that the shrimp vessel was carrying marijuana. The Coast Guard boarding party arrested the captain and crew and directed the *Star Trek* toward Guantanamo Bay, Cuba. The *Star Trek* met the Coast Guard cutter *Mesquite* shortly thereafter, and the *Mesquite* began towing the *Star Trek*. Around 7:00 p.m. on February 25, a fire broke out on the seized vessel. Officials removed all people from the *Star Trek*, and towing continued until 6:40 p.m. the next day when officials used .50 caliber machine guns to sink the shrimp vessel.

The *Star Trek* was owned and operated by B & F Trawlers, Inc., which allegedly had reported to the Coast Guard prior to the above events that the shrimp vessel had been stolen and was missing. According to B & F Trawlers, *Star Trek* was valued at $200,000 and was uninsured. * * *

[B & F] alleged under the [SAA and PVA] that the Coast Guard failed to use due care in the care, custody, and control of the *Star Trek* and deliberately and intentionally sank the vessel. * * * The district court dismissed the action. * * *

Vessels which are used, or are intended for use, to transport any controlled substances are subject to forfeiture to the government, and all right, title, and interest in the forfeited vessels vest in the government upon commission of the act giving rise to the forfeiture. 21 U.S.C. § 881(a)(4), (h). Statutes under which property used in the commission of criminal offenses is forfeited have consistently been held constitutional. [ ]

Normally we would rely on the above authorities to affirm * * * the district court's decision, for it seems anomalous that Congress would take away all property interests in forfeited property and replace them with a tort action. Here, however, the appellants have alleged that they had informed the Coast Guard that the vessel had been stolen. If appellants can prove that the narcotics violation occurred while the *Star Trek* "was unlawfully in the possession of a person other than the owner in violation of the criminal laws of the United States," then the *Star Trek* is not subject to forfeiture. * * *

Regardless whether the *Star Trek* was stolen, the Government alleges that appellants do not have a private cause of action for any or all of four reasons. First, it contends that the law enforcement exception to the Federal Tort Claims Act ("FTCA") should be incorporated into the SAA and PVA to bar this suit. Second, the constitutional doctrine of separation of powers bars this suit. Third, the SAA and PVA do not waive the government's immunity because the government was performing a function (law enforcement) in which private parties cannot engage. Fourth, the FTCA discretionary function exception, already incorporated into the SIAA and PVA, bars this suit. For reasons which follow, we accept only the last reason as creating an arguable limit on the government's liability.

A. *Law Enforcement Exception*

The FTCA law enforcement exception preserves governmental immunity from suit for "[a]ny claim arising in respect of the detention of any goods or merchandise by any officer of customs or excise or any other law enforcement officer." 28 U.S.C. § 2680(c). The provision is relevant here because Coast Guard officers are also considered customs officers, 14 U.S.C. § 143, and law enforcement officers, 14 U.S.C. §§ 2, 89.

Neither the Supreme Court nor any other circuit court has been asked to incorporate the FTCA law enforcement exception into the SAA and PVA. Until we are persuaded otherwise, we decline to do so. Congress enacted the SAA and PVA in 1920 and 1925, respectively. When Congress enacted the FTCA * * *, it did not incorporate the numerous liability exceptions therein into the SAA and PVA. Forty more years have elapsed since the FTCA became law, and Congress still has not modified or amended the SAA and PVA to incorporate any FTCA exceptions. Confronted with such a lengthy period of legislative silence, we hesitate to rewrite the SAA and PVA as requested by the government. If the law enforcement exception is to be engrafted into the SAA and PVA, then the grafting should be done by legislative surgeons, not judicial surgeons.[4] * * *

B. *Separation of Powers*

The government argues that imposition of liability for damage to property seized pursuant to statutorily prescribed customs enforcement duties would offend the separation of powers doctrine. We acknowledge that the threat of pervasive damage suits under the

4. The strength of today's reasoning is not undermined by our previous incorporation of the FTCA discretionary function exception into the SIAA and PVA. As we recently noted in *Wiggins v. United States*, 799 F.2d 962, 965–66 (5th Cir. 1986), historical evidence suggested that Congress, when it passed the FTCA, expected that the judiciary would create a discretionary function exception to liability even absent legislative articulation. Such historical evidence pertaining to a law enforcement exception is noticeably absent.

SAA/PVA could affect the government's ability to stem the illicit maritime trade in narcotics. Yet, we can also foresee certain situations in which imposition of maritime tort liability would not cripple law enforcement efforts. For example, assume that in their zeal to board their vessel and apprehend a nearby drug-running vessel, Coast Guard crewmen accidentally injure a pedestrian walking on the dock; while leaving the harbor, the Coast Guard vessel brushes against a fishing trawler and causes damage; upon returning with the seized vessel, the tow line breaks and the boat crashes into the dock, causing more property damage and personal injury. The government, cloaked with separation of powers protection, could avoid liability in such scenarios if we held here in broad terms that the tortious conduct occurred as a by-product of the government's protected law enforcement function. Although the facts of our case and the above hypotheticals present far different situations, they illustrate that not all government conduct should be protected under an "end-objective" analysis. We believe the better decision is to avoid cloaking all "law enforcement" activity with protection that is too broad and undefined under a separation of powers analysis.

C. *Uniquely Governmental Function Exception*

The SAA waives immunity from suit ["in a case in which, if a vessel were privately owned or operated, or if cargo were privately owned or possessed, or if a private person or property were involved, a civil action in admiralty could be maintained." 46 U.S.C. § 30903(a).] This provision is incorporated into the PVA. [See 46 U.S.C. § 31103 (a suit under the PVA "is subject to the provisions of [the SAA] except to the extent inconsistent with this [Act].")]. * * * [T]he government contends that the SAA and PVA do not waive immunity from suit by the plaintiffs because private individuals could not engage in law enforcement on the high seas. * * *

Despite its superficial appeal, we cannot accept this contention. The Supreme Court rejected a similar argument based on comparable language of the FTCA in *Rayonier Inc. v. United States*, 352 U.S. 315 (1957). There the petitioners alleged that the Forest Service's negligence in fighting a fire caused damage to petitioners' property. The Supreme Court rejected the government's assertion that the uniquely governmental function of fire fighting precluded suit under the FTCA. [See also *Indian Towing Co. v. United States*, 350 U.S. 61 (1955) (operation of lighthouse); *United States v. Muniz*, 374 U.S. 150 (1963) (negligent prison operation); *Yates v. United States*, 479 F.2d 878 (10th Cir. 1974) (negligence by air traffic controllers); *Downs v. United States*, 522 F.2d 990 (6th Cir. 1975) (negligence by FBI agent attempting to prevent airplane hijacking); *Canadian Transport Co. v. United States*, 663 F.2d 1081 (D.C. Cir. 1980) (national security and foreign affairs).] Under the above case law, we must reject the Government's "uniquely governmental function" argument.

D. *Discretionary Function Exception*

The discretionary function exception expressly preserves governmental immunity under the FTCA for "[a]ny claim based upon an act or omission of an employee of the Government, exercising due care, in the execution of a statute or regulation, whether or not such statute or regulation be valid, or based upon the exercise or performance or the failure to exercise or perform a discretionary function or duty on the part of a federal agency or any employee of the Government, whether or not the discretion involved be abused." 28 U.S.C. § 2680(a). We and other circuit courts have for some years incorporated this exception into the SAA and PVA. [ ] The district court did not rule on this ground of governmental immunity, but it is jurisdictional and therefore may be raised at any stage of the proceedings. [ ]

The Supreme Court has held that "it is unnecessary—and indeed impossible—to define with precision every contour of the discretionary function exception." [*United States v. Varig Airlines*, 467 U.S. 797, 813 (1984).] From legislative and judicial materials, however, the Court has gleaned two factors useful in determining whether the discretionary function exception protects particular government acts from liability. "First, it is the nature of the conduct, rather than the status of the actor, that governs whether the discretionary function applies in a given case. [T]he basic inquiry concerning application of the discretionary function exception is whether the challenged acts of a Government employee—whatever his or her rank—are of the nature and quality that Congress intended to shield from tort liability. Second, whatever else the discretionary function exception may include, it plainly was intended to encompass the discretionary acts of the Government acting in its role as a regulator of the conduct of private individuals." *Id.* at 813–14 (footnote omitted).

We construe the general discretionary function in this case as the apprehension and custody of drug-running vessels. To board, search, and seize any vessel suspected of smuggling narcotics is a sovereign prerogative that has taken on paramount significance in light of the epidemic encroachment of illegal drugs into our country. * * * Mindful of these facts, we seriously doubt that Congress intended to expose the government to tort liability, on the alleged facts of this case, that would not only inhibit Coast Guard enforcement efforts but would also effectively reallocate scarce law enforcement resources from drug interdiction to custodial care for seized vessels. * * *

* * *

[There is a qualification] on our holding as to the scope of the discretionary function [that necessitates our remand of this case to the district court]. We assume that some Coast Guard regulations may govern the agency's operations in regard to boarding, searching, arresting and transporting vessels found to contain contraband. It is possible that [the destruction of the *Star Trek*] may have been caused by a violation of Coast Guard regulations. In such an event, [nothing in the Supreme Court's or this circuit's FTCA jurisprudence] would shield the government from liability. The immunity preserved for employees' acts by the discretionary function exception assumes that those acts fulfilled, rather than ignored or abused, the appropriate regulations. A subsidiary point to this analysis is that if the regulations themselves "specifically empowered [the Coast Guard officers] to make policy judgments, [they] necessarily took certain calculated risks, but those risks were encountered for the advancement of a governmental purpose and pursuant to the specific grant of authority." *Varig*, 467 U.S. at 820. [The case is accordingly remanded for the district court to first determine if the Coast Guard was notified that the *Star Trek* had been stolen. If so, then the district court must analyze the Coast Guard's conduct under any applicable Coast Guard regulations governing the agency's boarding, searching, arresting and transporting vessels found to contain contraband.]

Notes

1. **The discretionary function doctrine.** The court's opinion is a useful indicator of the potency of the discretionary function exception. See also *Baldassaro v. United States*, 64 F.3d 206 (5th Cir. 1995) (dismissing a Jones Act/SAA suit by a government-employed merchant seaman who fell from a defective bunk on the view that decisions on the design of vessels' bunks and sea rails are within the government's discretion); *Mid-South Holding Co. v. United States*, 225 F.3d 1201 (11th Cir. 2000) (indicating that turning off a vessel's

bilge pump—causing the vessel to sink—during a Coast Guard/Customs Service search for illegal drugs was unchallengeable because discretionary).

2. **A bevy of defensive doctrines.** The *B & F Trawlers* opinion also shows that there are a bevy of other defensive doctrines available to the government. For another useful demonstration, see *Aktepe v. United States*, 105 F.3d 1400 (11th Cir. 1997).

3. **No juries.** Sovereigns naturally mistrust jury trial. See 28 U.S.C. § 2402, providing for nonjury trial of FTCA cases. SAA and PVA cases, being within the exclusive admiralty jurisdiction, are also tried only to the bench.

4. **Government employees also immunized.** 46 U.S.C. § 30904 provides: "If a remedy is provided by [the SAA or the PVA], it shall be exclusive of any other action arising out of the same subject matter against the officer, employee, or agent of the United States or the federally-owned corporation whose act or omission gave rise to the claim."

B. State and Local Governmental Immunity

The Eleventh Amendment provides: "The judicial power of the United States shall not be construed to extend to any suit in law or equity, commenced or prosecuted against one of the United States by citizens of another state, or by citizens or subjects of any foreign state." In a series of decisions the Supreme Court has extended state sovereign immunity far beyond the amendment's limited language.

In re Magnolia Marine Transport Co.

United States Court of Appeals, Tenth Circuit, 2004
366 F.3d 1153, 2004 AMC 1249

SEYMOUR, Circuit Judge:

* * *

On May 26, 2002, the M/V *Robert Y. Love*, a tugboat owned and operated by Magnolia and piloted by Captain William Joe Dedmon, was pushing two empty barges up the Arkansas River in Oklahoma. As the tugboat neared the Interstate 40 bridge, Captain Dedmon suffered a form of cardiac arrhythmia that caused him to lose consciousness for several minutes. While Captain Dedmon was unconscious, the tugboat pushed the barges into the bridge, causing the bridge to collapse into the river. Several vehicles plunged off the damaged overpass. Fourteen people died and five suffered injuries. The subsequent search and rescue, repair, loss of use, and clean-up costs required the State of Oklahoma to expend more than fifty-eight million dollars.

One week after the accident, Magnolia filed a petition in federal district court in Mississippi invoking the procedures of the Limitation of Shipowners' Liability Act. The next day, the State filed suit for damages in Oklahoma State court. After removal of the State's suit and transfer of Magnolia's limitation petition, the parties' legal actions were consolidated in federal district court in Oklahoma. Positing "that under the United States Constitution, the State of Oklahoma cannot be prohibited from [pursuing] its claim against Magnolia in the courts of Oklahoma, nor can the State be forced, without its consent, to pursue its claims in federal court," the State claimed it was "entitled to sovereign immunity from this limitation proceeding and from the Limitation Act." We now consider the State's appeal from the district court's denial of its motion to dismiss on immunity grounds.

* * *

The State of Oklahoma insists its constitutional sovereign immunity from suit prevents Magnolia from invoking the procedures of the Limitation of Shipowners' Liability Act as to the State's claim for damages. The logical starting point for our analysis of this proposition is the text of the Eleventh Amendment to the United States Constitution.

The Eleventh Amendment mandates that "[t]he Judicial power of the United States shall not be construed to extend to any suit in law or equity, commenced or prosecuted against one of the United States by Citizens of another State, or by Citizens or Subjects of any Foreign State." The question we must first answer, therefore, is whether Magnolia's limitation petition constitutes a suit "commenced or prosecuted against" the State of Oklahoma. For reasons we explore below, the answer to that question is no.

The State advocates a different starting point for our analysis. Oklahoma would have us begin with "the two-prong test enunciated by the United States Supreme Court" in *College Savings Bank v. Florida Prepaid Postsecondary Education Expense Board*, 527 U.S. 666 (1999). In that case, the Court "recognized only two circumstances in which an individual may sue a State": (1) where Congress has authorized the suit pursuant to its enforcement power under [§ 5 of the] the Fourteenth Amendment, and (2) where the State has waived its sovereign immunity. In urging these two exceptions to sovereign immunity as this court's analytical starting point, the State misses a crucial distinction between *Florida Prepaid* and the case before us. In *Florida Prepaid*, College Savings Bank sued Florida Prepaid Postsecondary Education Expense Board, an arm of the State of Florida, for [allegedly false and misleading advertising in violation of the] Lanham Act. Clearly, the Bank's suit was a "suit against a state" * * *.

Here, to the contrary, the State of Oklahoma has sued Magnolia for damages. Magnolia neither named the State as a defendant in its limitation proceeding nor served process upon the State. The limitation proceeding merely provides a forum for establishing a shipowner's right to limitation of liability and managing disbursement of a limitation fund to claimants who prove Magnolia is liable to them. The limitation proceeding thus lacks the traditional characteristics of a suit against the State.

* * *

The State derides as mere "semantics" any emphasis on the Eleventh Amendment's application only to suits "commenced or prosecuted against" a state, and insists the Supreme Court has carried state sovereign immunity beyond the "literal wording of the Eleventh Amendment." The Supreme Court has undeniably extended the protections of state sovereign immunity beyond the text of the Eleventh Amendment. See *Alden v. Maine*, 527 U.S. 706, 713 (1999) (holding that "the sovereign immunity of the States is [not] limited by [ ] the terms of the Eleventh Amendment"). The State cites eight cases in which the Supreme Court has arguably broadened the Eleventh Amendment's reach and urges us to broaden it yet again in the case before us. The cases the State cites are unhelpful, however. Although the cases involved new parties or fora beyond the literal language of the Eleventh Amendment,[2] each case is unquestionably *a suit against a state.* [ ] Oklahoma

2. See *Fed. Mar. Comm'n v. S.C. State Ports Auth.*, 535 U.S. 743, 754 (2002) (citing the cases the State relies on as holding Eleventh Amendment immunity applies to suits by Indian Tribes, foreign nations, and federal corporations, as well as to suits by private parties in state court, in admiralty proceedings, and by a state's own citizens under federal question jurisdiction).

points to no case in which the Supreme Court has extended Eleventh Amendment immunity beyond suits against a state, and we decline to do so in this case.

We return, therefore, to the question of whether Magnolia's limitation petition constitutes a suit against the State of Oklahoma. We agree with every court that has addressed this issue: the limitation proceeding is not a suit against the state. [ ] The Limitation of Shipowners' Liability Act creates a defense which * * * may be pled in a limitation petition invoking the procedures established in Rule F or in a shipowner's answer to a suit brought in state or federal court. [ ] If a shipowner chooses to file a petition for limitation under the federal court's admiralty jurisdiction, any claimant (including a state) must file its claim against the shipowner in the same court or risk taking none of the limitation fund as damages. [ ] But this federal proceeding for administering a limited fund does not transform the shipowner's defensive position under the Act into an offensive one.

* * *

[T]he State's invocation of sovereign immunity stands the relationship between the parties on its head: it is the State that seeks recovery from Magnolia in this case. Because Magnolia's limitation proceeding does not implicate the State's immunity from suit under the Eleventh Amendment, the district court properly denied the State's motion to dismiss. We affirm.

Notes

1. **State immunity is much broader than the Eleventh Amendment.** The Supreme Court cases Oklahoma relied on show how far beyond the text of the Eleventh Amendment state sovereign immunity has been taken. The most dramatic case is *Alden*, holding that the Tenth and Eleventh Amendments and the "structure of the original Constitution itself" combine to preclude a private party's suit against a state in the state's own courts. 527 U.S. at 728. Compare *Nevada v. Hall*, 440 U.S. 410 (1979) (holding that nothing in the Constitution prevents California citizens from suing the State of Nevada in California state court). The Court in *Alden* did not overrule *Nevada v. Hall*, but it did suggest that the California court should "respect Nevada's sovereignty as a matter of comity." 527 U.S. at 738.

2. **Waiver of state immunity.** States can consent to be sued. Many have statutes that waive governmental tort immunity, at least in significant part; normally they do not expose the state to suit in any other courts than its own. Consent may also be given in other ways. And it can be inferred: when a state files a lawsuit, it has generally effectively consented to counterclaims that arise out of the same transaction or occurrence on which it has sued.

At one time a state's operating a maritime venture was thought to constitute implied consent to liability for tortious conduct. But *Welch v. Texas Dept. of Highways*, 483 U.S. 468 (1987)—holding that a state can operate a ferry without subjecting itself to Jones Act liability to its employees—changed the law on that point.

3. **In rem actions.** *Ex parte New York*, 256 U.S. 503 (1921), stands for the general proposition that state-owned and -operated vessels cannot be subjected to in rem liability. But under certain circumstances in rem actions against property claimed by a state—but not in the state's possession—can sometimes be maintained. See *California v. Deep Sea Research*, 523 U.S. 491 (1998); *Florida Dept. of State v. Treasure Salvors, Inc.*, 458 U.S. 670 (1982).

4. **Congressional abrogation of state immunity.** Congress has a narrowly limited authority to abrogate state sovereign immunity. *Seminole Tribe of Fla. v. Florida*, 517 U.S. 44 (1996), held that nothing in Article I of the Constitution authorizes Congress to abrogate state immunity. But the Court has several times held that legislation enacted under § 5 of the 14th Amendment can overcome state immunity. See, e.g., *United States v. Georgia*, 546 U.S. 151 (2006); *Tennessee v. Lane*, 541 U.S. 509 (2004).

Northern Insurance Co. of New York v. Chatham County, Georgia

Supreme Court of the United States, 2006

547 U.S. 189, 126 S. Ct. 1689, 164 L. Ed. 2d 367, 2006 AMC 913

Justice THOMAS delivered the opinion of the unanimous Court.

* * *

[Respondent Chatham County, Georgia] owns, operates, and maintains the Causton Bluff Bridge, a drawbridge over the Wilmington River. On October 6, 2002, James Ludwig requested that the bridge be raised to allow his boat to pass. The bridge malfunctioned, a portion falling and colliding with Mr. Ludwig's boat. As a result of the collision, Mr. Ludwig and his wife incurred damages in excess of $130,000.

The Ludwigs submitted a claim for those damages to their insurer [petitioner Northern Insurance Company of New York], which paid in accordance with the terms of their insurance policy. Northern then sought to recover its costs by filing suit in admiralty against the County in the [United States District Court for the Southern District of Georgia, alleging negligence of County employees.] The County sought summary judgment, arguing that Northern's claims were barred by sovereign immunity. The County conceded that Eleventh Amendment immunity did not extend to counties, but nonetheless contended that it was immune under "the universal rule of state immunity from suit without the state's consent." The District Court agreed, * * * [holding] that sovereign immunity extends to counties and municipalities that, as here, "exercis[e] power delegated from the State."

The Eleventh Circuit * * * affirmed. The Court of Appeals acknowledged that the County did not assert an Eleventh Amendment immunity defense, which would fail because, under Circuit precedent, the County did not qualify as an arm of the State. The Court of Appeals nonetheless concluded that "common law has carved out a 'residual immunity,' which would protect a political subdivision such as Chatham County from suit." We granted certiorari to review the judgment of the Court of Appeals.

* * *

This Court's cases have recognized that the immunity of States from suit "is a fundamental aspect of the sovereignty which the States enjoyed before the ratification of the Constitution, and which they retain today ... except as altered by the plan of the Convention or certain constitutional Amendments." *Alden v. Maine*, 527 U.S. 706, 713 (1999) [ ]. Consistent with this recognition, which no party asks us to reexamine today, we have observed that the phrase "'Eleventh Amendment immunity'... is convenient shorthand but something of a misnomer, for the sovereign immunity of the States neither derives from, nor is limited by, the terms of the Eleventh Amendment." *Alden, supra*, at 713.

A consequence of this Court's recognition of preratification sovereignty as the source of immunity from suit is that only States and arms of the State possess immunity from suits authorized by federal law. [ ] Accordingly, this Court has repeatedly refused to extend sovereign immunity to counties. * * *

The County argues that this Court's cases recognize a distinct "residual" immunity that permits adoption of a broader test than we apply in the Eleventh Amendment context to determine whether an entity is acting as an arm of the State and is accordingly entitled to immunity. But this Court's use of that term does not suggest the County's conclusion; instead, this Court has referenced only the States' "residuary and inviolable sovereignty" that survived the Constitution. *See* The Federalist No. 39, at 245 (C. Rossiter ed. 1961) (J. Madison); *Federal Maritime Comm'n v. South Carolina Ports Authority*, 535 U.S. 743 (2002).

Because the County may claim immunity neither based upon its identity as a county nor under an expansive arm-of-the-State test, the County is subject to suit unless it was acting as an arm of the State, as delineated by this Court's precedents, in operating the drawbridge. [ ] The County conceded below that it was not entitled to Eleventh Amendment immunity, and both the County and the Court of Appeals appear to have understood this concession to be based on the County's failure to qualify as an arm of the State under our precedent. * * * Moreover, the question on which we granted certiorari is premised on the conclusion that the County is not "an 'arm of the State' for Eleventh Amendment purposes," and we presume that to be the case. Accordingly, the County's concession and the presumption underlying the question on which we granted review are dispositive.

As an alternative ground for affirmance, the County asks the Court to recognize a distinct sovereign immunity against in personam admiralty suits that bars cases arising from a county's exercise of core state functions with regard to navigable waters. Recognition of a distinct immunity in admiralty cases cannot be reconciled with our precedents. Immunity in admiralty, like other sovereign immunity, is simply an application of "the fundamental rule" that "the entire judicial power granted by the Constitution does not embrace authority to entertain a suit brought by private parties against a State without consent given." [ ] Accordingly, this Court has resolved sovereign immunity questions in admiralty by relying upon principles set out in this Court's sovereign immunity cases, rather than by examining the history or jurisprudence specific to suits in admiralty. [ ] Indeed, the Court applied the general principle that sovereign immunity does not bar a suit against a city to an admiralty suit as early as *Workman v. New York City*, 179 U.S. 552 (1900), which held that such immunity "afforded no reason for denying redress in a court of admiralty for the wrong which ... [had] been committed" by the city of New York.

* * *

Because the County has failed to demonstrate that it was acting as an arm of the State when it operated the Causton Bluff Bridge, the County is not entitled to immunity from Northern's suit. Accordingly, the judgment of the Court of Appeals is reversed.

Notes

1. **Arms of the state.** The Court might be read to suggest that its decisions have "delineated" criteria for determining whether particular governmental entities are arms of the state, but the delineation is hard to find in Supreme Court jurisprudence. In *Vierling v. Celebrity Cruises*, 339 F.3d 1309, 1314 (11th Cir. 2003), the court laid out that circuit's view:

> In deciding whether a state agency or instrumentality may invoke the state's immunity as an arm of the state, we have recognized three factors: (1) how state law defines the entity; (2) what degree of control the state maintains over the entity; and (3) from where the entity derives its funds and who is responsible

> for satisfying the judgments against the entity. Although no single factor is dispositive, the third factor ... is of considerable importance. Thus, when an action is in essence one for the recovery of money from the state, the state is the real, substantial party in interest and is entitled to invoke its sovereign immunity from suit. [Citations and internal quotation marks omitted.]

For cases addressing whether port authorities and similar entities are arms of the state, see *Puerto Rico Ports Authority v. M/V Manhattan Prince*, 897 F.2d 1 (1st Cir. 1990) (PRPA is arm of state); *Jacintoport Corp. v. Greater Baton Rouge Port Comm'n*, 762 F.2d 435 (5th Cir. 1985) (Baton Rouge Port Commission is not); *Kamani v. Port of Houston Authority*, 702 F.2d 612 (5th Cir. 1983) (Houston Port Commission is).

2. **"Governmental" vs. "proprietary" functions.** In many states, municipalities and other local governmental units are immune from tort liability under state law only if the injury in suit arose from a "governmental" (as opposed to "proprietary") activity. See Prosser & Keeton on Torts 1053–54 (5th ed. 1984); cf. *Thacker v. Tennessee Valley Authority*, 139 S. Ct. 1435, 1444 (2019). The governmental/proprietary distinction is famously difficult to draw.

3. **In rem actions.** *Workman* v. *New York City* was an in personam suit against the City for damages its fire boat caused in colliding with plaintiff's vessel. The Court equivocated on whether the fire boat could have been subjected to in rem liability, deeming that point "unnecessary to determine in this case." 179 U.S. at 572. According to 2 Schoenbaum, Admiralty and Maritime Law § 20:2, at 558 n.20 (6th [Practitioner Treatise Series] ed. 2018), "*[i]n rem* liability exists with respect to [city] property that does not serve an essential governmental function" (citing *The Lisbon*, 3 F.2d 408 (9th Cir. 1925), and *The West Point*, 71 F. Supp. 206 (E.D. Va. 1947)).

C. Foreign Governmental Immunity

Argentine Republic v. Amerada Hess Shipping Corp.

Supreme Court of the United States, 1989
488 U.S. 428, 109 S. Ct. 683, 102 L. Ed. 2d 818, 1989 AMC 50

Chief Justice REHNQUIST delivered the opinion of the Court.

[On June 8, 1982, the *Hercules*, a crude oil tanker owned by respondent United Carriers, Inc., a Liberian corporation, and chartered to respondent Amerada Hess Corp., also a Liberian corporation, was severely damaged and ultimately sunk when it was attacked in international waters by Argentine military aircraft during the war between Great Britain and Argentina over the Falkland Islands off the Argentine coast. United and Amerada brought separate actions against petitioner, the Argentine Republic, in the United States District Court for the Southern District of New York for the damage they sustained in the attack. United sought \$10 million in damages for the loss of the ship. Amerada sought \$1.9 million in damages for the fuel that went down with the ship. United and Amerada alleged that Argentina's attack on the neutral ship in international waters violated international law. They claimed subject matter jurisdiction under 28 U.S.C. § 1333 and under the Alien Tort Statute. The Alien Tort Statute was enacted by the First Congress in 1789. It presently appears as 28 U.S.C. § 1350, which is captioned "alien's action for tort" and provides:

> The district courts shall have original jurisdiction of any civil action by an alien for a tort only, committed in violation of the law of nations or a treaty of the United States.]

[The district court dismissed both complaints for lack of subject matter jurisdiction, ruling that the suits were barred by the Foreign Sovereign Immunities Act (FSIA), 28 U.S.C. § 1330 et seq.[1] A divided panel of the United States Court of Appeals for the Second Circuit reversed.] The Court of Appeals held that the District Court had jurisdiction under the Alien Tort Statute, because respondents' consolidated action was brought by Liberian corporations, it sounded in tort ("the bombing of a ship without justification"), and it asserted a violation of international law ("attacking a neutral ship in international waters, without proper cause for suspicion or investigation"). [ ] Viewing the Alien Tort Statute as " ... a jurisdictional grant based on international law," the Court of Appeals said that "who is within" the scope of that grant is governed by "evolving standards of international law." [ ] The Court of Appeals reasoned that Congress' enactment of the FSIA was not meant to eliminate "existing remedies in United States courts for violations of international law" by foreign states under the Alien Tort Statute. The dissenting judge took the view that the FSIA precluded respondents' action. We granted certiorari and now reverse.

We start from the settled proposition that the subject-matter jurisdiction of the lower federal courts is determined by Congress "in the exact degrees and character which to Congress may seem proper for the public good." * * * [The enactment of the FSIA in 1976] added a new chapter 97 to Title 28 of the United States Code, 28 U.S.C. §§ 1602–1611, which is entitled "Jurisdictional Immunities of Foreign States."[1] Section 1604 provides:

> Subject to existing international agreements to which the United States [was] a party at the time of the enactment of this Act[,] a foreign state shall be immune from the jurisdiction of the courts of the United States and of the States except as provided in sections 1605 to 1607 of this chapter.

The FSIA also added § 1330(a) to Title 28; it provides:

> The district courts shall have original jurisdiction without regard to amount in controversy of any nonjury civil action against a foreign state ... as to any claim for relief in personam with respect to which the foreign state is not entitled to immunity under sections 1605–1607 of this title or under any applicable international agreement.

We think that the text and structure of the FSIA demonstrate Congress' intention that the FSIA be the sole basis for obtaining jurisdiction over a foreign state in our courts. Sections 1604 and 1330(a) work in tandem: § 1604 bars federal and state courts from exercising jurisdiction when a foreign state *is* entitled to immunity, and § 1330(a) confers jurisdiction on district courts to hear suits brought by United States citizens and by aliens when a foreign state is *not* entitled to immunity. * * *

---

1. Editors' note: The FSIA is scattered through Title 28, at §§ 1330, 1391(f), 1441(d), and 1602–11.

1. From the Nation's founding until 1952, foreign states were "generally granted ... complete immunity from suit" in United States courts, and the Judicial Branch deferred to the decisions of the Executive Branch on such questions. [ ] In 1952, the State Department adopted the view that foreign states could be sued in United States courts for their commercial acts, but not for their public acts. [ ] "For the most part," the FSIA "codifies" this so-called "restrictive" theory of foreign sovereign immunity. [ ]

The Court of Appeals acknowledged that the FSIA's language and legislative history support the "general rule" that the Act governs the immunity of foreign states in federal court. The Court of Appeals, however, thought that the FSIA's "focus on commercial concerns" and Congress' failure to "repeal" the Alien Tort Statute indicated Congress' intention that federal courts continue to exercise jurisdiction over foreign states in suits alleging violations of international law outside the confines of the FSIA. The Court of Appeals also believed that to construe the FSIA to bar the instant suit would "fly in the face" of Congress' intention that the FSIA be interpreted pursuant to "'standards recognized under international law.'" [ ]

Taking the last of these points first, Congress had violations of international law by foreign states in mind when it enacted the FSIA. For example, the FSIA specifically denies foreign states immunity in suits "in which rights in property taken in violation of international law are in issue." 28 U.S.C. § 1605(a)(3). Congress also rested the FSIA in part on its power under Art. I § 8 cl. 10 of the Constitution "[t]o define and punish Piracies and Felonies committed on the high Seas, and Offenses against the Law of Nations." [ ] From Congress' decision to deny immunity to foreign states in the class of cases just mentioned, we draw the plain implication that immunity is granted in those cases involving alleged violations of international law that do not come within one of the FSIA's exceptions.

As to the other point made by the Court of Appeals, Congress' failure to enact a pro tanto repealer of the Alien Tort Statute when it passed the FSIA in 1976 may be explained at least in part by the lack of certainty as to whether the Alien Tort Statute conferred jurisdiction in suits against foreign states. * * * The Court of Appeals did not cite any decision in which a United States court exercised jurisdiction over a foreign state under the Alien Tort Statute, and only one such case has come to our attention—one which was decided after the enactment of the FSIA [and in which the jurisdictional requirements of the FSIA were arguably met. *Von Dardel v. U.S.S.R.*, 623 F. Supp. 246 (D.D.C. 1985)].

* * *

We think that Congress' failure in the FSIA to enact an express pro tanto repealer of the Alien Tort Statute speaks only faintly, if at all, to the issue involved in this case. In light of the comprehensiveness of the statutory scheme in the FSIA, we doubt that even the most meticulous draftsman would have concluded that Congress also needed to amend pro tanto the Alien Tort Statute * * *.

Respondents also argue that the general admiralty and maritime jurisdiction, 28 U.S.C. § 1333(1), provides a basis for obtaining jurisdiction over petitioner for violations of international law, notwithstanding the FSIA. But Congress dealt with the admiralty jurisdiction of the federal courts when it enacted the FSIA. Section 1605(b) expressly permits an in personam suit in admiralty to enforce a maritime lien against a vessel or cargo of a foreign state. Unless the present case is within § 1605(b) or another exception to the FSIA, the statute conferring general admiralty and maritime jurisdiction on the federal courts does not authorize the bringing of this action against petitioner.

Having determined that the FSIA provides the sole basis for obtaining jurisdiction over a foreign state in federal court, we turn to whether any of the exceptions enumerated in the Act apply here. These exceptions include cases involving the waiver of immunity, § 1605(a)(1), commercial activities occurring in the United States or causing a direct effect in this country, § 1605(a)(2), property expropriated in violation of international law, § 1605(a)(3), inherited, gift, or immovable property located in the United States, § 1605(a)(4), noncommercial torts occurring in the United States, § 1605(a)(5), and maritime liens, § 1605(b). We agree with the District Court that none of the FSIA's exceptions applies on these facts. [ ]

* * *

We hold that the FSIA provides the sole basis for obtaining jurisdiction over a foreign state in the courts of this country, and that none of the enumerated exceptions to the Act apply to the facts of this case. The judgment of the Court of Appeals is therefore reversed.

* * *

Justice BLACKMUN filed an opinion concurring in part which Justice Marshall joined.

Notes

1. Governmental immunity is traditionally viewed as defeating the courts' subject matter jurisdiction. Generally the requirements of waiver statutes are also treated as "jurisdictional" and thus not subject to relaxation no matter how compelling the case.

2. The FSIA is detailed and complex. The above version of the *Argentine* opinion omits an extended discussion of the FSIA exceptions to foreign sovereign immunity. Justices Blackmun and Marshall, specially concurring, argued that, rather than deciding whether any of the FSIA exceptions applied, the Court should have remanded the case to the Court of Appeal to conduct that inquiry.

3. **Actions in rem.** The FSIA precludes proceedings in rem against foreign-government-owned ships except to foreclose a preferred ship mortgage. See 28 U.S.C. §§ 1605(b), 1610(e). It also precludes using Rule B to attach the property of a foreign state to obtain jurisdiction (although it permits attachment to secure satisfaction of a judgment). See *id.* §§ 1609–1611.

4. **Jury trial precluded.** "There is no jury trial under the FSIA, and a demand for a jury will be struck."[2]

5. **State court jurisdiction.** "Plaintiffs [in FSIA actions] have an election whether to proceed in federal or in state court; however proceedings in state court are subject to removal."[3] 28 U.S.C. § 1441(d).

---

2. Schoenbaum, Admiralty and Maritime Law 1047–48 (4th [hornbook] ed. 2004).
3. *Id.* at 1047 n. 13.

Chapter XIV

Forum Shopping

Perhaps hoping to neutralize the negative connotations of the term *forum shopping*, a British jurist has noted that the term "is only a pejorative way of saying that, if you offer a [litigant] a choice of jurisdictions, he will naturally choose the one in which he thinks his case can be most favourably presented: this should be a matter neither for surprise nor for indignation."[1] When used pejoratively—as it frequently is—the "forum-shopping" designation implies that it is a "breach of professional etiquette"[2] for a lawyer to pursue the client's best interests. The negative connotations are misleading and regrettable. Lawyers who fail to maximize their clients' forum-selection and choice-of-law options are not providing adequate counsel.

Forum Shopping by Maritime Plaintiffs

In the version championed by the Supreme Court's *Romero* decision, *supra* at 102, the saving-to-suitors clause is a dramatically potent forum-selection device. Particularly when it is used to take a maritime case to state court in the hope of avoiding unfavorable maritime-law pronouncements by the local federal court of appeals—see *supra* at 115 note 3—the saving clause seems a unique benediction on forum shopping.

There are numerous other forum-shopping tools for maritime plaintiffs. As we saw in Section I-G-10, *supra* at 90–101, a maritime plaintiff can often establish a defendant's amenability to personal jurisdiction in more than one court. And in Section I-G-11, *supra* at 101, we made passing reference to the lack of any general venue restrictions on U.S. admiralty courts. At this juncture we need to elaborate on the subject of venue. *In re Louisville Underwriters*, 134 U.S. 488 (1890), stands for the proposition that, in the absence of an applicable statutory restriction,[3] venue in a federal court exercising admiralty jurisdiction is proper wherever personal jurisdiction can be had. The Court's explanation (*id.* at 493):

> Courts of admiralty are established for the settlement of disputes between persons engaged in commerce and navigation who, on the one hand, may be absent from their homes for long periods of time and, on the other hand, often have property

1. *The Atlantic Star*, [1974] A.C. 436, 471 (H.L.) (Lord Simon of Glaisdale, dissenting).
2. Juenger, *Forum Shopping: Domestic and International*, 63 Tul. L. Rev. 553, 564 (1989).
3. There are special venue rules for shipowner's petitions for limitation under the Limitation of Liability Act (Fed. R. Civ. P. Supp. R. F(9)) and for suits against the United States under the Suits in Admiralty Act (46 U.S.C. § 30906) and the Public Vessels Act (46 U.S.C. § 31104).

> or credits in other places. * * * To compel suitors in admiralty, when the ship is abroad, and cannot be reached by a libel in rem, to resort to the home of the defendant, and to prevent them from suing him in any district in which he might be served with a summons or his goods or credits attached, would not only often put them to great delay, inconvenience, and expense, but would in many cases amount to a denial of justice.

Federal Rule of Civil Procedure 82, providing that "[a]n admiralty or maritime claim" is not subject to the general federal venue statutes, makes it clear that *Louisville Underwriters* remains good law. See also 28 U.S.C. § 1390(b).

The Supreme Court has emphasized that venue is a quintessentially procedural (as opposed to substantive) matter.[4] Procedural matters are controlled by the law of the forum. Thus, maritime claims brought under the saving-to-suitors clause on the "law side" of federal court are subject to the venue rules set forth in 28 U.S.C. §§ 1390 et seq. Maritime claims brought under the saving-to-suitors clause in state court are controlled by the venue rules of the state.

Defensive Forum-Shopping

More often than not, the pejorative usage of "forum shopping" is meant as a criticism of plaintiffs' lawyers' litigation tactics. But maritime defendants also engage in forum-shopping maneuvers.[5] They have to. "In committing their ships to the general maritime trade, owners and operators run an unusual risk of being sued in venues with little or no connection to the subject matter of the suit. * * * [They must find ways] to avoid vexatious litigation on ... distant and unfamiliar shore[s]." *American Dredging Co. v. Miller*, *supra* at 113, 510 U.S. at 463–64 (Kennedy, J., dissenting).

The law provides defendants with a formidable array of doctrinal devices for such purposes. These include the limitations on subject matter and personal jurisdiction that are treated in Chapter I; doctrines restricting the venue in which particular actions can be brought;[6] the federal courts' removal jurisdiction; the discretionary authority of a federal court in which subject matter jurisdiction, personal jurisdiction, and venue are proper to transfer the case to another federal court (see 28 U.S.C § 1404(a)); doctrines upholding the validity of forum selection clauses and arbitration clauses in maritime contracts; the general-law doctrine of forum non conveniens; and the availability under certain circumstances of antisuit injunctions.[7]

Choice of Law

This chapter's primary choice-of-law perspective is *horizontal* choice of law, i.e., the choice between or among competing substantive laws of co-equal countries or states.

---

4. See *American Dredging Co. v. Miller*, *supra* at 113, 510 U.S. at 453: "[V]enue is a matter that goes to process rather than substantive rights—determining which among various competent courts will decide the case. Uniformity of process (beyond the rudimentary elements of procedural fairness) is assuredly not what the law of admiralty seeks to achieve, since it is supposed to apply in all the courts of the world."

5. See *Pain v. United Technologies Corp.*, 637 F.2d 775, 793 (D.C. Cir. 1980) (referring to a defendant's "reverse forum-shopping"); *Liaw Su Teng v. Skaarup Shipping Corp.*, 743 F.2d 1140, 1149 (5th Cir. 1984) (characterizing the "forum-selection maneuvers" of both parties as "gamesmanship").

6. See *supra* note 3.

7. See, e.g., *Rationis Enterprises*, *supra* at 90.

(But we also need to keep an eye on the pervasive *vertical* choice-of-law issue that is peculiar to U.S. admiralty, i.e., the choice between federal and state law.) These horizontal choice-of-law issues cut across the entire maritime field. The maritime law of the United States is subject to frequent criticism for multiplying them. One treatise singles out the areas of maritime liens,[8] collision,[9] and limitation of liability[10] for special disapproval.

Choice-of-law concepts that guide courts in choosing the applicable law in cases with multi-jurisdictional dimensions are functional parts of the law of forum shopping. A court presented with a case that it believes should be governed by the law of the forum will generally not be particularly motivated to find itself lacking in jurisdiction or to use its discretion to divest itself of jurisdiction. Conversely, a belief that the governing law should come from another system can often lead a court to look for ways to avoid entertaining a case.

A. Forum Selection, Arbitration, and Choice of Law Clauses in Maritime Contracts

Historically, the U.S. courts did not favor forum selection clauses. As the Supreme Court explained in *The Bremen v. Zapata Offshore Co.*, 407 U.S. 1, 9 (1972), "Many courts, federal and state, have declined to enforce such clauses on the ground that they were 'contrary to public policy,' or that their effect was to 'oust the jurisdiction' of the court." By the 1940s, however, a more receptive attitude began to develop. In *Krenger v. Pennsylvania R.R.*, 174 F.2d 556, 560–561 (2d Cir. 1949), Chief Judge Learned Hand wrote, in a concurring opinion, that he did "not believe that, today at least, there is an absolute taboo against such contracts at all."

The real turning point in judicial attitude came over twenty years later in *The Bremen*, in which a U.S. company had concluded a towing contract with a German company. As part of their negotiations, the two companies (with comparable bargaining power) had agreed that any dispute would be resolved "before the London Court of Justice." When the tow was damaged en route, the U.S. company brought suit in Florida and the German defendant invoked the forum selection clause. The district court refused to enforce the clause, instead following binding circuit precedent that "agreements in advance of controversy whose object is to oust the jurisdiction of the courts are contrary to public policy and will not be enforced." The Court of Appeals affirmed.

The Supreme Court concluded that forum clauses should generally be enforced. In reaching that conclusion, it rejected the "parochial concept that all disputes must be resolved under our laws and in our courts," which it found inconsistent with the needs of modern international business. "We cannot have trade and commerce in world markets

8. 1 Schoenbaum, Admiralty and Maritime Law § 9:8, at 820 (6th ed. [Practitioner Treatise Series] 2018) ("Because [U.S.] law on maritime liens differs from international practice and the laws of other countries, significant problems of conflicts of law arise.").

9. 2 *Id.*, § 14:10, at 181 ("Regret[ably], the United States goes its own way on many questions of marine collisions and casualties without regard to the international conventions in this area.").

10. 2 *Id.*, § 15:1, at 189 ("There is great need to revise the [U.S.] law of limitation of shipowners' liability to bring it into accord with international practice and modern policy concerns.").

and international waters exclusively on our terms, governed by our laws, and resolved in our courts." Henceforth, a "forum clause should control absent a strong showing that it should be set aside." The burden would be on the plaintiff to show that enforcement of the clause "would be unreasonable and unjust, or that the clause was invalid for such reasons as fraud or overreaching."

The Court supported its decision to enforce the forum clause by stressing the compelling facts of the case before it:

> We are not here dealing with an agreement between two Americans to resolve their essentially local disputes in a remote alien forum. In such a case, the serious inconvenience of the contractual forum to one or both of the parties might carry greater weight in determining the reasonableness of the forum clause. The remoteness of the forum might suggest that the agreement was an adhesive one, or that the parties did not have the particular controversy in mind when they made their agreement * * *.
>
> This case, however, involves a freely negotiated international commercial transaction between a German and an American corporation * * *. [S]election of a London forum was clearly a reasonable effort to bring vital certainty to this international transaction and to provide a neutral forum experienced and capable in the resolution of admiralty litigation. Whatever "inconvenience" [the plaintiff] would suffer by being forced to litigate in the contractual forum as it agreed to do was clearly foreseeable at the time of contracting. In such circumstances it should be incumbent on the party seeking to escape his contract to show that trial in the contractual forum will be so gravely difficult and inconvenient that he will for all practical purposes be deprived of his day in court. Absent that, there is no basis for concluding that it would be unfair, unjust, or unreasonable to hold that party to his bargain.

In *Carnival Cruise Lines, Inc. v. Shute*, 499 U.S. 585 (1991), the facts were very different: a U.S. consumer had accepted a contract of adhesion from a U.S.-based company that included a standard clause requiring disputes to be resolved in the company's home courts. The consumer did not even see the clause until she had already paid for her non-refundable ticket. In a 7–2 decision recognizing the "key factual differences," the *Carnival Cruise* Court nevertheless applied the *Bremen* analysis to enforce the forum selection clause. It also rejected the argument that the clause violated 46 U.S.C. app. § 183c(a)(2), now recodified at 46 U.S.C. § 30509(a), which prohibits provisions in passenger tickets that tend to weaken a passenger's right to a trial by a court of competent jurisdiction.

The *Carnival Cruise* decision inspired a firestorm of criticism. See, e.g., Mullenix, *Another Easy Case, Some More Bad Law: Carnival Cruise Lines and Contractual Personal Jurisdiction*, 27 Tex. Int'l L.J. 323 (1992). In 1992, Congress evidently "overruled" the decision's holding as it applies to passenger tickets by amending § 183c(a)(2). But the following year, Congress reversed field and restored the statute to its pre-*Carnival Cruise* version. On the basis of some evidence of legislative intent, it was argued that *Carnival Cruise* "is as dead [after the Congressional about-face] as it was under the 1992 amendment." See Franklin & Weldy, *Dark of the Night Legislation Takes Aim at Forum Selection Clauses*, 6 U.S.F. Mar. L.J. 259, 266 (1993). That interpretation seems unlikely. As things stand, *Carnival Cruise* is the authoritative interpretation of 46 U.S.C. § 30509(a).

In any event, the 1992–93 congressional flip-flop related only to passenger tickets. Regardless of that legislation, "the broad[er] implications of *Carnival Cruise Lines* remain with us." Sturley, *Forum Selection Clauses in Cruise Line Tickets: An Update on Congressional Action "Overruling" the Supreme Court*, 24 J. Mar. L. & Com. 399, 401 (1993). The following case and notes demonstrate the influence of the *Carnival Cruise* decision across the entire field of maritime contracts.

Vimar Seguros y Reaseguros, S.A. v. M/V Sky Reefer

Supreme Court of the United States, 1995

515 U.S. 528, 115 S. Ct. 2322, 132 L. Ed. 2d 462, 1995 AMC 1817

Justice Kennedy delivered the opinion of the Court.

[Bacchus Associates, a New York partnership, purchased a shipload of Moroccan oranges and lemons and arranged for shipment aboard the *M/V Sky Reefer*, a refrigerated cargo ship owned by M.H. Maritima, S.A., a Panamanian company, and time-chartered to Nichiro Gyogyo Kaisha, Ltd., a Japanese company. The bill of lading included Clause 3, entitled "Governing Law and Arbitration," that provided:

> (1) The contract evidenced by or contained in this Bill of Lading shall be governed by the Japanese law.
>
> (2) Any dispute arising from this Bill of Lading shall be referred to arbitration in Tokyo by the Tokyo Maritime Arbitration Commission (TOMAC) of the Japan Shipping Exchange, Inc., in accordance with the rules of TOMAC and any amendment thereto, and the award given by the arbitrators shall be final and binding on both parties.]

[The fruit sustained over $1 million in damage during the voyage. Vimar Seguros y Reaseguros, Bacchus' cargo insurer, paid part of the loss and became subrogated pro tanto to Bacchus' rights. Bacchus and Vimar filed an action in the United States District Court for the District of Massachusetts, in rem against the *Sky Reefer* and in personam against Maritima.]

[Maritima moved to stay the action and compel arbitration in Tokyo pursuant to Clause 3 of the bill of lading. Bacchus and Vimar argued that the clause was unenforceable under a line of cases stemming from *Indussa Corp. v. S.S. Ranborg*, 377 F.2d 200 (2d Cir. 1967) (en banc), holding that foreign forum selection clauses are void under § 3(8) of COGSA, which provides:

> Any clause, covenant, or agreement in a contract of carriage relieving the carrier or the ship from liability for loss or damage to or in connection with the goods, arising from negligence, fault, or failure in the duties and obligations provided in this section, or lessening such liability otherwise than as provided in this chapter, shall be null and void and of no effect.

The *Indussa* court held that foreign forum selection clauses are necessarily invalid under § 3(8) because they "put[] a high hurdle in the way of enforcing liability, and thus [are] an effective means for carriers to secure settlements lower than if cargo owners could sue in a convenient forum."]

[The district court held that the arbitration clause was enforceable, granted Maritima's motion for a stay pending arbitration, and certified the following question for interlocutory appeal pursuant to 28 U.S.C. § 1292(b): "[W]hether [§ 3(8)] nullifies an arbitration clause contained in a bill of lading governed by COGSA." The Court of Appeals for the First Circuit answered negatively. The court of appeals suggested that *Indussa* may not have survived our holdings in *Bremen* and *Carnival Cruise* but assumed arguendo that it did, i.e., that foreign forum selection clauses are invalid under § 3(8) of COGSA. It then turned to § 2 of the Federal Arbitration Act (FAA), 9 U.S.C. § 2, which provides:

> A written provision in any maritime transaction ... to settle by arbitration a controversy thereafter arising out of such contract ... shall be valid, irrevocable, and enforceable, save upon such grounds as exist at law or in equity for the revocation of any contract.

Reasoning that the FAA—having been reenacted in 1947—was both more recent and more specific than COGSA, the court of appeals held that "the FAA alone governs the validity of arbitration clauses, both foreign and domestic, and consequently removes them from the grasp of COGSA." [ ] Because of a conflict between the decision below and that of the Eleventh Circuit in *State Establishment for Agricultural Product Trading v. M/V Wesermunde*, 838 F.2d 1576 (11th Cir. 1988) (declining to enforce a foreign arbitration clause because that would violate COGSA), we granted certiorari.]

* * *

The parties devote much of their argument to the question whether COGSA or the FAA has priority. * * * [But there] is no conflict unless COGSA by its own terms nullifies a foreign arbitration clause, and we choose to address that issue rather than assume nullification arguendo, as the Court of Appeals did. We consider the two arguments made by petitioner. The first is that a foreign arbitration clause lessens COGSA liability by increasing the transaction costs of obtaining relief. The second is that there is a risk foreign arbitrators will not apply COGSA.

A.

The leading case for invalidation of a foreign forum selection clause is the opinion of the Court of Appeals for the Second Circuit in *Indussa*. * * * Following *Indussa*, the Courts of Appeals without exception have invalidated foreign forum selection clauses under § 3(8). [ ] As foreign arbitration clauses are but a subset of foreign forum selection clauses in general [ ], the *Indussa* holding has been extended to foreign arbitration clauses as well. See *State Establishment for Agricultural Product Trading* [ ]. The logic of that extension would be quite defensible, but we cannot endorse the reasoning or the conclusion of the *Indussa* rule itself.

The determinative provision in COGSA, examined with care, does not support the arguments advanced first in *Indussa* and now by petitioner. Under § 3(8) of COGSA * * * [t]he liability that may not be lessened is "liability for loss or damage ... arising from negligence, fault, or failure in the duties and obligations provided in this section." The statute thus addresses the lessening of the specific liability imposed by the Act, without addressing the separate question of the means and costs of enforcing that liability. The difference is that between explicit statutory guarantees and the procedure for enforcing them, between applicable liability principles and the forum in which they are to be vindicated.

The liability imposed on carriers under COGSA § 3 is defined by explicit standards of conduct, and it is designed to correct specific abuses by carriers. In the 19th century it was a prevalent practice for common carriers to insert clauses in bills of lading exempting themselves from liability for damage or loss, limiting the period in which plaintiffs had to present their notice of claim or bring suit, and capping any damages awards per package. [ ] Thus, § 3, entitled "Responsibilities and liabilities of carrier and ship," requires that the carrier "exercise due diligence to ... [m]ake the ship seaworthy" and "[p]roperly man, equip, and supply the ship" before and at the beginning of the voyage, § 3(1), "properly and carefully load, handle, stow, carry, keep, care for, and discharge the goods carried," § 3(2), and issue a bill of lading with specified contents, § 3(3). Section 3(6) allows the cargo owner to provide notice of loss or damage within three days and to bring suit within one year. These are the substantive obligations and particular procedures that § 3(8) prohibits a carrier from altering to its advantage in a bill of lading. Nothing in this section, however, suggests that the statute prevents the parties from agreeing to enforce these obligations in a particular forum. By its terms, it establishes certain duties and obligations, separate and apart from the mechanisms for their enforcement.

Petitioner's contrary reading of § 3(8) is undermined by the Court's construction of a similar statutory provision in *Carnival Cruise Lines v. Shute.* There a number of Washington residents argued that a Florida forum selection clause contained in a cruise ticket should not be enforced because the expense and inconvenience of litigation would "cause [ ] plaintiffs unreasonable hardship in asserting their rights" [ ] and therefore "lessen, weaken, or avoid the right of any claimant to a trial by court of competent jurisdiction on the question of liability for ... loss or injury, or the measure of damages therefor" in violation of the Limitation of Vessel Owner's Liability Act [quoting 46 U.S.C. app. § 183c, now recodified as 46 U.S.C. § 30509]. We observed that the clause "does not purport to limit petitioner's liability for negligence" [ ] and enforced the agreement over the dissent's argument, based in part on the *Indussa* line of cases, that the cost and inconvenience of traveling thousands of miles "lessens or weakens [plaintiffs'] ability to recover." [ ]

If the question whether a provision lessens liability were answered by reference to the costs and inconvenience to the cargo owner, there would be no principled basis for distinguishing national from foreign arbitration clauses. Even if it were reasonable to read § 3(8) to make a distinction based on travel time, airfare, and hotels bills, these factors are not susceptible of a simple and enforceable distinction between domestic and foreign forums. Requiring a Seattle cargo owner to arbitrate in New York likely imposes more costs and burdens than a foreign arbitration clause requiring it to arbitrate in Vancouver. It would be unwieldy and unsupported by the terms or policy of the statute to require courts to proceed case by case to tally the costs and burdens to particular plaintiffs in light of their means, the size of their claims, and the relative burden on the carrier.

Our reading of "lessening such liability" to exclude increases in the transaction costs of litigation also finds support in the goals of the Brussels Convention for the Unification of Certain Rules Relating to Bills of Lading, 51 Stat. 233 (1924) (Hague Rules), on which COGSA is modeled. Sixty-six countries, including the United States and Japan, are now parties to the Convention [ ], and it appears that none has interpreted its enactment of § 3(8) of the Hague Rules to prohibit foreign forum selection clauses, see Sturley, *International Uniform Laws in National Courts: The Influence of Domestic Law in Conflicts of Interpretation*, 27 Va. J. Int'l L. 729, 776–796 (1987). * * * [We] decline to interpret our version of the Hague Rules in a manner contrary to every other nation to have addressed this issue. See Sturley at 736 * * *.

It would also be out of keeping with the objects of the Convention for the courts of this country to interpret COGSA to disparage the authority or competence of international forums for dispute resolution. Petitioner's skepticism over the ability of foreign arbitrators to apply COGSA or the Hague Rules, and its reliance on this aspect of *Indussa* [ ], must give way to contemporary principles of international comity and commercial practice. As the Court observed in *The Bremen* [ ] when it enforced a foreign forum selection clause, the historical judicial resistance to foreign forum selection clauses "has little place in an era when ... businesses once essentially local now operate in world markets." * * *

B.

Petitioner's second argument against enforcement of the Japanese arbitration clause is that there is no guarantee foreign arbitrators will apply COGSA. This objection raises a concern of substance. The central guarantee of § 3(8) is that the terms of a bill of lading may not relieve the carrier of the obligations or diminish the legal duties specified by the Act. The relevant question, therefore, is whether the substantive law to be applied will reduce the carrier's obligations to the cargo owner below what COGSA guarantees. [ ]

Petitioner argues that the arbitrators will follow the Japanese Hague Rules, which, petitioner contends, lessen respondents' liability. * * *

Whatever the merits of petitioner's comparative reading of COGSA and its Japanese counterpart, its claim is premature. At this interlocutory stage it is not established what law the arbitrators will apply to petitioner's claims or that petitioner will receive diminished protection as a result. * * * The District Court has retained jurisdiction over the case and "will have the opportunity at the award-enforcement stage to ensure that the legitimate interest in the enforcement of the ... laws has been addressed." *Mitsubishi Motors* [*Corp. v. Soler Chrysler-Plymouth, Inc.*, 473 U.S. 614, 638 (1985)]; [ ]. Were there no subsequent opportunity for review and were we persuaded that "the choice-of-forum and choice-of-law clauses operated in tandem as a prospective waiver of a party's right to pursue statutory remedies..., we would have little hesitation in condemning the agreement as against public policy." *Mitsubishi Motors, supra*, at 637, n.19. Cf. *Knott v. Botany Mills*, 179 U.S. 69 (1900) (nullifying choice-of-law provision under the Harter Act, the statutory precursor to COGSA, where British law would give effect to provision in bill of lading that purported to exempt carrier from liability for damage to goods caused by carrier's negligence in loading and stowage of cargo); *The Hollandia*, [1983] A.C. 565, 574–575 (H.L. 1982) (noting choice-of-forum clause "does not ex facie offend against article III, paragraph 8,"[1] but holding clause unenforceable where "the foreign court chosen as the exclusive forum would apply a domestic substantive law which would result in limiting the carrier's liability to the sum lower than that to which he would be entitled if [English COGSA] applied"). * * *

Because we hold that foreign arbitration clauses in bills of lading are not invalid under COGSA in all circumstances, both the FAA and COGSA may be given full effect. The judgment of the Court of Appeals is affirmed, and the case is remanded for further proceedings consistent with this opinion.

Justice O'CONNOR, concurring in the judgment.

I agree with what I understand to be the two basic points made in the Court's opinion. First, I agree that the language of [COGSA] and our decision in *Carnival Cruise* [ ] preclude a holding that the increased cost of litigating in a distant forum, without more, can lessen liability within the meaning of COGSA § 3(8). Second, I agree that, because the District Court has retained jurisdiction over this case while the arbitration proceeds, any claim of lessening of liability that might arise out of the arbitrators' interpretation of the bill of lading's choice-of-law clause, or out of their application of COGSA, is premature. Those two points suffice to affirm the decision below.

Because the Court's opinion appears to do more, however, I concur only in the judgment. Foreign arbitration clauses of the kind presented here do not divest domestic courts of

1. Editors' note: Hague Rules article 3(8), cited by the House of Lords as "article III, paragraph 8," corresponds to COGSA § 3(8).

jurisdiction, unlike true foreign forum selection clauses such as that considered in *Indussa* [ ]. That difference is an important one—it is, after all, what leads the Court to dismiss much of petitioner's argument as premature—and we need not decide today whether *Indussa*, insofar as it relied on considerations other than the increased cost of litigating in a distant forum, retains any vitality in the context of true foreign forum selection clauses. Accordingly, I would not, without qualification, reject "the reasoning [and] the conclusion of the *Indussa* rule itself" * * *.

Justice STEVENS, dissenting.

The Carriage of Goods by Sea Act (COGSA), enacted in 1936 as a supplement to the 1893 Harter Act, regulates the terms of bills of lading issued by ocean carriers transporting cargo to or from ports of the United States.

* * *

Section 1 of the Harter Act makes it unlawful for the master or owner of any vessel transporting cargo between ports of the United States and foreign ports to insert in any bill of lading any clause whereby the carrier "shall be relieved from liability for loss or damage arising from negligence." [ ] In *Knott v. Botany Mills*, 179 U.S. 69 (1900), we were presented with the question whether that prohibition applied to a bill of lading containing a choice-of-law clause designating British law as controlling. * * * The [*Knott*] Court's holding that the choice-of-law clause was invalid rested entirely on the Harter Act's prohibition against relieving the carrier from liability. [ ] Since *Knott*, courts have consistently understood the Harter Act to create a flat ban on foreign choice-of-law clauses in bills of lading. [ ] Courts have also consistently found such clauses invalid under COGSA, which embodies an even broader prohibition against clauses "relieving" or "lessening" a carrier's liability. Indeed, when a panel of the Second Circuit in 1955 interpreted COGSA to permit a foreign choice-of-law clause, *Muller v. Swedish American Line Ltd.*, 224 F.2d 806 (2d Cir. 1955), scholars noted that "the case seems impossible to reconcile with the holding in *Knott*." Eventually agreeing, the en banc court unanimously overruled *Muller* in 1967. *Indussa Corp.*, 377 F.2d at 200.

In the 1957 edition of their treatise * * *, Gilmore and Black had criticized not only the choice-of-law holding in *Muller*, but also its enforcement of a foreign choice-of-forum clause. They wrote:

> The stipulation for suit abroad seems also to offend COGSA, most obviously because it destroys the shipper's certainty that COGSA will be applied. Further, it is entirely unrealistic to look on an obligation to sue overseas as not "lessening" the liability of the carrier. It puts a high hurdle in the way of enforcing that liability. [ ]

Judge Friendly's opinion for the en banc court in *Indussa* endorsed this reasoning. * * *

* * *

[Our] interpretation of maritime law prior to the enactment of the Harter Act, our reading of that statute in *Knott*, and the federal courts' consistent interpretation of COGSA, buttressed by scholarly recognition of the commercial interest in uniformity, demonstrate that the clauses in the Japanese carrier's bill of lading purporting to require arbitration in Tokyo pursuant to Japanese law both would have been held invalid under COGSA prior to today.

The foreign-arbitration clause imposes potentially prohibitive costs on the shipper, who must travel—and bring his lawyers, witnesses, and exhibits—to a distant country in order to seek redress. The shipper will therefore be inclined either to settle the claim at a discount or to forgo bringing the claim at all. The foreign-law clause leaves the shipper who does pursue his claim open to the application of unfamiliar and potentially disadvantageous legal standards, until he can obtain review (perhaps years later) in a domestic forum under the high standard applicable to vacation of arbitration awards. * * * Yet this Court today holds that carriers may insert foreign-arbitration clauses into bills of lading, and it leaves in doubt the validity of choice-of-law clauses.

* * *

The Court's decision in this case is an excellent example of overzealous formalism. By eschewing a commonsense reading of "lessening [of] liability," the Court has drained those words of much of their potency. The result compounds, rather than contains, the Court's unfortunate mistake in the *Carnival Cruise* case.

* * *

Notes

1. Did anything survive of *Indussa*? Most courts have held that *Sky Reefer* validates not only foreign arbitration clauses but also foreign forum selection clauses in bills of lading subject to COGSA. See, e.g., *Mitsui & Co. v. Mira M/V*, 111 F.3d 33 (5th Cir. 1997); *Fireman's Fund Ins. Co. v. M/V DSR Atlantic*, 131 F.3d 1336 (9th Cir. 1998).

2. The *Sky Reefer* Court cited *The Hollandia*, a decision of the British House of Lords (which has recently been reconstituted as the British Supreme Court), to illustrate a situation in which "the choice-of-forum and choice-of-law clauses operated in tandem as a prospective waiver of a party's right to pursue statutory remedies." In *The Hollandia*, a cargo claimant showed that the chosen court would apply a lower package limitation than would a British court. The choice-of-forum clause was accordingly invalid. After *Sky Reefer*, a few U.S. cargo claimants used the *Hollandia* analysis to avoid the enforcement of choice-of-forum clauses. See, e.g., *Y-Tex Corp. v. Schenker, Inc.*, 2011 AMC 2512, 2516–24 (W.D. Wash. 2011); *Kanematsu USA, Inc. v. M/V Ocean Sunrise*, 2003 AMC 2200, 2204–07 (E.D. La. 2003). But the effort has more often failed. See, e.g., *Liberty Woods International, Inc. v. M/V Ocean Quartz*, 889 F.3d 127 (3d Cir. 2018).

3. In *Atlantic Marine Construction Co. v. United States District Court for the Western District of Texas*, 571 U.S. 49 (2013), the Supreme Court established the procedure for enforcing forum selection clauses. Although *Atlantic Marine* was a non-maritime case (despite its name), lower courts have regularly followed the case in the maritime context.

4. The Rotterdam Rules, see *supra* at 284–85, would partially restore the *Indussa* principles. Under optional chapter 14 (which would apply only in those nations that "opt in" when they ratify the convention), a cargo claimant would have the right to bring suit against the carrier in any of a specified list of places having a connection with the transaction (e.g., the place of receipt, the port of loading, the port of discharge, the place of delivery). For shipments to or from the United States (when *Indussa* would have applied), the cargo claimant would have access to a U.S. forum. The principal exception to this new proposal would be for larger transactions defined as "volume contracts," in which the parties would have greater freedom of contract, including the ability to agree on forum selection clauses under certain conditions. See M. Sturley, T. Fujita & G. van der Ziel, The Rotterdam Rules: The UN Convention on Contracts for the International Carriage of Goods Wholly or Partly by Sea 333–373 (2d ed. 2020).

5. The foregoing trilogy of cases—from *The Bremen* to *Sky Reefer*, but especially *Carnival Cruise*—persuaded most lower courts to hold that forum selection and arbitration clauses in seamen's employment contracts are valid (if bargained for and not otherwise unconscionable). See, e.g., *Bautista v. Star Cruises*, 396 F.3d 1289 (11th Cir. 2005); *Marinechance Shipping, Ltd. v. Sebastian*, 143 F.3d 216 (5th Cir. 1998); but see *Abuan v. Smedvig Tankships*, 717 So.2d 1194 (La. App. 1998) (refusing to enforce such a clause against a cadet seaman who was not a member of the labor union that negotiated the clause with the shipowner). In *Sabocuhan v. Geco-Prakla*, 78 F. Supp. 2d 603, 606–607 (S.D. Tex. 1999), the district judge said he was bound to follow *Marinechance* and enforce a forum selection clause requiring litigation in the Philippines of a Filipino seaman's claim that arose from seismic operations near Galveston, Texas, but he found *Marinechance* a deplorable holding:

> Were this Court at liberty to decide the issue, it would unhesitatingly hold unenforceable the kind of maritime forum-selection clauses at issue in this case. It is axiomatic that seamen are wards of the Admiralty court. This Court finds it truly shameful that the United States, the greatest and most prosperous nation on the face of the earth, would deny an injured seaman a remedy within its court system. This refusal is all the more appalling when the seaman is injured in the course of conveying goods right to the very shores of this nation. These seamen often labor aboard dilapidated vessels in deplorably dangerous working conditions, and yet at considerable risk to life and limb they assist in bringing products to this country which inure to the benefit of all United States citizens. Denying an injured seaman a United States forum is utterly contrary to the beneficent attitude towards seaman that has for centuries characterized the Admiralty courts of the English speaking world.

6. A central part of the *Sky Reefer* Court's rationale for enforcing the arbitration clause before it was that the district court retained jurisdiction over the case and at the award-enforcement stage could ensure that the plaintiff's statutory rights were protected. How would that procedure work in practice, particularly in cases in which the foreign arbitrators made no award that could be enforced? The following case, in which you can read excerpts of both the district court and court of appeals decisions, explores some aspects of that question.

Asignacion v. Rickmers Genoa Schiffahrts

United States District Court, Eastern District of Louisiana, 2014
2014 AMC 713

JAY C. ZAINEY, District Judge.

I. *BACKGROUND*

Plaintiff, a citizen of the Republic of the Philippines, was employed by Defendant, a German corporation, to work as a fitter in the engine room of the *M/V Rickmers Dalian*, a vessel owned by Defendant and flagged in the Republic of the Marshall Islands. Plaintiff and Defendant entered into a written employment contract that was executed by the Philippine government through the Philippine Overseas Employment Administration ("POEA"). The employment contract incorporates the Philippine government's Standard Terms and Conditions Governing Employment of Filipino Seafarers On Board Ocean-Going Vessels ("Standard Terms"). The Standard Terms require that all employment claims must be resolved through arbitration in the Philippines. Specifically, Section 29 of the Standard Terms states that:

> In cases of claims and disputes arising from this employment, the parties covered by a collective bargaining agreement shall submit the claim or dispute to the original and exclusive jurisdiction of the voluntary arbitrator or panel of arbitrators. If the parties are not covered by a collective bargaining agreement, the parties may at their option submit the claim or dispute to either the original and exclusive jurisdiction of the National Labor Relations Commission (NLRC), pursuant to Republic Act (RA) 8042 otherwise known as the Migrant Workers and Overseas Filipinos Act of 1995 or to the original and exclusive jurisdiction of the voluntary arbitrator or panel of arbitrators.

Disputes submitted to the NLRC are resolved by arbitration. As a result, all employment disputes subject to the POEA's Standard Terms are resolved by arbitration. In addition, Section 31 of the Standard Terms provides that all claims arising out of a seaman's employment shall be governed by Philippine law.

On October 26, 2010, Plaintiff was working aboard the *M/V Rickmers Dalian*, as it was docked in the Port of New Orleans, when a cascade tank in the vessel's engine room overflowed and splashed scalding water on Plaintiff who was standing nearby. Plaintiff was immediately rushed by ambulance to West Jefferson Medical Center in Marrero, Louisiana. After receiving emergency medical attention and evaluation, Plaintiff was transferred to the burn unit of Baton Rouge General Medical Center in Baton Rouge, Louisiana, where he stayed and received treatment for nearly a month. Plaintiff was then repatriated to the Philippines, where he continued to receive medical attention.

As a result of the accident aboard Defendant's vessel, Plaintiff sustained severe burns to 35% of his body, including his abdomen, upper and lower extremities, and genitalia. On May 7, 2012, Plaintiff underwent plastic surgery in the Philippines, where a significant amount of scar tissue was removed from Plaintiff's lower abdomen. Plaintiff's burns resulted in an insufficiency of skin in various areas of his body, affecting his body heat control mechanism. Furthermore, Plaintiff experienced the formation of multiple skin ulcerations and sexual dysfunction.

Plaintiff filed suit in state court on November 12, 2010, against Defendant to recover for his injuries pursuant to the Jones Act and the general maritime law of the United States. Defendant filed exceptions to enforce the arbitration clause in Plaintiff's employment contract. On May 16, 2012, the state court granted Defendant's exceptions, stayed litigation of Plaintiff's claims, and ordered arbitration to take place in the Philippines, pursuant to the arbitration clause in Plaintiff's employment contract.

Arbitration commenced before the Department of Labor and Employment, National Conciliation of Mediation Board in Manila. On February 15, 2013, the Philippine arbitral panel issued a decision finding that United States law would not be applied, that Philippine law controlled and accordingly, that Plaintiff was entitled only to scheduled benefits based on his level of disability resulting in an award of $1,870.00.

On March 4, 2013, Plaintiff filed a motion in state court requesting that the court order Defendant to show cause as to why the stay of litigation should not be lifted and why the decision of the Philippine arbitrators should not be set aside as being against public policy of the United States. On April 3, 2013, Defendant removed the action to this Court. In addition, Defendant filed [a separate action] seeking to have the Court enforce the award. The Court consolidated [the two actions].

In the instant motion, Defendant moves for the Court to recognize and enforce the award. Plaintiff opposes Defendant's motion, arguing that enforcement of the award would violate the public policy of the United States. For the reasons that follow, Defendant's motion is denied.

II. *APPLICABLE LAW*

The United States and the Philippines are both signatory States of the New York Convention on the Recognition and Enforcement of Foreign Arbitral Awards ("the Convention").[2] "Among the Convention's provisions are jurisdictional grants giving the federal district courts original and removal jurisdiction over cases related to arbitration agreements falling under the Convention." This Court has previously established that the international arbitration agreement between the parties in this case falls under the Convention. Thus, the Convention governs this Court's consideration of the award.

The Convention provides a carefully structured framework for the review and enforcement of international arbitral awards. When an award is rendered in a signatory country, courts in that country have primary jurisdiction over the award, giving them the exclusive authority to annul the award. Courts in other signatory countries have secondary jurisdiction over the award, which limits them to consider only whether to enforce the award in their country. Since the award was rendered in the Philippines, this Court has secondary jurisdiction over the award and the authority to consider only whether to enforce the award in the United States.

Article V of the Convention enumerates the seven exclusive grounds on which a court with secondary jurisdiction may refuse enforcement of an international arbitral award. Under the Convention, if the court having secondary jurisdiction does not find any of the Article V grounds to be applicable, it must enforce the award.

The party defending against enforcement of the arbitral award bears the burden of proof that one of these defenses applies. "Absent extraordinary circumstances, a confirming court is not to reconsider an arbitrator's findings." Furthermore, courts "may not refuse to enforce an arbitral award solely on the ground that the arbitrator[s] may have made a mistake of law or fact."

The only Article V ground for refusal that Plaintiff invokes is the public policy defense found in Art. V(2)(b). The public policy defense provides that recognition and enforcement of an arbitral award may be refused if the competent authority in the country where recognition and enforcement is sought finds that "[t]he recognition or enforcement of the award would be contrary to the public policy of that country." The public policy defense is to be construed narrowly and applied only where enforcement of an award would violate the forum state's most basic notions of morality and justice.

III. *ANALYSIS*

Defendant has filed the instant [motion] to have the Court recognize the award rendered in the Philippines. Defendant argues that there exist no grounds for the Court to refuse enforcement of the award and that the Court must enforce the award pursuant to the Convention.

In opposition, Plaintiff argues that enforcement of the foreign arbitral award would violate the public policy of the United States due to the arbitral panel's refusal to apply United States law, depriving him of his rights under United States general maritime law,

2. Editors' note: The Convention is implemented by 9 U.S.C. §§ 201–208.

as well as his statutory rights under the Jones Act. For this reason, Plaintiff argues that the Court should refuse to enforce the award pursuant to Article V(2)(b) of the Convention.

Plaintiff argues that enforcement of the award violates public policy under the Supreme Court cases of *Mitsubishi* [*Motors Corp. v. Soler Chrysler-Plymouth, Inc.*, 473 U.S. 614, 629 (1985)] and [*Sky Reefer, supra* at 531]. In these cases, the Supreme Court contemplates condemning arbitration awards as being in violation of public policy when the choice-of-forum and choice-of-law clauses operate in tandem as a prospective waiver of a party's right to pursue certain remedies they are entitled to under law. This has been referred to as the "prospective waiver" defense. Plaintiff argues that by providing for the arbitration proceedings to take place in the Philippines and to apply Philippine law, the arbitration agreement prospectively waived his right to pursue the rights he was entitled to under United States law.

In *Mitsubishi,* the Supreme Court expressed the importance of enforcing forum selection clauses under the Convention, finding that:

> [C]oncerns of international comity, respect for the capacities of foreign and transnational tribunals, and sensitivity to the need of the international commercial system for predictability in the resolution of disputes require that we enforce the parties' agreement, even assuming that a contrary result would be forthcoming in a domestic context.

The Supreme Court in *Mitsubishi* concluded that an agreement to arbitrate claims in Japan arising under the Sherman Act was enforceable because United States law would be applied and the federal policy favoring arbitration supported arbitration. Although it was clear that American law would be applied, the Court made the following observation: "We merely note that in the event the choice-of-forum and choice-of-law clauses operated in tandem as a prospective waiver of a party's right to pursue statutory remedies for antitrust violations, we would have little hesitation in condemning the agreement as against public policy."

Following the *Mitsubishi* decision, the Supreme Court also upheld a foreign arbitration clause in [*Sky Reefer*]. In [*Sky Reefer*], the plaintiff argued that a foreign arbitration clause in a bill of lading, which provided for arbitration in Japan, was unenforceable because there was no guarantee that the foreign arbitrators would apply the Carriage of Goods by Sea Act ("COGSA").

The Supreme Court in [*Sky Reefer*] found the plaintiff's argument to be premature given that the plaintiff failed to establish that the foreign arbitrators would not apply COGSA and that there would be no subsequent opportunity for review. As a result, the Court enforced the arbitration agreement. Nevertheless, the Court quoted *Mitsubishi,* stating that "[w]ere there no subsequent opportunity for review and were we persuaded that 'the choice-of-forum and a choice-of-law clauses operated in tandem as a prospective waiver of a party's right to pursue statutory remedies ... we would have little hesitation in condemning the agreement as against public policy.'"

Mitsubishi and [*Sky Reefer*] gave rise to the "prospective waiver" defense. They also have led to much confusion about when this defense is to be applied. To help understand this timing issue, it is useful to recognize the two-stage process for a federal district court dealing with actions falling under the Convention.

The first stage is the "arbitration-enforcement" stage. This is when the court must determine whether or not to compel arbitration pursuant to an arbitration agreement between the parties. In this case, this stage was complete when the parties were ordered to conduct arbitration proceedings in the Philippines.

The second stage is known as the "award-enforcement" stage. This is when the court must determine whether or not to confirm an award that has been rendered by an arbitral tribunal. This is the stage at which proceedings in this matter currently stand.

Mitsubishi and [*Sky Reefer*] provide that when there will be subsequent opportunity for review of the foreign award, a court should enforce the arbitration agreement at the agreement-enforcement stage, despite the appearance that arbitration under the terms of the agreement will likely result in a deprivation of rights. This is because at the agreement-enforcement stage "it is not established what law the arbitrators will apply to petitioner's claims or that petitioner will receive diminished protection as a result." Even though the arbitration agreement may provide that a certain country's law will be applied, the Supreme Court contends that it is proper "to reserve judgment on the choice-of-law question," since this "must be decided in the first instance by the arbitrator."

The liberal enforcement of arbitration agreements at the agreement-enforcement stage is justified by the district court's retention of jurisdiction over the case. Since the district court retains jurisdiction, it "will have the opportunity at the award-enforcement stage to ensure that the legitimate interest in the enforcement of the ... laws has been addressed." Thus, it is at the award-enforcement stage of proceedings, where this case currently stands, where the court is to apply the prospective waiver defense to ensure that the award has addressed the plaintiff's legitimate interest in the enforcement of the laws. The Court will now conduct that review.

As an initial step of the Court's review of the award, the Court must address the choice-of-law issue. [Applying the *Lauritzen-Rhoditis* test, see *infra* at 550, the court concluded that the law of the vessel's flag should be applied. The Marshall Islands, however, has by statute adopted "the non-statutory general maritime law of the United States" as its general maritime law.]

[The court then examined the remedies available to an injured seaman under the general maritime law and reviewed the arbitral proceedings to determine whether the Plaintiff's interests in the enforcement of the law were properly addressed.]

In conducting a non-intrusive inquiry into the foreign arbitration, as this Court is permitted to do, it is obvious that the rights Plaintiff was entitled to under the general maritime law of the United States were not available to him in the arbitration. The arbitral panel did not consider, nor did Philippine law require or allow that it consider, any evidence pertaining to Plaintiff's lost wages and medical expenses or the moral and compensatory damages and punitive damages [that] he had a right to seek.

It is clear to the Court that the arbitral proceedings and the award of $1,870.00 did not address Plaintiff's legitimate interest in the enforcement of United States general maritime law. The arbitral panel did not take cognizance of these claims and decide them.

Next, the Court must determine whether Plaintiff's prospective waiver and deprivation of his rights under general maritime law constitutes a violation of United States public policy. The Supreme Court in *Mitsubishi* and [*Sky Reefer*] contemplated a violation of public policy when arbitral awards result from the prospective waiver of one's rights in the context of United States antitrust law and COGSA. This Court must determine whether this reasoning should extend to a seaman's rights under the general maritime law of the United States.

The Fifth Circuit has stated that the twin aims of maritime law include: "achieving uniformity in the exercise of admiralty jurisdiction and providing special solicitude to seamen." The Fifth Circuit has cited Justice Jackson's rationale for treating seamen more favorably than other types of laborers:

> From ancient times admiralty has given to seamen rights which the common law did not give to landsmen, because the conditions of sea service were different from conditions of any other service, even harbor service.... While his lot has been ameliorated, even under modern conditions, the seagoing laborer suffers an entirely different discipline and risk than does the harbor worker. His fate is still tied to that of the ship. His freedom is restricted.

The Fifth Circuit has long recognized the special solicitude afforded to seamen and the need to protect them as wards of admiralty. * * *

The Court finds that based on the aforementioned precedent, as well as similar notions found in many decades of binding court decisions, the deprivation of the rights and protections that injured seamen are afforded under United States general maritime law constitutes a violation of this country's public policy. The Supreme Court has stated that a public policy must be well defined and dominant, and is to be ascertained by reference to the laws and legal precedents rather than from general considerations of supposed public interests. The Court finds these requirements to be satisfied.

The Fifth Circuit has stated that public policy is not offended simply because the body of foreign law upon which the judgment is based is different from the law of the forum or less favorable to plaintiff than the law of the forum would have been. However, in this case, the Philippine law applied by the arbitral panel did not simply provide less favorable remedies than United States general maritime law would have. Instead, the Philippine law provided *no such* remedies. Accordingly, the remedies available under Philippine law were not less favorable, but rather were nonexistent.

* * *

The Court reiterates that its finding of a public policy violation lies neither in the arbitral panel's failure to apply United States law nor its decision to apply foreign law. Rather, what forms the basis of the public policy violation is the effective denial of Plaintiff's opportunity to pursue the remedies to which he was entitled as a seaman that resulted from the panel's application of Philippine law. Had the panel applied a set of foreign laws which provided a basis for pursuing similar rights and protections, public policy would have been satisfied. However, such a basis was absent under Philippine law, as evidenced by the proceedings.

Defendant also argues that whatever United States laws the Marshall Islands might "borrow," those laws must still be viewed as being of the Marshall Islands. For this reason, Defendant contends that the arbitral panel's failure to apply Marshall Island law cannot constitute a violation of the public policy of the United States. However, as before, a proper characterization of the Court's finding renders this argument unpersuasive. The Court's public policy finding is based on the following: this country's strong policy of protecting seamen; the substantive rights to which Plaintiff, as a seaman, was entitled under the applicable law (albeit of the Marshall Islands); and the unavailability of those rights in the law applied by the arbitral panel. For these reasons, Defendant's argument is unavailing.

The Court notes that the violations of public policy identified by the Supreme Court in *Mitsubishi* and [*Sky Reefer*] involved the deprivation of statutory rights in the contexts of antitrust law and COGSA. The Court further notes that antitrust law and COGSA are both typically applied to govern business disputes between sophisticated parties, whereas the general maritime law of the United States protects seamen. Having already established this country's public policy in favor of seamen, the Court sees no reason why the substantive rights provided by United States general maritime law should be categorically precluded from the prospective waiver defense created by the Supreme Court in *Mitsubishi* and [*Sky Reefer*].

After considering the foreign arbitral award in this matter, as well as this country's strong public policy in favor of protecting seamen, the Court finds that enforcement of the award would violate this country's most basic notions of morality and justice. As such, the Court refuses to enforce the award on public policy grounds pursuant to Art. V(2)(b) of the Convention.

Asignacion v. Rickmers Genoa Schiffahrtsgesellschaft mbH & Cie KG

United States Court of Appeals for the Fifth Circuit, 2015
783 F.3d 1010, 2015 AMC 913

PRISCILLA R. OWEN, Circuit Judge:

* * *

We have held that the Convention's "public policy defense is to be 'construed narrowly to be applied only where enforcement would violate the forum state's most basic notions of morality and justice.'" In the context of domestic arbitral awards, the Supreme Court has recognized a public-policy defense only when an arbitrator's contract interpretation violates " 'some explicit public policy' that is 'well defined and dominant, and is to be ascertained by reference to the laws and legal precedents and not from general considerations of supposed public interests.'" The Eleventh Circuit has held that the "explicit public policy" requirement applies with the same force to international awards falling under the Convention. We see no reason to depart from that standard here.

The parties do not dispute these standards. Rather, they disagree whether Asignacion's case provides the narrow circumstances that would render the arbitral award unenforceable under the Convention because it violates United States public policy.

A

Asignacion's public-policy defense primarily turns on the adequacy of remedies under Philippine law. But at oral argument, Asignacion's counsel also urged that United States public policy requires that foreign arbitral panels give seamen an adequate choice-of-law determination; he argued that the arbitrators' exclusive reliance on the choice-of-law provision in Asignacion's contract did not constitute a choice-of-law determination, let alone a fair one.

To the extent that Asignacion's defense turns on the Philippine arbitrators' exclusive reliance on the contract's choice-of-law provision, courts are unable to correct this sort of unexceptional legal error (if one was in fact made) when reviewing an arbitral award. Applying Philippine law to a Filipino seaman in Philippine arbitration, by itself, is not cause for setting aside the award, even if American choice-of-law principles would lead to the application of another nation's law.

B

Asignacion has the burden of proving that the Convention's public-policy defense applies. The Philippine arbitrators awarded Asignacion $1,870. Were he to prevail in a suit under United States general maritime law, we have little doubt his recovery would be greater. * * *

Asignacion's arbitral award does not represent the sum total of Rickmers's obligation to Asignacion under the POEA Standard Terms contract. Section 20(B) required Rickmers to pay Asignacion's medical costs until he was repatriated to the Philippines and his disability level was established. There is no dispute that Rickmers met its obligations under Section 20(B). At oral argument, Asignacion's counsel represents that he has incurred medical expenses after Rickmers's Section 20(B) obligation terminated. But our careful review of the record has found no evidence that the Philippine arbitral award was inadequate relative to Asignacion's unmet medical needs, let alone so inadequate as to violate this nation's "most basic notions of morality and justice." We conclude that the district court erred in determining that Asignacion's award violated the public policy of the United States.

C

Finally, Rickmers contends that the district court erred by also relying on the prospective-waiver doctrine to refuse to recognize the Philippine arbitral award. We agree.

In [*Mitsubishi*] the Supreme Court addressed a district court's enforcement of an agreement to arbitrate, which forced an auto dealer to arbitrate its antitrust claims under the Sherman Act [ ] in Japan. The Court commented, in dictum, that "in the event the choice-of-forum and choice-of-law clauses operated in tandem as a prospective waiver of a party's right to pursue statutory remedies for antitrust violations, we would have little hesitation in condemning the agreement as against public policy." Similarly, in [*Sky Reefer*], the Court, again in dictum, suggested that *Mitsubishi's* prospective-waiver doctrine might apply to contracts under [COGSA]. In both cases, the Court declined to apply the doctrine, in part, because it would be premature to do so; each case addressed the enforceability of an agreement to arbitrate, as opposed to awards in which the arbitrators actually failed to address causes of action under American statutes.

The present case is at the award-enforcement stage, unlike *Mitsubishi* and [*Sky Reefer*], and the district court applied the prospective-waiver doctrine. The district court noted that the antitrust laws in *Mitsubishi* and COGSA in [*Sky Reefer*] applied to "business disputes between sophisticated parties." Because seamen are afforded special protections under United States law, unlike sophisticated parties, the district court concluded that the prospective-waiver doctrine prevented the enforcement of the Philippine arbitral award.

However, the prospective-waiver doctrine is limited to statutory rights and remedies. From *Mitsubishi* onwards, the Supreme Court has referred only to "statutory" rights and remedies when discussing the doctrine. The Court recently continued that phrasing in *American Express Co. v. Italian Colors Restaurant,* where the Court refused to apply the doctrine to a waiver of class arbitration. The Supreme Court has not extended the prospective-waiver doctrine beyond statutory rights and remedies. The district court therefore erred when it relied on the doctrine to afford Asignacion an opportunity to pursue his claims under the general maritime law. * * *

For the foregoing reasons, we REVERSE the order of the district court and REMAND for the district court to enforce the arbitral award.

Notes

1. What rationale might there be for limiting the prospective-waiver doctrine to statutory rights and remedies?

2. The Federal Arbitration Act does not "apply to contracts of employment of seamen, railroad employees, or any other class of workers engaged in foreign or interstate commerce."

9 U.S.C. § 1. Most courts have held that this exclusion applies only to 9 U.S.C. chapter 1, the original Federal Arbitration Act, and does not apply to 9 U.S.C. chapter 2, which implements the New York Convention.

B. Forum Non Conveniens, Venue Transfer, Choice of Law

Sinochem Int'l Co. Ltd. v. Malaysia Int'l Shipping Corp.

Supreme Court of the United States, 2007
549 U.S. 422, 127 S. Ct. 1184, 167 L. Ed. 2d 15, 2007 AMC 609

Justice GINSBURG delivered the opinion of the unanimous Court.

This case concerns the doctrine of forum non conveniens, under which a federal district court may dismiss an action on the ground that a court abroad is the more appropriate and convenient forum for adjudicating the controversy. We granted review to decide a question that has divided the Courts of Appeals: "Whether a district court must first conclusively establish [its own] jurisdiction before dismissing a suit on the ground of forum non conveniens?" We hold that a district court has discretion to respond at once to a defendant's forum non conveniens plea, and need not take up first any other threshold objection. In particular, a court need not resolve whether it has authority to adjudicate the cause (subject-matter jurisdiction) or personal jurisdiction over the defendant if it determines that, in any event, a foreign tribunal is plainly the more suitable arbiter of the merits of the case.

I.

The underlying controversy concerns alleged misrepresentations by a Chinese corporation [Sinochem International Co.] to a Chinese admiralty court resulting in the arrest of a Malaysian vessel in China. * * * [The vessel, owned by Malaysia International Shipping Corp., transported steel coils from Philadelphia to Sinochem in China. When the vessel arrived in port, Sinochem had it arrested by the Guangzhou Admiralty Court, alleging that Malaysia International had defrauded Sinochem in transactions related to the bill of lading. The Guangzhou court] rejected Malaysia International's jurisdictional objection, and that ruling was affirmed on appeal by the Guangdong Higher People's Court.

On June 23, 2003, shortly after the Chinese court ordered the vessel's arrest, Malaysia International filed the instant action against Sinochem in the United States District Court for the Eastern District of Pennsylvania. Malaysia International asserted in its federal court pleading that Sinochem's [petition to the Guangzhou court was based on misrepresentations, resulting in an unlawful arrest of the ship. Malaysia International sought compensation for the loss it sustained due to the delay caused by the ship's arrest. Sinochem moved to dismiss the suit on several grounds, including lack of subject-matter jurisdiction, lack of personal jurisdiction, and forum non conveniens.]

The District Court first determined that it had subject-matter jurisdiction under 28 U.S.C. § 1333(1) (admiralty or maritime jurisdiction). The court next concluded that it lacked personal jurisdiction over Sinochem under Pennsylvania's long-arm statute [ ]. Nevertheless, the court conjectured, limited discovery might reveal that Sinochem's national contacts sufficed to establish personal jurisdiction under Federal Rule of Civil Procedure 4(k)(2). The court did not permit such discovery, however, because it determined that the case could be adjudicated adequately and more conveniently in the Chinese courts. No significant interests of the United States were involved, the court observed, and while the cargo had been loaded in Philadelphia, the nub of the controversy was entirely foreign: The dispute centered on the arrest of a foreign ship in foreign waters pursuant to the order of a foreign court. Given the proceedings ongoing in China, and the absence of cause "to second-guess the authority of Chinese law or the competence of [Chinese] courts," the District Court granted the motion to dismiss under the doctrine of forum non conveniens.

A [divided] panel of the Court of Appeals for the Third Circuit agreed there was subject-matter jurisdiction under § 1333(1), and that the question of personal jurisdiction could not be resolved *sans* discovery. Although the court determined that forum non conveniens is a nonmerits ground for dismissal, the majority nevertheless held that the District Court could not dismiss the case under the forum non conveniens doctrine unless and until it determined definitively that it had both subject-matter jurisdiction over the cause and personal jurisdiction over the defendant.

* * *

II.

A federal court has discretion to dismiss a case on the ground of *forum non conveniens* "when an alternative forum has jurisdiction to hear [the] case, and ... trial in the chosen forum would establish ... oppressiveness and vexation to a defendant ... out of all proportion to plaintiff's convenience, or ... the chosen forum [is] inappropriate because of considerations affecting the court's own administrative and legal problems." *American Dredging Co. v. Miller* [*supra* at 113], 510 U.S. at 447–448 (quoting *Piper Aircraft Co. v. Reyno*, 454 U.S. 235, 241 (1981), in turn quoting *Koster v. (American) Lumbermens Mut. Casualty Co.*, 330 U.S. 518, 524 (1947). Dismissal for forum non conveniens reflects a court's assessment of a "range of considerations, most notably the convenience to the parties and the practical difficulties that can attend the adjudication of a dispute in a certain locality." [ ] We have characterized forum non conveniens as, essentially, "a supervening venue provision, permitting displacement of the ordinary rules of venue when, in light of certain conditions, the trial court thinks that jurisdiction ought to be declined." *American Dredging*, 510 U.S. at 453; [ ].

The common-law doctrine of forum non conveniens "has continuing application [in federal courts] only in cases where the alternative forum is abroad" [ ] and perhaps in rare instances where a state or territorial court serves litigational convenience best. [ ] For the federal-court system, Congress has codified the doctrine and has provided for transfer, rather than dismissal, when a sister federal court is the more convenient place for trial of the action. [28 U.S.C. § 1404(a).] * * *

A defendant invoking forum non conveniens ordinarily bears a heavy burden in opposing the plaintiff's chosen forum. When the plaintiff's choice is not its home forum, however, the presumption in the plaintiff's favor "applies with less force," for the assumption that the chosen forum is appropriate is in such cases "less reasonable." *Piper Aircraft Co.*, 454 U.S. at 255–256.

III.

Steel Co. v. Citizens for Better Environment, 523 U.S. 83 (1998), clarified that a federal court generally may not rule on the merits of a case without first determining that it has jurisdiction over the category of claim in suit (subject-matter jurisdiction) and the parties (personal jurisdiction). * * * While *Steel Co.* confirmed that jurisdictional questions ordinarily must precede merits determinations in dispositional order, [*Ruhrgas AG v. Marathon Oil Co.*, 526 U.S. 574, 584 (1999)] held that there is no mandatory "sequencing of jurisdictional issues." In appropriate circumstances, *Ruhrgas* decided, a court may dismiss for lack of personal jurisdiction without first establishing subject-matter jurisdiction.

Both *Steel Co.* and *Ruhrgas* recognized that a federal court has leeway "to choose among threshold grounds for denying audience to a case on the merits." [ ] Dismissal short of reaching the merits means that the court will not "proceed at all" to an adjudication of the cause. * * *

IV.

A forum non conveniens dismissal "den[ies] audience to a case on the merits" [ ]; it is a determination that the merits should be adjudicated elsewhere. See *American Dredging*, 510 U.S. at 454. * * * A district court therefore may dispose of an action by a forum non conveniens dismissal, bypassing questions of subject-matter and personal jurisdiction, when considerations of convenience, fairness, and judicial economy so warrant.

* * *

Statements in this Court's opinion in *Gulf Oil Corp. v. Gilbert*, 330 U.S. 501 (1947), account in large part for the Third Circuit's conclusion that forum non conveniens can come into play only after a domestic court determines that it has jurisdiction over the cause and the parties and is a proper venue for the action. [ ] The Court said in *Gulf Oil* that "the doctrine of forum non conveniens can never apply if there is absence of jurisdiction" [ ], and that "[i]n all cases in which ... forum non conveniens comes into play, it presupposes at least two forums in which the defendant is amenable to process" [ ].

Those statements from *Gulf Oil*, perhaps less than "felicitously" crafted [ ], draw their meaning from the context in which they were embedded. * * * *Gulf Oil* did not present the question we here address: whether a federal court can dismiss under the forum non conveniens doctrine before definitively ascertaining its own jurisdiction. * * * [W]e find in *Gulf Oil* no hindrance to the decision we reach today.

The Third Circuit expressed the further concern that a court failing first to establish its jurisdiction could not condition a forum non conveniens dismissal on the defendant's waiver of any statute of limitations defense or objection to the foreign forum's jurisdiction. Unable so to condition a dismissal, the Court of Appeals feared, a court could not shield the plaintiff against a foreign tribunal's refusal to entertain the suit. [ ] Here, however, Malaysia International faces no genuine risk that the more convenient forum will not take up the case. Proceedings to resolve the parties' dispute are underway in China, with Sinochem as the plaintiff. Jurisdiction of the Guangzhou Admiralty Court has been raised, determined, and affirmed on appeal. We therefore need not decide whether a court conditioning a forum non conveniens dismissal on the waiver of jurisdictional or limitations defenses in the foreign forum must first determine its own authority to adjudicate the case.

V.

This is a textbook case for immediate forum non conveniens dismissal. The District Court's subject-matter jurisdiction presented an issue of first impression in the Third Circuit [ ] and was considered at some length by the courts below. Discovery concerning personal jurisdiction would have burdened Sinochem with expense and delay. And all to scant purpose: The District Court inevitably would dismiss the case without reaching the merits, given its well-considered forum non conveniens appraisal. Judicial economy is disserved by continuing litigation in the Eastern District of Pennsylvania given the proceedings long launched in China. And the gravamen of Malaysia International's complaint—misrepresentations to the Guangzhou Admiralty Court in the course of securing arrest of the vessel in China—is an issue best left for determination by the Chinese courts.

If, however, a court can readily determine that it lacks jurisdiction over the cause or the defendant, the proper course would be to dismiss on that ground. In the mine run of cases, jurisdiction "will involve no arduous inquiry" and both judicial economy and the consideration ordinarily accorded the plaintiff's choice of forum "should impel the federal court to dispose of [those] issue[s] first." *Ruhrgas*, 526 U.S. at 587–588. But where subject-matter or personal jurisdiction is difficult to determine, and forum non conveniens considerations weigh heavily in favor of dismissal, the court properly takes the less burdensome course.

For the reasons stated, the judgment of the Court of Appeals is reversed, and the case is remanded for proceedings consistent with this opinion.

Notes

1. **The Supreme Court's forum non conveniens cases.** The doctrine of forum non conveniens has been quite important in federal-court transnational litigation, but the Supreme Court has paid only sporadic attention it. The *Sinochem* opinion cites all of the cases in which the Court has directly addressed the doctrine: *Gulf Oil* (1947) (holding that a federal court in Manhattan had discretion to refuse to hear a negligence action against a Pennsylvania-based corporation for causing a warehouse fire in Virginia); *Koster* (1947) (holding that a federal court in Brooklyn could decline to hear a shareholders' derivative action against an Illinois corporation); *Piper Aircraft* (1981) (holding that a federal court in Pennsylvania had discretion to refuse to hear a products liability action by Scottish air crash victims against the Pennsylvania company that manufactured the allegedly defective aircraft); and *American Dredging* (1994) (*supra* at 113) (holding that state courts are not obliged to follow the federal forum non conveniens doctrine in saving clause cases).

2. **The transition from Gulf Oil to Piper Aircraft.** The federal doctrine of forum non conveniens had a modest beginning in *Gulf Oil*, where the Court said that dismissals for forum non conveniens should be "rather rare," characterized the plaintiff's lawsuit as an "imposition" on the Manhattan federal court's jurisdiction, suggested that the action was brought there for purposes of "harassment," and stated:

> [T]he plaintiff may not, by choice of an inconvenient forum, vex, harass, or oppress the defendant by inflicting upon him expense or trouble not necessary to his own right to pursue the remedy. But unless the balance is strongly in favor of the defendant, the plaintiff's choice of forum should rarely be disturbed.

330 U.S. at 507–509 (internal quotation marks omitted). Thirty-five years later, the doctrine had transmogrified into a surprisingly broad authorization to federal district courts to guard against congestion of their dockets by foreign litigants. The *Piper Aircraft* Court stated:

> The forum non conveniens determination is committed to the sound discretion of the trial court. It may be reversed only when there has been a clear abuse of discretion; where the court has considered all relevant public and private interest factors, and where its balancing of these factors is reasonable, its decision deserves substantial deference.

3. For critical studies of the federal courts' forum non conveniens jurisprudence, see Robertson, *The Federal Doctrine of Forum Non Conveniens: "An Object Lesson in Uncontrolled*

Discretion," 29 TEX. INT. L.J. 353 (1994); Robertson & Speck, *Access to State Courts in Transnational Personal Injury Cases: Forum Non Conveniens and Antisuit Injunctions*, 68 TEX. L. REV. 937 (1990); Robertson, *Forum Non Conveniens in America and England: "A Rather Fantastic Fiction*," 103 L.Q. REV. 398 (1987).

Camejo v. Ocean Drilling & Exploration

United States Court of Appeals, Fifth Circuit, 1988
838 F.2d 1374

GOLDBERG, Circuit Judge:

[Joao Camejo, a Brazilian citizen and resident, was employed in Brazil by a Brazilian entity, Superpesa Transportes Maritimos, Ltd.] as a diver in connection with mineral exploration. He died in a diving accident in Brazilian waters on February 22, 1984. At the time of his death, Camejo was diving from a Panamanian flagged rig, the *Zephyr II*, drilling for the Brazilian national oil company * * *. [He was wearing a diving helmet designed and manufactured by U.S. Divers Corp. and Diving Systems International, Inc., both U.S. corporations. Camejo's widow (Shirlei Camejo) and children, who live in Brazil, brought this wrongful death action against Superpesa, U.S. Divers, and Diving Systems in Texas state district court. Superpesa did not enter an appearance in the state court. Defendants U.S. Divers and Diving Systems removed the action to the U.S. District Court for the Southern District of Texas.[1]] Superpesa never appeared in the district court or in this court.

Shirlei Camejo based her claims on the general maritime law of the United States [and] the Jones Act, [46 U.S.C. § 30104. The district court dismissed the Jones Act claim on the basis of 46 U.S.C. § 30105. Section 30105 was added to the Jones Act in 1982. It] denies a Jones Act remedy and any other remedies under general maritime law to foreign seamen in the offshore drilling industry when they are injured in another country's territorial waters, unless neither the country where the injury occurred nor the seaman's home country provide any remedy. The district court recognized the applicability of § 30105 but misinterpreted its import. [The district court's ruling stated:]

> As a preliminary matter, the Court would note that Plaintiffs' claims for relief under the Jones Act must be dismissed. The incident which gives rise to this cause of action occurred after 1982, when Congress amended the Jones Act to exclude from its coverage certain aliens.
>
> The pleadings make clear that Plaintiff's decedent was an alien employed by an enterprise engaged in the production of off-shore energy resources in territorial waters off of Brazil. Because Plaintiff has not shown that no remedy was available to her so as to fit this case within one of the exceptions to [§ 30105's] exclusion provision, she has failed to state a claim for relief under the Jones Act, and that portion of the case must be dismissed.

[W]e agree that this [ruling] was correct. The district court, however, failed to realize the full import of [§ 30105]. The section does not just deny Shirlei Camejo, and similarly situated plaintiffs, relief under the Jones Act; the section also denies relief under * * * the general

1. Editors' note: There was no apparent basis for personal jurisdiction in Texas over U.S. Divers and Diving Systems, but evidently neither defendant contested the issue. Camejo did challenge the district court's removal jurisdiction; the challenge was rejected on grounds that need not concern us here.

maritime law of the United States . [Therefore, the district court should have dismissed Mrs. Camejo's general maritime law claims on the merits, along with the Jones Act claim.]

[Instead, the district court dismissed the general maritime law claims on the grounds of forum non conveniens. The forum non conveniens dismissal was subject to the conditions listed in the margin.[4] For the reasons set forth below, we believe that the forum non conveniens ruling was correct.]

* * *

For many years, in many admiralty cases, this court held that, before addressing the issue of forum non conveniens, the district court should decide whether American or foreign law applied. To determine the choice of law question the court used the eight factors set out by the Supreme Court in *Lauritzen v. Larsen,* 345 U.S. 571 (1953), [*Romero v. Int'l Terminal Op. Co.*, 358 U.S. 354, 381–84 (1954),] and *Hellenic Lines Ltd. v. Rhoditis,* 398 U.S. 306 (1970). [The seven *Lauritzen* factors are: (1) the place of the wrongful act; (2) law of the flag; (3) allegiance or domicile of the injured; (4) allegiance of defendant shipowner; (5) place of the contract of employment; (6) inaccessibility of foreign forum; and (7) law of the forum. 345 U.S. at 583–98. The eighth factor, added in the *Rhoditis* decision, is the shipowner's base of operations. 398 U.S. at 309.] This court held that if American law applied, the district court should generally retain jurisdiction and proceed with the case. On the other hand, this court held that, if the district court determined that foreign law applied then the district court should proceed to an analysis of the *forum non conveniens* factors set forth in *Gulf Oil Corporation v. Gilbert,* 330 U.S. 501 (1947).

In 1981, in *Piper Aircraft Co. v. Reyno,* 454 U.S. 235 (1981), a products liability action under diversity jurisdiction, the Supreme Court held that a choice of law analysis is only tangentially relevant to the *Gulf Oil forum non conveniens* analysis and that a court need not perform a choice of law analysis before its *forum non conveniens* analysis. * * * [In the aftermath of *Piper Aircraft v. Reyno,* this court handed down *In re Air Crash Disaster Near New Orleans, Louisiana on July 9, 1982,* 821 F.2d 1147, 1164 n. 25 (5th Cir.1987) (en banc), stating:]

> We * * * can discern no * * * justification for refusing to apply *Reyno*'s principles * * * to forum non conveniens issues in Jones Act and general maritime cases. We believe that a single and uniform approach to the analysis and application of the forum non conveniens doctrine best serves litigants and the courts. We therefore, expressly disapprove of and overrule our Jones Act and general maritime caselaw that utilize[d] a modified forum non conveniens analysis. Henceforth, all cases, including Jones Act and maritime actions, are governed by the dictates of *Reyno* and this opinion.

Even though this court issued the *Air Crash* opinion after the district court decision in this case, we must apply the *Air Crash* holding as we consider this case. We note at the outset, however, that "[a]n appellate court may reverse the decision of a district court on a motion to dismiss on *forum non conveniens* only if it constituted a clear abuse of discretion." "Simply stated, our duty as an appellate court in reviewing forum non conveniens decisions is to review the lower court's decisionmaking process and conclusion

4. The [forum non conveniens] dismissal was subject to the following conditions: (1) That Defendants submit to service of process and jurisdiction in the appropriate Brazilian court; (2) The Defendants waive any running of the statute of limitations from the date on which the ... lawsuit herein was filed until the date of this Order; (3) That Defendants agree to participate in discovery in accordance with Brazilian law; and (4) That Defendants agree to satisfy any final judgment.

and determine if it is reasonable; our duty is not to perform a de novo analysis and make the initial determination for the district court." *Air Crash,* 821 F.2d at 1167.

* * * In *Air Crash* this court said: "A defendant of course bears the burden of invoking the doctrine and moving to dismiss in favor of a foreign forum." The defendants here clearly met this burden. The *Air Crash* court continued:

> This burden of persuasion runs to all the elements of the forum non conveniens analysis. Therefore, the moving defendant must establish that an adequate and available forum exists as to all defendants if there are several. If the moving defendant carries this initial burden, it must also establish that the private and public interests weigh heavily on the side of trial in the foreign forum. The Supreme Court has held that a moving defendant need not submit overly detailed affidavits to carry its burden, but it "must provide enough information to enable the district court to balance the parties' interests."

The defendants submitted detailed motions for dismissal on the grounds of *forum non conveniens* to the district court. The defendants' motions discussed the relevant facts and applied the *Gulf Oil* factors to these facts. Shirlei Camejo did not submit any pleadings, motions or memoranda of law that controverted any of the defendants' statements regarding the *forum non conveniens* issue. As a result none of the relevant facts alleged by the defendants in their *forum non conveniens* motions are in controversy. We therefore conclude that, if these uncontroverted facts are sufficient to support the district court's *forum non conveniens* decision, the defendant has met his burden of persuasion.

* * * In *Air Crash* this court said:

> The district court must first decide whether an available and adequate foreign forum exists. This is a two-part inquiry: availability and adequacy. A foreign forum is available when the entire case and all parties can come within the jurisdiction of that forum.... A foreign forum is adequate when the parties will not be deprived of all remedies or treated unfairly, even though they may not enjoy the same benefits as they might receive in an American court ...

In this case the district court found that Plaintiff Shirlei Camejo did not dispute the existence of an adequate alternative forum.

* * *

We now proceed to review the federal district court's balancing of the public and private convenience factors that the Supreme Court set forth in *Gulf Oil Corp. v. Gilbert.* The *Gulf Oil* opinion listed the following private interest factors:

> Important considerations are the relative ease of access to sources of proof; availability of compulsory process for attendance of unwilling, and the cost of obtaining attendance of willing, witnesses; possibility of view of premises, if view would be appropriate to the action; and all other practical problems that make trial of a case easy, expeditious and inexpensive. There may also be questions as to the enforceability of a judgment if one is obtained. The court will weigh relative advantages and obstacles to a fair trial.

The *Gulf Oil* opinion also listed the following public interest factors:

> Administrative difficulties follow for courts when litigation is piled up in congested centers instead of being handled at its origin. Jury duty is a burden that ought not to be imposed upon the people of a community which has no relation to the litigation. In cases which touch the affairs of many persons, there is reason

> for holding the trial in their view and reach rather than in remote parts of the country where they can learn of it by report only. There is a local interest in having localized controversies decided at home.

The absence of the actual employer in this jurisdiction and the greater interest of Brazil in deciding a controversy involving one of its citizens are significant factors which support the district court's action, as they did in *Piper,* especially since Shirlei Camejo has not demonstrated any connection at all with Texas. Compulsory process for Brazilian witnesses is unavailable in a Texas forum. The cost of bringing Brazilian witnesses to Houston is very high. All the information regarding the Plaintiff's damages is in Brazil. The rig was and still is in Brazil. The local interest of Brazil in determining a case involving the death of one of its citizens is great; Texas courts have no comparable interest in the case.

Although *Gulf Oil* counsels that courts should not disturb the plaintiff's choice of forum unless the balance strongly favors the defendants, *Piper* held that a foreign plaintiff's choice deserves less deference. In this case the balance so strongly favors the defendant that we have no trouble in concluding that the district court did not abuse its discretion in declining to exercise its jurisdiction to decide [this case].

* * *

Notes

1. The *Camejo* court's treatment of some state-law issues has been edited out of the opinion above.

2. For a full analysis of 46 U.S.C. § 30105, see Robertson & Kelly, *Protecting U.S. Oil Companies from Lawsuits Brought by Foreign Offshore Oil and Gas Workers: A Report on the Effects of the 1982 Amendment to the Jones Act,* 21 Rev. Litig. 309 (2002).

3. For additional demonstrations of the interplay between choice-of-law issues and choice-of-forum issues, see *Gonzales v. Naviera Neptuno, S.A.,* 832 F.2d 876 (5th Cir. 1987) (reversing judgment for plaintiff and ordering forum non conveniens dismissal of action for death of Peruvian blue-water sailor aboard Peruvian-flag vessel in Port Arthur, Texas); *Miller v. Philips Petroleum Company Norway,* 537 A.2d 190 (Del. 1988) (applying federal maritime choice-of-law principles and state forum non conveniens law to disputes arising from the capsizing of a semi-submersible drilling rig in the Norway sector of the North Sea); *Marriott v. Sedco Forex Int'l Resources,* 827 F. Supp. 59 (D. Mass. 1993) (denying motion for forum non conveniens dismissal of action by four seamen—one U.S., three British—alleging exposure to AIDS from hepatitis vaccinations administered by their employer on oil rig off the coast of India, and holding that the U.S. citizen's case would be determined under U.S. law and the British seamen's cases under Indian law).

4. In *Piper Aircraft,* the defendants made three highly successful forum-shopping moves. The plaintiffs initially filed suit in a California state court. (a) Defendants removed the case to federal court (C.D. Cal.). (b) They then used 28 U.S.C. § 1404(a) to have the case transferred to the Middle District of Pennsylvania. (c) They then successfully moved for forum non conveniens dismissal, effectively sending the case to Scotland.

5. *Piper Aircraft* is explicit in approving the application of the forum non conveniens doctrine in such a way as to favor U.S. litigants over foreigners:

> [The district court in this case] held * * * that the presumption [in favor of retaining jurisdiction] applies with less force when the plaintiff or real parties

> in interest are foreign. [This] distinction between resident or citizen plaintiffs and foreign plaintiffs is fully justified.

454 U.S. at 255. Moreover, the Court emphasized the desirability of restricting litigation by foreign plaintiffs against U.S. manufacturers, stating that otherwise:

> The American courts, which are already extremely attractive to foreign plaintiffs, would become even more attractive. The flow of litigation into the United States would increase and further congest already crowded courts.

Id. at 252.

6. Despite the *Piper*-approved bias in favor of U.S. resident plaintiffs, courts do grant forum non conveniens dismissals against U.S. residents. *Alcoa Steamship Co. v. M/V Nordic Regent*, 654 F.2d 147 (2d Cir. 1980) (en banc), was a particularly dramatic example. Alcoa, a New York corporation, owned an ore transfer pier in Trinidad. A Liberian ship struck the pier, causing about $8 million in damages. When Alcoa libeled the ship in rem in the Southern District of New York, it was met with a successful defensive motion to dismiss for forum non conveniens on the view that Trinidad was the proper place for trial. Alcoa's showing that the Trinidad court would apply a liability limit of $570,000—leaving Alcoa holding the bag for the remaining $7.43 million—left the court wholly unmoved.

7. As is true with forum non conveniens, most of the successful defensive invocations of the *Lauritzen-Rhoditis* choice-of-law framework have been against foreign plaintiffs. But see *Schexnider v. McDermott International, Inc.*, 817 F.2d 1159 (5th Cir. 1987) (relegating a U.S. seaman to Australian law); *Bilyk v. The Vessel Nair*, 754 F.2d 1541 (9th Cir. 1984) (relegating a U.S. seaman to Mexican law).

8. **When is *Lauritzen-Rhoditis* the correct choice-of-law approach?** *Lauritzen* and *Rhoditis* (and *Romero*, *supra* at 79, 102) were cases in which foreign seamen sought to apply the Jones Act against their employers. The choice-of-law approach emanating from those cases has come to be used in many other contexts as well. See SCHOENBAUM, ADMIRALTY AND MARITIME LAW § 3-18 at 193 & n.725 (6th [hornbook] ed. 2019); *Rationis Enterprises Inc. v. Hyundai Mipo Dockyard Co.*, 426 F.3d 580 (2d Cir. 2005) (suit by cargo interests, damaged when ship broke into two sections, against Korean shipyard that had welded the sections together); *Perforaciones Maritimas Mexicanas, S.A. v. Grup TMM, S.A.*, 2007 WL 1428654 (S.D. Tex. 2007) (allision in Bay of Campeche between Mexican flagged supply vessel and Mexican flagged mobile drilling rig). But see *Dresdner Bank A.G. v. M/V Olympia Voyager*, 446 F.3d 1377, 1381–82 (11th Cir. 2006) (stating that "the proper analysis for choice-of-law problems in maritime contract cases [is not *Lauritzen-Rhoditis* but instead] the Second Restatement of Conflicts of Law, Sections 6 (Choice of Law Principles) and 188 (Validity of Contracts and Rights Created Thereby), as well as governmental interest analysis").

9. When application of the *Lauritzen-Rhoditis* factors (or of some other choice-of-law methodology) calls for the application of foreign law, the proper ruling is to dismiss *on the merits* the portions of plaintiff's complaint that rely on U.S. law. (Frequently, that means dismissal of the whole complaint.) Scattered cases dismissing for lack of subject matter jurisdiction in this situation are not well reasoned on this point. See the explanation in *Neely v. Club Med Management Services, Inc.*, 63 F.3d 166, 174–78 (3d Cir. 1995) (en banc).

10. **International comity.** The term "international comity" has many meanings. See generally *Hartford Fire Ins. Co. v. California*, 509 U.S. 764 (1993); *Mujica v. AirScan, Inc.*, 771 F.3d 580 (9th Cir. 2014). In forum non conveniens disputes in which foreign governmental interests are arguably implicated, defendants seeking forum non conveniens

dismissal sometimes urge a somewhat vague "rule of international comity" as a separate argument—standing alongside but not part of the forum non conveniens analysis—for dismissal. See, e.g., *Perforaciones Maritimas Mexicanas S.A. v. Seacor Holdings, Inc.*, 443 F. Supp. 2d 825 (S. D. Tex. 2006); *Sector Navigation Co. v. M/V Captain P*, 2006 WL 2946356 (E.D. La. 2006). It has been hard to tell when—if ever—this "international comity" concept adds anything to the *Gulf Oil* "public interest" forum non conveniens factors. A recent nonmaritime decision shedding some light on this matter is *GDG Acquisitions, LLC v. Government of Belize*, 749 F.3d 1024 (11th Cir. 2014). The court began its analysis by describing a doctrine of "retrospective international comity" whereby a U.S. court should often defer to a prior or ongoing adjudication in a foreign country. That doctrine is legitimate; it is separate from forum non conveniens; and it is rarely in play in the normal forum non conveniens arena. Another doctrine, which the court termed "prospective international comity," seems to lack legitimacy; it is another phrasing of forum non conveniens; and:

> [W]e have reserved prospective international comity abstention for rare (indeed, often calamitous) cases in which powerful diplomatic interests of the United States and foreign sovereigns aligned in supporting dismissal. We decline to transform prospective international comity into a forum-selection tool for sovereign litigants to wield in common breach of contract actions.

Id. at 1034.

Index